Other books by Aaron Wildavsky
Budgeting: A Comparative Theory of Budgetary Processes
The Politics of the Budgetary Process
How to Limit Government Spending
The Private Government of Public Money
(with Hugh Heclo)
Planning and Budgeting in Poor Countries
(with Naomi Caiden)

A HISTORY OF TAXATION AND EXPENDITURE IN THE WESTERN WORLD

Carolyn Webber
and
Aaron Wildavsky

SIMON AND SCHUSTER
New York

Published by Simon and Schuster
A Division of Simon & Schuster, Inc.
Simon & Schuster Building
Rockefeller Center
1230 Avenue of the Americas
New York, New York 10020
SIMON AND SCHUSTER and colophon are registered trademarks of
Simon & Schuster, Inc.
Designed by Irving Perkins Associates
Manufactured in the United States of America
2   4   6   8   10   9   7   5   3   1

Library of Congress Cataloging-in-Publication Data

Webber, Carolyn.
A history of taxation and expenditure in the Western world.

Bibliography: p.
Includes index.
1. Taxation—History. 2. Expenditures, Public—
History. I. Wildavsky, Aaron B. II. Title.
HJ2250.W42   1986   336.2′009   86-3863
ISBN: 0-671-54617-1

*Grateful acknowledgment is made to the following museums, societies, and publishers
for permission to include the following material:*

The Curtis Publishing Company: Cartoon, "Billions of Deficit, Billions of Debt," by Herbert Johnson. Reprinted from *The Saturday Evening Post* © 1946 by The Curtis Publishing Company. Used with permission. (PLATE 25)

Herblock Cartoons: Cartoons, "The Mini-And-Maxi Era," from *Herblock's State of the Union* (Simon & Schuster, Inc., 1972) and "Idol Must Have Human Sacrifice," from *Straight Herblock* (Simon & Schuster, Inc., 1964). Used with permission of Herblock Cartoons. (PLATES 29, 31)

King Features Syndicate, Inc.: Cartoon, "Home on the Range," by Rube Goldberg. © King Features Syndicate, Inc. Used with permission. (PLATE 28)

Los Angeles Times Syndicate: Cartoon by Dan Wasserman, for *The Boston Globe*. © 1986 by Los Angeles Times Syndicate. Reprinted with permission. (PLATE 33)

Metropolitan Museum of Art: Wall painting of Nubians bringing tribute. The Metropolitan Museum of Art, New York. (PLATE 5)

Octopus Books: Bas-relief from Noviomagus, painting of chamberlain, woodcut of mint operated by Maximilian I, from *Coins* by John Porteous
(*continued on page 710*)

For Melvin and Mary

CONTENTS

Preface   13
Chapter One: BUDGETARY CULTURES   17
  BUDGETS AND SOCIAL ORDERS   17
  COPING WITH COMPLEXITY   22
  WHERE PREFERENCES COME FROM   24
  THE BUDGETARY BASE AS A MANIFESTATION OF SOCIAL
    ORDER   31
  REGIMES ARE PART OF WHAT WE SELECT IN CHOOSING
    RATIONALITY   32
  MODELS AS MAPS   34
**Chapter Two: FINANCE WITHOUT MONEY: BUDGETING IN THE
  ANCIENT WORLD**   38
  BACKGROUND CONDITIONS   40
    The Societies 40
    Priest-Kings 45
  THE CENTRALIZED STATE, BUREAUCRACY, AND FINANCIAL
    ADMINISTRATION   49
    Egypt 54
    Mesopotamia 57
    China 59
    India 62

7

8   Contents

GOALS OF THE ANCIENT KINGS AND HOW THEY ACHIEVED
   THEM   65
DIRECT AND INDIRECT REVENUES: TAXES AND CORVÉE   68
   Taxation and Morality: Favoritism and Exemptions 74
FISCAL MANAGEMENT IN THE ANCIENT WORLD   77
   Control of Corruption 82
   An Evaluation 87
APPENDIX: TRANSACTIONS IN BARTER AND MONEY   90

**Chapter Three: FROM REPUBLIC TO EMPIRE: TAXING AND
SPENDING IN CLASSICAL ATHENS AND REPUBLICAN AND
IMPERIAL ROME**   **93**
BACKGROUND   93
   Social and Economic Conditions 93
   Political Institutions 95
FINANCE AS TECHNOLOGY   101
   Innovation and Change 101
   The Liturgies 102
REVENUE   107
   Taxes 107
   Tax Administration: Tax Farming 113
SPENDING IN REPUBLIC AND EMPIRE   119
   The Treasuries and Earmarking 119
   Financial Accountability 127
   The Athenian Audit 128
   *Delegated Financial Management in the Roman
      Republic* 131
   Centralization Under the Emperors 133
   *Coping: Making Ends Meet Versus Evading Punitive
      Taxation*   139
THE CONCEPT OF PUBLIC INTEREST   142

**Chapter Four: FINANCE IN THE PRIVATE GOVERNMENTS OF
MEDIEVAL EUROPE: POOR KINGS**   **148**
BACKGROUND   153
   Time Frame 153
   The Barbarian Invasions 154
   Administrative Decline 156
   The Scarcity Economy of the Early Middle Ages 158
   Economic Revival Begins in the Eighth Century 160
   Recentralization in the Feudal Kingdoms 164
REVENUES AND EXPENDITURES OF MEDIEVAL GOVERNMENTS   167
   The Early Middle Ages 167
   The Feudal Contract 171

Pity the Poor King: Feudal Financial Institutions   174

Revenue Strategies of Late-Medieval Governments   181

    Chartering Towns   183

    Support from the Church   185

    Purveyance   188

    Borrowing with Tallies   189

    Currency Debasement   190

    Borrowing to Cover Deficits   192

    Forced Sale of Royal Assets   196

    Legalized Taxation   197

    Public Loans   203

FISCAL CONTROL: MEDIEVAL ADMINISTRATIVE STRUCTURE
AND THE POVERTY OF KINGS   204

    Medieval Financial Control: The Audit   209

    The Meaning of the Middle Ages: Theories of Change   221

**Chapter Five: POOR PEOPLE, RICH KINGS: GETTING AND
SPENDING IN EARLY-MODERN EUROPE**   **228**

    *Evolution and Revolution, Continuity and
       Change*   228

THE CONTEXT   231

    *Technology, Productivity, Population Growth, and
       Economic Expansion*   231

    The Theory and Practice of Absolutism   235

    The King and His Ministers: Evolution of a Role   241

    Enlightenment and Reform   243

    The Emergence of "Public" Government   247

FINANCING GOVERNMENT   250

    The Market for Capital   250

    Private Loans   251

    Government Borrowing   252

    Short- or Long-Term Debt?   254

    Market Administration Provides Credit   255

    The Public Capital Market   256

    Public Banking in the Dutch Republic   257

    The Bank of England   259

THE REVENUES OF NATIONS: ENLARGING THE BASE   259

    Ordinary and Extraordinary Revenue   262

    Direct Taxes on Land and Its Produce   262

    Confiscation of Property   264

    Colonial Exploration and Exploitation   265

    Devaluation   265

    Sale of Offices   266

The Joint-Stock Companies 268
Market Taxes: Customs Duties 269
Internal Excise Taxes 271
Market Taxes and Equity 272
Food Riots and Tax Revolts 273
STATE GOVERNANCE FOR PRIVATE PROFIT: MIXED ADMINIS-
TRATIVE SYSTEMS IN THE TRANSITIONAL ERA   274
Centralization Under Absolutism 276
*Decentralization: Earmarking and Market
   Administration* 276
*Decentralization Was Costly for Governments and
   Profitable for Administrators* 277
*Private Prerogatives of Public Office Inhibit
   Accountability* 279
Financial Control Through Threat and Example 282
Early Government Budgets 283
*Public Government, Public Finance, and Public
   Administration* 286
*Professional Administration Replaces Market
   Administration* 288
Reform and Reformers 292
CONCLUSION: ACHIEVEMENTS OF AN ERA   296

**Chapter Six: THE WAYS AND MEANS OF PUBLIC GOVERNMENT:
TAXING AND SPENDING IN REPRESENTATIVE STATES OF THE
EARLY INDUSTRIAL AGE**   **299**
CHANGING PARADIGMS OF GOVERNMENT FINANCE   299
THE CONTEXT FOR CHANGE   310
EFFICIENCY, RATIONALITY, AND THE IDEA OF THE BAL-
ANCED BUDGET   323
WAYS AND MEANS: TAXES   332
Taxation and Welfare Spending 349
THE NINETEENTH-CENTURY LEGACY FOR MODERN TAXING
AND SPENDING   355

**Chapter Seven: BALANCED REGIMES, BALANCED BUDGETS:
WHY AMERICA WAS SO DIFFERENT**   **358**
THE COLONIAL PERIOD   361
THE FIRST AND SECOND AMERICAN REVOLUTIONS   366
PUBLIC DEBT AND BALANCED BUDGETS   370
INTERNAL IMPROVEMENTS   377
THE AMERICAN MYSTERY: BUDGETING WITHOUT A BUDGET   388
AN END TO BUDGETARY EXCEPTIONALISM? THE REEMER-
GENCE OF HIERARCHY   400

THE EXECUTIVE BUDGET   411
RAISING REVENUE IN THE AMERICAN FEDERAL SYSTEM: DI-
    VISION OF LABOR   416
THE END OF EXCEPTIONALISM   425

**Chapter Eight: STABILITY AMIDST TURBULENCE: THE HALF
CENTURY AFTER 1914**   **428**
TWENTIETH-CENTURY FINANCE: AN OVERVIEW   430
TAXING AND SPENDING IN THREE WESTERN DEMOCRACIES
    DURING WORLD WAR I   436
DEBT AND IMMOBILITY IN THE 1920s: A STUDY OF FRANCE,
    GERMANY, BRITAIN, SWEDEN, AND THE UNITED STATES   445
        Spending in the 1920s   448
        Taxation in the Twenties   451
THE DEPRESSION AND THE WELFARE STATE IN WESTERN
    EUROPE AND THE UNITED STATES   453
MILITARY EXPENDITURES BETWEEN THE FIRST AND SECOND
    WORLD WARS   464
        *Britain in the 1920s and 1930s (with Comparisons to
        Nazi Germany)*   465
        The Domestic Impact on Britain   466
        The United States   471
        France   471
EFFECTS OF WORLD WAR II IN THE UNITED STATES AND
    BRITAIN   472
THE ASSUMPTIONS OF POST–WORLD WAR II BUDGETING   476
        Coordination by Role   478
WHY THE LINE-ITEM BUDGET LASTED, AND SOME RECENT
    COMPETITORS FOR ORGANIZING BUDGETS   480
UNIT OF MEASUREMENT: CASH OR VOLUME   482
        Time Span: Months, One Year, Many Years   483
        Calculation: Incremental or Comprehensive   485
APPROPRIATIONS VERSUS TREASURY BUDGETING   486
WHY THE TRADITIONAL BUDGET LASTS   487

**Chapter Nine: THE GROWTH OF THE WELFARE AND TAX STATES:
FROM THE 1960s UNTIL TODAY**   **490**
BUDGETING IN TURBULENT TIMES   490
GROWTH OF THE WELFARE STATE   493
MILITARY SPENDING FROM THE END OF WORLD WAR II
    THROUGH THE MID-1960s   506
THE DEFENSE BUDGET–MAKING PROCESS   511
BRITAIN, FRANCE, AND GERMANY AFTER WORLD WAR II   512
        A Note on Technology   517

12   **Contents**

Defense as a Function of Regime   519
THE POLITICAL CULTURE OF TAXATION   521
CORPORATE TAXATION AND TAX PREFERENCES   523
FOR BETTER OR FOR WORSE: INCOME TAXATION AS A MIR-
   ROR OF DEMOCRACY   526
GERMANY: THE POLITICS OF GROWTH   535
SWEDEN: THE POLITICS OF STABILITY   539
CLASS POLITICS IN BRITAIN   544
TAXATION IN POSTWAR FRANCE   547
A CULTURAL EXPLANATION OF TAX DIFFERENCES   550
WHY PROGRESSIVE STATES TAX CORPORATE INCOME LOW,
   AND LOW AND MIDDLE INCOMES HIGH   552
THE EMERGENCE OF SPENDING LIMITS   555

**Chapter Ten: A Cultural Theory of Governmental
Growth and (Un)balanced Budgets**   **560**
PROBLEM SUCCESSION   562
WHY GOVERNMENT GROWS   567
WAGNER'S LAW   569
WILENSKY'S LAW   571
MARXIST THEORIES   574
TAX HYPOTHESES   576
OLSON'S LAW AND OTHER POLITICAL HYPOTHESES   578
TESTING CULTURAL THEORY   584
APPLYING CULTURAL THEORY   585
PELTZMAN'S LAW, OR CULTURE RECONSIDERED   587
EGALITARIAN PROGRAMS GROW FASTEST   588
IS THE DEFICIT IN THE BUDGET OR IN SOCIETY?   590
BUDGETARY BALANCE AS A FUNCTION OF REGIME   594
THE TRANSFORMATION OF BUDGETARY NORMS   598
BALANCED BUDGETS AND UNBALANCED REGIMES   607
Notes   **615**
Bibliography   **677**
Index   **711**

PREFACE

A project extending over eighteen years has its own history. Early in 1968, Aaron Wildavsky asked Carolyn Webber to explore the history of budgeting with him. The search unearthed a vein so rich we have been mining it ever since.

At first we meant to write only a monograph on ancient finance. Something so remote was interesting for its own sake, we believed, but it wasn't likely to hold lessons for the present. Then we thought of studying financial history worldwide, but, though our spirits were willing, in the end strength proved weak. We had wanted to include chapters exploring the legacy of Byzantium for governments of eastern Europe, and of Arab civilization for governments in North Africa, Spain, the Near East, and Southeast Asia. We settled just for taxing and spending in Western nations.

As the years passed and our knowledge of taxing and spending processes accumulated, we came across events that might command headlines in today's newspapers. Yet we were not always certain that, with the apparent advantages of modern financial technology, our contemporaries would find these ancient historical practices worth discussing.

Then, as New York City's financial crisis began to unfold in 1975, the pattern of ad-hoc borrowing to pay for past spending and to support future expansion recalled the kings of early-modern Europe, whose financial troubles we were studying. The absolute monarchs of early-modern states lacked permanent revenue sources to support their lavish spending, so they borrowed from any available lender. When loans came due, they refinanced them if possible. As the debt expanded beyond their ability to repay, early-modern kings could either declare a moratorium on interest, imprison their creditors, or, by declaring royal bankruptcy, erase obligations by fiat. Such default could (and did) bankrupt lenders; but, unlike present-day governments and the bankers who hold their debts, early-modern kings did not need to worry about repercussions on an interlocked national or world banking system.

Now that American deadlock over budgets competes for news with European gridlock, and when taxes, debt, and deficits are staples of worldwide discussion, the accounts reported in *A History* seem almost contemporary. Because, in retrospect, "they" didn't do so badly and "we" are not doing so well, aspects of budgetary history appear quite modern.

The most important acknowledgment we wish to make is to each other: for forbearance and friendship. It is hard for us to remember when we were not working on *A History* or to imagine what it will be like when we are not.

Along the way, we have incurred many debts. The National Endowment for the Humanities and the Sloan Foundation provided major financial support. Over the years, the following institutions helped out with typing, research assistance, and work space: the Institute of International Studies, the Graduate School of Public Policy, the Political Science Department, the Institute of Urban and Regional Development, the Survey Research Center, the Childhood and Government Project, and the Children's Time Study, all at the University of California, Berkeley; the Russell Sage Foundation; and the Western Regional office of the Environmental Defense Fund. In the early years we were helped by talented research assistants: Ruth Battle, Naomi Caiden, Jane Cajina, Carol Chamberlain, Thomas Lennox, Mari Malvey. Students in Wildavsky's budgeting seminars who wrote papers on financial history surveyed literatures we had yet to explore: John Gilmour, Richard Gunther, Yong-Chool Ha, Benno Marx, Benny Miller, Ernest Notar, Carl Patton, Alex Radian, Aran Schloss, Robin Silver, Sven Steinmo, Joe White. Mappie Seabury and Robert Asahina edited and improved our text.

Doris Patton, Aaron Wildavsky's secretary, may well believe that she has been mired in this history as long as we have. Thanks are not sufficient commendation for her care and dedication, her eagle eye for error.

No one or two persons know enough to write a book of this scope. Jan-Eric Lane read and criticized the entire manuscript; Thomas Bisson and Peter Marris, large sections. If there were a reader's medal of honor, they would deserve it. Many others helped by criticizing individual chapters: James Alt, Douglas Ashford, Jesse Burkhead, Rufus Davis, James Fesler, R. I. Frank, Peter Garnsey, Walter Hettich, Ronald King, Richard Netzer, Alan Peacock, Sam Peltzman, Clare Penniman, Richard Rose, Geoffrey Vickers, Harold Wilensky. Their aid in suggesting different interpretations and in correcting our errors has been indispensable.

Our division of labor was straightforward. Webber wrote initial drafts of chapters two through six, Wildavsky, chapters one and seven through ten. We then each modified the other's drafts, sometimes extensively. We each revised and rewrote each other's drafts so often and over so long a period of time that more than two people were really at work; neither of us was the same when re-revised as we had been on the previous series of revisions or the ones before that. Thus, although careful readers will no doubt detect our respective styles and approaches, we are both equally responsible for each of the parts as well as the whole.

Melvin Webber and Mary Wildavsky must have wondered if this work would ever be completed; so did we. Yet their support was continuous and we are grateful for it.

CAROLYN WEBBER
AARON WILDAVSKY

Chapter One

BUDGETARY CULTURES

There are ... those who are looking to see if there is one thing that can be understood, and those who keep saying it is very complicated and that nothing can be understood. You must study the simplest system you think has the properties you are interested in.

—CY LEVENSON

To tax and to please, no more than to love and be wise, is not given to men.

—EDMUND BURKE

Numeration and writing emerged when early societies began to mobilize and allocate resources. In deposits scattered along major lines of communication in the ancient Near East, archaeologists have found over two hundred hollow clay spheres dating from the fourth millennium B.C. The surfaces of these tennis-ball-size spheres display embossed or incised markings of cones, disks, paraboloids, and other geometric shapes; these symbols resemble pictographs known to represent animals (horses, sheep, goats) and ancient measures of grain. The spheres rattle when shaken, and, if broken, release small clay objects shaped like the exterior symbols. Other such objects, without clay enclosures, have been found at sites ranging from Egypt to the Indus Valley; some date back to the ninth millennium B.C.

An archaeologist speculates that these ancient artifacts—fabricated before writing or abstract conceptions of numbers are known to have existed—functioned as receipts.[1] The clay spheres served as envelopes, the interior tokens as symbols of things given in exchange. Thus the entire artifact—clay sphere, interior tokens, and external markings denoting the number and shape of tokens inside—represented either the consummation of a commercial transaction or the discharge of a financial obligation. Ancient governments assessed and collected taxes in kind: the same grain, animals, and labor service represented by the cuneiform symbols.

BUDGETS AND SOCIAL ORDERS

The mobilizing and allocating of resources in past ages bears small resemblance to how modern governments get and spend money. In the

17

decentralized, private market administrations of ancient, medieval, and some early-modern governments, for example, taxing, spending, and borrowing were fused. Over the centuries, when revenue was tribute, received in kind (grain and animals for consumption; scarce commodities—rhino horns, ostrich feathers, jewels—for gratification), receipts and expenditures were determined together. For most of history there were no formal budgets as we know them today.

Nevertheless, for ease of exposition, we shall call borrowing, taxing, and spending, taken together, "budgeting." In this sense of the term, the budgets we have grown accustomed to in our own age are not natural to man or society. Each age has had its own patterns of budgeting consonant with its cultures and technologies.

In its broadest definition, budgeting is concerned with translating financial resources into human purposes. Since funds are limited and have to be spent on different purposes, budgetary processes are mechanisms for making economic and political choices.

Budgets are also moral orders, regulating relations among people through commands and prohibitions. "There is no money" may not be the saddest sentence of all, but it is one of the most conclusive (along with the other great justifications for decisions—there is no time, it is unnatural, and God forbids it).[2] Even the form of budgets (as in the family practice of providing envelopes for this or that expenditure) suggests priorities.

The desire to control a budget is not the same as having the technical or organizational capacity to do so. A central treasury into which all funds flow not only has to be conceived, but must be facilitated by double-entry bookkeeping, the conceptualization of a uniform system of accounts, and other devices for keeping track of revenues and expenditures. The preference for a centralized and comprehensive budget also followed the development of adequate transportation networks connecting a state's center with its provinces. For budgetary reformers within governmental hierarchies in the late eighteenth and nineteenth centuries—Turgot and Necker, followed by Louis Thiers in France, Stein and Hardenberg in Prussia, Gladstone in England—a budget, based on a single central treasury, was a means not only of keeping track of all of government's revenues and expenditures, but of relating one to the other to attain a rough equivalence (balance, as it is still longingly called) between a government's resources and its commitments.

The invention of Arabic numerals, line items, statistical sampling procedures, and computerized tax returns over the centuries has made all the difference in governments' capacity for control. Market-oriented regimes may desire to devote public resources to more productive uses; without national or international capital markets or easy access to credit, however, they may not be able to do so. Egalitarian regimes may prefer an annual budget to enforce accountability to the citizenry; but, with accounts in chaotic conditions, audits years behind and separate funds of uncertain size, they may not be able to enforce their will. Oliver Cromwell's Puritan Commonwealth in England during the mid–seventeenth century, for example, aimed to replace the personal financial administration of the Duke of Buckingham, the deposed King Charles I's hated Finance Minister (and paramour), and his venal officials, with a government administration accountable to the citizenry. Under the bookkeeping methods used by most governments in those days, however, accounts inevitably were difficult to decipher. Separate revenue funds existed for each of the many taxes collected by a government; current fund balances could never even be estimated, nor future balances predicted; and government audits of tax collectors stood years in arrears. Although Cromwell's new professionalized administrators did try to introduce some order into financial management, the combination of technology and social circumstances necessary to implement reforms did not exist in England at that time. Lacking the crown's patrimonial revenue, and with a polity divided into rival sects (Diggers, Levellers, Ranters, Muggletonians, etc.) unwilling to grant authority to levy new taxes, Cromwell's commonwealth faced continuous financial emergency. Strapped for funds to pay the militia, it could scarcely enforce its writ beyond three miles of the palace.

Yet technology alone cannot specify what is done with the opportunities it offers. Enhancing the ability to extract resources, for example, does not determine who will pay how much, or what the funds will be used for. Whether the technology will be used to redistribute income from richer to poorer, or the other way around, or whether expenditures and revenues will be reduced, or vice versa, depends more on what people do to technology than on what technology does to people.

Making ends meet does not appear to have been easy at any time, except for brief periods (which is why we include a chapter on American exceptionalism). Nowadays industrial societies are wealthier than ever before and governments are better at extracting resources, yet their ability to spend has more than kept pace. More people pay taxes and more receive benefits, but revenue often fails to meet society's increased demands on government. Audits, central banks, electronic data processing, and other devices of modern technology facilitate calculation of future revenues and expenditures. But it would be optimistic to say that modern peoples are better able to control their financial destinies.

Since much can be said about every society and its budgetary behavior, we will be imposing an element of uniformity to make each period coherent in its own terms: the patterns of taxing, spending and borrowing we find in each time and place will be explained by analyzing political regimes. Whatever else may and does change, we will argue, the societal cultures and the political regimes that express them are limited in number and powerful in their consequences for budgeting. These cultural categories will serve as analytic instruments for ordering events in disparate periods, divided not only by time but also by tradition and technology.

Our theory is that there are three major types of societal organization: hierarchical, market, and sectarian cultures. From commitments to these cultures come the formulation of preferences about what is worth having.

Of course, no society we know about is organized according to a single principle. Hierarchical orders have existed in governments spanning the ages, with society divided into higher and lower ranks, linked by traditions and formal rules specifying who can do what. Market elements have also permeated societies in all ages and places. Self-regulation provides an alternative answer to the question of how to live with other people. Long before social theorists in early-modern Europe praised the market for its capacity to generate beneficent outcomes, individuals in diverse societies bartered and bought and sold goods and services. When a society is organized in order to reduce the need for authority by fostering exchange for mutual benefit, we would call its lifestyle of bidding and bargaining "market individualism."

A third, ever present way of life, which represents forces dissenting from an established authority that allows some men to choose for others, we call "egalitarian sectarianism." It is sectarian because it rejects authority, egalitarian because to live a voluntary life without one man dominating another it is necessary to diminish differences among people. By their nature, such purely voluntary associations tend to be small and short-lived. How can they maintain equality of power except by face-to-face relations? And how will they keep the group together when there is no authority? Sects leave traces permitting analysis of their history only when dissent is organized and it manages to change society to fit the iconoclasts' image of how life should be lived.

Sects are associated with heterodoxy, the antinomy of orthodoxy. From the Essenes of Biblical days to the Jansenists in late-medieval France and the Diggers, Levellers and Plymouth Brethren of the Puritan Revolution in England, to various nineteenth-century utopians, to the Student Non-Violent Coordinating Committee in 1960s America, sects have embraced a separate and ascetic life, censoring the corrupt world outside. Nowadays, nineteenth-century dissenters' prescriptions for reorganizing society have become public policy in all the welfare-state democracies of the Western world. Other kinds of sects are manifestly with us today. A prime example is the Green Party in Germany, which protests against existing authority. Everywhere in the Western world there are other sectarian movements to reduce differences among people: feminism, the civil-rights movement, gay rights, anti-poverty activism, the movement for the "deinstitutionalization" of the mentally ill, and so on.

More than one social order may exist in one country at a time. Before the modern era, for instance, elements of individualism merged with hierarchical norms and structures in the practices of tax farming and the sale of offices. Tax farming was common in diverse governments for millennia, from the city-states of Mesopotamia in the third millennium B.C. until the first revolution in France in 1789. In the absence of a capital market to provide advances against long-delayed revenues, pre-modern governments often contracted with private entrepreneurs to collect some or all of their taxes, securing badly needed, short-term funds. Private holders of contracts to collect such taxes amassed personal fortunes while wielding delegated government authority.

Market, sectarian, and hierarchical regimes wax and wane throughout history, though not according to any known cycle. Rather, these alternative ways of organizing social life are always present. History, as we conceive it, is about the consequences of people's choices of political ways of life—regimes and combinations of regimes—at particular times.

In the late eighteenth century, for example, two nations—one old, the other new—challenged existing ways of taxing and spending. Both the United States and France had been ruled by hierarchical regimes; the U.S. moved toward market individualism, while, for a short time, sectarians ruled during the radical phase of the French Revolution. Viewing with concern the American colonies' resistance to Britain's stamp taxes, Edmund Burke worried that "instead of a standing revenue, you will have, therefore, a perpetual quarrel."[3] In 1789, when

Benjamin Franklin wrote of the inevitability of death and taxes, he was no doubt alluding to his nation's recent tax revolt and its financial embarrassments. He did not say that no mode of taxation would have suited a people bent on rejecting a distant hierarchy.[4] To think that taxes on stamps and tea precipitated a revolution is to confuse the straw that broke the camel's back with the entire load.

When we say that budgeting is part of social order, we are not saying that budgeting lacks all autonomy. Nor are we saying that political regimes within any society can do whatever they want—only that budgeting, like ruling, is part of the dominant political regime in a given society.

Ask how budgets should be made and you will be asking how social life ought to be lived. Cultural organization requires social support. People must be able to do things for others. They must be able to act together to support their way of life, to oppose other ways, and to hold one another accountable for things that go wrong. Getting and spending by governments is an important mode of collective action and accountability.

COPING WITH COMPLEXITY

The objects of spending, from harems to hospitals, are virtually unlimited; the possible means of raising revenue, from gifts to expropriations, hardly less so. Yet the awesome variety of revenue devices and spending practices that will be described in this book is deceptive. A closer look reveals that most forms of financial management in government belong to only a small number of categories.

For generations on end, governments collected only a few types of taxes. They levied direct taxes on part of the produce of the land: those who grew crops paid by the bur of millet, the catty of rice, or the bushel of oats; or in livestock, lambs and kids, salmon or herring. Governments also assessed head taxes. For millennia, the otherwise untaxable poor paid their dues in compulsory labor service. In ancient Egypt, China, Central America, Europe during the Middle Ages and in the early-modern era, and colonial Africa during this century, people without money gave the government so many days each week or each year in compulsory labor service, most of it spent building and maintaining public works. In the Soviet Union today, the *sabotnik,* a periodic day of contributed labor service, is a throwback to this ancient practice. From the earliest time, public service has also been donated by citizens of city-states in ancient Mesopotamia and classical Greece, the municipalities of the Roman Empire, and cities in medieval Europe; state and local governments have formed public commissions since the mid–nineteenth century; "dollar-a-year" men served the United States government during the Second World War.

Although the wealthy were spared the pain of paying regular taxes throughout most of history, they did not get off scot-free. Governments, pressed for funds, repeatedly levied taxes on the external manifestations of wealth. When a man's home is a castle, it denotes not only who he is but what he is worth. Governments have levied taxes not just on houses but also on supporting columns, doors and windows, fountains, and other signs of affluence. Just as citizens of England in the late eighteenth century paid an annual tax on horses and hackneys, so do car owners in most jurisdictions today pay purchase taxes and registration fees commensurate with a vehicle's value.

Taxes and markets have been interrelated throughout history. Market taxes have been a significant revenue source, from the customs, excise, and stamp taxes of the early-modern era to sales taxes and value-added taxes today. And from the earliest times, the exchange process enabled governments to impose taxes on transactions: outsiders entering a fortified jurisdiction paid a tax as they entered or departed. Governments have always raised revenue by taxing mass-consumption staples—grain and salt, beer and wine. Indeed, market taxes are found in all periods and places, perhaps because exchange itself is universal, perhaps because transactions localized in markets are easy to tax.

As individuals have devised ingenious methods for avoiding taxes and siphoning off tax receipts for personal use, governments have tried to counteract loss of revenue with equally cunning controls. Usually, the methods were awkward and ineffective—a source of constant difficulty for both governments and their people. But again and again, neither taxpayers nor governments ever quite succeeded in attaining their financial goals; or, if limited success was achieved, it rarely endured.

Taxing and spending are repeatedly subverted by unanticipated consequences. Britain's medieval Exchequer, designed to control others, itself became stultified as ritual impeded action. Closer to our own time, goals have become displaced. During the nineteenth century, reformers believed that eliminating corruption would permit governments to do what they had always done, but more cheaply. Instead, as governments have been enlarged to do much more than before, honesty has become the best policy for spending ever increasing amounts. Government officials have learned how to raise revenues and to allocate resources more efficiently, but, in a vastly different climate of social expectations, they have also learned to make government much bigger than before. This process helps explain why the rise of capitalism was followed so soon by the welfare state. Over centuries and civilizations, the only certainty in governments' taxing and spending behavior is the absence of an ultimate solution.

WHERE PREFERENCES COME FROM

Where do the preferences for a given way of life come from? What sort of social glue holds people together? What are the consequences for budgeting of living according to the principles of the various political regimes?

If there were an infinite and unrelated number of cultures, no intelligible answer could be given except "It depends." History is uniqueness. But, if social organizations are limited in number and interconnected, a comprehensible answer can be given: people's preferences emerge from defending or opposing different ways of life.

Our premise is that people express their preferences as part of constructing—building, modifying, rejecting—their social institutions. The values people prefer and their beliefs about the world are woven together through their cultures. Political cultures are called regimes.

The important decisions individuals make are simultaneously choices of culture. People discover preferences by deciding whether to reaffirm, alter, or abandon their way of life. They continuously construct and reconstruct their culture through decision-making.

Who is to blame when things go wrong? Sectarian regimes blame "the system," the established authority that upholds unnatural inequality. Hierarchies blame deviants who harm the collective by failing to follow its rules. Market regimes fault the individual for failing to be productive, or for restricting transactions (not allowing the best bargains to be made). Suppose there is then a new development. Without knowing much about it, those who identify with each particular way of life can guess whether it will increase or decrease social distinctions; their guesses will be shaped by observing what like-minded individuals do. Just as political party identification enables individuals to cut their information costs during elections, people decide for or against existing authority as external circumstances change. It does not take much for members of a market or a sectarian regime to figure out whether they oppose or approve of a progressive income tax, or for a member of a hierarchical regime to surmise that a central treasury will strengthen the state more than a fragmented system of finance will.

Each culture seeks to promote certain values and practices: collectivism seeks to maintain social differences, egalitarianism to diminish them, and individualism to allow them to grow large. The key question is: What sorts of people, sharing which values, legitimating what practices, would repeatedly act in a certain way to keep their own regime together and to discomfort their adversaries?[5]

Political regimes are based on answers to two questions: "Who am I?" and "How should I behave?" The answer to the question of identity is that individuals may belong to a strong group (a collective that makes decisions binding on all members), or their ties to others may be so weak that their choices affect only themselves. To answer the question of action: individuals' behavior is subject to many or few social prescriptions. The strength or weakness of group boundaries and the constraints on individuals (see Table 1) are the social components of their political regimes.

TABLE 1

EIGHT MODELS OF SOCIAL ORDERS AND THEIR POLITICAL CULTURES (REGIMES)

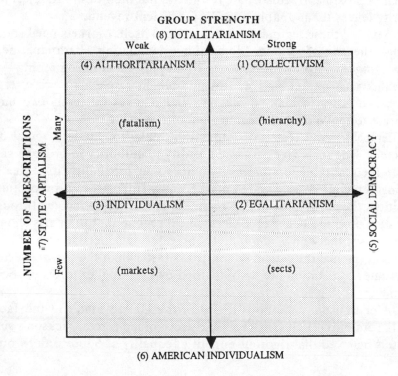

Strong groups with numerous prescriptions combine to form a hierarchical regime. Strong groups with few prescriptions form a sectarian regime—a life of voluntary consent, without coercion or inequality. The bidding and bargaining of market regimes—which unite few prescriptions with weak group boundaries, thereby encouraging endless new combinations—create a self-regulating substitute for hierarchical authority. When boundaries are weak and prescriptions strong, so that decisions are made by people outside the group, the regime is authoritarian and fatalist.

Just as an act is socially rational if it supports one's way of life, budgetary processes are rational if they maintain the political regimes in which they are imbedded. In market regimes, for instance, budgets reflect opportunity for gain by bidding and bargaining. Under hierarchical regimes, budgets reflect the detailed division of people and their activities by rank and status. And, under a sectarian regime emphasizing purely voluntary organization, budgets are devoted to distributing equal shares. According to our theory, hierarchical regimes, which strive to exert authority, spend and tax high in order to maintain each rank and status. Market regimes, preferring to reduce the need for authority, spend and tax as little as possible. Egalitarian regimes spend as much as possible to redistribute resources, but their desire to reject authority leaves them unable to collect sufficient revenues.

No one of these regimes is sufficient unto itself. Markets need something—the laws of contract—to be above negotiating. Hierarchies need something—controlled masses—to sit atop. Sects need something—an inegalitarian market and an inequitable hierarchy—to criticize. It takes two poles to make a magnet, and it takes (at least) two half-regimes to make a whole regime.

Hierarchies and sects in combination make for modern social democracy. The sects give up some hostility to authority in order to gain greater equality. Hierarchies give up some inequality in order to strengthen consensus. Though markets may still exist in a subordinate position, the desire of sectarian regimes to redistribute income through the state, and the belief of a hierarchical regime that the parts should sacrifice for the whole, combine to increase the collective role of government. Hence the public sector grows faster than the private sector; high rates of taxation are accompanied by even higher levels of social spending.

Under unusual conditions found in the United States in the Jacksonian era of the 1830s, markets and sects joined forces. Jackson's supporters believed that rigorous pursuit of equality of opportunity would result in greater equality of outcome. When private wealth is seen as the source of inequality, such an alliance cannot be established. However, the Jacksonians believed that governmental hierarchy was the major source of inequality. Thus market and sectarian regimes, allied under Jackson, organized against the state apparatus by enforcing low levels of spending and taxing. Because we know of no similar examples, we call this hybrid "American individualism."

Instead of combining with sects to foster equality, hierarchical regimes may move toward greater separation between top and bottom, accentuating power differences. People beneath the ruling groups lose their role in the system and become fatalistic. Budgeting is done for them but not by them; loss of autonomy accounts for their fatalism. In such a despotic regime, the distinction between public and private never develops, because everything (and everyone) belongs to the hierarch. Taxation is virtually confiscatory, but spending on behalf of the people is kept on a tight rein.

In social-democratic regimes, both taxing and spending rise because the hierarchical elements increase revenue while the sectarian element demands redistribution. By contrast, both revenues and expenditures are small in a regime of American individualism, with the market elements demanding low taxes and the sectarians determined to reduce the coercive power of government.

When big competitors force out rivals in market regimes, leaving only a few players in the game, everyone else becomes fatalistic, accepting whatever life offers without exerting independent initiative. This combination of individualism and fatalism we will call, following modern fashion, "state capitalism." Though it allows independent power centers, the state directs all major activities. State capitalism's appetite for spending and taxing is moderated by the need to convince capitalists to stay in the coalition, and by the inclination to limit coercion of its own citizens; unlike despotism, state capitalism does not seek to control everything. The government budget is large but not so large as in a totalitarian regime, because there is no effort to mobilize the entire society. Thus, as in Nazi Germany in the early 1930s, taxes are moderate, but state spending is large.

Another combination of cultures—substantial though not necessarily equal proportions of hierarchy, markets and sects yoked in uneasy harness—is more complex than either hierarchy or markets alone, or both regimes together. It is not so often found historically, but it dominates present-day Western democracies.

Such a coalition can come about in several ways. Once market competition and social hierarchy become an established team, there is bound to be a loosening of constraint. Freedom of contract can hardly be guaranteed without allowing other liberties as well, including the right to refuse contract—that is, to criticize and propose alternatives. Emerging simultaneously during the seventeenth and eighteenth centuries, representative government and unregulated markets are political and economic manifestations of individualism. Sects, whose activities as political critics cannot be readily separated from a competitive regime's need to transact business without external coercion, may spring up in such a permissive context. Alternatively, sects may help to establish regimes, as they did in America. With no hereditary hierarchy, with settlement by Protestant sects, and with wide-open spaces to absorb dissident elements, circumstances in America were uniquely favorable for the emergence, and then growth, of an egalitarian social order.

What interests us (see Table 2) are the kinds of budgetary behavior produced by such cultural pluralism. Spending and taxing patterns under political pluralism depend, we hypothesize, on the relative

TABLE 2

BUDGETARY CONSEQUENCES OF HYBRID REGIMES

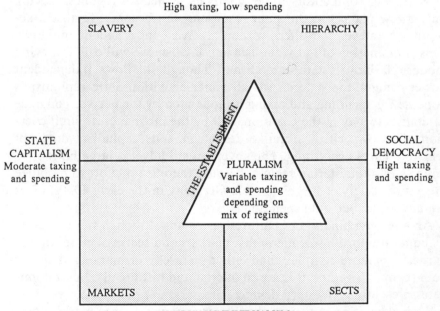

DESPOTISM
High taxing, low spending

SLAVERY   HIERARCHY

STATE   SOCIAL
CAPITALISM   DEMOCRACY
Moderate taxing   PLURALISM   High taxing
and spending   Variable taxing   and spending
                         and spending
                         depending on
                         mix of regimes

THE ESTABLISHMENT

MARKETS   SECTS

AMERICAN INDIVIDUALISM
Low taxing and spending

strength of the primary regimes that make them up: the stronger the market forces, the lower the taxing and spending; the stronger the sectarian regime, the higher the spending and the lower the taxation; the stronger the hierarchical element, the more both revenue and expenditure go up.

Whenever governments in past ages could insure that taxes would be collected—in ancient China, India, and Egypt, in the early Roman Empire and Byzantium, and in the European nations from the late Middle Ages on—organizations within government manifested the prescribed differentiation of function characteristic of hierarchy. Audits of local tax collectors by central government agents exemplified hierarchical principles. Yet the repeated breakdown of hierarchy over the centuries reflects how maladapted rigid prescriptions are to changing contexts.

Centralized capacity to plan and control spending did not exist in any government until the nineteenth century. Governments from the earliest times administered taxing and spending by earmarking: revenue from each tax went into a specific independent fund; in turn, fund balances defrayed predetermined classes of expenditure. Because independent administrators had jurisdiction over each fund, those who dealt with governments' finances neither comprehended the scale of spending or deficits nor exerted much influence over the disposition of state assets.

Whereas earmarking represents a merger of individualism with hierarchy, the program budgeting and zero-base budgeting of the 1960s and 1970s reflect different social orders. By erasing lines of authority in favor of activities supporting broad objectives, program budgeting is designed to facilitate competition. The costs and benefits of alternative programs are presented, and, ideally, the most effective arrangements, in terms of their return, are chosen. It is not the mix of resources that matters—any combination is acceptable—but only effectiveness. Resources have no intrinsic merit but only an instrumental value—the rate of return. It is no secret—indeed, this is its avowed rationale—that program budgeting is based on economic models embodying market processes. Program budgeting is part of the rationale for a society of competitive individualism whose political manifestation is in a market regime.

The ideal budgetary form for sectarian regimes, by contrast, is zero-base budgeting. For one thing, this approach—taking nothing for granted, as if the budget were born yesterday—is perfectly suited for attacking existing relationships. In concept, all the products of social understandings reached over long periods of time are to be swept away. No ancestors, no dead hand of the past imposing distinctions (read "line items") on the future, no social order. What could be better suited to sectarians who wish to reject established order than a budgetary form presupposing that the world is to be made anew every year?

A society organized on a voluntary basis would have to reject line-item budgeting as redolent of hierarchy. A major innovation in the history of finance, dating back to the nineteenth century, the line-item budget is still the most common method of expenditure budgeting. The lines have sums attached and contain separate items specifying the object of the proposed spending. Each line may be a different expenditure. Currently the main criticism of this approach is that the items reflect organizational needs, such as operations, maintenance, and personnel, rather than the broad purposes the spending is supposed to serve. But this is to confuse hierarchies with markets. For line-item budgeting is the form par excellence of the hierarchy. The more lines there are, the finer the differentiation among them, the better they mirror the division of labor within the bureaucracy and, by extension, the roles and statuses the regime is trying to maintain.

Each political culture generates its characteristic budgetary objectives—productivity in market regimes, redistribution in sects, and detailed procedures in hierarchies. Under *exploitative budgeting* in a fatalistic regime, rulers seek to maximize the surplus of revenue produced by their fatalist subjects. In *productivity budgeting* within a market regime, it is the ability of money to make money, or to spend the least for a given objective, that counts in decision-making. *Redistributive budgeting* in sectarian regimes aims not at a substantive outcome, but at the equalization of society's goods. And the *procedural budgeting* common to hierarchies seeks the correct form, based on the belief that the proper division of labor and specialization alone will produce the right results. In a hierarchy, how budgeting is done (how the game is played) matters as much as what is accomplished (who wins). Budget rituals, such as the medieval rite of the exchequer, with its minuetlike moves, reinforce the rightfulness of a hierarchical regime by encapsulating its principles.

Members of market regimes favor economic growth, so long as they can compete for the benefits; participants in a sectarian regime favor equal shares, even if everyone receives less than under an alternative budgetary process. Whereas sectarian regimes are interested in promises of equality (pre-audit in modern parlance), hierarchies care more about post-audit to determine whether rules have been followed, and market regimes are in perpetual audit for productivity. Budgetary procedures in market regimes are flexible, but the demand for productivity is not: "What have you done for me lately?" is the perennial query.

THE BUDGETARY BASE AS A MANIFESTATION
OF SOCIAL ORDER

If a budget both reflects and justifies its political regime, as we contend, then its boundaries should guard that order. This is the significance of the budgetary base, the largest part of the budget, the bulk of which is protected from serious scrutiny. Outside the base, everything is up for grabs, except for small additions or subtractions.[6] On the budgetary base, therefore, rest the political pillars of society. An across-the-board attack on the budgetary base is equivalent to a revolution. Breaching the budget is equivalent to opening the boundaries of the social contract to renegotiation. The fundamental priorities of the regime—who will be taxed how much for which purposes—are turned upside down. Governments, therefore, seek to sanctify major sources of revenue and items of expenditures.

In modern governments there are three kinds of budgetary boundaries: between the size of the state and the size of the economy, between revenue and expenditure, and among sources of income and items of spending. Let us begin with items of spending, because the dividing lines are clear—drawn in, as it were, since mankind first learned to write.

The base is nondiscretionary spending, a manifestation of social agreement on essentials. But if that is all there is, no more and no less, budgets would be predetermined; last year's budget, a rough approximation of the base, would be the same as this year's. Resource allocation, however, rests on discretionary income and expenditures, monies that might be raised or spent, or not, depending on circumstances. This slack (as resources in excess of immediate needs are called in the organizational literature) has to be given relative ranking. These increments are the stuff of ordinary budgetary dispute.

There are regimes, however, whose members lack discretionary income, and who, therefore, do not budget in the ordinary sense of acquiring or allocating resources. In fatalistic regimes, the rules are not made by the members but for them. Just as there are no social boundaries for them to maintain, there are no boxes or niches or line items of revenue or expenditure. The people take what comes. Their culture is timeless; there is no marked separation between the days and the year, no past or future, only the present. There is no saving, no anticipation of tomorrow. The social experience necessary to make a budget, i.e., periodically to relate income to outgo or to divide each into component parts, is missing. Therefore, we cannot describe these nonexistent budgetary processes.

From no real budgeting under the grip of fatalism, we move to the competitive budgets of market regimes. Their form is to be formless: all transactions are permissible. The base shifts with each new bargain. Programs compete, and winners attract more discretionary resources. Budgeting in market regimes is like riding a roller coaster—fun if you stay on, awful if you fall off.

Boundaries make good budgets, we might say with apologies to Robert Frost, but a lack of internal rules does not. Because the division of labor elevates some people above others, and specialization suggests that some people know more than others, sectarian regimes reject all social demarcations except those separating the good (i.e., the equal shares) from the bad (the hierarchical or market budget). Sects oppose the budgetary base in total and by item because it conserves the existing order.

Hierarchy is the home of the budgetary base. Interaction in society establishes a base that is as well defined as its social structure. There ought to be and there is a list of priorities for taxing and spending. Hence the entire base, each and every item, is supported. But if hierarchy cannot be reevaluated, resources cannot be reallocated. Absent adaptation, the economy runs down. Conflict accumulates. The budget becomes petrified. If hierarchy clones itself, social rigidity may lead to rigor mortis of the budgetary process.

REGIMES ARE PART OF WHAT WE SELECT IN CHOOSING RATIONALITY

We postulate a variety of societal objectives attached to different ways of life, objectives that change as the composition of political regimes changes. To say that revenue is maximized is to say nothing about who pays or whether the proceeds will go mainly to certain private individuals, or will be distributed to equalize citizens' income, or will accrue largely to those who control government. Since who pays and who receives matter a good deal, the allotment of revenue and expenditure reacts upon budgetary objectives. Minimizing revenue may be the most rational course for sectarians who fear that governmental power will be used against them or who are concerned that they cannot distribute the proceeds evenly enough to avoid rampant envy—a disintegrative force in an egalitarian social order. Not knowing whether they will have equal opportunity to claim government funds, members of a market regime, by contrast, may choose to diminish the role of collective authority so as to leave more resources in private hands. To allow only a single budgetary objective is to impoverish political as well as budgetary life.

One can, as many do, conceive of government as run by a single ruler, or set of rulers, who seek to maximize revenue. The task then is to get other people to support the ruling authority in the style to which he or they would like to be accustomed. In the cut-and-thrust of budgetary maneuver, this ruler-versus-ruled, two-person game has a certain plausibility. But as soon as the constraints imposed by mutual interaction become evident, simplicity yields to complex social games. What can our ever hungry rulers do? As with expansive ancient empires or nations in Europe during the mercantilist era, they can seek to increase national wealth so as to have a larger revenue base. But then they must restrain their appetites lest they devour the goose before it delivers its gold. Rulers can reduce costs of revenue collection. Whichever way they go, however, whether toward multiplying the number of state collectors (who themselves have to be supported), or by farming out taxes to others (who may become rivals or generate tax revolts), the anticipated effects on the regime through which they rule restrains their behavior. Even in subsistence economies, rulers can increase revenue sources through conquest. Yet wars often cost more than they bring in.

Enforcing compliance is costly; thus rulers seek voluntary compliance. Another term for such consent is *legitimate authority*. Certainly, if citizens vest rulers with the right to tax and spend in their behalf, without demanding special privileges, the budget game is easier. How to achieve beneficial mutuality is the subject of social-contract theories.

The most cursory account of expenditure and taxation at virtually any period of history (pick a page in the following chapters and see) reveals frustrated rulers and distressed citizens. There is hardly an equivalence between benefits received and taxes paid, or, at least, few will admit to it. Yet the inequities, for the most part, are accepted; tax revolts are relatively rare. Either the alternative, if one exists, is regarded as worse or members of polities do accept the right of others to rule over them. How can this be?

In an effort to rescue rational-choice theory in public finance, Margaret Levi observes that

> The recognition of exploitation, that is, the recognition that the contract is unfair, does not in itself precipitate efforts to redress the

wrong. Action is possible only when the exploited party perceives a way to do better, when it has both an alternative vision of the distribution of goods and when it has the capacity to act to attain that vision.[7]

An advance has been made: "alternative vision[s] of the distribution of goods" have been introduced into the picture. This is not far from, indeed it is very close to, meaning different ways of life.

The postulate of revenue maximization cannot explain why people stick so long to what social critics perceive as bad bargains.[8] We think people make smaller choices in the context of larger ones; they see that their budgetary choices are intertwined with their choices of how to govern and be governed, i.e., how to live. Alternatives are important because the choice is not between something and nothing but between rival regimes. The scope of what is being pursued has widened; the "interests" of the actors now include their political regime.

MODELS AS MAPS

Why is a budgetary process the way it is at a certain time and place? Because, we will answer, political regimes are the way they are. No one, we hope, will expect us to provide a universal theory of social and political change. Rather, we will try to relate changes in regime to changes in budgeting. By employing a common form of cultural accounting throughout the book, we hope to make changes in one era comparable to those in another.

The fact that the primary political cultures can be found virtually everywhere does not signify that they are equally important at any specific time and place. Religious sects emerged during the Middle Ages, for instance. As doctrinal deviations from the dominant hierarchy, such sects (whose members were labeled heretics by the prevailing social order) either rejected society or were rejected by it, so that they exercised no substantial political power. (In time, however, some heresies did provoke change in hierarchy's ways.)

Hierarchy has always been with us, apparently, but the ever present, life-encompassing hierarchies of ancient societies are a long way from the barely recognizable, limited, secular hierarchies Tocqueville found when he visited the United States in the 1830s. And while market relationships are ubiquitous even when formally outlawed, there is a big difference between their dominant role in, say, the United States after the Civil War, or among Scottish entrepreneurs of the eighteenth and nineteenth centuries, and their sub-rosa existence in socialist states of eastern Europe today. Fatalism is not common in highly developed societies in which affluence and diversity create abundant options for individuals, but when linked with hierarchy in past ages, it was the dominant way of life for most people.

Our models allow for change over the long run. But the models do not predict where change will occur, or what that change will be. Any specific culture *may* or it *may not* be strong at particular times and places. The variety of thought and behavior encompassed by the cultures serves to accommodate the diversity of political regimes—wherever and whenever these occur. In this way, while allowing for different combinations of cultures at specific moments in time, a single set of categories can be used to characterize social life in all historical periods.

The terrain we will traverse in this book is detailed; the reader badly needs a map. Look at these models of political regimes and budgetary processes as guides to the historical canvas that follows. When the directions are reasonably accurate, we will know where we are and why. When they lead us astray, we will ask whether we have failed to follow the map, or whether it needs to be redrawn.

The plethora of detail inherent in a history of taxation and expenditure, albeit limited merely to the Western world, does make one wonder what can be learned from so fine-grained an account, other than the fact that taxing and spending are complicated. For each period, the reader can find out how governments raised revenues, what they did with the income, and what, so far as the record will allow, the consequences were for the regimes involved. We will lay out the historical context so as to offer understanding of how the participants in budgeting perceived their situation and, therefore, why they may have behaved as they did.

Since we do not claim privileged access to the minds of the dead, any more than do the historians on whom we rely, our imaginative reconstruction may well be challenged. Certainly it is only one of many possible interpretations. Scholars with interests different from ours might well find another meaning.

We have superimposed on historical events a theory of the relationships between budgets and regimes. Yet there are no sects or hierarchies lying thick on the ground, any more than there are masses or classes. The world as we know it consists of individuals. We see them as making choices, when they are allowed, between existing authority and some alternative, the aggregate result being patterns of budgetary action that occur as if the individuals were implicated in one or another political regime.

Here it is, then, three times removed from reality: a history woven of

TABLE 3

BUDGETARY CULTURES

	Individualism	Egalitarianism	Collectivism
Social Order			
Criterion of Judgment	productivity	equality	legality
Type of Equality	opportunity	result	before the law
Blame	individual	system	deviant
Economic Growth:			
Desirability and Achievement	yes, high	no, low	yes, but medium
Political Regime	**Markets**	**Sects**	**Hierarchies**
Power	noncentralized	shared	centralized
Authority	avoided	rejected	accepted
Objective	to increase differences	to reduce differences	to maintain differences
Budgetary Process			
Criterion of Choice	results	redistribution	procedure
Agreement on Base	high on totals; low on items	low on totals and items	high on totals and items
Taxes	low	medium	high
Spending	high personal, low public	low personal; high public	high on public and personal
Responsibility	by program	by system	by position
Auditing	perpetual audit	pre-audit	post-audit
Strategy	minimize expenditure and revenue	redistribute resources	maximize revenue and expenditure
Deficits	low	high	medium

events, some of which may be wrongly reported and others that were probably omitted; reconstructions that in other hands would look somewhat different; and analysis by means of intellectual constructs. Surely, we change history as we write it. Our imposition upon history, hypothesizing relationships between budgetary patterns and political cultures, is summarized and expanded in Table 3. The question is whether this threefold alchemy turns a golden subject into brass or whether it offers some advantages in interrogating history.

Chapter Two

FINANCE WITHOUT MONEY: BUDGETING IN THE ANCIENT WORLD

The king was the state. He was its ruler, spiritual, temporal and financial. Between royal private pocket and public purse there was but small distinction. "The Treasury is the root of kings,"[1] speaks an ancient maxim of Hindu political theory. Another maxim hammers home that "the Treasury, and not the physical body of the king is . . . the real king."[2] Financial administration and government, therefore, are inseparable.[3] The ruler cannot survive without getting—and spending. Many basic conflicts of financial administration are already visible in ancient times. Because taxation and budgeting are ubiquitous state functions whose character can be traced through different ages, cultures, and polities, the problems of getting and spending are among the best-known to mankind.

In the beginning there was no money. Taxes were paid in kind—grains, cattle, cloth, labor, and valuable objects—to support the priest-kings, their families, attendants, armies, and officials. Goods were transported to the king's treasury by primitive means—riverboats, and the backs of animals and men. The royal storehouses were watched over by hordes of officials who weighed, measured, and stole whenever they could. When money appeared, a new, dual economy of coin and kind involved the state in systematic assay. It also demanded a standardized basis of exchange and a method of converting from one system to another.

The king could not live without taxes, and his subjects could not easily live with them. Although a wise ruler should draw a fine line between sufficient income and intolerable demands on those who bear the brunt of his exactions, there is no evidence that ancient kings did so. But kings do need trustworthy men as tax collectors. Now, a tax collector's very function tempts him to cheat. Therefore ancient kings developed complex devices for assuring honesty in their officials —mechanisms that also might make it hard for honest men to perform their task expeditiously.

To check administrative excess, the king might multiply officials to watch over one another. The result could be an unwieldy bureaucracy—with a spirit of its own resisting the royal will—so large and complex that the king has difficulty understanding what is going on. The extent to which he governs it or it governs him becomes problematic.

If everything actually reaches royal storehouses, the king is better able to control his income and its disbursement. Primitive transportation, however, results in extensive spoilage and pilfering. When goods are needed back in the provinces, it may be difficult to move them in time or to avoid the double losses inherent in coming and going. The alternative to centralization was to establish provincial government storehouses and appoint officials to guard them. Problems of transportation and spoilage might then be eased, but decentralization itself makes for new woes. If external attack threatens, state-appointed local officials may not be able or willing to provide adequate defense and the province might be lost. The weakened central government then would be subject to attack. Also, provincial officials could easily slough off dependence on and fealty to the king. They might become advocates of the local inhabitants against the king, or feel they can steal with greater impunity. Having sent a servant to outlying regions, the king one day might find himself faced with a rival for power. Despotism contains the seeds of hierarchy if the government stays together, or of a competitive regime if it splits apart. The ancient king's men either became part of his hierarchy, accepting his rule but imposing constraints upon it, or they refused his rule, bargaining for themselves, by themselves.

The structure of financial administration that appeared repeatedly in the ancient civilizations we have surveyed resulted from parallel efforts to solve such problems, common to them all. Governments of the Mesopotamian city-states beginning in the third millennium B.C., ancient Egypt and Crete (3100–1100 B.C.), Mauryan India (300 B.C.–A.D. 200), China during the Shang (1523–1027 B.C.) and Han (200 B.C.–A.D. 200) dynasties, Japan up to the nineteenth century, the Bronze Age civilizations of sub-Sahara Africa (A.D. 300–1500), and the classical Inca civilization in Peru (A.D. 1200–1532) all had well-developed and quite similar systems of financial administration. Widely dispersed in space and time, these governments produced similar solutions to the problems of supporting monarchs. Similar kinds of taxes were levied, administered in similar ways; the funds were used for like purposes; and similar attempts were made to guard against fraud and theft. With a common political culture of despotism—a regime of arbitrary rule by masters over fatalistic subjects—these ancient civilizations had similar patterns of budgeting.*

How did government financial policy reflect a monarch's goals? To what extent did taxpayers, tax collectors, and financial officials act successfully on their own terms or those of their rulers (which were not necessarily the same)? Where were the points of tension in administrative structures, and what were the means by which conflict was resolved? We shall describe financial administration in the centralized governments of the ancient world, as well as the decentralized, partly autonomous administrative system that repeatedly appeared as the central authority collapsed from internal overload and/or external attack.

BACKGROUND CONDITIONS

THE SOCIETIES

Against the dominant Neolithic pattern of small settlements populated by farmers and herdsmen, man's first town or city civilization arose in the Near East about 3600 B.C.[5] The fertile valleys of the Nile and the Tigris and Euphrates rivers produced several societies based on the productivity that resulted from using bronze. The civilizations of Egypt and the various Mesopotamian city-states, characterized by specialization of function and division of labor, achieved a high level of artistic, material, and cognitive achievement, in representational art, monumental architecture, and written language and literature.

Despite an active trade among the ancient Near East civilizations,

* There is no monograph on financial administration in the ancient world. For the earliest period, the available information is scattered and fragmentary. The raw data for historians and archaeologists consist in part of monumental evidence, carvings and inscriptions on the temples and pyramids that have either survived or been excavated. A limited amount of documentary evidence exists in the form of cuneiform tablets and papyrus documents of state. Scholars have deciphered and interpreted these materials, to reconstruct a general image of government in those ancient times. Our coverage of the financial practices of ancient governments is derivative, based solely on these secondary sources. But since our purpose is to study general trends, to explore the evolution of financial administration in different countries under roughly similar conditions, our work does not require complete information about any single empire.[4]

TABLE 4
CHRONOLOGY FOR ANCIENT FINANCE[6]

Civilization	Dates
Ancient Near East	
City-States	
Sumer	c. 3500 B.C.
Lagash	c. 2300 B.C.
Uruk	2700–2500 B.C.
Akkad	3000–2400 B.C.
Empires	
Babylonia	1800–1600 B.C.
Assyria	1100–600 B.C.
Egypt	
Old Kingdom	3100–2181 B.C.
Middle Kingdom	2150–1786 B.C.
New Kingdom	1561–1166 B.C.
Crete	
Minoan	2100–1400 B.C.
Mycenaean	1400–1100 B.C.
Indus Valley	
Mohenjo-Daro and Harappa	2500–1500 B.C.
Mauryan India	300 B.C.–A.D. 200
Hebrew Kingdoms	1020–925 B.C.
China	
Shang Dynasty	1523–1027 B.C.
Chou Dynasty (western)	1027–771 B.C.
Chou Dynasty (eastern)	770–256 B.C.
Warring States period (feudal)	403–221 B.C.
Chin Dynasty	221–207 B.C.
Han Dynasty	200 B.C.–A.D. 200
Tang Dynasty	600–900 A.D.
Central and South America	
Inca	A.D. 1200–1532
Aztec	A.D. 1300–1500
Central African Kingdoms (various)	A.D. 300–1500

their economies were essentially agricultural.* The city-states and empires of Old Kingdom Egypt (3100–2181 B.C.), Sumer and Lagash in Babylonia (3500–2300 B.C.), Assyria (1100–600 B.C.), Mycenaean Crete (1400–1100 B.C.), Shang China, and Mauryan India consisted of a number of loosely connected agricultural settlements (each one no larger than a small village), joined by tribal and religious allegiance or

* Hartmut Schmoekel notes that over nine-tenths of the cuneiform documents from ancient Mesopotamia known today are concerned with economic matters, attesting to the liveliness of the commercial life.[7]

by the bonds of political submission to a central settlement where the ruler lived. By modern standards the capital cities were small, with probably no more than thirty thousand persons.* Populations of noblemen, priests, warriors, and slaves in such cities were supported by agriculture enhanced by irrigation. Building and maintaining dikes and canals were important state-supported activities in Egypt, China, the civilization of the Indus Valley, and the Mesopotamian city-states.[10] Many scholars attribute the social and economic differentiation in the Bronze Age civilizations, and even the emergence of governmental institutions, to the organization necessary for developing suitable irrigation systems.

Most people lived on the land. Where there was no irrigation, peasants and slaves tilled the soil for a meager output; at best their efforts yielded only a small annual surplus, and all too often there were crop failures that brought real famine.[11] The population was young; infant mortality was high; illness and accident were common; and life expectancies were low.[12] Housing was primitive, and most men lived mean, hard, and hazardous lives, close to the edge of subsistence.

Time was conceptualized as circular. Life was lived from day to day under the protection of the primal deity, represented by the priest-king, and by a panoply of lesser, local gods believed to determine each man's fate. Ancient kings were quasi-religious figures akin to gods on earth; a pervasive belief in the supernatural clothed them with authority.

Communication between various parts of the ancient empires was limited. Navigable waterways, where they existed—in Egypt, parts of Mesopotamia, and China—were the principal means of communication between provinces and central capital. When drought or flood impeded navigation, communication was disrupted. Invention of the spoked wheel during the second millennium B.C. made very little difference. Wheeled vehicles could be used to transport tax grain from one district to another—as in China and India during the first millennium B.C.—only in dry seasons. When rain or snow mired the rutted

* Schmoekel estimates that the average population of the earliest Mesopotamian towns of the mid–third millennium B.C. was 17,000.[8] Other scholars have based their estimates on textual references and on projections that assume an occupancy ratio of six to ten persons per occupied dwelling in excavated areas (the present density in Middle Eastern cities). This technique produces reasonable estimates for the smaller cities. For Ur, estimates have yielded populations of 24,000; for Sumer, 36,000; Lagash, 19,000; and the provincial towns Umma and Khafajah, 16,000 and 12,000. Frankfurt's estimate of 360,-000 for Ur seems unreasonable in view of the supply technology that existed then.[9]

wagon tracks, outlying districts were isolated for long periods. With physical isolation came loss of control; often a government tax collector was the only regular contact between provinces and center.*

A surplus was essential to support the government. Some ancient monarchs, like the Egyptian pharaohs of the Old Kingdom, who were richly endowed with fertile land, could live off their estates and were relatively self-sufficient. If personal holdings also included mines, precious metals could fortify a king's independence.

Although the relationship between crown and temple changed over time, the early priest-kings and the temples profited from monopolies over foreign trade; from domestic enterprises, such as stone quarrying, that provided raw material for major construction; and from sale of such essential commodities as salt and oil. In the ancient Middle Eastern civilizations and in Mauryan India, palace and temple also conducted a large lending business. In Mesopotamia, beginning in the third millennium B.C., the temples and the kings regularly leased seed, cattle and surplus land to cultivators in exchange for interest, paid in kind, of one-sixth to one-seventh of the harvest.[14]† Besides these conventional businesses, Mesopotamian kings derived a regular income from temple prostitutes.[15] Victory in war frequently yielded lavish tribute to supplement royal wealth. The indemnities—paid in food, textiles and furs, precious metals and jewels, draft animals, and prisoners who became slaves—helped to maintain the king's extensive religious and household retinue, and the army that insured his control of the population.[16]

Because not all kings were wealthy and not all wars were successful, very early in the history of civilization ancient kings came to rely on tax payments. Offerings of personal service or of food and supplies, as occasional voluntary gifts to propitiate the gods, in time became systematic contributions supporting the temples and the imperial household. These offerings were the taxes of the ancient world.[17] In districts where money was unknown or uncommon, taxes were assessed as a proportion of the produce of the land and paid in kind. At first these payments supplemented the king's income from his own lands and

* In China, early in the Han Dynasty, the length of wagon axles was standardized to permit wagons bearing grain paid as taxes to travel from outlying districts to the provincial centers where the emperor's storehouses were located. Since the ruts the wagons created varied with axle width, and this differed by district, standardization facilitated transport.[13]

† In the languages of ancient Mesopotamia and Egypt the same word signified *calves, to give birth,* and *interest.*

mines, and from the profits of royal monopolies over production and sale of essential commodities. Later these taxes came to be the priest-king's principal source of support.

In an economy without money a man also could discharge his tax obligation by providing a ruler with personal service. Ancient kings who accepted such payment in human labor were solving several problems at once. Corvée, the compulsory-labor tax of the ancient world, was first of all a visible demonstration of personal loyalty to the king. But more important, corvée provided a dependable method of recruitment: the king always was assured of men to serve as soldiers, to labor on the royal estates or in the king's mines, and to build and maintain dikes and canals for irrigation, and temples and monuments to the king and the gods. By providing a steady flow of personnel to the palace, corvée reduced uncertainty for the king and helped to insure his control.

This picture of a government that manages its financial affairs solely through personal obligation combined with barter is somewhat over-simplified. Archaeological evidence indicates that in several Mesopotamian city-states a parallel economy of money and barter existed as far back as the third millennium B.C. While barter or exchange of services prevailed in agricultural districts, various types of money did simplify transactions in cities and towns.* During the reign of Hammurabi of Babylon, the state levied taxes in coin in the cities, and at equivalent rates measured in kind in rural districts.[18] As a circulating coinage of stable value became established throughout the ancient world by the middle of the first millennium B.C., parallel payment of money and kind became common.

Many different civilizations—the Bronze Age civilization of Egypt during the Old (3100–2181 B.C.) and Middle (2150–1786 B.C.) kingdoms; China during the Shang and Han dynasties; Minoan Crete (2400–1400 B.C.); Mycenaean Greece; the Sumerian city-states of southern Mesopotamia; and the more recent Bronze Age cultures of pre-Columbian Central America (A.D. 300–1500) and sub-Sahara Africa (A.D. 300–1500)—operated under this barter-plus-service mode of budgeting. But even in the ancient civilizations where money existed, agriculture remained predominant. For this reason we treat government finance of this period as if the state received its entire revenue in kind.

Fiscal management was cumbersome and costly. Where taxes were paid in commodities, the government had to establish common units of

---

* See the appendix to this chapter, "Transactions in Barter and Money."

measure[19] and determine equivalent rates for one commodity in exchange for another. At any time and place, rates of exchange—in commodities or from commodities to money—might be the result of custom; yet, in an economy of periodic scarcity, there was a tendency for rates to rise or fall over time along with variations in agricultural productivity. Powerful kings, such as Hammurabi of Babylon, intervened to stabilize rates by issuing decrees of compulsory valuation.[20] Whether the price and wage maxima established by various ancient kings did help commerce is problematic, but they did protect government revenues against loss due to inflation.

Food grains were the commonest medium for tax payments; in the civilizations we have surveyed, taxes were levied on produce of the land at traditional rates in each locality. Taxes also were paid in other commodities—at different times and places, furs, felt, linen and silk cloth, fruit, honey, salt, base and precious metals, jewels, horses, cattle, and produce of merchants and artisans.[21] The initial function of regular levies was to reduce uncertainty by providing a constant supply of grain for the imperial household, for the army that defended it, and for the rest of the population, in the event of famine. With the surplus accumulated during periods of peace and prosperity, the monarch enhanced his wealth by trading in the markets that grew up around temple and palace, at first exchanging surplus grain for scarce commodities, later for money.[22] As a result, fiscal management in the ancient world was largely logistical. It dealt with collection, storage, distribution, and sale of a variety of commodities. Product management, warehousing, handling, and merchandising were distinctive features of much ancient government finance.

PRIEST-KINGS

Early ancient governments were organized around a priest-king, believed to be (like the first kings of Egypt) a god himself or (like kings of the ancient Mesopotamian cities or princes of the Chinese provinces) the chief representative of the local patron god.* The king stood at the

---

* As long as the territory governed by Bronze Age states of the ancient world was geographically limited, as in Minoan Crete, or physically isolated, as in Egypt, the priest-king's divinity remained unchallenged. In the Mesopotamian city-states, where attack from barbarian tribesmen or rival cities always threatened, and in the city civilizations of the Indus Valley and China, the king could not maintain his position merely by symbolizing the gods' authority; kingship there was relatively unstable. Even in Egypt, isolated by desert from external attack for most of its history, the state's collapse during the first Intermediate period (Sixth–Tenth Dynasty, c. 2263–2050 B.C.) accelerated reassessment of the magical-divine quality of the king. After this period the pharaoh was viewed more as a political functionary than as a god.[23]

apex of a truncated pyramid of state and society. Assisted by a small group of priests and personal favorites drawn from the nobility, the king ruled over a small population of artisans and merchants and a broad base of landless laborers, many of them slaves. As deity, religious leader, chief civil official, and giver and interpreter of laws, ancient priest-kings were the earliest dictators ruling over a theocratic-authoritarian state. Laws, based on traditional practices, could be modified only by powerful monarchs with undisputed authority. The earliest ancient governments made no distinction between the king's private role and his function as high priest of the sacred temple and/or head of state. According to his skill and strength the king supervised administration, established and executed policy, and was principal beneficiary of the government's accomplishments. King and state were so interlinked that the king's private welfare and the public good were synonymous. Nor was there any distinction between his private wealth and the public purse. The wealth of the realm and all taxes and tribute owing to it belonged to the gods, the temple, and the king. This is the pure version of the despotic regime.

The power of the ancient priest-kings varied with their personalities, the skill of their advisers, the valor of their armies, the extent of external attack, and the exigencies of climate and local agricultural output. The legendary kings of the ancient world—Urukagina of Lagash (early twenty-third century B.C.); Sargon of Akkad (2350–2300 B.C.); Hammurabi of Babylon (1792–1750 B.C.); the Egyptian Pharaohs Harmhab (1349–1319 B.C.), Thutmose III (fifteenth century B.C.), and Amenhotep III (1417–1379 B.C.) of the Eighteenth Dynasty; and the Emperor Asoka (274–232 B.C.) of Mauryan India—were strong monarchs who governed during periods of expansion and internal prosperity.

All the ancient civilizations we studied had to defend their borders repeatedly against neighboring tribes and migrating people, sometimes succumbing to invaders. Most ancient civilizations went through a period of imperialistic expansion. Some ancient governments were more militaristic than others; the Assyrians engaged in continuous warfare, for example, while the ancient Egyptians waged few wars of external conquest.* Old and Middle Kingdom Egypt evidently had only a

* Unlike their Assyrian conquerors, Babylonian kings seldom engaged in warfare. Their stone cylinder seals record and extol their peaceful accomplishments—construction of temples, canals, walls, and monuments. Assyria, in contrast, was highly militarized, with an army of over 200,000 warriors.[24]

small mercenary army–police force of Libyans and Nubians, led on military expeditions, when necessary, by civil officials. Only under the New Kingdom Empire did the state develop a full-fledged standing army and officer corps. Most ancient monarchs stood at the head of large standing armies that insured continued control of the government when it was not actually engaged in war. Support of the military in food and supplies was the ancient government's principal expense.

Crimes against society were viewed as crimes against the gods as well as the king,[25] as were treachery against the king's person or theft of his personal or state property. Offenses were punished by retribution; men who stole from kings faced punitive fines, torture, or execution by harsh methods.[26]

Land was the basis of wealth in all ancient societies, and in principle all land belonged to the gods and their chief representatives, the priest-kings. Palace and temple were therefore the largest landowners in ancient civilizations, their holdings at first not distinct from one another.

The temple, in early theocratic governments, was a financial center as well as the center of worship.[27] Its economic activities resulted in revenues that substantially increased the priest-king's wealth. Elements of competitive individualism existed. Temple lands were rented to small cultivators to produce a regular income. Within their walls the temples formed self-sufficient economic units where artisans practiced their crafts and traders bought and sold commodities. The king and the priests commanded a share of each transaction for the temple treasury in exchange for protection and trading privileges. As ancient governments developed a system of money, kings sometimes also served as bankers. To the unfortunate subjects whose need was pressing enough for them to pay the normal interest of 20 to 30 percent a year, the temple and the king would willingly lend surplus funds.[28]

Over the millennia, at different times and places, a gradual separation of temple and palace came about; and with this began the distinction between the temple's wealth and the king's private hoard.[29] The city-states of Mesopotamia, early in the third millennium, gradually established separate treasuries. Since land was the primary source of wealth, this meant separating palace lands from temple holdings. The Mesopotamian priest-kings slowly secularized extensive portions of communal land that earlier had belonged to the gods and the temple. This land was cultivated to supply food only for the palace. The king could also use his holdings to reward faithful service with grants. As land grants were divided among heirs in parts of Mesopotamia, private ownership became common and land later became a marketable commodity.[30]

Kings often demanded contributions of food and supplies from temple stores after palace and temple holdings were separated; in time these contributions became a regular tax. Division of financial authority between the two separate storehouses—in effect two treasuries, the temple's and the king's—made for periodic tension. Although priest-kings continued to act as the temple's chief administrators, the lesser priesthood tried repeatedly to obtain exemptions from royal demands. (Occasionally pious kings such as Urukagina and Gudea of Lagash tried to reduce taxes and reunite temple and palace holdings, but their efforts were exceptions to the general trend.[31]) At the same time, the minor landowners who were independent of temple and king sometimes attenuated the king's newfound authority. While they usually supported the king, ambitious noblemen sometimes aligned themselves with the lesser priests to gain exemptions from the king's taxes or even to usurp control. During the last half of the second millennium B.C., several cities in Babylonia and Assyria obtained royal charters of exemption from corvée and taxes.[32]

In Egypt, unlike Mesopotamia, separation between palace and temple resulted from steady enlargement of temple holdings. In theory the divine pharaoh owned all the land of Egypt. But successive generations of pharaohs, trying to secure their position in the afterlife, made generous gifts of land to the temples built adjacent to the pyramids that would entomb their bodies.[33] The distinction between the government treasury and the monarch's private wealth, as well as between temple and state, appeared by the middle of the second millennium B.C. Early in the Twelfth Dynasty of Middle Kingdom Egypt, for example, a provincial prince had relations with three independent treasuries—the temple's, the province's and his own—and three separate contracts specifying the treasures he wished buried with him.[34]

By the end of the second millennium B.C., about one-fifth of the country's land had been given to the temples in this way. By then the Temple of Amon at Thebes had become the country's second-largest landowner, rivaling the crown itself in wealth.[35] Though the Egyptian priesthood was formally subservient to the king, the high priest repeatedly intervened in court affairs and tried to win exemptions from royal taxes. A regime of despotism ruled by a single, simple hierarchy began to be modified by relationships among more complex (because more numerous) hierarchies.

The Centralized State, Bureaucracy, and Financial Administration

At* any one time, governmental institutions, like the monumental sculpture surviving from ancient Egypt and Mesopotamia, appeared to be unchanging. Once established, administrative techniques tended to persist for centuries with only minor alterations.[36] Yet just as water and wind gradually eroded ancient structures, so, too, did administrative practices of ancient governments change—slowly, on a time scale calibrated in centuries and millennia.

Although change was slow, during much of their history all the ancient governments we studied were internally unstable, and all were continuously vulnerable to external disturbances. The sporadic innovations in financial administration were attempts to establish a stable basis of expectations in an environment that had recently changed.[37]

How an administrative system is organized depends on what must be accomplished to support the regime and what can be done with existing technology. In early Egypt and Mesopotamia when temple and government were synonymous, a highly organized system of financial administration was unnecessary. The priest-king maintained himself, the lesser priests and his followers with produce of the royal domain. Voluntary donations brought to the temple by residents of nearby land supplemented royal production.* Temple priests had only to collect the offerings from the altar. Perishable gifts doubtless were consumed immediately, the remainder deposited in storehouses for later use. During prosperous times offerings were regular, predictable, and sometimes so plentiful as to produce a surplus. When harvests failed, however, the king could reverse the direction of contribution, drawing on stored surplus to provide food for the hungry or seed grain for the next sowing. Even after voluntary contributions had become compulsory taxes, the financial administration of ancient theocracies was inseparable from either the temple or the king's household; it was simple, personal and direct.

---

* In remote parts of the world ancient practices persist today and men still bring gifts of food to the gods. In a small Catholic church in the Guatemalan highlands one of the authors watched an Indian woman kneeling over an improvised altar where she had laid out an offering of maize, squash, and fruit shaped to represent a child. There, as in isolated districts throughout the world, the church's conventional ritual is a thin veneer over native people's animistic beliefs and practices, and "formal Catholicism reaches only to the eighth row." Demonstrating its flexibility, the church accepts devotion however it is offered and permits native people to follow the ways of their ancestors with only minor changes.[38]

The territorial range a ruler can govern effectively depends to a considerable extent on existing technology. The essential requirements are conceptual and mechanical. Legal codes and bureaucracy are both based on prior invention of written language. A system of numeration and mathematical calculation, enabling governmental officials to maintain administrative and historical continuity by keeping written records, was a prerequisite of bureaucratic control.[39] Simple mechanical inventions in communications, and improved methods of transporting people and goods from one place to another also affected an ancient government's effective administrative domain. Records written with quill on papyrus or parchment were easier to prepare, lighter, and more durable than those incised with stylus onto clay tablets; and records written with pen or brush on paper were simpler yet, although not always more durable. When improved methods of transportation shortened the time distance between settlements, ancient kings could control a wider territory. The spoked wheel, saddles and harnesses for pack animals, the lightweight chariot, and the parallel development of stable, broad-beamed sailing ships, all may not have increased contact immediately; but the combined effect over hundreds of years, diffusing slowly from place to place, was increased accessibility among previously isolated regions.[40]

Administrative techniques for financial management of government were first invented, we surmise, when the range of fiscal tasks increased beyond the king's personal capacity to control them. With the primitive transportation and communications available, a monarch's effective geographic control was limited by the distance a man could walk in a day. Beyond that range men would not carry gifts to the temple. If the king needed contributions, he would have to send agents out into the countryside to claim them.

When the king separated himself from the temple and established an independent power base, he was often able to enlarge the territory he controlled. If the king had a strong army, territorial expansion might result from successful forays against weaker city-states nearby. The conquered people then would live too far from the new king to bring him gifts, and, in any case, they might prefer to maintain allegiance to their traditional gods and would continue to deliver offerings to local priests who had granted them favors in the past.[41]

If a government grew beyond its effective communications range, there were several possible outcomes (which we can reconstruct only by conjecture, since no records survive). In some cases, physical expansion may have so reduced voluntary donations that the king was forced to adopt a compulsory tax system. But such a geographically dispersed territory required a far greater organization than the relatively few officials needed to handle collection, storage and distribution of voluntary offerings from a limited area. If the subject people spoke a different dialect or language, collection might be further complicated by the need for interpreters.

Archaeological evidence from Mesopotamia reveals that the earliest compulsory taxes were tithes, levies assessed on a fixed proportion of the total crop, based on some official's estimate of what a man had harvested. A man who took gifts to the temple gave only what he could spare; but when the king demanded regular payments of a specified amount, a reluctant subject's compliance could be achieved only by coercion. Thus a compulsory tax policy demanded multiplication of officials to assess and collect the crop.

Transporting produce from outlying districts to the capital created other new problems. Besides supporting a horde of officials along the way, the king needed to provide pack animals or ships. Compulsory taxation generally brought increased and more varied revenue, overloading existing granaries. To guard against mildew, rats or theft, the king was forced to enlarge both his storage capacity and the number of officials who watched over the warehouses. The early priest-kings at first may not have anticipated the effects of such new taxes, especially the administrative overload. But a conceptual adaptation began to come about; governments gradually invented new devices to maintain control of finances. Administrative organizations are the tools a government uses to accomplish its essential tasks. One might say that the ancient kings invented bureaucracy in an attempt to cope with overload; whether the bureaucracy enabled the king to govern or became the government is not known.

Yet bureaucracy in government is hardly possible without a model of stratified social relations in society. Centralized administrative structures were organizational manifestations of the hierarchical social and political structure of ancient societies. In the highly stratified New Kingdom Egyptian society, for example, "every individual was bound by the function prescribed for him within the social organization . . . in principle no one was free."[42]

Whether these hierarchical regimes were simple or complex depended on the structure of their societies. To describe the extreme examples, a powerful king of a small, isolated, and ethnically homogeneous society could maintain personal control of a centralized bureaucracy with a limited number of officials. Settlement along a limited number of navigable channels (such as are revealed by Landsat imaging of southern Iraq) served both to maintain a hierarchy of places in ancient Mesopotamia and to facilitate central governments' efforts to collect taxes.[43] Rulers of territorially dispersed, ethnically diverse territories often governed through intermediaries, adopting loosely organized administrative structures in which central control was weak or nonexistent.

Governmental bureaucracies deal with increasing environmental complexity by means of functional and geographic differentiation. When work load increases, performance may be maintained or enhanced by dividing the work among several persons. In horizontally organized systems, each official may be responsible for accomplishing all the tasks in a specific territory. Vertical organization divides administration into many subtasks, each assigned to a specialized official. He may accomplish a job alone or supervise subordinates who do the work.

In the earliest ancient governments, the first functional specialization we know about began with irrigation. In the Sumerian temple communities of southern Mesopotamia early in the third millennium B.C., in predynastic Egypt, and in Shang China, temple priests organized the human energy that created the agricultural base for city civilization.[44] Provision of irrigation facilities was an essential secular function of the ancient kings; the oldest and main job of the kings of Babylonia, for example, was to dig canals.[45] Lesser temple priests assumed a variety of specialized roles. Serving both as terrestrial intermediaries with the gods and as the king's organizing agents in the real world, such priests, so far as is known, were the first officials of ancient governments.[46]

The priest-kings of the early Mesopotamian city-states headed a varied bureaucracy. The chief administrative official, with power second only to the king's, was the *sukkal,* in charge of all civil and religious functions. Immediately beneath him were two specialized offices of equal rank. The *sanga* (high priest) was the chief religious official, responsible for the temple's sacred functions. His secular counterpart was the *nubanda,* or economic administrator, whose domain encompassed the temple's many practical problems.

The nubanda directed lesser priests whose work was still more specialized. Some acted as hydraulic engineers, directing and supervising the crews of corvée labor mobilized each year to clear the canals of silt and strengthen the dikes.[47] When the nubanda negotiated leases for temple lands, other priests who served as scribes wrote out the leases. Still others collected rent. Some priests managed temple granaries where produce from the king's own land was deposited along with payments in kind for temple leases and devotional offerings brought to the temple altar. Serving as intermediaries between the king and the people, granary priests distributed the stored surplus to the population in times of need. When the temple began to assess compulsory taxes, priests served as *maskim* (tax collectors).[48] As the king gradually established a secular government he replaced priests with a civil bureaucracy.

A bureaucracy calls for organizational procedures—to select officials and subordinates and, next, to specify what each should do. Then there must be a way to teach each person his job, and to transmit the operational and social content of each occupation from one generation of bureaucrats to the next.[49] Where authority is delegated, there must be reliable devices for insuring that each official actually accomplishes his assigned task. If an organization is to continue administering effectively, solutions to these problems must be developed and institutionalized. The problems are closely related; several are mutually interdependent. In the earliest bureaucracies of the ancient world, selection, acculturation, and training were accomplished simultaneously by co-opting officials from the noble class.

After priests, the earliest government officials were the king's close relatives. Religious doctrine dictated the ruler's choice of assistants in the theocratic government of predynastic Egypt. Because the pharaoh was believed to embody the divine spirit, only his sons were allowed direct contact with him. Egyptian princes, therefore, acted as intermediaries between the king and lesser palace attendants who communicated royal commands to the people.[50]

A ruler's religious motives for employing his own kinsmen as administrators sometimes were reinforced by expediency. When the Sumerian King Naram-Sin (2267–2230 B.C.) deposed local Mesopotamian chieftains and installed his own relatives, he was trying to make his authority acceptable to the conquered people by providing substitute rulers who might be judged to share his divinity.[51] Similarly, the Sumerian King Shulgi (2112–2052 B.C.) of Ur's Third Dynasty cemented his alliance with conquered states by marrying off his daughters to local rulers.[52] Trustworthiness was the main criterion for choosing financial officials. In the Mesopotamian kingdom of Ur, for example, the king first wrested control from temple priests by appointing his own kinsmen to the priesthood. After priests and relatives, whom else could the king trust but men from his own class? So officials of early civil bureaucracies were noblemen in the palace's inner circle.

EGYPT

The foundations of Egyptian bureaucracy were laid by the Pharaoh Djoser at the beginning of the Old Kingdom's Third Dynasty (2800–2700 B.C.). Until then princes of the royal line had performed the separate functions of religious, military, and financial administration under the king's personal supervision. Djoser enlarged the number of officials and the territory his government could control by creating a horizontally organized administrative system. He divided the kingdom into nomes (provinces), but maintained centralized control by appointing provincial representatives to the court. Some were literate men from the noble class; others were temple priests. (Unlike Mesopotamia and China, where responsibility for financial administration was secularized very early, temple priests filled important bureaucratic posts throughout ancient Egyptian history.)[53] To unify control of separate administrative functions Djoser created a supervisory role, that of grand vizier, with broadly based authority over the kingdom. Like the sukkal of early Mesopotamia, the vizier was a generalist responsible for managing the king's land and personal household as well as for judicial and financial administration. Possessing ultimate financial authority, the vizier supervised production, collection, and allocation of commodities that flowed into the monarchical treasury as taxes. Initially, princes filled the position. By the Fifth Dynasty, men not from the royal line began to be appointed as viziers and to many subordinate positions.[54]

How were noblemen chosen to serve the king? Under Old Kingdom dynasties, sons of important families were named to important posts during childhood and educated at court with princes of the royal family. By this method the kings aimed to create class solidarity and unflagging loyalty to the throne. They were not always successful, as a papyrus document from the Middle Kingdom attests: Entrusting a commission to his chief treasurer, Pharaoh Sesostris III concluded his orders with the plea "My majesty sendeth thee, my heart being certain of doing everything according to the desire of my majesty; since thou has been brought up in the training of my majesty and the sole teaching of my palace."[55] That the king found it necessary to remind his treasurer in writing of his allegiance indicates that hand-picked officials did not always serve with devotion.

In Egypt, as in other ancient states, the bureaucracy provided a partial index of the relative strength of the three groups holding power in the society—nobility, priesthood, and crown. With passage of time, recruitment and training methods changed. More and more officials and scribes were needed as the bureaucracy became established in Egypt. Soon trainees exceeded the palace school's capacity. Noblemen administrators in outlying provinces took on themselves the acculturation and training functions. Instead of sending their sons to court, provincial officials kept them at home to learn how to manage the local administration. Claims on the jobs became hereditary as offices passed repeatedly from father to son, eventually attenuating loyalty to the central government.[56] Within each district, as the various hierarchies had to adjudicate their differences, relationships among the masters of the despotic regime became more complex.

With its internal authority undermined, the weakened central state collapsed at the end of the Sixth Dynasty (2181 B.C.).[57] Authority became further decentralized during the Intermediate period and the early Middle Kingdom (2100 B.C.). Acting autonomously, noblemen continued to supervise provincial offices—the court of justice, the land office, a service for conservation of dikes and canals, the militia and its equipment, and the provincial treasury—much as they had done since the Fourth and Fifth dynasties.[58]

By the end of the Twelfth Dynasty (1991–1786 B.C.), the central government had reasserted control of the provinces. Mayors (*nomarch*) appointed by the crown lived in the capital of each nome and administered the central government's judicial system.

Territorial expansion during the New Kingdom enhanced decentralization; supervisory authority as well as managerial authority became differentiated by geographic area. Instead of one vizier, two were appointed to oversee the central government's provincial interests, one for Lower and Middle Egypt, the other for Upper Egypt. During the Eighteenth Dynasty (1567–1320 B.C.) still another supervisory official, the vice-king of Kusch, was added to administer the southern colonial areas.[59]

During all periods of Egyptian history, management of finance entailed a large and complex administration. The local tax collector was only the first level in the hierarchy of specialized officials—draymen, warehousemen, stewards, overseers, and scribes*—involved in collecting and distributing all commodities and services that comprised the government's revenue. In provincial villages and towns during the Old

---

* Throughout the ancient world, literacy was the exclusive privilege of priests and nobles. In ancient Near Eastern societies, and in India and China, the ability to read, write, and cipher was both a mark of honor and an indication of social status. Special schools trained selected boys from Egypt's noble families to be scribes. Beginning in early childhood, they learned to write the elaborate hieroglyphic script used in official documents.[60]

and Middle Kingdoms, the "scribe of the field" collected the corn tax after each harvest, three times a year. After he weighed the corn at the riverbank, draymen loaded it onto barges and took it to state granaries.[61]

For an economy subject to periodic famine, the volume of goods transported must have been enormous. Records from the Middle Kingdom report that it took an entire fleet of riverboats to carry grain and other commodities from the provinces to the capital at Thebes,[62] where the king's officials stored the raw materials until used by the court or sold. A list of the Old Kingdom treasury's subdepartments specifies the variety of commodities and indicates what a complex task management of in-kind revenues must have been. There were separate granaries for barley and wheat; separate storehouses for dates, fresh vegetables, wine, and flax; and workshops for processing the raw materials—oil presses, bakeries, a mat-making shop, a linen-weaving and clothing-manufacturing workshop, and a laundry.[63] A distinguished French scholar's description of the Old Kingdom treasury delineates functional divisions in its organizational structure:

> ... The substance of the tax assuming all forms, it took an inexpressible quantity of special agents to receive it, in addition to appropriated buildings, herdsmen, stables, containers, granaries, wine-keepers, wine cellars, beer cellars, oil cellars. Twenty classes of laborers contributed their skills and services to the needs of the Treasury. If it was a question of cattle, grains or textiles, this tax was led to the meadow, sometimes to the butcher shop, to the currier's; it was sifted; it was reduced to flour. It was made into bread, into pastry. It was ironed, folded, relegated to a garment or a bolt of cloth.[64]

Taxes were apparently paid in gold and silver as well as in commodities and labor during the Middle Kingdom. Men without property paid the king in labor service (corvée) during all periods of Egyptian history. The "white house" (state treasury) appears to have been somewhat separate from the king's household. In addition to divisions for granary and royal herds, treasury subdivisions included the "double gold house" and the "double silver house." Presumably these were storage vaults for the king's metallic treasure.[65]

Assessment procedures remained "immensely laborious and complicated" well into the Ptolemaic period (when Egypt was a province of Athens, then of Rome). Under the Ptolemies, land in each village had to be classified by ownership (royal or private), size of plot, and name and status of occupant. Taxes on the yields from each plot varied with the cultivator's status, with the crop cultivated, and with the current level of the Nile flood. To prevent cultivators from harvesting crops without surveillance, the government had to station guards in each village. As growers brought grain to a central location for threshing, collectors commanded the government's share.[66]

MESOPOTAMIA

Like Egypt, early Mesopotamia and China also alternated between centralized administrations with strong internal controls and noncentralized systems with fragmented authority. Unlike Egypt (where centralized control was established during the Old Kingdom, very early in its history), the Mesopotamian city-states were seldom united under a single ruler for long. For a brief period during the Third Dynasty of Ur (2050–1950 B.C.) Sumer and Akkad were united into a loose federation under a Great King, and the *ensi* (appointive district governors of the separate city-states) were required to contribute regular gifts from local temple revenues to his central treasury.[67] But even then there was no uniform administrative pattern. In some districts *ensi* were closely controlled by the central government, while in others they were virtually autonomous.[68] Until the separate city-states were united by Hammurabi during the First Babylonian Dynasty (c. 1750 B.C.), and again during the Kassite period that followed his reign, local rulers owed neither allegiance nor taxes to a central authority.

The highly organized administrative system that existed briefly during Hammurabi's reign combined centralized control with the areal administration we call decentralization. Hammurabi created the illusion of local autonomy by permitting an assembly of elders, drawn from the wealthiest men in each city, to administer local matters.[69] At the same time Hammurabi exercised tight central control over his appointive bureaucracy of functionally-specialized district governors, judges, garrison commanders, local officials, and scribes; it operated throughout the empire.[70] Although citizens of all cities had to pay taxes to the central government, the civil bureaucracy itself did not collect the taxes. This task was delegated to each city's assembly of elders, who in turn handed the job to local merchants and bankers, who were, if not the world's first tax farmers, at least the first whose traces historians have found.*

---

* Cuneiform tablets from the Babylonian city of Sippar during this period seem to indicate that the city's chief administrative official was appointed from a small group of

The tax-farming arrangement came into existence in Mesopotamia as increasing secularization of property created a private economy separate from that of temple and state. In exchange for a fixed fee, negotiated in advance and paid to the assembly of elders each year, merchants who acted as tax farmers contracted to collect local taxes. By leasing out the tax franchise, the assembly guaranteed a certain amount of tax receipts, much as the central government had by delegating tax collection to the cities. At the same time, the assembly avoided the unpleasant task of confronting reluctant taxpayers. While potentially profitable, tax farming always entailed risk. If a tax farmer's hired agents did not collect enough to pay the contract fee, he was still liable for the full amount; and in years when the harvest failed, he might incur losses. The incentive for enterprise—as in any new business—was the ever present possibility of collecting more than the contract fee. Whatever this amounted to in any year was the tax farmer's profit, and, like any present-day businessman, he tried to increase it. In Mesopotamia, near the end of the second millennium B.C., the traditional tax on land was 10 percent of the crop, payable in kind. In practice, tax farmers collected much more. Seeking to guarantee in good years against possible losses from poor ones, the average tax farmer demanded one-fifth to half the crop from reluctant peasants.[72] A mixed regime was created: hierarchy was joined by markets.

Although the central government delegated the collection function, a division of the royal bureaucracy headed by the *makisum* (tax director) received and allocated revenues. During Hammurabi's reign the makisum of Babylon traveled through the whole kingdom to bring in taxes on time. If payments were late, this official sent dunning notices to local assemblies: "Why have you not yet sent to Babylon the 30 lambs as your tax? Are you not ashamed of such behavior? I am now sending you a [letter]; as soon as you have had sight of my letter send the 30 lambs as your tax to Babylon. If you do not send them, you will have to pay one shekel of silver for each lamb."[73] To make payment

---

wealthy noblemen who held the office in rotation, one year at a time. An Oriental scholar speculates that "perhaps the city's 'mayor' was elected by lot from among citizens whose personal financial status could guarantee the king the payment of taxes imposed on the city." While he served as mayor, the "overseer of merchants," as the chief official was called, was entitled to a share of the produce from the king's fields, perhaps as partial compensation for services. Like the Greek liturgy of a later period, liability for the office was rotated among wealthy citizens, probably to assure equitable distribution of the burden and risk of service.[71] At this early date, decentralized collection procedures merged elements of competitive individualism with hierarchy.

easier, the tax director stationed "the clerk of the gate" at the city entrance or on the municipal wharf to relieve taxpayers of their load as soon as they arrived. After the *mussadinim* (collectors) received the produce it was sent to the treasury's various subdepartments—divisions of grain, wool, sheep, goats, etc. No doubt these departments were little more than temporary corrals or warehouses. Perishable goods were either consumed in the king's household or, as in Egypt, sold or lent to merchants at regular rates of interest. Wool and other unprocessed raw materials went to state factories.[74]

During the late second millennium, "river and land officials" in Mesopotamia collected taxes from provincial governors, who were relatively independent of the weak Kassite kings. In such periods of deteriorating central control, the forcible collection procedures of provincial officials approached confiscation. When taxes were due, the collector and his assistants would enter a city. To insure compliance, the canal inspector first would close the main sluice gates. Then the collector would demand payment of all money taxes and one-tenth of all cattle, asses, and small livestock. Citizens were forced to provide grain to feed the caravan of horses brought to carry tax receipts back to the provincial capital, and sometimes to contribute horses and wagons for the army. At collection time troops stationed in the city by the provincial governor rounded up town dwellers and peasants to serve on labor gangs or in the army.[75] In the face of such extortionate collection procedures, it is not surprising that Babylonian cities and temples tried to obtain tax exemptions.

CHINA

Like Mesopotamia, China had decentralized governmental institutions for much of its early history. For a relatively brief period, toward the end of the western Chou Dynasty (ninth–eighth centuries B.C.), a strong ruling family governed a loosely organized feudal monarchy—ancient China's closest approximation to a centralized state. Unlike Egyptian and Mesopotamian religions, the animistic religion of early China had no priests. Each man communicated directly with the gods in personal rites at outdoor shrines or at home.[76] Since there was no priestly class, early emperors installed their relatives as administrators; in turn, these kinsmen delegated authority for local administration to feudal vassals. Noblemen-officials were doubtless chosen to compensate them for military aid they had given the emperor, but also because of their wealth.

In a scarcity economy, only men of property could afford to educate their sons. During the Chou Dynasty, the chief provincial nobles, like those of Egypt during the Old Kingdom, began to send their oldest sons to a special school in the capital where the heir to the throne was educated. The curriculum encompassed everything a provincial administrator might need to know. The boys learned archery and chariot driving, ceremonies and rites, and writing and arithmetic. Younger sons of great nobles and sons of minor provincial noblemen studied at provincial schools with a similar curriculum. Ten years of training shaped the young men to a uniform pattern. More important, ten years of close association with the crown prince built an enduring personal loyalty to the ruling family.[77] By creating the educational means for cultural reproduction, hierarchy had begun to institutionalize itself.

The Chou emperor had a centralized bureaucracy, as well as a feudal retinue to assist him in governing the provinces. Although not much is known about it at that early period, the chief administrative officer's organizational role, like that of the Egyptian vizier or the Mesopotamian sukkal, changed over time. Originally, the chamberlain was the emperor's household manager. "He was overseer for the butchers, the cooks, preservers of food, tailors, shoemakers, furriers, dyers, storekeepers and treasurers. He [managed] the palace and commanded the eunuchs and domestics."[78] By the first half of the seventh century B.C., the chamberlain had become the emperor's principal civil administrator, responsible for collecting taxes and supervising the royal domain. Several cabinet-level administrators assisted him. Although the other ministers' specialized duties can only be assumed, since there is no record of them, we know that there were two financial officials: a grand treasurer and a general controller. The treasurer (much like the Babylonian makisum) supervised many lesser agents involved in collecting and delivering government revenues. The controller represented an early attempt to achieve financial accountability; he functioned as chief scribe, keeper of records, and auditor.[79]

When barbarian invaders sacked the capital at Anyang in 771 B.C., central authority, never strong even at its peak, disintegrated. For centuries thereafter feudal princes governed the Chinese provinces. This long period of autonomy created a tradition of independent provincial administration that persisted through much of China's history. After the separate provinces were reunited under the Han Dynasty's emperors (200 B.C.–A.D. 200), local administration remained in the hands of noble families who were still relatively independent of central control. Within each locality, hierarchy ruled; among nobles and the emperor, relationships were marketlike—i.e., based on exchange.

Local autonomy, of course, was partly the result of China's great size. Since outlying provinces were physically isolated from the capital for much of the year, local administrators were free to collect taxes and disburse revenues. Although emperors and financial officers of later dynasties tried to impose constraints on provincial tax administration, imperial rule always was minimal. Local officials did not even have to account for receipts and expenditures.[80]

Their aristocratic origin had much to do with local officials' autonomy. Throughout China's history, government service was a privilege reserved for the wealthy; only upper-class families were acceptable members of its hierarchy. The mass of common people lacked autonomy and wealth, and descendants of merchants failed to meet social criteria. Even after emperors of the Han Dynasty had developed formal methods of recruitment to the imperial civil service by competitive examination, only sons of the wealthiest noble families could afford the long years of literary education needed to prepare for them. Moreover, judgment tempered choice among noble candidates for office. An ancient document of Chinese statecraft differentiates between "capable" aristocratic candidates and those merely "worthy." Important positions within the internal administration should go to those deemed capable, it specifies, while worthy candidates "may be entrusted with leadership positions externally."[81] During the Tang Dynasty (A.D. 600–900)* need for officials and clerks increased, and the government developed special examinations for "meaner peoples and mandarins of lower rank." But control was still concentrated at the top; selection procedures for the highest positions in the imperial civil service (reserved for the sons of great officials) bypassed civil-service examinations. Preference for the highest classes was justified because "from their childhood they have been accustomed to this type of function [civil administration], because their eyes are used to the affairs of the court, and because the rules of palace etiquette are known to them without their having to be taught, whereas a man of common birth, even if he is gifted with exceptional talent, will not necessarily be able to get used to it."[82]

A man's "moral character, his accomplishments, and his practical talents" should serve as guidelines for selecting officials, the document differentiating worthy from capable candidates advises. Accomplishments and practical talents are easily ascertained, but how can moral character be known in advance?[83] Restricting the highest offices to a limited social class did not necessarily protect the king against treachery. Congeries of hierarchies left open the possibility that a strong ad-

---

* Synchronous with the late Roman Empire and the early Middle Ages in Europe.

ministrative official or military leader would try to use power for personal gain. According to a scholar of China's legalist school (mid–second century B.C.), whose views influenced later emperors, if a ruler wishes to maintain control of government, he should not cede much power to ministers. If he does, the document advises, "this will be the ruin of government . . . [for then] the interests of the prince and the ministers will become different and the ministers will no longer be loyal. . . . [The ministers' interests] will be strengthened and . . . the prince['s] will be destroyed."[84]

INDIA

A classic document of Hindu statecraft, the *Arthasastra,* advises kings of Mauryan India in the third century B.C. to maintain personal control of government finances in order to protect themselves from treachery: "Internal troubles are more serious than external troubles, which are like the danger arising from a lurking snake. Troubles due to a minister are more serious than other kinds of internal troubles. Hence the king should keep under his own control the powers of finance."[85] For students of organizational structure in despotism, Kautilya's *Arthasastra* is indispensable. Much like Machiavelli's *The Prince,* yet composed over one thousand years earlier, the *Arthasastra* is a detailed handbook of practical advice on how a king should manage a hierarchy. The *Arthasastra* is the best description that we have found of the goals and methods of ancient kings.[86]

Mauryan India was contemporary with the empire of Alexander the Great. After the Hellenistic armies invaded India there was periodic contact between India and the older monarchies to the north and west. Some scholars believe that the *Arthasastra* reflects the influence of Egyptian, Persian, and Hellenistic ideas of the monarch's central authority and role in government.[87] Certainly by comparison with China's government at the same period, the administrative structure described in the *Arthasastra* is more centralized and the offices more specialized.

At the local level, a single official performed multiple tasks associated with financial administration. This was the *gopa,* an unspecialized officer whose tasks resembled those of the village headman in tribal societies, except that the territorial domain was larger: it included eight to ten adjacent villages. The gopa conducted the local population census and cadastral (land-ownership) survey that determined what each man owed the king, and he collected taxes when they were due.

By comparison with early Chinese emperors who had no effective checks over local financial administration, the kings of Mauryan India tried to exercise control through a chain of supervisors. The Greek idea of administrative control through audit (see pages 128–31) clearly had reached India by the time Kautilya wrote,[88] since the principal task of the superior offices he described was financial control. Local officials accounted to district officers (*sthanika*) for all receipts. These men accounted to a central government auditor (*pradestara*), who, in turn, accounted to the king's principal minister of finance (*samaharta*), who himself reported directly to the king. Audit had become a specialized governmental function.

At the ministerial level, financial management was more specialized than in Egypt, Mesopotamia, or China. Two ministers of equal status, the collector general (samaharta) and the chamberlain (*sannidhata*), served the king, reflecting a partial separation between management of the king's personal household and that of state finances. Of the two offices, the chamberlain's was more specialized. Although his work included managing the palace grounds and prisons, his main job was to supervise the vast bureaucracy associated with the king's storehouses. A corps of weighers, measurers, and sweepers received revenue paid in as taxes, stored it in underground chambers, and disbursed the proceeds to meet the king's obligations. Always subject to the chamberlain's surveillance, these workmen controlled the quality of commodities paid into the treasury and kept complete records of receipts and expenditures.[89]

Like the Egyptian grand vizier, the Mauryan collector general (samaharta), second in authority over finance, had various administrative functions—superintendent of police and finance minister. His task was to provide information to help the king formulate financial policy: "what is to be done" (decision-making), "what is done" (implementation), "what remains to be done" (planning).[90] The periodic accounts of "income and balance" presented to the king no doubt were intended to assess the financial state of the realm as well as give the king an instrument of control.

The collector general, also responsible for financial control, supervised local revenue collectors, district supervisors, and the government auditor. As chief of police, the collector general tried with the help of spies to insure that collectors did not exact too much from taxpayers, siphon off more than their share of receipts or make fraudulent reports to the king's auditors.[91]

Even with periodic audit, there was always danger that officials would try to cheat the king. Kautilya advised the king to set aside time every day to confer with ministers and examine their accounts. Each minister was required to produce a surplus; if not, he was fined. By this means the king aimed to force men at the top to assume personal responsibility for what went on below, because so many levels of authority multiplied the chances of fraud. To circumvent collusion or conspiracy, Kautilya admonished the king to see the district accountants separately when they convened to report to the chief auditor,[92] and to make each one wait in a different place.

The centralization of authority and specialization of function in the Mauryan administrative system was intended to reduce uncertainty by increasing organizational control. The hierarchical structure, the audit, and the ubiquitous network of spies that Kautilya advised the king to employ were designed to achieve administrative stability. But, as always, there was a price to pay: the layers of checks upon checks were expensive and cumbersome.

Furthermore, stability imposed by coercion from above could be won only at the cost of rigidity when conditions changed. When favorable conditions produced abundant harvests, a centralized system enabled kings to capture large proportions of its produce. But deterioration of collected produce, pilferage, and the bureaucracy's salaries were a real cost to the ancient king. And when harvests failed, not only did he face small revenue collections, but his chief financial administrator might become a rival.

Whether it was conducted by trusted noblemen, or by tax farmers under contract, a decentralized financial administration balanced income against certainty. The central power delegated the implementation of its decisions to officials in other locales. Central authority was sharply circumscribed, with certain areas of decision, such as tax collection, in the hands of semi-independent units. Aiming to maintain contact with district governors, kings in Assyria in the first millennium B.C. established a network of posting stations along the main caravan routes.[93] When employed by governments whose control of outlying territory already was weak, a noncentralized administration invested an unstable environment with a small measure of certainty. The revenue produced would be less than under a centralized system but tax collection did not entail outlay of limited resources; the king was often guaranteed a small amount of revenue by advance payment. Whereas kings could not totally control abuses by remote collectors, they made the best of it by getting what they could while the getting was good.

GOALS OF THE ANCIENT KINGS AND HOW THEY ACHIEVED THEM

Egyptian and Mesopotamian kings wrote (or had written for them) broad statements of purpose to accompany their laws and regulations. Intending wide distribution, rulers had these pronouncements inscribed on tablets and stone monuments in public places. In them and in private correspondence with administrative officers, the kings communicated a common conception of purpose and of the king's role as head of state.[94] Like their modern successors, ancient kings framed goals in broad language. Government existed to provide safety, justice, and welfare for all the people. Within that government, the king's role was as a benevolent father. By righteous deeds he was to set a good example for the people. His strength would protect the population; his wisdom would bring justice; and his foresight would result in prosperity throughout his domain. A king shall "endear himself to the people by bringing them into contact with wealth and doing good to them." By so doing "he shall never be devoid of happiness. He may enjoy in equal degree the three pursuits of life, charity, wealth and desire, which are interdependent upon each other." This worthy statement defined the goals of the kings of Mauryan India.[95] Writing in the last years of his reign, the Babylonian King Hammurabi summed up his accomplishments with the satisfaction of a man who has done his life's work well:

> I made an end of war;
> I promoted the welfare of the land;
> I made the people rest in friendly habitations;
> I did not let them have anyone to terrorize them.
> The great gods called me,
> So I became the beneficent shepherd whose scepter is righteous;
> My benign shadow is spread over my city.
> In my bosom I carried the people of the land of Sumer and Akkad;
> They prospered under my protection;
> I have governed them in peace;
> I have sheltered them in my strength.[96]

Hammurabi's Code enjoined the king to see that "the strong do not harm the weak."[97] Even the Egyptian pharaoh's autocratic power was tempered by the obligation to maintain order and provide justice for all people.[98] If he was strong and wise, a king could expand the state's borders and increase its wealth. Within these broad goals, rulers distributed state resources in traditional ways. Whether he was strong or weak, whether his empire was poor or prosperous, the king had to meet regular fixed expenses before considering anything new. For that reason "wealth and wealth alone [was] important."[99]

The regal image created by a monarch's wealth was a significant source of his power.[100] So, too, were large-scale public constructions, one way hierarchy demonstrated its potency. The colossal pyramids of Egypt, the monuments of Babylon, and the tombs, temples, and pagodas of China and India—embodying such large expenditures of life and labor—tangibly demonstrated the power and wealth of the king and symbolized his role as high priest of the state religion.[101] The costs to the king's authority of raising revenues for these displays must have been considerable, but on this the records are silent.

Ancient monarchs also used wealth to build an infrastructure largely for the purpose of defending the realm against attack. Beginning with the ancient Mesopotamian city-states, strong kings fortified their cities with walls.* When wheeled vehicles became common, kings built roads to connect distant parts of their kingdoms with the capital, to expedite troop movements in military emergencies, and to facilitate transport of tax receipts to the capital.† The roads were passable for only part of the year. "When we went away, the millets were in flower. Now that we are returning the snow falls and the roads are all mire," wrote an anonymous soldier-poet of China's Chou Dynasty.[104]

---

* If a king was weak, he might be unable to mobilize labor to maintain the walls, and his capital would then be vulnerable. In China at the end of the sixth century B.C., the king was so poor that he could not repair the walls. Fortunately for him, he was able to command contributions from his feudal vassals.[102]

† The first Emperor of unified China, Shih Huang Ti, was a vigorous creator of hierarchy. Centralization was enforced by standardization of written language, weights and measures, sizes and shapes of currency, and even road widths and wagon axles. Between 220 and 215 B.C. he joined a network of defensive walls in the northern provinces into China's Great Wall and had a road built on top; the wall extends 2,000 miles. A stone rampart twenty or more feet high and as deep at its base winding up and down steep mountain ridges, the restored segment of this ancient wall north of Beijing conveys vividly to modern visitors the overwhelming power of ancient despotism. Corvée labor and prisoners of war built the wall and other public works. Under this Emperor a road network expanded throughout the empire to facilitate troop movements and insure remission of tax receipts to the capital. Corvée labor built the Emperor's palace and his tomb, recently discovered near Xian. "Everything is set in order . . . ," reads his proclamation, but not everyone agreed; "the empire was taxed heavily without regard for the cost," a contemporary observer records. Forced labor and oppressive taxation exacted a heavy toll from slave subjects. Three years after the Emperor's death, a rebellion ended his heirs' rule.[103]

Water transport was more reliable than roads; in mountainous districts the first Han Dynasty Emperor had a deep canal cut through rocky terrain to connect the Yellow River with the Wei and thus facilitate transport of troops.[105] In Mesopotamia the major irrigation canals were wide enough to permit navigation in small boats.[106]

The most powerful kings used external conquest to enlarge and enrich the state. To defend kingdoms some rulers also maintained large standing armies. Warrior kings delegated the command function to feudal nobles and recruited troops by means of corvée—an early form of taxation that combined in one contribution a family's liability for both taxes and military service. During wars soldiers supported themselves by looting in conquered territory, but in peaceful interludes the king had to feed the armies or disband them.[107] Ancient Mesopotamian kings resolved this dilemma by paying troops with land grants that could be passed on to a man's decendants.[108] This land-grant device served two purposes; it provided a permanent army, and it insured the troops' loyalty.

A king's wealth permitted him to engage in charitable acts. Kings took with one hand and gave with the other. One monarch of Middle Kingdom Egypt had inscribed on his tomb a record of his bounteous aid to the people:

> ... there was none wretched in my community; there was none hungry in my time. When years of famines came I plowed all the fields of the Oryx nome, as far as its southern and northern boundary, preserving its people alive and furnishing its food, so that there was none hungry therein. I gave to the widow as to her who had a husband; I did not exalt the great above the small in all I gave. Then came the great Niles, rich in grain and in all things, but I did not collect the arrears of the field.[109]

Minor state officials could also perform good works. An assistant treasurer of the Theban nome during the Eleventh Dynasty, who resided at a place called Gebelen, describes his foresight with evident satisfaction:

> I sustained Gebelen during unfruitful years, there being four hundred men in distress. But I took not the daughter of a man, I took not his field. I made ten herds of goats, with people in charge of each herd; I made two herds of cattle and a herd of asses.... I brought grain for Esneh and Tuphium, after Gebelen was sustained.[110]

Throughout ancient Egyptian history, grants to temples were a continuous expense for the pharaohs.[111]

Kautilya advised the kings of Mauryan India that "finance is the chief means of performing virtuous acts."[112] Because Vedic law forbade Brahmin priests to engage in commerce,[113] Indian kings contributed land to the temples and exempted them from taxation; money contributed to Brahmins was looked upon as "an imperishable treasure."[114] Widows and orphans of men killed in the king's service were paid subsistence in food or were granted forest products, cattle, land, and occasionally money.[115] During famines a king was expected to give away food and seeds, forgive taxes, and initiate construction projects to provide work for the people.[116] Kings of India were enjoined to "support like a father the blind, the dumb, the defective in limb as well as those who have renounced the world."[117]

While such acts of virtue presumably would bring happiness in the present life and salvation in the next, hedonism and avarice would lead the king to damnation. From a text in the *Sukraniti* we learn that

> maintenance of troops and subjects, and for the performance of sacrifice, confers happiness upon the king both here and hereafter, while its collection for other purposes causes suffering to him: what is accumulated only for wife and children and for personal enjoyment leads to hell and does not produce happiness hereafter.[118]

It was unnecessary for the ancient kings to forgo pleasure to insure salvation, for their resources were large. The power to command corvée from the population made possible massive public works without direct cost, and regular tax revenues supported the king and his household in luxury, with an ample margin for charity.

DIRECT AND INDIRECT REVENUES: TAXES AND CORVÉE

Corvée, the mandatory contribution of personal labor to the state, was the earliest form of taxation for which records exist; indeed, in the ancient Egyptian language the word "labor" was a synonym for taxes. In the Mesopotamian city-states of the third millennium B.C., able-bodied men had to give a specified number of days of labor to the priest-king each year. During peacetime the laborers built and maintained irrigation systems, the temple, and the city walls, and cultivated and harvested the king's fields. When the king went to war with another city-state, laborers served as soldiers. Throughout the ancient world, and a few parts of the modern world until today,* forced labor served government. During periods of strong central authority, ancient kings conscripted huge battalions of corvée labor for long periods, building great monuments and extensive public works. The Pharaoh Cheops, for example, is reported to have forced 100,000 men to work three months each year for twenty years to build the pyramid that surmounted his tomb.[120] Acording to legend, construction of the first Chinese emperor's palace and tomb occupied over 700,000 men;[121] almost 800,000 men labored to build a provincial highway for a later emperor of the Han Dynasty.[122] Even if these ancient manpower statistics are legends, they illustrate both the scale of ancient enterprise and the extent of the ancient kings' (nontax) income from corvée. The temples, palaces, capital cities, and pyramids of the ancient world were built at far lower money cost than would have been possible in later eras, because manpower was virtually free.

If a man served the king where he lived, he provided his own subsistence. When an Inca emperor commandeered a labor gang for highway construction, for example, the men were obliged "to come with their food and tools."[123] For large projects, however, the king would recruit men from a distance.[124] If the government had to transport them from one locality to another, the treasury provided food and clothing. Provided with "4 lb. bread, 2 bundles of vegetables and a roast of meat daily, and a clean linen garment twice a month," over one thousand men worked for many years to build the tomb of King Seti I of second-millennium Egypt.[125] Seti reigned sixty-three years, time enough to have a magnificent tomb hewn from a limestone mountain in the Valley of the Kings across the Nile from the capital at Thebes. The tomb contains ten large rooms off a central corridor more than one hundred yards long. In all but a few rooms (apparently in-

* Over the course of history, various governments have conscripted men to build public works when the state's money income was inadequate to pay them, or when labor was in short supply. Corvée labor built local roads in England and Scotland from the sixteenth to the nineteenth century, and was used on public works in colonial America and pre-revolutionary France. Although an International Labor Organization convention outlawed compulsory labor in 1946, until the early 1950s all able-bodied men in Belgian and French colonial territories were required to provide fifteen days of labor each year on the roads, or to pay a specified sum of money. Authoritarian states still use forced labor to punish political dissidence, as well as to promote economic development. In the Chinese People's Republic until recently, citizens could be drafted to spend ten days a year on road repair and maintenance, and political dissidents may be assigned permanently to construction brigades. There are periodic charges of the use of forced labor in the Soviet Union. In developed countries of the Western world, compulsory labor survives only in prisons.[119]

complete at Seti's death), walls and ceilings are completely covered with brightly painted carvings of god figures and hieroglyphic accounts of royal achievements (interspersed with funerary texts). Slave artisans, who lived near the necropolis, were forbidden to cross the river to the world of the living.

In tribal societies that preceded the ancient city-states, communal labor was the shared responsibility of all able-bodied men; but in ancient governments, those who owed the king service had nothing else to give—landless peasants, convicts, and prisoners of war. Priests and nobles were exempt from corvée, and men of means could buy an exemption with payments in money or in kind.[126] Corvée could not have been practiced in a regime that valued equality of condition.

Evasion was likely when the central government was weak. During the Kassite period in Mesopotamia, the cities sought and received exemptions from the obligation to provide men for corvée and military service.[127] When the state was at war, registration machinery might break down; during the unsettled feudal period of the late Chou Dynasty (eighth century B.C.), many Chinese men left their ancestral homes and wandered from province to province. By this means they could evade corvée, but provincial governments found other ways to tax them.[128] Successive Egyptian governments continued to exact compulsory labor service from peasants until the late seventeenth century of the modern era; but in other parts of the ancient world a head tax or household tax payable in kind or money gradually replaced corvée as a source of revenue. In China, after the Tang Dynasty (A.D. 600–900), in feudal Japan (until 1868), and in Mauryan India, an annual tax was levied on each able-bodied man or each eligible household.

Local representatives of provincial governors administered the labor census and conscription in Egypt and Mesopotamia. During the Han Dynasty (200 B.C.–A.D. 200) in China, gentry families in each district kept track of each household's contribution. Each adult male had to give a month of labor every year, and more during emergencies or for special conscriptions. Those aged nineteen to twenty-one built public works near their homes; twenty-two- to twenty-four-year-olds spent a month in the local militia. At twenty-four and twenty-five years of age, a man could be sent to a remote district with the army.[129] Village headmen in feudal Japan and Mauryan India kept records of compulsory labor service; they took a census of the eligible population and called each man to work for the required time as his turn came due. In rural Japan in the nineteenth century A.D., for example, each family furnished the equivalent of 40 man-days per year—10 days for labor tax, 10 days for materials-produced tax, and 20 days for land tax.[130] Each male in a Chinese family during the Tang Dynasty was required to provide 20 man-days of labor on public works each year and two additional days in leap years; if one member volunteered for 30 days, however, the entire family was exempt from further service for a year.[131]

Apart from labor service, the basic tax in the ancient world, and the one producing the largest revenue, was the tithe, an assessment of a fixed proportion of agricultural produce. Although we have no tax statistics for ancient times, one Oriental scholar has estimated that during the Tang Dynasty in China, 80 to 85 percent of the government's tax revenues were paid in grain.[132] Kautilya advised the Mauryan kings to collect revenue from the people as a farmer would harvest a crop. "Just as fruit are gathered from a garden as often as they become ripe, so revenue shall be collected as often as it becomes ripe."[133] In Mesopotamia, after calving and shearing time, the government ordered herdsmen to travel to the capital to settle their accounts; various towns were ordered to send specific quotas of calves, lambs, and wool, or a substitute payment in money. Fishermen and hunters paid proportions of their catch, and peasants gave a fixed share of their produce. In the other ancient societies the tax came due after the harvest* and was paid mainly in the staple grain of the region—rice in China and Japan, wheat in Egypt, and a variety of cereals and agricultural products in India.

Rates were high. According to the Bible, Egyptian peasants paid the pharaoh one-fifth of the produce of the land.[135] Kings of Mauryan India claimed one-fourth of each crop.[136] Percentages were lower in Mesopotamia; the government took one-tenth of the harvest and the natural increase of each herd, although, on occasion, it did raise the rates to one-fifth, one-fourth, one-third, and sometimes half.[137] During the Chou Dynasty in China there was regional discrimination;[138] those who lived in or near the capital paid relatively little (one-twentieth of the produce), while in distant provinces feudal vassals were obliged to collect from one-fifth to one-fourth of the district's produce for the

---

* In Egypt the tax was collected every two years until the Middle Kingdom, when there was a changeover to annual collections. The original practice stemmed from the king's personal voyage up the Nile every second year to collect his levies. Collection through provincial officials then proved more practical, which was probably part of Djoser's rationale for setting up the provincial structure. As the administrative organization became established, the government was able to collect taxes after each of the year's three harvests.[134]

central government.* A poem dating from the western Chou Dynasty evokes peasant cultivators' resignation to tax collectors' demands:

> Big rat, big rat,
> Do not gobble our millet.
> Three years we have slaved for you,
> Yet you take no notice of us.[140]

In Mesopotamian towns the ruler also levied a regular tax (paid in money) on merchants and artisans. Merchants' guilds were a rich source of income to Babylonian kings, who demanded and got from one-third to half the merchants' gross receipts; perhaps that is why those rulers could afford to tax peasants and herdsmen at lower rates than did other ancient governments.[141]

Although the basic tax in the agrarian civilizations of the ancient world was grain, obligations could also be met in staple commodities, textiles, jewels and precious metals, and in early forms of money. The treasury accepted payment in gold, silver, jewels, cattle, and linen in Eighteenth-Dynasty Egypt.[142] Merchants paid in coin in Mauryan India. Storehouses of the kings also held a wide array of foodstuffs: wheat, rice, pulses; sugar and salt, oil, clarified butter, honey, fruits, vegetables, and spices.[143] In China during the Chou Dynasty, payments could be made either in silk or in coin,[144] while residents of mountain districts paid in more exotic commodities—skins of wild animals, rhinoceros horns, ivory, and rare-bird feathers.[145] Kings of China's ancient Shang Dynasty (late second millennium B.C.) did not simply wait in the capital for tribute to flow in. As kings did during the Middle Ages in Europe, these rulers went on "hunting expeditions" into their provinces, living off subjects and collecting gifts as they traveled.[146]

When finances ran short, or during emergencies, the king might impose a selective increase in normal taxes in kind. Kautilya advised Mauryan kings to demand, on penalty of fine, an additional contribution of one-fourth to one-third of the crop and also to make the peasants cultivate an extra crop for the government. His advice reflects the pragmatism of one who would expedite large enterprises, yet also derive income from human frailties. Men who performed useful state functions—construction of fortifications, gardens, buildings and roads, colonization of wastelands, and exploitation of mineral resources— and those who lived on the kingdom's borders were exempted from the

---

* Later, during the Han Dynasty, peasants paid a smaller share, one-fifteenth, and then one-thirtieth.[139]

increases, while actors and prostitutes paid half their wages to the king. Hostility toward moneylenders served also as rationalization for profit; Kautilya recommended that the entire earnings of goldsmiths be confiscated, "for they carry on their fraudulent trade while pretending to be honest."[147]

Besides regular and extraordinary levies, ancient rulers assessed imposts on persons and goods moving from one place to another; they levied tolls within their kingdoms, and customs duties on imported commodities.[148] Subjects also made regular contributions to the temples and had to pay special taxes on such state occasions as the birth of a prince[149] or the king's visit to their locality.[150] Ancient governments also had several nontax revenue sources. If a man died without an heir, the ruler confiscated his property, as he did if a man was convicted of a crime.[151]

Where they were not entirely confiscatory, taxes varied with an individual's assets. Much later (during the eighteenth and nineteenth centuries of the modern era) this principle of social differentiation would reappear—in the principle of liability for taxes according to an individual's *faculty*, or ability to pay. In ancient times governments appear to have invoked a parallel principle: taxes varied according to a government's capacity to make people pay.

The similarity among the tax systems that evolved in several civilizations of the ancient world results at least partly from technological diffusion. When Alexander the Great conquered India, contact between previously isolated societies may have facilitated transfer of Egyptian administrative techniques into the Mauryan Empire. The Chinese system of financial administration was exported to Japan. It is also possible that forms of taxation that emerged independently in Egypt, Mesopotamia, China, and the pre-Columbian civilizations of Central and South America only represented the simplest solution to the problem of revenue collection in an agricultural society with rudimentary technology and organizational capability and only limited use of money. Spanish conquerors in the sixteenth century found in Mexico a compulsory-labor tax very like the corvée of the Chinese Han Dynasty in the second century B.C.[152] Men without property in the Aztec Empire worked one day a week for Montezuma. The Códice de Mendoza, a cadastral survey itemizing contributions in kind from each village in his domain, is displayed in the Museo de Antropología in Mexico City. (See illustration number 7 for a facsimile page.) In these civilizations, far removed in space and time, similar administrative devices provided government services.

TAXATION AND MORALITY: FAVORITISM AND EXEMPTIONS

The burden of supporting government in the highly stratified, agriculturally based societies of the ancient world fell disproportionately upon the poor. Bound to the soil in peonage or slavery, peasants paid the largest share of taxes in kind and provided all compulsory labor service. Year after year peasants contributed from one-tenth to one-half their produce to the king's agents, who levied the tax as the crop was brought to the threshing floor. When such calamities as floods, drought, or plagues of insects reduced the crop, arrears in payment were postponed, to be collected in full with the next good harvest. If a man had nothing for the collectors, he might have no recourse but to sell his wife or his daughters into slavery to raise the tax.[153]

Payment of taxes must not have been voluntary. On a stone bas-relief from an Old Kingdom Egyptian tomb, we see the king's deputies, armed with cudgels, driving unwilling taxpayers to a reckoning with treasury officials (see illustration number 6).[154] (Even as late as the nineteenth century of the modern era, Egyptian peasants would boast of the number of blows they endured before they would render payment.[155])

Ethical precepts transmitted from lore of ancient China and India embody egalitarian principles. Thus, the administration of a wise king should be tempered with mercy; in principle, the obligation of subjects to serve and support the ruler should be tempered by considering a subject's ability to pay. When Mauryan kings demanded extra taxes, only owners of irrigated land had to pay more: The king "shall never demand an increase of such of his subjects who live on land of middle or low quality, ... nor who have not enough subsistence."[156] Indian merchants paid more if they were wealthy; dealers in luxury goods paid at higher rates than sellers of common household articles and foodstuffs.[157] But in most ancient civilizations, certain favored classes were exempt from taxation altogether. In China, for example, filial sons and grandsons, devoted husbands and constant wives, and those "whose modest and virtuous lives were an object of the loving respect of their neighbors" were not required to pay. The aged, the sick, the exiled, and the barbarous were also exempt, as well as children of "meritorious subjects" and profound scholars.[158] We do not really understand the function of these extraordinary categories. Perhaps they served merely as a cover for favoritism.

Royal decrees in Old Kingdom Egypt granted the temples immunity from the taxes and obligations of other subjects. The list of these immunities is instructive, for it illustrates what the people were required to provide the king: corvée labor for royal construction projects, and for field work on domain lands; feeding and housing royal envoys and their retinues as they traveled through the kingdom; taxes on cattle, leather, trees, and water holes.[159] Although the pharaohs donated lavishly to the temples throughout ancient Egyptian history, the temples occupied a particularly favored position during the New Kingdom. The holdings were exempt from all taxes, and any official who tried to infringe on temple properties faced punitive sanctions. All misappropriated property had to be returned to the temples, and sometimes offenders were forced to make a hundredfold restitution to placate priests and gods.[160] With priests and nobles exempt, the burden of supporting the king fell upon the rest of the population.

Realizing that punitive taxation eventually would harm the polity, Indian kings levied penalties and fines against officials who collected too much. From Kautilya we learn that "whoever doubles the revenue eats into the vitality of the country. If he brings in double the amount to the king, he shall, if the offense is small, be warned not to repeat the same; but if the offense be grave he should be proportionately punished."[161] Harmhab, an Eighteenth-Dynasty pharaoh, imposed severe punishment for extortion. A tax collector found guilty of demanding excessive payments from the poor was sentenced to have his nose cut off and was banished to a desolate frontier settlement in the Arabian desert.[162] In Babylonia, where collectors at times raised the rates to one-third or even one-half, a decree of the king Ammisaduqa during the sixteenth century B.C. forbade use of force by tax collectors, and canceled taxpayers' debts. The reforms of King Urukagina of Lagash during the second half of the third millennium also were directed against the extortionate rates of "parasitic" tax collectors, and were intended to "restore freedom" to his subjects.[163] "From one end of the land to the other," an ancient scribe recorded, "there was no tax collector."[164]

Although the Indian kings tried to protect taxpayers from extortionate collectors, they were not above raising revenue by a variety of illicit stratagems that ranged from simple misrepresentation to elaborate subterfuge, espionage, and outright confiscation. Morality in Mauryan public finance was blatantly opportunistic. The end of maintaining the ruler in power justified any means of providing revenue. Kautilya lists a variety of devious ways of obtaining revenue; if one did not work, another might. The list encompassed negative sanctions, positive rewards and appeals to the full range of human emotion—vanity, avarice, lust, ignorance, superstition, and fear. It is so evocative of the times that we have included it in glorious detail.

Kautilya's List of Devious Mechanisms for Raising Revenue in Time of Need

The collector general shall seek subscriptions from citizens and country people alike under false pretenses.... Persons ... shall publicly pay handsome donations, and with this example the king may demand [the same] of others. . . . Spies posing as citizens shall revile those who pay less ... Those who, of their own accord, or with the intention of doing good, offer their wealth to the king shall be honored with a rank in the court, an umbrella, or a turban or some ornaments in return for their gold. . . .

Or having on some night set up a god or an altar, or having opened a sacred place of ascetics, or having pointed out an evil omen, the king may collect subsistence under the pretense of holding processions and congregations [to avert calamities]. . . .

Or by causing a public panic owing to the arrival of an evil spirit on a tree in the city, wherein a man is hidden making all sorts of devilish noises, the king's spies, under the guise of ascetics, may collect money [with a view to propitiate the evil spirit and send it back].

Or spies may call upon spectators to see a serpent with number-less heads in a well connected with a subterranean passage, and collect fees from them for the sight. Or they may place in a bore hole made in the ... corner of a temple, or in the hollow of an ant-hill, a cobra, which is, by diet, rendered unconscious, and call upon credulous spectators to see it [on payment of a certain amount of fee]. As to persons who are not by nature credulous, spies may sprinkle over, or give a drink of, such sacred water as is mixed with anesthetic ingredients, and attribute their insensibility to the curse of the gods. . . .

Prostitute spies, under the garb of chaste women, may cause themselves to be enamored of persons who are seditious. No sooner are the seditious persons seen within the abode of the female spies than they shall be seized and their property confiscated to the government. Or whenever a quarrel arises between any two seditious parties of the same family, poisoners previously engaged for the purpose may administer poison to one party; and the other party may be accused of the offense and deprived of their property.[165]

Yet the dilemma for kings remained: taxing too low left the state poor; taxing too high left their subjects impoverished. And the golden mean remained elusive.

FISCAL MANAGEMENT IN THE ANCIENT WORLD

Although collection of taxes in kind and payment of debts in commodities are not budgeting in the modern sense, financial administrations of the ancient world employed several decision criteria used in modern fiscal systems. Modern budgeting is allocation plus control. Control may not be achieved, but this has always been true. In the short run, modern governments allocate resources for roughly the same purpose each year; since many obligations are fixed, the proportions of available resources for various uses remain relatively constant. Budget administrators usually attempt to maintain "slack"—excess funds that may provide a cushion against unanticipated contingencies—in their operating accounts. Budgetary decisions are informed (though, then and now, they are not necessarily influenced) by forecast of anticipated revenues.

Centralized financial administrations of ancient governments appear to have operated according to similar decision rules. To protect their populations against the ever present threat of famine, kings and financial administrators tried to accumulate a surplus. Concerned with agricultural production, they tried to forecast revenue. And they tried to maintain accounts of receipts and disbursements to limit losses from corruption. In Egypt, Mesopotamia, China, Japan, and India, local officials kept detailed records of population, land ownership, and productivity of each plot of land. Local census records and cadastral surveys enabled the government's representatives to make rough predictions of anticipated income from each district. The records also insured maximum revenue, for if a taxpayer tried to claim a meager crop, officials could cite the records of his productivity in previous years in order to establish a lien on his produce in the present.

During the New Kingdom in Egypt, and in Mauryan India, the treasury cumulated local records in order to anticipate income. As the prospective tax liability from each village became known, government accountants totaled the village accounts into a national registry* that

---

* While record-keeping in the ancient world must have required enormous labor, the cumulated tallies could not have been very accurate. The Egyptian hieratic numerals, and the system of numerals used in ancient China and India, were cipher systems in which the first letter of the word for each number was used as a symbol for the number. Without the concept of zero, these systems of numerals used many different symbols.

Ancient scribes used an abacus to simplify calculation. It was originally a sand-strewn board into which lines were drawn to form columns for units, tens, hundreds, and thousands. Pebbles, shells, sticks of bamboo, or glass bead counters placed in each column indicated the number of units, which could be added or subtracted as calculations were

was presented to the king at regular intervals so that he could assess the realm's financial strength. When the cumulated accounts were matched against the treasury's detailed records of commodity inventories and disbursements, the revenue predictions enabled ancient kings to formulate crude budgets. As a further aid to prediction the Egyptian kings kept track of the water level in the Nile, and, according to Kautilya, the *sannidhata* (chamberlain) of Mauryan India measured rainfall. Thus, he decreed: "In front of the storehouse, a bowl with its mouth as wide as an aratni [twenty-four angulas, a measure of distance] shall be set up as a rain gauge."[167]

Agricultural taxes varied with the quality of land in India, Egypt, Mesopotamia, China, and Japan. Different rates were levied on irrigated and dry plots, fertile soils, barren land, and forests and orchards. To determine liability for land tax, the village official conducted an annual agricultural census that measured and registered the total area under his jurisdiction—the quality of all plots within the administrative unit, land ownership, and revenue assessments.[168] Such cadastral surveys were conducted differently in each civilization. When the corn began to ripen in Egypt, "the fields were measured by two scribes, the 'holder of the cord' and the 'stretcher of the cord,'" and on the data obtained an assessment would be made of bushels or sacks of corn per aurora (100 square cubits, about two-thirds of an acre).[169] In India, where the tax was paid in a wide variety of crops, the land-classification scheme was more detailed. To insure that all revenue due the state was collected, the gopa counted all land by "numbering cultivated and uncultivated plots, the upland and lowland plots, the gardens, fruit-gardens, the sugar-cane gardens, [the village] jungle, the homestead land, the sacred sites, the shrines, the embanked reservoirs, the cremation grounds, the site for the distribution of alms and drinking water, the grazing grounds and the roads."[170] Information was entered on a roll that became a permanent record of land ownership and tax receipts.

Local officials also conducted an annual head count to determine liability for corvée and head tax. The Indian gopa registered the number of people in each household: sex, age, and occupation (whether cultivator, herdsman, peddler, artisan, workman, or slave); the number of domestic animals; and each household's previous annual contribution

made. In time, a wax-covered tablet and later a table with lines incised into the surface replaced the sand. The abacus was used in parts of Europe until the seventeenth century of the modern era and is still used in the Orient.[166]

of taxes in cash, unpaid labor, tolls, and fines.* In Egypt, the king's agents also took a census of cattle to determine liability for taxes in kind.[172] There, and in Mesopotamia, the annual census was the most important event of the year.[173] The Chinese took regular censuses from the Chou Dynasty on.[174]

In Egypt, the grand vizier supervised all aspects of financial administration. The country was divided into two administrative regions during the New Kingdom, and revenue from all sources flowed to the treasury of the southern vizier at Memphis, whose financial functions are described by a noted Egyptologist:

> The amount of all taxes to be levied and the distribution of the revenue when collected were determined in his office, where a constant balance sheet was kept. In order to control both income and outgo, a monthly fiscal report was made to him by all local officials, and thus the southern vizier was able to furnish the king from month to month with a full statement of prospective resources in the royal treasury. The taxes were so dependent, as they still are, upon the height of the inundation and the consequent prospects for a plentiful or scanty harvest, that the level of the rising river was also reported to him.[175]

The grand vizier received revenue from all sources: land tax and head tax, payments from temple treasuries, and tribute from conquered people. With the help of scribes, the vizier tried to forecast prospective revenue and regulate disbursements. During the reigns of the strong monarchs of the New Kingdom, the grand vizier, and his subordinate, the chief treasurer, were in daily contact with the pharaoh, who participated actively in financial administration.[176]

Supervising administration of finance was one of the chief duties of the kings of Mauryan India. Kautilya advised the king to be "ever wakeful,"[177] and to set aside part of each day to examine the accounts of receipts and expenditures, to hear ministers, and to receive gold.[178] "He shall have so thorough a knowledge of both the external and internal incomes running even for a hundred years that, when ques-

---

* "... Having numbered the houses as taxpaying or nontaxpaying, he shall not only register the total number of inhabitants of all the four castes in each village, but also keep an account of the exact number of cultivators, cowherds, merchants, artisans, laborers, slaves, and biped and quadruped animals, fixing at the same time the amount of gold, free labor, tolls, and fines that can be collected from [each house]. He shall also keep an account of the number of young and old men that reside in each house, their history, occupation, income, and expenditure."[171]

tioned, he can point out without hesitation the exact amount of net balance that remains after expenditures have been met with."[179]

Management of government finance in ancient India exhibits several characteristics of modern budgetary systems. Just as the chamberlain's primitive rain gauge represents a crude attempt to forecast revenue, so, too, do his hundred-year records represent past efforts to control expenditure. Kings of Mauryan India allocated resources more or less systematically to traditional uses. They paid a fixed share of the revenue (see list below) to the "body of state expenditure."

   Budget Categories in Mauryan India include funds for:
   1. The chanting of auspicious hymns during worship of gods and ancestors and on the occasion of giving gifts.
   2. What is given as a present on occasions of auspicious prayers by the priests.
   3. The royal seraglio.
   4. The royal kitchen.
   5. Expenses for . . . messengers.
   6. The royal storehouse.
   7. The armoury.
   8. The warehouse for merchandise.
   9. The storehouse for forest products.
   10. The state workshops.
   11. Forced labor.
   12. Maintenance of infantry, cavalry, chariots, and elephants.
   13. The state herds.
   14. Museums of beasts, deer, birds, and snakes.
   15. Storing places for firewood and fodder.[180]

Kings of Mauryan India had a formal budget that allocated fixed proportions of revenues to the principal expenses. According to the *Sukraniti,* a medieval treatise on political theory, one-half the revenue should be paid to the army; one-twelfth for gifts; one-twelfth for salaries of principal officers; one-twelfth for salaries of heads of government departments; and one-twelfth for the king's personal expenditures. The remaining one-sixth was to be retained in the treasury as a surplus.[181]

During the Han Dynasty in China, imperial officials tried to insure adequate revenues by drawing up a rough expense budget before they established head-tax rates. With an ancient allocational technique that resembles modern budgetary earmarking, Chinese officials assigned special classes of revenue—duties levied on mountains and waterways, parks and lakes, and markets and shops—to specific persons, probably in payment for services.[182]

Because ancient kings had little control over a hostile environment, they accumulated large surpluses to safeguard against the ever present threat of famine. The Biblical story of Joseph in Egypt illustrates one king's (or, at least, his advisers') foresight. Ancient and medieval Chinese emperors maintained a network of provincial *granaries of constant equalization,* with branches located at strategic points along major roads and waterways and at the empire's borders. Although the principal goal was to reduce uncertainty by providing a constant supply of food grain for the army and for the population in the event of famine, the emperors also wanted to influence the price of grain.

When the harvest was abundant the state bought grain at a low price and stored it, thus raising the price that producers would receive in the market. In times of scarcity the government released part of the stores in charitable contributions to the starving, and sold the remainder at less than the current market price. Though emperors may have intended only to make food available to the people at reduced cost, their market operations must also have been a source of profit to the treasury, for the grain was sold for more than its original cost. As long as these economic activities were carried on as separate enterprises within the king's bureaucracy, subject to its division of labor, they remained hierarchical. Only if royal grain purchase and resale produced a class of moneylenders independent of the crown would market relations modify hierarchy.

Gradually the granaries' main function changed. As surpluses accumulated in good years, officials began to make interest-bearing loans to the unfortunate producers who had consumed grain they would need for the next season's planting. By the ninth century A.D., the granaries of constant equalization had been transformed from institutions of public charity into agricultural banks.[183]

To maintain a large surplus was a primary tenet of Mauryan public finance. Kautilya admonished: "Of the stores . . . collected, half shall be kept in reserve to ward off calamities of the people, and only the other half shall be used. Old collection shall be replaced by new supply."[184] Through a system of rewards and punishments the king tried to provide an incentive for economy. A wise collector general shall "increase the revenue and decrease the expenditure,"[185] selling the king's stores to realize a gain when prices increased, and writing off expenditures on "the relics of wretched undertakings" that brought irreversible losses.[186]

Kautilya advised Indian kings to budget one-fourth of the total revenue for servants. Salaries in kind were to be fixed at a scale commensurate with each man's service. The detailed classification of occupations provided remuneration at a scale calculated both to instill enthusiasm for work and to maintain continuous loyalty.*

Tenets of economy governed management of revenue collected in kind. A detailed system of quality controls specified the kinds and amounts of food dispensed from warehouses to support the king's human and animal servants.† Kautilya's advice embodies organizational principles for fiscal management, providing instructions for resource control. The line-item budget he describes and prescribes—so much for this position, so little for that—is an imitation of hierarchy.

CONTROL OF CORRUPTION

The ancient kings believed human nature to be base. Without control, man, self-serving by nature, would appropriate more than his share of the king's revenue. "Just as it is impossible not to taste the honey or the poison that finds itself at the tip of the tongue, so it is impossible for a government servant not to eat up at least a bit of the king's revenue."[189] These rulers tried to devise a structure of incentives and a network of control to guard against avarice. A panoply of institutions was essential, they believed, for controlling the appetites.

Careful selection of government servants was the essential first step in a control structure. By appointing men of wealth, selected and

---

* Here are a few examples of Mauryan job classifications:

"The sacrificial priest, the teacher, the minister, the priest, the mother of the king, and the queen shall [each receive] 48,000 [panas per annum]. With this amount of subsistence, they will scarcely yield themselves to temptation and hardly be discontented.

"The prince, the nurse of the prince, the chief constable, the officer in charge of the town, the superintendent of law or commerce, the superintendent of manufactories, members of the council of ministers, the superintendents of country parts and of boundaries, 12,000. With this they will be loyal and powerful supporters of the king's cause.

"The chiefs of military corporations, the chiefs of elephants, of horses, of chariots and of infantry and commissioners, 8,000. With this amount they can have a good following in their own communities.

"The foreteller, the reader of omens, the astrologer, . . . the storyteller, the bard, the retinue of the priest, and all superintendents of departments, 1,000.

"Trained soldiers, the staff of accountants and writers, musicians, 250. Of these, the trumpet blowers shall get twice as much wages as others. . . .

"The honorable playmate of the king, the elephant driver, the sorcerer . . . shall have honorarium ranging from 500 to 1,000 [panas] according to their merit. . . ."[187]

† ". . . ten adhakas of rice will be fit to be the food of young elephants; eleven adhakas for elephants of bad temper; ten adhakas . . . for elephants trained for riding; eleven . . . for chiefs of the army; six . . . for queens and princes; and five . . . for kings. . . ."

"One-sixth prastha of supa for a man; and half the above quantity of oil will form one meal for low castes.

"The same rations less by one-fourth the above will form one meal for a woman; and half the above rations for children."[188]

trained from their youth to administer government finances, monarchs hoped to guard against self-seeking at their expense. Ever fearful of conspiracy or treachery that might weaken their control, kings were not content merely to appoint finance ministers from the nobility,* but were ever on the alert for tests of fidelity. Kautilya advised the Mauryan kings to use the "lust test" in selecting a finance minister. It was executed as follows:

> A woman spy, under the guise of an ascetic, and highly esteemed in the harem of the king, may allure each prime minister, one after the another, saying, "The queen is enamored of thee and has made arrangements for thy entrance into her chamber, besides this, there is also the certainty of large acquisitions of wealth." ... If they discard the proposal, they are pure.... Those whose purity has been tested under monetary allurements shall be employed in the work of a revenue collector and chamberlain.[191]

A man who could resist a seductive queen's advances could be trusted to manage the king's wealth. The Chinese and late Roman emperors left even less to chance and often employed eunuchs as finance ministers.

When the imperial Chinese civil service was established in the Han Dynasty, administrative officials got little or no salary, but were allowed to appropriate a proportion of in-kind revenue for personal use. The gopa, local officials of Mauryan India, also received a proportion of the collected produce as reward for service—a one-sixteenth, one-eighth, or one-sixth share depending on the district's productivity.[192] The Japanese, who adopted the Chinese system of financial administration, rewarded hereditary local officials (daimyo) in proportion to the rice collected from each household. The emperor supplemented this subsistence payment with periodic grants of silk cloth.[193] Payment of a fixed and substantial proportion of tax receipts to local collectors in Mauryan India and feudal Japan was a device to forestall misappropriation. And, apparently, so it did, but these payments also fostered a spirit of independence.

Such irregular methods of compensation had other disadvantages. In a multilayered bureaucracy like the Chinese, little was left for the central government after all state officials had taken their share. Hierarchy is expensive. Payment in kind also had disadvantages for collec-

---

* Political analysts, who wonder if their studies make them conservative, might ponder this bit of advice: "employ as ministers such new persons as are proficient in the science of policy ... such new persons will regard the king as the real scepter-bearer and dare not offend him."[190]

tors, for in time of shortage rewards were sharply reduced. The imperial Chinese bureaucracy made a unique adaptation to the modest compensation of its officials. When money became the normal medium of exchange, payments in kind were eliminated, leaving only small salaries as a reward for service. Imperial officials then compensated themselves in a currency known as "squeeze." At each step of the tax collection—local, provincial, and national—each official exacted an irregular, extralegal payment from taxpayers. This combination of fee-for-service and institutionalized bribery became a regular feature of Chinese financial administration.

As with any system of remuneration based in part on personal initiative, the Chinese method provided multiple opportunities for officials to defraud the people, and favored the wealthy over the poor. A landowner could buy a reduction in his liability, or an outright exemption, leaving the tax burden on those who could not afford a bribe. The resulting corruption characterized Chinese financial administration over the centuries.[194]

To serve the king in an administrative capacity was a highly personal act in ancient governments. An appointive official was equally responsible to the king for performing or failing to perform assigned duties adequately. Higher officials were accountable for subordinates' actions. Yet as imperial expansion extended the territory of the ancient kingdoms of Egypt, China, and India, appointed officials were unable personally to answer to the king. Primitive transportation and communication networks impeded contact. By what strategies could a king insure an honest and reliable administration? To supplement incentives for honest administration, ancient rulers devised a system of controls to protect themselves against embezzlement.

The most common control mechanism was redundancy—duplication of function. Where communication was imperfect an appointed official was more likely to give the king's interests top priority if he knew that his honesty was being checked by another official performing the same task. Large numbers of clerks, scribes, weighers, and overseers were needed to handle the sheer volume of commodities paid in as taxes; but proliferation of officials also served as a financial control, as one functionary checked on the work of another.

As the tasks of financial administration became increasingly specialized, ancient rulers tried to check malfeasance by granting supervisory authority to government inspectors. During the Middle Kingdom in Egypt the pharaohs sent supervisors from the central government to live in provincial headquarters of the Egyptian nomes.[195] Itinerant inspectors traveled through the provinces of Han China and carried back to the capital reports of provincial administrators' integrity and honesty.[196] Pyramiding authority was built into financial administration of Mauryan India.[197] The mere presence of government inspectors, however, did not always insure honesty, for these men had no actual power. As agents of the central government, their function was only to induce honesty by threatening to tell the king.

To insure that provincial administrators represented imperial interests, local financial officials in China during the Han Dynasty were not permitted to serve in their home areas.[198] And the powerful Pharaoh Harmhab of Eighteenth-Dynasty Egypt provided special incentives to keep his staff of traveling inspectors from becoming corrupted:

> ... Harmhab had them provided for with great liberality. They went out on inspection several times a month, and on these occasions either just before their departure or immediately after their return the king gave them a sumptuous feast in the palace court, appearing himself upon the balcony, addressing each man by name, and throwing down gifts among them. They were also given substantial portions of barley and spelt [a grain] on these occasions, and "there was not found one who had nothing."[199]

Harmhab tried to control corruption among provincial officials by drafting a series of laws imposing punitive sanctions for common offenses—embezzlement of tax receipts, appropriation of court fines, and issuance of falsified wage vouchers for soldiers and army officers.[200] The Pharaoh traveled throughout the kingdom to see that the new laws were enforced.

Kings of Mauryan India attempted to induce sound fiscal management by both offering rewards and exacting penalties. An official who increased the revenue of a government department was rewarded by being given eight times the increase; if revenues fell he paid a fine of eight times the loss.[201] Kautilya enumerates the causes of mismanagement; among them are ignorance, weakness, idleness, timidity, and greed.[202] His edicts provided that fines for mismanagement should be proportional to the amount of guilt.[203] An official could be fined for "scraping off" or "eating up" the king's revenue,[204] or for any of forty varieties of embezzlement. Among these, Kautilya lists a variety of simple errors in bookkeeping and techniques to appropriate funds by misrepresentation.

> What is realized earlier is entered later on (such as rice); what is realized later is entered earlier (such as the late crops, wheat, etc.);

what is hard to realize (taxes from Brahmins) is shown as realized; what is collected in full is entered as collected in part; . . . incongruity in representing the work turned out (as in the case of the superintendent of boats misappropriating ferry dues under the false plea that only Brahmins crossed the river on a particular day); making use of false weights and measures; deception in counting articles [etc.][205]

For "enjoying" the king's gems or other valuable articles, an official could be executed.[206] Judging government servants to be "naturally fickleminded, and like horses at work, [to] exhibit a constant change in their temper," Kautilya recommended daily examination of the work of the king's chief officials.[207] Trade with the king's stores presented many opportunities for fraud.

How was defalcation detected? It took ingenuity: "Just as the fish moving under water cannot possibly be found out either as drinking or not drinking water, so government servants . . . cannot be found out [while] taking money for themselves."[208] Each department of the Mauryan government had a staff of accountants to keep detailed records of receipts, expenditures, and net balance. Accounts were kept according to a prescribed form; any clerk who diverged was fined, as was his superior.[209] Cumulated daily accounts from each department and net receipts for the year were presented to the king for audit on the first day of the new year. Through that audit, which exemplified hierarchy, Mauryan kings aimed to implement an effective system of control.[210]

During the middle and late dynasties the Egyptian pharaohs also had a system of financial management and a comprehensive audit; the Mauryan system of financial management appears to have been based on the Egyptian model. But controls exercised by the Indian kings went a step further, for the accountants' totals were verified or challenged by a network of espionage agents penetrating every level of administration and reporting back to the king. The king appointed several varieties of spies who—in disguises of recluse, fraudulent disciple, merchant, scholar, ascetic, or mendicant woman[211]—traveled through the kingdom investigating every appointed official. Ministers, priests, army commanders, the heir apparent, officers in charge of the harem, the collector general, the chamberlain, superintendents and heads of government departments,[212] local tax collectors,[213] all came under scrutiny. Trying to assure certainty, Mauryan kings invoked the principle of redundancy. Each official was investigated by three spies (each in a different disguise and none of them known to the others). Each spy reported to the institute of espionage, whose officials had spies of their own to spy on the spies. "When the information thus received from these three different sources is exactly of the same version, it shall be held reliable."[214] In despotic regimes, such as that of Mauryan India, fear of detection and reprisal was intended to force compliance. Yet the very existence of such a network indicates widespread corruption.

The existence of a rich central treasury is a sure sign of hierarchy. A market regime would not permit any government (as distinguished from successful private entrepreneurs) to become wealthy. Only collectives organized on principles of hierarchy, such as the despotic governments we have described, have a central treasury. Hierarchies encourage central accumulation, and attempts by those who collect and distribute society's wealth to siphon it off are deviations from proper behavior.

AN EVALUATION

Whether the threats of intimidation and violence that pervaded financial administration in the kingdom of Asoka brought in much additional revenue is questionable. In the ancient world the financial structure supporting any government was fragile. Because income depended mainly on agricultural output, fortunes of ruler and individual cultivator alike were dominated by uncertainties that have plagued agriculture since time immemorial. Neither farmer nor king could count on regular and recurring income. Events could be anticipated only as far ahead as the next harvest.

So ancient kings accumulated huge surpluses as a safeguard against the unexpected. Yet in societies in which most people lived on the edge of subsistence, such surpluses were essentially wasteful. Even where transportation was adequate to transfer the king's share to central storehouses, distribution methods often were inadequate for allocating stores where needed. In China during the Han Dynasty, piles of grain lay rotting in the capital while famines ravaged the provinces.[215] Stores of commodities were costly and cumbersome; collection, storage, and distribution of revenue in kind involved the state in an enterprise impossible to manage.

There was a seemingly simple solution to the problem of allocation. Tax receipts could be stored where collected, and distributed to meet the king's local obligations. This could minimize losses from transporting produce to central warehouses but the king then faced a different and equally difficult problem: how to prevent distant local officials from setting up shop on their own.

Corruption was accepted as a normal adjunct of financial administration in China and Japan. In the small-scale society of feudal Japan, a weak king—or one with few ambitions and a limited territory—could tolerate small diversions of revenue if remissions were regular and adequate to support the royal household in proper style. Rulers of the large and physically dispersed empire of ancient China had a different strategy. Han Dynasty emperors sent ambitious noblemen (who might threaten royal control) to govern distant provinces with virtual administrative autonomy. By accepting only a token revenue, or none at all, as a cost of administering a large, far-flung territory,[216] the emperor effectively removed the threat to his control that an ambitious interloper might pose. Throughout Chinese history, however, efforts to control corruption were largely ineffective.

In Egypt and India the attempt to control receipts and audit expenditures involved the government in a costly enterprise that yielded variable returns for the amount of effort required. The Mesopotamian alternative, collection by tax farmers, made much smaller demands on the ruler's ability to administer and control. With tax farming the government needed only a relatively modest administrative capacity to negotiate contracts and enforce payment of the contract fee. Tax farming proved to be such a workable alternative to a large centralized bureaucracy that it was adopted in Egypt late in the New Kingdom[217] and was used in many different governments until the late eighteenth century of the modern era.

Histories, or even data, from "the bottom up" do not exist for ancient times. If we ask what the populace got out of ancient finance, we have little more than conjecture to go on. Perhaps ordinary people got military protection. Or, equally plausible, they were the main victims in wars they cared nothing about. Perhaps they were protected against famine. We do know that taxes and low productivity prevented them from accumulating surpluses. "Voting with their feet" was not possible, for there were no places to go. What we can say is that government grew, extending its scope, dividing and subdividing its functions. Moral codes may have limited government's greed. Necessity—the need for labor and produce—may have limited its extortion. But in the main in those days, either you were in the government or you were out of luck.

As far as the ordinary person was concerned, all ancient regimes were despotisms. The common man did not make the rules he lived by, nor could he alter them. In no way could the actions of his rulers be limited. If "the people" were not legally slaves, they might as well have been. The differences among regimes of slavery, hierarchy, and markets, as these came and went over the course of history, were differences among masters.

Budgetary mechanisms in ancient despotisms mirrored societal organization; ancient regimes were steeply hierarchical, consequently power relationships in budgeting (who takes from and gives to whom) were entirely asymmetrical.

Why do we have no record of taxing and spending in market or sectarian regimes? Perhaps such regimes did not exist. Yet even in modern times the work of anthropologists has brought to light societies based on bidding and bargaining in New Guinea, India, and Africa.[218] No, we suspect that only the large, hierarchically organized states left records. This does not imply that hierarchy came first in human history, that it was the original regime from which all others are derived or into which they decomposed. As we have seen, ancient hierarchy did sometimes utilize market methods.

A variety of social orders is possible, but, when they appear, hierarchies are larger and hence more visible than other structures, and they keep better records for posterity. In ancient states, to be sure, hierarchy appears to be the main, if not the sole, solution to the problem of maintaining social order. Even such marketlike activity as lending by temples or granaries is mediated through and limited by hierarchical priestly and bureaucratic relationships. It also appears that in recorded history hierarchy has been found more frequently than any other political culture. Even so, there is more than one way to build a collective upon the principle of structured inequality.

In a caste system, domination is achieved by separation. The Brahmins, to whom Kautilya directed advice, for instance, separated themselves not only from subordinate castes but also from the direct exercise of political power. Members of the priesthood relied on social as well as financial support from the lower orders; and the principles of subordination that Hindu doctrine inculcates, in turn, helped shore up the governing authorities. More than one hierarchy existed, but they reinforced one another rather than competing for the favor of excluded groups. (In other ancient kingdoms the priesthood did govern, presumably making manifest the gods' will in secular life.) The financial implications of such stratification are high levels of taxation on subordinate castes, and even higher levels of spending on upper castes to maintain social differences.[219]

All forms of hierarchy—class and caste, simple and complex—seek glory for the collective, and that costs money. But complex hierarchies, containing distinct strategies for different spheres of life, cost the most because they have more finely graded positions to support. The line-item accounts we impute from the patterns of expenditure give each level its due. Expenditures are difficult to reduce because the status and function of the occupants of each position (and hence their relationships to other occupants and statuses) are simultaneously a product and a measure of what the government spends on them.

There are the beginnings of differentiation. Tasks within the king's household were divided up; specialization emerged. The temples of the priesthood generated their own treasuries and carried on economic activities. They too could live off their own. The crown's functionaries (whether they served on a geographic or a functional basis or both) systematized their tasks. They developed some expertise and some autonomy. These bureaucratic instruments of royal power extended its reach but also added to its expense, siphoned off its revenues, and wove a web of restraint around its prerogatives.

Revolution and conquest merely put different people in place without challenging the principles of hierarchy. Rivalry among hierarchies had begun.

APPENDIX: TRANSACTIONS IN BARTER AND MONEY

The earliest money is thought to have been associated with religious rituals. In Bronze Age deposits throughout Europe and the Near and Far East, archaeologists have found collections of cowry shells and various types of metal rings and spirals suitable for personal ornamentation. The regular occurrence of these objects in many societies suggests that they might have served a dual purpose, as a store of value in exchange transactions as well as for personal decoration. Any object that serves as a store of value may also serve as a primitive form of money. By force of custom it may become a standard of value against which other goods are measured.

In an economy of pure barter, goods are exchanged for one another in proportions equivalent to their value in use. The awkwardness of valuing different commodities, even in simple exchange transactions, leads to adoption of a common standard against which to measure the value of goods. Cuneiform tablets from Mesopotamia in the third millennium B.C. indicate that at that early date transactions were being conducted as if an independent standard of value existed. The various goods to be traded were valued separately in reference to a common standard that appears to have been established by the temple and maintained by the government.

In Mesopotamia the standard was the *gur*, a volume equivalent to a bushel of barley, the staple grain of that region. Other commodities were valued in terms of the number of *gur* of barley they would bring in exchange. In any transaction involving several items, only the difference in the aggregate value of goods involved would change hands. In other societies at different times various staple commodities have served as the standard of value. In the Congo during the mid–sixteenth century, for example, it was salt. A block of salt of specific dimensions (fifty-five centimeters square and a hand's breadth in thickness) was worth three capons. Three blocks could be traded for one goat or sheep, fourteen or fifteen blocks for a cow, and twenty blocks for a slave. Shells, being more durable than salt, were used as the standard in exchange transactions over long distance. Cocoa beans served as money in the Mayan temple city of Chichén Itzá at the same period. A pumpkin was worth four beans, a rabbit ten, and a slave one hundred.

When any society established such a customary unit of exchange, whether a standardized measure of barley, salt, or some other perishable substance, exchange was greatly simplified. Commodities could be valued against the standard and bought and sold in markets. The standard also made it easier for the government to command regular payments of taxes in kind. The value of these payments could be assessed according to the customary ratio of various commodities measured against the common standard.

With metal as a standard, transactions were further simplified. Commodities offered for sale or in payment of taxes could then be valued either in terms of each other, in terms of the common standard in kind, or against the common standard in metal. Early Bronze Age archaeological deposits have yielded pieces of copper, lead, brass, gold, and silver formed into bars, disks, ingots, and lumps of a similar size and weight. These pieces of metal were suitable for exchange and may have been the earliest metal money.

Various cuneiform and hieroglyphic texts indicate that the pieces of metal were weighed or measured out under official control of a temple or a city. Just as the standard measure of grain of a particular temple, for payment in kind, might be accepted in its immediate territory, a standard of weight for the pieces of metal used in transactions might also have been established by a temple or a city and then become generalized over the surrounding territory. If the issuing temple or city stamped its seal on the bags of grain or pieces of metal, its officials, in effect, guaranteed the weight of grain or the quality of assay.

Bars of silver, copper, and lead stamped with the city's seal were widely used in Babylon, Assur, Kanish, and other Mesopotamian cities during the second millennium B.C. One shekel of silver weighing eight grams was worth one *gur* of barley or dates (weight 120 liters) or two and a half sheepskins.

Thus, although the metal-bar money had relatively high value and could be used only for large payments, it simplified transactions in temple markets where men who had traveled long distances made their transactions. A passage from the Bible illustrates the favorable effect of money on trade: ". . . if the way be too long for thee, so that thou art not able to carry it; or if the place be too far from thee, . . . then shalt thou turn it into money, and bind up the money in thine hand, . . . and thou shalt bestow that money for whatever thy soul lusteth after, for oxen, or for sheep . . ."[220]

Copper small change in denominations suitable for ordinary transactions appeared during the middle of the first millennium B.C. Issued first by the Lydian and Ionian cities, copper coins spread rapidly over the Greek region. In Mesopotamian trading cities, copper and silver had a decimal relationship: one hundred pieces of copper were worth one silver shekel. While coinage was used in the cities from that time on, the money economy was rarely found in rural areas where a dual economy of money and kind continued to exist for centuries.

Chapter Three

FROM REPUBLIC TO EMPIRE: TAXING AND SPENDING IN CLASSICAL ATHENS AND REPUBLICAN AND IMPERIAL ROME

BACKGROUND

SOCIAL AND ECONOMIC CONDITIONS

By the sixth century B.C., several small, autonomous city-states were established on the Attic peninsula at the eastern end of the Mediterranean, and two centuries later another emerged at Rome on the Apennine peninsula. Political institutions differed significantly from those of the ancient kingdoms, for in these new city-states, power was delegated by the people to a governing council of tribal elders. The social structure remained like that in the ancient monarchies. There was a limited landowning aristocracy; a military class; a small group of independent landowners and merchants; and a large number of craftsmen and unskilled laborers, many of whom were slaves. Although in theory the power to govern was diffused among all the people, in practice property ownership was a requisite of citizenship; neither women nor slaves could claim the privileges or assume the obligations of citizenship. Status was fixed by birth; social mobility upward or downward was seldom possible.

As in the ancient monarchies, life was hard for the entire population. In classical Athens nobles and slaves alike lived in small windowless huts lining the narrow, rutted dirt streets below the Acropolis. The mountainous terrain and arid summer climate meant that food was never abundant; the threat of famine was real and continuous. Whether from wars, from high child mortality, or from famine, illness, or accident, most people died young. With average life expectancies between twenty and thirty years,[1] populations remained stable.

Men's faith in local gods provided an element of stability in a life filled with uncertainty. Each city-state had at least one patron deity, along with a temple and its priestly overseers. Personal sanctification could be assured by worshiping there and contributing money or services, and by participating in the many festivals. Olympic games and theatrical spectacles honoring local gods dominated public life.

Religion and the state were closely linked in the Greek city-states and in Rome, but not synonymous as in the ancient monarchies. The Temple of Athena and the seat of government and politics in the Athenian *agora* (marketplace) were physically adjacent on the Acropolis, but each had a separate organizational identity. There, as in Rome, temple and secular government maintained administrative and fiscal autonomy. Athens violated that autonomy only occasionally in emergencies,[2] by borrowing from the Temple of Athena, but the Roman Republic had a legal prohibition against lending to temples or borrowing from them.

Such symbiosis between religion and government as existed was manifested in use of state funds to provide food and entertainment for the urban poor during religious festivals.* The bread and circuses of imperial Rome were paralleled in Athens by lavish expenditures for theatrical performances, and free food distributed at games and festivals honoring the local gods.

Limited agricultural productivity made the city-states dependent on trade or conquest for survival. To support the concentrated population of classical Athens (estimated at nearly 250,000 persons),[4] food had to be imported from subject territories.[5] Overcultivated and eroded land in Italy produced a limited food supply, and feeding the city of Rome was a continuous problem from the late republic on. As Rome's population grew to over a million, the increasing quantities of grain needed to sustain residents came from conquered territory, first from Sicily, then from North Africa, Egypt, and Spain.[6]

Just as now, stable currency was essential for overseas trade. Though small-denomination coins had been used commercially in Egypt and the Near East before the sixth century B.C.,[7] the Athenian city-state was the first government in the ancient Mediterranean world to main-

---

* Several Athenian statesmen protested this extravagant use of state resources. Thus, Demosthenes complained, "The Panathena, the Dionysia are always celebrated at the proper time, festivals on which you expend more money than on any naval enterprise . . . but when you send out a fleet, it always arrives too late." Plutarch agreed: "If it were calculated what sum each play cost the Athenians, it would be found that they had spent more treasure upon . . . Oedipuses and Antigones and the woes of Medea and Electra than upon wars undertaken for empire and freedom against the barbarians."[3]

tain a stable currency over time. Silver from the mines of Laurion near Athens backed the Attic drachma, which became the standard of value throughout the eastern Mediterranean basin after the fifth century B.C. As military victories were won over surrounding city-states, Athens used its currency as an instrument of economic autarchy. Subject states had to replace their currencies with Athenian silver coinage bought at rates favorable to the Athenians.[8] When the Roman Republic's armies occupied territory controlled by the Greeks, the Roman Senate introduced its own coinage.

POLITICAL INSTITUTIONS

For a brief period in history, Greek and Roman city-states were organized in republican form to suit preferences of powerful groups among their citizens rather than a single monarch's will. An unprecedented style of governance—one joining the strict social stratification with competitive political relationships—supplanted the rigid truncated hierarchy of despotism. In ancient despotisms all power and authority radiated down from the apex. In both these republics, in contrast, while a council of high officials selected from the hereditary landholding class formulated alternatives and implemented the chosen policies, there was also some diffusion of authority. People ordinarily voiceless in a political culture of fatalism—peasants, craftsmen, and small landowners—also shared in decision-making.[9] In some uncertain proportion, they ratified or chose policies. According to legend, both representative councils, the Athenian Areopagus[10] and the Roman Senate, were formed when landowning aristocrats usurped kings' power. The transition occurred in Athens sometime during the sixth century B.C., in Rome about a century later.

A small corps of government officials assisted the councils and were directly accountable to them. These councils enacted laws and decrees that specified what services the state would provide: military defense; civil administration and justice; construction and maintenance of public buildings; provision of essential infrastructure such as harbors, roads, and aqueducts; and periodic contributions to religious festivals.[11] By contrast with the ancient despotisms, in which a king's will was unchallenged law, the republican councils sometimes adjudicated, altered, and reversed their actions in response to pressures from citizens. In both Athens and Rome the councils had power to grant tenure on state-owned lands, to control the courts and the military, and to manage state finances.

Government in classical Athens rested on the Greek concept of *pólis,* community of citizens. Unlike modern representative governments, place of birth was not the only criterion of citizenship; women, slaves, and persons without any land could not participate in public life. Yet within the boundaries defining its citizenship, Athenian democracy was an ancient precursor of the New England town meeting; the government was a popular assembly of all male citizens over eighteen years of age. A quorum of six thousand citizens (the Ekklesia) was required to vote approval of important state policies—declaring war or peace, granting citizenship to individuals or states, a vote of ostracism against any person—and of financial matters, such as authorizing secular use of temple funds or imposing a tax. The ancient city-state's institutions of governance served limited purposes: to supply collective services that individual citizens could not provide for themselves, and to be a source of moral authority in resolving conflicts between individual citizens, or between citizens and government.

Because a large body could do no more than vote consensus on general policies, in Athens a smaller executive council handled routine affairs. In the democratic reforms of the mid–fifth century B.C., the popular assembly created a revolving council of five hundred citizens, the Boulé, which then became its executive arm. Selected annually by lot from all male citizens over thirty years of age, members of the Boulé represented a proportional cross section, not only of the ten tribes (*demes*) of Athens, but of the entire Athenian community, for there were no property requirements for membership.

The Boulé, although formally advisory and administrative, effectively formulated policy. Its principal task was to prepare an agenda for the large council; unless the Boulé had passed a formal resolution on a topic, the Ekklesia could not consider it.

Financial powers of the Boulé were considerable. While the Ekklesia had to sanction all but routine expenditures, the Boulé proposed what these would be and spent the money when it was authorized. With financial authority over the temple cults, the Boulé supervised temple treasury officials. It negotiated leases on temple lands, paid for the new temple buildings and for religious festivals. The Boulé had independent authority to fine state debtors up to five hundred drachmai—a very large sum for Athenians. It also controlled tax collection[12] by approving and administering contracts with tax farmers.

Administrative officials appointed by the council were directly accountable to it in an annual audit, while delegated officials—councilors and magistrates—were accountable to the entire *pólis* at the end of their terms. Although the requirement for public accountability did not always insure honesty, it enabled the community to exercise control over its officials and helped to insure that public and private roles and responsibilities did not become confused. (There were no similar institutions in the Roman Republic.)

Stability of the Athenian city-state in the Golden Age of Pericles derived from the conservatism of its governing council and from a prosperous economy. Council members shared a common interest in maintaining the existing order; most disagreements could be adjudicated within the council. And throughout the classical period, Athens was a busy commercial center. Profits from trade enabled merchants to contribute abundant state support in the form of liturgies (see page 102), while the treasury also profited from customs and excise taxes levied on foreign imports.

Athens gained control of the surrounding region after the Graeco–Persian Wars. While serving as treasurer of the Delian League (a regional military-defense federation), Athens confiscated League funds, doubling its revenues and thereby stabilizing its finances.[13] As in its domestic affairs, the Athenian assembly exercised final authority over finances of the Athenian Empire. The assembly could exempt a satellite state from taxes or authorize harsh provincial tributes. Money flowing into Athens from provincial cities created a comfortable surplus that reduced the risk of injudicious decision.

To what degree were Athenian representative institutions tinged with, or distorted by, elements of despotism, hierarchy, and competitive individualism? The centuries-old disagreement over Athenian political institutions follows from the intermingling of these elements in its political culture. Political equality among Athenian citizens rested on a slave base. Nevertheless, despite slavery, and despite a nobility that shaped and executed choice, Athens manifested substantive elements of participation.

This was not the case in the Roman Republic. There (as in Athens, before its democratic revolution in the fifth century B.C.), the governing council was drawn from the landowning class, but the Senators had life tenure instead of serving one-year terms. Although wealthy members of nonsenatorial orders occasionally were elected to the Senate, as early as the fourth century B.C. and throughout most of the republic, the controlling offices of *consul* (leader of the Senate) and *magistrate* (chief military official) were closely held by a group of twenty ruling families. This oligarchy gained control of the Senate and managed to perpetuate its dominance by means of political alliances and arranged intermarriages. As the Roman Senate controlled chief magistracies as well as leases for public land, the wealth and power of these families steadily increased. Their hierarchical world-view explains the republic's unenlightened revenue system and cumbersome financial policies.*

As Rome gradually embarked on a course of imperialistic expansion, the Senate had to confront disagreements over domestic and provincial policies. Political life continued to become more complicated; pure regimes of a single type were left behind. Rival hierarchies formed: the more extreme found support among patricians from the Senatorial order, and Equestrians, or knights, who commanded the Roman legions. A more moderate group sought mass support by proposing modestly egalitarian policies, including redistribution of state income. The two hierarchies competed for the favor of poorer soldiers and veterans. Factionalism broke the oligarchy's control of the Senate and eventually led to civil war. Continuous insurrection fomented by rival groups eventually brought about the end of the republic.

In the last two centuries of the republic (second and first centuries B.C.), the Senate divided into two rival groups—the Optimates, representing the old ruling oligarchy, and the Populares. Favoring moderate change in the Senate's policy of leasing public land, the Populares tried to form alliances with lower orders in order to wrest control of the Senate from the old oligarchy. Differences between the two groups initially focused on a land-redistribution scheme proposed by Tiberius Gracchus in 133 B.C.[15]

Military expansion in the late republic created yet another rival faction: generals who had first assumed state authority when they created their own law in conquered territories. When civil government was reestablished, these generals stayed on to command provincial garrisons. Assisting civil governors sent out from Rome with day-to-day administration, these military men established a power base for enhancing their personal political fortunes.

A large and expanding population of poor veterans also created difficulties for Roman government as its military power increased. Many men drafted in the late republic were former peasants, independent farmers with holdings of no more than three to five hectares. Returning from war to find their land reverted to desert, they abandoned farming and settled in the cities. But Rome's conquests in the eastern Mediterranean had produced a large captive population of skilled, literate slaves, a far more attractive labor supply than the displaced veterans.

* Very few—ten—families alone supplied half the 200 consuls who served during the 100 years before Tiberius Gracchus' tribunate; 159 of the consuls were recruited from twenty-six families.[14]

Without resources or prospects for employment, they then became a potentially volatile nucleus within the cities. Worried about these veterans' threat to domestic stability, some conservative Senators among the Populares revived the Gracchi scheme for redistribution of public land on the Italian peninsula.

Tension within the Senate was compounded when ambitious military men took sides in the escalating internal turbulence. During the civil wars of the first century B.C., a power-hungry general named Sulla gave support to Optimates in the Senate. He warned the Senate that troops under his command would rebel if land reform was approved. Then, buying off his men with land and money confiscated from rich provincials, Sulla brought his army back to Italy to fight against the Populares and dislodge them from control of the Senate. Julius Caesar and then Augustus, when they assumed control of the Roman government at the end of the republic, restored the army's loyalty by raising soldiers' wages and granting small plots of land to demobilized veterans.*

The two-hundred-year-long struggle between Senatorial factions was further complicated by demands of the rising Equestrian order. Like the Senators, the *equites* (knights) belonged to the landed class, although wealth requirements for membership were lower than for Senators. (Just as birth conferred fixed social rank in Roman society, so, too, did it determine each group's economic role.) Because Roman law did not restrict equestrians from engaging in business, as it did Senators, many knights became involved in banking, moneylending, and the thriving trade growing out of Rome's territorial expansion.

Experienced in business and finance, the Equestrians were able to manage economic development and overseas administration for the Roman state. As early as the second century B.C., Equestrians (later called Publicans) contracted with the Senate to build public works, operate state-owned mines, provide food and supplies for the army, and, as tax farmers, to collect provincial revenues. Out of this competition between rival hierarchies came elements of a marketlike regime, more explicitly based on bargaining.

A functional interdependence between the two propertied orders de-

* In modern, welfare-oriented democracies, policymakers have learned to be wary of the potential fiscal threat of small programs that gradually grow larger and consume more resources. Like so many policy problems that governments face, this one is not new. When the Caesars established military pensions, they unknowingly created a precedent that would cause serious fiscal difficulties several centuries later, in the turbulent late empire, when over 100,000 men were eligible to be pensioned off.[16]

veloped, although their legal status remained nominally unequal. The Senate soon came to rely on Publicans for entrepreneurial services. And while at first the Publicans may have had other sources of wealth than state contracts, the more they specialized in service to the state, the more they became economically dependent on the Senate. Politically subordinate to the Senate in the early republic, the Equestrian order could not bring cases before civil and criminal courts, and thus had no recourse against unfavorable treatment.

Although they never achieved social status equal to the Senators', the knights' position gradually improved as new wealth made them desirable allies in the struggle within the Senate. Several *equites* were named Senators after the Second Punic Wars (216 B.C.); they replaced old Senatorial families whose male descendants had been killed in battle. After that a few exceptional Equestrians were occasionally admitted to the Senate. Then, during the civil wars of the late republic, Sulla tried to pack the Senate with Optimates; he appointed three hundred more *equites* as new members. They did not penetrate the Senate's inner circle; none was ever appointed to the body's highest offices. But as a group, the Equestrians were chief beneficiaries of the political and economic developments of a century of conflict among rival factions in Rome's government.

During the first two centuries of empire, as the Senators' role in Rome's government was attenuated, the Equestrians' grew steadily. The first Emperor, Augustus, increased property requirements for Senators; this act cut the Senate's membership back to six hundred, while permitting Equestrians to remain members.[17] And then, because the early emperors did not wish to risk restoring Senators' capacity to cause trouble, they filled positions in the new imperial civil service with Equestrians.[18]

Whether the political and social context was one of dissension and turbulence (Rome during the late republic and the late empire) or stability (Athens in the time of Pericles, and Rome under the early emperors), government always had problems in raising revenue. A society's financial institutions manifest its past and present political and social values and the current development of its economy and technology. Above all, rudimentary technology and low productivity established the context for taxing and spending in the classical world. During the eight or nine centuries encompassed by this chapter (from about 600 B.C. to A.D. 400), citizens of the republics and empires of Athens and Rome always lived close to the margin. Since a surplus was never assured, representative, oligarchical, and tyrannical governments alike established moderate norms for taxes levied on citizens. If local taxes failed to produce requisite revenue, states with powers over limited territory turned to outsiders for financial support, externalizing the burden. In time, the tribute of empire supplanted each republic's moderate taxes on its citizens.[19]

Market methods constituted an appropriate administrative technology for governments of the classical world, which were constrained by poor transport and minimal knowledge of accounting and record-keeping procedures. Relying on others (volunteers or contractors) to administer finances reduced a small state's management burden and consumed relatively little of its resources. Yet in Athens and Rome, as in the ancient empires, financial administration by market methods entailed problems of accountability and control. Like the ancient empires, governments of Athens and Rome under republic and empire oscillated between market and hierarchical financial management. Each mode worked well enough for a time. Yet eventually the changes in government, economy, and society we have sketched here caused the prevailing mode to become dysfunctional. Whether market or hierarchy, it either collapsed of its own weight or was slowly modified by internal reforms, and was eventually replaced by its opposite. Centralization followed decentralization; decentralization replaced centralization.

FINANCE AS TECHNOLOGY

INNOVATION AND CHANGE

Over the past two thousand years there have not been many large changes in techniques for managing government finances. Separated by centuries and millennia, major innovations in raising and allocating revenue came about at a glacial pace. Some spread into geographically adjacent areas, only to be abandoned and then reintroduced at a later date in slightly different form and altered context. Several innovations appeared more than once, separated by intervals so great that they could only have occurred independently.

The representative governments of classical Athens and the Roman Republic produced several significant new methods of taxing and spending that differed from the practices of the ancient monarchies' centralized bureaucracies. Both voluntary giving by the wealthy few and market methods to tap the lesser resources of the mass public typified each republic's early financial management. Several of their techniques—the liturgies and administration of all taxing and spending by funds—are not familiar today, or even comprehensible in terms of modern thinking about finance in analytic categories that differentiate between taxing and spending.

In Athens and Rome a citizen's giving and the state's getting were dual aspects of a single process, at once religious and honorific. The contributions wealthy individuals made to both republics show an emerging conception of public responsibility. Early in both republics' history, when contributions were freely given, norms of fairness and mutuality regulated what, and how much, individuals would give. During the turbulence of the late Roman Empire, coercion enforced contribution; only the myth of voluntarism remained.

There was no functional division between taxing and spending in early Athenian and Roman financial administration. Whether they were public tax collectors serving the governing council, or private individuals holding tax-farming contracts with the state, those with authority to collect revenue also had authority to disburse it for specified purposes. Compared to the ancient monarchies', administrative techniques were simple and consumed few resources.

THE LITURGIES

In Athens and Rome, institutions for managing government finances were both an expression and a result of the young state's limited power and authority. The governing councils had power to tax, but not too much—for direct taxation connoted tyranny and was viewed as inconsistent with liberty.[20] Moreover, as free citizens comprised only a small proportion of each city-state's population, and as the landowning classes by tradition were exempted from taxation altogether, direct taxation would have yielded limited revenue.

Liturgies, goods or services contributed to the state by wealthy individuals in classical Athens, and *munera,* the adaptation of the Greek liturgy in Rome, permitted these small states to govern unburdened by the elaborate bureaucracies of the ancient empires, when temple and state were synonymous. Then, a liturgy was a periodic voluntary contribution of goods or services to the temple or the priest-kings, given to secure personal sanctification. As the distinction between temple and state evolved, sporadic giving became institutionalized and provided a regular source of support that the state could anticipate and regulate by law.

The Greek meaning of *liturgy* is public service.[21] Even before the sixth century B.C., when Solon first codified Athenian law, wealthy citizens of Athens were expected to contribute support for essential state functions. In the early days most contributions paid for festivals honoring local gods; the religious meaning of *liturgy* survives. But the Athenian liturgy was not simply a ritual. Its performance was honorific, a demonstration of citizenship. Wealthy citizens tried to draw public attention to their generosity; a defendant in a lawsuit in the late fifth century B.C., for example, claimed to have spent nearly ten talents (56,000 drachmai) on liturgies—more than three times the required amount. Public boasting was common and the sum was no doubt exaggerated, but it represents a very large contribution indeed.[22] Although some types of liturgy retained a voluntary character in classical Athens, and later in the municipalities of the Hellenistic Empire and the Roman Republic, the threat of confiscation or imprisonment rendered the state's demands virtually compulsory.[23] In one sense, then, the liturgy was the substantive equivalent of compulsory labor service, or corvée.[24]

The regular contributions of wealthy Athenians mainly defrayed costs of religious festivals held often throughout the year. These "ordinary" liturgies paid for the chorus in theatrical productions; for athletic events, games, and the municipal gymnasium; for torch races; and for religious processions. Grain that was donated fed the masses attending the festivals.[25]

The state also made periodic demands during emergencies to defend against aggressors. These "extraordinary" liturgies, at first sporadic, were later regularized. Well before the sixth century B.C., the state forced wealthy Athenian citizens to perform the *trirarchy*—to assume personal responsibility for the operation of a warship *(trireme)* for one year. Although the ship was provided by the state, the *trirarch* had to maintain it and provide all necessary equipment; to muster a crew and provide its food and salary; and to take personal command.[26]

This "voluntary" procurement had deficiencies, especially in wartime, for the state had no control over the standard of performance. Intermittent service meant that trirarchs often lacked skill managing ships and men. Finding a competent steersman to navigate unfamiliar waters and command the crew was problematic. Sometimes labor shortage in Athens forced trirarchs to recruit rowers from distant islands, and if the ship returned to the crew's home before a trirarch's service ended he might face mass desertions.[27] To reduce the burden, individual trirarchs might be tempted to cut corners, or to avoid personal involvement altogether, paying a contractor to provide the service.[28] By the third century B.C., when the Athenian economy

functioned with a stable currency, the trirarchy was no longer an effective allocative device, but had become purely honorific.[29] Instead, a
tax on capital assets of the wealthy, the *eisphora,* provided funds for
the state itself to build, equip, and operate the ships. Occasionally the
state collected forced loans, much like an extraordinary liturgy, from
wealthy citizens.

When the Romans occupied Egypt and the city-states of the Hellenistic Empire during the third century B.C., they simply adopted existing methods of local administration and installed Roman supervisors.
Municipal administration by voluntary liturgy suited Rome's needs
admirably, for it left the state's resources untouched. During the last
two centuries of the republic (second and first centuries B.C.), the
Romans adapted the Greek liturgy to public management of provincial cities in Italy and their western provinces.[30] There voluntary contributions of private citizens were called *munera,* the Latin word for
public service.

Besides helping pay for local religious festivals, Olympic games, and
local gladiatorial shows, the wealthiest people in Rome's provincial
cities performed many day-to-day tasks of municipal administration
and donated additions and repairs to public facilities. At regular intervals elected magistrates of the western municipalities chose some
wealthy citizens to supervise municipal agencies—police, water, public
records—and others to defray the expense of heating public baths and
repairing roads, drains and sewers, public buildings, and city walls.[31]
During the first two centuries of the republic, municipal demands were
not excessive and wealthy citizens gave generously to the cities, particularly if they had been honored by election to public office. In the
Greek city of Lycia, for example, a man named Opramoas donated
millions of drachmai to improve his own city and nearby settlements.[32]
In Egypt, where there was no tradition of local self-government, a state
official selected liturgy holders annually from a census of eligible property owners in each village, men whose wealth ranged between two
hundred and four thousand drachmai.[33]

A body of law governed the Athenian liturgies to insure equitable
distribution of the burden. No one had to perform more than one liturgy at a time, or any liturgy for more than two successive years. Orphans, invalids, the aged, and women were exempt, as were citizens
who colonized and administered Athenian provincial cities. Exemptions from ordinary liturgies might be granted as a reward for public
service, but exemption from the trirarchy was prohibited by ancient
law.[34]

A special body of law regulated the extraordinary liturgies. The trirarchy was limited to one year; a citizen could be compelled to serve again only after two years had elapsed. While serving as trirarch he was exempt from all other liturgies. A citizen who refused might be imprisoned and his property confiscated, but if he considered the financial burden excessive he could request exemption. A marketlike legal procedure known as *antidosis* provided tax relief; it was apparently designed to discourage evasion. The liable citizen who could find another person willing to assume his obligation would be excused. But the state compelled him to place all his possessions at the substitute's disposal and to accept the substitute's property in exchange.[35]

There were no such laws or customs governing allocation of municipal or imperial liturgies in territory under Roman control. The Romans adopted the liturgy solely in order to simplify provincial administration and reduce administrative costs. Ethical principles embodied in Athenian liturgies—the citizens' personal responsibility to the state, and the state's corresponding responsibility to protect them and assure equity—were not incorporated into Roman law or administrative practice. Except for Egypt, where Athenian practices had been introduced earlier, those liable to the Roman liturgies had little legal protection against excessive demands on property, and no effective channel of appeal. At best, a liable subject could petition the emperor for exemption, a practice that cities tried to curb with communications urging emperors to deny such favors.[36]

During the late republic and the early empire, within each Roman municipality, elected magistrates—and, in Egypt, state officials—were responsible for collecting the tribute and remitting it to Rome. Since the empire was prosperous, this obligation entailed little burden. These citizens saw their obligations as *honores,* public recognition of high status in the community.[37] Decurions continued to give even after municipal expenses began to rise during the early empire (second century A.D.);[38] perhaps they wished to dispel envy among fellow citizens.[39] In a sense, the early emperors ruled by collusion with the provincial upper class. Imperial grants of municipal autonomy and the principate's moderate taxes fostered cohesiveness among municipal elites. Mutual emulation promoted voluntary giving.[40] But also, as long as citizens paid their taxes, the *decemprini* or *decuriones* (as holders of liturgies were called at different times and places) would willingly collect; for, in addition to public honor, collectors could often gain a private profit from short-term personal use of tax funds (equivalent in the modern world to the "float" that dispensers of traveler's checks use to their advantage before the checks are cashed).

The voluntary arrangement worked reasonably well during the first two centuries of empire. With the anarchy and economic disorganization of the third century, however, tax collections fell off sharply; wealthy men who served as collectors were forced to draw on personal assets to make up the deficits. After the third century, the obligation became, in effect, a form of selective taxation, for the liturgies nearly always entailed a direct charge on the holder's estate.[41] Successive emperors demanded increased services and contributions in kind as the empire fell apart. Decurions had to furnish horses and mules for the imperial post and mounts for the army, and to feed and house troops stationed in the cities.[42] Since the emperors continued to hold local collectors personally responsible for these services and all expected revenues, irrespective of amounts collected, the decurions became reluctant to serve voluntarily.[43]

Legal codes of the late empire (third and fourth centuries A.D.) indicate a policy designed to prevent citizens from evading the liturgies. Its ineffectiveness may be judged from successive revisions of the codes; the law set down ever more specific standards of performance together with liability for liturgies.[44] Initially the emperors invoked the principle of collective accountability to deter an individual decurion from evading responsibility; if one member was delinquent, the others paid his share. Eventually liturgies were made compulsory for all propertied citizens except nobles, military men, and clergy. Honor turned to burden as the wealthy had to draw on private assets to meet the state's incessant demands.

Yet there were a few loopholes. A rich man could enlist in the army or try to buy a post in the imperial service in Rome for himself and his sons. If the officeholder stayed in Rome long enough or attained a high enough rank, the position might even become hereditary and effect permanent exemption for his heirs.[45] Men in public-service occupations—teachers, physicians, actors, athletes, and priests of the pagan cults, all requiring wealth and leisure for preparation—were exempt also.[46] When the Emperor Constantine was converted to Christianity early in the fourth century, he excused members of the Christian clergy from all municipal taxes and liturgies. To evade them, many citizens fled their native cities. Others joined the priesthood or entered monastic orders, and some even lived as hermits in the desert of southern Egypt.[47] Affectations of piety must have let too many wealthy men escape, for shortly afterward Constantine rescinded this immunity and forbade decurions from taking holy orders. If a man wished to enter the priesthood, he was required to demonstrate his faith by surrendering one-fourth of his property to the state.[48] When Rome's subjects moved to avoid liturgies, successive emperors issued edicts rendering all citizens liable to liturgies of their native place as well as their present residence.[49]

With only limited authority to enforce compliance, late Roman emperors adopted the policy most likely to insure it. Early in the fourth century an imperial edict decreed that henceforth membership in the curial order—to which men who provided administrative, logistic, and fiscal services belonged—would be hereditary.[50] Born into a family of decurions, a man could never escape his obligation. Confiscation of property was the penalty for default. During the fourth and fifth centuries many wealthy men evidently achieved noble (Senatorial) status by bribing palace officials to grant titles. To prevent loss of revenue, the emperors gradually restricted Senators' immunity from the liturgies and taxes, and finally abolished it.[51]

As long as government's claims on wealthy citizens were relatively few and simple, the liturgy effectively simplified provincial administration. But when external pressures forced the state to greatly enlarge its demands on donors' personal resources, provincial citizens became less and less willing to contribute, and voluntary procurement failed. States then turned to taxation to provide needed resources.

REVENUE

TAXES

In the persistent struggle to make ends meet, governments throughout the world and over the course of history have relied principally on increased taxation. When revenues fell, new taxes were added or rates of existing taxes increased. Governments also have often used citizenship or social status as a justification for demanding additional taxes. In Periclean Athens,[52] for example, only *metics,* merchants who were legal residents of Athenian provincial cities, bore the burden of rate increases. Finding revenue from provincial taxes too low, the third-century Roman Emperor Caracalla extended Roman citizenship to all residents of the empire wherever they lived, thus making residents of provincial cities liable for Roman taxes as well as for the local taxes they had previously paid.[53] Citizenship became a means of supporting the state, as well as of (hopefully) influencing it.

Like most governments through history before the modern era, Greece and Rome derived revenue where wealth was visible. While maintaining tax exemptions for elite groups, both taxed the commercial classes heavily. Special edicts compelled merchants to provide supplementary services and additional taxes. Often, in emergencies, governments made forced drafts on funds held by commercial classes.[54]

Athens and Rome levied few direct taxes in the early period when both enjoyed adequate revenue (from public lands inherited from the ancient kings) to support their limited activities. Initially, each republic's finances rested on rents paid to cultivate state-owned land or to extract mineral resources from it, or to use markets, gymnasia, baths, and other public structures.[55] A variety of indirect taxes on commerce supplemented this revenue, including customs duties at the ports of Piraeus and Ostia, market taxes on commodities imported overland (collected at city gates, and again at point of sale), and special taxes levied on sale of personal property such as land and slaves.[56] Rates were low, varying between one and 5 percent of the value of goods taxed.[57]

To be taxed directly symbolized dishonor, incompatible with the ideal of a free citizen. In Athens, for example, only low-status residents, such as prostitutes and aliens, paid direct taxes.[58] Financial emergencies caused by prolonged wars eventually forced both Athens and Rome to abandon this prohibition against taxing free citizens, and to adopt a direct tax on capital assets. During the Peloponnesian Wars, the Athenian council reactivated the *eisphora,* an ancient tax on capital assets. Assessed at progressive rates and initially paid by the wealthy as an extraordinary liturgy during military emergencies, it was used regularly to supplement revenue during the Hellenistic Empire.[59]

Thus elements of three different political orders were found in classical Athens; their coexistence may account for controversy over the extent of Athenian egalitarianism. The least powerful residents—those without a voice or capacity to influence the rules—paid direct taxes. They lived under a slave regime for tax purposes, even though they did not have the legal status of slaves. During the republican period the principle of equality for the nobility governed policy decisions; then Athens levied indirect taxes at low levels. As need for revenue increased because of war-induced fiscal stress, elements of hierarchy appeared. Athens adopted direct taxes. Although administered initially by citizens, the new taxes were levied on all property owners.

When the Roman Republic began paying soldiers wages, in the fourth century B.C., it adopted the *tributum,* a direct tax on property. Each year the Senate determined the amount of revenue required, then prorated that sum among the taxpaying population in proportion to the value of each taxpayer's capital assets, determined in a special census of assessment. Rates were low, less than one percent of the tax-payer's property.[60] Those without property paid *tributum in capita,* a personal tax similar to the poll taxes of the ancient monarchies. The burden fell solely upon the commercial and plebeian orders, for Senators, who comprised the landowning aristocracy, paid no direct taxes.[61]

As the Roman Republic annexed territory at the end of successful wars, it took over taxes already being levied in each district before the conquest.[62] Provincial revenue derived mainly from land and its produce. To cultivate public land *(ager publicus)* confiscated by the republic, provincial citizens paid a rental fee, or *stipendia.* In addition, each year the cultivators owed a tithe, a direct tax on produce of the land, paid in kind at varying rates—those traditional in each locality before the conquest.[63] In Spain and Sicily taxes were nominal.* The fertile provinces of Asia paid at higher rates, generally one-tenth of perishable crops and one-fifth to one-sixth of grains.[65] Ore from Spain's silver mines also contributed wealth to Rome's coffers; it was extracted by gangs of slaves managed by contractors.[66] By the first century B.C., the provinces had become so productive that the Senate stopped collecting direct taxes from all citizens of Rome and the Roman cities of the Italian peninsula.[67] When Cicero observed, ". . . government cannot possibly be maintained without taxes,[68] [for] revenues are the sinews of the republic," [69] he was commenting on Rome's financial security at that time. Rome was the master in a regime of slavery.

The empire's use of hierarchy is manifested in its financial administration as well as in other aspects of political life. Markets reinforced hierarchy as imperial financial administration in Roman provinces gradually became professionalized. During the peace and prosperity of the early empire, the provinces continued to make regular remittances to Rome. Early emperors abandoned the tithe, substituting the *tributum soli*—a uniform fixed tax on land, payable initially in kind and later in money. Shifting to taxes paid in coin may actually have created prosperity as subjects in remote provinces traded goods formerly bartered or consumed locally, to raise money to pay taxes. Development

---

* From backward regions such as Gaul, Britain, and Spain, the Romans exacted tribute in compulsory labor for building and maintaining roads and aqueducts. Except for Roman Egypt, where peasants had provided conscript labor on dikes and canals for thousands of years before the Roman conquest, corvée was an uncommon form of taxation in most of the territory governed by Athens, and in Rome during the republic and the early empire. Corvée was unnecessary because many public facilities were built by wealthy citizens who contributed the money and materials, and provided their personal slaves to do the work.[64]

of internal trade networks, in turn, helped to tie the far-flung empire together.[70] Although tax rates were low and remained unchanged during the entire period of empire, efficiency of collection increased in the imperial provinces when civil servants selected by the emperors replaced tax farmers who had collected provincial revenues for the Senate during the late republic.[71]

While Roman citizens still paid no direct taxes, the Senate continued to levy a variety of indirect taxes on them, as it did on provincials. Rome had collected *portoria* (customs duties on commodities traded overland and by sea) since the early days of the republic. During the early empire, rates were low, 2.5 percent of the value of goods traded in Gaul and Asia, and probably 5 percent in Africa and Illyricum.[72] Whenever a master freed a slave, the state levied a manumission tax ranging between 2 and 5 percent of the slave's value; from one to 4 percent was charged on sale of slaves at auction.[73] A variety of other transactions taxes brought in additional revenue.[74]

During the second and third centuries A.D., fixed expenses climbed as the imperial bureaucracy and army expanded. But, although commitments had increased sharply, direct taxes remained at traditional low rates. The imperial hierarchy began to be squeezed between rising costs and a fixed income, while rapid inflation, caused in part by its debasements and its spending, reduced the value of money revenue. During the second century the denarius fell to 10 percent of its value during the previous century.[75] By A.D. 301, when Diocletian issued his edict specifying maximum prices, the price of wheat was fifty to one hundred times higher than representative prices during the second century.[76] The emperors searched desperately for alternative revenue, yet still did not raise direct taxes.[77] Because agricultural methods in those times fixed productivity at a low level, the emperors believed taxes had reached an upper limit. When provincial revenue became insufficient to support the state, citizens of Rome and the Italian cities lost their tax exemption; once again Roman citizens had to pay all imperial taxes, direct and indirect.[78]

As the empire grew in size and internal complexity, it became progressively more difficult for a single ruler to maintain control. With rapid accession of one weak ruler after another to the throne,* there

* Historians refer to the middle fifty years of the third century of the Roman Empire as "the anarchy." The rapid turnover in leadership is an index of political instability. Between the death of Severus Alexander and the accession of Diocletian, there were about twenty legitimate emperors; each reigned on an average about two and a half years; all but two died by violence—murdered by conspirators or killed in civil wars.[79]

was no continuity in fiscal policy and no internal control over expenditures. Successive emperors tried to reduce deficits by levying a proliferating variety of indirect taxes on property, residence, occupation, and sale of commodities.[80] On top of regular taxes, all citizens had to pay irregular emergency taxes, varying in amount from one year to another according to political and economic circumstances; the new levies became an onerous burden as government made increasing ad-hoc demands. An Egyptian document conveys the urgent tenor of appeals for funds: "The King has repeatedly issued orders for crown gifts; do all you can, and in haste. . . . The gifts must reach Alexandria within three days. . . . Also send what is due . . . for the King's birthday." [81] Special levies included the crown gold, a large gift of gold coins to each new emperor for his inauguration, and the *annona,* a periodic contribution of grain or money to provide food for the growing population of Rome (and, after the third century, for the army).[82]

Emperors in the second and third centuries relied on the army to maintain law and order; soldiers' wages were the largest single expenditure. Soldiers also helped the Roman governors collect taxes[83] when wealthy provincial citizens (who had performed these duties as voluntary liturgies during the early empire) tried to evade the imperial government's demand that they make up the deficit from personal wealth. To maintain the army's loyalty and to mitigate the effects of inflation, the emperors gradually increased military wages and granted generous pensions to soldiers returned from the provinces.* After the third century—with the imperial treasury in perpetual deficit and the currency depreciated—the emperors could pay neither regular wages nor pensions. Taking the law into their own hands, soldiers foraged the provinces for food and supplies.[85] If the hierarchy's propensity toward lavish spending is not matched by equivalent revenue, a regime is in real trouble. As the government lost its ability to command revenue to sustain traditional obligations, it lost control of the empire.

Tax reforms initiated by the Emperor Diocletian were implemented by coercive tactics common to all branches of imperial administration during the late empire. Just as in the ancient monarchies, the army and the imperial civil service combined to police the population and force compliance with the law.

With the goal of restoring the empire's failing authority, Diocletian adopted a policy designed simultaneously to increase the state's reve-

---

* Caesar and Augustus had paid the soldiers 150 denarii a year; Tiberius, 225; Domitian had raised the stipend to 300; there it remained for a century. Then Commodus raised it to 375, Severus to 500, Caracalla to 750.[84]

nue and to augment its power. According to most historians, Diocletian's famous tax edicts of A.D. 301 did not introduce new practices; but they did improve methods of collecting the irregular taxes common during the previous century.[86] Because the edicts provided that most taxes and all government debts be paid in kind, historians of the period have dismissed Diocletian's reforms as a retrogressive return to natural economy. But compared to the fiscal chaos of the previous century, these tax edicts reflected a pragmatic approach in a time of rapid change and instability within government and society. The reforms attempted to marshal the empire's resources to meet its primary obligations—wages for the large civil and military bureaucracy needed to keep the government in power. By increasing tax yields, Diocletian tried to create a fiscal cushion against contingencies.

To provide food for the army, Diocletian combined the previous century's irregular taxes into one tax on agricultural output (the *annona*), payable at regular intervals.[87] To simplify administration, he established a uniform rate throughout the empire, but provided a hedge against uncertainty by building in a flexible rate structure that could be adjusted each year to meet government's needs and yet conform to changing provincial supplies (see pages 125–26). Like the earlier Roman land tax, the *tributum,* the annona rested on a comprehensive agricultural census that classified all land in the empire according to productivity. Combining the characteristics of the ancient head tax and the traditional direct tax on land, the annona was assessed according to a hypothetical measure of average productivity. That measure, the *iugatio-caput,* represented the amount of land of any quality that one man aided by an ox could cultivate and live on.[88]

Administered by an enlarged corps of civil servants, backed by the army, the annona was expensive to collect, for it entailed all the administrative complexity of the fiscal systems of ancient kings—tax census, cadastral survey, state collectors, state granaries, and a network of spies to report evasion.[89] Hierarchy proliferated. As in the ancient kingdoms, revenue collected in kind in each administrative district was used locally to pay troops and civil servants. With more than ten thousand civil servants estimated in the eastern provinces alone,[90] and over 400,000 soldiers as provincial garrisons,[91] little was left for central government when fixed expenses had been met. To supplement revenue in kind, Diocletian levied the crown gold every five years and, like the ancient kings, charged fees for granting local monopolies on production and sale of commodities. Collecting revenue in kind depressed economic activity. Trade within the empire withered; the money supply shrank.[92]

The centralized system of taxing and allocating receipts established by Diocletian remained essentially unchanged for several centuries. With minor modifications by the Eastern Roman Emperor Constantine early in the fourth century, the *iugatio-caput* provided support for the early Byzantine state.

TAX ADMINISTRATION: TAX FARMING

Early in their history, the Athenian and Roman republics got their income from the same source the ancient kings did—periodic rental of state-owned land. Financial officers (*tamiai*) of the Athenian council appointed agents to collect and remit rents at regular intervals. When limited taxation was imposed to supplement this income, the councils appointed additional officials who were directly accountable to the councils—collectors as well as inspectors to insure that collectors did not cheat the state.[93] This division of authority and accountability was similar to administrative organization in the ancient monarchies. As each new tax was imposed, and the bevy of officials needed to collect and distribute revenue increased, the structure became more complicated and more cumbersome. By the middle of the fourth century B.C., the council had adopted an entirely different, and greatly simplified, arrangement for collecting some local taxes and all revenue from distant provincial cities. As hierarchy reached its limits, it was supplanted by market methods.

As the use of money became common, the Athenian council turned to tax farming to simplify financial administration: it began collecting taxes on a fee-for-service basis. Each year the council contracted with private businessmen known as *telonai* (buyers of taxes) to collect revenue. As self-made men whose wealth came from business, tax farmers normally had social status inferior to the governing aristocracy's. (Elite opinion characterized one tax farmer as "vulgar in character, lacking any decency, and without principle." [94]) The Boulé granted short-term franchises for each indirect tax to individual tax farmers, and also contracted with individuals or tax-farming syndicates (*telonarches*) to collect tribute from provincial cities.[95] Businessmen (either individuals or syndicates) who wished to become state fiscal agents submitted competitive bids to the council[96] specifying how much they were willing to pay for the privilege of collecting taxes.

Ideally, the highest bidder was to win the council's choice. But, to guard against possible default from an agent's lack of capital, Athens imposed stringent conditions that effectively discouraged all but rich men from competing for a contract. When a bid was entered, the state demanded a deposit; a bidder who won the contract had to pay half the fee in advance and the remainder six months later. Since local taxes came in at irregular intervals, these requirements for venture capital prevented the marginally wealthy from entering bids.

To protect further against possible losses, Athens threatened harsh sanctions for default in payment of the second half of the contract fee. Violators might be sent to prison and lose voting rights; these penalties connoted *atimia*, civic dishonor. Those still delinquent after nine-tenths of the fiscal year would suffer a doubled obligation and confiscation of property, and would also forfeit their deposit. To compound the hardship, atimia was transferred to a prisoner's children until the debt was paid. On occasion, however, the citizen assembly could also grant relief; in the event of a major crisis like war or plague, the assembly could vote to cut the contract fee in half.[97]

By contracting with the telonai, the council at once simplified internal administration of finance, insured a certain income from each specific tax or territory, and eliminated possible losses from calamities of nature, war, or fraud. But there were several disadvantages in the arrangement. In exchange for a guaranteed income, the state had to sacrifice some revenue, for in a good year the contract fee might be lower than the revenue the state could have collected on its own (even after deducting costs of collection). Further, by agreeing to confer state authority on private individuals, who did not necessarily share such other goals as maintaining legitimacy and administering effectively, the councils thereby also weakened their control over the government.

In return for sums paid to the council, the telonarch had the potential for gain limited only by the effectiveness of his collection. The tax farmer also assumed a significant risk—the same risk the state was avoiding. As an independent agent of the state, he had only minor police power to enforce compliance: he was entitled to search ships and containers, to confiscate goods smuggled through customs, and to bring charges against smugglers; beyond these powers, a tax farmer could rely only on intimidation or on coercion to insure payment. Threatened with losses from poor harvests, wars, and the ever present drain on receipts from his hired collectors' embezzlement, the average agent earned relatively modest rewards,[98] sometimes operating so close to the margin that he was forced to rely on anticipated profits of a new contract to pay off debts of an old one.[99] As an inducement to perform this risky but essential government function, the council guaranteed tax farmers immunity from compulsory military service.[100] Yet the fact that contracts found ready buyers marks them as reasonable investments. When optimum conditions prevailed, an Athenian tax farmer might earn more than 12 percent a year, the normal rate of return on invested capital in Athens in those days.[101]

As long as the tax farmer paid the second half of his contract fee on time, there was no attempt to regulate his performance. But if rumors of a tax farmer's cheating became widespread, the Boulé would not renew his contract. Although there were some instances of collusive bidding to push up the contract price, Athenian tax farmers operated too close to the source of power to abuse their franchises.[102]

As Athenian territory expanded during the Hellenistic period, tax farming became established in Greek colonies in Egypt and on the Italian peninsula.[103] Athenian provincial cities and cities of the Hellenistic Empire were distant from Athens; there, in no danger of close surveillance, tax farmers were free to eliminate competitors for the franchise by bribery[104] and to exact tribute from the natives by every conceivable means. Tax farmers' avarice is amply documented. A wealthy lady in the Hellenistic city of Cos, for example, speaking for her class, complains in a letter to a friend: "Every door now trembles against the tax farmers." [105]

As the Roman armies conquered surrounding territories, the Roman Senate, like the Boulé, simplified its administrative responsibilities and avoided a large, uncontrollable financial bureaucracy by contracting with Publicans, wealthy members of the commercial Equestrian order, to collect provincial revenue. In the Roman *municipia*—the towns of the Italian peninsula—and in Sicily, Rome's moderate taxes brought in modest revenues. The Senate awarded short-term, one-year contracts for each tax to several small tax farmers in each municipality. There, as in Athens, the contractor's function was limited and, although his profits were modest (0.6 percent to one percent of the crop), he seldom tried to cheat taxpayers or the state.[106] In Egypt the Romans adopted a system of financial administration inherited from the Ptolemies, which was in turn a modified version of the centralized administration established during the New Kingdom. Tax farmers in Roman Egypt were closely controlled, and they functioned as little more than an arm of the bureaucracy. A network of government inspectors supervised small contractors in each district to make sure that profit from each franchise was no more than 10 percent of the contract fee.[107]

Tax farmers had far greater autonomy and power in distant territories. The Senate could exert only a minimum of control through provincial governors whose personal interests sometimes diverged sharply from the state's. At least one Roman governor, the notorious Verres, used his post in Sicily to enrich himself by pocketing funds, accepting bribes, and entering into collusive agreements with local tax contractors.[108] Even honest governors lacked adequate means to supervise collection. With no other way to collect provincial taxes, the Senate often was forced to ignore graft and to grant special concessions to tax farmers.

As early in the republic as 215 B.C., for example, a consortium of three Equestrian companies (whose nineteen members had become wealthy from providing services to government) contracted with the Senate to ship grain and supplies on credit to armies in Spain. Because the Senate had no other way to transport supplies, the syndicate could specify contract conditions to minimize risk. It would carry the cargo only if the Senate would reimburse members for loss in a storm of some dilapidated ships bearing worthless cargo.[109] As a further reward for service, syndicate members demanded exemption from military service.[110]

During the Roman Republic and Empire, travel between Rome and Roman provinces in the eastern Mediterranean took at least six weeks overland for specially picked runners, and somewhat longer by sea for the fastest ships in good weather.[111] To simplify leasing revenues, the Senate negotiated a single contract for all direct and indirect revenues from each distant province. In the wealthy province of Asia during the last century of the republic, tax farmers collected both fixed taxes (tithes, head taxes on man and beast, and rental payments on the public lands) and indirect taxes (such as tolls, customs dues, municipal taxes, and special levies on doors, windows, and columns, and on salt).[112]

Farming revenues in a productive province was a large-scale enterprise demanding substantial capital. The syndicate holding contracts in Bythnia during the first century B.C., for example, had tens of thousands of employees.[113] Early in the republic several Equestrians in Rome formed joint-stock companies, the *societates publicanorum,* to pool their capital and share the risk of doing business at long distance.[114]

The syndicates sometimes operated as holding companies which in turn delegated their authority to small local contractors in exchange for a flat fee. Local contractors' ambitions guaranteed only slightly reduced profits, yet eliminated the need for an elaborate system of internal control. The syndicate had a network of warehouses for storing taxes collected in kind, and a fleet of ships for transporting part of the produce to Rome. In good years, when revenue exceeded the contract fee, the syndicate enhanced receipts by trading. At the great market on the island of Delos, syndicate traders exchanged grain at a favorable rate for spices and cloth, which they shipped to Rome and sold at a profit.

Publicans also performed other services for the Senate. They bought mining contracts, built roads and public buildings under contract, and provided postal service.[115] In occasional emergencies Roman syndicate members supported the Senatorial treasury by lending it money. But their principal subsidiary function was to provide Rome with a flexible method of allocation. Tax farming was a simple way for the Senate to discharge provincial financial obligations without running the risk of transferring provisions or coins for long distances under uncertain conditions.

The syndicates paid their contract fee to the Senate at the end of the year after taxes had been collected, and, as a consequence, provincial syndicate agents usually held large stocks of grain or coin. Early in the republic the Senate adopted the practice of drawing against these stocks to meet local expenses. The Senate would issue warrants on tax-farming companies, who then paid the state's local debt in money or in kind (deducting the amounts advanced locally from annual contract fees). In this way most transactions between the Senate and the tax farmers were negotiated on paper with no need for physical transfer of large amounts of money, always a risky venture under ancient conditions.* As the republic became involved in wars of conquest, it spent more than it collected in most provinces; and only a small amount of local collections ever reached Rome.

Only the Asian taxes produced an annual surplus.[116] In that fertile province abundant agricultural output produced large revenues, and the tax franchise was highly remunerative. As an incentive to serve so far from Rome, the Senate granted a long-term (five-year) contract,[117] and therefore demanded a large fee. Armed with the security of a long-term franchise, the syndicates could punitively exact taxes from the population with little risk of cancellation by the Senate.

The principal opportunity for extra gain stemmed from the absence of a market mechanism for converting agricultural produce into money. As a barter economy still existed in the agricultural districts, local subcontractors profited by converting taxes paid in grain into the money payments demanded by the Roman Senate.

---

* The Greeks and the Romans used small, shallow-drafted vessels propelled by oarsmen and fragile sails. They had rudimentary knowledge of navigation, and always feared sailing out of sight of land. Long distances were negotiated by moving from point to point along the Mediterranean shore, setting out each morning, making for land at night. Since Greek and Roman sailors would travel only during spring and summer, when storms were not likely, a round trip from, say, Athens to Alexandria might take a year and a half, six months in each direction, with a six-month layover.

Writing in the first century B.C., Cicero reported that corrupt governors instructed tax farmers to collect in-kind taxes at remote places where taxpayers were ignorant of the market value of their produce. Agents could convert grain into money at less than the going rate, then profit later from its sale. In suitable circumstances, the syndicate could hold the grain until the price increased, then reap a speculative profit. In some districts, tax farmers could actually corner the market and set prices.[118]

Syndicate agents in Roman Asia exacted a tithe of 10 percent of the crop from all landowners, unmercifully and irrespective of personal circumstances. If a landowner could not pay, the syndicate—acting as an agricultural bank—offered to lend funds at interest rates that ranged from 12 percent (the legal but unenforceable maximum) up to 48 percent.[119] When the landowner could not pay tax arrears plus accumulated interest, the tax-farming syndicate confiscated his land.*

The Senate repeatedly tried to control these extortionate practices by cajolery and threats to prosecute or cancel contracts. But since the Senate was dependent on tax farmers to collect the Asian revenue, and the Asian province was so remote, its hands were tied.[121] Or perhaps Senators had no incentive to control the syndicates. There is evidence that some Senators, though prohibited by law from making personal investments in a business, nevertheless aimed to participate in syndicate profits by buying unregistered shares in tax-farming companies.[122] With a share of the proceeds at stake, why try to interfere? In an establishment composed of market and hierarchic elements, a mutually beneficial symbiosis may sometimes come about: each social order can contribute services essential for the other. Hierarchy provides the organizational boundaries needed to strengthen defense, while competitive individualism increases productivity. But if the hierarchy becomes too rigid, or if individualists are too venal, such developments may force a change in the terms of accommodation between the two groups.

Loss of revenue from tax farmers' usurious profits, and accumulation of large landholdings in Asia (on which, as Roman citizens, tax farmers paid no taxes), caused the first Roman Emperor, Augustus Caesar, to look for a better way to collect imperial revenues. Early in his principate, Augustus stopped selling tax-farming contracts in the

* Yet we must not go too far; tax farming *was* risky. Some rapacious governors extorted so much from provincial cities that they bled the residents dry. For one five-year period during the late republic, for example, tax farmers in Cilicia sustained losses; because the governor had been there before them, the syndicate could not collect any revenue.[120]

imperial provinces for all but indirect taxes.* Augustus replaced the
tithe paid in kind with a fixed money tax collected by state servants.
That this change reduced the Asian province's tax burden by one-
third, while presumably sustaining Rome's revenues, indicates the
scale of tax-farming profits there.[124] Tax farmers operating in the Senatorial provinces during the early empire were gradually forced out
everywhere but in North Africa as the emperors developed their own
bureaucracy.

An effective device for a small or weak state, or a loosely linked empire with limited internal communication, tax farming, by harnessing
private enterprise to perform a perennially unpopular task, guaranteed
the state a secure, if limited, revenue without necessitating either an
elaborate bureaucracy—difficult to control at long distance—or enforcement mechanisms to counteract the citizenry's perennial reluctance to pay. In an age before banking, tax farming provided an easy
way to handle tax receipts and government payments for services
without shipping bulky commodities and money from place to place.
As with spending by earmarking, tax collection and spending was a
one-step process. Because of these advantages, tax farming reappeared
in Byzantium, and it was used by most governments in Europe during
the Middle Ages and the early modern era.

SPENDING IN REPUBLIC AND EMPIRE

THE TREASURIES AND EARMARKING

The balanced government budget is a recent invention, no more than
125 years old. In the republics of Athens and Rome—as in the empires,

* New evidence from Palmyra, an oasis along a caravan route between Asia and the
Mediterranean, illustrates imperial efforts to systematize local market taxes and control
tax farmers responsible for collection:

"Since in former times most of the dues were not set down in the tax law but were exacted by convention ... and it frequently happened that disputes arose ... between ...
merchants and ... tax collectors, it is resolved that the magistrates in office and the [mu-
nicipal tax board] should determine the dues not set down in the law and write them into
the next contract, and assign to each class of goods the tax laid down by custom. ... When
[the taxes] have been confirmed ... they should be written ... on the stone column opposite the temple. ... [Moreover] the magistrates ... should ... see that the contractor does
not exact any excess charge."

This edict specifies market taxes on food staples (olive oil, salt fish, animal fat), luxuries
(unguent in alabaster vessels, in goatskins), clothing (purple-dyed fleece, clothes workshops, clothes merchants traveling about the city), services (taxes on prostitutes, on loading and unloading pack animals), and on sale of slaves. The heaviest tax levied in this
desert settlement (800 denarii per year) was paid by water users, either for irrigating cultivated plots or for watering camels.[123] Apparently custom in the desert embodied the
market principle, no longer common, of pricing water relative to its scarcity.

feudal states, and monarchies that followed them—equivalence of income and expenditure, even when it was sought, was an accident as often as it was a result of deliberate intent. In Athens and Rome throughout the classical period—as in the ancient empires—when strong leadership coincided with peace and good harvests, or if conquest yielded abundant tribute, there was little need for additional revenue.[125] But when bad weather or losses in war combined with weakness at the top, the government, like its people, faced hardship. In the ancient world any unanticipated event forcing governments to contribute from fixed resources created an excess burden for state treasuries. But the level at which balance occurred, or the size of a surplus or deficit, was not merely happenstance. Budgetary balance or deficit is related to political regime.

Two precepts, economy and moderation, provide the best guidelines for state financial management; so spoke Aristotle, who thought the state should be run like a well-managed house:

> [He who gives] advice on ways and means should be acquainted with the nature and extent of state resources, so that if any is omitted it may be added, and if any is insufficient it may be increased. Further, he should know all the expenses of the state, that if any is superfluous it may be removed, or if too great, may be curtailed. For men become wealthier, not only by what they already possess, but by cutting down expenses.[126]

But the goal of economy was hard to attain. If revenues met expenditures and provided a modest surplus—as happened in Athens during the time of Pericles, and during the reigns of the Roman emperors Augustus,[127] Nero, Nerva, and Hadrian—although government's power and autonomy were greatly enhanced thereby, such stability was short-lived. If wars depleted the surplus or if revenues dwindled, governments of Athens and Rome were forced to adopt a variety of often desperate, and usually ineffective, expedients to attain a rough correspondence between revenue and expenditure.[128] Historians viewing financial practices of ancient Athens and the Roman Republic and Empire from a modern perspective have perceived them as unnecessarily chaotic.[129] Yet the limited opportunities for control suggest that the few brief periods of stability and financial adequacy were the abnormal circumstances.

The governments of classical Athens and the Roman Republic were small and provided very few direct services, relying instead on voluntary contributions or service provided under contract to accomplish a few essential functions. They did not need complex accounts.

Instead of the cumbersome administrative machinery required to receive and process state revenues paid in kind (as in ancient Mesopotamia, China, and India), state finances in Athens—and later in Rome—were managed with a device that greatly simplified collection and distribution of revenues: earmarking. Surviving records of state finances show that earmarking and tax farming partially achieved what is accomplished today through the budget. By requiring tax farmers to pay franchise fees before taxes were collected, the republics tried to assure payment of at least minimal revenues over the short run. Though ineffective in controlling the flow of funds over time, earmarking made it possible to keep track of current receipts and expenditures.

Regular state revenues were paid into separate funds; each fund could be used only to meet a specific expenditure. For a state with limited financial and administrative resources, assigning receipts from specific revenue sources to special funds with particular uses is budgeting in a straightforward way. With earmarking there is no question about how resources will be used, because the use is specified. Availability of funds determines amounts spent; unless there is a large surplus in an earmarked fund, balances act as a check on spending, for when revenues are depleted, expenditure for the fund's specified purpose must stop.

Generally speaking, a centralized treasury goes along with centralized rule. Regimes with strong boundaries—large hierarchies or small equities—aim to allocate resources for everyone all at once. Now, in past ages earmarking has often been used simply because there was no other way to achieve collective allocation—no better technology existed. But when earmarking is not mandated by absence of financial technology, its use indicates strong tendencies toward competitive individualism. Separation of revenue by source and allocation of receipts by function in modern governments in effect convert collective goods into individual ones, for such specificity permits calculation of losses and gains by private people.

Earmarking simplifies financial administration. In the ancient world, this was directly accomplished by physically separating funds.[130] The Athenians had several public treasuries at various places on the Acropolis. Each treasury had its own staff of administrators, clerks to receive payments, and a strongbox to lock up receipts. Officials made disbursements and kept records of amounts received and spent. During the preclassical period there were separate treasuries for military defense, capital construction, and civil administration, but, as these functions were provided largely by liturgy, the amounts in each treasury were probably small.

By the sixth century B.C., money had come into general use in Athenian commerce,[131] and the few taxes levied on commercial dealings were paid to the governing council in coin. When Athens began to demand taxes in money, rather than in personal service or in kind, a large number of separate treasuries appeared.[132] Each received revenue from a separate source and made disbursements for specific purposes. At one time revenue from harbor duties was allocated for improvements to port facilities at Piraeus; any surplus was used for repairs to the city's walls.[133] Receipts from court fees and fines paid salaries of judges and jurors.

After the Athenian Republic assumed responsibility for civil defense, military expenses were paid from a separate fund, the *theorica,* which contained receipts from the tax on capital assets. Its evolution illustrates how an allocative technique like earmarking may be adapted to changing conditions. The theorica was originally established to replace the trirarchy as a source of support for the Athenian navy; its funds were used to build warships and to pay salaries of the fifty or more rowers on each vessel. Since the state collected the tax on capital assets annually, whether at war or not, balances in the theorica built up rapidly during peacetime.

By the middle of the fourth century B.C., this surplus was used to pay for popular entertainment and food distributed during religious festivals; thus was manifested the principle of equity. Control over the theorica gave the fund's administrators great power, for it permitted them to court the people's favor. During the mid–fourth century B.C. the fund's commissioner, Eubulus, persuaded the Boulé to adopt a flexible method of earmarking. This increased his power still further, by providing that all surplus revenue be deposited in the theoric fund during peacetime, or into a newly created military fund, which Eubulus also administered, in the event of war.[134] Centralized power was in the making.

The principal expense in Athens during the Hellenistic period, and in the Roman Republic, was wages for the army, which were paid in kind to soldiers in the provinces, using the grain received from direct taxes on provincial land. Expenses for civil administration were moderate for both governments. Officials appointed by the governing councils served voluntarily or for a low salary, and their personal slaves performed the day-to-day work.[135]

In the Roman Republic the principal source of state revenue, the tax on public land, was deposited into a treasury fund, the Aerarium Saturnii, so named because it was located in the basement of the Temple of Saturn in the Roman Forum. The Aerarium became the republic's principal treasury. Revenue from all sources flowed into it—rental payments on the public lands, taxes on its produce, tribute from subject territories, and contract fees paid by tax farmers. The Senate appointed Aerarium officials, who made disbursements to the army, to the Publicans who contracted with it to provide internal improvements, and for the modest costs of civil administration. Rome's expanding resources fostered acquisitive tendencies. "I need a quaestor or magistrate who will supply me with gold from the state's moneybags," a man named Lucilius asserted.[136]

The republic's affluence became visible as the spoils of conquest supported Rome's building boom during the second half of the second century B.C. Huge volumes of captured treasure flowed there to pay for (and decorate) new public buildings that transformed the city. An aqueduct built at the same time cost 45 million denarii. By contrast, Athens spent only two million denarii to build the Parthenon, the cult statue of Athena, and the monumental entrance to the Acropolis.[137]

During the early Roman Empire, state expenses increased sharply. Aiming to appease the gods, create personal monuments and provide employment for the city's expanding population of poor immigrants, the early emperors built imposing public buildings in the large cities, aqueducts to bring pure water to growing city populations, and a network of good, hard-surfaced roads throughout the empire.[138] The ruling hierarchy began to build a bureaucracy. Emperors gradually created a salaried civil service to perform the tasks of civil administration and collect taxes; its wages eventually became a large item of state expense.[139]

The early emperors established personal dominion over state finances by founding their own treasuries. During the early empire there were at least three major treasuries in Rome. The Aerarium continued to serve as the treasury of receipt for the Senatorial provinces until the mid–first century B.C., when Claudius usurped the Senate's power to appoint Aerarium officials.[140] Early in the principate Augustus used his personal fortune to buy control of the army. Donating 170 million sesterces, Augustus established a separate military treasury, the Aerarium Militare, specifically to pay soldiers' wages and pensions.[141]

To hold revenues from the newly annexed imperial provinces, the emperors established separate provincial treasuries—called *fisci,* from the Latin word for "basket"—administered by their *procurators.* Early emperors also kept personal wealth *(patrimonium)* separate from imperial funds. This geographic separation of funds was not a manifestation of decentralization, but of the extension of central control to the provinces. The financial power of most of the early emperors, derived from the enormous patrimonium, made it possible for them to supplement inadequate state revenue with personal wealth. It was largely a strategy of political expediency in his struggle with the Senate that prompted Augustus to contribute over two billion sesterces to the state during the forty years of his reign, a sum equivalent to seven times the Republic's total revenues in the year 62 B.C., thirty-five years before he took office. Once the precedent for emperors' contribution to the state was established, his successors continued to contribute their private funds to the imperial treasury until the distinction between emperors' private revenues and state revenue was gradually obscured.[142]

As happened with the early division between Senatorial and imperial revenue, earmarking the emperor's own wealth was gradually abandoned as the fiscus became the sole imperial treasury.[143] Like revenue from the public lands during the republic, the patrimonium was a reliable source of funds for public purposes and a reserve for emergencies.[144]

During the early empire the emperors drew mainly on funds in provincial treasuries. The emperors could withdraw funds from the Aerarium for limited expenses in Rome—wages of the imperial guard and food given to the Roman population on feast days. But since disbursement from the Aerarium was so slow, being constrained by bureaucratic procedure, most emperors preferred to use their personal wealth instead. As surplus revenue resulted from tightened administrative controls in the imperial provinces, provincial balances were transferred to Rome and deposited into local branches of the provincial fisci. Revenues from new imperial taxes were also paid into new earmarked funds. By the middle of the first century A.D., there were at least five fisci in Rome.*

The fiscus was no longer a collection of earmarked funds by the beginning of the second century A.D., but had become the principal treasury of the empire. Like the Athenian state treasury and the Roman Republic's Aerarium, the fiscus received imperial revenue from all sources; and its army of officials and clerks paid out funds on demand to meet expenses of maintaining the army, the civil bureaucracy, the imperial household, and the cost of public works.[146] But activities of the fiscus extended far beyond the traditional functions of a state trea-

---

* Two fisci held surplus revenue from Asia and Egypt; a third fiscus, the emperor's personal funds; a fourth, proceeds of the Jewish poll tax; and the last contained revenue from a new tax, the annona, allocated to military wages.[145]

sury, in many ways resembling those of a modern business conglomerate. There is no doubt that the fiscus loaned money for a profit; it was probably the largest banker in the empire.[147] The fiscus was also involved in merchandising. During Vespasian's reign the fiscus began to rent stalls in the imperial Forum to traders and to market goods there—metal from state mines, produce from imperial estates, and grain from provinces that still paid taxes in kind.[148]

The army continued to be the largest imperial cost, as it had been during the republic. When the use of money became common throughout the empire, emperors began to pay the Roman legions in coin. While a soldier was stationed abroad, the fiscus kept a running account of his accumulated wages and his expenses for supplies. Often by the time the soldier returned from a long campaign, his expenses were so large that when these were deducted from his accumulated wages, the treasury did not have to pay out much.[149] During the first two centuries of empire, the Roman army had between twenty-eight and thirty legions, or about 150,000 to 160,000 men. In addition, there were cavalry, light-armed troops and the forces stationed in and around Rome, totaling another 150,000.[150] Although prices had increased steadily during the first two centuries of empire, soldiers' wages lagged, having been raised only at century-long intervals, first by Caesar (to 900 sesterces), then Domitian (1,200 sesterces), and finally Septimus Severus (1,800 to 2,000 sesterces).[151] To maintain the troops' loyalty and compensate them for their long service, the emperors granted each soldier supplemental bounties by providing severance pay in land or cash. For the ordinary foot soldier, the supplements were modest (12,000 sesterces), but for an officer such as a senior centurion (*primus pilus*), the payments might be enough to give him Equestrian rank on retirement (400,000 sesterces or 100,000 denarii).[152] * When aggregated and combined with wages for the late empire's swollen bureaucracy, the state's fixed cost in wages and pensions must have been enormous.

During the third century, when invasions, economic disorganization, and political alienation had caused revenues to dwindle, the imperial treasury was forced to discharge its obligations through barter. With proceeds of the military annona collected in kind, soldiers once again could be paid.[154]

Diocletian's reforms of A.D. 301, systematizing collection of revenue

* Until the late second century, the denarius' value was relatively stable in real terms. One denarius would buy 17.5 liters of corn; the average daily wage for common laborers was 0.75 denarius. From these figures we can judge the lavish scale of the retirement benefits for senior officers.[153]

in kind, had a subsidiary outcome important for this history. To insure adequate supplies for the armies, the Emperor instructed officials in each district to make an annual estimate of needed supplies—such as food (wheat, barley, meat, oil, wine), uniforms, horses—and of fresh recruits. According to new procedures, the number of combined units of labor and land (*iugatio-caput*) was set down in the district's cadastral survey. By dividing estimates of each of the needed supplies by the number of taxable units, administrators could arrive at district tax quotas for each commodity for that year. This annual quota *(indictio)* was equivalent to a tax rate; it was explicitly related to, if not determined by, anticipated expenditure.[155]

This process relating resources to needs was highly fragmented. As with earmarking, the early emperors' accounts *(rationes)* (see pages 137–38), or the cadastral surveys of ancient empires, enumeration was carried out district by district, and within districts, for each commodity and unit of cultivation. Such balancing of a district's resources against its prospective needs, as far as we know, had not happened before. Although procedures adopted under Diocletian appear to manifest the future-oriented, means-ends–related mind-set associated with modern expenditure budgeting, centuries were to pass before any government possessed either technical capacity or political authority permitting allocation among uses of total expenditure.

After the third century, imperial expenses in the provinces increased as citizens tried to evade the liturgies; the imperial government was then forced to assume some defense costs, such as repairs to walls surrounding municipalities, that heretofore had been paid by their residents.

Early in the third century, the emperor Septimus Severus greatly enlarged his private wealth by confiscating property from Senators who opposed his policies, and from citizens of Gaul and Spain who were unable to raise the heavy tribute levied upon them.[156] For income from the confiscated estates, Septimus established a new treasury, the *res privata*. Its revenues were so extensive that eight procurators were required in Italy alone, as well as numerous others in the provinces, to administer the fund. When Septimus died the res privata passed on to his heirs, leaving them a larger fortune than any emperor had ever bequeathed.[157] This treasury remained the private property of the emperors until the fourth century, when, under the early Byzantine emperors, it was merged with the state treasury, and the private imperial income was once again used for public purposes.[158]

If a ruler is weak or the governing council disunited, financial management by earmarking makes it hard for the state to control corruption. With many treasuries, the governing council has trouble overseeing the internal finances of each. Officials and clerks are tempted to engage in bribery or to appropriate revenues by other collusive practices. In a government of dispersed power, such as that of Athens or the Roman Republic, the existence of a number of separate treasuries—each with an autonomous bureaucracy and regular access to funds—created independent power sources that in time challenged the governing council. It was not the excesses of hierarchy, but its half-formed character, that characterized Athenian and Roman finance. In both polities hierarchy was tempered by market forces—by a competing order of competitive individualism.

FINANCIAL ACCOUNTABILITY

Governments have always tried to guard their resources against theft. To administer its finances effectively, a state needs trustworthy officials, but how can it find such men? The Roman Republic gave up collecting harbor taxes at Ostia for a time because it could not prevent officials from accepting bribes.[159]

Fiscal-management practices in Athens and Rome, as in other governments at different times and places, represented two approaches to the problem of control. One was personal, internal to the system, and based on voluntary compliance. Rulers or governing councils appointed presumably trustworthy men from their own class to administer state finances, and made them personally accountable. In small governments, like the ancient monarchies, a single, multipurpose official was personally accountable to the king. The republican councils of Athens and Rome had another management technique: the councils administered state finances through several specialized financial officials appointed from the governing class and responsible to the entire community. These men served without payment, for the Greeks believed that salaries would corrupt public officials.[160]

When a single official was named to supervise all receipts and disbursements, internal administration could be simplified. Administrative confusion created by numerous treasuries probably forced the Athenian council to consolidate management of its finances. During the third century B.C. it delegated power over the public purse to a single specialized financial official, the state treasurer, who received all revenues and disbursed funds to the separate treasuries. That office became the prototype for financial administration in the Hellenistic kingdoms and during the Roman period. The *strategos* of the Hellenistic Empire and the quaestor, the censor, the *praetor,* and the *a rationibus* of the Roman Republic and Empire modeled their duties on the Athenian treasurer's. Each of these officers supervised the hierarchy of officials engaged in collecting and distributing public revenue.

From time to time this single official was a strong man who imposed sweeping reforms to improve efficiency of revenue collections and allocation. Athenian and Roman reformers had several distinct, sometimes contradictory, and often overlapping goals. Some tried to simplify administration to reduce the burden of management, while others tried to clarify the locus of responsibility, thereby tightening administrative control of tax receipts and spending. All reformers worried about the ever present threat of losses from corruption, and worked to devise better ways of insuring accountability within government.

Concerned with public morality, the earliest reformers tried to control the state's funds by making politicians accountable for expenditures. In the fifth century B.C., the Athenian Cleisthenes established control by separating receipts and distribution. He vested control of state finances in the Apodectae, a body of ten members selected by lot from the Senate; it was to receive all payments to the state and keep records of their source. Together with the Senate, the Apodectae distributed receipts to the various treasuries for disbursement; but there is no evidence that the treasurers were required to account for those funds.[161]

THE ATHENIAN AUDIT

By the beginning of the fourth century B.C., Athenian statesmen were held accountable for expenditures as well as receipts through the public audit, an invention of the ancient Greeks. Established during the preclassical period, the audit had grown out of the gradual democratization of Athenian political institutions. It expressed the governing philosophy of the *pólis*—the reciprocal responsibility and liability of citizen and state. Before being discharged from office at the end of his year of service, an Athenian official was forced to submit to formal public examination. No official was exempt. All state officials, members of the Areopagus, the Boulé, priests of the sacred temples, and even trirarchs were required to account for all receipts and expenditures.[162] As public information, treasury accounts were chiseled into stone tablets and mounted on public buildings.[163]

The audit had two parts: a general hearing of an official's competence while in office *(euthynia),* and (if he had handled public funds) a separate financial audit *(logos)* by public accountants. The governing council chose the board of ten general examiners from its members.

If financial irregularities were uncovered by the accountants, they could bring charges against the offender in a special public court—one that the accountants also presided over. And, if the general examiners found valid evidence of crimes or misdemeanors against the people, they could pass it on to the Areopagus or (after the democratic reforms of 462 B.C.) to one of several popular courts where the evidence would be heard and a judgment pronounced.[164]

In order to safeguard revenues, governments throughout history have also provided sanctions to hedge against losses. In a government with weak legitimacy, such as that of Egypt during the Middle Kingdom or the late Roman Empire, sanctions were punitive, entailing loss of life, mutilation, or imprisonment. In a stable government like that of Periclean Athens, sanctions were usually moderate, entailing only fines and the dishonor that accompanied them or, at worst, confiscation of property. An official who would not submit to audit was barred from the courts, prevented from making religious offerings to the gods, and forbidden to travel outside Athens.[165] If his accounts showed discrepancies,* the official was brought to trial; if convicted, he was fined and forced to restore the amounts in question. If an official did not pay, the state would imprison him and confiscate his property.[167] An officeholder's personal liability for public funds explains why Athenians preferred to use public slaves, rather than free citizens, as clerks. If a discrepancy in the accounts was discovered, a slave could be tortured to elicit a confession, and his superiors could then be exonerated.[168]

But close examination of an official's behavior after the fact did not satisfy the Athenians. The state tried to forestall malfeasance in office before it occurred by holding special hearings *(dokimasia)* to screen elected candidates before they could take office. All *archons*—magistrates— and the five hundred members of the newly elected governing council were subject to confirmation in hearings conducted by the retiring Boulé. Initially, if the Boulé disqualified a candidate, the decision was final; later, probably before the end of the fifth century B.C., a rejected candidate had the right of appeal to a citizens' court.[169]

The conceptual basis of the Athenian audit lies in a sharp distinction

---

* Accounting technology in ancient Greece was rudimentary at best. Athenian building accounts indicate that financial records were kept in narrative form and were often rudimentary. Receipts and payments were intermingled, and there was no attempt to strike a balance. Doubtless many officials were convicted and fined simply because some items of receipt or expenditure had been lost, or because of errors in arithmetic.[166]

between officials' public and private roles. Athens was not the first state in the ancient world to mark this distinction; the ancient monarchs also, by encouragement or coercion, had tried to induce such awareness in financial officials. But in the economically stable and politically conservative environment of classical Athens, the public audit tended to create a climate of morality in the public service. (Or so, from our distant vantage point, are we led to believe.) In the localized environment of Athens, an official's reputation for honesty or dishonesty was widely known long before he came up for audit. The official was likely to have behaved circumspectly while he served, to avoid prejudgment and possible public embarrassment.

This does not mean that all officials were honest, or even that honest men were always irreproachable. The Greek commentator Polybius reports that if "the state entrusted to anyone a talent [an amount equivalent to six thousand drachmai, a very large sum for the Greeks], and if it had ten checking clerks, and as many seals and twice as many witnesses, it could not insure his honesty." [170]

As a matter of fact, bribery may have been as common in classical Athens as in modern governments. If an Athenian official could not account for all funds, collusion was suspected. Even Pericles was known to have mishandled public funds.[171] Still, the accepted Athenian model of the public servant as a man who subordinated his desire for personal acquisition while in office probably resulted in a more honest administration of state finances than if the public audit had not existed.

But among the many financial administrators of ancient Athens and Rome, a few exceptional men do stand out. The fourth-century B.C. Athenian statesman Lycurgus was a prototype of the trusted public servant who was also an effective financial reformer. So honest that Athenian citizens deposited their private funds with him for safekeeping, Lycurgus managed public funds with economy for fifteen years. On a tablet mounted on a façade of the riding school built during his term of office Lycurgus proudly set forth the results of his careful management: four hundred ships built and repaired; fifty thousand darts stored on the Acropolis; golden statues erected throughout the city to celebrate victory in war; construction of a gymnasium, docks, armories, and a theater; and the total revenue increased.[172] Whether those who paid were as pleased we do not know.

Lycurgus' reputation for good management is matched by that of the Roman reformer Cato, who was elected censor (chief financial officer) of the republic in 184 B.C. Cato's enumeration of things he did not do while serving as governor of Spain elaborates his conception of public morality, apparently uncommon in his day:

> I have never placed garrison commanders in your towns . . . to seize their goods and their families. I have never divided booty . . . nor spoils among . . . my friends, so as to deprive those who have won it of their rewards. I have never granted permits to requisition at will so my friends can enrich themselves. . . . I have never distributed the money for the soldiers' wine among my attendants and friends, nor made them rich at public expense.[173]

During his term as censor, Cato increased public revenue by raising taxes paid by the wealthy, and by trying to enforce stringent economy both in public and in private life. Cato exacted the highest fees from the tax farmers, but, to conserve funds, he would pay only modest contract fees for improvements to the city's roads, sewers, and aqueducts. Showing a conception of public morality uncommon for the times, Cato limited the use of public money for private purposes by cutting the pipes that brought water into private houses and gardens.[174]

As the territory governed by a state increases in size, internal control through direct liability and accountability of one person to another becomes impossible. The ruler or council gradually diffuses its authority to unknown men whose honesty may be questionable. The semivoluntary methods of financial administration in Athens and the Roman Republic—liturgies and tax farming—made it possible for these governments to avoid problems inherent in delegating authority. Since the liturgy and tax farming were largely self-policing, Athenian and Roman governments could administer a large territory with only a modest civil bureaucracy, and there was no need for an elaborate control apparatus.

DELEGATED FINANCIAL MANAGEMENT IN THE ROMAN REPUBLIC

Although the Romans also used a public audit, it was not their principal control technique. During the last two centuries of the republic, the Senate controlled expenditures for public works and for repairs to public buildings in Rome by voting a definite sum for each building, road, or aqueduct, then letting a construction contract to the Publicans for that amount.

To meet military expenses and administrative costs, the Senate voted block grants to military commanders and to each provincial governor at the beginning of his term.[175] To award contracts and administer grants, the Senate delegated its authority to the quaestors. These specialized treasury officials exercised considerable power in the late republic, for the law gave them control of all public disbursements by contract, and responsibility for expenditures under the grants. An official who was required to justify his expenditures presented his accounts directly to the quaestors rather than to the Senate.

Military commanders of the late Roman Republic did not have to account for their spending; and provincial governors had to submit accounts only at the end of their terms, though these accounts were often inexact or cursory.* If a grant had not been completely spent at the end of a term, it was common for the governor to distribute the balance to his staff or pass it on to his successor. Since often many months passed before he returned to Rome, an unscrupulous official could easily appropriate public funds by conspiring with the provincial quaestor or his successor in office to share the balance, and then pad his accounts to cover the deficit.[177] Even if discrepancies were discovered, the Senate was powerless to recover any funds.

While delegating power to administer finances to a single official such as the quaestor may have reduced confusion, it did not insure that corrupt practices would be curbed. Even if he were inclined to be honest, the average quaestor, appointed only for a limited time, often had difficulty controlling minor Aerarium officials who held permanent appointments. During the late republic there was an active market for these clerical jobs. A scribe from the Equestrian class who had been appointed to the treasury could easily sell his position to anyone with enough money, irrespective of the applicant's qualifications. The scribes were paid small official salaries which they supplemented by charging fees. Each time one of them submitted a bill or collected a tax he added a small personal charge. Many scribes undoubtedly also accepted bribes. The posts must have been profitable, or the incumbents would not have been willing to pay for them.[178] In the mid–second century (159 B.C.), the Roman Senate passed several laws against bribery; apparently the laws were ineffective. Twenty-five years later, one foreign potentate advised another that in Rome everything was for sale.[179] A flurry of reform occurred about forty years later when a man named Mucius Scaeveola was sent out from Rome to govern a prov-

---

* Accounts submitted by Verres, the corrupt governor of Sicily during the late republic, were so brief that they induced a tirade from Cicero, self-appointed guardian of public morality:

"... Let us see how he gave in his accounts. ... First of all, note their brevity—'I received,' says he, '2,235,417 sesterces; I spent, for pay to the soldiers, for corn, for the legates, 5,417 sesterces. ...' Did ... anyone ever give in his accounts in this manner? ... What precedent is there in all the accounts that have ever been rendered by public officers?"[176]

ince in Asia. According to his chronicler (Diodorus), Scaeveola performed exemplary service:

> ... He decided that his staff and he should pay all their expenses from their own pockets. By the simplicity of his life style and ... incorruptibility he restored the province from its previous misfortunes. For his predecessors ... had taken the tax farmers into partnership ... He curbed ... lawless practices [by finding] tax farmers guilty [of extortion] and compelling them to reimburse financial losses [of] those who had been wronged.[180]

Delegated financial management did not control corruption in the late Roman Republic; the Senatorial audit was merely a formality. Only an official who acted in flagrant violation of the idealized norms of public morality inherited from Athens attracted attention. Having delegated authority for financial control to quaestors, the Senate often could not control them, for it had no effective sanctions. And, with the Senate divided into irreconcilable factions, a corrupt official could always find a like-minded Senator to defend him.

Perhaps the problem with delegation in the late republic grew more out of factionalism and instability than out of management deficiencies, for delegation did have advantages. Letting officials charge fees for services, for example, is a rational compensation method for a state with modest resources and limited administrative capacity. Like tax farming, with which it has been associated, administration by fees enabled the state, by delegating authority, to accomplish an essential function at low cost, for the taxpayers footed most of the bill. Administration by fee might also result in increased public revenue. Since the official's personal reward depended on the amounts collected, he was likely to work hard in the state's behalf. But administration by fee has the same disadvantages as tax farming, because when the state abrogates control over minor officials, it must condone excessive zeal in collection of fees, and close its eyes when officials take bribes or commit other irregularities.

CENTRALIZATION UNDER THE EMPERORS

The early emperors achieved internal financial control through gradual development of centralized management structures. Having attained power through a conspiracy, the early emperors did not trust their peers from the Senatorial order to administer finances. To recapture revenue lost to tax farmers in Rome's eastern provinces, Julius Caesar and his successor Augustus gradually phased out existing contracts for collecting direct taxes in the imperial provinces. The emper-

ors replaced provincial tax farmers with procurators, appointive officials who were private agents of the imperial household. Understanding that tax collection entailed organization and expertise, the
emperors chose as procurators the same businessmen and financiers
from the Equestrian order who had served the republic as tax farmers.
But instead of being private entrepreneurs with personal discretion, the
Equestrian administrators became the first members of the Roman
civil service—a centralized administrative corps accountable to the
emperors. Competitive individualism was supplanted by hierarchy, at
least for a time.

Not that it was easy to find incorruptible Equestrians. Seldom was a
man's reputation for honesty the criterion for selection; instead, emperors' choices rested on knowledge that a candidate was less avaricious than other contenders. The early emperors tried to retain
personal control of appointees: "The subjects should be sheared but
not shaved," Augustus' successor, Tiberius, reprimanded a prefect in
Egypt before removing the man from office.[181]

To make sure that Equestrian civil servants would serve with integrity, Augustus and later emperors appointed a few clerks who had been
slaves of the imperial household (imperial freedmen) to the civil service for the routine work of financial administration. Devoted to the
emperor who had granted them freedom, these imperial freedmen
served with honesty. The emperors provided management continuity
by selecting successive generations of minor administrators from
freedmen's descendants.[182] A few exceptional freedmen even reached
the highest administrative levels.*

At first the emperor tried to centralize financial management only in
the imperial provinces, where procurators directed tax collection and
disbursed public money to resident military forces. In the Senatorial
provinces, procurators acted as the emperor's business agents, manag-

* The poet Statius has left a description of one of them in a eulogy written to honor his
father, a financial officer under an early emperor. If we are to believe Statius' effusive
language, his father was a prototype of Weber's rational administrator, an ideal public
servant who devoted himself selflessly to a task that might have overwhelmed a lesser
man:

". . . To thee alone is given the governance of our holy ruler's wealth. In thy sole charge
are the riches all nations render, . . . the bullion that Hibernia casts from her mines of
gold, the glistening metal of the Dalmatian hills; all that is swept in from African harvests
or ground on the threshing floors of sultry Nile or gathered by the divers in eastern waters. . . . Lighter than thy task would be to number the forest leaves or the raindrops in
winter. With quick brain thou reckonest what sums are demanded by the Roman
armies. . . . Thou wast seldom at peace; thy heart was closed to pleasure; thy fare was meager, and never did draughts of wine dull thine industry."[183]

ing the patrimonium—an emperor's private estates, mines, and commercial interests. As the emperors gradually did away with tax farming in the Senatorial provinces, the imperial procurators became responsible for tax collection there as well.[184] Careful management of provincial finances during the early empire produced a surplus that was used for investments in public buildings and facilities.[185] Hierarchic orders gain support by making visible expenditures in the collectivity's name.

The imperial Roman civil service evolved through several centuries. The reorganization initiated by Augustus, and built upon by his successors, eventually produced a complex organization of paid professionals skilled in all tasks of imperial administration, including management of government finance. The Roman civil service came into being slowly, for both Augustus and his successor Tiberius tried to conduct a personal government and appointed relatively few officials. To cope with an expanding empire, the Emperor Claudius, who reigned fifty years after Augustus, enlarged the civil service and developed a small central cabinet of specialized officers to administer law and finance in the provinces. Over the next century, successive emperors built on Claudius' innovations to increase central control; they expanded the power, the number, and the functional specialization of offices in the imperial service, tending to promote from within the ranks. As the civil-service positions came to command increased power, prestige, and higher salaries, the emperors appointed fewer imperial freedmen; by the second century, under Hadrian, the corps consisted largely of men from the higher-ranking Equestrian order. Administrative development was relatively complete by the end of that century; there were 136 different offices in the imperial service, graded and ranked in four classes on the basis of salary—no doubt commensurate, as today, with an officeholder's responsibility and competence.*

Expansion of the imperial administration made for a gradual, but considerable, enlargement of the emperor's power at the expense of the Senatorial aristocracy. As the imperial bureaucracy developed effective management techniques, financial control gradually shifted from Senate to emperor. During the republic it had been vested in the Senate. Early emperors assumed control and initiative in financial matters, although the Senate still maintained formal responsibility. To maintain the illusion of joint control, Augustus and his successors continued

---

* By Commodus' reign the four rankings commanded annual salaries of 60,000, 100,-000, 200,000, and 300,000 sesterces.[186]

to consult the Senate, and established commissions on financial issues. But the Senate's power of the purse was so eroded by expansion of imperial power that, by the end of the first century, when the state treasury was depleted and the Emperor Vespasian was traveling outside Rome, the Senate had to wait for the Emperor to return and decide how to provide the needed resources. By that time the procurators in the Senatorial provinces had acquired control over public finance as well as management of the imperial estates.

When the early emperors took control of the state treasury the Senatorial audit was abandoned. But as the emperors established control over financial administration, they did begin to regulate spending in all parts of the empire. At first in the imperial provinces, and later in the Senatorial provinces, Roman procurators received revenues collected locally, and disbursed these funds to pay the occupying armies and imperial officials stationed there.

As the emperors sent agents out into the empire, the federal system of administration that had functioned effectively during the Roman Republic began to break down. Although provincial cities were still in principle autonomous (as they had been during the late republic), the procurators began to interfere in the finances of provincial cities, with the idea of preventing citizens from making unwise investments that might jeopardize imperial revenue. Much the same practices are followed by unitary European governments today in regard to loans sought by localities.

Letters written to the Emperor Trajan by Pliny the Younger, while governor of the province of Bythnia, provide evidence of central-government constraints on municipal expenditure. The people of Nicaea had nearly completed a theater and a gymnasium that were badly built; Claudiopolis had put up a public bath on a poor site; Nicomedeia had built an aqueduct and then abandoned it. Pliny asked Trajan's advice for ways to prevent the recurrence of such incompetence. For the city of Prusa, Pliny petitioned the Emperor's permission to build a bathhouse. Amastris asked to cover a sewer, the free city of Sinope to build an aqueduct.[187] Later, during Hadrian's reign, the city of Alexandria Troas started to replace its rainwater tanks with an aqueduct, but the expenses greatly exceeded the cost estimates, and the local procurator protested to the Emperor, who stopped the project.[188]

Although all these investments in municipal facilities were donated as provincial liturgies, the emperors' local agents felt obliged to protect imperial interests by limiting amounts spent. In some provincial municipalities, imperial officials tried to limit extravagant spending for private observances like weddings and festivals. In others, those agents violated the tradition of local autonomy by auditing municipal accounts.[189] Hierarchy expanded its prerogatives. Since each position carries its own requirements, however, hierarchical regimes sometimes pass sumptuary laws to restrain by fiat what is commanded by custom.

Concern for economy did not stop at the provinces. The early emperors also tried to reduce operating expenses at home. *De Aquaeductibus,* a famous text by Frontinus, administrator of public works for the Emperor Trajan, describes his attempts to reduce the cost of maintaining the fountains of Rome. Frontinus' statement displays all the rectitude of a modern economy-minded administrator who specializes in cost containment; it reflects a universal theme in public pronouncements on financial control.

> It remains to speak of the maintenance of the conduits. . . . There are two [gangs of slaves established for this purpose] . . . , one belonging to the state, the other to Caesar. . . . Both of these large gangs, which regularly were diverted by . . . favoritism, or by negligence of their foremen, to employment on private work, I resolved to bring back to some discipline . . . by writing down the day before what each gang was to do, and by putting in the record what it had done each day. The costs of the state gang are paid from the state treasury, an expense which is lightened by the receipt of rentals from water rights. . . . This income [was] formerly lost through loose management. . . . I took pains to bring it under fixed rules . . . that it might be clear what . . . fell under this tax.[190]

From a perspective of intellectual history, the early emperors' most remarkable achievement was to develop an information base for managing imperial finances. The *rationes imperii,* the tabulation of imperial resources and expenditures that Augustus' officials compiled, was not a budget, for it was an accounting only of *past* revenues, resources, and commitments. But, like the cadastral surveys of the ancient kings,[191] the rationes represented an attempt to conduct a systematic inventory of the empire's resources. When one considers the poorly developed bookkeeping techniques of the ancient world, where Roman scribes kept their records in Roman numerals, which were very difficult to cumulate, it is amazing that any effort was made to compile the imperial accounts.[192]

The impetus behind these efforts was an interest in the past, aimed at connecting it to what was hoped would be a collective future. Budgeting is not merely prospective, it is retrospective, justifying what has happened in the past—to legitimize a regime. The balance sheets of the early Roman Empire served the latter purpose.

The imperial balance sheets that Augustus submitted to the consul

Piso in 23 B.C., and periodically thereafter, included separate counts for each province of (1) the number of troops stationed there; (2) revenues; (3) expenditures and cash balance in the Aerarium; (4) cash balances in the emperor's provincial treasuries (fisci); and (5) amounts due from tax farmers who still collected fixed taxes in the Senatorial provinces. Before his death Augustus also left a summary balance sheet. This *breviarium totius imperii* cumulated the provincial rationes and listed by name the imperial slaves and freedmen (who were significant capital assets of the crown). Augustus' successor Tiberius continued to publish the rationes; Caligula, who followed Tiberius, kept up the accounts for only a short time. Thereafter the practice lapsed, perhaps because it became too difficult to maintain the accounts as the empire expanded, or because the distinction between public and imperial finances became more and more blurred.[193] Each successive emperor's private property was merged with the imperial patrimonium and passed on to the next ruler; thus the imperial property gradually assumed a character similar to that of the public lands *(ager publicus)* of the Roman Republic or the temple properties of the Greek city-states.

Imperial control of municipal expenditures in the Roman provinces persisted well into the late empire as decurions were required, under penalty of flogging, to account for revenues collected and expenses incurred.[194] But the concept of a central government's accountability disappeared with the rationes imperii of the early emperors; throughout the turbulent late empire there was neither control of nor accounting for the imperial establishment's lavish expenditures.

By the late empire the civil service, consisting largely of Senatorial and Equestrian officials, had become demoralized and corrupt. Adopting an ancient Oriental practice, the emperors appointed eunuchs to administer state finances; these castrated males could have no legitimate claim to power and no heirs and, so it was believed, might therefore be trusted not to tamper with state funds.[195] Yet, like some imperial freedmen, a number of palace eunuchs of the late empire did amass large personal fortunes. Whether these were acquired through sale of influence or other illicit means it is impossible to tell.[196]

The emperors tried to cope, aiming to control finances through duplication of function combined with intimidation and threat of punitive sanctions.[197] Several officials were appointed to perform the same task, with the expectation that one would check on another and report any irregularity. But trying to achieve morality in government during the late Roman Empire by creating a climate of fear was hopeless, and such strategies did not succeed. Requiring continuous surveillance of civil officials and the population, control of corruption by intimidation was cumbersome; it was also expensive, for it entailed a widespread, costly network of spies drawn from the army, or a secret police. And when the emperors tightened control, taxpayers found new ways to evade.

COPING: MAKING ENDS MEET VERSUS EVADING PUNITIVE TAXATION

The low productivity of ancient economies created similar pressures on governments and taxpayers. Subject to hazards beyond man's control—plague, flood, drought—agricultural production in Athens and Rome was limited and always unpredictable. Since the resources consumed to support the governments of subsistence economies left a smaller share for those governed, ancient states did not have many options. A government such as that of Athens could maintain legitimacy by invoking altruism, drawing on gifts given by the people to demonstrate allegiance. If its needs were small (and as long as no catastrophe occurred), private philanthropy might even sustain such a government. But if resource requirements grew, ancient governments either had to adopt coercive methods to collect taxes or had to look for other support.

As a first step, governments might devalue currency. Ancient governments coated bronze coins with a wash of silver or issued new coins with inferior weights or metal content.[198] For example, Rome's coins were 98 percent silver in the early empire (mid–first century A.D.). By the mid–third century (A.D. 250), coins were only 40 percent silver, and during the next twenty tumultuous years, repeated debasements reduced silver content to 4 percent.[199] There was an inherent disadvantage to such strategies, for, as price inflation generally followed devaluation, additional revenue received as taxes was canceled out by increased costs for essential services.[200] In republican and imperial Rome the largest expenditure—more than half of revenue—was military wages.[201] When soldiers in distant provinces were paid in depreciated Roman currency, their generals avoided widespread mutiny either by coining their own currencies[202] or, more commonly, by letting troops supplement their wages by looting.[203]

A government might also urge moral restraint, issuing decrees prohibiting citizens from lavish spending on personal adornment; the money saved was to be contributed to the state. In the Greek city-state of Ephesus during the fourth century B.C., women were forced to give jewelry to the state treasury.[204] Aristotle related that the citizens of Sparta provided financial aid to their neighbors, the Samians, by requiring all citizens, slaves, and cattle to fast for one day and then contribute the food that would have been consumed.[205] To pay for the Punic Wars during the second century B.C. in the Roman Republic, Cato the Censor imposed a luxury tax on furniture, chariots, jewelry, and clothing, and tried to limit the amount of meat served at banquets.[206]

When social hierarchy coexists with economic individualism, there is a conflict between public and private splendor. Hence the public condemnation of private luxury and the difficulty in making it stick. As the Romans loved public magnificence (as Cicero observed fifty years later), in accord with the norms of hierarchy, they claimed to abhor private luxury. The government was to glorify Rome, not to grant private privilege. Aiming to allocate sacrifice more or less equally among the populace, Cato manifested egalitarian traits; he spoke out also against public distribution of grain to the poor.[207] Apparently sacrifice was not popular; Rome tried to enforce six different sumptuary laws during the second century B.C.[208]

Because few governments that enacted such sumptuary laws had the authority to enforce compliance, several Roman emperors adopted a more direct strategy, confiscating land and personal property from Senators and wealthy citizens in an attempt to obtain the grain and animals needed to pay the army and feed the urban poor.[209] In such turbulent times as the anarchic third century A.D., this policy had a desirable side effect: it reduced opposition.

When all else failed, as a last resort a ruler could draw on his personal financial resources, providing support to the state through sale or rental of crown lands, contributing his private wealth, or even auctioning off crown jewels or royal house furnishings. The merging of king and state that had disappeared briefly in the Athenian and Roman republics thus reappeared in the Hellenistic and Roman empires. Nevertheless, for a ruler to subsidize the state with his personal funds (as Augustus and Nero did[210]), or to sell off royal furniture and heirlooms (as Marcus Aurelius did[211]) was far less common than its opposite. More often, Hellenistic and Roman rulers, like the priest-kings of the ancient monarchies, augmented their private hoards by drawing funds from the public treasury, no matter what its condition.[212] What subjects paid, the hierarchy consumed.

In the late Roman Empire—when wars, the economic disorganization caused by invasion, and extensive state confiscation of private landholdings had reduced receipts to a trickle—the Emperor Diocletian revived the budgeting practices of the ancient priest-kings. A series of edicts reimposed the compulsory payment of taxes in kind, forcing all men to continue cultivating the land they lived on in order to produce the tax. The edicts provided that, as in the ancient monarchies, land be classified according to yield, with a fixed proportion of each crop paid to state tax collectors. Diocletian sent spies out into the empire to intimidate taxpayers and force compliance with his edicts.[213]

Under such circumstances, what could a citizen do to protect himself? By what strategies could he evade the tax collector and preserve his personal wealth? Heavily burdened taxpayers of the late Roman Empire—and citizens of other states, widely dispersed in space and time—adopted remarkably congruent tactics.

Taxation may be inconvenient and even burdensome for men of property, but is rarely so punitive as to deprive them of subsistence. Rich men found ways to evade the tax collector in the late Roman Empire, just as they have done throughout history. During the third century, many wealthy Romans buried their jewelry or stocks of gold coin.[214] (The location and content of buried hoards provide data for modern economic historians of the ancient world.[215]) Evasion was not difficult for mercantile members of the Equestrian order who held such intangible property as mortgages and loans. If businessmen kept no records of transactions, the state could not tax them on additions to their assets. It was largely to avoid taxation that in the late empire all but a few merchants and bankers stopped keeping accounts.[216] Landowners had more trouble evading taxes, for their assets were hard to hide. Except for falsely reporting their holdings in the cadastral survey that provided an estimate of taxable assets, landowners could hope to keep the tax collectors off their land only by force.

During the fourth century, tradesmen and artisans who provided essential services and supplies to the state were exempt from taxation. Merchants providing food and supplies for the army, and services and supplies for the imperial household,[217] were immune, as were shipowners whose vessels carried grain from the provinces to Rome.

A poor man had less choice. If he could not pay, his only legal recourse was to join the army. Rather than paying taxes, many small farmers holding marginal land in poor districts preferred to abandon it; they went to Rome or Constantinople, where they could live on the imperial dole. Flight from small holdings led the Emperor Diocletian to adopt a policy that taxed labor and land as a single unit; if a man moved away, he was still liable for the tax on his land. Occasionally small landowners took illegal steps to evade taxes. During the third century, the citizens of some eastern provincial cities joined together to get help from resident troops. The provincials offered the soldiers gifts of money or food in exchange for help in driving away the tax collectors.[218] Finally, a small landholder could sacrifice his independence and place himself under the protection of a powerful landowner whose resources were adequate to defy the collectors.[219] In exchange for giving protection, the landowner took part of the produce; often the rich landowner confiscated the poorer man's land.

As rich and poor alike tried to evade taxes, successive rulers of the late empire adopted more stringent enforcement and control methods. Since taxes remained constant, when the strategies of the wealthy succeeded, the tax burden fell on the poor. Just as in the ancient empires, those least able to pay were deprived of all property and, in provinces where land had low productivity, subsistence as well.[220] Writing in the fifth century, early in the Byzantine period, Salvian the Presbyter, a man of God, described the miserable plight of the common people:

> But what else can these wretched people wish for, they who suffer the incessant . . . tax levies? To them there is always imminent a heavy and relentless proscription. They desert their homes. . . . They seek exile . . . [for] the enemy is more lenient to them than the tax collectors. . . . This very tax levying, although harsh and inhuman, would nevertheless be less heavy and harsh if all would bear it equally. . . . Taxation is made more shameful and burdensome because all do not bear the burden of all. They extort tribute from the poor man for the taxes of the rich, and the weaker carry the load for the stronger.[221]

THE CONCEPT OF PUBLIC INTEREST

It is not surprising that overburdened citizens tried to evade taxes. Rulers and financial officials alike normally served themselves before the state. Any behavior while in office, however self-serving, was fair play. Whenever and wherever it is found, punitive taxation enforced by corrupt officialdom obliterates the concept of public interest. For without an interactive public to respond to and protect, hierarchy becomes despotic.

The public-interest idea is a fragile one. It is slow to emerge; and a polity must nurture it carefully to sustain it. Financial practices in classical Athens and the early Roman Republic mark a distant beginning of the public-interest idea—as in Athens' ritualized audit of officeholders. And as idealized norms of fairness governed the assignment of the liturgies in Athens and the provincial municipalities

of the Roman Republic, so, too, did they govern individuals' performance of the liturgies.

For the individual to be willing to submerge private interests to collective interests by paying taxes, and by serving government with integrity, several conditions must exist, for ethical norms and high
standards of individual behavior emerge only from a particular context. There must be strong and stable government with the legitimacy
to establish, and then to maintain, norms of fiscal equity. Citizens will
more willingly support government if its taxes are moderate, and if
taxes are administered evenhandedly by officials who maintain high
standards of honesty and accountability while holding public office.
Public laws require consistent enforcement before individuals will
limit personal acquisitive impulses to enhance the commonweal. Only
when restraints on individuals operate continuously for long periods of
time, therefore, is there a chance for honesty among taxpayers and
within government to become institutionalized. Public officials must
learn to maintain, and to respect, a distinction between private, personal interests and the collective interest embodied in a public office.

During periods of peace and prosperity in classical Athens and in
early imperial Rome, the state was strong enough to enforce a distinction between the public and private roles of statesmen and administrators. During the Hellenistic Empire and the late Roman Republic and
late Roman Empire, the state lacked authority to perpetuate the distinction, and the public-interest concept foundered as corruption in
government became the norm.[222]

A materialist explanation is not hard to find. Men must live one way
or another. If public service is not reserved to the wealthy, honest administration cannot exist unless public servants receive a living wage.
Public controls, then, were strongest during periods of peace and prosperity. When wars, inflation, and famine depleted the surplus so that
the state could not pay its officials, or when the voluntary administrators' personal wealth was threatened by confiscatory liturgies and extortionate taxes, as happened during the Hellenistic and late Roman
empires, the public-interest idea, so briefly seen in classical Athens and
in early imperial Rome, disappeared. But, if we ask why the response
to adversity emphasized private rather than public interest, there are
cultural explanations.

What sort of social relationships would generate a sense of public
obligation? Which political cultures would motivate their adherents to
respect the distinction between public and private, and give voluntary
support to the public domain?

Were the question solely about the size or extent of government, market regimes of competitive individualism would have to be ruled out. Valuing private opulence more than public splendor, such cultures aim to reduce society's need for public institutions, not to increase dependence upon them. Members of market cultures choose autonomy; dealing face to face, negotiating bargain by bargain, they seek reciprocity. Making sacrifices for public purposes interferes with acquisitive impulses. Still, if government's role could be limited by being circumscribed, preventing the public domain from consuming private resources, then its tax take might be diminished. In market regimes, a well-institutionalized distinction between public and private would prevent the public domain from encroaching on the private.

In a society based solely on market principles, however, there would only be a slim public sector, largely for maintaining rules for holding, buying and selling property. As with the Condottiere in the Italian city-states during the Renaissance, or mercenary soldiers in Africa in recent years, even defense would be provided by negotiating contracts, by bidding and bargaining. Serving to defend government only when circumstances warrant, such mercenaries are rewarded for their efforts, but are expected to fade away until recalled. If only its market elements established the structure of society, most of it would be in essence private.

Similarly, were a society based entirely on hierarchical principles there would be no place for private perspectives and interests. With a sacrificial ethic subordinating the parts to the whole controlling society, the public sector would engulf the private sector (if, indeed, a private sector existed).

The distinction between public and private we seek to explore presumes a conception of each in relation to the other; in government the very ideas of public and private are interdependent. Thus a distinction between public and private is barely discernible in the ancient empires discussed in the previous chapter, because everything and everyone belonged to the ruler. Monopolistic, tightly structured, ancient societies served the collectivity by serving the ruler; as those societies were organized, there was little differentiation among social orders. Without a combination of cultures, the distinction between public and private had no basis in social life.

A strong sense of public duty typifies egalitarian societies. Individual citizens vote to arrive at consensus on collective actions; that consensus then serves as a moral sanction against deviance. If the meaning of being equal is equality of condition, classical Athens left much to be desired; slaves, women, poor people, and outsiders could not be citizens. But by the standards of the time (the Golden Age of Pericles in the third century B.C.), rule through Athenian assemblies, albeit often honored in the breach, was exceedingly egalitarian. Hierarchies based on social and economic criteria existed, but were not all-inclusive or all-powerful. Thus differences among social orders provided the possibility of differentiating between what belonged to the collective and what belonged to the citizen.

The city-state republics in which the first stirrings of a public–private distinction emerged may be described as a combination of hierarchic and egalitarian regimes. Purging the term *social democracy* of its modern connotations (especially its devotion to social-welfare programs), we can give it a more rudimentary objective: republican government should not act so as to increase existing inequalities. Government should be run by the active participation of citizens. With the development of citizenship based on consent comes also the sense of collective obligation, first reflected in voluntary donation (the liturgies) and then superseded by taxes—devices to enforce common contribution to the city-state.

Rome was different. There egalitarianism was much weaker, hierarchy much stronger, and its norms of differentiation pervaded government. When the Senatorial order could attain consensus, it voted policy, but indirect participation in government was extended also to the Equestrian order; its members performed marketlike functions for government and were often generously rewarded for their risk and effort. The forums of Rome and provincial cities were indeed markets as we know them, but, since Roman law prohibited Senators from engaging in market activities, if a Senator did wish to buy or sell he acted through an intermediary—a personal slave, a freedman, or a member of the Equestrian order; presumably all these groups stood to benefit from market activities.

Republican Rome built upon the emerging distinction between public and private by extending rule in an oligarchical manner through the great Senatorial families. Since government was shared among those eligible, the public purse could not belong to a single ruler. The "public" domain was small, but it did exist. Although the empire took back much that the republic had given, it gradually leavened its royal hierarchy with social strata subject to market principles (again, the Equestrians, and the civil service staffed by imperial freedmen). As duty to the emperor who embodied the state was attenuated by strata adept at mixing his business with private gain, it became worthwhile for him to separate a bit more of his patrimony from the collective resources. The variety embodied in the public–private distinction has to be based upon a similar diversity in social, and hence political, relationships. As the distinction between the public and private property and prerogatives of the ruler gradually broke down, so, too, did the internal administration of the western empire.

A rationale for the inequality embodied in a hierarchy is that such inequality safeguards the collective. Hierarchy in an organization—as in the army—does more than protect against foreign invasion. If a society operates by hierarchical principles, so the rationale runs, eventually everyone will be better off, even though the extent of each individual's improvement is directly related to his social rank. Sacrifices made by past and present generations, then, can be redeemed in a brighter collective future.

The fine social gradations so characteristic of hierarchies (running back to notable ancestors, and forward to future reproduction of the same relationships) can be adapted to organizing other aspects of governance. (Thus in recent times hierarchical principles have guided division of government accounts into functional categories, and formulation of budgets for specific units of time. Judgments of hierarchies have justified government investment, and have served to rationalize high taxes that force citizens to postpone present consumption to achieve future goals.)

But if the privileges accorded to rank in a hierarchy are not accompanied by corresponding obligations, as was the case in the late Roman Empire, individualism replaces collectivism. Then the center cannot cohere. When people understand that actions of those who govern are aimed at serving only private interests, rather than serving the collectivity, their rationale for remaining within the social order is undermined. "Each man for himself" is not a behavioral norm of collectivism. Threatened by individualism, collectivism may preserve hierarchy by embracing some version of despotism. Fear induced by brute force then becomes the dominant means of social control. Or, alternatively, small groups such as the early Christians in Rome may break off from the collectivity. Maintaining independence, such groups may for a time try voluntarily to live up to the collective ideal.

Just as collectivism's economic promise is that it will generate a surplus of future financial resources—to keep pace with demands imposed by society's yearning for improvement—so its moral premise is that the system can work only if each individual assumes the moral obligations commensurate with his social role. Show that the center does not know best in its allocation of duties, or that social division of labor is determined by anticollectivist principles (such as purchase of position), and the edifice will crumble, breaking down because its moral foundations are undermined.

When the struggle for control of the state in late imperial Rome caused it to become a factional preserve, norms of fairness and honesty evaporated. By the fourth century, men responded to disorder by screening it out. Mosaics and public statuary from the fourth and fifth centuries recently excavated in Ostia near Rome, and in Ephesus in Asia Minor, depict inward-looking men, turned from public to personal preoccupations.[223] The dimensions of individuals' social and political allegiances contracted from empire to village to manor. The concept of public interest, of common enterprise shared equally by all citizens, no longer had meaning. The stage was set for the transition to the localized, personal, and private governments of Europe in the early Middle Ages.

Chapter Four

FINANCE IN THE PRIVATE GOVERNMENTS OF MEDIEVAL EUROPE: POOR KINGS

There have been many governments without a center throughout history, both before and after the European Middle Ages.[1] There were feudal periods in China during the Chou, late Han, and late Tang dynasties, in Japan between the ninth and eighteenth centuries, in ancient Egypt during the Middle Kingdom, in ancient Mesopotamia during the Kassite period, in the Byzantine Empire from the tenth to the twelfth century, and so on. Over the course of history governmental authority has been fragmented among multiple local jurisdictions more often and for longer periods than it has been centralized. The conditions that permit centralized control—abundant resources or control of a critical resource (like irrigation), internal social and political stability, freedom from external pressures, and strong leadership by powerful governing officials—have not been maintained indefinitely in a capricious world, either singly or in combination. Indeed, the very absence of such circumstances has generated pressure for centralization. Even in governments that have maintained a strong center for a long time, financial administration has fluctuated between central control and local autonomy. Our analysis of the practices by which ancient governments obtained and allocated resources has so far focused almost entirely on periods when central government was strong. The rudimentary, nearly nonexistent government of the multiple jurisdictions of Europe in the early Middle Ages provides a polar contrast to the centralized administrative organization of the ancient monarchies, the later Roman Empire, and early Byzantium.

In early-medieval government, as in the ancient empires, there was virtually no distinction between the private legal and fiscal preroga-

148

tives of local authorities (whether civil or religious) and public authority. Likewise, management of public services and facilities was indistinguishable from management of private holdings by powerful men. During the feudal and pre-feudal periods of medieval Europe, government was equivalent to one man's personal rule of a limited territory. On land under his jurisdiction, public economy and the fiscal obligations related to it were identical with the domestic economy of his private household.

As long as men were bound to the land by feudal constraints there was no distinction in custom or law between public and private authority. But after the twelfth century, when peasants began to settle in towns developing all over Europe, early-medieval concepts of private governmental authority changed. As with the Athenian liturgies or the *decurionate* of the early Roman Empire, private merged with public roles. The symbiotic relationship between merchant guilds and town government found in the Hanseatic and northern Italian communes of the late Middle Ages often yielded public benefit. The guilds collected taxes from members to support construction and maintenance of public facilities—market buildings, town clocks, roads and bridges; the donations benefited all town citizens as well as the guildsmen.[2]

The interdependence of business and government so prominent in the tax farming of classical Athens, the Hellenistic Empire, and the Roman Republic reappeared in the late Middle Ages when Italian merchant-capitalists served as financial advisers to feudal kings, sometimes (also as tax farmers) collected their taxes, and loaned kings money when they were strapped for cash. Often there was a tenuous distinction between public and private, for the fiscal power of feudal kings and of merchant-capitalists was closely linked. As in Athens and Rome, government and business shared a common interest in the state's financial stability. Feudal kings tried to raise money for fighting wars—the normal business of government organized along military lines—while merchants were willing to provide capital in exchange for the trade concessions feudal monarchs had power to grant. As there was always a severe discrepancy between revenues and expenditures of medieval feudal governments, mutual advantages arose from amalgamating collectivism and individualism.

Yet, similarities between ancient and medieval governments are far fewer than their differences. In scale, and in organizational form, the private, manorial governments of the early Middle Ages, and the feudal monarchies that succeeded them in England and France, were smaller and simpler than the large, specialized bureaucracies of the ancient empires, or of late imperial Rome. And although religion was the strongest integrating element in society throughout the Middle Ages, and the church's influence dominated all activities, there were no medieval equivalents to the ancient priest-kings who were at once ruler and deity. According to political doctrine developed during the Carolingian period (771–987), feudal kings transmitted God's will to man, but they were not viewed as gods incarnate, and they were not worshiped or protected by priests, as in the ancient theocratic monarchies. Among the multiple governments of early-medieval Europe, the church came to be the most powerful by far, but public authority was largely secular. Although local bishops provided public services during the pre-feudal period (sixth to tenth centuries) and the church has always fulfilled some quasi-public functions, like providing relief to the poor, the administrative organizations of church and state evolved separately.

But, like the public/private distinction, the differentiation between church and state was very hazy between the end of centralized authority in the West and its revival five centuries later. Beginning in the sixth century, popes performed all civil government functions in the city of Rome, as local bishops did in the hinterland. Until the twelfth century, local feudal rulers reserved the right to appoint one of their lay vassals as bishop. Their purpose was less to secure repose of their soul in the next world than to enjoy income from the church's extensive landholdings in the present. Throughout the twelfth century there were bitter conflicts between popes and feudal kings over whether the bishop (as the pope's representative) or the local secular ruler was entitled to revenues from ecclesiastical property.

After the Investiture Controversy (1075–1122), as this dispute between kings and popes has been labeled, it was no longer possible to maintain that the king's body represented the holy spirit. With the Gregorian reforms of the twelfth century, feudal government and its law, as well as the kingship itself, became progressively more secular. As study of Roman law was revived, it gradually constrained rulers' authority; in all legal matters except state finance, the king was no longer the only person qualified to pass judgment on his peers.[3] When a class of professional jurists began to define and elaborate the king's role as head of state, the distinction between the public and private roles of men in power, dormant since the fourth-century-B.C. Athenian Republic, was likewise revived.

The separation of roles, the expectations attached to positions, embodied in legal and constitutional developments of the twelfth and thirteenth centuries, revived earlier hierarchy. But the idea that both ruler and ruled had specific rights and obligations with respect to the state as a *public* entity was new. In both the early-ancient and early-medieval periods the state's fiscal and administrative apparatus existed to serve a ruler whose public and private roles were indistinguishable. Because the twelfth century marks the beginning of a conceptual distinction between public and private roles and prerogatives of rulers and ruled, it may be viewed as a distant beginning of the modern era.

Ancient financial practices changed as they passed through the Middle Ages into the modern era. For example, the idea that land is the primary source of wealth and that governments should derive support from taxing its produce has deep roots in the agrarian life of the past. In the Middle Ages the land tax of the ancient world changed from a levy of a fixed proportion of produce paid in kind into a money payment based on an estimate of land's productive value. Taxes on the land are with us still. Local governments in the United States and in most rich countries derive their operating budgets largely from property taxes.*

In the evolution of financial institutions, controversy over methods rarely results in radical change.† Instead, innovations coexist with

---

* There is an interesting parallel between budgetary problems of modern American cities and those of capital cities of the late Roman Empire. In both instances fiscal problems appeared because of the inelasticity of a fixed revenue base. After the third century, Rome and Constantinople had large indigent populations that depended on the emperor's generosity for food. The imperial annona, a regular tax on the land, was collected in kind, earmarked for the imperial dole, transported to both cities, and distributed daily to the urban poor. As Rome and Constantinople depended heavily on imported food, political stability was linked to agricultural productivity throughout the empire. By tradition the annona was paid at a fixed rate; therefore a decline in productivity or in efficiency of collection meant reduced imports, a smaller dole, and eventually urban riots, which the emperors tried at all costs to avoid. Although modern American cities do not collect taxes in kind as the Roman emperors did, they must finance an increasing variety of social services out of the relatively fixed revenues derived from taxes on land. Even before the tax revolts, municipal revenues from property taxes, in states like California and Michigan, did not keep up with inflation, or with increases in fixed costs resulting from local welfare programs. Everywhere in the United States assessments continue to be set at a nominal proportion of market value of most urban land.[4]

† Some archaic fiscal and administrative practices have been retained deliberately by governments so as not to offend or displace established interests, while others survive long after their original purpose has been forgotten. The goldsmith's balance—found on the U.S. Treasury's seal, and used to weigh out coins in European banks—is an example of such an anachronism. It was a vital tool of financial administration during the late Middle Ages, when impecunious feudal magnates often used currency debasement to increase revenues in the short run; no local currency was accepted elsewhere without first determining its intrinsic value.

rearguard actions to defend the status quo. Thus an account of feudalism introduces few new financial institutions to this history, for fiscal mechanisms in local jurisdictions of Europe in the early Middle Ages resembled financial operations in the ancient monarchies. In a stagnating economy producing only bare subsistence, with a rudimentary local currency, men met their obligations to governing authorities as they did in poor economies since time immemorial—with personal labor or periodic contributions of goods. Financial history also repeats itself in the devices used for financial control. The ritualized audits of early feudal kingdoms in Normandy, Flanders, and England after the eleventh century bear a strong resemblance to the treasury audit of classical Athens.

According to a distinguished contemporary political philosopher, J.A.G. Pocock,

> Western historiography has always been fundamentally ambivalent concerning the nature of feudalism . . . [There is incongruity] between the pyramid of dependence which its juristic structure implies and the independence which the feudatory employs in practice . . . between the perception that the tenant holds of a Lord and the perception that his tenure is hereditary and nearly indefensible.[5]

Thus, as feudalism emerged, the collectivism associated with hierarchy was invaded by or combined with individualism, and both were real. In the ancient orders, collectivism dominated individualism. In the feudal social order, collectivism was limited in two important respects: no feudal lord could control all or most of the other lords, nor could he maintain his own authority without resources provided by subordinates, each of whom ruled independently over land within the lord's domain. Within each individual domain hierarchy was still stringent, but over time its rules controlled fewer areas of life. Personal spaces that could not be occupied by others gradually emerged.

Modern interest in feudalism does not occur only for its own sake. The combination of individualism and hierarchy found in feudalism is the source of political liberty, capitalism, and science—all based on competition, whether of rulers, money, or ideas. It is to absence of central coercive capacity, and the independence of participants—two conditions of competition—that we must look for clues to the context and content of feudalism. Some scholars have traced the causes and consequences of modern society back to material or military or financial changes occurring during the Middle Ages, such as improvements in agricultural productivity, invention of the stirrup and the crossbow, or invention of double-entry bookkeeping. We seek the roots of these changes in the social orders where they first appeared.

The fiscal innovations that appeared in commercial communes in northern Italy after the eighth century, and in Hanseatic trading towns along the Baltic coast from the twelfth century on, reveal the spread of the individualism existing in feudal relationships. Revival of business created a small surplus above subsistence that permitted town governments to levy more taxes. Commercial revival created a fertile environment for innovation in government administration and finance. Growing diversity—resulting from contacts between cultures—and steadily increasing affluence from trade created a suitable organizational milieu for rapid social and economic change. Fiscal practices invented in the northern Italian communes—the income tax, the property tax, administration by an impersonal salaried bureaucracy serving for a limited term, and double-entry bookkeeping—foreshadowed government financial practice in the modern era by several centuries and provided a bridge to it.

BACKGROUND

TIME FRAME

Measured against similar epochs in the ancient world, when governmental institutions changed very slowly if at all, there were sharp contrasts during the thousand years of the European Middle Ages. Between collapse of the centralized Roman administration in the west in about the fifth century and reestablishment of strong central government in the European nation-states by the fifteenth, there are at least three overlapping subperiods, each with a somewhat different mode of government, and hence different ways of handling finances. The early Middle Ages (the time between the fifth and seventh centuries that historians used to call the Dark Ages) were a period of nongovernment, or, more accurately, of minimum government. Compared with the powerful Byzantine Empire, western Europe in the early Middle Ages was a backwater. Except for a short time in the sixth century under the Merovingian kings and the ninth century under Charlemagne, governmental authority in western Europe outside Italy was purely local, extending for only a few miles around small settlements that remained from Roman occupation, or that had grown up around manors of powerful landowners or the bishop's palace. Between the fifth and seventh centuries mutual need for protection provided the organizational impetus for government, as it did between the tenth and thirteenth centuries when feudalism was the predominant governmental form.

THE BARBARIAN INVASIONS

Even after the most drastic political dislocations, there is continuity; many of the economic and social relationships in early-medieval society had roots in conditions that had begun to appear in Rome in the third and fourth centuries. In the Western Roman Empire landowner-ship was becoming steadily more concentrated, and after Diocletian's tax edict of A.D. 301 cultivators were legally constrained from leaving their land.

From the time of the early Christians, men have speculated about the causes of the decline of imperial Rome. Although attacks on the empire's outposts following large-scale migration of barbarian tribes became more numerous after the third century, Germanic tribes already had been filtering into the empire since before Caesar's time (first century A.D.). The gradual decline of the Roman Empire in the west extended over several centuries. But, measured by the failure of effective administrative control from the center, the fifth century marks the end of the Western Empire even though Roman administrative *forms* were observed by the German kings well into the seventh century.

Commentators have attributed this failure of Roman government to such diverse reasons as mysticism, moral degeneracy, dilution of its racial stock, climatic change, population decline because of lead poisoning, and a host of other factors.[6]

The invasions did result in sometimes cataclysmic discontinuity in local social and economic life. Yet Roman social and economic institutions, and Roman law and administrative practices, continued to function effectively in parts of Gaul and Italy even after the German kings began to govern there in the fifth century.[7] In spite of episodic interruptions, barbarians were gradually assimilated into Roman society in Italy,[8] and life went on much as before. But in northern and western Europe, where the invasions gradually disrupted local economic life, the tribal institutions of the conquerors sometimes replaced Roman practices in once flourishing provincial towns. Over the long run, and throughout the territory governed by the late empire, tendencies toward change by evolution and revolution coexisted.

From the middle of the third century on, the western half of the empire was subjected to relentless pressure. Germanic tribesmen were at first drawn by the wealth of Roman provincial towns; during the third century successive invasions of Huns, Avars, and Slavs migrating from east of the Danube pushed deep into imperial territory. From then on the barbarians were a continuous threat to the Western Empire's military outposts and a steady drain on its fiscal resources. Successive emperors levied punitive taxes to pay the growing army of mercenaries mobilized to combat attacks on the western frontiers, which stretched along the entire length of the Rhine and the Danube. By the fifth century, in spite of heroic efforts, the empire's defenses had collapsed. The barbarians marched through the eastern provinces and into Gaul and Italy, looting and burning towns.

In the wake of these invasions, city populations declined. Once flourishing provincial towns drew in on themselves during the third and fourth centuries, and rebuilt walls to encompass a reduced territory. Bordeaux in southern Gaul shrank from 175 to 56 acres, and Autun even more drastically—from 500 acres to 25.[9] While not as cataclysmic as legend allows, the sack of Rome by Alaric the Hun and his followers in 410 symbolized the physical destruction and social disorganization produced by the conquests.

The local character of early-medieval economy was closely linked to agricultural conditions in the Western Empire during the third and fourth centuries. As inflation progressively reduced the value of money income, land—the traditional source of status and power in ancient society—became an ever more attractive investment. From the second century on, landholdings of wealthy Romans steadily increased in size. Owners did not necessarily live on their estates; and only in a few exceptional cases were they interested in agricultural productivity or estate management. When the supply of slave labor began to decline in the west after the second century, landowners employed contractors to supervise peasant cultivators—part slave, part propertyless rural poor—who worked the land as share tenants in exchange for a meager subsistence.

With the invasions of the third and fourth centuries, estate owners moved from city to country. There they built magnificent villas that formed the core of virtually self-contained economic units, and lived off the surplus produced by the peasant labor. In spite of the invasions, their lives were largely unchanged.

The poor were less fortunate. In districts where attacks were continuous, men of modest means, independent artisans, and craftsmen fled the cities and begged protection from manor owners, exchanging the uncertain freedom of town life for the greater likelihood of survival on the land. Likewise, some smallholders pledged their land to the wealthy in exchange for protection, while others abandoned the land entirely to escape the oppressive tax burden, and large landowners often added these holdings to their own estates.

From the third to the fifth century the landed wealth of men who paid no taxes increased steadily. Since imperial revenue derived largely from land taxes, abandonment of smallholdings meant reduced state income as its fixed expenses were rising. The emperors tried to impede nobles' consolidation of land into tax-exempt estates by enacting laws that tied men to the land. But the legislation only benefited large landowners. In a time of declining population and generalized labor shortage, large landowners were thereby insured a dependable supply of labor.

The Roman class structure in the west became polarized by the fifth century; the skewed distribution of income, status, and power that had always existed in Roman society was intensified. Instead of the social class mixture that had existed in the late republic and the early empire—of landed aristocrats, wealthy businessmen, independent smallholders, free urban artisans and laborers, and rural and urban slaves—Roman society in the fifth century came to be made up of two groupings: the extremely rich and the very poor.[10] As usual, those least able to help themselves—the poor and the alien—were the chief victims of rapid social and economic change, revolt, and turmoil. It was during the late empire that conditions typical of early-medieval economy and society emerged.

ADMINISTRATIVE DECLINE

When Constantinople became the Roman Empire's capital (following partition in A.D. 364), the imperial center shifted east; Italy and Gaul gradually became provincial outposts. Even though the eastern emperors tried at first to maintain centralized control, it took a minimum of a month to send a runner from Constantinople to Rome,[11] and with the fluctuating conditions of the fourth and fifth centuries, contact between eastern and western bureaucracies gradually declined. In the Eastern Roman Empire the proliferating state bureaucracy was top-heavy and filled with abuses. But the requirement that a man must spend his lifetime in the imperial service before he could achieve the highest posts did provide a corps of specialized administrators. In the west the *praetorian prefects* who served as district governors were appointed from the senatorial aristocracy. Neither by training, temperament, nor prior experience were these men qualified for administrative responsibility. From the more stable times of the early empire on, all of them had depended heavily on subordinates. The languor of the upper classes provided other men's opportunities.

Accustomed to personal tax exemptions, these aristocratic administrators were always willing to grant similar privileges to others of their class. Whether because of this favoritism, corruption at lower levels, or reduced productivity after the invasions, revenue in the west declined to the point where it became impossible to pay either civil-service personnel or troops.[12] The eastern emperors were unwilling to divert eastern revenues to defend the west; thus when the Germans moved into Italy in the fifth century they met little organized opposition.

From the third century on, the western emperors had adopted a strategy of absorbing the Germans into Roman society. As invaders populated the outermost provinces, the Roman generals drew up treaties with their chieftains. The generals proclaimed the tribes *foederati* (allies), then enlisted them in the Roman armies. The Germans were paid with land grants from the res privata (the emperor's private treasury) or with land confiscated from the church or the local aristocracy. In most cases the Romans ceded local tax revenues to the conquerors.[13] Although the German chieftains were loyal to the Roman state and some of them eventually intermarried with the local Roman aristocracy, the tribal leaders were illiterate for the most part, and their training in guerrilla warfare did not equip them to administer. So they depended on the local nobles, who were also poorly qualified for the task. With incompetence squared, so to speak, it is not surprising that the Roman administrative system gradually fell apart. Since communications links to the center—roads, way stations, and troops to defend them—were financed by local revenue from each province, contact between outlying districts[14] and the center was reduced. By the sixth century, when German kings governed Italy, the Western Empire, once united in law and administration from the Mediterranean to the North Sea, had become a fragmented collection of local jurisdictions governed fitfully, if at all, by occupying chieftains, by the local bishop, or by powerful landowners of Roman stock—with help from the few remaining literate priests.

Within each region, inhabitants gradually became subject to eclectic local laws, combining vestiges of the old Roman law with customary practices of the governing tribes.[15] During the late empire the distinction found in Roman law between an owner's preeminent right to dispose of private property and the subordinate rights of his tenants became blurred. When merged with Germanic tribal norms of communal ownership, such attenuation of individual property rights underlay the legal distinction between ownership and use of property later found under feudalism.[16] Meanwhile, pre-feudal law emerged from day-to-day decisions of powerful landowners, which tended to establish precedents for similar actions in the future, accounting for the regional legal differences in Europe throughout the Middle Ages.

THE SCARCITY ECONOMY OF THE EARLY MIDDLE AGES

There are large gaps in men's knowledge of economic life in western Europe between the fifth and ninth centuries. As with Sherlock Holmes's dog that didn't bark, the important evidence was what did not happen. Interregional trade, always an index of economic activity, did not stop altogether, but it fell off. From the sixth to the eighth century, especially in Italy, there was still some local trade conducted with local currencies. But since relatively few men had money, people (like populations of the ancient empires) mainly consumed what they produced themselves or exchanged it at standardized ratios for goods or services their neighbors could provide.[17] In frontierlike districts of northern Europe, the natural environment supplemented the produce of small farms: men trapped game, collected edible roots and berries, and kept bees.[18]

As in less developed economies of the modern world, limited resources, poor technique, and a general scarcity of means limited all men's options. Early-medieval economic life was local and predominantly rural. Walking to cultivate his fields each morning and returning at night were the extent of a man's travel. With rare exceptions, ordinary men lived out their lives where they were born; inhabitants of adjacent villages might never meet.[19]

Production on the early-medieval manor was organized much as it had been on the Roman *latifundia*. The dry-farming techniques practiced in Italy and southern Gaul in ancient times were labor intensive, but without crop rotation, fertilizers, or artificial irrigation where water existed, the land yielded a limited crop. During classical times it had always been necessary for the Roman goverment to import food to maintain its population. During the late Roman Empire, when increased productivity meant that a cultivator would be liable for higher taxes, there was little incentive to alter the practice of centuries.

North of the Alps, where rainfall was abundant, biennial crop rotation may have produced higher yields, but under the German tribes' equal-inheritance laws there was a gradual fragmentation of landholdings, and it brought a corresponding reduction in output.[20] By the ninth century, moreover, a large proportion of the land in Europe was not in cultivation—half or more in France, two-thirds in the Low Countries and Germany, and four-fifths of the land in England[21]—having been abandoned during the invasions and never reclaimed. As with abandoned buildings in central cities today, when people give up what they earlier fought to obtain and defend, it is a sign of disruption, or of the existence of perverse incentives.

Between the sixth and tenth centuries climatic change plus a series of technological improvements gradually caused agricultural output to increase;[22] but, for the mass of the population, living conditions were not much different in the early Middle Ages from the scarcity economies of the ancient past, or even some undeveloped and overpopulated parts of the world today. There was an absolute population decline in western Europe in the late Roman Empire.[23] Although there are no statistics to document early-medieval demographic patterns, in all likelihood the high infant-mortality ratios and low life expectancies revealed by analyzing thousands of Roman tombstones[24] existed in the lower Middle Ages also. Children died young and men lived short lives in all social classes, but especially among the peasantry, weakened by chronic malnutrition and endemic disease.[25]

There was likewise very small distinction between the tied tenancy of the late empire and the villeinage and serfdom of medieval Europe. Like the tenant cultivators of Roman *latifundia,* the medieval peasant was bound to the land by personal, political, and economic constraints. He was not entirely without rights (unlike the slaves found on manors in Italy and Gaul well into the ninth century). In exchange for a house and a small plot of land, he was guaranteed the lord's protection and a minimum level of subsistence. He could marry, accumulate possessions, and convey them to his heirs. But he was bound to the land by an obligation to provide his personal labor and his family's on the landowner's holdings for a prescribed number of days each week (as in England) or each year; and to pay the owner's collectors the rents and customary feudal payments in kind that drained away whatever surplus he might occasionally produce.[26]

The economic underpinning of feudalism as it developed in western Europe between the sixth and eighth centuries under the Merovingian kings rested on the manorial system of agriculture, in which the serf was the lowest productive link. ("Manorial" is the term applied to agricultural organization in England. The feudal economy on the Continent is labeled "seignorial.") The relationship between land tenure and the obligation to provide service was the basis for the interlocked network of mutual dependency that was the essence of the feudal relationship at all social levels—from the lowest, that of serfdom, to the intermediate but economically unproductive rank of knighthood, to the highest aristocratic levels of feudal nobility.[27] The exchange of services that we now regard as an intrinsic attribute of private business (a contract ranking labor before leisure) was, under European feudalism, the only basis for social interaction to promote collective concerns. In those days conceptions of public had meaning only in terms of a reciprocal obligation arising from dependency, and enforced by coercion.

ECONOMIC REVIVAL BEGINS IN THE EIGHTH CENTURY

Increased production of food and fibers was essential to transform the rural subsistence economy of the fifth–seventh centuries into the flourishing commercial economy of the medieval towns, just as it also was to maintain a large unproductive class of feudal knights and nobles. Between the seventh and tenth centuries several technological improvements adopted in northern and western Europe greatly increased agricultural productivity. When employed in combination, the three-field system that allowed one-third of the cultivated land to remain fallow each year and the moldboard plow drawn by horses instead of oxen created the agricultural surplus that was the base of the medieval economic revival.[28]

This surplus gradually transformed man's traditionally passive attitude toward nature: he became its master rather than the hapless recipient of whatever fate bestowed. During the Carolingian period of the eighth century, the circular, repetitive conception of time found in ancient civilizations was replaced by an agricultural calendar that created a progressive, linear conception of time. For each month of the farmer's year—from March, when winter rains stopped and allowed him to prune dead wood from the vines, through October, when he gleaned the last sheaves of grain from the fields and processed them into beer—his tasks were specified.[29]

Increased production provided more food for all segments of society, but especially the lowest. Compared with the emaciated figures of early medieval woodcuts, the well-padded people portrayed in early Renaissance paintings testify to improved living standards. As the population began to grow, pressure on settled land caused men to undertake vast schemes to develop virgin territory; medieval development schemes may be compared in scale with colonization of the American West, the Soviets' development of Siberia, or the land-reclamation movement in Israel. From the tenth century on there was an extensive effort to develop new farmland. Men cleared forests, drained swamps, and built dikes to reclaim land from the sea, and there were several organized efforts to colonize unsettled territories.[30]

Improved farming methods often left the peasant with a surplus after he had paid his rents and feudal dues. As in China today, he could sell surplus produce; local markets attached to cathedral or castle took place once a week from the ninth century on. Coinage issued by local nobles gradually replaced barter; by the ninth century money was used in parts of England and Gaul; and in northern Italy during the tenth century money was common even in rural districts.[31] By increasing men's options, surplus created a suitable environment for change in nonagricultural roles and activities as well. Slowly an economy of money and trade based on regional specialization superseded the primitive agrarian economy that had existed in northern Europe for nearly half a millennium.[32] And where there was money there was movement.

In the complex, interlocked causal nexus of large-scale social and economic changes, economic revival gradually altered settlement patterns. Where horses, with their greater speed and mobility, replaced oxen in cultivation, peasants could live in villages and make daily journeys to the fields and back. In parts of Germany, northern France, and England between the tenth and thirteenth centuries, rural populations gradually clustered as peasants abandoned isolated hamlets and moved into towns, drawn by the attractions that settlements have always provided—the church, schools, markets, and chances for diverse experiences.[33] Over several generations, rapid population increase fragmented agricultural smallholdings in districts where equal division of property among heirs was the rule, and younger sons of free peasant families began to leave the land. With labor in surplus, serfs also began to leave the land in steadily increasing numbers for the towns; according to customary law well developed by the twelfth century, a serf became a free man if he lived in a town for a year and a day.[34]

As the economy revived, small towns grew from immigration and natural increase. In time, larger populations began to press on town walls. Congestion, in turn, led to physical expansion. In rapidly growing districts of Flanders and northern Italy the boundaries of fortified towns were moved outward, often several times, as settlements spread beyond existing walls into the surrounding countryside.[35] Pisa in Italy, for example, multiplied the territory within its walls by a factor of six between the eleventh and fourteenth centuries, from 74 acres to 456, while Florence, whose development was later but more rapid, enclosed 197 acres at the end of the twelfth century but an additional 1,300 by the middle of the thirteenth, to provide space for future growth.[36] In the ninth century there had been only a handful of towns in western Europe with more than five thousand inhabitants. By the end of the thirteenth, hundreds of small and medium-sized towns existed. Many grew spontaneously from a location at river junctions or along active trade routes. Other towns were chartered in the eleventh and twelfth centuries by kings, local magnates, and bishops. Perceiving the prosperity of mercantile settlements, these men gave part of their land to merchant settlers in exchange for a pledge of tax revenue from trade.

It was in the coastal cities of the Italian peninsula—Venice, Naples, and Amalfi, where trading contact with the Arab and Byzantine worlds had never been entirely broken—that commercial revival was at first most vigorous.* There by the ninth century, and in the Lombard communes of Genoa and Pisa after the eleventh, merchants traded local raw materials—timber and iron—for fabrics, exotic spices, and jewels from the Far East. As the economy of northern Europe revived after the tenth century, Italian merchants carried specialty products over the Alps to exchange for cash in local markets. The Crusades also stimulated trade by exposing northern Europeans to products of the Orient. By the twelfth century an active exchange between northern and southern Europe had grown up.[38]

Feeling the pinch of inflation as rising prices eroded the value of customary feudal revenues in kind, still paid at traditional rates, some nobles in northern France saw in trade the prospect for cash income. The fairs in Champagne, held six times each year from the twelfth century, began as attempts to derive revenue from tolls and market taxes, but quickly became important instruments of economic development and cultural exchange. Located centrally—between Italy, France, and Germany—the Champagne fairs became outlets for specialized goods produced throughout Europe. As commerce revived, smaller fairs were established at favorable locations. Foods, grains, spices, metal products, leather, and, above all, textiles, woolen and linen, were traded.[39] The fairs served also as interregional financial clearinghouses where Italian merchant-bankers earned profits from

---

* Venice played somewhat the same role in medieval and Renaissance Europe as does Japan in today's world. Before a culture of competitive individualism had become widespread, Venice was a trading state preeminent. It was a republic and, like modern Japan, was governed by an oligarchy whose members put collective interests before personal interests. Unlike nobility elsewhere, members of its two hundred noble families worked to increase familial wealth by actively engaging in the city's thriving commerce linking east and west.[37]

arbitrage—exchanging the multiple local currencies of medieval Europe for each other.

Italian merchants were as ingenious in finding ways to circumvent the church's prohibition against moneylending as they were in devising schemes to cushion their investments against risk.* The merchants used a variety of techniques ranging in sophistication from formal contracts of mutual indemnity to outright fraud. For each round-trip trading voyage there were two or more contracting parties. A single large investor, or sometimes a consortium of small investors, supplied the capital. In exchange for a one-quarter share of the profits, a noninvesting partner accompanied the goods in transit, conducted the exchange, and returned to the original port with a cargo of vendible goods. The investor received disguised interest equivalent to three-quarters of the profit, but bore all the risk if the ship failed to make port. This pooling of financial and entrepreneurial resources served as a kind of maritime insurance and, if the transaction was completed, produced substantial gain for both parties; 150 percent seems to have been the average rate of return.[40]

After the thirteenth century, when (by a succession of edicts) the church clamped down on profitmaking, merchants often resorted to subterfuge to protect investments. In one-directional trade with neighboring communes, a Genoese merchant would write a contract (*cambium maritimum*) specifying payment only in foreign currency. By deliberately undervaluing the currency of payment, merchants could obtain higher returns on capital than the church allowed. Contracts involving foreign exchange might also serve as a cover for moneylending, often at extortionate rates.†

Italian merchants developed new techniques for internal business

* The medieval church was not the first institution to prohibit lending money for interest. In scarcity economies of past eras as well, most personal loans were made to finance consumption in times of hardship. From ancient times, therefore, governments and religious orders have condemned usury (charging interest, or excessive interest) as socially harmful at best, and at worst as a crime. The church's prohibition against moneylending was strengthened in the early Middle Ages, a time of severe scarcity.

† The kind of dealing the church tried to prohibit is illustrated by the following transaction. Early in the thirteenth century a Genoese banker loaned a sum of money to a local merchant, to be repaid the following month at the fair in Provins. Their contract specified that the funds be repaid in the currency of Provins, which was undervalued in terms of the current exchange rate with Genoa's currency. If the merchant could not pay at the specified time, he could extend the loan until the next fair, or the succeeding one, but could pay only in the foreign currency, discounted by an additional 3 percent for each extension. If the borrower were to have renewed the loan at each of the six annual fairs he would have paid annual interest of 335 percent![41]

management. Invention of double-entry bookkeeping in Genoa in the twelfth century, and its diffusion into the other Italian communes by the thirteenth,* enabled merchants to keep continuous track of inventories, assets, outstanding debts and payments due. As availability of current information permitted better-informed decision about business transactions, the scale of enterprise gradually increased. By the thirteenth century, Italian banker-merchants—the Bardi of Lucca, and the Riccardi, the Frescobaldi, and the Peruzzi of Florence—were shipping capital and commodities to northern Europe and profiting from both. By that time they had become the principal entrepreneurs of medieval Europe and a source of credit to merchants and feudal kings.

The dynamic growth of the communes reshuffled traditional status conceptions and class alignments, and changed the ancient attitude that business was no occupation for a man of high status. By the twelfth century a new class of merchant oligarchs had emerged as the source of economic and political power in northern Italy. While the infant kingdoms of northern Europe were still private, fragmented feudal baronies, the Italian communes had established autonomous governments and developed financial institutions to sustain them. In Venice, Genoa, Florence, Milan, and countless smaller towns, a small group of merchants and artisans successfully wrested governing power from church and rural feudal nobility, and consolidated their influence in communal governments that for a time were independent of both. It was in the communes, rather than in the young nation-states (whose methods of fiscal management retained an archaic character well into the modern era), that modern government finance began.

RECENTRALIZATION IN THE FEUDAL KINGDOMS

"The heathen from the north wrought havoc in Christendom and grew greater in strength. . . . A mighty army of them collected. . . . Some . . . towns were besieged, others burned, and most terribly did they oppress

---

* The conceptual basis of double entry appears to have been drawn from algebra, which was known in northern Italy in the late Middle Ages, possibly through contacts with Arab traders. The essential elements of double entry were dual recording of each transaction as an item of expense (debit) and as an amount due (credit), and periodic summation of the two categories, to arrive at a total that, if correct, would be identical for each. Compared to the haphazard accounts of ancient scribes—a partial running list of amounts spent and received, kept in Roman numerals and in paragraph form—the new accounting method significantly systematized methods and facilitated orderly work habits. The first printed treatise on double entry, Luigi Pacioli's *Summa de arithmetica,* appeared in 1494, but historians feel that the principles Pacioli enunciated were a compendium of practices developed over the two preceding centuries by countless clerks working in banks and countinghouses all over northern Italy. There is an extensive literature on the origins of double entry, which we have sampled only partially.[42]

the Christians."[43] Throughout the ninth century, invaders once again disrupted settled life in northern Europe. From their shallow-draft vessels, marauding Scandinavian tribes made sporadic attacks on coastal settlements of England, Ireland, Germany, and France and penetrated inland as far up the major rivers as their ships would sail. The almost total absence of written records in parts of continental Europe from the ninth to the twelfth century is a single measure of the extensive depredations.[44]

Like barbarian invaders of the Roman Empire six centuries before, the Norsemen settled in Normandy (the part of northern France that bears their name) and, through intermarriage with the resident population, gradually became assimilated into local society. They adopted some local customs, and gradually altered local political and social institutions to conform with their own.

As attacks diminished, order and stable government slowly returned to northern Europe. To be sure, political organization based on need for military defense—an essential element of feudalism—produced a situation of chronic low-level warfare. When the invasions ended, underemployed knights and barons continued to exercise the specialized skills they had spent a lifetime learning. There were continuous armed disputes between rival barons of equal power, and even strong feudal magnates were often unable to prevent vassals from fighting against one another.[45] (In our time too, though on a smaller scale, we might add, public police powers are selectively supplemented by private protective agreements.) But, compared to the absolute dissolution of authority that accompanied the invasions, there was a gradual return of political control. Between the tenth and twelfth centuries in Europe, partial, creeping centralization, and feudal decentralization existed side by side.

In several territories a new type of small-scale central government grew out of feudal institutions. In an age when to rule at all was to rule by force, ability to command men slowly brought order and organization. By the late twelfth century in England and the thirteenth in France, strong feudal monarchies had maintained control for nearly two hundred years. By means of military conquests, political alliances through strategically arranged marriages, and coalition with the church, the territory each kingdom's ruler could command gradually grew. The feudal kingdoms were founded on personal authority of strong military leaders, but successive rulers gradually built an organization to regulate civil affairs as well. Where no central government had existed for centuries, feudal kings established order.

French and English kings succeeded in suppressing fighting among feudal magnates. From the fortified outposts they erected in territory consolidated under their rule, kings tried to protect their interests while discouraging castle-building by potential rivals. The kings tried to maintain order by formulating legal codes and developing a mechanism for enforcement. They appointed trustworthy men to act as their local agents, then gradually built a civil bureaucracy of lay officials, with checks to insure obedience to the royal will. Feudal monarchs acquired a monopoly over coinage; the superior intrinsic value of the king's coinage sometimes made it preferable to local currencies. Although not always stable, feudal kings' coinage provided more reliable standards of value than had existed before.

With political stability and reliable coinage, trade and industry prospered. To supplement the customary in-kind revenue from the royal domain, feudal kings levied market taxes payable in coin. As medieval Europe moved from barter to money economy, feudal kings' power to command money revenues (when lesser magnates could obtain only feudal service and payment in kind) gave them the surplus to hire mercenary troops, which in turn helped to further consolidate their political control. The process of recentralization in England and France is well understood. It was gradual and not without incident, but on the whole the trend was toward ever more effective, if small-scale, central government.[46]

Elsewhere in Europe, centralization came later. The Germanic half of the Holy Roman Empire, torn by disputes among rival barons, and racked throughout the twelfth century by a controversy with the church over control of ecclesiastical revenues, remained feudalized for several centuries longer. Except for Norman territory in Italy and Sicily, political control of the Italian peninsula remained fragmented throughout the Middle Ages. Because such noncentralized governments—"ordered anarchies," as Evans-Pritchard called them—do not sit still long enough to make recorded history, our analysis of administrative and fiscal practices in the late Middle Ages will focus mainly on the feudal monarchies of England and France, and the independent communal governments of the northern-Italian city-states.

While the pattern of development was roughly similar in both states, France lagged behind England by nearly two centuries.[47] Nominal centralization was abruptly achieved in England with the Norman Conquest. The French monarchy became an important political force in feudal Europe only after gradually acquiring territory, influence, and organizational capacity, over more than two hundred years. Both of these feudal states perpetuated the centralized monarchical governmental model of the Carolingian era, Byzantium, imperial Rome, and the ancient monarchies before them. In contrast, the political forms that emerged in city-states of northern Italy between the eleventh and thirteenth centuries both revived the democratic *pólis* of classical Athens and foreshadowed self-governing municipalities of the present.

REVENUES AND EXPENDITURES OF MEDIEVAL GOVERNMENTS

THE EARLY MIDDLE AGES

The earliest Frankish kings of Roman Gaul collected all the taxes their subjects would pay, but, as there was no longer a public treasury, they melted down the tax receipts and added the bullion to their private hoards.* But Merovingian kings' efforts to collect taxes were destined to be short-lived. Recent converts to Christianity, Frankish kings equated tax collection with evil.

Gregory of Tours, a sixth-century bishop, describes an episode, perhaps apocryphal, that illustrates the Germanic rulers' view of the Roman revenue system, and documents its collapse. During the reign of King Chilperic two of his children became seriously ill. Viewing their condition as the act of a vengeful God, the Queen pleaded with her spouse to "burn the wicked tax registers" in the hope of inducing a miraculous cure.[49]

The burning of the cadasters—if, indeed, it took place—accelerated the administrative disintegration that had already gained momentum. As Roman organization in western Europe collapsed, receipts from the land tax gradually declined, then disappeared altogether. In some districts men still paid local tolls and market taxes, but, as trade was minimal, so, too, were tax receipts. Often the local nobleman kept the collections for his personal use, or to support public facilities he now provided for those who lived under his protection.[50] With public money appropriated for personal use by men who governed, the private, local character of medieval government and economy had appeared.

By the seventh century, if not before, government had become iden-

---

* Under conditions of uncertainty (in the medieval world just as in the modern era), men have chosen to hold personal wealth in liquid form. Epic literature of the early Middle Ages describes richly ornamented clothing and weapons of the German warriors— gold and silver rings, armbands, and belt buckles; swords, shields, and spears inlaid with gold and silver; and gilded and jeweled saddles and harnesses. A small object made from precious metal must have had substantial intrinsic value in an age of depressed prices and minimal circulation of money. When measured against the purchasing power of its equivalent in coin, a sword, a saddle, or a piece of jewelry must have represented a large capital asset, the bulk of the owners' personal wealth. Accumulation of precious metal in private hoards no doubt contributed to the stagnation of the Merovingian era.[48]

tical with estate management; there was no longer a distinction between manorial rights and political authority.[51] The Frankish kings'
revenues, like those of the local landowning nobility, derived from
their private estates.[52] The holdings provided their owners a subsistence in agricultural commodities somewhat analogous to the in-kind
revenues of the ancient monarchies. Yet, because the lands were not
contiguous but were physically dispersed, there was a significant difference in the manner of procurement.

Without an administrative organization to collect the produce, or
transport networks to move it from outlying estates to the center, medieval kings and nobles, of necessity, adopted a peripatetic lifestyle.
Throughout the year, accompanied by a sizable retinue of horses and
men, kings traveled from place to place to consume the produce of
their scattered holdings. The traveling court was a ubiquitous feature
of medieval government, an organizational result of the turbulent
times.

In addition to subsistence, medieval rulers traveled to maintain political control. In an age of impaired communications, localism, and
personal government, a ruler's periodic appearance in various parts of
his domain was good public relations, for it assured the population,
first of all, that he actually existed. And repeated visits tended to solidify the authority of his reign.* In Marc Bloch's colorful language, medieval kings "positively killed themselves by travel." The Holy Roman
Emperor Conrad's travels in 1033 were fairly typical. He traveled some
1600 miles as the crow flies, and many more on the winding roads of
the times, from Burgundy to the Polish frontier, back to Champagne,
and then to Lusatia in north-central Germany to spend the winter.[53]
Several hundred years later, between August of 1298 and October of
the following year, Edward I of England followed a complex route of
over 1300 miles, extending from one end of his small kingdom to the
other.[54] Just as in the ancient empires, when rain or snow made roads
impassable, kings and nobles alike settled down where provisions and
forage were adequate; they set out on the road again in the spring.†

---

* Rulers of ancient governments moved about with an entourage for the same reasons
as did medieval kings. China's rulers during the Shang Dynasty held an itinerant court.
The early Roman Emperor Hadrian traveled throughout his domain also; after the anarchic politics of the late Roman Republic, his royal progress conveyed to Rome's people
the enhanced authority of empire.

† As an instrument of political control, the traveling court persisted well into the Renaissance. In 1535 a Venetian ambassador to the court of Francis I of France wrote to his
superiors: "My tenure as ambassador lasted forty-five months.... I traveled con-

There was another similarity between the fiscal economy of early-medieval regimes and of the ancient empires. In a subsistence economy with minimal circulation of money, tenants discharged whatever obligations they owed to nobles largely in the currency of heavy and continuous labor. From the lord's point of view, it was more economic to give each peasant family a parcel of land to produce its own subsistence, and then to demand a regular quota of compulsory labor service in exchange, than it was to maintain a large staff of field hands throughout the year when his need for labor was seasonal and irregular and he had no money to pay them.[56] A regular period of compulsory labor service on the lord's land was the way slaves, serfs, and free tenants without money paid for the land they cultivated, and for whatever services in lieu of government the lord might provide.

The period and type of labor varied with the tenant's status; requirements were heavier and more onerous for unfree men. Free laborers might be required to furnish a cart and a horse for manorial errands, or a plow team and a driver for four or five weeks each year, or to provide specialized skills like carpentry or horseshoeing. The lord might demand up to three man-days of labor each week of the year from each family of serfs, and more during periods of intensive activity. Since the servile tenants owned no horses and had no skills, the men worked as manual laborers—cutting wood, shearing sheep, guarding the manorhouse at night, or building roads and bridges; their wives and daughters wove cloth for the manorial household, did laundry, and provided other domestic services.[57]

Medieval forced labor was heavier than ancient corvées, both in absolute terms and because it was impossible to evade. Forfeiture of a peasant's holding was the penalty for noncompliance, a risk no man would run in an age of scarcity. The relationship between a nobleman and his armed retainers in the early Middle Ages still retained some of the voluntarism that typified the German chieftain's interaction with his tribesmen, but as feudal institutions developed, custom gradually established the lord's right to demand a specified number of days of military service each year. While the knight might prefer to remain at home to tend his holdings rather than follow the lord into battle for the customary forty days each year,[58] he too had little choice. But however

---

stantly. . . . Never during that time did the court remain in the same place for as long as two weeks." Elizabeth I of England used the royal progress to reduce opposition to her policies; confronted with a costly visit by the Queen and her extensive entourage, critics would quickly come around to the Queen's views.[55]

burdensome, whether to nobles or peasants, medieval corvées were less exploitative than those of the ancient world because they involved an element of reciprocity. In the miniature governments of the early Middle Ages, men exchanged labor for land, or the right to its use, while in the ancient monarchies men served government under duress for long periods and received nothing in return.

Even after the Roman land tax remained little more than a hazy memory, the lord's quasi-governmental role empowered him to make demands that resembled a tax, regularly requiring peasants to bring gifts of produce, small animals, or a few coins to the manorial household. Custom gradually transformed such voluntary gifts into compulsory obligation that was sometimes even codified by law.[59] The tenants of ten "hides"* of land owned by Ine, an eighth-century Saxon king of Wessex in England, for example, regularly contributed "10 casks of honey, 300 loaves of bread, 12 buckets of Welsh ale, 30 of clear ale, 2 full-grown oxen, 2 wethers [castrated male sheep], 10 geese, 20 chickens, 10 pieces of cheese, one bucketful of butter, 5 salmon, 20 pounds of fodder, and 100 eels."[60] Each tenant's payments were modest; some historians have equated them with rents paid for use of land. Yet in-kind contributions provided a regular income for the lord in addition to labor service he could command.

A third source of manorial income resulted from the lord's monopoly over essential capital facilities. When the peasant brought grain to the lord's mill to be ground into flour, he left a proportion in payment. When he made the flour into bread, he was obliged to bake it in the lord's ovens, for he had none of his own, and again he left a loaf or two behind. Since the peasant had no alternative, the *banalités* (as these charges were called on the Continent) were a continuous drain on his slender resources. Some lords reserved monopoly right to sell wine or beer, others to provide animals for stud service at a cost, still others to provide for a price the horses used to thresh the community's grain.[61]

Heavy as they might have been in a scarcity economy, medieval manorial taxes were never so extortionate as the land tax of the ancient world. Men were never forced to sell their kinsmen to pay medieval taxes in kind, and the immediacy and interdependence of the manorial-feudal relationship made the lord a forgiving landlord in times of famine or personal hardship. Restrictions on a man's liberties that seem unreasonable by modern standards—such as the near-universal requirement that a serf obtain his master's permission before he could

* The hide was a medieval measure of land area usually equivalent to 120 acres.

marry[62]—were accepted as normal, just as similar restrictions might be in traditional societies of modern times. Under conditions of scarcity and extreme deprivation men will tolerate the most onerous conditions because these are customary.[63] Once custom established the lord's rights to labor service and payments in kind, successive generations of tenants accepted them without question as long as the contributions weren't increased. In addition, in the chaotic world of those days, Christian doctrine was strongly stabilizing. The church taught that God made the world in his image and that it would always remain as it was. Since life on earth was merely a prelude to the afterlife—with its reward of perpetual bliss in Paradise if one followed ecclesiastical rule—men discounted hardship in the present world against the expectation that conditions would be better in the next.[64]

Although religious and secular authority were at times intermingled and at times separate during the Middle Ages, church and state had equivalent social orders. With one lord or king, one God or pope, both structures were hierarchies. But, if individualism proved to be attractive in social life, change could eventually come about in political and religious life as well.

THE FEUDAL CONTRACT

European feudalism was, first of all, a system of mobilizing resources for military defense. Just as the manorial economy grew out of the land-tenure relations of the late Roman villa, so, too, the personal, political, and military network of feudalism had its origins in the declining years of the Roman Empire, when nearly every aristocrat maintained a force of armed men on his estate to protect against invading German tribes. Under the egalitarian norms of German tribal custom during the Merovingian period, the hired strong-arm men of the late empire gradually became companions-in-arms who lived in the master's house, shared his fortune, and often served him for most of their lives.

The Merovingian warrior was no longer the rude peasant foot soldier of the Roman era, but was becoming a specialized professional. With invention and spread of the horseshoe and the stirrup in northern Europe, mounted shock combat gradually became the predominant military technique. To obtain a war-horse and equipment for battle a man needed wealth. By the mid–eighth century, a horse, sword, spear, shield and armor were worth twenty oxen, or the plow teams of ten peasant families. Moreover, fighting with a lance on a charger entailed a long apprenticeship that few ordinary freedmen could afford in a subsistence economy. By the Carolingian era in the eighth century the companionate military service of the Merovingian period was a thing of the past. Under the institutions of feudalism that replaced it, military service became the specialized prerogative of an aristocratic elite.[65]

When the warrior lived in his master's house, subsistence and group camaraderie were the only rewards for service, since the relationship derived from mutual need and advantage. As the expense of armed service grew, it became customary for the master to reward his vassal (as the warrior had come to be called) with a grant of land to hold for the vassal's lifetime, for the master had no other resources to give. Carolingian emperors granted vast estates to their vassals from the royal domain and also from lands confiscated from the church's vast holdings.[66] In exchange, vassals still gave armed service, by old German custom forty days in each year.[67] With the unsettled conditions following the ninth-century invasions, vassalage acquired a secondary, political function. On the land of his fief a vassal possessed authority to govern—to administer justice, collect taxes, build roads and bridges, and even raise his own army—as well as rights to produce of that land.[68] After the Carolingian monarchy collapsed, local fiefdoms were the only government.

Once the vassal had power to govern his fief, the lord could no longer control him, save for reclaiming the land. By the tenth century, when most fiefdoms had become hereditary, a formal ritual of homage and fealty invoked the church's superior authority to safeguard the lord's rights. The vassal pledged faith to his lord on relics of saints or a Bible. He promised to fight in the lord's army, send knights to his aid, garrison the lord's castle, attend him at court, and extend the hospitality of his manor to the lord and his retinue whenever they passed by.[69] To meet the terms of his contract, a vassal with large holdings of land would divide it, giving over use of the land to men of lower rank, and these men, in turn, would further subdivide their estates, until, after a succession of partitions, the smallest holding belonged to one knight. With subinfeudation, as this process is now called, each level of the hierarchy owed fealty and service to the lord directly above him, until, at the highest levels, the chief vassals owed both to the crown. In these relationships hierarchy was balanced by some measure of reciprocity.

The feudal contract differed in various parts of Europe, but its essential quality of mutuality entailed inherently weak control, which has led political scientists to characterize feudalism as an extreme case of decentralization. As with the Athenian liturgies, the decurionate of the Roman provincial municipalities, or any other political contract based on good faith, there were no guaranteed standards of performance once immediate needs of both parties were met. When common defense and law and order—traditional prerogatives of government—depended solely on private authority deriving from ownership of land, it mattered how land was transferred from one holder to another. If a fief was granted for the recipient's lifetime, the lord possessed effective sanctions, for he could always repossess it, but when feudal tenure became hereditary the lord lost this option.

To back up mere promise, the customary law of feudalism gradually established the lord's right to influence the terms of succession so that he might still protect his rights emanating from the land. And insofar as his rights protected those under him, they also gained from the lord's ability to guarantee his commitments into the future. Feudal law insured that land passed intact to heirs by the rule of *primogeniture*—inheritance by the oldest son—which gradually was adopted throughout Europe.* Feudal law contained two further checks that enabled the lord to maintain control over the fief's identity. If the holder of a fiefdom died without an heir, or if he had produced an heir that the lord judged to be incompetent, the lord possessed the power of *escheat*, which permitted him to reclaim the fief and assign it to another. If a vassal died before his heir had reached maturity (always a likely possibility), the lord held the power of *wardship*, which enabled him to repossess the fief and govern it until the vassal's heir was old enough to take the oath of fealty. The lord's control over succession and inheritance included the right to approve a widow's remarriage, and to select suitable mates for his vassals' daughters.[71] A final safeguard of the lord's rights was his power of *entail*. By this rule, at least theoretically, the lord could reclaim a fief if his vassal's performance failed to meet his requirements, whatever they might have been.

These customary powers served to stabilize the feudal relationship. Perhaps their existence indicates the most common ways vassals tried to evade their obligations. The terms of the feudal contract *were* one-sided, for the lord gave fewer promises. He was obliged only to give military aid if the vassal's land was attacked, and, when the vassal required it, to provide "good and speedy justice," either in court or on

* Only the oldest son of a noble family was permitted to marry. The dowries given to daughters upon marriage represented their ultimate share of family assets. Donations to the church or to monasteries bought ranked places in religious orders for second and later sons.[70]

the battlefield.[72] There is a sense in which subinfeudation served as a stabilizing influence. A principal vassal might hesitate to violate his feudal contract with the king because his actions would set an unfavorable example to men who in turn owed him feudal service.[73]

From their holdings of land all feudal magnates, whatever their rank, derived incomes from labor service and payments in kind.[74] The difference in their revenue was simply a matter of scale, for under the political economy of feudalism a man's wealth and authority were directly related to the size of his holding.

PITY THE POOR KING: FEUDAL FINANCIAL INSTITUTIONS

The basic fiscal problem of feudal monarchs in the reviving economy of Europe between the eleventh and fourteenth centuries was to develop nonfeudal revenue sources. As the medieval economy expanded, prices increased; kings and lesser feudal magnates alike then found it steadily more difficult to live off the produce of their holdings. Yet their efforts to enlarge the revenue base met with repeated frustration, for it had been so long since men had paid taxes to a central authority that the custom no longer existed.

If ability to command and collect taxes was a measure of effective centralization, France was the only kingdom in Europe to emerge from the Middle Ages with a strong, centralized fiscal system. By the fourteenth century, French kings had established a productive revenue system and were regularly collecting a variety of taxes from nonfeudal sources. English kings were not successful in reestablishing the power to tax. Throughout the later Middle Ages and beyond, they were forced to live from hand to mouth as they faced chronic revenue shortages. Their financial problems were not a result of inadequate resources; the kingdom's real wealth grew steadily.[75] The problems stemmed from a source that had not appeared before in the history of governments' efforts to mobilize resources: limitation of a ruler's unconditional power to levy taxes. Political developments between the eleventh and early thirteenth centuries mark the turning point between ancient government by monarchical fiat and modern government by consent. After the thirteenth century, English kings faced continuous conflict with their baronial councils over royal authority to levy new taxes that would tap the kingdom's growing wealth. Although the English baron expected tenants on his personal domain to observe rules of hierarchy, he was not willing to be similarly constrained by rules made by others. Outside his own territory he practiced autonomy.

French kings convened their baronial councils at irregular intervals from the thirteenth century on; like the ancient monarchs, they levied taxes solely on the basis of their own authority.[76] The English barons, by contrast, had firmly established their right of joint control of revenue procurement by the end of the same century. After 1215, when the barons forced King John to sign the Magna Carta, the principle that the king could not levy taxes without Parliament's consent was affirmed repeatedly. The barons defined and elaborated the reciprocal rights of king and subjects with respect to taxation in a succession of later thirteenth-century charters that reiterated the Magna Carta's principles.[77] Despite the narrow focus at the time they were drafted, these documents have become a source of basic liberties in the Anglo-American political tradition; by establishing the principle that the king must obtain his subjects' consent before he could levy new taxes, the barons declared that, like all other men, the king was subject to law. The limited competition between barons and king then diffused among other groups. At least as far as the power to tax is concerned, England emerged from the Middle Ages as a limited monarchy.

Throughout northern Europe the period between the eleventh and thirteenth centuries was marked by gradual transition from feudal-manorial to market economy. In the undeveloped feudal monarchies of the eleventh century, customary manorial revenues were adequate to maintain the king and his servants as he traveled from place to place; his expenses (like those of Kautilya's kings in Mauryan India) entailed little more than providing for the physical needs of his personal household. Fortunately for students of financial history, eleventh- and twelfth-century kings of Norman England acted as if they followed Kautilya's advice to a wise monarch: they kept track of expenditures.

A twelfth-century document tells us that King Henry I paid his staff money and a modest food allowance, which he supplemented with a regular ration of whatever commodities were needed to perform a given task. Thus, his chief household officer was paid at the rate of "five shillings a day, and one lord's simnel loaf [fruit cake] and 2 salted simnel loaves [wheat bread] and one sextary of clear wine and one sextary of ordinary wine and one fat wax candle and 40 pieces of candle."[78] Lesser personnel were paid at lower rates; wages were lower if a servant lived in the king's house.*

* Alongside Kautilya's elaborate roster of specialized offices (which encompassed such exotic and specialized tasks as "superintendent of the harem," "reader of omens," and "keeper of the elephant forests") the medieval king's household seems pedestrian: its only purpose was to provide for the king's personal needs. The king's servants included cooks,

English kings' manorial revenues amounted to £11,000 each year at the time of the Norman Conquest.[80] Since a king paid modest wages for his household staff and did not need to maintain and equip an army—this service was provided by his vassals—kings of the eleventh and twelfth centuries in England (and the other feudal monarchies as well) did not have to spend much. Besides his household, the king's principal expense was occasional contributions to church or charity. His treasury was typically so modest—a few chests of coins, jewelry, and personal valuables—that the king could carry them as he moved. In medieval French *la bougette* meant little purse; the king's budget was originally the leather pouch in which he carried his fortune.[81]

As use of money became widespread during the twelfth century, feudal magnates of England and France manipulated payment of manorial dues to their advantage. Like tax farmers in rural districts of Roman Asia in the late republic (when a transition from barter to money economy was also occurring), feudal kings and nobles controlled the rate by which commodities were evaluated for conversion into money and the terms of payment—whether in money, commodities, or a combination of the two. When their currencies were stable, feudal rulers asked payment in money. If a monarch's currency happened to be depreciated—a relatively normal condition for medieval governments—he asked for payment in kind instead.[82] But when feudal magnates converted payments in kind into money equivalents, a general practice after the twelfth century, they instructed their stewards to evaluate commodities at a fixed scale—one well under the current market price.[83] Perhaps kings hoped to compensate for rising prices that were gradually eroding the value of customary manorial dues—either by evaluating commodities low and then asking for more or by selling the surplus for a profit. The market economy created incentive to hold commodities like grain in hope of a better price in the near future.[84]

In addition to manorial dues and armed service, feudal custom had established the lord's right to request extraordinary contributions in money from vassals and retainers on special occasions such as the knighting of their sons, marriage of their daughters, payment of a ransom if they were captured in battle, and other occasions the lord might specify at will.[85] These irregular payments, known as aids, were given

---

bakers, butlers, porters, trumpeters, grooms, huntsmen, and a personal attendant to the king himself, the *ewerer*, "who shall receive a penny a day for drying the king's clothes, and when the king takes a bath he shall have four pence."[79]

willingly in recognition of personal interdependence. Perhaps legitimation of aids provided legal rationale for feudal kings to impose regular taxes on subjects as they searched for methods to enlarge the revenue base.

It was during the twelfth century—when feudal kings wished to demonstrate their piety by leading an army to the Holy Land—that they first needed to supplement ordinary revenues. Even in the first few Crusades, when kings could marshal a feudal army, they needed money for poor knights who could not afford to pay their way, and to transport the army by sea.[86] At the end of the twelfth century, Philip Augustus of France paid the consul of Genoa 5,850 marks of silver (the equivalent of over a year's revenue from the prosperous fiefdom of Flanders) to carry his army of 650 knights, 1300 squires, 1300 horses, and their arms, baggage, and provisions over the sea to the Holy Land.[87]

Religious fanaticism no doubt motivated Crusaders who hoped to free the Holy Land from unbelievers and so insure their salvation. But knights who survived their holy quest could reap substantial material gain along the way. During the last quarter of the eleventh century, for example, a weak emperor of Byzantium bought off the Norman nobleman Robert Guiscard and his followers with gifts, titles, and public offices.[88] Henry IV of Germany made out equally well: the Emperor Alexius Comnenus awarded him 100 pieces of silk and promised 16,000 more, 144,000 nomismata (the bronze coinage then current), and 200 offices.[89] Largely ceremonial, such offices nevertheless paid holders an annual salary. (If the offices had been sold to Byzantine citizens, the salaries would have represented interest on the purchasers' invested funds.) If an office did entail work, a holder, whether a native or a foreigner, could derive further gain from fees levied on natives of Byzantium for whatever services were provided. A younger son of a noble family thus had a good reason for going on Crusades: by traveling to the Holy Land, he could become wealthy.[90]

To finance their Crusades feudal kings borrowed money and levied extraordinary aids.[91] As the twelfth century progressed, they also asked more and more frequently for aids to finance local feudal wars.

By the thirteenth century, money had become abundant throughout Europe. With continued economic growth, traditional knight service was becoming an inconvenient and costly method of mobilizing resources for donor and recipient alike. And once again, changes in financial arrangements followed changes in the social order. Just as growth of a money economy brought some differentiation in society as merchants in towns were accorded social status, so, too, did it bring new ways of meeting feudal obligations.

At the beginning of the thirteenth century most knights would still serve their lords when called, merely for the glory of battle. By the end of the century many had become sedentary men of property, more interested in increasing the productivity of their holdings than in fighting. Many English knights refused to serve at all, especially if an overseas campaign threatened to keep them abroad for longer than the mandatory forty days. A feudal contract between a late-thirteenth-century king of France and his vassals specifies mutual obligations. Though the vassal was committed to the traditional period of knight service, the King was unable to detain him longer without payment.* The contract further provided for the vassals' exemption from long-term service abroad.

> The Baron and all vassals of the king are bound to appear before him when he shall summon them, and to serve him at their own expense for forty days and forty nights, with as many knights as each one owes; and he is able to extract from them these services when he wishes and when he has need of them. And if the king wishes to keep them more than forty days at their own expense, they are not bound to remain if they do not wish it. And if the king wishes to keep them at his expense for the defense of the realm, they are bound to remain. And if the king wishes to lead them outside of the kingdom, they need not go unless they wish to, for they have already served their forty days and forty nights.[93]

A knight's reluctance to fight also stemmed from the expense of equipment. As the technique of mounted shock combat became ever more elaborate, with both knight and his costly war-horse in a full suit of armor plate, only the wealthiest knights could afford armor.[94] As far as the king was concerned there was no sense in conscripting someone lacking arms and equipment, and so as the thirteenth century progressed there was a gradual tendency to substitute money payments for feudal service.

---

* Fourteenth-century kings paid for knight service but could still command vassals' attendance at court. By the fifteenth century in England elements of individualism permeated the ritual associated with hierarchy. A high-ranking noble aiming to demonstrate his potency could travel with a retinue of two or three hundred persons if he wished. Followers no longer volunteered to go along (as in the old days) but would come if they were paid. The fifteenth-century retainer thus was no longer a manifestation of collective needs and obligations; he was a paid member of a feudal entourage. Subsequent usage has modified the term's meaning: the retainer became fee paid for professional advice, or for professional services contracted for in event of need.[92]

In England the payments took two forms—*scutage,* a special aid in lieu of service, and *distraint of knighthood,* a fine levied against a liable knight if he did not appear when called. While the payments and fines came into existence as sanctions against evasion, the money collected could also, at least in theory, enable the king to pay mercenaries who would provide a controllable and dependable army. In practice the proceeds were never enough, because of widespread evasion coupled with losses that resulted from complex patterns of land tenure, and equally complex networks of personal obligation produced by subinfeudation.[95]

By the twelfth century, the original Norman land grants had been subdivided so many times that at the lowest levels of the feudal pyramid the average tenant held only a fraction of a knight's fee (the original unit of land that was to provide a single fighting man for William the Conqueror's feudal army). By the thirteenth century these "ordinary" knights had become equivalent to free tenants—a rudimentary country gentry—for although such ordinary knights still possessed the social status that knighthood conferred, their holdings were too small to produce the surplus needed for battle equipment.

Because the records of feudal land tenure were not updated as subinfeudation occurred, there was a cumulative discrepancy between the number of knights a tenant-in-chief (as the principal vassal was called) was required to provide to the king and the much larger number of vassals who owed the tenant-in-chief feudal service. If tenants-in-chief were systematic in collecting fines and scutages, they could obtain much more from their vassals than the king demanded from them. While an earl or baron might be obligated to provide three or four armed knights each year (or the money equivalent of their service liability), he might collect payment in lieu of service from as many as ninety men and could pocket the difference. Likewise, in France at the end of the eleventh century, the Bishop of Bayeux had over one hundred vassals but was required to provide only twenty knights to his immediate lord, the Duke of Normandy.[96] When French kings levied extraordinary aids, their chief vassals were their collection agents, and, like the English tenants-in-chief, French chief vassals gained personal advantage from the collector's role, retaining the surplus over amounts legally due the king.

Although the Exchequer made several attempts during the mid–thirteenth century to correct for the discrepancy between actual and recorded feudal obligations, efforts to increase yields from scutage were unsuccessful because of widespread passive resistance. By the fourteenth century it was no longer worth the trouble and expense of trying to collect, and, as more productive revenue sources were developed, the tax, along with the feudal army, gradually disappeared.[97]

By the end of the thirteenth century, when scutage was just about gone in England, money payments in lieu of feudal service still provided substantial royal revenue in France. From the early part of the thirteenth century a nobleman could exempt himself from feudal service by paying the crown half his annual revenues.[98] The strong, well-organized King Philip the Fair (whose rule spanned the late thirteenth and early fourteenth centuries) first levied a series of temporary taxes on income and property to supplement these substitute payments for feudal service. For the great feudal levy of 1304, for example, noble vassals could if they wished send armed knights. Alternatively, for each mounted knight he owed, a nobleman could pay one hundred livres for each five hundred livres of his income. By the fourteenth century, the obligation had been extended to the entire population. Thus in 1304 peasants were to provide six foot soldiers (later reduced to four) for each group of one hundred hearths.[99]

During the eighth century, Saxon kings of England had levied an annual tax (the Danegeld) on the island's population to protect against invading Danish tribes. Thus, when the Normans invaded England in the eleventh century, they found a rudimentary fiscal system already in existence. With an established precedent for regular taxes, and a functioning organization for assessment and collection, the Normans could increase amounts collected without much resistance by improving administrative methods.

But French kings had to start from scratch, and they established their power to tax income and property through a process of negotiation and conciliation that extended over several centuries. As Capetian kings tried to consolidate control over widely dispersed territories, they used their discretionary taxing power as leverage in bargaining with the church, recalcitrant feudal barons, and townsmen. During the twelfth century, subjects in several different towns in the kingdom agreed to pay periodic tallages, initially in commodities (bread and wine) and later in coin, in exchange for the king's written pledge to maintain a stable currency during his lifetime.[100] Establishment of firm taxing power during the fourteenth century resulted from military necessity: France had to resist armed invasion from Flanders and England. When the king called his advisory council of barons, townsmen, high-ranking clerics, and bureaucrats together to ask for temporary aids to pay for defense, council members could understand the crown's need for money. No doubt they were still unwilling to pay direct taxes, but, as council members, they had to agree to collect them from others.

As volunteer feudal armies gave way to mercenary forces, the normal military activity of the first feudal age became steadily more expensive. At the end of the thirteenth century the cost of an English foray into France might run to over £50,000, which was more than half the crown's annual money revenue from the royal domain.[101]* Nonmilitary expenses were going up also. As the feudal monarchy solidified its authority and control during the late thirteenth and early fourteenth centuries, an enlarged corps of paid officials increased the crown's direct costs. The price of order was rising.

Pinched between increasing costs and stable or declining incomes, late-medieval monarchs adopted a variety of fiscal strategies that ran the full gamut from deliberate efforts to enhance available resources by traditional means to spur-of-the-moment improvisations generated by a desperate shortage of funds.

Late-medieval kings of England and France tried roughly similar tactics in marshaling resources to sustain their political ambitions. Sometimes merely opportunistic, sometimes exploitative in the ancient sense, and sometimes truly innovative, their revenue strategies buffered the short-term deficits, but were not uniformly successful in providing permanent revenue sources. At the end of the fourteenth century, our somewhat arbitrary cutoff point, financial institutions of medieval governments, like the governments themselves, were in a state of transition between private and public government. Although the end of the fourteenth century marks the end of the Middle Ages in western Europe, except in the small autonomous governments of the northern-Italian city-states, financial institutions bear small resemblance to those of modern government.

REVENUE STRATEGIES OF LATE-MEDIEVAL GOVERNMENTS

The unformed, small-scale personal feudal monarchies of the eleventh century had developed into stable governmental organizations by the middle of the thirteenth. Though the monarchy was still a personal government, it was becoming less personal; late-medieval kings were re-creating administrative and fiscal instruments by which large territories could once again be controlled from the center. As feudalism

---

* Just as some modern city governments accept market principles when contracting for such services as refuse collection and fire protection, so does deployment of mercenaries suggest at least a limited acceptance of competitive individualism.

withered away, a distinction that had not existed before (except briefly in classical Athens and the Roman Republic) gradually emerged: a separation between public and private roles of kings and subjects with respect to each other.

Within the Western political tradition, development of a conception of public government has involved conceptual, legal, and administrative innovation and adaptation extending over many centuries and still under way. At the same time that a vassal's "private obligations to a personal king were gradually being converted into public service . . . to an impersonal state,"[102] the king's sovereignty was coming to rest on symbolic, legal, and administrative foundations rather than on the affective relationships of the earlier feudal age. The men who controlled the governments of England, France, and the rapidly growing communes of northern Italy during the thirteenth century were inventing new governmental roles and experimenting with a variety of novel devices for providing services and generating revenue.

Germanic ideals of kingship had accorded a ruler an implicit power of trusteeship over his people's rights under customary law. A king's duty was to maintain justice and peace within his domain. Mutual obligation and mutual consent established a framework for relationships among such kings and their subjects. But when feudalism developed as a network of contractual obligations, earlier customary relationships among kings and people changed. Under feudalism a king's rights were preeminent only if his rights did not conflict with his subjects' rights. Yet late-medieval jurists soon recognized that a king's authority could be sustained only if private rights were constrained to some extent.[103]

From the thirteenth century on, then, feudal kings faced two principal tasks, closely interconnected, although nominally distinct. The first was to create a new conception of political loyalty and organization— the abstract idea of realm—expressing the collective interests of kings and people. The second task was more concrete, yet in many ways harder to accomplish. As feudal service became obsolete the monarchies had to find new, nonfeudal revenue sources to support their growing governments.

Unlike the earlier principle that a ruler derived authority largely from military control of specific territory, the late-medieval conception of realm transcended both the paternalism and the localism of the earlier feudal age. As defined by thirteenth-century legal theorists, the realm was a community of subjects united, not primarily by contractual obligation, territorial proximity, or personal allegiance, but by common observance of a body of law.

Although the king enunciated laws with the advice of his council, their legitimacy did not rest solely on his personal or religious authority. It derived from the king's right as recognized sovereign to determine policy "for the common good." Drawing on revived Roman legal doctrine, thirteenth-century political theorists postulated that within his kingdom the king was "emperor in his own realm."[104] The king had power to "state the law or . . . , where the law failed to give the solution to a problem," to make policy decisions.[105] In France (though not in England) the king's power to legislate for the common good was interpreted liberally. By the fourteenth century the French king was entitled to "use any property, moveable or immoveable, . . . for the public good and defense of the kingdom"[106] and therefore was able to impose regular taxes on his subjects as feudal services gradually disappeared. The need for order has often led to legalized abuse.

Kings developed diverse approaches to resource mobilization—through compulsion deriving from royal prerogative and through individualism stemming from perception of mutual advantage. To derive support, kings employed monetary and nonmonetary, fiscal and nonfiscal, calculated and improvised strategies—singly, sequentially, or in combination, whatever proved expedient. All these revenue strategies of late-medieval governments had a common aim of tapping a growing reservoir of mercantile wealth. Having found ways to circumvent constraints of religious doctrine, rulers found appealing the idea that more was better—as they had since time immemorial.

Chartering Towns

Establishing new towns on unoccupied land best exemplifies an indirect revenue strategy. Between the eleventh and thirteenth centuries feudal nobility and landowning clergy undertook urbanization with such vigor and enthusiasm that their movement to charter towns assumed proportions of a speculative boom. Their intentions were clear. Compared to manorial holdings, an equivalent amount of land given to establish a town constituted a highly productive source of revenue that could be collected in money without the inconvenience of handling revenue in kind. Town markets enabled founders to profit from indirect taxes on trade. As a condition of a town's charter, nobles and clergy often required residents to pay an annual tax; the town councils agreed to pay such taxes because town life provided personal liberty and an immunity from feudal exactions.* When feudal kings chartered

* The charter of the small village of Lorris granted by Louis VI of France in the twelfth century served as a model for others; it illustrates the advantages of town residence. ". . . the man who elects to reside at Lorris is to pay only six deniers for his house and . . . land.

towns, they granted more than lesser nobles or clergy; since kings had greater need for revenue, there was more to gain from concessions.

The mutual give-and-take that developed between kings and town councils—of land in exchange for autonomous governments, and freedom to trade in exchange for a promise to pay taxes—marks an early emergence of the norm of reciprocity. For competitive political and economic systems to operate, not only must there be adequate inducements for all participants, but each must have some sphere of independence from the other. At any moment the existing system reflects a balance among various actors' preferences, each behaving in accordance with an appraisal of what it is expedient to give in exchange for what will be received in return. In a political context, conceptions of reciprocity and competition become meaningful when bargaining among the leading actors begins.

But there is more. Systemic change may be accompanied by an easing of systemic restrictions. Just as tax farming was used to support ancient monarchies (and private plots now produce food in the Soviet Union and China), so the disabilities of enterprising monarchs might have been mitigated a little by sharing power with townsmen, even though sharing did entail some loss. There is a sense in which the autonomy that kings granted to the governing councils of the royally chartered towns made their council members counterparts for local administration of the high feudal magnates whose authority derived from hereditary ownership of land.[108]

During the twelfth and thirteenth centuries, French and English kings could not levy taxes on town residents without first obtaining their governing councils' agreement about the rates to be charged. When monarchs wished to raise the rates of existing taxes or to impose new ones, English kings summoned representatives from the towns to London, and French kings sent agents out into the provinces to negotiate changes. Because power to levy taxes was not yet firmly established, thirteenth-century kings were unable to sustain outright demands, and so they adopted a bargaining strategy. If a community refused to pay what they asked, kings were forced to modify demands or else to grant subsidiary concessions; they knew that the longer bargaining went on, the lower the ultimate yield would be. On different occasions kings lowered tax rates, accepted payment of taxes in install-

If he lives there peaceably for a year and a day he is henceforth free and cannot be claimed by a previous master. He is to be quit of all . . . forced exactions; of watching service, and corvées . . . Whenever he pleases the man of Lorris can sell his possessions and go elsewhere. He cannot be tried outside the town, and there according to specified rules of procedure. Fines and punishments are strictly limited."[107]

ments, promised to restore a debased currency or to grant exemptions from military service, and agreed to let the town merchants serve as tax farmers.[109] When agreement would produce some revenue, even though less than kings asked for, flexibility was expedient.

But late-medieval kings did not rely upon bargaining alone. To create and then sustain support for new taxes, kings adopted a parallel strategy of persuasion. When treasuries ran dry from expenses of feudal wars, late-medieval kings became their own advocates and traveled through their kingdoms to ask subjects for gifts, loans, and temporary war subsidies. If kings were unable to travel, they sent out subordinates. Thus, in 1282 Edward I of England, who was himself busy fighting against a rebellion in Wales, sent his treasurer around the kingdom to beg for funds; the journey netted over £16,000.[110] Philip the Fair of France, in December 1303 and January 1304, made the long trip from Paris to southern France to announce his intention to levy a tax.[111] These trips were exceptional events, arising from unusual financial straits, but they reflected the opportunism of every aspect of late-medieval governments' financial activities.

Support from the Church

Observing lagging contributions, medieval kings derived extraordinary income by exercising traditional royal prerogative. When financial pressures built up, it was always tempting and convenient to tax the great wealth of the church. During the Merovingian era, newly converted pagan kings had donated vast reaches of imperial Roman lands to the church. In the ninth and tenth centuries, when the Papacy was weak, local feudal magnates, seeking to appropriate the produce of church lands for their own use, began to appoint laymen who were their vassals as bishops. A revived Papacy reasserted its power to appoint ecclesiastics as bishops by the twelfth century, but feudal kings still maintained some control over the clerical hierarchy within their territories. Appointment of lay bishops was slow to die out, in part because the king was permitted to vote with the church hierarchy when an election for bishop was in dispute.[112] Especially in England—where Norman feudal doctrine had established the king's right (as principal vassal) to claim ultimate custody of all land in the kingdom whether it was held by laymen or clergy—as well as in France,[113] the king continued to exercise some control over revenue from church land.[114] From the twelfth to the fourteenth century, English kings asserted their right to appropriate income from church land for the period between a bishop's death and appointment of his successor. Since land held in ecclesiastical tenure consisted of productive manors that often yielded up to £1,000 money income each year, a king had strong incentive to delay appointment* of a new bishop for as long as he could.[116] When a bishop died, the king might conveniently neglect to notify the pope, or he would find pretexts for delaying election of a new bishop as long as possible. If the king disapproved of an elected bishop, he could exercise his veto power to force another choice.[117] Vacancies of from six to eighteen months were common; some wealthy bishoprics remained empty for as long as six years.[118] During royal custody of church lands, the king claimed ordinary manorial revenues and could collect in full whatever scutages and aids were due from the bishop's vassals.[119]

In addition to irregular appropriations of ecclesiastical income, English and French kings levied direct taxes on the church. When kings needed money to pay for wars, it was more expedient to tax clergy than laity, for by the late Middle Ages there were no more fighting bishops and the church could offer little threat or resistance to royal demands. Early in the twelfth century English kings occasionally levied money taxes on lands of vacant bishoprics. By the thirteenth century, taxation of tenants of church land was common in England, and by the fourteenth regular taxes of one-tenth of the value of church property had become a standard source of revenue to English and French monarchies.[120] In the mid–thirteenth century, sometimes without notifying the orders, Edward I of England pledged property of monasteries in his kingdom as security for loans from his Italian bankers.[121]

Kings and church were not always fiscal adversaries. In the late twelfth century, when kings were trying to raise money to finance the Crusades, the Pope gave his permission to levy a tax on clerical income; it established a precedent for regular taxation of the clergy in succeeding centuries. During the reigns of Henry II of England in the thirteenth century and Philip VI of France in the fourteenth, the Papacy made outright gifts to the crown.[122] In the latter case a friendly pope at Avignon loaned over one million florins, more than a year's normal expenses, to pay for the extraordinary expense of French defense in the Hundred Years' War.[123]

---

* Within each kingdom bishops were chosen (elected) by church hierarchy and kings from a slate of high-ranking clerics—usually second or lower sons from noble families within the kingdom. Since an elected bishop required the pope's formal confirmation, replacing a bishop took a long time even if a king did not hold up the process. Possessing more power than any secular ruler, twelfth-century popes had their own agenda: to make sure that bishops in distant dioceses would represent church interests, popes tried to appoint Italians to foreign bishoprics.[115]

As an independent governmental authority, the Papacy also possessed power to tax, but very little of local collections appears to have reached Rome. From the ninth century the church had levied an annual hearth tax (called Peter's Pence) on all households in Christendom, but total annual receipts from England in the twelfth century were only the token amount of £200.[124]

Thirteenth-century kings found diverse uses for money garnered from the church. When they were reasonably solvent, both Henry III of England and his son Edward I used receipts from vacant bishoprics in ways that appear to have been calculated to increase the monarchy's symbolic influence. They built castles, contributed money for construction of cathedrals and churches, gave to charity, and established sinecures for friends.* In wartime, when expenses normally outran revenues by a large margin, both kings appear to have established priorities for the funds. Employing a modern mode of budgetary calculation, they earmarked revenues from specific vacant bishoprics for block grants to royal officials, to repay loans contracted to maintain their armies, and as security for further borrowing.[126] When financial pressures were extreme both these kings sometimes assigned anticipated revenues from vacant bishoprics to creditors long before a bishop's death.[127]

Just as expediency governed kings' calculations about procuring revenue from the church, so, too, did opportunism often determine how the produce of vacant bishoprics would be allocated. Entertaining visiting royalty made inordinate demands on the royal larder; an English monarch might issue urgent orders for "hundreds of eggs, eels, bream, does, and pigs for the royal household," and his stewards "had to arrange for the necessary fishing, hunting, salting, packing in barrels and carriage to Windsor, Westminster, Gloucester [or] wherever the king might be."[128] The king had wood cut from ecclesiastical forests and

* An analysis of government expenses, written by an experienced administrator of the late-twelfth-century English treasury, evokes the spirit of the age, recalling goals of righteous monarchs of earlier eras (righteousness apparently is retrospective): ". . . The abundance of resources, or the lack of them, exalts or humbles the power of princes. For those who are lacking in them become prey to their enemies, whilst those who are well supplied with them despoil their foes. Money is necessary, not only in time of war, but also in time of peace. For in the former case, revenue is expended on the fortification of towns, the payment of wages to soldiers, and in many other ways; . . . In the latter case, although weapons of war are laid aside, churches are built by devout princes, Christ is fed and clothed in the person of the poor, and the Mammon of the world is distributed in other acts of charity. The glory of princes consists in mighty deeds, both in peace and war, but it excels in those where, in return for an earthly outlay, there follows an eternal and blessed reward."[125]

requisitioned food for the feudal army from the church's manors. During the mid–thirteenth century, for example, Edward I used produce from vacant bishoprics to provision his forces in Gascony. In March 1242 he ordered the stewards of Winchester to send "1,000 carcases of bacon, 1,000 quarters of wheat," and the same quantity of oats to the port at Portsmouth "by Easter at the latest against the king's voyage beyond seas." Again near the end of the century he commanded that grain be sent from the same bishopric to supply his army in Wales.[129]

Purveyance

To provision a feudal army fighting far from home was a difficult logistical problem for thirteenth- and fourteenth-century kings. An army could live off the land while it fought, but equipment and food were needed to get it to the battle site. To convey troops overseas and obtain supplies, late-medieval kings used their power to command purveyance from subjects. A late-medieval equivalent of kings' earlier privilege of claiming hospitality from vassals, the right of purveyance enabled medieval kings to requisition fishing and merchant vessels from owners, and food and supplies from local merchants. When an expedition was being planned or if logistical emergencies arose during battle, French and English kings commanded local tradesmen to bring their goods—usually grain, meat, salt, and beer—to battlefield or embarkation point. There merchants were obliged to sell at whatever price the king's agents might specify; if the king paid, it was usually well below what the goods would command in the market. English shipowners in the five Channel ports were collectively required to supply fifty-seven vessels for forty days each year. Though shipowners were paid for use of their vessels, the king's practice of requisitioning a ship long before it was needed was costly and inconvenient for owners. When the king had no money he offered credit, a practice that usually amounted to outright confiscation. On other occasions kings demanded labor service for construction of royal buildings, roads, and bridges.[130]

That a clause in the Magna Carta is devoted to the king's right to command purveyance in goods and services indicates that the practice aroused enmity among liable subjects. The burdens of supply were especially onerous during long wars; then hundreds of little men bore the cost of provisioning the government. The scale of royal confiscation in England is indicated by the fact that near the end of the thirteenth century, when Edward I had accumulated huge debts to local merchants, the church intervened in the merchants' behalf; the Pope threatened to excommunicate the King's ministers in charge of purvey-ance.[131]

Borrowing with Tallies

English kings' indirect-borrowing strategies became much more so-phisticated over time. If funds were inadequate to pay for purchases, as was often the case, treasury officials issued wooden *tallies of receipt* on anticipated revenues instead of paying cash. The tallies, artifacts of the pre-literate twelfth-century Exchequer, were notched wooden sticks that originally served as receipts for manorial revenues paid into the treasury or for sums it paid out.[132] During the twelfth and thirteenth centuries tallies were used in Flanders as well as in England.

Although payment of debts by issuing sticks of wood appears to be a primitive method of financial management, the device possessed a number of advantages for a government that had only modest admin-istrative capacity and was chronically short of funds. At a time when knowledge of banking procedure was rudimentary in England, the tal-lies, by enabling the king to postpone payment of debts, anticipated the funded debt of a later age. From an administrative perspective, payment of debts by issuing tallies was a form of earmarking. Tallies were issued for income expected from a specific revenue source, and were valid only if all the conditions marked on the tally were in effect at the time of collection. If, as often happened, the king issued a tally on receipts of a specific customs collector at a given port, a creditor could not enforce payment if the collector lost his post before the credi-tor could go there to demand payment. Under such conditions tallies became financial instruments—an equivalent of informal contracts—and, as with any contract, the burden of collection lay with the credi-tor. If the tallies became invalid—whether because of a clerical error or because of a change in the specific conditions under which they were issued (as, for example, the death of a king)—the tallies became forced loans without interest. This was true because invalid tallies seldom were redeemable, or, if they were, it was at less than face value. When a king died, his successor rarely honored his predecessor's tallies, but if he did, he invariably paid less than the dead king owed. Even when the state's promise to pay could be redeemed, prompt payment was un-usual; before a creditor could collect from the crown he might wait anywhere from two to ten years. Thus, issuance of tallies in lieu of payment pushed back the king's time horizons and gave him time to develop alternative fiscal strategies.

It was to reduce the creditor's risk of holding the state's uncertain promise to pay that tallies gradually became negotiable instruments, an informal equivalent of a fiduciary currency. Because the creditor's name was not inscribed on the tally, it could be sold in the market for whatever it would bring. But when the king's creditors accepted partial payment to shorten a wait of indefinite duration, they unknowingly reversed their relationship to the crown. By selling tallies at a discount, the king's creditors became inadvertent lenders to the state.[133] In order to compensate for the discount at which tallies sold, creditors also forced up the price kings had to pay.

Currency Debasement

Payment of debts by issuing tallies was an indirect monetary strategy, qualitatively similar to another device poor medieval governments sometimes used in emergencies to supplement revenue. From the tenth century on, just as in the late Roman Empire, the multiple local currencies of Europe had been repeatedly debased.[134] Monetary strategies of ancient and medieval governments appear to have been founded on a simple linear model of economic causality.[135] When the stock of precious metal was fixed and more money was needed to pay government debts, ancient and medieval governments often gathered the existing coinage at the mint, melted it down, had new dies made, and issued new coins with reduced precious-metal content. Without an understanding either of the reciprocal relationship between the value of money and prices or of the direct relationship between the amount of money and the price level, ancient and medieval governments operated as if an increase in the volume of currency in circulation, whether its value was stable or not, would automatically increase the ruler's wealth. No doubt their presumption was true in the short run, for in the Middle Ages (just as with international currency devaluations under fixed-parity exchange rates), there was generally a time lapse before a change in the money supply was reflected in increased local prices. If a king's treasury was depleted, rather than involving himself in the lengthy process of negotiation and conciliation required to gain approval for new taxes so that he could pay his debts, it might have been simpler to issue new coinage.

By depreciating coinage a king could earn a profit. After paying for collection of old coins and reissue of new ones, the king could retain in his coffers the remaining precious metal. The yield from recoinage varied from 4 or 5 percent of the strike in the early Middle Ages to more than 8 percent in the eleventh and twelfth centuries.[136] Although late-medieval kings may have known that bad money drives out good, they appear to have understood that money would be used within their kingdoms no matter what its precious-metal content. There was still another advantage to currency depreciation: with profits from recoinage kings could pay debts in cheap money. Conversely, if a king wanted to levy a tax, he had a real incentive for reforming the currency by issuing new coins with increased precious metal content. Then subjects would pay him sound coin.[137]*

Yet debasement had disadvantages for rulers also: when subjects feared devaluation, they became restive. In 1103 in Poitou in France, "there was great tribulation ... [when] silver coins were exchanged and minted for bronze."[139] As reciprocal obligations under feudalism became formalized at fixed money exchange values, even high-level subtenants had reason to be wary. While their subtenants' feudal pay-

---

* Merchant oligarchs of the communes of northern Italy during the thirteenth century adopted a sophisticated strategy to deal with fluctuations in local currency values. With introduction of a double metallic standard in gold and silver, merchants accepted payments of debts owed to them only in sound gold coinage, while they paid their own bills in silver that was depreciating steadily.

Modern historical commentary on debasement of ancient and medieval currencies appropriately reflects notions of economic causality that existed then. Chief among these is a conception of the intrinsic value of money. If a currency was devalued, the price rise that normally followed was attributed to reduced gold or silver content of the new coinage, rather than to the increased amount of circulating coinage. This is an important consideration if we wish to explain why prices changed in response to alterations in metallic content of money.

Economists agree that prices within a country fluctuate in relation to the amount of money in circulation and in relation to the stock of goods. When the money supply increases and the stock of goods does not, competition for goods in the market forces prices up. This explanation appears to fit the medieval context. Inflation followed debasement in the Middle Ages because both the supply of bullion within a monarchy and the stock of goods were relatively stable. If the government happened to be at war and the king also exercised his power of purveyance—buying for himself at a fixed price below the prevailing market price, or confiscating goods from merchants—prices went up because less remained for everyone else. Rising prices then led late-medieval governments to adopt policies that anticipated the economic mercantilism of a later age. A shortage of food coupled with inflation caused French kings, in the fourteenth century, to fix the price of food in Paris and its environs. During the same century the English monarchy prohibited export of essential commodities to keep the home price low.

Modern commentary on medieval currency debasement sometimes exhibits elements of a quantity theory of money. During periods of rapid economic expansion, such as occurred throughout Europe during the thirteenth century, the rate at which the existing money supply moves from hand to hand (velocity of circulation) increases even if there is no associated growth in the amount of money in circulation. If the money supply increases for any reason, the stock of goods remains fixed or expands slowly, and the velocity of circulation remains high, inflation also occurs. Thus when impecunious medieval kings made loans, whether informally by issuing tallies or by borrowing large sums from abroad, the expansion in the money supply that the loans created also caused domestic prices to increase.[138]

ments remained fixed, devaluation in effect increased the amounts the magnates owed the king.[140] During the late twelfth and early thirteenth centuries, numerous feudal magnates throughout Europe signed charters (confirmations) proclaiming their intention to maintain a stable currency. An early signal of an emerging culture of individualism, confirmations of currency were granted by kings and dukes in exchange for subjects' promise to pay nominal taxes.

Although debasement occurred less often after the thirteenth century, it was still a useful measure in emergencies. In the late thirteenth century Philip the Fair of France obtained two-thirds of his government's treasury receipts (over one million livres) through devaluation.[141] A successor, John the Good, in the mid–fourteenth century, appears at times to have employed debasement as the sole source of revenue. In the thirteen years between 1337 and 1350 he altered the currency twenty-four times; eighteen of the changes occurred in a single year.[142]

Under the best conditions currency revaluation rarely provided more than temporary relief for any fiscal crisis. To collect the existing currency and melt it down was an awkward and costly expedient. As late-medieval governments generally lacked administrative capacity to carry out recoinage, their limited resources were further strained by the cost of hiring currency farmers (private agents who were often bankers) to undertake the task.

Borrowing to Cover Deficits

A much more productive revenue strategy, one commonly employed by late-medieval governments, was borrowing. In the late twelfth century, kings of England and France and the count-kings of Catalonia began to make loans to meet the growing expenses of their monarchical households. Sporadic at first, by the thirteenth century borrowing had become a routine method for providing a fiscal cushion in ordinary circumstances; it was an especially valuable resource in emergencies. Merchants and moneylenders, domestic and foreign, were the principal sources of credit.

There were several repeated scenarios whereby kings obtained support from private lenders. Overlapping at their boundaries and shading one into another, they depict the behavior of borrowers and lenders relative to each other under varying conditions. Mutual advantage is the keynote of the first; it typically occurred when borrowers were weak in relation to lenders. When kings needed money they looked for sources of credit, either individuals or institutions with surplus funds.

Borrowing randomly, the twelfth-century kings of England and France obtained small advances from lay and clerical sources—Jewish money-lenders, bishops, religious houses, the Knights Templars and Hospitalers—and from wealthy noblemen, merchants, and citizens of towns.[143] In exchange for loans, the kings granted concessions to lenders, such as freedom to trade or collect local taxes, or they paid interest disguised as a gift.

Lending to kings was profitable business when from 26 to 50 percent interest was repaid with the principal.[144] By the late thirteenth century and well into the fourteenth, prosperous Italian banking houses regularly loaned large sums of money to kings of England and France. Advancing funds before royal revenue reached the treasury, the bankers helped to regulate cash flow. There was an explicit understanding between Edward I of England, the first English king to negotiate private banking arrangements with a single Italian firm, and the Riccardi of Lucca. Whether the monarch had funds on hand or not, his bankers were expected to pay his bills "out of the king's money or their own." Sometimes the firm advanced small sums to cover household expenses ("the king not having money in hand at present"), but on one occasion Edward I owed the Riccardi £23,000.[145]

In addition to gifts in lieu of interest paid to their bankers, kings provided incentives to assure that loans would be granted and later renewed. When a king entered into an agreement with a foreign banking house he might grant it a banking monopoly within his kingdom; the fourteenth-century King of England Edward III did exactly this in his negotiations with the Bardi firm.

Late-medieval bankers were involved in diversified commercial activities in addition to finance; the bankers exported unprocessed English wool to continental markets, French wine to England, and they served as tax collectors for the pope.[146] Kings in need of money could make the prospect of lending to them attractive by helping to create a favorable climate for their lenders' business. Again Edward III's dealings with the Bardi provide an example. On several occasions, eager to grant concessions for the vast sums of money he needed for his wars against France,* Edward authorized the Exchequer to collect the Bardi's private debts. Edward I had a similar arrangement with the Riccardi.[148] Thus a relationship founded in business could develop into one in which interests of both parties were so close that it was hard

---

* In a speech before Parliament, the king's treasurer dramatized his mentor's need for loans. "All the revenues of the realm," he declared, "would not cover half the king's expenses."[147]

to tell where business ended and government began. At one period in the fourteenth century when England and France were at war, the Bardi paid spies in the bank's Normandy branches to report to the English King on deployment of the French navy.[149] After the late thirteenth century when Parliament granted English kings authority to collect customs duties on wool exports, successive kings borrowed on the security of forthcoming customs revenue. The kings then appointed their bankers as tax farmers for the customs duties, thereby insuring that the tax would be collected, and guaranteeing an additional profit on the bankers' wool-export business.[150] During the late fourteenth century, French businessmen who became farmers of indirect taxes in France also made loans to the crown.[151]

A relationship founded in mutual advantage could be maintained indefinitely as long as benefits to both parties were approximately equal. As long as royal concessions provided a stable climate for business and kings repaid their loans, bankers were willing to lend. But when kings (or bankers) overextended their credit and then defaulted on loans, or if kings saw their financial position improved or found alternative sources of funds, a temporary coalition between monarchs and merchants could be broken off as readily as it was entered into.[152] Under such circumstances the king held the trumps and the bankers were powerless to alter the outcome; the mutual-advantage scenario would then shade, imperceptibly or abruptly, into one of confiscation-exploitation.

By the late Middle Ages, governments had come to rest on firm legal foundations. Both customary law and revived Roman law granted steadily increasing legal authority to kings even when they could not yet command regular financial support from populations. Outsiders were vulnerable to a king's fiat, for they had no legal recourse when confiscation occurred. Among the earliest lenders to the English crown were Jewish moneylenders like the financier Aaron of Lincoln, who, in the late twelfth century, before Italian bankers had become established in England, provided periodic loans to the crown.[153] Since Jewish merchants were not bound by the church's prohibition against charging interest, they could accumulate a surplus by clipping coins or lending money. Though their activities were essential in the expanding mercantile economy of the late Middle Ages, as outsiders in the larger society Jews were helpless when a hostile government set out to appropriate their wealth. By the early thirteenth century, instead of borrowing from Jews the English began to levy fines and taxes against their property. Having taxed away their wealth and found alternative sources of loans by the end of the thirteenth century, the monarchy expelled Jews from England.

A similar sequence—borrowing, default, and confiscation of the lender's property followed by territorial exclusion—characterized the French monarchy's relations with its lending sources throughout the late Middle Ages. Like the English, the French borrowed from Jewish moneylenders, then subjected them to harsh discriminatory taxes and eventually expelled them from France. Before French kings had a treasury of their own they deposited state funds with the Paris branch of the Knights Templars, a crusading religious order similar to modern mercenary soldiers of fortune. The Templars became skilled in managing assets and developed a network of banks throughout Europe and the Near East.[154] In the late twelfth century Louis IX borrowed money from the Paris Templars, a practice continued by his successors for over a century. (Kings of Aragon and Catalonia, territories now in northern Spain, used the Templars to manage their finances in the twelfth and thirteenth centuries also.[155]) Early in the fourteenth century while the French treasury was still under the Templars' management, Philip the Fair had nearly all the Templars in France arrested and charged with heresy; their high officials in Paris were burned at the stake. Needing money to wage war, and having developed a French financial bureaucracy, Philip no longer needed the Templars. Just as he had confiscated property of Jewish subjects expelled from his kingdom, Philip sought to appropriate the Templars' vast wealth. After their holdings in France yielded less than he hoped for, Philip persuaded a weak pope to dissolve the order.[156]

During the fourteenth century Italian lenders to French and English kings received the same cavalier treatment. In France various Italian bankers to whom the king owed money were accused of usury, imprisoned, and released only after their firms had paid large fines. Other bankers, less fortunate, died in prison.[157] During the thirteenth and fourteenth centuries English kings defaulted repeatedly on their loans. With capital exhausted by the crown's refusal to pay, Italian firms were forced to declare bankruptcy. When a bankrupt bank could no longer advance funds, kings withdrew subsidiary concessions as well; then, biting the hand that fed them, kings expelled their former supporters from the country and turned to other firms that would lend on more favorable terms.* It would be fair to say that in the Middle Ages

---

* The Italian lenders must have been aware that they operated abroad in a risk-laden environment. A poetic member of the Frescobaldi family of Florence, whose firm sus-

the relationship between kings and financiers, as well as the half-cooperative, half-conflicting cultures these relationships represented, was ambivalent on both sides. Each needed the other. Each feared the other.

At the end of the Middle Ages kings did not need to look abroad for loans. By the fifteenth century the Company of Staple (a merchant guild that had obtained a monopoly over English wool exports to France) had accumulated an adequate surplus to lend money on terms the crown could specify.[159] Late-medieval French kings sometimes had to rely on their administrative officials' ability to obtain personal loans from private sources. On occasion both English and French kings also borrowed from town governments, wealthy merchants, and landowners.[160]*

Forced Sale of Royal Assets

But there were times when abuse of the borrowing privilege destroyed monarchical credit ratings and no one would lend to kings. Under such conditions they pursued desperate strategies for obtaining money—by selling crown land or pawning jewels. Thus in the late fourteenth century, shortly after his accession to the throne, Richard II of England raised over £9,000 by selling crown jewels. Collapse of French royal credit early in the fifteenth century forced the King to have several large clusters of gems removed from the crown to deposit in Italy as security for loans, which were for smaller amounts than the jewelry's value. Henry IV of England, early in the fifteenth century, forced his military commanders to assume the state's costs by pawning

---

tained the English monarchy during the early fourteenth century, advised its personnel assigned to posts in England to tread gently in dealing with foreign clients:

> *Wear no bright colours, be humble;*
> *Appear stupid but be subtle in act.*
> *Spend freely and do not show yourself mean.*
> *Pay as you go; collect your debts courteously, pleading your need;*
> *Do not be too inquisitive;*
> *Buy as good occasion offers, but have no dealings with men of the court.*
> *Be obedient to the powerful, keep on good terms with your fellow countrymen,*
> *and bolt your door early.*[158]

* A different borrowing pattern existed in the emerging fiscal administration of Catalonia. Instead of borrowing primarily from merchant-bankers, in the late twelfth century the count-kings both feudalized and commercialized revenue collection. They granted and sold territorial fiscal rights in exchange for the recipients' help in arranging loans to the crown. Lenders who were third parties advanced cash against the security of forthcoming revenue; repeated transactions suggest that revenues were never adequate to meet the crown's needs.[161]

jewels or pledging their private estates as security for state borrowing.[162] As real feudalism was gradually disappearing, Philip the Fair hit upon a novel technique for raising revenue in emergencies. He made knighthood salable. For a price, rich merchants of humble birth could buy a noble title from the state; on other occasions the new rich paid to conceal their social origins.[163] But such strategies were mere stopgaps, for they did not exploit their realms' real resources.

Nearly all revenue strategies we have enumerated—bargaining with residents of towns, advocacy, appropriation of church property, currency manipulation, exercise of the power of purveyance, royal borrowing, and confiscation—were only temporary solutions to medieval kings' problems of revenue procurement. Except for chartering towns, the strategies were designed to relieve short-term pressures for funds and were not taken with an understanding of their consequences for royal income or the general economy, or, in some instances, of political costs. To the extent that any given strategy reflected an opportunistic appraisal of what was feasible at the moment (an evaluation that is impossible to reconstruct), medieval kings acted with similar expediency as do modern statesmen. Especially in England, where Parliament continued to reject the kings' demands for funds well into the transitional era that followed the Middle Ages, whatever revenue grants the kings obtained were the outcome of fortuitous circumstances or temporary political alliances.

Legalized Taxation

Although a political climate that would permit permanent taxing power was not to exist in England until several hundred years after the end of the Middle Ages, late-medieval monarchs occasionally did acquire legal authority to tax. There was little political cost in levying a tax as long as it fell only on outsiders. Largely because Italian merchants working in England held a monopoly on exporting raw domestic wool to continental processors, the English Parliament, in the late thirteenth century, authorized the king to levy a tax on wool shipped from English ports. Known as the "Ancient Custom," this duty—at first only the token amount of six shillings per bag of wool—established the precedent for later taxation of the wool crop at up to 25 percent of its value. Eventually all commodities exported from England, whether by native merchants or by foreigners, were subject to customs duties. The Ancient Custom was easy to enforce because nearly all wool was shipped from five major Channel ports. Duties on wool exports became the "chief richesse" of England, the largest wool producer—its most productive and predictable revenue source until the end of the Middle Ages.[164]

Taxes on exports were designed to tap new mercantile wealth indirectly by laying the burden on foreign buyers. The French required a purchased license for all goods shipped out of the country.[165] From time to time late-medieval kings also acquired temporary authority to tax their own population's growing income from trade. Occasionally the baronial councils gave English kings power to levy a *lay subsidy* (a small direct tax on income and personal property). Unlike the ancient land tax or earlier feudal revenues in kind, lay subsidies were potentially elastic revenue sources, because the value of the tax base generally lagged only slightly behind changes in the price level. Lay subsidies were never a significant source of income, for rates were low, varying between one-thirtieth, one-fifteenth, or, at the most, one-tenth of the value of liable citizens' personal assets; and property was not assessed comprehensively nor at its full value. But the subsidies are interesting, for, even at that early date, unprecedented principles of equity governed their assessment and collection.

Because the king was forced to bargain for taxes, he could not ask for too much or place the whole burden on the men who voted to grant the subsidies. Thus noblemen were partially exempt. But so, too, were the poor: persons with little or no property did not pay lay subsidies. This provision may have resulted from a pragmatic appraisal of subjects' inability to pay or, perhaps, even from a concern for their welfare. Whatever the reasons, the tax burden thus fell on those who were benefiting from economic growth—merchants, landowning gentry, and propertied peasants.[166]

English kings did not succeed in institutionalizing a direct tax on mercantile wealth; each subsidy was enacted for a limited time to buffer emergencies and was then discontinued. The French rulers had no need to levy lay subsidies; by the late fourteenth century they had established the king's right to receive a regular tax from all men in their kingdom except noblemen. This was the taille, a levy of regressive incidence—in substance similar to the ancient hearth or poll tax. Each year, the king's agents collected a fixed charge on each person or household in his domain. No one liable to this tax could ever be exempt, no matter how great his fortune might be, or how modest his resources. The taille was productive; by the middle of the fifteenth century it represented about two-thirds—and near the end of the same century about 85 percent—of French royal revenue.[167]

In some cities of northern Italy during the thirteenth and fourteenth centuries, direct taxation of mercantile property provided substantial income to communal governments—Milan, Sienna, Perugia, Florence, and Lucca, to name some that have been studied. These direct taxes are worth study: at a time when no other governments in medieval Europe were systematically balancing expenditures against resources, Italian communes were trying to pay their way by taxing mercantile wealth.

The property taxes, levied in order to cover deficits in the previous year's communal accounts, appear to have been budgeting by hindsight. Like lay subsidies, the direct taxes (called *dazio* or *libra*), were collected irregularly as need for money became pressing. During wars between communes, when expenditures were large, a commune might levy a dazio several times in a single year; sometimes three to five years or longer might elapse between collections. If a deficit occurred, or appeared to be in the offing, communal fathers would determine how much they needed, then raise the amount by proportional allocation among liable citizens. Each man's percentage equaled the proportion his property represented of the community's total assessed wealth. Unlike the ancient head tax or the French taille, which extracted the same payment from all men, such a direct tax embodied equity. In declarations that prefaced each announcement of a new dazio, communal fathers of Sienna stated the principles on which the tax stood. More than empty rhetoric, their pronouncements expressed concern that "a greater equality will be maintained among the citizens." Thus each citizen was asked to bear his proportionate share of the burden; a poor man paid nothing, the wealthy paid a lot.[168] A man who was asked to pay more than what he judged his fair share could invoke appeals procedures to reduce his liability.*

---

* The medieval conception of equity as fairness focuses on *equality of opportunity*, a value most often found in a political culture of individualism. Two present-day expressions of egalitarian ideas, both income redistribution and setting limits on consumption by taxing away income, emerged much later, in the social-democratic political cultures of the early industrial age. Redistribution was an ever present aspect of medieval life nonetheless; the modes of redistribution reflected both individualistic and hierarchical elements. Religious doctrine clothed individual acts of philanthropy with sanctity; those with a surplus were *expected* to share their wealth with the vast multitude of poor. In a world marked by violence at all social levels, insuring one's passage through the pearly gates was a pervasive concern. Seeking to underwrite the repose of their souls, wealthy persons donated land to the church and they endowed chapels and monasteries. Large donations to church or monastery might be made conditional on the religious order's support of the donor's heirs (becoming, in effect, a contemporary equivalent of life insurance or social security). In late-medieval England, rich persons made bequests to churches to buy masses and prayers upon their death or that of specified individuals. Some noblemen left

Assessment of property determined liability for direct taxes. Although the property tax varied greatly among the communes—and even within each commune, from one dazio to another—citizens paid a percentage of the value of visible items of personal property, of local real estate, and sometimes of intangible goods such as mortgages and contracts. Like property subject to tax, the rates were variable. On different occasions, depending on urgency of need, direct tax rates ranged between a low of one or 2 percent in Florence to a high of 20 percent in Sienna, the average rate being 5 or 6 percent.[170] As rates varied, so, too, did amounts collected. When a dazio was levied at a higher rate, the yield might be considerable.[171] Thus, in 1289 the commune of Florence collected 72,000 lire, 6 percent of an assessed base of 1,152,000 lire.[172] One scholar has estimated that direct taxes brought in in about half of most communal revenues during the second half of the fourteenth century.[173]

In order to be productive, a tax based on the value of property required a sophisticated organizational capacity to determine how much each man should pay. Communal governments lacked administrative and technical ability to maintain a continuing record of property ownership; therefore new property surveys and assessments were needed before each successive dazio could be collected.

Various procedures, from simple to complicated, were used to value property: self-assessment; valuation by neighbors and by a group of community elders whose individual appraisals were averaged to determine the assessment;* and costly and complex property surveys. Some communes used a zero-base technique to simplify administration. The commune of Pistoia, for example, cut administrative costs in politically effective fashion by burning the old tax registers before each new assessment was made.[175] Others—Sienna, Lucca, Florence, and Prado among them—experimented briefly with a permanent register of prop-

---

funds to pay alms to the poor (who were expected to say prayers for the donor's soul); others set aside money to buy new clothing for the paupers rounded up to walk in their funeral procession. The church mediated charitable giving. Like modern philanthropy performed for its tax benefits, motivation for such redistribution was primarily personal.[169]

* The procedure used in Florence during the mid–thirteenth century illustrates an administrative application of the equity norm. In each section of the city five men were chosen as property assessors. Each of the five, acting on personal knowledge of residents' wealth, made an independent judgment of the value of all residents' property. The high and low evaluations for each citizen were thrown out and the middle three averaged to determine a man's assessment, which was then subject to taxation at a specified rate. Nowadays some international sports contests are judged by a similar method.[174]

erty ownership, but abandoned the effort because it was too difficult to maintain the records as property changed hands.[176] With limited organizational capacity in the thirteenth and fourteenth centuries, communal governments, even in a stable environment, would have been hard pressed to keep comprehensive records. When administrative deficiencies were compounded by political instability and continuous price fluctuations, the communes found it impossible to maintain the books.

Difficulties of property assessment eventually led the communes to abandon direct taxes on income and property. But as time passed the taxes also became less productive. Because payment was voluntary and a man's liability often rested on self-assessment, there was large potential for successful evasion. Men would hide movable property outside the district or donate local real estate to monasteries, in an effort to shelter land from taxes while retaining its use. The communes threatened fines and imprisonment to deter tax evasion and on occasions forced religious orders to submit to an audit when collusion with evaders was suspected.[177] During the fourteenth century, Florentine law compelled businessmen to submit profit-and-loss statements along with their direct tax returns.[178] Even in the smaller democratically governed communes where political life was grounded in consent, a man who was asked to reach into his pocket too often might become alienated even from a benevolent government. Egalitarian regimes have rarely been good at tax collection. In the communes—as in the infant states of northern Europe or in modern American cities and states—the high visibility of direct taxes rendered them unpopular and politically costly. By the mid–fourteenth century the yield from direct taxes had fallen to about 15 or 20 percent of most communes' revenues.[179]

Communal governments bridged the gap with indirect taxes. From the late thirteenth century the communes levied a complex array of taxes on market exchanges. These incremental taxes, known as *gabelles,* were levied on every possible commodity or service at every stage of production and marketing. The communes left no stone unturned; one commentator has asserted that they taxed "all but air and water."[180] An eclectic combination of modern customs, excise, sales, value-added, and luxury taxes, the gabelles represented fiscal pragmatism in an urban mercantile environment. Since the communes depended almost entirely on imported goods, indirect taxes drew revenue from the entire population and could not be evaded. Taxes were imposed on imports by sea or through city gates; on production and sale of food and clothing; on wages of soldiers and city officials; and for performance of services. (In the latter cases gabelles were effectively a direct tax on income.) Compared to direct taxes, gabelles deflected the tax incidence downward; imposts on food staples—salt, grain, bread, meat, and wine—were highly productive and rates were revised upward with passage of time.[181] The wine gabelle in Florence illustrates the trend: it was first imposed at the end of the thirteenth century at 6 percent of the sales price; by the mid–fourteenth century the rate had been increased to 50 percent; thereafter it fluctuated between 40 and 66 percent of the market price.[182]

For collection of the innumerable indirect taxes (there were thirty-four in Florence at the mid–thirteenth century[183]), the communes relied on tax farmers whose personal interests lay in exploiting their franchises to obtain the maximum yield. Farming taxes increased certainty in revenue; when the tax farmer paid part of his fee in advance, the communes had guaranteed income. Or, the income could be systematically allocated to pay government debts. The latter practice was common in Venice, where the government borrowed regularly from citizens; receipts from specific gabelles were earmarked to amortize loans. In the late twelfth century Venice allocated anticipated income from rental fees for stalls in the Rialto market, and from several gabelles to pay back a loan of forty thousand lire.[184] The governing council of Florence went to the opposite extreme in the mid–fourteenth century; it behaved as if it had joined the "tax-of-the-month club": Florence paid for a war by using proceeds of the gate gabelle (customs) in July 1336, the salt monopoly in October, and the sales tax on wine in December of that year.[185]

Sales taxes did have a built-in deflator, taking less from the people as the market price fell, but in the depressed environment of the late fourteenth century the heavy burden of the multiple gabelles aroused increasing hostility. The burden on the poor became greater as the wealthy found ways to evade indirect taxes. Rich Florentine merchants, for example, established permanent residences outside the city to avoid paying taxes; the communal government reacted by extending the city boundaries out into the countryside to include all territory within three thousand paces of the city walls.[186]

Plugging the loopholes when consensus was lacking was at best a defensive strategy. In the late fourteenth century, throughout mercantile Europe as well as in Italy, the social stability characteristic of feudalism was giving way to turbulence and unrest. An aftermath of the plague that killed over a third of the population of Europe was economic depression.[187] Falling wages, rising prices, and unemployment affected the poor first. But instead of resignedly accepting their fate as their ancestors had done from time immemorial, peasants and city workers, anticipating the future, tried to cope with their environment so as to alter their circumstances. As in more recent times when the poor were led to expect more from government than they could receive, discontent led to protest. There were tax riots in Florence and Lucca, in the communes of Flanders, and peasant revolts in France and England when governments tried to collect too much from the poor.[188] Leaders of the English peasant revolt of 1381 invoked tradition to legitimate their demands. They protested against the government's attempt to collect a poll tax, taking the same amount from all men in the kingdom irrespective of their means, and they demanded that thereafter no tax should be levied "save the fifteenths which [our] fathers and forebears knew and accepted."[189] New normative canons of tax incidence were transformed into ideological instruments justifying slightly broader sharing of power. Once bargaining between barons and the king had been accepted, other groups could seize on the same principle, all the while maintaining that the privileges so recently gained had been theirs from time immemorial.

Having failed to acquire power to tax by the end of the Middle Ages, English kings fell back on indirect techniques for mobilizing resources. During the fifteenth century they took large forced loans from London merchants. To maintain the monarchy without having to ask Parliament for funds, these kings adopted a strategy of agricultural self-sufficiency. To enlarge royal income, they tried to enhance productivity of crown estates;* at midcentury, Edward IV pledged to the Commons, "I purpose to lyve uppon my nowne."[190]

Public Loans

Of all the revenue strategies employed by late-medieval governments, the most creative do not properly belong in this chapter, for their character is modern. Foretelling the future, the north-Italian communes financed government partly by borrowing, then funded and managed their debt in an orderly fashion. In emergencies like famines or wars, the wealthy were forced under threat of fine to lend specified amounts to the city for short periods of time.[191] To allocate forced

---

* Improving agricultural productivity was a forward-looking act that presages the emergence of modern rationality concepts. By the fifteenth century most landowners (kings included) had become interested in new farming techniques and improved methods of estate management. (Such techniques had been developed on monastic estates from the twelfth century on.) Once feudalism died out, landowners could direct energy and resources formerly spent on battle toward improving management of their holdings.

loans among liable citizens, the communes followed the same norms
and procedures developed to assess direct taxes: a man's share of the
debt was proportional to the value of his property. During the fourteenth century the communes regularly borrowed from citizens when
revenues were short; rich men with surplus funds were only too happy
to lend because the communes guaranteed repayment plus an increment that ranged between 10 and 60 percent of the principal.[192] Also,
from the late twelfth century the communes had utilized an ingenious
device for borrowing over long term, which circumvented the church's
prohibition against interest. On security of land owned by citizens,
communal fathers borrowed money for long, but indefinite, periods
that varied with the length of the lender's lifetime. Instead of paying
interest throughout the period of the loan, the communes repaid principal plus an amount specified as "rent." Repayment occurred on the
death of the lender, or in some cases on the death of his heirs. Because
the church viewed the additional payments as life insurance the interest disguised as rent escaped ecclesiastical censure.[193]

    To schedule repayments some communes kept accounts by double
entry.[194] Some appointed special agents to keep track of creditors.
Some offered rewards to informants to discourage fraudulent claims
for repayment.[195] Often forthcoming receipts from specific gabelles
were earmarked to pay back loans.[196] The need to borrow, and then to
plan and schedule repayment, involved communal governments in a
future-oriented activity that anticipated both the funded debt and the
consolidated-fund budget of a much later age. As early as the thirteenth century, the modern attitude that man could successfully shape
his environment was expressed in techniques for managing communal
finances. When fiscal institutions of the northern-Italian communes
are compared to the crude revenue systems of feudal monarchies of
England and France, these developments are all the more remarkable,
for the innovations appeared at least five hundred years ahead of their
time. The social orders of these communes, in fact, were far closer to
the competitive individualism of capitalism during the Industrial Revolution than to the collectivism of the feudal kings.

FISCAL CONTROL:
MEDIEVAL ADMINISTRATIVE STRUCTURE AND THE
POVERTY OF KINGS

Medieval men understood that financial administration was critical to
the state's prosperity and strength. Employing an organic metaphor,

John of Salisbury, a twelfth-century English political theorist, compared the tasks of state "treasurers and financial experts" to the stomach and intestines of the human body, which "if they become clogged through excessive indulgence of appetite and remain stubbornly constipated, engender manifold and incurable disorders and bring ruin on the whole body."[197] To be aware of the many difficulties associated with financial administration, however, was not to resolve them. Although medieval kings may have recognized their serious problems, they did not know what to do or, if they did, were unable to do much.

The poverty of kings in the late Middle Ages resulted not only from inability to mobilize resources as feudalism waned, but also from the nature of the feudal institutions used to collect and disburse what revenues the king had. Just as there was a disparity between the kingdom's real wealth and the monarch's capacity to tap it, so, too, was there an institutional deficit. Because their financial and administrative institutions were unsuited to their expanding needs, late-medieval governments could not even effectively use the resources they had. The devices they tried were too fine-grained for their minimal technical-administrative capacity. Where routine existed, procedures tended to become formalized and inflexible; if there was none, each transaction with the treasury demanded an administrator's attention. Cumulative incoherence in administrative institutions for collecting, accounting for, and disbursing revenue resulted from all the improvisational methods by which resources were mobilized.

In organizational structure, as well as in the kind of revenue obtained, there is a marked parallel between early-medieval financial administration and that of the ancient empires. Starting with a simple two-level structure of collectors and receivers, organization for government finance had, by the end of the Middle Ages, evolved into a complicated patchwork of overlapping instrumentalities and officers—collectors, receivers, auditors, supervisors, and adjudicators. Roles were duplicated and tasks overlapped. At different times private agents (feudal officials or foreign bankers who served the state as tax farmers) and public servants (salaried administrators in a newly formed monarchical bureaucracy) administered finance.

Administrative systems, like revenue sources, were often in flux. During the late eleventh and twelfth centuries (when background conditions were reasonably stable), established organizations with elaborate procedures and numerous officials and clerks replaced earlier informal management by a few of the king's personal servants. Staffed at first by amateurs at central and local levels, medieval treasuries later became professionalized at the top. Although, as external conditions changed, fixed procedures often made it difficult to keep up the records, the men responsible for financial operations, as need arose, could be as flexible in administrative matters as they were in their search for revenues. Piecemeal adaptation of procedures in the late Middle Ages was intended to simplify control and distribution of funds, but, as with the modern income tax, the cumulative outcome of many small changes was often a greater complexity and incoherence than had existed before. Medieval regimes were hierarchical in intention, but not in accomplishment.

"Where the treasury is, there shall be thy heart,"[198] said the commentator FitzNigel, alluding to his government's cameral administration of finance. The early medieval state treasury, just as in the ancient empires, was identical with that of the king's private household. Feudal kings kept their wealth in the chamber or tent where they slept. A single official (a personal servant who became known as the *chamberlain*) stood guard over the king and his treasure. Serving as custodian of the king's funds, the chamberlain granted gifts as the king wished, and accepted whatever offerings the king's subjects brought in.[199]

At the top, early-medieval administrative structure was small and personal. Thus an official separation between the monarch's private finances and state finance did not occur during the Middle Ages. But an administrative distinction gradually evolved between the king's personal household expense and all other costs of government. This separation was accompanied by a shift from cameral administration to more differentiated administrative modes.

The development was neither linear nor homogeneous; change came about in different ways in England and France. When administration is viewed narrowly—as a technical instrument—the variety of devices medieval governments employed at different times reflected the opportunism with which kings and their counselors approached fiscal problems. Before governments had developed administrative capacity, private agents served as substitutes for a state treasury. The Paris branch of the Knights Templar was the sole central agency for receipt and distribution of French royal revenues until Philip the Fair established the Chambre des Comptes (as the medieval French treasury was known) early in the fourteenth century. Throughout the Middle Ages various private individuals or organizations—local sheriffs and Italian bankers—served as governments' tax collectors.

Changes in administrative organization reflect contemporary ideas about how the men who serve government relate to it. When the king was merely one of many local feudal magnates, his agents were at once his friends and comrades-in-arms, his vassals, and his personal servants. Although the king still chose friends as advisers in the late Middle Ages, administration of finance was becoming less personal. While the relationship between government and the individuals who served it was not the contractual relation of a public official to the modern state—since a strong element of personal loyalty persisted—nevertheless the modern concept of professionalism was beginning to emerge.

By the fourteenth century, salaried men, trained for the work, served as administrators; and the organizational structures typical of the transitional era following the Middle Ages had evolved. At the top, financial administrations of England and France were quite similar: in both countries, simple cameral administration had been elaborated into a central state treasury whose paid personnel received and audited regular revenues and paid the king's bills.[200]

The major difference between the central financial administrations of these two kingdoms in the late Middle Ages was the social background of the administrative class. From the twelfth century on, high officials of the English Exchequer were noblemen—bishops or laymen who were barons of the king's court, selected from "the most important and prudent subjects of the realm."[201] But Philip the Fair staffed his new central state treasury in the Louvre with middle-rank knights rather than clerics. Well educated and trained in law and accountancy, such "ordinary" knights had modest personal resources and expectations.

Unlike their English counterparts, fourteenth-century French administrators were not bound by the cumbersome practices of the twelfth-century Exchequer. When they set up the French treasury, state administrators adopted the newest managerial techniques: as experience increased, so did efficiency. As with professional public servants everywhere, the salary the king paid was only partial reward. The nonpecuniary benefits—personal satisfaction with a job well done, and proximity to power—were rich compensation.[202]

Professionalization of public service occurred only at the top because, for most of the Middle Ages, private agents handled local revenue collection. Although French and English local officials held different titles, they performed similar tasks. The Anglo-Norman *sheriff* and the French *prévôt* were generalized offices of an ambiguous status that changed over time. In the seventh and eighth centuries the landowner's manorial steward, a free peasant cultivator, was the local administrator.[203] As agent of a small private government, he resolved disputes, allocated and supervised compulsory labor service on the lord's land, collected feudal payments in kind, and made sure all of it was ready when the lord appeared at the manor. In France by the ninth century the steward's office could be sold for a limited term to whoever might bid highest. With emergence of feudalism, local offices tended to become hereditary property—of nobles in England, and of men of humbler origins in France.[204]

As private agent of a nonexistent or weak central government, the local officer's role somewhat resembled the tax farmer's. Whether the posts were bought or inherited, local agents kept a portion, perhaps one-third or more, of the profits of justice and feudal dues from the king's land.[205] Without supervision from the center, as with tax farming, there was great potential for abuse; an avaricious agent could exact more than customary feudal dues from the king's tenants, and enrich himself by retaining the surplus.[206] An eminent medievalist speculates on the extent of the practice: "How many taxes and labour services were extorted from the villeins . . . by this petty rural tyrant; how many chickens . . . from their poultry yards; how many casks of wine . . . from their cellars, or . . . bacon from their storehouses; how much weaving imposed on their wives." The Abbé Suger, a twelfth-century bishop who served the French king, must have reflected contemporary sentiment when he advised: "An estate abandoned to serjeants [manorial stewards] is an estate lost."[207]

To curb local collectors' greed, French kings, in the mid–twelfth century, added an intermediate, supervisory level to field administration. They sent salaried officials (known as *baillifs* (bailiffs) in the north and *seneschals* in the south) from Paris as their representatives in the provinces to check on the *prévôts*. Like traveling inspectors of the Chinese civil service during the Han Dynasty, these officers established authority over the *prévôts* by repeated appearances, and could thus curb their abuses.

As the kingdom grew larger, permanent representatives of the central government gradually replaced itinerant inspectors. By the mid–thirteenth century a resident supervisor served in each bailiwick (territorial administrative division) for a term of from three to five years.[208] The bailiffs effectively subordinated the *prévôts,* brought stability to provincial administration, and thereby helped to unify France. With jurisdiction over military, judicial and financial administration, the bailiffs also helped spread new ideas about administration by installing common practices in territories where they served. Seneschals and bailiffs carried dissimilar legal and administrative conceptions of northern and southern France back to the center, where amalgamation slowly occurred.[209] Making their rounds from one bailiwick to another, these men gradually created the administrative homogeneity that served to mold the heterogeneous French provinces into a unified state.

In England the foundations of late-medieval local financial administration were laid in the twelfth century when Henry II reasserted his right to appoint and remove sheriffs at will. Instead of the noblemen who had served as local administrators since the time of the Saxons, Henry chose middle-rank knights, more easily controlled than barons. Since the new men might not have sufficient wealth to carry out their tasks, Henry instituted an expense allowance. Every six months when sheriffs turned in their receipts to the Exchequer, they could deduct all legitimate expenses exceeding the allowance.

The sheriffs (who collected only manorial payments from crown land, the equivalent of customary feudal payments) became less important when manorial dues were a declining proportion of government revenues. As new revenue sources were added after the twelfth century, other organizational roles gradually emerged to handle assessment and collection. Whether handled by clergy or laymen, the new offices were for the most part unpaid. The commissioners who supplanted the sheriff in property assessment after the twelfth century were local notables with sufficient wealth to support such a public duty and to advance funds to the treasury every six months whether taxes had been collected or not. (In practice, the second requirement was seldom fulfilled.) The only permanent paid local financial officials in England were the escheators, who managed land repossessed by the crown (and held until a new feudal tenant could be found). After the late twelfth century, kings appointed paid officials in each port to administer customs—weighers, collectors, comptrollers, searchers for contraband, and supervisors.[210] To collect property taxes in towns, the king relied on merchants who had agreed to serve as one condition of the town's charter; later, guilds assumed the task.

In an age of localism the English sheriff, along with the French *prévôt,* could abuse his office, but not for long; if the king heard complaints as he traveled through the land a corrupt officer could be replaced by a more honest man. In addition to this leverage, the Exchequer had a formal procedure to check on local agents. This was the audit, held twice each year from the twelfth century on.

MEDIEVAL FINANCIAL CONTROL: THE AUDIT

Faced with the problem of choosing officials to carry out his will, the king would select men whose character he knew, whose responses were predictable, and whose judgments he respected. In a twelfth-century English document, for example, there is reference to the "faithful and intimate subjects who are ... engaged on the secret business of the king ..., whose hands direct the royal councils and the affairs of the kingdom."[211] But the more men he had to choose and the farther away they were, the more difficult the king's task became.

The importance of the king's choice was directly related to the scale of the medieval system. Personal control through incessant travel became physically impossible as the territory to be governed increased. Scale is also a function of the number of officials. When layers in a bureaucracy were multiplied, trust became the most important criterion of choice, not only for those who served close to the king but for successively lower echelons as well.

In all matters of government, but especially where finance is concerned, a man must be trustworthy. The Abbé Suger put the problem neatly. "There is nothing more dangerous," he advised the French kings, "than to change the personnel of government without due thought. Those who are discharged carry off with them as much as they can, and those who take their place are so fearful of receiving the same treatment as their predecessors that they proceed, without loss of time, to steal a fortune."[212] Top-level jobs—treasurer, counselor, judge, and auditor—at first were filled by high-ranking clerics or noblemen, men educated uncommonly well for the age, who came from the king's social class. Because these men had ample personal wealth they appeared to warrant trust. As in the ancient empires, however, control of local financial officials was not an easy matter. If poor, such men stole from necessity; if rich, from avarice.

Ancient governments often dealt with the problem of trust with espionage networks designed to create parallel channels of information and control. Kautilya's words to a wise king illustrate the method. "... having encouraged ... a spy with honor and money rewards, the minister shall tell him ... 'Thou shalt inform us of whatever wickedness thou findest in others.' "[213] In Byzantium, a despotism of the Middle Ages, emperors aimed to reduce drains on the treasury by buying off state officials. By contributing lavish stipends of food and clothing to holders of titles and offices, and by paying large salaries whether or not an office entailed work, the emperors aimed to discourage thievery.* As financial officials' duties entailed inordinate respon-

---

* A man named Liudprand who served as ambassador to Byzantium from the modest court of the Holy Roman Empire during the mid–tenth century appears to have been overwhelmed by the fortunes conferred on Byzantine officeholders:

"The week before ... Palm Sunday, the emperor distributed ... salaries. I was invited to the ceremony, which someone thought might interest me. Things happened as follows:

sibility while subjecting the holders to constant temptation to steal, they received the highest salaries.[215] Although lacking resources for bribery, and without organizational capacity for espionage, governments in medieval Europe did have several effective devices to substitute for trust.

Compared to the ancient monarchies' draconian methods of control by intimidation, the medieval audit was a more effective deterrent; its existence alone tended to create a climate of relative honesty.

From the long-range perspective of intellectual history, the medieval audit is an example of conceptual reinvention; in many of its elements it resembled the treasury audit of classical Athens. From the viewpoint of modern social science, the audit may be viewed as an administrative institution; the social context in which an institution appears affects how its underlying impetus is expressed. When the audit is viewed narrowly, as administrative innovation or technical device, the procedure's appearance in various parts of medieval Europe between the eleventh and thirteenth centuries demonstrates the process of technological diffusion.*

In essence, both ancient Athenian and medieval audits were rituals, symbolic representations of a ruler's legitimacy. Both had the same purpose: to control the government's officials. Both were personal, entailing an individual's declaration of integrity and capacity to execute

---

A large table, ten cubits long and four wide, was covered with bags full of gold, the insignia on each ... indicated whom they were for. The latter began to file by the emperor ... They were called in succession according to the rank of their offices. ... the multitude of objects [each] received was so great that they could not carry them on their shoulders. Not without some effort and the support of their entourage, they dragged the goods behind them ... I observed file past ... an immense crowd ... Each received ... according to his rank. Moreover, the ceremony was not over in a single day. Beginning the fifth day of the week of Palm Sunday, and lasting from one o'clock to four, it was repeated the sixth and seventh day."[214]

* The Normans conducted an audit in England and in their territory on the Continent; a similar procedure was carried out by the counts of Flanders after the thirteenth century. An audit appears in France during the last decade of the twelfth century (1190–94); it was well established there ten years later. From the late twelfth century (1178–80), the count-king of Catalonia conducted a regular audit. The surviving records of Catalonian manorial receipts, and deductions for expenses made in the count-king's behalf by his bailiffs, are more like the treasury records of classical Athens than the summary documents surviving from northern-European audits. The manorial accountings took place in each bailiwick, at irregular intervals; the findings were set down in paragraphs. These decentralized inquiries, one scholar speculates, may represent an early stage in development of the audit. Yet, even where centralized, the procedure did vary. Clerks of the French treasury kept systematic records of receipts and expenses, but, so far as we know, they did not issue wooden tallies as receipts for payment.[216]

his office. By requiring a financial officer to make a public statement summarizing his receipts and expenses (during or at the end of his term of office), these governments aimed to check on officials, deter them from wrongdoing, and thereby create a climate of honesty in financial administration.

The Athenian audit, however, was control of the top by the citizens. Since Athenian law judged treasury receipts to be public property, the chief financial officer faced the assembled populace at the end of his term to proclaim honest management of public funds. When the audit first reappeared in northern Europe in the late eleventh century, a conception of public government did not exist. Because government under feudalism was small, personal, and private, the medieval audit became control of the bottom administrative level by an intermediate group for the benefit of the top. When the audit was first adopted, hereditary agents in each district, not tax farmers, collected feudal dues from the king's land. Feudal monarchs used the audit to protect against theft of their property, which, as in the ancient empires, was identical with the state's. Unlike classical Athens, there was no financial control of the top layer of government throughout the Middle Ages. Compelling a king to account for his expenditures did not accord with the medieval conception of monarchy. The idea of accountability *to* and *in* government was partial; it applied only to local collectors and revenues—both from the king's land and from the profits of justice (fines paid by subjects for disturbing the king's peace).[217] Not until the fifteenth century did the idea of financial accountability at the top reappear briefly, and then again disappear. In England, where effective control of the purse was first institutionalized, Parliament's struggle to make the king account for his expenses lasted several centuries longer.

Although the medieval ceremony of the audit contained ancient elements, no one knows how these elements reached northern Europe or how they were combined. There is good reason to believe that medieval men reinvented the audit, combining the resurrected idea of personal accountability with the ancient practice of cadastral surveys, which were occasionally made during the Carolingian era (tenth century). The medieval auditor's calculations were made with an abacus, a tool used by scribes since the time of the pharaohs; perhaps the Normans brought the abacus to northern Europe from Sicily after their forays into Mediterranean territory during the tenth century.

The next most important tool of the medieval audit was the wooden tally of receipt.[218] Although it was also used in China during the tenth century[219] and may have been carried to Europe by traders, we are unable to find a link between the two; therefore we assume its widespread use in Europe after the eleventh century to be still another example of conceptual re-invention.

The medieval audit also included several original components: from a conceptual and technical standpoint it synthesized old and new elements. The idea of balance—that there should be a rough correspondence between receipts and expenses—was not part of the Athenian ritual, possibly because ancient accounting technique did not allow such comparison. The Athenian ritual was an audit of spenders in an era when the Attic drachma (the Athenian coinage) was the hard currency of the ancient world. Because many different currencies of widely fluctuating value might be paid into a medieval treasury, and because medieval men held a conception of intrinsic value, it was important for medieval kings' auditors to determine the metallic content of taxes paid in coin, through sampling and assay.[220] From each collector's remittance, auditors selected a few coins at random; if the sample appeared to be depreciated, the entire payment was melted down for analysis. When the silver content of a remittance was less than the prevailing standard, the tax collector was required to make up the deficit.

The principal medieval contribution to the audit was juridical. Whenever a medieval government conducted an audit—whether in Normandy, England, Flanders, Catalonia, or France—a selected panel of noblemen sat in council to adjudicate possible disputes between collectors and receivers. If a discrepancy could be proved, the judicial council determined what sanctions were needed.

Best-known of the medieval audits is the English ritual of the Exchequer; rich documentation describes it in detail.* At least part of the procedure had Anglo-Saxon origins: a well-developed system of accounting for produce of royal estates already existed at the time of the

---

* Compared with previous epochs, there is an abundance of primary source material for study of late-medieval government finance. The wealth of sources is at least a partial result of medieval record-keeping techniques. Unlike the papyrus, or the clay or wax tablets used by Egyptian, Babylonian, and Roman scribes, medieval clerks wrote on parchment, thinly stretched animal skins. When suitably tanned and prepared, parchment provided a firm, durable writing surface. There is a large literature on medieval administration, and, since the tasks of the medieval state were limited, studies of financial administration are a substantial part of it. The primary source for the Exchequer audit is "The Dialogue of the Exchequer" (*Dialogus de Scaccario*), a delightful discussion of the Exchequer's operations during the twelfth century, written in the form of a catechism by Richard FitzNigel, Bishop of London and an "experienced fiscal officer of the crown" during Henry II's reign.[221]

Norman Conquest. Twice each year, local collectors of feudal payments from crown land were required to travel to wherever the king held his court. Each collector was obliged to turn in his receipts, then to make an accounting of expenditures. Each sheriff in turn was called before the assembled auditors. Standing before a table covered with a black cloth marked into squares, a sheriff paid in his collection. The auditors counted the payments, then compared total receipts and expenses the sheriff claimed as deductions against treasury records of the previous audit, to determine whether the collector's claim of expenses was reasonable, and to see how much he still owed. The total amount due was entered with counters in the squares of the Exchequer board (as the checkered table was called), and the current payments were subtracted. Next, the total was compared with the accounting submitted by the sheriff in the previous audit; if the two were comparable, the sheriff received a cut tally as a permanent receipt. Referring to the semiannual audit as a game, a financial historian describes its conduct:

> And now the "game" has been opened. The treasurer ... asks his adversary if he is ready to render his account. The latter replies in the affirmative, and is immediately challenged upon the first item of his reckoning. Hereupon a general commotion ensues. The clerks turn the membranes of their rolls to compare the entries of the previous years, and the chamberlain's serjeants heap upon the table rouleaux of silver, counter-tallies,* and warrants, representing the accountant's credit in the treasury. Then the calculator, rising in his place, prepares to make the moves of the game as they are dictated from the contents of the great roll.
>
> The sum of each separate entry of the farm of the county being announced, he ... arranges the amount quoted, in specie or in counters, within the appropriate columns. Next he sorts out the credit before him into heaps in the same columns below this dummy treasure, and, when everything is complete, subtracts pence from pence, shillings from shillings, and pounds from

* Medieval tally sticks were seven or eight inches long, divided by a mark into two unequal parts. Specialized treasury clerks cut notches into both sides of the tally, thereby representing in standardized notation the amount each sheriff had paid into the treasury. When each sheriff's business with the treasury was concluded, the tally cutters severed the two parts. The larger piece of each tally (the countertally or *counterfoil*) was stored at the treasury. The smaller part (the *foil*) was given to the sheriff as a receipt. The British monarch's revenue officers continued to furnish the wooden tally until 1832. The first law of finance is inertia. Modern usage of the term "counterfoil," however, illustrates how the meaning of specialized language changes over time. In modern banking terminology, a counterfoil is a receipt or check stub, while "foil," the medieval term for a receipt, is no longer used.

pounds, till the corresponding pieces on both sides are exhausted by the exchange. Then, unless the accountant is quit,* so much as is left on either side represents the advantage or loss of each respectively, the deficit being made good or the surplus allowed. . . .

Meanwhile, the tallies held by the sheriff's servants have been carefully compared with the foils preserved in the Exchequer, to guard against forgery, or even a slip of the knife, and woe betide him if any such flaw be discovered, for then he would be forthwith handed over to the marshal for safe custody in the Fleet, unless he could fasten the fraud upon his deputy or attorney. . . .

The contest is slowly waged, the piles of silver, gold, and metal counters, sticks and scrolls, being marshalled, advanced, and swept off the board . . . till the account of the farm is concluded . . . for another six months at least.[222]

The audit appears to have been an effective method of control, for it created a salutary atmosphere of compliance. Although the Exchequer's sanctions for mismanagement or embezzlement were limited—small fines or at worst short-term imprisonment—the threat appears to have kept peculation to a minimum. Beyond the mid twelfth century, when his tenure in office became subject to annual reappointment, the Anglo-Norman sheriff collected what was due and his profits were modest. When abuses occurred, it was during unstable periods, such as the transition from payment in kind to payment in coin, when the king was abroad, or when central authority weakened.

Periodic administrative reforms tightened up control of the sheriffs. Even before Henry II had asserted his right to reappoint sheriffs each year, his predecessor had tried to make the office less profitable by doubling the purchase price. To increase yields from royal land, the crown also tried to rationalize local administration by creating new offices that would permit sheriffs to specialize in revenue collection.[223] In a series of public inquests held in the last half of the thirteenth century, local property was revalued to take account of inflation, thereby increasing feudal revenues.[224]

The inquests had a secondary purpose: they provided a forum for citizens to vent their ire against dishonest sheriffs. Like most administrative reforms, the results were less than the king hoped for; according to a contemporary commentator, "The king sent his commissioners everywhere to inquire how his sheriffs and bailiffs had conducted themselves; but no good came of it."[225] Nevertheless, by the end of the

* When a sheriff's accounts were quit, he paid in exactly the amount owed, no more or less.

thirteenth century the king had enlarged the Exchequer's prerogative; his vassals' stewards were liable for audit along with the king's sheriffs. When barons of the Exchequer could prove that a sheriff had defaulted on payments to the crown (whether directly to the king or indirectly to one of his vassals), the barons could send the unfortunate to prison, where he would "be held in safe keeping in irons and . . . remain . . . at [his] own cost until [he had] fully satisfied their lords of their arrears."[226]

During the eleventh and twelfth centuries, when medieval governments were small and feudal payments were largely in kind, the audit appears to have been conducted in an orderly fashion. A king's main source of support was the produce of his domain, and the audit enabled the king's agents to keep track of what was due him. As the king traveled from place to place, members of the king's court consumed part of his revenues in kind; much of the remainder was paid out locally by the sheriffs. Though sheriffs were required to account for their receipts and expenses item by item, little money changed hands in the semiannual audit. With gradual conversion to payment of feudal dues in money, the auditing process became much more complicated. Payment in coin necessitated an assay to determine whether money paid in was of acceptable quality. Sometimes payment was partly in coin and partly in kind; if so, the need to maintain parallel records, or to convert from one means of payment to the other, involved local collectors and central recorders in more administrative detail than they could handle.*

Strict regulations governed how Exchequer books were kept. For permanence, manorial records were written on strips of parchment—tanned, stretched, cut to uniform dimensions, and stitched together to form a linear scroll. This financial document was known as the Pipe Roll, perhaps because when rolled and tied it resembled a tube. For each semiannual accounting of the great number of feudal payments from the king's many manors, his clerks wrote separate entries in ink on the roll. Line-item accounts with a vengeance, these records were extraordinarily detailed. Although Arabic numeration was known in northern Europe by the twelfth century, treasury clerks noted each

---

* Records submitted for audit by bailiffs collecting the Catalonian count-kings' revenues illustrate the difficulty of administering such a mixed revenue system. The parchments stated balances in kind, in coin, and in money of account. To simplify evaluation of tax receipts in kind (counted in Roman, Germanic, and Moorish systems of measure), bailiffs converted perishable commodities into grain equivalents, and then converted grain equivalents into money of account.[227]

entry in Roman numerals because the practice was traditional, and because it was hoped thereby to prevent fraud.[228] Since Roman numerals occupied more space than Arabic notation, a clerk would have difficulty changing an entry by writing over it. No erasures were permitted once an entry was made; if he made an error a scribe could repair it only by inserting a correction between lines of the scroll.

Designed to permit administrative control, the specificity of medieval manorial records came to overwhelm not only the illiterate collectors, but also the king's educated auditors, whom the records were created to enlighten. Hard enough to carry out when conditions were stable, these accounting procedures were inflexible and unresponsive in an environment of change. Complexity far beyond capacity to deal with it resulted in overload. With changes in land ownership, feudal tenure, and customary obligations, the Exchequer rolls fell years in arrears;[229] they were not brought up to date until long after the Middle Ages ended.

Detail in entries was useful for control of collectors, but was a handicap if overall totals were needed. Medieval kings never knew what they had, because their records were fragmented. Treasury scribes kept separate sets of books for manorial revenues from each district, for lay and clerical subsidies, and for income from tax farmers. Tax-farming revenue was a relatively certain amount; the contracts were negotiated in advance for a fixed fee. Manorial revenue was fixed and theoretically predictable, but to calculate its real value when prices were rising presented difficulties, which medieval men lacked analytic capacity to confront even if the idea had occurred to them. Income from lay and clerical subsidies granted at irregular intervals was uncertain; productivity varied with the king's popular image, with his reason for collecting a subsidy, and with economic conditions. The main cause of uncertainty was late-medieval governments' lack of conceptual and technical-administrative capacity for synthesis. Cumulation and summation of accounts lay far in the future; the practice of earmarking— creation of autonomous funds—was to cause more confusion before government accounting was simplified. The Exchequer's role was only to try to keep track of the parts. Our twelfth-century informant states its perspective: ". . . the business of the Exchequer is different from other business . . . in many cases it may be said that 'explicitness does harm and generalities are harmless': but, here, on the contrary, 'explicitness helps and generalities are a source of trouble.' "[230]

Complexity in record-keeping was only part of the problem; disbursement procedures were equally cumbersome. Each small payment from the treasury required the king's scribes to prepare a writ (a document granting permission to pay money out), and then to obtain the king's or his chamberlain's signature. To assure legality, each document was stamped with the king's seal.* The process was awkward and time-consuming, and there was a constant risk of embezzlement from counterfeit of the royal seal.[231]

Whether the king was at home or abroad, there were always logistical problems. Although the Knights Templars and later the Italian banker served as transfer agents for long-distance payments, local disbursements in money involved moving large quantities of coin. As the king traveled from place to place, the chamberlain and his clerks carried along manorial records and containers of coins. Medieval documents evoke the confusion. The chamberlain first had to find wagons and horses, then to insure safe conveyance of the precious contents as the king's entourage moved across a sparsely settled countryside, where roads were little more than ruts and bandits might lie in ambush around the next bend. From treasury records of the late twelfth century, for example, we learn that its officers paid six pounds "for the hire of carts which carried the [king's] treasure from London to Winchester and part of the same treasury to Salisbury and again to Dorchester, and for the many businesses of the treasury while the king was sojourning on the coast."[232] The chamberlain and his knights packed the money—silver pennies, the only currency of the times—in barrels; each barrel contained £100 worth of coins. Then they guarded the money in transit, enlisting aid from the sheriff of each county the procession passed through.[233]

The treasury had permanent headquarters in London by the mid–thirteenth century, but problems of disbursement were no less complex. When the king was fighting some distance from London—abroad, or in Scotland or Wales—the treasury organized convoys to transport money for supplies and to pay troops. On the battle site, treasury agents dispensed money in bulk, "by the sack and the barrel," like any common commodity. Thus, in the early thirteenth century King John wrote the following instructions to his paymaster in France: "Pay the dealers for the horses out of the £700 cask from which £100 has already been taken ..."[234] To speed payment in the hinterlands, John established a number of provincial treasuries in fortified castles throughout the kingdom. Details about the opening of a branch at

---

* The customs seal had two parts: the collector kept one half, the king's port supervisor held the other. Double stamping of each voucher might have discouraged exporters from trying to bribe customs collectors.

York have survived; to convey money and records from London there were

> twenty-three carts, each drawn by five horses, ... a company on horseback, ... a number of other Exchequer officials, their clerks and servants, the purveyor of the carts, the purveyor of the food, the crier of the bench [to announce their passage through the land], and grooms for the horses, fifty in all. There was the guard of foot and horse under the command of the sheriffs of London and Middlesex.[235]

The treasury notified the sheriff of Lincolnshire in advance to have waiting at Torksey "four good strong small ships each able to bear the weight of eight winecasks and tackle and sailors needed to man the vessels."[236]

Without a network of banks, disbursement was cumbersome even when the king had money on hand. By the end of the Middle Ages, and until deposit banking became common, problems of transferring funds were somewhat reduced when the Exchequer began to issue tallies on receipts of provincial tax collectors. In addition to their importance as a method of deficit financing, the tallies—as they gradually came to substitute for coin—simplified disbursement as well.

Between the eleventh and fourteenth centuries, as medieval governments developed administrative arms, the components came to be interrelated and interdependent. As in any complex organization, single changes often had unexpected repercussions; a change suitable for one purpose might be unsatisfactory for another. With increasing pressure to raise and spend money for an expanding state, medieval governments enlarged their central bureaucracies; and the English created decentralized treasuries. Administrative expansion sometimes led to loss of control of personnel as new, untested men became administrators. In the late thirteenth century, for example, an unknown Exchequer representative in London, one Adam of Stratton from Wiltshire, became wealthy by lending the poor money he had embezzled from the king. He forged royal seals, charters, and even the deed to a Cluniac monastery in Gascony (which he hoped to confiscate for his personal estate).[237]

But only the worst abuses led to prosecution and imprisonment, for the modern conception of conflict of interest did not exist in the late Middle Ages. A financial official normally conducted his private business and his service to the state simultaneously; indeed, wealth was a prerequisite for holding office. After the fourteenth century, French kings capitalized on their officials' business connections: drawing no distinction between officials' public and private roles, or between the state's and their officials' personal resources, French kings borrowed money from them whenever possible. These officials, in turn, made personal loans at high rates of interest in order to lend to the king. This practice seriously undermined the king's authority over his treasury men, for if the monarch wished to continue to borrow, he was forced to disregard their corruption.[238]

The French monarchy's financial affairs and those of its treasury officers were closely interlocked during the fifteenth century. For example, while acting as financial counselor to the king, the merchant Jacques Coeur conducted a thriving import-export business. In his private capacity Coeur raised large sums for the crown but, as partial compensation for this service, used crown revenue to finance his own trading.[239] Governing elders of the northern-Italian communes in the thirteenth century had a similarly ambiguous role in formulating and executing their governments' financial policies. In their public capacity as city officials, these Italian officials authorized communal borrowing. Then, in their private capacity as merchants or bankers, and with superb rationality, the same men loaned money to the commune at interest rates they were free to specify. Next, in their public capacity, they authorized tax collection to pay interest on the loans, and later they determined priorities for repayment of the principal. (Inflation caused by the borrowing must have contributed to prosperity within communes while wage earners' real incomes fell.) A similar confusion of public and private roles, if discovered in the modern world, would result in ostracism, prosecution and imprisonment, but in the rapidly changing late Middle Ages norms had not yet developed to differentiate between public and private activities of government officials. The behavior we describe was a practical way to conduct government business, and, unless the king needed a scapegoat, no one objected to it.

Establishment of provincial treasuries in England eased the currency-transfer problem but created new difficulties. Dispersal of personnel, records, and wealth made it harder than ever to keep track of medieval kings' resources. Royal confusion also resulted partially from the way the extraordinary revenues—lay and clerical subsidies and customs—were administered.

Right to collect such subsidies had been granted to kings incrementally; each subsidy was enacted for a specific financial emergency. With no previous organization, and without much advance notice, kings had to improvise administrative methods. In England, bishops administered the first few clerical subsidies. The king specified which prelates should collect the subsidies, ordered that the bishops store the coin in monasteries with especially thick walls, and, when collection was completed, that they move the money to the Exchequer in London. Before long, salaried Exchequer agents took over collection of clerical subsidies. By the thirteenth century, Exchequer clerks were officially in charge of collecting lay subsidies also,[240] but since these subsidies were property taxes, just as in the Italian communes, the task of property assessment created serious problems. The English used the same techniques as the communes did. Taxpayers voluntarily declared their property's value, or local committees of twelve men determined property values. Just as with the modern property tax before computer assessment, undervaluation must have been the norm. There was general consensus by the mid–fourteenth century that revaluation of property for each subsidy was more than the Exchequer could cope with; appraisals were fixed, and did not change for three centuries thereafter.[241]

The French used tax farmers, private businessmen, or Italian bankers to collect both lay and clerical subsidies.[242] Because the French kings had no central administrative capacity for finance until the fourteenth century, they were forced to use tax farmers to collect the extraordinary revenues; but, by so doing, they received less than the potential yield, and tax farmers pocketed the difference. Although medieval men never thought in these terms, their opportunity costs of administration under contract were exceedingly large. Until long after the Middle Ages ended, the same was true for the English kings who used tax farmers to collect the customs, the most dependable source of royal income. Perhaps medieval monarchs were trying to recoup some losses when they defaulted on loans from Italian bankers who served them as tax farmers, promptly expelled the bankers from their kingdoms, and then confiscated bank property.

THE MEANING OF THE MIDDLE AGES: THEORIES OF CHANGE

Europe during the Middle Ages provides a provocative history for scholars to explain; within it an ancient social order of despotism became an order with elements of political, social, and economic individualism. The thousand years of the medieval era successively encompassed political and administrative noncentralization (fragmentation of authority), decentralization (dispersal of authority), and recentralization (concentration of authority).

Generalizing from the dearth of empirical evidence about central government's administrative organization in the Western Roman Empire after the fifth century, some historians have judged mutual need for defense in the absence of effective central authority to be sufficient reason for emergence of feudalism. Spread of feudal relationships has been attributed to technological innovations in waging war (the stirrup and the crossbow); the improved living standards that came about concurrently with feudalism are explained by diffusion of new farming methods—the horse collar, the moldboard plow, selective planting, and crop rotation.

In recent years concepts drawn from economic theory have been used to explain feudalism: efforts to attain individual and collective advantage under conditions of extreme uncertainty provided impetus for feudal relationships. By the fifth century, so the argument runs, the costs of the superstate (the Roman Empire) had exceeded its benefits. As organized imperial defenses collapsed in the west, people in the empire's periphery—subject to intermittent attack from marauders, and without any way to settle disputes—were willing to buy defense and justice from an individual, who became their protector.

The protector's compensation was the labor service given by peasants for farming his holdings, and the military service furnished by men of higher station to defend his domain. Collapse of the Roman imperial army brought an end to recruitment of captives to serve as slaves; together with the short life expectancies engendered by deprivation and disease, this contributed to a shortage of labor. For those who sought sanctuary in this time of instability and hardship, the coercive character of the private governments (which were, in effect, local monopolies) was somewhat mitigated by the security given by the fortified enclosure the protector maintained.

A few of the private governments eventually were able to enlarge both their domains and, to some extent, their authority. As recurrent epidemics of plague prolonged the labor shortage, one outcome was emergence of competition for labor. (In the jargon of economists, the terms of trade for labor worsened.) At the top of the emerging feudal pyramid, very weak kings competed for allegiance of the large landowners who would become their feudal vassals. And, as labor grew scarcer, feudal landowners lower in the hierarchy tried to interpret the laws of property in such a way as to bind their peasant labor to the land. With emergence of the feudal contract, landed vassals were bound to the king in the same way as peasants on each feudal tenant's land were obligated to serve their masters.

But then, as feudal rights became hereditary, the king who aimed to defend his fragile authority against potential challengers became obligated in turn to the large landowners who were his tenants-in-chief. When assembled, the armed knights who served a king's supporters could provide an army to defend the king's cause. When relationships among near-equals are maintained to achieve both individual and collective advantage, decisions are often arrived at by bargaining. From our analytic perspective, there was apparent dissonance in feudal relationships, for within the feudal hierarchy elements of individualism emerged. A social order of pure hierarchy (such as existed in the ancient despotisms) was dissolved to some extent; it was supplanted, in part, by the reciprocal relationships characteristic of individualism.

How did recentralization of government at the end of the Middle Ages come about? According to an economic explanation of change, there was a shift in the terms of trade for labor. Either feudal relations contained the seeds of their own destruction (as Marx might have put it), or, if we use different language, feudalism's very success transformed society's economic base. Explanation must take account of exogenous factors as well. Recovery from the devastating plague of the fourteenth century brought an increased birth rate, and after the disastrous floods and freezes near the beginning of the century, the improved weather, together with heightened productivity of new farming methods, yielded enough food to support an expanding population. In territories like England's, with no unsettled land to expand into, labor became relatively plentiful in relation to land. Interregional exchange of specialized products was common by the fourteenth century; economic growth generated further expansion and fostered specialization.

Innovations in waging war—the longbow and the pike by the fourteenth century, and gunpowder during the fifteenth—permitted armies to attack and defend large territories; the armored knight and the fortified castle, both of them static and immobile, were no longer needed. In time, an army paid by the king replaced the feudal warriors. As feudal relations were being attenuated, wars between rival territories stretched out over several monarchs' lifetimes. According to an economic explanation of centralization, it became increasingly profitable for kings to appropriate the profits of the enlarged territory in which trade could be conducted once peace had been made. Tapping the resources created by economic growth, kings levied new taxes on land and trade.

Although still honorific, feudal service was no longer voluntarily given by the fourteenth century. Where feudal tenants-in-chief could bargain with more than one potential protector, competition forced the king to share the revenue from growth with subordinates; his taxing power remained limited. If substantial economies of scale in defense were possible (whether because of new technology or locational advantages), costs of war might remain commensurate with available resources. In these circumstances, kings did not need to obtain consent for increased taxation, and feudal relationships could be maintained.

Such an explanation of the rise and decline of feudalism has been set forth by two economists, Douglas C. North and Robert Paul Thomas. Since their theory subsumes regional differences in both the manner and the rate of change from a static economy founded in mutual obligation to one in which attainment of individual advantage resulted in rapid growth, it has provoked lively controversy among historians. Changes in relative prices between land and labor and shifts from local to foreign trade are North and Thomas' key variables. Their theory seeks to identify the reasons for the shift from a zero-sum view of the economy, in which participants seek the largest share they can get from a fixed pie, to a positive-sum view in which rising productivity yields greater returns for everyone, however unequally such produce may be distributed. The thesis best fits relationships in the feudal economy of England.*

Economic theory has two aspects that may usefully be distinguished. A materialist side explains human behavior in terms of each individual's desire to get more of whatever is valued. Behavior is also explained as rationality, or instrumental calculation; under prevailing

* North and Thomas state their central thesis:

"The rise of the Western world was [caused by] the redirection of incentives as a consequence of the development of institutions which made it more profitable to attempt to increase productivity within any economic activity. The fundamental institutions of feudalism had developed because of the scarcity of labour relative to land, which made it imperative to capture from labour the rents not existing from a ubiquitous supply of land. Population pressure undermined the economic basis for the institutional organization of feudalism by reversing the relationship of prices as a result of diminishing returns and by expanding the size of markets. Increases in population relative to a fixed supply of good land led to agricultural prices rising relative to nonagricultural prices; this in turn increased the value of land and decreased real wages as the output per labourer fell. Growing population, colonization, and consequent different regional factor endowments led to expanding trade. The result was that landlords now found it to their interest to commute labour dues to payments in kind and in cash, and to lease the demesne lands in return for rent.

"... The effects of the long decline in population were striking. Relative prices reversed. Land now relatively more abundant became less valuable; labour became more scarce and, as a consequence of competition between lords to acquire labour, more dear. To recapture the loss in rents from the now more valuable labour, the lords attempted to use their political power to reimpose feudal obligations. Peasants and labourers, on the other hand, saw freedom from these obligations as a chance to capture more fully the returns of their own labour, which had now risen strikingly in terms of real wages."[243]

circumstances people presumably try to improve their condition. When mankind lives at the edge of subsistence, the materialist view is sufficient explanation of behavior; where the means for sustaining life are truly limited, an individual will always want enough to live on. But if a surplus exists above subsistence, this view fails to explain why material gain is preferred to values such as friendship, autonomy, amenity, or group support. In short, economic rationality tries to explain how people attempt to get what they want, not why they want it. We are interested in the formation as well as the realization of preferences.

Economists' efforts to expand the scope of material values to encompass all human preferences join man's acquisitive impulse (materialism) with his wish to attain individual advantage (rationality). The relative prices so often used by economists as measures of value encode this sense of advantage. Societies are centralized or decentralized, imperial, feudal, or capitalist, so the argument runs, because those members of society whose choices influence outcomes think they will be better off under specific conditions. If one set of arrangements is compared with another, taxes may be lower, or more protection is given, or disputes are resolved to the protagonists' satisfaction.

Technology also serves to shift relative advantage. Because it is difficult to differentiate between cause and effect of any specific innovation, technological influences on social change are harder to isolate than are economic factors. If the scope of innovation goes beyond specific inventions to encompass institutions (such as tax farming or new ways of supporting government), then the distinction between innovation and all other social practices is blurred.

We prefer a broader explanation of change than those deriving from economy or technology; it arises from differences among alternative social orders. Choice among collectivism, individualism, egalitarianism, or some combination means much more to people than a choice of occupation or income. Reflecting a society's values and practices, the social order in which a person lives affects all aspects of his existence: his daily life, his familial relations—in short, his world-view. If people seek to make their lives consistent, as we think they do, it seems unlikely that an open, fluid social structure based on competition will be found in a hierarchical society. Nor, for that matter, will such a society easily foster a climate conducive to experimentation—say in science or the arts, which might eventually give rise to new systems of thought. No doubt creative individuals exist in all social orders, but their ideas stand a better chance of being disseminated in a culture that positively values competition than in the others.

Instead of economic and technological explanations for the broad social changes of the Middle Ages, we see change as an interpenetration of social orders. Except for the church, no strong central authority existed throughout the Middle Ages, but this fact does not preclude all choices. As relationships among near-equals in the feudal pyramid gradually became established, bargaining based in reciprocity did emerge. As coalitions between one local notable and another formed, dissolved, and formed again over time, mutuality penetrated hierarchical relationships. Give-and-take among individuals and groups is one characteristic of individualism.

The new individualistic patterns of governance manifested both strengths and weaknesses. Within each territory, economic activity quickened, and populations grew over time. Because the temporary coalitions of notables could not simultaneously maintain internal order while defending their combined holdings against external attack, each territory's external relations were unstable. The task of creating a viable central authority therefore involved the ability to sustain a delicate balance between hierarchy and individualism. Local notables had to oversee rules of hierarchy in their own territories to preserve their internal order. Yet, to maintain his dominance, an aspiring ruler had to foster a measure of competition among supporters who were his near-equals in territory and power. By trial and error over the centuries, those tenants-in-chief who aspired to be kings bid for support among their peers by extending hierarchical relationships upward. Building an authority structure from the bottom up, as it were, was not likely to re-create the despotic relationships found in the ancient empires.

The process by which the feudal monarchy emerged was not really centralization as we understand it. Having lived through several centuries of political fragmentation (or noncentralization), the feudal monarchs of the later Middle Ages in effect created decentralized kingdoms. Local notables' jurisdiction over administration of justice and defense was supplanted by the central authority's. Yet within each feudal tenant's personal domain, scope still remained for individual variation, and for personal autonomy. Compared to the immediate past, then, the feudal monarchy was recentralized to some extent. But, since every constitution is likely to have been written against the last usurper, the new kingdoms were decentralized compared to the political systems of the ancient empires. Bit by bit, feudal monarchs negotiated a workable combination of collectivism and individualism. Eventually hierarchy came to dominate the polity. Yet its formal structure coexisted with elements of economic individualism, and over time these elements grew ever stronger.

Both capitalism and Protestantism are, in their respective spheres, forms of individualism. Both reject collective control in favor of individual relationships, whether maintained with the divine or with competitors. Capital accumulation, after all, existed long before the Middle Ages. In earlier times, nearly all resources went into collective consumption, either by rulers or by priests, building castles or cathedrals. What has to be explained, in our view, is why hierarchical collectivism—one church, one empire, each run from the top—gave way to competitive individualism: private markets and personal consciences. Protestantism cannot explain capitalism because, socially speaking, they are much the same thing. That is why we have tried to explain how competition among feudal magnates spread into other areas of society so there was less collectivism and more individualism.

Chapter Five

POOR PEOPLE, RICH KINGS: GETTING AND SPENDING IN EARLY-MODERN EUROPE

During the Middle Ages in Europe both kings and their people were poor; in the early-modern era (fifteenth through eighteenth centuries) most people remained poor, but kings began to get rich as the fortunes of their governments improved through enhanced revenue-raising capacity. Shrewdly assessing the tolerance of their subjects, rulers imposed a steadily increasing burden of taxes, singly or a few at a time. Harvesting the fruits of rising productivity, rising revenue yields allowed kings to live in splendor and to wage wars of national aggrandizement. But in some states the burden became heavier than their people would tolerate.

EVOLUTION AND REVOLUTION, CONTINUITY AND CHANGE

The financial practices of governments of seventeenth- and eighteenth-century Europe are closely linked with the great political revolutions that created the representative state, ending government and administration by medieval methods. No longer was government to be, by right, the private domain of the wealthy and privileged. Revolutionary ideology revived the ancient Athenian conception that government, its administration and the money it commands, should belong to all the citizens. A ruler's untrammeled power to treat the state and its fisc as his own was to be abridged by national legislative assemblies. Henceforth government would be public, a joint venture between the crown and its citizens as represented in legislatures. Revolution implemented ideas about organizing the world that have been joined hand in hand ever since: legislative control of the purse, and the twin conceptions of public administration and public finance. But the subjects who became citizens discovered that liberty had its own price: they still had to pay taxes.

Never before in the course of recorded history had an abrupt shift in the group holding power in society produced such large changes in methods of managing state finances. The profound changes in men's attitudes toward and relationships with the state in the seventeenth and eighteenth centuries ended the centuries of oscillation between centralized and decentralized administration and control of state finance. Modern financial institutions developed slowly and at different rates throughout Europe, and administrative structures varied from country to country. Yet, their common properties overshadow the differences. Centralized, productive revenue-expenditure systems began to emerge during this era; by the end of this period the essential building blocks had been created.

Until the early-modern era, the only significant alteration had been a tightening or loosening of financial control; the same modes of management appeared, disappeared, and reappeared again and again. State officials, selected largely by favoritism, collected the direct taxes; the same officials paid for local spending out of revenue collected in each locality. If governments did try to make officials accountable for funds in their care, self-interest, combined with poorly developed accounting procedures, guaranteed that efforts would be ineffective. When revenues were inadequate and/or slow to reach the center, states obtained advances on anticipated taxes by borrowing at high interest rates from selected private lenders—bankers, financiers, and tax farmers. And as in previous periods, an important source of state revenue was the market for titles and offices, which were a quick road to social respectability for aspiring, upwardly mobile mercantile families.

Although national governments' strength increased steadily from the sixteenth century on, states managed their finances by repeatedly expanding and patching medieval structures. Though at first government activities did not extend beyond medieval precedents, the scale of government increased, and rising prices raised the cost of existing activities. Compared to poor medieval kings, early-modern monarchs lived in splendor, and needed lots of money to support their extravagant courts and to pay for the warfare by which their nations were built. Early-modern wars entailed salaried armies, fleets of ships to protect commerce, and an enlarged corps of officials to represent the national government in the provinces and to extract resources to stabilize and enhance its power.

For these purposes, governments grated new, centralizing structures on top of the old, decentralized ones and created the mixed administrative system typical of the age. Following strategies of expediency inherited from the past, early-modern governments used market taxes and market administrative methods to raise and spend money. They increased revenues by taxing the poor, who could not complain, and accomplished all the tasks of financial management at once by employing tax farmers to collect a proliferating variety of indirect local taxes and to pay for local expenditures. In the absence of a developed market for capital, tax farmers provided critically important, short-term credit to the state while nonmarket taxes trickled slowly into the treasury. The borrowing potential inherent in private financial administration caused some states to cling to it long after its high cost had led other states to create centralized management.

The strategies hard-pressed governments of the baroque age employed to raise and spend money gradually created a mixed public/private system of financial administration so complex that its administrative fragmentation, financial cost, and lack of equity became apparent to all. In a time of rising literacy, widespread popular awareness of the differences in taxes levied on geographic regions, on town residents and country dwellers, and among social classes pitted segments of society against one another. The siphoning of state revenues into private pockets—more and more visible as private administrators enhanced their grip on the state's financial machine—exacerbated tensions created by the states' incessant demand for money. The ultimate results were explosions that brought about abrupt shifts in power. One outcome of the great political revolutions, to which financial pressures contributed so appreciably, was a climate well suited to major innovation in state finance.

Like so many others before and after them, early-modern rulers and their advisers must often have thought that *their* financial problems were unprecedented. Seeing accountability defeated by complexity, their subjects might easily have agreed. But both were wrong. Government *could* be simpler and still make large demands. It had not yet occurred to anyone that subjects would learn to tolerate bearing arms and paying taxes when they became citizens.

Opportunistic, shifting, segmented—the ad-hoc methods of finance found in early-modern Europe suited that turbulent time. The variety of taxes and modes of collection are almost as confusing now as states' financial structures must have been then. The choice of methods may be seen as retrogression—crude throwbacks to practices in earlier times. But the methods were effective; they did raise large sums. And perhaps their very inefficiency and confusion gave a little protection to subjects against a state whose centralized government was rapidly learning how to extract an ever greater share of subjects' personal resources.

THE CONTEXT

TECHNOLOGY, PRODUCTIVITY, POPULATION GROWTH, AND ECONOMIC EXPANSION

For generations European populations remained nearly stable. Between the fifteenth and eighteenth centuries, as in preindustrial societies throughout the world today, if a child survived to adulthood, average life expectancy was about forty years. Beyond normal attrition from diseases whose causes were not understood, lack of sanitation, poor diet, squalid dwellings and periodic catastrophe—war, plague or famine—took their toll. Each year births balanced deaths at about forty per thousand.[1]

As in all previous periods of man's history, most of Europe's population was desperately poor. Seventeenth-century man's passion for counting and cataloguing has provided crude statistical measures to document its conditions. Comprising 80 percent of the population of sixteenth-century Spain, and, in the late seventeenth century,[2] more than half of France and half of England, men without property lived just at the margin. If, as has recently been suggested, the laboring class spent 80 percent of its income for food, 10 percent for housing, and the remainder for clothing,[3] little was left to fall back on when the inevitable emergency occurred.

Peasants were more vulnerable than townfolk in a monetized economy, for they had no dependable cash income. When bad weather occurred in some districts for several years in a row, populations died by the thousands because there was no food (like men in subsistence economies of earlier eras, or certain underdeveloped parts of the world today). Peasants consumed seed grain, then sold their possessions, but the proceeds of distress sales staved off starvation for only a short time. The poor "eat bread only three times a week," reports a witness in southwestern France. "Several inhabitants have gone fourteen whole days without eating."[4] A mid-seventeenth-century chronicle describes conditions in one of the worst places: "The people of Lorraine and other surrounding lands are reduced to such extremities that, like animals, they eat the grass in the meadows . . . and are black and thin as skeletons." Ten years later the same observer recorded that famine had killed over seventeen thousand people in a district of Burgundy and forced inhabitants of some towns to eat wild plants. "Some people," he reported, "ate human flesh."[5]

By the late seventeenth century, because of increased agricultural productivity and innovations in household technology, a limited group—perhaps 5 to 15 percent of European society, depending on the locale—enjoyed a rising standard of living. Yet between the beginning of the fifteenth century and the beginning of the nineteenth, despite the continuing hardship for most people, the population of Europe more than doubled; from about 80 to 85 million it increased to 190 million inhabitants.[6] Although mortality (especially of infants) remained high for nobles and commoners alike, birth rates began to rise slowly.

Introduction of new crops and new methods of cultivation that increased agricultural production was one cause of population growth. The waning of feudalism meant that landowners stayed home; many became interested in enlarging the output of their patrimonial land. After the fifteenth century, kings, nobles, and commoners adopted innovative agricultural techniques. Crop rotation, use of manure for fertilizer, and irrigation and drainage projects produced higher yields.[7] Corn and maize, brought from the New World, supplemented the traditional barley and millet. With an emerging market economy and its corollary, improvement in overland transport (the building of roads and canals), the specter of localized famine gradually receded.

Europe in the early-modern era was a rural society. Seven out of ten men lived on the land.[8] The cyclical pattern of cultivation and harvest governed existence, as it has for peasants in agricultural societies throughout history. Brief periods of intense activity counterbalanced long spells when nothing needed to be done. As long as routine tasks were performed, there was ample time for the myriad of festivals, religious and secular, that marked the transition from season to season, from one life stage to the next. Well might righteous Protestants exhort against the twin sins of idleness and drunkenness, when, in the mid–seventeenth century, saints' days, feast days, christenings, weddings, and funerals consumed over one hundred days of each year on the average, in town and country alike.[9]

Two more of each ten lived in villages or small towns.[10] The large wave of urbanization that accompanied industrialization had yet to occur. By the late seventeenth century there were only three large cities—London, Paris, and Constantinople—with populations of more than 400,000 persons. The modal size of large urban settlements—national capitals as well as trading centers—was between 40,000 and 100,000 inhabitants.[11] These cities were scattered at random across the

Continent at the beginning of the early-modern era. By the end of it modern patterns of city location had appeared; along major trade routes, small cities—in northern Europe and northern Italy especially—increased in population and size.[12] For those who think that "small is beautiful," this was a golden age.

Within the cities, physical, social, and economic organization was much like that found in urban areas of developing regions today. Large cities were aggregations of separate villages unified by roads and bridges. Gradually, open land was filled in by the contemporary equivalent of suburban development, where the rich lived side by side with the poor, because, from the late Middle Ages, apprentices and journeymen had traditionally shared their masters' homes. Numerous domestic servants also lived in the cities; in mid–seventeenth century even a middle-class London household such as Samuel Pepys's had at least four. In districts where noblemen and rich merchants had built fine large houses, a quarter or more of the local population might be servants.[13]

Local business greatly resembled the "bazaar" economy of modern Asian cities analyzed by Clifford Geertz.[14] Local markets, once they ceased to be held only on special days of the week, were collections of small stalls or shops run by merchants who dealt in specialized commodities.[15] Performing most operations by hand, manufacturers and artisans labored in small workshops; similar activities were concentrated in the same street or district. Throughout the cities, but especially where people congregated, street hawkers sold food. Because houses of all but the rich were squalid and cramped, streets and alleys teemed with people at all hours of the day. Before the clock came to govern men's lives, men and women spent their days going and coming with intermittent purpose, as observers and participants in a changing urban scene. Most people traveled on foot; draymen pulled handcarts laden with goods through the streets; the horse-drawn carriages of the wealthy splashed mud or dirt, and refuse, on those who walked. Going out alone was unsafe after nightfall: brigands and thieves might lurk in dark places.

Trade with the rest of the world was mainly in luxuries. To be sure, within Europe there was regional specialization in producing and selling primary goods. England had exported wool, then finished cloth, to the Continent since the late Middle Ages. The Baltic States sold lumber, valued for construction, shipbuilding and fuel. After the seventeenth century, Sweden exported minerals—copper and iron. France sold wine; Spain, oil and sherry. Italy sent alum, used for dyeing textiles. Poland shipped grain westward; the Dutch sold herring and other salt fish. The high cost of overland transport meant that bulk goods traveled on navigable rivers or by sea. From more distant places—the Orient, and colonial America—European traders imported luxuries consumed only by the wealthy: spices, silks, porcelains, sugar, tobacco, and tea.

By the seventeenth century, a small, new middle class, seeking to emulate the nobility's opulent consumption, supplemented the demand, creating a market for luxury goods manufactured in Europe. Chief among these were products used to make and decorate clothing: silk, fine wool cloth, velvets, and lace. Household artifacts such as tapestries, inlaid furniture, porcelains, silver plate, and mechanical clocks and toys became items of pride and status. Because there were few capital instruments and no savings banks to secure a small surplus, buying costly decorations for one's home was a good investment as well. By mid–seventeenth century, for a few men at least, the standard of living was rising. In at least one city in France by the late eighteenth century, social leveling among nobility and upwardly mobile professionals and merchants was creating a common lifestyle involving lavish consumption of artifacts and art, but only within the private domain of home and family. As Molière gently reminds us, lavish public consumption connoted vulgarity.[16]

Yet until the mid–eighteenth century, when industrialization of northern Europe began, most laboring men continued to live, as had their ancestors, in near-destitution. Like pavement dwellers in large cities in modern India who spread their meager possessions on a few square feet of sidewalk, the poor owned next to nothing. Some pots and pans, a chest, a bed, feather pillows and quilt, and a few pieces of clothing comprised their household inventory.[17]

Though aggregate income did rise slowly in early-modern Europe, the increase accrued only to a narrow segment of society composed of merchants, fine artisans, professional men, and government servants, living mainly in northern Europe. Farther south on the Continent, income distribution was still very unequal. The laboring population derived a living as it could; most people worked at farming, an increasing proportion at low-paid wage labor in towns. Some lived on charity. Subsisting at the margin of society, growing numbers became vagrants, moving from town to town whenever local authorities discovered and evicted them.*

---

*Everywhere in Europe where poverty forced peasant populations to leave their homes to forage for subsistence, vagrants' pilferage plagued those more affluent. The homeless

The working poor, who were barely capable of supporting them-selves, bore the burden of supporting the absolutist state. When early-modern governments, seeking to raise revenue by all possible means, imposed a bewildering variety of indirect taxes on goods sold in the market, the poor paid in greater measure than the rich because their entire income was spent for consumption. And then the state de-manded their labor service on road construction and maintenance, military service, and, sometimes, food and housing for troops.

As a political constituency, the poor often have been mute. Since ancient times, popular riots have been exceptional. Yet the potential for popular uprising remained latent, especially if governments were too weak to promise rapid and severe suppression. When most men in society live at the margin, protest may result from seemingly small causes—a small increase in the price of staple food items, or a new tax. For this reason the most despotic of ancient rulers tried to maintain civic order through regular donations of food to the poor.

The rising frequency of food riots, peasant revolts, and other lower-class protests in early-modern Europe attests to a social and political environment that gradually was changing.[19] Though governments, cit-ing their own poverty, did not hesitate to heap new taxes on old in-juries, the groups directly affected were beginning to cry out. The combination of widespread poverty, rising food prices, new taxes on food, and local administration of taxes by agents of tax farmers—whose zeal in collection was often excessive—proved to be politically explosive.

In the short run, most food riots (think of the Polish and Moroccan protests of the 1980s) succeeded by provoking governments to inter-vene in the market to increase supply. The French riots of 1790 had far greater consequences: they triggered a chain of events that profoundly changed the nature of government itself.

THE THEORY AND PRACTICE OF ABSOLUTISM

Political absolutism is synonymous with centralization. No longer peri-patetic feudal monarchs, kings successfully asserted power over pe ripheral elements in society to enhance their control. Through the conflict by which power was recentralized, the weak feudal monarchy became the nation—a cohesive governmental unit whose population

---

poor "raided chicken coops, milked untended cows, stole laundry drying on hedges, snipped off horses' tails. . . . They became smugglers, highwaymen, pickpockets, prosti-tutes."[18]

gradually came to be united in language, custom, and law, and to devote its allegiance to the person of the king. Still, we must be clear that rule was absolute only compared to what had gone before. The term *absolutism* is not to be taken literally. For beneath the new kings stood entrenched local forces; these did not always (or sometimes even often) go along with the royal will. Cromwell, the Protector, for example, could hardly make his writ for collecting taxes good three miles beyond his palace.

The movement to centralize developed momentum in the early sixteenth century, when a series of strong rulers in Spain, France, and England were able to subordinate provincial nobilities' powers. In the Middle Ages, local nobility had claimed the right (through local councils of notables) to execute the central tasks of government—to interpret the law, to allocate traditional taxes among local populations, and to appoint local officials. When kings reclaimed these powers, absolutism had its beginnings.

The justification invoked by these strong kings was not new: the doctrine of divine right of kings was a variant of ancient doctrines of theocratic kingship. Seeking to resolve conflicts between kings and church, as well as to clarify their respective jurisdictions, late-medieval jurists tried to differentiate between a monarch's worldly and religious roles. To retain the king's allegiance as an arm of the church, late-medieval legal theorists resurrected the idea that a king could claim political authority because, of all men in society, he alone had a direct line to God. No longer a personified deity, as ancient god-kings were believed to be, the king's person nevertheless symbolized the unity of church and state. While the church's voice became preeminent in religious matters, the king held supreme temporal power.

In practice, absolutism entailed progressive concentration of authority in the king's name, if not his person, As government grew larger, it took a strong hand to keep the ship of state on even keel. Some weak kings expressed their will through personal agents. Others came to the throne as children, leaving control of the state in the hands of regents. A few lacked the intellect to confront any problem. Still others were lazy, preferring aristocratic pastimes—the banquet, the hunt, the romantic imbroglio, and court rituals that became steadily more elaborate—to the hard work of personal rule.

Without royal competence, the balance of center, against periphery, always unstable when social and governmental institutions are changing rapidly, would tend to slip. Yet, in spite of a transport technology that hampered internal communication, from the late sixteenth century on, absolutist governments built up an apparatus of central control.

France, the largest European state, took the lead in time and in the scale of efforts to centralize. French kings faced greater problems in overriding local autonomy than did rulers of small states; they also spent more money. Although it was the wealthiest state in Europe during the early-modern period, France seldom succeeded in raising sufficient money (for a variety of reasons we will explore in detail). The Dutch Republic, England, and Prussia were more successful in developing methods for managing their rising expenditure. It was not, we hasten to add, that French kings did not raise more money year by year; rather, it was that their spending grew faster than their revenues. If the trappings of court and the spread of bureaucracy were not enough, such an imbalance would suggest to us a collectivist social order.

To some modern observers, the French methods of control appear to be an uneasy, inconsistent combination of local and central administration. The traditional prerogatives of local aristocrats merged with the market methods of earlier eras. Overriding both these influences, yet sometimes interchangeable with them (for at times kings used market techniques to recruit and reward state officials), was the central government bureaucracy. Serving both as umbrella and as counterweight, it barely maintained its claims against dissident, local interests.

The ever changing combination of authorities and roles—local and central, state and private—meant that the same individual could represent both local interests and central government while he feathered his own nest by serving the state. We believe that these arrangements, rather than being inconsistent, reflected the different standards of an age when government and society were in flux. Such apparent dissonance was found in all governments of Europe in the Ancien Régime. Both the plurality of roles played by the same actors and the variety of controls employed by absolutist governments represent a pragmatic effort to create new governing devices consonant with the state's rising scale.

Through a process of diffusion, the structures that French governments developed—the hierarchical pyramid of local administrators (*intendants*) and central government supervisors (*surintendants*), with the king at the apex—became the paradigm for absolutism in less developed states. An active king at the center ruled through competent subordinates who built personal networks of information and control. Louis XIV's astute Finance Minister, Colbert, and the Sun King himself served as role models. In the late seventeenth century, when bureaucratic absolutism had become well established in France, a new breed of kings emulated French methods in order to subordinate their provincial aristocracies. Emissaries of the French government went to Sweden, Prussia, Russia, and Spain to teach kings and councilors how central government should be organized.

Enhancement of state power was the goal, and the absolutist state came actively to intervene in the development process. As capitalist institutions took shape, states derived power from controlling markets; hence there was a continuing series of wars for commercial and territorial dominance. To tap new markets abroad, states shared with private capital the risk and cost of colonial exploration and settlement, by means of a new legal device, the joint-stock company. Joint ventures also underwrote development at home—construction of roads and canals to improve internal communication and trade, land drainage, installation of streetlights, and piped water in large cities.

Absolute monarchs established state industries so governments could profit from the growing market for luxuries. Collectors and museums throughout the world now treasure products that came out of seventeenth- and eighteenth-century state workshops—fine tapestries, porcelains, and richly decorated glass. The elaborate ritual and ostentatious display of the baroque-age courts has left, in addition, a rich artistic legacy: by their patronage, absolute monarchs supported the most creative men of the age—painters, sculptors, poets, musicians, inventors, and scientists.

Luxury expenditure by and for government multiplied during the age of absolutism. The mid-sixteenth-century French King Francis I, for example, spent somewhat more than three million livres for his household in 1542. Under Louis XIV over one hundred years later, court expenditure averaged nearly twenty million livres.[20] The traditional financial policies and ineffective administrative practices inherited from the past were inadequate to sustain even a fraction of the absolutist state's lavish spending for consumption and war.

In retrospect, we see that the central task for early-modern governments was to achieve a regular flow of funds to the fisc. By the seventeenth century, large-scale warfare had become an institutionalized means of enlarging national power. Expenditures of all states in Europe consequently rose sharply to support paid armies and navies that steadily grew more costly. During the Thirty Years' War in the early seventeenth century, for example, between 100,000 and 200,000 men fought under arms. Twenty years later 450,000 to 500,000 men fought on both sides in the War of the Spanish Succession.[21] The Prussian

Army, barely a fighting force of 2,000 men in 1640, had swollen to 200,000 by 1786.[22] English expenditure for wars grew from about £4,000 a year in the late sixteenth century to between £4 million and £9 million a year (estimates vary) at the beginning of the eighteenth.[23] In the early seventeenth century (1607) the French war budget was 4.5 million livres; one hundred years later (1706), 100 million.[24]

Financial policies were calculated to support nations' drive for dominance. Absolutist governments subsidized exports but taxed imports heavily. Because wars were expensive, governments taxed goods produced for internal consumption as well. The heavy hand of state regulation reached everywhere by the early eighteenth century. In the absolutist paradigm, no demand made on the population could be too strenuous to turn the state from its goal.[25]

If implementing new modes of governance is judged to be creative, the seventeenth century, when kings and their councilors were forging centralizing instruments, was European absolutism's dynamic phase. But, unlike earlier eras when life was static, intellectual life, which did not stand still, affected government's and society's institutional structure. By the late eighteenth century, absolutist institutions had become inappropriate for the environment surrounding them.

In the literate eighteenth-century world, government became the prime target of criticism. Those who spoke out against absolutism invoked concepts of individualism developed by John Locke. The new doctrines foreshadowed political participation in the representative state. The economic counterpart of Locke's ideas was the individualism of the French Physiocrats (Quesnay, Cantillon, and Turgot) and of David Hume and Adam Smith, whose free-market theories set forth a promising alternative to state regulation.

Paradoxically, the success outside government of ideas associated with market institutions had created contrary pressures for changes within government. In an age of centralized control the decentralized market-administrative methods inherited from the past—sale of office, patronage, sinecures, contracts for state services—were no longer considered appropriate, because of their high cost. Yet the centralized structures of absolutism were also judged costly.

The significance of the criticism is its focus on cost. Rulers and their councilors well understood the need to cut costs. Starting in the late Middle Ages, management skills and cost consciousness increasingly governed use of privately held assets. Producers aimed to reduce costs while either holding constant or increasing output—what we call efficiency. After the sixteenth century, agricultural handbooks and practical business manuals circulated widely, communicating the latest techniques to responsive readers. At times kings and nobles tried to increase profits from their own holdings by following such advice.

But controlling costs on an estate, however large, or in a business was child's play in comparison to introducing new methods into national government. It was hard enough to conceptualize improved modes of financial management for so vast an organization. Yet improved productivity in the private sector provided evidence that, if anyone cared enough, government too could be more efficient. The hidden assumption that state spending would be held constant while increased efficiency reduced cost was not examined. It was enough to get away from the bad old days.

Where those who held power depended financially on men with a strong vested interest in maintaining old ways, problems of implementation proved to be formidable. Unless government adopted draconian methods, indifference or, worse still, internal sabotage would inhibit all efforts to innovate.

In England, nobles' control of the state's financial apparatus weakened during the seventeenth-century Puritan Revolution; tax farming was abandoned there when the Stuarts were restored to power in 1660. The Hapsburg state and Prussia, each modernizing administration in different ways at different times, maintained royal dominance in modified form. Some poor and undeveloped states—Italy, Spain, Sweden, and Poland—proved impervious to change. And in France, where an alliance of conservative nobles and profit-seeking private financiers perpetuated an antiquated, ineffective financial administration, revolution occurred.

The recentralization that took place at the end of the Middle Ages was converted into absolutism during the two centuries that followed. In the rationale for absolutism, echoes of ancient despotism resound, but the hue and cry over the divine right of kings was but a feeble recapitulation of the overarching powers of theocratic kingship. Aspiration was not matched by achievement during the early-modern era. States grew larger to oppose still larger states. No one knows what might have happened had any one state been able to overcome the others (as did some ancient theocracies at one time or another), thereby converting its problems of international conflict into those of domestic management. Lacking means of redress and bereft of alternatives, the less productive states might have been absorbed by the more productive ones, much as autonomous territories like the duchy of Burgundy merged with France at the beginning of this era.

As things turned out, no international monopoly emerged; there was, instead, an oligopoly of nations, each holding the others in check, competing for economic as well as military advantage. To succeed in international competition, states needed to accumulate economic resources. Involving strong elements of state control of the economy, mercantilist policies represented efforts by absolutist regimes to acquire wealth in a manner consonant with a despotic social order. In their overseas colonies, governments managed to maintain political dominance while extracting resources needed to compete, but within Europe the same states could not exert control beyond their borders. Modeled on the quasi-autonomous organizations administering colonial territories, joint-stock companies were established to develop domestic economies. As these companies revealed their worth in economic competition, centers of internal power became somewhat more pluralistic. Despotism shaded back to collectivism and accommodated growing elements of economic individualism. A working alliance between principles of hierarchy in the state and competition in the economy was in the making; we call such a combination "the establishment." In this alliance, which was ultimately labeled capitalism, individualism at first coexisted with collectivism. Soon enough, however, there would be attempts to separate the two orders by confining each to its respective domain.

THE KING AND HIS MINISTERS: EVOLUTION OF A ROLE

Developing over the course of two centuries in response to the growth environment of the early-modern world, the ministerial role evolved from an unspecialized personal deputy in action to a sophisticated technical specialist, equally capable of conceptualizing and designing new policies and then of implementing them with appropriate political measures.

In Europe, ministerial government and absolutism emerged hand in hand. For advice on the many problems of managing the state, medieval monarchs had turned to the *curia regis* (royal council), a circle of thirty or more clerics and noblemen who were a king's personal retainers and (hopefully) his friends. As it followed the king on his rounds, the council was available if urgent matters called for decision. But when the state grew larger, and its problems more numerous and complicated, so large a council proved too unwieldy for decision and action.

Throughout the sixteenth century as absolutist institutions were taking shape, kings came to rely on a smaller number of advisers. In this transitional interval, kings continued to rely on well-known, trusted associates—courtiers, friends, paramours, and spouses. When the state's problems came to transcend the king's ability to cope, he looked outside his intimate circle—to men with proven ability to convert thought into action. Such new men, who became the king's ministers, were sometimes high-level clerics with administrative experience gained by overseeing the church's hierarchical structure. As time passed, the king more often picked ministers from a growing pool of successful merchants and financiers—self-made men with practical experience in worldly affairs.

From the beginning, kings selected ministers who roughly specialized in foreign affairs, defense, justice, and finance. If, as often happened, the king came to rely more on one minister than on others, it was most likely, at first, to be the foreign-affairs minister; in a world pervaded with diplomatic intrigue, expertise at conciliation was critical to achieving national dominance.

Throughout the seventeenth century, whenever negotiations between foreign ministers broke down, the outcome was armed conflict that steadily increased in scale and expense. Before states had access to the growing market for capital, whichever government ran out of money first had to surrender. Without funds to pay its sailors, and unable to borrow, England's navy met defeat in the Anglo–Dutch War of 1667. Paid standing armies and innovative tactics based on siege, march, and maneuver steadily drove up costs of war, even as such forces permitted continuous involvement in wars. Public resistance to the taxes levied to support its army contributed to France's defeat in the War of the League of Augsburg (1697) and the War of the Spanish Succession (1713). As the seventeenth century gave way to the eighteenth, the finance minister's skill in finding ways and means to maintain the state and its activities gradually elevated his status among ministers.

The late-seventeenth- and early-eighteenth-century finance minister was a designer of institutions and often, too, a sophisticated, innovative technician. If we were to construct a composite from leading finance ministers of the age, it would embody, first of all, the forcefulness of Colbert, who introduced a semblance of balance between income and expenditure, order, and honesty (however temporary) into the chaotic state of late-seventeenth-century French finance. A series of late-seventeenth- and early-eighteenth-century English financial officials conform to an emerging professional prototype with their ability to create and then implement methods for the state to borrow money from the public. Sir George Downing vigorously transmitted administrative technology. As ambassador to the Dutch Republic during the Stuart Restoration, he observed the successful operation of Dutch public banks; subsequently he introduced into England the idea of public debt guaranteed by Parliament. Sidney Godolphin—First Lord of the English Treasury under four monarchs before and after the Glorious Revolution—represents the pragmatic administrator who implemented new programs. He made the Bank of England operational by overseeing the series of experiments that determined how the newly created bank would borrow money from the public. By drawing up annual estimates of expenditures and balancing these against proposals for taxes, William Lowndes, his successor, effectively created the first parliamentary budget.

By contrast to finance ministers who spent their efforts developing centralizing structures, the prototypical late-eighteenth-century finance minister addressed himself to reform. Both Turgot (who served briefly as finance minister for Louis XVI) and William Pitt the Younger (under George III) tried to introduce methods of centralized control that would reduce losses from market administration. Turgot's task was greater of the two: he tried to implement ideas developed during and after the seventeenth-century revolutions in the Netherlands and England. Because his proposed reforms entailed fundamental shifts in tax incidence and in managerial mode, he alienated powerful people around the King who stood to lose from the changes. As a result, Turgot's reforming efforts foundered, and he soon lost his post. In England, Pitt adopted an incrementalist reform strategy. He was willing to let time work to achieve the goal of administrative cost reduction. Instead of sweeping out holders of sinecures in the Treasury, Pitt waited until they died, and did not replace them.

Under absolutism the minister was first and always a personal servant to the king; later, in response to growing pressure from many new interests and constituencies, the government minister came to view his task broadly. Besides serving the person of the king, by late eighteenth century he also served an abstract collectivity, the nation. Though its nominal head, the king was becoming but one man among many. Where the absolute monarch had been forced to conciliate influential rivals for power—nobles in some states, parliamentary factions in others—the eighteenth-century king became a titular ruler whose power derived more from his people's consent than from a divine imperative. And where the king's absolute power was attenuated, the minister's increased.

ENLIGHTENMENT AND REFORM

Ideas generated by European thinkers in the seventeenth and eighteenth centuries are fundamental sources of the organizing principles of representative government. Ways of thinking that emerged during this period—about man's nature, his relationships to his society and economy, and government's role in reconciling individual and collective interests—still shape our thinking about man's relationship to government. A catalogue of the conceptual metaphors found in the speculative writing of that era sounds familiar because the men who designed the United States government—Franklin and Madison, Jefferson and Jay—held opinions shaped by the dominant intellectual currents of their age. Natural rights, natural order, balance, individual rights, general welfare, human improvement achieved through exercise of reason, the separation of public and private interests in government, economic efficiency, administrative rationality—all these ideas, and more, were their lexicon.The basic documents of American government, the Declaration of Independence and the Bill of Rights of its Constitution, embody most of these principles.

Late-eighteenth-century French thinkers gave a name to this period of intellectual history, which they believed to be a century of light following a long interval of darkness and arising from the power of human intelligence: the Enlightenment. By exercising reason, unconstrained by outmoded ideas, man could, without limit, improve his condition on earth. Purposeful men could alter existing modes of organization, which were the product of nature's law (an ordered, beneficent nature), modified by cumulative tradition.

As Enlightenment philosophers saw them, modes of thought and organization surviving from the recent past—the Middle Ages and the Ancien Régime—were as the darkness of barbarism compared to the light shed by reason. Their numerous targets ran the full gamut of practices and institutions, particularly the superstition perpetuated by medieval religion; the deficiencies of authoritarian rule by monarchical absolutism; and constraints against development that resulted from absolutist monarchies' mercantilist economic policies. To continue such policies, these thinkers believed, inhibited man's capacity to improve his condition. Dominant Enlightenment ideas dignified man's present life.

Enlightenment theorists drew optimism from the achievements of seventeenth- and eighteenth-century science. The powerful explanations of Descartes and Newton assured them of the intrinsic orderliness of the universe. If man could discover nature's order by scientific experiment, by analogy he might also experiment to change existing social organization and thereby improve man's condition on earth. Hence social change was both desirable and possible. Man was not intrinsically evil, as the heritage of medieval thought would have men believe; man was good in essence, but had been corrupted by evil institutional structures. Condemning existing institutions for suppressing good and inducing bad behavior embodies elements of an egalitarian social order.

With few exceptions, Enlightenment theorists enunciated the linear conception of progress that led to nineteenth-century social reforms and is still found in modern social-policy proposals. Faith in human perfectibility produced demands for improved universal education that would bring about man's enlightenment by appealing to sensory experience. In an age when public execution for minor crimes provided idle entertainment for the masses, Enlightenment theorists saw the exercise of brutal power over men as corrupt. They pressured governments for changes in criminal procedures and for prison reform. Because they believed that society was responsible for improving the condition of individuals whose lives were debased, some Enlightenment men advocated state relief for the destitute, and abolition of slavery.

As for government, Enlightenment thinkers felt that all the people of a nation would benefit if, by following their advice (as Joseph II, the Hapsburg emperor, listened to Voltaire), absolutist monarchs could become enlightened rulers. Government's effectiveness would be enhanced if the power of reason replaced traditional practice in determining state organization and administration. Although they decried the wastefulness and brutality of market administration, not all had ideas about what would be better. Some who did saw the possibility of simplified tax systems administered for governments by intelligent men for the public's benefit.

The most powerful paradigm of the Enlightenment amalgamated Newtonian concepts of balance with altruistic individualism. It provided theoretic justification for a representative state whose structure, as well as the composition of its legislative body, represented a nation's citizens in balanced proportion. When applied to the economy, the same amalgamation of conceptual elements produced the simple yet potent model of the self-organizing, self-regulating market in equilibrium.

Elements of representative government had existed in Europe since medieval times, when an alliance of local nobility against the center produced a representative government of landed aristocracy. The representative commonwealth John Locke outlined, and then proclaimed the most desirable form of government, served to rationalize the widened political participation that was one outcome of England's two seventeenth-century revolutions. At the time he was writing (immediately after the Glorious Revolution of 1688) Locke's work, like the Federalist papers, was a polemical tract as well as a political theory. In his ideal commonwealth, lawmakers could be selected from all segments of society. By analogy, Locke justified the abrupt changes that had occurred in England's political institutions—changes that expanded suffrage and political representation beyond the nobility to include some men of modest wealth. On the Continent representative government emerged more than a hundred years later.

Unlike Locke's approach, which rationalized changes in government that had already come about, eighteenth-century economic ideas emerged, by a dialectical process, as reaction against the mercantilist policies then being followed by governments. Mercantilism represented a union of collectivism and individualism, or, better still, the absorption of individualism by collectivism. The state, rather than the individual entrepreneur, became initiator and central director of economic activity. Now, central control did have a hoary lineage; it was as old as the ancient empires. Eclectic as it was, mercantilist theory justified state intervention in markets on grounds that a nation, by having more commodities, and by keeping most of them at home, could and would become wealthy.

The mercantilist state actively intervened in markets in many different ways. Some states (France and the Hapsburgs') monopolized production and sale of essential commodities like salt, ores, and fuel. Governments that did not exploit such resources often granted monopolies, in exchange for gifts or loans, to noble court favorites. If these men exploited the grants, they did so ineffectively and at high cost. In France and Prussia, state-owned industries, organized to produce luxury products, siphoned capital and skilled labor from other productive activities. Everywhere in Europe restrictions on imports and exports deprived manufacturers of raw materials, and sellers of markets. Government fiscal policies—direct taxes on landed income, and hundreds of indirect taxes on production and sale of commodities—discouraged private investors and inhibited trade by interposing a heavy-handed tax collector between merchants and landowners and their laborers, and between buyers and sellers.

The self-organizing market model was a common eighteenth-century idea; it emerged as a reaction against mercantilism. As men struggled to conduct their affairs, hampered by their governments' restrictive economic policies, it became obvious to the thoughtful ones, theorists and practitioners alike, that less regulation was desirable. But in the late eighteenth century, state control of the economy was so well entrenched that the now familiar self-organizing, self-regulating market system seemed a desirable but unattainable ideal. Nearly a century passed before eighteenth-century ideas about economic policy were fully implemented. Eventually these ideas provided theoretic rationale for the laissez-faire policies of the minimalist nineteenth-century state.

THE EMERGENCE OF "PUBLIC" GOVERNMENT

As the role of ministers evolved, new normative standards gradually came to govern their actions. Sixteenth- and seventeenth-century ministers saw little if any distinction between their personal obligations to king and state and their private benefit. The merger of state and personal interests, found in all pre-modern governments using market-type structures and incentives to organize and reward personnel, reached its peak in the Ancien Régime. With patronage to dispense, contracts to let, and offices to sell beyond all previous scale, ministers easily could line their pockets while serving the state. Alternatively, when the state's creditors pressed hard for payment and no other source of money was available, these same men had to borrow in their own names, then extend personal funds to king and state.

By the late eighteenth century an abstract conception of "public" government had begun to emerge. In our own time the concept is so basic to our shared understanding of what government does and how it is organized, that we rarely ask what it means. But this unanimity is a recent development. A multifaceted concept that has been modified over time, "public" in its simplest connotation means collective. As the writers of the American Constitution formulated the idea, a government by and for the public derives its power from the consent of the governed—it is made of, and responsive to, no single figure such as a minister or a king, but to an abstraction, the people of a nation.

The public idea derived from multiple sources. When Renaissance intellectuals looked for historical analogies to justify a government with wider authority than the king's alone, they did not hark back to the medieval representative assemblies (the *parlements*), which still existed in some form in most states of Europe. Theorists who criticized absolutism understood that the parlements represented a narrow segment of society, the privileged orders, and even their members objected to kings' increasing authority. With the blurring effect that passage of time seems to have on perception of reality, early-modern political theorists found an idealized image of a government by and for the people in governmental structures of classical Athens and Rome. The power of the people in, and on, government (illusory as it was in

the ancient world) possessed compelling attraction for seventeenth-
and eighteenth-century minds.

As we have seen, ideas about public government also derived from a
body of thought antithetical to those ancient conceptions. A new perception of the individual, and of the nature of social and political
order, derived from the hypotheses of Copernicus and Newton, with
their general theses of order through balance, which suggested that
government, like the universe, could be the same for all men.[26]

Doctrines of individual salvation through work and achievement
also contributed to an emerging distinction between public and
private, deriving from changes in social norms that accompanied
the embrace of Protestantism. Christopher Hill, historian of
seventeenth-century England, characterizes English revolutionary
Protestants as "the industrious sort of people."[27] Protestants did not
live out their lives preparing for sanctification in some future Paradise.
They could achieve a state of grace on earth by doing society's useful
work every day. More than elsewhere in Europe, work replaced leisure
in Protestant societies. As productivity increased, interest rates fell.
Because learning was valued, education spread widely. A free press
emerged. An educated middle class became influential in, and over,
governments. Of course such changes did not take place all at once,
nor were all members of society affected equally. But gradually, as a
consequence of all these developments, innovation occurred in many
aspects of life.

Though no amount of argument can provide conclusive answers to
an open-ended question like the influence of Protestantism upon capitalism, we think it useful to consider the influence of both social movements on the social order we call individualism. The pope of the
Catholic Church presided over a collectivist religious order. From the
pope down, its principles were hierarchic. Had they been followed to
their logical conclusion throughout Europe, something like the Holy
Roman Empire, headed by a single emperor, would have governed
everywhere.

Clearly, this would not do for the emerging European nation-states,
at least not for all of them. At a time of deep religious belief, a doctrine
emphasizing the individual's ability to maintain a direct relationship
with the Almighty, without intermediaries, had its uses for princes who
would be kings, and kings who would retain their independence. And
then within each state there were papal lands and revenues that might
be diverted to secular uses.

From the viewpoint of religious sensibility, the abuses of the church (such as sale of indulgences, a neat parallel to the venal sale of governmental offices), suggested that collectivism had been corrupted by individualism. The private interests of churchmen had assumed priority over the general interest—of believers in salvation. How was this glaring anomaly—selling souls for profit—to be overcome? One way, the first way, was through reform of the Catholic Church. Aside from the difficulties of penetrating the hierarchy (it would have been necessary to start from the top and touch all bases down to the lowest level), in the end collectivism would have had to be reaffirmed.

It was Martin Luther's genius to see another way. His doctrine of justification by faith rather than works (or in addition to works) provided the believer with a direct relationship to God. No authority figure—neither Luther's father, as Erik Erikson argues in *Young Man Luther,* nor the Holy Father—could stand in the way.

What we need to understand, however, is not Luther's road to salvation, but why his doctrines attracted so much support. If we posit a pre-existing disposition to an individualistic culture—a culture that selects doctrines as appropriate rationalizations of its values, beliefs and practices—we may be able to better understand the relationship between Protestantism and capitalism. Instead of seeking to reform collectivism (the Papacy, state economic control), the Protestants and the new capitalists sought to reform individualism by restricting it to the domain they cared most about.

A firm advocate of social hierarchy, an opponent of economic leveling, Luther reserved his individualism for the realm of faith, where it could be purified without attacking (or being attacked by) collectivism. Budding entrepreneurs were content to stick to commerce, trading support of the state and its bureaucracy for enlarged ability to bid and bargain. Instead of joining the collectivist camp, Protestants and capitalists established personal enclaves of individualism. And, for this purpose, a conceptual as well as practical separation of public and private, collectivist and individualist roles, was essential.

These influences all shaped ideas of men who proclaimed, ever more stridently, the idea of government by and for the public. As the nineteenth century began, the stage was set for reforms that, over the next century, would create representative government.

The role separation that the idea of public government embodies is not complete even now. Some state officials still view high office as a hunting license. The diverse reaction around the world to disclosure of bribes paid to high government officers is a crude index of how firmly the public idea has taken root.

By the late eighteenth century a theory of public government had been enunciated; practical implementation had barely begun.

FINANCING GOVERNMENT

THE MARKET FOR CAPITAL

Emergence of a stable public market for state debt is the major institutional achievement of this era in financial history. Accustomed as we are to the smoothly functioning modern market for public debt, it is hard to imagine the less effective arrangements of an earlier age. Only occasionally, when the normal market for capital breaks down, as in the New York City financial crisis of 1975, can we glimpse a modern counterpart of how the market for state debt must have operated under the tempestuous conditions of an earlier era.

When (in mid–eighteenth century) Adam Smith attributed to market institutions the unique capacity to harmonize individual and collective interests as if "by an invisible hand,"[28] a market for capital had existed in Europe for nearly two hundred years. For an institution to serve such purposes, several conditions must be met. If the commodity is capital, there must be borrowers who need money enough to pay for its use, and lenders with surplus funds and a willingness to provide them for a negotiated fee. If capital is to be freely forthcoming, mutual benefits from each transaction ultimately rest on trust—that the lender will deliver what he promises, and that the borrower will meet his obligation to repay debt plus interest at agreed-upon rates when it comes due. When confidence underlies capital transactions, as Smith noted, debt agreements between individuals may serve a social purpose that neither borrower nor lender intended. If both parties are credit-worthy, for example, debt may be sold on the secondary market for a small discount, thereby enlarging the money supply.

Modern cities, states, and highly developed nations routinely borrow money on the open market to finance deficits and to defray expenses before normal revenues come in. Because government credit in developed nations is stable and secure, state debt is a highly attractive investment in its original issue, and then is freely negotiable on the secondary market. Subject to changing market conditions that determine the present market value of a given debt issue, government securities are a nearly liquid commodity, virtually interchangeable with money.

In the mature, modern capital market, national government debt is floated routinely by state treasuries through central banks, their issuing agents. By buying and selling state debt in the open market, central banks not only control the money supply, but also influence interest rates by maintaining the market value of state debt within tolerable limits. Central banking procedures associated with management of state debt have become so routinized that we often take them for granted, but it should be evident by now that they did not always exist in their present form. Modern state banking techniques are the outcome of several centuries of trial, error, and modification of method— the way so much technical innovation has come about.

PRIVATE LOANS

Transcending deeply rooted moral constraints against deriving profit from lending, the earliest experiments built up a market for trading in private capital. Because poverty was so widespread, the Catholic Church censured moneylending well into the seventeenth century and beyond. So, too, did Protestant theologians. In the mid–sixteenth century, Luther praised those who made low-interest loans to small farmers. In Geneva, Calvin tried to maintain low-interest rates to benefit the poor.[29]

By the late sixteenth century in southern Europe, and with increased use in northern Europe by the mid–seventeenth, a variety of new arrangements enabled individuals to lend or borrow money, and then to enlarge the money supply by trading debt instruments on the secondary market. Circulating at a discount until retired or renewed, private loan documents served as fiduciary currency long before states issued paper money. Besides the bill of exchange (which became more common as time passed), traders in capital could deal in promissory notes, bank checks, mortgages or pawn pledges on real or personal property, certificates of specie deposit with silversmiths or goldsmiths, and bills obligatory, the domestic equivalent of the bill of exchange. Because coined money was in short supply throughout the early-modern period, such debt instruments were essential for an expanding commercial economy. The increased money supply supported economic growth, and finance capitalism flourished in Catholic and Protestant states alike.

In the dynamic environment of seventeenth-century Amsterdam, after the Dutch revolt against Spain, a market for discounted debt emerged. By paying a small proportion of the final value of a bill of exchange to bankers, merchants converted future claims into present assets. Private entrepreneurs had no trouble at all raising money on the Amsterdam market. Bills of exchange flowed there for discount from all over Europe, providing capital for the Dutch Republic's extraordinary growth and prosperity during the seventeenth century.

GOVERNMENT BORROWING

While solvent, credit-worthy individuals could borrow money easily, a market for state debt was slow to develop. Under late-medieval and early-modern conceptions of monarchy, the identity of king and state made state finance the king's personal responsibility. Until the concept of a nation as a collective governmental unit of its citizens emerged, states could not command credit. When states needed money, kings and their financial agents had to borrow in their own names from private lenders.

Early in the Renaissance there were still bankers, merchants, and moneylenders with a surplus adequate to lend large sums of money to kings. The center of loan activity gradually shifted north from Italy to southern Germany, when the Fugger and Welser mercantile and banking families began to grant loans to royalty. By the seventeenth century the center of lending activity had shifted to Antwerp and Amsterdam; Flemish and Dutch merchants and financiers provided credit, and often administrative services under contract, to a diverse clientele of European kings.[30]

From the king's point of view, it was more desirable to borrow at home than abroad; his power of governance then would permit him, rather than the bankers, to dictate terms. As economic development led to private capital accumulation, kings gradually did find domestic sources of loans.

When kings borrowed from domestic lenders, royal authority to coerce all too often determined loan conditions. A stable market for state capital was slow to develop, because borrowers and lenders lacked confidence in each other. Because kings could not be prosecuted when they failed to pay up, men with money hesitated to lend to royalty.[31] And kings were notoriously bad debtors. Whether because of monarchical caprice, insufficient revenue to support rapid expansion of spending, the high cost of war, ineffective methods of financial administration, or, as was usually the case, a combination of these causes, kings seldom could meet their obligations.

So kings invoked absolutist powers to stay solvent. Sometimes they repudiated debts through massive state bankruptcies. At other times monarchs arbitrarily lowered interest rates and lengthened time periods of loans, thereby reducing lenders' return. A king who owed large amounts to a single individual might trump up legal charges against him. In the late Middle Ages, Louis IX of France accused his financier, Jacques Coeur, of trying to poison the Queen. After Coeur's imprisonment, torture, and secret trial, the king fined the former minister, confiscated his extensive property, and expelled him from France.[32] In 1627 Francis I of France accused his Finance Minister, merchant-banker Beaune de Semblançay, of malfeasance. Three years before, Semblançay had faced inquest and managed to clear his name, but this time he was not so lucky. Aiming to rid the king of an embarrassing creditor, the court found him guilty as charged; two days later he was hanged.[33] Throughout the early-modern period, French kings employed the *chambre de justice* (as a royal trial on vague charges was called) to obtain forgiveness of their debts.[34]

Because royal promises to pay were worthless all too often, an informal secondary market for state debt emerged in the late Middle Ages, long before a stable primary market for state capital existed. When kings borrowed on the security of forthcoming revenues (by issuing tallies or notes to creditors assigned to specific revenues coming due), lenders tried to recover funds by selling the primitive debt instruments for whatever they could get. Just as in the late Middle Ages the secondary market value of tallies and notes depreciated steadily, the instruments moved from hand to hand at higher discount rates with each successive sale.

Observing the burgeoning market for private capital, kings and their ministers tried to tap into it by inventing new loan devices, capital instruments of short and long term. Similar to the tally in conception, but less awkward to negotiate, was the revenue-anticipation note, in theory a short-term instrument. Kings sold these notes (called *rescription* in France and *censo* or *asiento* in the Hapsburg empire—Austria, southern Italy, and Spain) to any willing buyer. Domestic and foreign bankers, merchants, and noblemen, all eager to obtain royal favors in exchange for the credit they could grant kings, risked their capital by investing. Like tallies, the notes circulated at a large discount that reflected the market's appraisal of their present value.

As long as kings entered the capital market as private individuals, borrowing on the strength of personal promises to pay, their poor credit rating insured that the market would grant loans at high interest rates that reflected risks lenders incurred. This was true even when the king put up his patrimony as security by selling long-term annuities or mortgages secured by revenue anticipated from the royal domain. Like the medieval life-rents on which they were modeled, these annuities provided buyers fixed revenue at an agreed upon interest rate for one or two lifetimes. In a period of secular decline in interest, the fixed rates, when paid, made royal annuities an attractive investment. As kings and their ministers came to understand the high cost of annuities, they defaulted on interest payments, then looked for other ways to borrow.

SHORT- OR LONG-TERM DEBT?

In those distant days the distinction between long- and short-term borrowing (like the vague distinction between private and state office) was seldom firm. Kings often borrowed at short-term, but were unable to pay when the principal came due. In such situations they might postpone redemption by renewing a loan or extending its term. Just as in the New York City debt moratorium of 1975, short-term notes became long-term bonds. Spanish terminology for state paper differentiated between *censos* (short-term bonds) and *juros* (long-term bonds). But to all practical purposes, all the Hapsburg state's borrowing, like that of the other states of Europe, ultimately became *juros* after repeated bankruptcies and postponements.[35]

Some analysts[36] have viewed conversion of short-term into long-term debt as a measure designed with rational foresight in order to stabilize state finances. Long-term loans, contracted for a specified period at a given interest rate, embodied a known, predictable claim on state resources. Short-term notes, often issued under conditions of severe financial duress, merely pushed back the time horizon of emergency, permitting the state to pay its most urgent debts before forthcoming revenue reached the treasury or new taxes were levied. In the parlance of modern financial analysis, long-term borrowing created a *funded debt,* while short-term notes, issued and reissued to pay the state's continuing expenses, were a *floating debt.**

Since the early-modern state entered the market for capital at a competitive disadvantage, its borrowing terms might be improved by con-

---

*Under conditions of severe financial uncertainty, Latin-American governments during the 1960s and 1970s often found themselves unable to pay creditors in full. When pressed, they would pay off obligations a few percent at a time. Hence their notes circulated at a discount. After a time, there arose a huge floating debt of unknown magnitude, which bedeviled weak governments and was abolished when the military took over.[37] More recently, Third World nations unable to service development loans from private banks have simply added interest owed to the loan principal. Because U.S. banks claim outstanding loans as assets, default by any large borrower might threaten a bank's capital structure, conceivably leading to insolvency. In July 1985, Peru's newly elected President threatened default, then limited interest payments on Peru's foreign loans to a percentage of the nation's export earnings, with unpaid interest to be added to the loan principal.

solidating short-term floating debt, issued at various interest rates, into long-term, fixed-rate obligations. Interest payments and redemption charges on long-term debt could then be *funded*—assigned in advance for payment out of receipts from a specified revenue source whose yield could be predicted.

In fact, as modern government bankers know, short-, medium-, and long-term bond issues are necessary tools of state financial management. Short-term debt—modern treasury bills or states' and municipalities' notes—defray ongoing expenses before normal revenues reach government treasuries. Medium- and long-term bonds, issued for terms from one to twenty or thirty years (in effect, one lifetime if we speak in medieval financial language), support deficits of nations, and state and municipal investments in facilities designed to be amortized over long periods of time.

In the early-modern era, state borrowing embodied no such regularity. During wartime, when one financial emergency often followed another in rapid succession, state financial behavior was sometimes, unavoidably, wildly erratic. During normal circumstances (mostly the intermittent intervals between wars) early-modern governments employed familiar, timeworn methods to stabilize state finances.

MARKET ADMINISTRATION PROVIDES CREDIT

What prompted kings to adopt, and then to maintain, contract forms of financial administration was the constant need for short-term credit to bridge the gap between revenue collection and its remission to the treasury (up to four years in the most extreme cases.[38]) Advances tax farmers paid into state treasuries when contracts were renewed were an effective source of short-term credit to states when the market would not grant it. By threatening to revoke a tax-farming contract or to exact harsh terms when it was renewed, kings could command additional short-term credit from contract holders. Thus, in 1638, faced with sudden need for money to finance war with the Scots, Charles I of England summoned Sir Charles Pindar, head of the syndicate of customs farmers, and asked for Pindar's help. The King could count on it; according to a member of the court, "Sir Charles never fails the king when he has the most need."[39] Hoping thereby to secure their investments, contract holders did whatever the King asked. With the administration by favoritism and patronage existing in early-modern governments, emergency financial aid often was a gift to the sovereign, an advance payment for favors the lender hoped would be forthcoming. A direct financial incentive buttressed a lender's willingness to bail out the king. If the loan was repaid (as it often was, if the crown wished to continue borrowing), the lender could count on a profit from the difference between the maximum permissible interest rate paid by the crown and the somewhat lower rate the lender himself paid to borrow the money.[40]

So, too, the practice of selling offices, common in all European states of the Ancien Régime, was effectively a way for governments to borrow at long term without entering the capital market. Though property-in-office lasted longest in France, venality was an adjunct of financial administration in all European states. It disappeared when nations gained access to the capital market, paying interest at rates equivalent to or lower than rates paid by private borrowers.

THE PUBLIC CAPITAL MARKET

The public concept, when applied to the capital market, rests on the notion of national issue and guarantee of state debt. State finance became public finance when a governing body representing the people of a nation, not the king alone, borrowed funds for the state. In its capacity as public representative, the governing body contracted loans. The legislature was legally liable to provide adequate tax revenue to pay interest on the public debt, and to redeem principal when it came due.

The development of a secure, regularized public capital market—one that permitted government to borrow from a wide spectrum of its people—took a long time. In the process by which the public capital market emerged, the conceptual bases of several separate but closely related late-medieval and early-modern financial institutions came together to create a new one: the state central bank, which then became the cornerstone of stable, modern, *public* finance.

In the late-medieval and early-modern periods, contrary to the present, cities had sounder credit ratings than any king's government. The dynamic environment of the northern-Italian city-states in the fifteenth century generated the idea of collective guarantee of municipal debt. Collective guarantee was first used to obtain funds for quasi-banking institutions created to make small loans to destitute citizens. Called *monte de pietà*, such city loan banks obtained operating capital from charitable donations of wealthy individuals.

Although philanthropic purposes of the monte never entirely disappeared, banks gradually assumed new roles. In some places the monte became a source of capital for private investors and government alike. To increase working capital, their governing bodies (selected from among the town's leading citizens) solicited deposits by promising to pay 4 percent interest. Because the councilors' collective liability stood behind bank capital and any outstanding loans, individuals had an incentive to deposit surplus personal funds.

There were eighty-nine monte in cities all over northern Italy by the early sixteenth century. Besides providing consumer loans, the monte assumed conventional private banking functions: they became savings banks, safety deposits, and outlets for capital seeking safe investment. The monte also came to serve as public banks, often acting as paymaster for the city and guarantor of municipal debt.* Some city banks were so adequately capitalized that they could lend money to kings. In the late sixteenth century, Florence's public bank turned a handsome profit when it loaned 300,000 ducats to Philip II of Spain.[41]

Observing investors' willingness to buy city debt, kings hit on the idea of using municipal credit to guarantee personal borrowing. Instead of selling bonds in their own names, kings issued debt underwritten by large municipalities with sound credit. State loans backed by municipal guarantee became common in England in the Tudor period when the Corporation of London was forced to underwrite royal debts.[42] At about the same time, French kings began to borrow against loan guarantees issued by Paris and Lyons.[43] The Hapsburgs made loans on the strength of credit ratings of small Spanish towns, superior to the crown's.[44]

PUBLIC BANKING IN THE DUTCH REPUBLIC

Although the idea of municipal banking did not immediately take root in other European nations, it fell on fertile ground in the affluent Dutch Republic. Early in the seventeenth century Amsterdam established its own municipal bank, modeled on the Bank of Venice.[45] The Amsterdam bank's success caused it to become the model for state banks of other national governments. The municipal fathers did not rely on charity to obtain capital, but funded the Bank of Amsterdam over long term by selling interest-bearing paper backed by municipal guarantee.

In time, Amsterdam's bank became the issuing agency for the Dutch nation's debt. By promising, and then by maintaining, a promise to redeem Dutch debt at par,[46] the bank attracted capital from all over Europe. As capital became freely available, the bank could borrow

---

*Cities could sell their bonds more readily than nations because their wealthiest citizens collectively guaranteed the loans. While these citizens' promises appear to embody the selfless motive for public service of the ancient Greek and Roman liturgies, guarantors no doubt had a material motive as well: they were the principal investors in city loans.

whenever it needed to, and at interest rates that fell steadily throughout the seventeenth century. In the latter part of that century, when the restored Stuart King Charles II of England was paying 10 percent for borrowed money and Louis XIV of France could not borrow for less than 15 percent, the Dutch were issuing debt by offering interest rates of 6.5 percent when the state was at war, and 3.5 percent in peacetime.[47] (The market apparently appraised the risk of war at 3 percent.)

The Dutch Republic's notes and bonds became such popular investments that "the security of men of modest means was inseparable from the security of state or city."[48] By creating and then maintaining investor confidence in the republic's obligations, Amsterdam's town councilors (all hardheaded businessmen), who determined the bank's policies, effectively created the first national public bank.

As an outcome of the bank's policies, a stable public market for state capital emerged. Foreign observers marveled at how the Dutch Republic, through the Amsterdam bank's access to the public capital market, had created a flexible, elastic source of funds for the state. Loans were freely forthcoming in times of war and peace alike. "When they pay off any part of the Principal," observed Sir William Temple, a state official in Restoration England, ". . . [investors] receive it with Tears, not knowing how to dispose of it to interest with such Safety and Ease."[49]

Late-seventeenth-century English merchants and financiers looked across the Channel with envy at their Dutch competitors who could borrow so cheaply. Such English mercantilist writers as Sir Josiah Childe and Thomas Yaranton pointed out that the Amsterdam bank "was of so immense advantage to them" (Childe, 1668),[50] because Dutch debt issues "go in Trade equal with Ready Money, yea better in many parts of the World than Money" (Yaranton, 1677).[51]

Nor was the lesson of Dutch finance lost on English government observers. Sir George Downing, England's ambassador to Amsterdam after the Stuart Restoration, convinced Charles II of England to try a new method of debt funding modeled on the Dutch. It merged the old principle of borrowing to anticipate forthcoming revenues with the notion of collective guarantee, and added a new element—administrative simplification. To finance the Anglo–Dutch War of 1667 the English Treasury issued bonds secured by Parliament's, not the King's, guarantee that interest and redemption charges would be paid from specified tax revenues at a given time. Bonds were numbered and dated in the order of sale, and, because the Treasury promised to redeem the bonds in the same order, the guaranteed debt became readily negotiable. The experiment in systematic debt funding proved to be temporary, but it established the precedent for orderly funding of long-term state debt.

THE BANK OF ENGLAND

When the Hanoverian William III, a Dutchman, was installed as England's co-ruler after its peaceful revolution of 1688, England implemented its version of a public bank. Modeled on the Amsterdam bank, the Bank of England was so successful at underwriting public debt that it soon became the prototype for public banks of other nations. Under direction of a series of astute financial innovators, England's new public bank quickly created investor confidence in government-funded debt, enabling England to borrow large sums at steadily declining interest rates. Writing in *The Spectator* in 1711 (a decade after the bank's establishment) Joseph Addison compared public credit to "a beautiful Virgin seated upon a Throne of Gold" possessed of the powers of a Croesus to "convert whatever she pleas'd into that precious Metal."[52] By the end of the first third of the eighteenth century, according to Samuel Barnard, a mercantile member of Parliament, public credit had become as essential to public and private economic activities and as dependable "as breath in man's nostrils,"[53] sounder even than private credit. The public capital market was firmly established in England. But it was not until after the cataclysmic events of the eighteenth century's last decade that a sound public capital market emerged in the other European states.

THE REVENUES OF NATIONS: ENLARGING THE BASE

Actors in the drama of nation-building understood that stable finance was the foundation of state power. The sixteenth-century political theorist Jean Bodin—like other Renaissance scholars who recalled classical precedents to legitimize their pronouncements—may have known of the Roman consul Cicero's assertion, "The revenues are the sinews of the republic."[54] Bodin enunciated a new version of this ancient organic analogy: "Financial means are the nerves of the state."[55] As with homilies of unknown origin, Bodin's declaration kept turning up. Hear, for example, a sixteenth-century Venetian official's elaborate metaphor: precious metals give government "its pulse, its movement, its mind, soul, and its essence and its very life."[56] Or the pithy aphorism attributed to Colbert: "Money is the vital nerve of war."[57] To

History of Taxation and Expenditure in the Western World

modern ears these two (of many) examples seem to have the hollow ring of truism.

The equivalence of money and stability is understandable when we remember that early-modern governments never had sufficient funds to support royal ambition. To statesmen calculating the power of their nations in this era of development, taxes and the money revenues these brought in were interchangeable indices. The chronic warfare associated with emergence of monarchical absolutism consumed revenues faster than a reluctant population could or would provide. State poverty was so common that it became a subject for satire, "Men screw, and scrape, and snatch and hoard, and pile, and our exchequer's empty all the while," sighs the treasurer in Goethe's *Faust* to his emperor.[58] Yet without money it was impossible to wage war; neither the mercenary armies hired under contract by the Renaissance state nor the paid armies of absolutism would fight for long without wages. "Our mercenaries restive grow, demand their hire with angry cry. Yet, if 'twere all paid up, we know they'd bolt and never say good-bye,'" the ruler's field marshal admits.[59]

While the private sector was becoming affluent, at least at the top, the public sector was not, especially at the top. Societies manifested contrary tendencies: the hierarchical regime spent, and the individualistic commercial regime saved. By the standards of their subjects, especially the lower and middle orders who paid taxes, governments were rich and spendthrift. They spent all they could tax and more. As aspiration outran achievement, rulers became more creative in finding and consuming the fruits of new sources of revenue.

The reasons for the early-modern state's perpetual deficiency of money are systemic, interdependent, and not all related to the taxes it tried to collect. The legacy of ancient and medieval ideas about government's fiscal prerogatives limited the state's power to tax, while the exemption of nobility from taxation, a legacy of feudalism, left only poor peasants and small merchants subject to taxes. Low productivity in real terms insured that the traditional direct tax on land would have small returns, for it is not possible to extract much from a population living at or near subsistence.

Apart from these factors deriving from an absence of economic development, early-modern states lacked technical capacity to determine which sectors to tax as production expanded, and to administer taxes to produce maximum yield. To some observers the hodgepodge of methods early-modern states used to raise revenue was little more than opportunism, spawned by continuous emergency:

—Ancient and medieval techniques persisted in direct taxes on land, the revived feudal wardships of sixteenth-century England, confiscation of land and money, currency debasement, sale of crown land and of offices for revenue.

—Individual and state interests were intermingled in the activities of new organizations, the joint-stock companies, that were intermediate—both in historical development and organizational structure—between medieval, private governments and the public government of the modern world. Joint-stock companies produced profits for private investors and revenue for states.

—To enhance revenue some states held monopolies over valued mineral resources—silver, tin, alum, and lead. Just as less developed nations now lease out mineral rights to private corporations, early-modern states granted exploitation rights to private contractors and then tried, sometimes successfully, to control price and terms of sale to achieve the maximum revenue.

—Indirect taxes gradually became the financial mainstay of early-modern states. Neither joint-stock companies nor mineral rights had the revenue-raising capacity of consumption taxes.

—Pressed by deficits from the Napoleonic Wars, states in the late eighteenth century revived the direct tax on incomes first used in Italian Renaissance communes. Imposed without recent precedent, the income tax was so unpalatable to taxpayers that when the wars were over it was once again abolished—for another thirty years.

Inconsistent as this variety of revenue sources must seem, when judging practices of this era it is important to remember that key institutions for conducting state finance, like the state itself, were still developing. For the first time in history, moreover, so far as we can tell, human intelligence was directed toward understanding the financial system, as a means of improving and redesigning state institutions. Clerics, businessmen, government servants, and academic intellectuals all contributed to a growing body of speculative thought and writing about government finance. As early as the late sixteenth century it was understood, for example, that currency debasement, an ancient device for improving revenue in the short run, was a futile strategy because of the price inflation that would result from it.

By the end of this era of financial history a rudimentary theory of public finance had come into existence. It was fragmentary, often more polemic than theory, and unsystematic. As with modern fiscal theory, theorists disagreed about what the state should do. The theories, however, were formulated precisely because early-modern state finance was so turbulent. The seminal concepts of modern public-finance theory—fiscal equity, economic efficiency, and fiscal productivity—received their first rough formulations in response to ineffective financial policies of governments during this period.

ORDINARY AND EXTRAORDINARY REVENUE

During the sixteenth and early seventeenth centuries the legacy of ancient and medieval ideas about state finance limited kings' abilities to raise revenue. The distinction between a king's *ordinary,* or patrimonial, revenue and *extraordinary* revenue that was obtained from all other sources persisted well into the early-modern era. Long after ordinary revenue had become inadequate to support the state, and supplemental taxes originally granted for short terms had become permanent, the distinction between ordinary and extraordinary revenue made it hard (but not impossible) for kings and their ministers to enlarge the revenue base.

Constrained by tradition from imposing new taxes and handicapped in collecting existing levies by undeveloped financial administrations, early-modern monarchs lived from hand to mouth. In the mid–seventeenth century, just after the Thirty Years' War, for example, Frederick William I, Elector of Brandenburg-Prussia, borrowed fifteen thaler* every two days from the municipal magistrates of Berlin to buy food for himself and his court.[60] Hierarchies must spend large amounts to discharge ceremonial obligations associated with organizational roles. When King Charles II of Spain died, his heirs had to borrow from Madrid merchants to pay for the lengthy and expensive ritual of a reigning monarch's funeral.[61] In those days, even for an ordinary noble family, not a king, appropriate rites entailed hundreds of masses, processions, and alms for the poor, which ate up the equivalent of a bourgeois family's annual income.[62] Strapped for funds and unable to obtain credit, in 1619 James I of England likewise was forced to postpone his Queen's final rites. Anticipating a long wait for their money (if the King ever did pay his bills), London tradesmen charged him double for whatever they delivered.[63]

DIRECT TAXES ON LAND AND ITS PRODUCE

Inadequate as traditional revenues were when demand for money increased, states continued to collect direct taxes on land, the chief revenue source of ancient and medieval governments. The French *taille*

---

*The unit of currency in Prussia at that time; etymological source of the word *dollar.*

réalle; English feudal aids; the tenths and fifteenths levied on English towns; the French *contribution;* and the Spanish crown's *servicios, moneda forera,* and *vecinos pecheros;* and even the assessments, England's land tax after Cromwell—all ultimately derived from land income. Although productivity, and hence land income and land values, went up slowly, land revenues did not increase fast enough because governments' appetite increased with the eating.

Centuries of incremental expansion of direct taxes, moreover, had produced an incoherent patchwork of incidence, exemptions, and rates. Although reliable data for this period are generally lacking, Turgot, when he served as *intendant* of Limoges, tried to estimate variations in rate and incidence of the taille in his province. In several parishes, those who worked the land paid 56.5 percent of their profit to the king; in others, 54 percent and 49 percent; a few favored parishes paid only 20 to 25 percent. Landowners, he found, paid an average of 48 to 50 percent of aggregate land income in taxes. Worse off still were the *métayers,* sharecroppers who cultivated leased holdings and paid, in addition to taxes, a proportion of their produce in rent. These "miserable poor," as Turgot called them, gave up about 80 percent of their earnings to landowners and the state.[64]

After the seventeenth century, when construction of roads and canals improved communication between regions, knowledge of regional inequities aggravated tensions that always had been associated with tax collection. As in the ancient past, the perennial resistance of taxpayers caused absolutist states to employ draconian collection measures, confiscating personal property and land when dues were not paid.* Throughout the seventeenth and eighteenth centuries, resistance to states' fiscal claims periodically erupted in tax revolts. To placate populations and maintain the flow of direct taxes, states sometimes were forced to modulate demands.

Even in regions where productivity was rising, yields of direct taxes were not easily improved because traditional power alignments and institutional arrangements were so deeply embedded. Fearing to alienate landowners whose support was crucial, governments hesitated to

---

*During the French Wars of Religion (late sixteenth century), both Catholics and Protestants—liable to heavy taxes and drafts of food and shelter for armies—complained that the state was taking from them "everything but the clay and rocky soil." Tightening the screw yielded negligible return if poor peasants had already sold their assets to buy food. Commissioned to seize property of tax delinquents, the bailiff of a poor district of southwestern France during the mid–seventeenth century reports on conditions: "In cases of distraint for debt, when I arrive at the houses, all I find are the four walls, stripped of all the movable goods, which the tenants say they have sold or pawned to buy bread."[65]

raise tax rates, while administrative problems involved in updating property assessment registers impeded capture of revenue from rising land values. Pressed by creditors, and unable to borrow, sixteenth- and seventeenth-century Spanish, French, and English monarchs, as a last resort, sold or mortgaged crown land to meet deficits.

CONFISCATION OF PROPERTY

As in ages past, confiscation from any vulnerable group supplemented normal revenue. We do not count forced loans that kings exacted from nobles, municipalities, and merchants as real confiscation unless, as sometimes happened, the state failed to pay interest, declared bankruptcy, or (by the king's whim) failed to pay back loans. The usual victims were, rather, individuals and institutions whose beliefs differed from the majority's at a time when there was very little toleration. Thus, during the Reformation, Protestant states seized property and income from the Catholic Church. When kings like Henry VIII of England, Gustavus Vasa of Sweden, and princes of assorted north-German principalities of the Holy Roman Empire each embraced their own versions of Protestantism, their governments obtained temporary relief from financial pressure by selling off property—land, buildings, and ceremonial objects made from precious metals and jewels—confiscated from the church. After a dispute with the Pope, Henry VIII withdrew from the church, then took over all the monasteries in England to pay for his wars. Again during the Puritan Revolution, Cromwell and his followers appropriated property of loyalists, the deposed Stuart King Charles I, and the Church of England. Sold to any willing buyer at half its appraised market value, confiscated royalist property bought at such a bargain became the nucleus of a few private fortunes,[66] but the proceeds of such sales were barely a pittance for a government forced for the first time to subsist solely on current income.

Apart from the fact that the Reformation abolished clerical exemption from taxes, no financial innovation occurred as a direct result of monarchical conversions.

The Counter-Reformation likewise provided only temporary financial respite for Catholic nations. Neither property taken from expatriate Huguenots after France's sixteenth-century Wars of Religion nor wealth extorted from Jews in the Hapsburg empire during the Inquisition ameliorated the finances of these states. (Kings who supported the pope—the French and the Hapsburgs—continued to derive regular, and sometimes substantial, revenues from taxes on church property, and could demand additional financial support from the church in emergencies.)* Confiscated royal and ecclesiastical property was placed on the auction block after the French Revolution in the revolutionary government's vain attempt to restore the state's solvency.

COLONIAL EXPLORATION AND EXPLOITATION

For a time plunder from abroad supplemented normal revenues. In a circular fashion, the rich spoils exploited from colonial territories simultaneously augmented state revenue and created need for more as competition among nations for control of resources of distant lands led to authorized piracy, and then to wars. Spain's booty from its American colonies amounted to 180 tons of gold and 16,000 tons of silver between 1500 and 1650, the period of maximum confiscation, according to Braudel and Spooner's rough estimates from records kept by the customs agency at Seville. Imported bullion increased the monetary stock of gold in Europe by 5 percent and doubled the stock of silver.[68] Spanish monarchs waited impatiently for arrivals of ships from the New World; the vessels carried bullion to pay off Genoese bankers who had loaned money to restore Spain's depleted treasuries. But the enlarged supply of coinage metal proved to be a temporary blessing, because inflation eroded the value of currencies while expenses were going up. By the seventeenth century, inflation was a fact of economic life in Europe.† No longer the simple outcome of price increases following upon currency devaluations, inflation resulted instead from printing or coining money in excess of revenue received by governments, and of growth of productivity in the society.

DEVALUATION

Though they may have known better, early-modern finance ministers still tried, on occasion, to use the ancient technique of currency devaluation to improve states' financial condition. Gradually the traditional devaluation techniques—calling in coins for adulteration with base metal or reissue in smaller sizes—gave way to formal devaluation of a

---

*At times the church's wealth was confiscated by Catholic states. In 1690, after Louis XIV had sent his silver tableware to be melted down at the mint, he learned "that there is much more silver in the churches than is necessary for the decency of divine services." Accordingly, he directed the Bishop of Paris to make an inventory of ritual objects that could be turned into coin. Soon afterward Louis demanded another cash contribution, a "gift" of twelve million livres, which the clerical hierarchy financed by selling church land.[67]

† An early-seventeenth-century commentator describes the inflation in vivid language:
"Before the voyages to Peru, one could keep much wealth in a little place, but now that gold and silver have been cheapened by abundance, great chests are required to transport what before could be carried wrapped up in a piece of drugget. A man could go a long way with a purse in his sleeve, but now he needs a trunk and a horse."[69]

nation's money of account. The early-modern equivalent of a fixed-parity currency, a nation's money of account was a bookkeeping device, a fictitious measure of worth employed by merchants and bankers for settling debits and credits in trade between nations. Because so much business was transacted with fiduciary instruments—bills of exchange, bank credit notes, and state and municipal bonds and debentures—the impact of devaluation was widespread and immediate. By arbitrarily altering the money of account downward, the state could buy goods abroad until domestic inflation wiped out the advantage. Such a strategy was especially useful when wars ended; demobilized troops then could be paid off in cheap foreign currencies.

As effective financial institutions gradually were invented and adopted, states stopped devaluing currencies when finances were tight. By the late eighteenth century, men in authority understood that the attractiveness of state debt to investors in a public capital market was directly related to a stable currency. Preferring secure credit to the temporary advantage a devaluation might bring, most nations abandoned the technique.

SALE OF OFFICES

Some historians count the ancient practice of selling titles and offices, so common in sixteenth- and seventeenth-century Europe, as among the more opportunistic methods by which early-modern states raised revenues. As a source of income from outside the tax system, sale of offices is pejoratively classified as a financial "expedient." In the institutional context of that era, venality was expedient for all parties to the transaction. Under early-modern conceptions of property-in-office, the market price of an office comprised the lender's investment. The status, fees, and perquisites exacted from an office constituted his return. Venal offices, like long-term annuities, proved to be profitable investments when their market value increased over time.

Lacking adequate revenues, states capitalized on the yearning of the new rich for titles that would, they hoped, bring them social status. For a moderate investment, a gift, or a loan to the state, a mercantile family could acquire a title whose venal origin might in time be forgotten. If an office had a potential for profit, so much the better; then its income might be invested in land that would provide means for legitimate entry into the traditional aristocracy.*

*In an age of large families and huge expenses for conspicuous consumption, a noble family of ancient lineage could bolster a declining fortune by marrying its sons to daugh-

Offices proliferated without any relationship to administrative tasks throughout the sixteenth and seventeenth centuries. Long before Parkinson had enunciated the principle that work expands in direct proportion to the personnel allotted to it, venal bureaucracies appear to have operated in accordance with his model. In 1621 the Castilian treasury was administered by one supervisor and three clerks. Twenty-five years later it employed three supervisors and eleven clerks, fourteen accountants, and forty councilors-at-war.[71] Nine governors general ruled over European and Asiatic Turkey in 1534; forty years later there were twenty, and fifteen years after that forty.[72] Yet proliferation of offices sometimes exceeded all efforts to find work for officeholders. Seeking to derive the maximum revenue from aspirants' wish for profit and prestige, the French crown sold so many offices in the late sixteenth century that it became impossible for buyers to hold their places at once: by agreement the two or more holders of each office served as administrators in alternate years.[73]

Even by the self-serving ethical standards of the age, contemporaries considered returns to venal offices excessive. Thus, in 1619, noting appointment of a hundred new officeholders, the noble Council of Castile complained to the King that these men (who they believed were recruited from inferior social classes) were cheating people.[74] The French nobility earlier had concurred with this view; an ordinance of 1504 declared that "by deceit, fraud, thievery, embezzlement and other evil means" venal tax officials were "enriching themselves from the public substance of the land."[75]

Sale of office contributed significantly to state income at some periods. In the late sixteenth century, and again during the second decade of the seventeenth when French society was torn by its Wars of Religion, from 30 to 40 percent of state revenue derived from venality.[76] By then the French government had learned to capture the inflated value of venal offices by requiring holders to pay an annual tax, levied as one-sixteenth of the office's value.[77] Payment of the *paulette,* as this tax was called, confirmed the holder's property rights in an office and assured his descendants' claim to any future fees and perquisites. When venal offices thus became hereditary, sale of office was no longer only a revenue-raising device. Because money paid for an office legally could

---

ters of merchants. Bringing a large dowry of money or land to the match, a daughter could serve as a rung in the ladder of a mercantile family's upward mobility. The climb took only one generation; if the pair proved fecund and the offspring survived, the grandchildren and all their descendants would be ranked as nobility.[70]

be held by government in perpetuity, sale of office became a primitive form of debt funding.

The private procurement of capital resulting from the sale of titles and offices fitted well with the personal, private character of the early-modern state. Even when states did not formally sell titles, kings liked to maintain secret patronage accounts for rewarding favorites. A gift of money or land, a grant of patent or monopoly, or appointment to a si-necure could serve at once as royal manifestation of esteem and reward for a favored subject's loyalty, an investment to buffer an uncertain fu-ture, and a source of regular income. At some future time when finan-cial stringency threatened, a subject's gratitude for royal largesse might permit the king to collect a deferred return from his generosity. Since the gifts created an implicit obligation to return the favor, recipients might be potential donors or lenders to the crown. Patent and monop-oly holders also paid an annual licensing fee to the state.

THE JOINT-STOCK COMPANIES

For a time, chartering joint-stock companies held the promise of rich rewards. Hoping to profit from a lucrative luxury trade with the New World and the Far East, kings subsidized the voyages of adventurers. Isabella of Castile, for example, paid seven-eighths of the cost of Co-lumbus' first two voyages, reserving the right to the same proportion of whatever profit might result.[78] In exchange for personal investment in the Africa Company, Elizabeth I of England was to claim a third of the profits. Henry IV of France personally negotiated with Dutch mer-chants for formation of the Dutch East India Company. Royal spon-sorship of chartered companies was a common revenue strategy by the late seventeenth century. The remaining capital came from private in-vestors who shared the crown's risk and reward. As European states established entrepôts, and then colonies, in the New World, Africa, and the Far East, the profits of colonialism supplemented early returns from trade in exotic commodities. Besides the trading monopolies granted in their charters, joint-stock companies were legally mandated to exercise the state's role of governance in those distant territories, in-cluding power to collect taxes for support of resident garrisons. The East India Company, the Africa Company, the Company of the South Seas, and the Hudson's Bay Company, to name but a few, enhanced national power through colonial exploration and trade. Tribute and booty confiscated by company agents, revenue from legitimate trade, and proceeds of taxes levied by the companies on colonial territories all contributed to the growing wealth of early-modern nations.

The joint-stock companies whose organizational structure and operational methods (as well as their source of capitalization) incorporated state and private elements were the one new organizational structure created in this transitional era. Their very form exemplifies a merger of individualism and collectivism. Company directors tried to achieve state goals of trade and political expansion while they worked to earn a profit for kings and private investors. (The mixing of state and private resources and power in an organization designed to achieve collective purposes is familiar enough in our age: the regional or national development corporation, for example, or the industrial conglomerate of the corporate state.)

In the administrative culture of the early-modern state, there was hierarchy in form, but not yet in substance, for private influence determined how all government's tasks would be executed. Not only were major and minor officeholders selected by patronage; when men sought to invest funds in the state, private influence determined who the investors would be. With few exceptions, holders of the limited shares in joint-stock companies were men close to the king. And when a public market for capital began to emerge during the seventeenth century, private influence determined who could invest in state debt. The Bank of Amsterdam sold its securities to the same group of wealthy businessmen who guaranteed the bank's loans. The Bank of England's earliest debt offerings, likewise, were not sold on the open market; its directors invited a limited number of financiers (known to be solvent) to buy up the securities. Such insider trading was common in those days; this risk-averting strategy, used in all business, was deemed prudent for successful operation of new state financial institutions.

In spite of the effort involved in procuring revenue, receipts never met state needs. Inflation and rising expenditures combined to keep state finance always in arrears; this, in turn, prompted a continuous search for new revenue sources. The state needed collectible taxes that could increase along with inflation and economic expansion. To tap their most productive economic sectors as trade increased, early-modern governments turned to market taxes. By the late eighteenth century, imposts on consumption provided about two-thirds of state revenues.[79]

MARKET TAXES: CUSTOMS DUTIES

Early-modern state officials did not invent consumption taxes, but they imposed them more intensively than states had ever done before.

270 A History of Taxation and Expenditure in the Western World

Throughout the early-modern period governments raised most of their revenue by taxing domestic and foreign trade. Generalizing from conditions of scarcity, mercantilist writers in the late Middle Ages had developed crude theoretic rationales for fiscal protectionism. Using the same household analogy as Aristotle nearly two millennia earlier, little-known writers advised governments to husband wealth with exchange controls to prevent loss of coinage metal.[80] When Europe's money supply expanded in the sixteenth and seventeenth centuries, this rationale no longer seemed tenable; but instead of fading away, old ideas about fiscal protectionism absorbed new intellectual currents. Protectionism was justified by the emerging norms of balance that permeated seventeenth- and eighteenth-century political and economic thought. Later mercantilists—Serra in Spain, Jean Bodin in France, and Thomas Mun, Sir William Petty, and Misseldon in England—enunciated the pivotal (and enduring) mercantilist concept of "balance of trade."[81]

Whether because of legitimation provided by this doctrine, or through strategies of expediency, early-modern governments adopted an increasing variety of import and export taxes. Not only did port taxes provide revenue; they became instruments of a burgeoning fiscal and economic autarky designed to promote national economic development. If it was harmful for states to lose currency by buying abroad, then why not avoid temptation by producing as much as possible at home? In the Hapsburg state, France, and Prussia, mercantilist doctrines led to establishment of state industries.

Yet, whether states levied duties on foreign trade or promoted domestic industry, policymakers of this era aimed always to enhance state power. (Even today, in Japan, as in less developed nations, protectionism is believed to be a necessary corollary of national economic development.) In fact, as Adam Smith, David Hume, and their nineteenth-century successors pointed out (demonstrating the reversal of ideas that has been so common in science and policymaking), customs duties were poor taxes, because they obstructed the trade between nations that could yield mutual benefits. High import and export taxes provided less revenue than proponents hoped for, and port taxes impeded, instead of promoting, economic development.*

---

*Anyone who has traveled up the Rhine from Rüdesheim to Mainz, stopping at the fortified castles spaced closely along the way, might understand how early-modern protectionism could inhibit development. Consider some mid-seventeenth-century Prussian estimates: The cost of loading and unloading cargo at sixty or more way stations along the Rhine, to determine the taxes to be levied at each one, trebled its price. The value of fifty-four out of each sixty planks floated down the Elbe went to pay customs duties. A

Customs duties failed to achieve their revenue potential because evasion was so widespread. Shippers ran goods illegally at night whenever possible, landing in remote places to bypass collectors. Until the eighteenth century, moreover, most states did not try to collect customs duties, but instead leased out franchises to syndicates of tax farmers. Those states that lacked adequate administrative capacity to collect customs duties were powerless when it came to intercepting smugglers. Sir William Petty, late-seventeenth-century actor in state financial dramas, as well as originator of statistics and probability theory,[83] calculated the scale of his government's loss. After twelve years of state collection under Cromwell, Charles II and his advisers had reinstated customs farming. Soon after the Stuart Restoration, Petty estimated that false customs declarations, and customs farmers' profits, deprived England's treasury of half its indirect-tax revenue.[84]

INTERNAL EXCISE TAXES

Low yields resulting from taxpayer evasion and market administration of customs prompted state officials to search for other things to tax. To supplement receipts from import and export taxes (collected by all governments since ancient times), all European states imposed a proliferating variety of indirect taxes on commodities and services traded in domestic markets from the seventeenth century on. In an age of growing commerce, internal taxes on commodities and services seemed a reasonable option. Wherever barter had been replaced by trading for money, states could count on local market taxes to bring in substantial revenue.

Imposing consumption taxes singly or a few at a time, governments opportunistically zeroed in on whatever people bought. Eventually so many consumer goods were taxed that even a partial list provides a good index of the standard of living. Consumers paid taxes on food (sugar, spices, grains, meat, malt, vinegar) and drink (chocolate, wine, cider, beer, ale, coffee, and tea). From the late Middle Ages, taxes on salt had provided dependable income for some states. Essential for food preservation in an age without refrigeration, it was a household staple for seasoning the bland cereals (oatmeal, polenta, farina, buckwheat, or rice) that constituted the basic diet of peasant populations. Heat, light, and cleanliness cost more because of taxes on coal, candles, and soap. Materials used to manufacture textiles (alum and ammonia)

---

boat trip from Dresden to Hamburg, normally of eight days' duration, took four weeks in a cargo-bearing vessel. Local tolls during the Renaissance could double or triple the price of goods transported on French roads and canals.[82]

were taxed; so, too, were silk and wool fabric, leather, hats, and whale-bone used in corsets. In England, where from the mid–seventeenth century on there was a deliberate attempt to tax luxuries, style-conscious citizens paid taxes on wigs, fashionable for men and women alike. No personal vice (or pleasure) went unnoticed; governments taxed tobacco, playing cards, and dice.[85]

The late sixteenth century saw the start of a boom in magnificent town and country houses built to reflect a family's wealth and social position. The nobility's passion for building was soon copied by the new rich—merchants, financiers, and tax farmers—emulating the aristocracy's opulent lifestyle. England's government reaped some revenue from this ostentatious display by imposing the closest approximation to progressive taxation existing during this era. The state taxed the houses, as well as materials used in construction—tiles, bricks, and window glass (then a luxury product manufactured laboriously by hand). A house already built was subject to a tax on the number of windows and chimneys it contained, assessed progressively, according to size. The French taxed common household artifacts made of pewter, and England taxed not only the silver rich men bought to embellish their homes, but also the carriages, horses, and hackney chairs kept by the wealthy.

MARKET TAXES AND EQUITY

Except for imposts on luxuries, market taxes were highly regressive. In the continental absolutisms especially, the poor—burdened also by direct taxes; in-kind exactions such as road corvée, confiscation of grain and draft animals in wartime; and quartering of troops—contributed far more in proportion to their means than did the rich. But policymakers of the age did not think so. Invoking emerging norms of universality, politicians and mercantilist theorists justified market taxes because, unlike the direct taxes of earlier eras, no man was exempt. In the seventeenth century, Sweden's Premier Oxenstierna expressed the prevalent belief that market taxes were "pleasing to God, hurtful to no man, and not provocative of rebellion."[86] In 1732, during parliamentary debate on extension of the salt tax, England's Prime Minister Sir Robert Walpole argued in its favor:

> Of all the taxes I ever could think of, there is not one [tax] more general nor one less felt than the duty upon salt. . . . Every subject contributes something; if he be a poor man he contributes so small a trifle, it will hardly bear a name; if he be rich, he lives more lux-

uriously, and consequently contributes more; and if he be a man of a great estate, he keeps a number of servants and must therefore contribute a great deal.[87]

In sum, it is a tax "least burdensome to the people, and which makes the tax fall equally upon the subjects in general."[88]

Walpole did not pause to reflect that the incessant search for revenue could hardly stop with those least able to pay.

FOOD RIOTS AND TAX REVOLTS

Throughout Europe ordinary men were becoming restive under the rising fiscal burden, as attested by the increased incidence of civil disorder after mid–seventeenth century. Precipitated by local shortages and price increases, consumer protests reflected a decline of feudal tenure and growth of cities and national markets, with consequent need for money to buy food and pay taxes.[89] Peasants and poor townfolk could not understand this large secular movement; they knew only than when prices of staple foods like bread and beer went up, their diet was threatened. Sometimes, when grasping collectors administered new taxes for tax farmers whose prosperity was blatant, populations erupted. People vented their anger by attacking local merchants, breaking in and looting stocks of food.

Although the riots did not cause state policies to change, unrest did focus thoughtful men's attention on the way market taxes were levied and collected. As the eighteenth century wore on, not all observers agreed with Walpole's contention that "a tax which is the most equal and the most general is the most just, and the least burdensome."[90] Fiscal justice—we call it fiscal equity—came to occupy men's minds.

In our age, conceptions of equity comprise the central core of fiscal theory. Equity of incidence manifested is one measure of the goodness of a tax. In the eighteenth century, fiscal equity meant that, without exception, all men should pay taxes. On this score market taxes did meet the equity criterion. But gradually, as the number of market taxes increased, Enlightenment theorists began to realize that the poor were paying more than their share. Turgot, appealing to Louis XVI for more equal taxation, eloquently poses the rhetorical question:

What is a tax? Is it a burden imposed by force upon the weak? If so, then government would rest upon no other principle than that of might, and the prince would then be regarded as a public enemy.

He goes on to make his case for what is now called "horizontal" equity:

The expenses of government, having for their object the interests
of all, should be borne by every one, and the more a man enjoys
the advantages of society, the more he ought to hold himself hon-
oured in contributing to these expenses.[91]

Governments did not change their tax policies, but new ideas were in
the air. Turgot's friend and colleague David Hume believed it imperative that taxes "be laid on gradually and affect not the necessities of
life," for "exorbitant taxes, like extreme necessity, destroy industry by
producing despair, and even before they reach this pitch, they raise the
wages of the labourer and heighten the price of all commodities."[92]

Perhaps, if market taxes had produced the income that rulers wanted
to sustain spending, Enlightenment theorists might have ignored the
effect on the poor. In the end, it was neither the absolute number of
market taxes nor their perceived insufficiency that caused the cumbersome machinery of state finance to bear down so heavily on those who
could least afford to pay as it ground erratically from one crisis to another. If taxes had all been collected, then sent in promptly to the
treasury, the early-modern state might have managed to remain solvent. But the methods used to administer tax collection and expenditure were inconsistent with such a seemingly simple canon of
administrative effectiveness.

It took several centuries before governments could create structures
to collect all the taxes due, remit all the proceeds to the center, and account for receipts and disbursements. Long before anyone understood
how to implement improvements, there was perceived need for better
ways of administering taxing and spending.

STATE GOVERNANCE FOR PRIVATE PROFIT: MIXED ADMINISTRATIVE SYSTEMS IN THE TRANSITIONAL ERA

The early-modern state's administration, like its taxes, embodied an
eclectic mixture of elements. Administratively autonomous local elites
remaining from medieval modes of governance shared control with a
small but increasing corps of government servants whose authority to
act in the king's name on complex matters sometimes gave them broad
powers. The tasks government lacked capacity to perform—mobilization of armies and administration of indirect taxes—were sold or
leased to private agents, individuals or syndicates of men whose wealth
and reputation for entrepreneurship provided some assurance that the
tasks would be accomplished.

According to some modern observers of the transitional state, coexistence within the same system of these three classes of actors—local elites, government servants, and private contract administrators—engendered an incoherence not matched in governments before or since. Most historians of early-modern state administration, implicitly comparing then current ideas about organization and administrative methods to the conventional wisdom of modern administrative science, critically enumerate the many deficiencies of the early-modern system: its incapacity to control either personnel or expenses; its pervasive corruption; the frequent breakdown of communication between the few levels that existed, or sometimes of the entire system.

To judge a system of one era by norms of a later one, we think, is not useful. Unlike modern governments of highly developed states, early-modern government was organized on market principles; it was largely private enterprise and private administration devoted to the king's personal service. In spite of changes occurring so rapidly, states clung to organizational principles and structures of their ancient and medieval predecessors, and did so long after a changing context had impaired the effectiveness of traditional methods.

Yet gradually new ideas about administration did emerge. In financial administration especially (for that was where costs of market administration were greatest) states gradually adopted innovative managerial modes that at first functioned alongside the old methods and then came to supplant them. If we look at early-modern financial administrations from the perspective of their development—as organizations endeavoring by the limited means then existing to cope with a government, an economy, and a society in the midst of rapid change—their confusion and incongruity may be understood, even appreciated, if not condoned.

The seminal ideas that give coherence and structure to modern state administration developed slowly to shape the views of the avant-garde in the seventeenth century (as well as today). Now familiar canons, these included such fundamental concepts as administrators' loyalty to the state as abstract entity, not merely an individual's personal obligation to the king's person or his role as head of state. Reemerging concurrently, long dormant from its Athenian origins, was the idea that the state is (or should be) an aggregation of a "public"—a collectivity of people for whom, ultimately, all government's work is performed. Both these ideas: (1) the professional administrator serving an administrative abstraction, the state, and (2) the state itself as an active, viable polity deriving powers of governance from its citizens' consent, emerged from the turmoil of seventeenth- and eighteenth-century revolutions.

CENTRALIZATION UNDER ABSOLUTISM

As governments gradually developed power, and then technical capacity, to impose controls on autonomous outlying jurisdictions, the evanescent principle of administrative centralization (quiescent in Europe since Byzantium had dissipated the organizational legacy of the late Roman Empire) became the basic tenet of seventeenth- and eighteenth-century administrative reforms. As is common in major reversals of paradigms, the new centralization was a reaction against the fragmentation of authority (both within and among organizations) that had survived from the decentralized government of the previous era. In the early-modern context, where the outcome of autonomous management was viewed as administrative chaos by those who sought to improve governments' management capacity through centralization, reformers came to believe that states as abstract entities could best serve the public of their citizens if power to decide and then to implement radiated outward from the center.

Consolidation was the watchword. Administration of both revenues and expenditures in early-modern states had been accomplished by earmarking, a decentralized method that made it difficult to maintain effective financial control from the center. To consolidate financial administration, early-modern governments first tried to combine autonomous units, then gradually to weed out unproductive officials who consumed state resources. If the tune sounds familiar, it attests to the tenacity of ideas about government reorganization and of their tendency to recur over and over again in the context of collectivism.

DECENTRALIZATION: EARMARKING AND MARKET ADMINISTRATION

How did early-modern states manage to administer finances by such diverse and decentralized means? As in financial administrations of previous ages, at first there was no separation between resource procurement and resource allocation. Getting and spending money was the job of the same organization, each one authorized to collect specific taxes. Revenue from each tax, in turn, was set aside to pay for specific classes of expenditures.

Whether state agents or private administrators—the venal officeholders and tax farmers—administered collection and disbursement made no difference to the outcome. Earmarking, invented long ago in ancient states whose revenue sources and varieties of expenditure were limited, was a simple way to handle receipts and disbursements. In theory, collectors for each autonomous fund or account had authority to seek out legally mandated revenue. If enough was collected, its clerks might be authorized to pay those with financial claims against the fund. Like the envelope technique for managing household finances, earmarking might work well enough if revenue was ample (it seldom was), if the number and variety of claims were limited (not common), and if the funds' officials did not withdraw much money for personal purposes (virtually unheard of).

The market methods used throughout this transitional era insured that managers of state finance could and would use funds collected with governmental sanction for personal purposes. By negotiating privately to make their resources available to the state, holders of tax franchises or venal offices claimed state authority for personal use in exchange. The incentive for investing funds in the state by buying an office, leasing a tax-farming franchise, or lending money to government against security of a specific revenue coming due was the profit that could be derived from it. Market administrators operated on the same principles as any modern businessman. When an early-modern investor paid a good price for an office or a tax franchise, or risked his capital by lending to government, self-interest assured that he would try to derive the maximum return. Diversion of revenue into private pockets—normal and legal with market administration—drained away much of collected revenue; the remaining resources quite often were not adequate to pay the state's bills.

Nor were state administrators immune from the self-aggrandizing drives that market administration engendered. Before Samuel Pepys took office as an Admiralty clerk, his patron, the Earl of Sandwich, cued him in on prevailing standards of probity in office. As an old Cromwellian, Pepys was one of Restoration England's emerging contingent of public-spirited administrators. Nevertheless, ". . . it was not the salary of any place that did make a man rich," Pepys's patron advised him, "but the opportunities of getting money while he is in the place."[93] Following his mentor's counsel, Pepys resolved "first to serve the king well, and next . . . how to cast to get a penny myself."[94] The diaries record a continuous struggle with his conscience to define the fragile boundary between deserved reward and peculation.

DECENTRALIZATION WAS COSTLY FOR GOVERNMENTS
AND PROFITABLE FOR ADMINISTRATORS

The ancient linkage of market administration with earmarking became steadily more confusing and costly for government as the number of independently administered taxes multiplied. Although quantitative estimates for this period are at best unreliable, some seventeenth-century French figures will illustrate the scale of government's loss. In 1627, soon after Richelieu had become France's chief minister, one of his subordinates estimated that the treasury could anticipate nineteen million livres that year from the taille. Only six million—about one-third—actually materialized. The remainder was consumed by state administrators' depredations plus fees paid to 22,000 local collectors, 160 regional supervisors and 21 supervisors general.[95] (During the 1630s there were three to four thousand officials in Normandy alone.[96]) Again in 1639 Richelieu's *surintendant* of finance predicted forthcoming revenue of 79 million livres. Thirty-two million—40 percent—eventually came in; collection costs ate up the remaining 47 million.[97] When Colbert took office as Louis XIV's finance minister, he too tried to estimate likely productivity of various revenue sources. To convey Colbert's calculations with simplicity, we present them in a table (which, we note again, should be interpreted with caution). But correspondence with earlier fiscal productivity ratios is unmistakable.

TABLE 5[98]

Revenue Source	Estimated Receipts	Actual Receipts	Actual Receipts as Percent of Estimate
	(in millions of livres)		
Taille	57	20	40
Aids (excise)	8	2.5	30
Gabelles	20	4	20
Tax Farms	37	11	30

State officials scored highest: they produced almost 40 percent of revenue anticipated from the taille. Privately administered indirect taxes (the aids) and tax farms yielded less: each brought in under a third of predicted amounts. And gabelles, the market taxes that since the Renaissance had been collected by state officials using clandestine and punitive strategies to trap potential evaders, yielded only a fifth of Colbert's expectations. Compare these low returns to fiscal productivity ratios in modern highly developed states. Administrative cost of the U.S. income tax, for example, presently averages about one-half of one percent of amounts collected.[99] Of course, were the costs of private accountants and tax lawyers figured in, the ratio would be higher.

In addition to such vast leakage from administrators' profits, losses were incurred from delays in remission to state treasuries. If balances remained after claims assigned against each fund were paid, administrators were expected to remit the remainder (*les restes,* the French called it) to the center. States counted on returned balances to defray expenses without an assigned revenue source. Because of a combination of factors, however, the requirement for remission of fund surpluses was impossible to enforce; governments seldom received much money from this source. A conception of government office as private business, together with inept or fraudulent bookkeeping and undeveloped banking institutions, kept earmarked funds in the provinces for long periods of time, beyond the state's claim.

PRIVATE PREROGATIVES OF PUBLIC OFFICE INHIBIT ACCOUNTABILITY

The potentiality for gain inherent in market administration reinforced tendencies, inherent in government, to resist innovation. In those days, when the form of action was as important as what actually was done, it was important not to deviate from precedent. Paradoxically, even as change was occurring so rapidly (and perhaps because of change), repetition of ineffective but traditional practice in financial administration was accorded legitimacy merely by long continuity. Men who held office through purchase or favoritism had an interest in sustaining the built-in conservatism precedent had created. If new management methods induced expansion in the administrative corps, fees and perquisites of officeholders could be reduced by transfer of their business to new men. Improved management techniques—like double-entry bookkeeping—that entailed comprehensive, timely, accurate recordkeeping aroused resistance among state and private administrators. It was not that these techniques were strange or hard to understand; double entry had been used in business since the late Middle Ages. By making it possible to trace diversion of revenue, comprehensive, analytic accounting would reveal how much officeholders siphoned off, and hence could reduce profits from fraudulent fees or excessive returns on investments in office.

Whether an office was acquired by purchase, inheritance, or appointment, ideas about holders' personal prerogatives influenced how state money was handled. Collectors retained state funds in their private custody between receipt of revenue and remission of undisbursed balances to the center. Stored in strongboxes in their homes or (after mid–seventeenth century) deposited with goldsmiths, the balances were readily available for an officeholder's personal use. Substantial, unremitted balances could be invested, loaned for interest, used as security for personal loans, or embezzled. Risk from malfeasance was multiplied because of the large number of autonomous revenue funds.

Governments had required custodians of state money to maintain accounts of receipts, disbursements, and balances from the Renaissance on. Some state financial documents surviving from this period tell us that records were kept. But they all too often represented a triumph of form over substance and lacked useful information for government. Administrators' neglect to maintain the accounts, which were kept by poorly trained clerks without supervision, made it hard for states to limit erosion of revenue. Abstracts from a mid-eighteenth-century English tax commissioner's report "on the unsatisfactory administration of the window tax" provide one insider's view of the problem:[100]

> Mr. Stanforth . . . [is] an entirely negligent officer who does not even answer the letters . . . exhorting him to his duty. . . .
> Barthw. Lynch . . . is so taken up in another employment that he has no leisure to perform any part of the . . . duty; he neither attends at appeals, the signing of the rates, nor the making up or settling the collectors' accounts, which occasions backwardness in . . . payment of duties, the money not being collected till near 2 years after . . . due, in which time many of the inhabitants die or remove; his books are crowded with errors and from his frequent employment of a deputy many inconveniences may arise. . . .
> Tho. Life . . . keeps no books, neither does it appear that he ever made a survey; he is by profession a surgeon. . . .
> In Wales the officers look upon their duty as a sinecure, for the most part they keep no books and those who do have no method.

If a man was determined to make his fortune in office, he could, in addition, doctor the books. A case of embezzlement notable even for this freewheeling era involved the seventeenth-century financier Barthelemy Hervart, who served as controller general (chief accountant) of France soon after the nation's credit had collapsed, as an aftermath of the Fronde, a mid-seventeenth-century tax revolt. Sparing no pains to siphon off money from state coffers, Hervart forged documents to obtain illegal interest payments on money he had advanced to his government, and altered legitimate payment vouchers so he could collect money due others. Under his jurisdiction a situation that had previously derived from ineptitude became formalized as policy. Because clerks were instructed to keep the books so as to obscure individual transactions, treasury accounts became incomprehensible to outsiders. After receipts and payments were entered, clerks burned the primary registers, making it impossible to identify Hervart's diversion of funds.[101]

Apart from establishing procedures and maintaining compliance, difficulties arose because the account books (like modern state papers) were officeholders' property. While a man held office he could shield accounts from scrutiny. If he left office during his lifetime, tax registers went with him; and if he died in office, the records passed on to his heirs. Because accounts were so numerous, and auditing procedures, detailed beyond reason, were cumbersome and slow, years might pass before authorities got around to examining a given account. In the late eighteenth century the English public-accounts commissioner discovered several Admiralty officials "whose accounts have not been prosecuted [audited] for upwards of seventy years,"[102] a normal situation in other states as well.

Custodians of state money could maintain autonomy because transfer of funds to the center still entailed inordinate risk. As the last defenders of usury doctrine, even Protestant states were slow to adopt fiduciary instruments for transferring funds. A late-sixteenth-century French fiscal manual details procedures for shipping money, unchanged from medieval methods. Packed in cannisters containing no more than five hundred livres in coin, balances traveled by mule train or wagon convoy, attended by clerks and armed guards. Delay added cost, therefore convoys should move along as quickly as roads would permit—"in summer ten leagues per day, in winter eight."[103] Crossing national frontiers compounded security problems. In the late seventeenth century, with sea routes between Spain and its armies in the Netherlands blocked, Philip II reluctantly had to ship money overland. To send his troops' wages of 100,000 crowns from Florence to Paris by convoy required seventeen wagons with an escort of two hundred foot soldiers and five companies of cavalry. If need for funds was extreme, trusted couriers would make their way across Europe with gold coins sewed into their clothing. Not all reached their destinations safely. In 1590, for example, robbers near Basle held up six messengers carrying money from Italy to Antwerp and relieved them of fifty thousand crowns.[104]

Until the late eighteenth century when the inland bill (a correspondent banking instrument, the domestic equivalent of the bill of exchange), was invented, governments had to move money in bulk, with all the inconvenience and risk this entailed. Without techniques for book transfer of funds, amounts retained in outlying districts varied directly with distance from the center. In 1786, when the English Treasury's finance commissioners looked into the problem, the minor gentry who served as tax collectors were, by convention, permitted to retain accumulated state funds for six months.[105] In practice very little came in the first year, not much more the second or third. On the average, seven years passed between tax collection and remission of balances to the center.[106] Meanwhile, as an earlier (1780–82) accounts commissioner put it, "the Public have been obliged to pay for want of the Use of their own money . . ."[107]

Long before the late eighteenth century, government money managers understood that losses accrued from market administration. A holder of several venal places (plural officeholding was common) who flagrantly neglected the duties of an office might occasionally be removed.[108] Governments always tried to obtain the maximum return possible in negotiations with tax farmers. Sixteenth-century French officials, for example, were instructed to auction off tax farms at night so that more people could attend. To prevent collusion that would keep bids low, an auctioneer was not to take early offers, but to prolong the bidding until a candle on his table burned out.[109]

FINANCIAL CONTROL THROUGH THREAT AND EXAMPLE

As long as governments depended on cash advances from market administrators to finance deficit spending, little could be done to reduce revenue lost through market administration. Periodically, however, kings and their ministers zeroed in on the worst offenders. Brought before a royal tribunal, accused of financial crimes against the state, liable administrators were lucky to escape with their lives. During the sixteenth and seventeenth centuries several French *surintendants* of finance were tried and imprisoned; one was hanged, another served eighteen years in prison before he died. By holding key figures in state finance up before their peers as examples of what might happen if a man claimed too much of the state's money, kings and their ministers instilled fear in the others and thus aimed to control erosion of funds. Lacking alternative means of control, states practiced intimidation; the "vague threat of terrible punishment" (Bosher's words) might induce the accused to pay fines levied against him, and perhaps even temporarily to curtail diversion of funds.[110]

When governments faced problems of any kind, private administrators of state finance provided good scapegoats to divert people's attention; throughout the early-modern era, men who supported the state by conducting its financial administration for profit aroused wide popular hostility. It was not only because tax farmers' agents performed the odious task of separating people from their money. In a traditional society, where wealth and social position derived largely from hereditary ownership of land, private administrators' rapid accumulation of property, and their ostentatious display, so men believed, was a visible manifestation of ill-gotten gains.[111] Since their services were necessary to keep the state functioning, market administrators did earn money for the effort and risk they incurred, but seldom social acceptance. Confronted with more than normal business problems, one venal officeholder was led to wonder if the return was worth the trouble. During the Dutch war against England (1667), after sailors' wives had sat in at the Admiralty for several days because their husbands had not been paid in months, Pepys's superior told him that "he wishes he had sold his place at some good rate to somebody or other at the beginning of the war, and that he would do it now but nobody will deale with him for it."[112] From the profit of an office, then, must be subtracted the cost in hostility, as well as any financial loss. Insofar as private collectors deflected anger they provided nonfinancial services for kings, too.

Absolutism brought out both the best and the worst of possible budgetary worlds. Half hierarchical, half market, it sometimes generated the least desirable budgetary outcomes implicit in each political culture. The bizarre amalgam of practices so characteristic of the age combined the rigidity of hierarchy with the propensity of markets to foster avarice among individuals. Proponents of hierarchy did not know how to manage a large bureaucracy with efficiency, while individualists did their best to take advantage of such opportunities for personal gain as came their way.

Yet, incoherent as it was, the interplay between the two regimes did eventually lead to innovation. The adverse consequences for the polity of mixed state/private financial administration were so evident to everyone touched by the system that they cried out for reform. Under appropriate conditions, when incompatibility between the two orders had generated high levels of stress, new men who held new ideas could move into the interstices. Enhancing hierarchy, yet creating a context favorable for spread of market ideas, reform in financial administration changed the distribution of power among social orders. Whether the nobility turned to business when forced to support government by paying taxes commensurate with their wealth, or members of the middle class who became government servants adopted aristocratic ways, innovation did engender social mobility. With its confusion of identities and growing substitution of roles, reform in financial administration may well have resembled a Restoration comedy at first—masks and all.

EARLY GOVERNMENT BUDGETS

States endeavored to cut administrative costs by the only means known to them. From the mid–seventeenth century on (although the northern-Italian communes began sooner), governments tried to manage their finances with an early version of budgeting. Budgeting involves allocating funds ahead of time by relating expenditure to income. Early-modern budgeting dealt mainly with the revenue side of this equation, for the earmarking technique predetermined allocation. When early-modern state officials talked of budgets they often meant proposals for taxes (as the term today connotes in England).

Seventeenth- and eighteenth-century state officials also referred to procedures for maintaining and reviewing government financial registers as budgeting. Records kept by custodians of autonomous funds provided a crude measure of revenue likely to be forthcoming from each source, no doubt with considerable error and delay. Revenue received in the most recent period for which audited records existed provided a base for predicting likely revenue in the current period. Never an exact procedure, even now with sophisticated forecasting techniques, the prediction by long-delayed hindsight of the early-modern era provided only a rough measure of forthcoming revenue. By comparing prior-period revenue against expenses assigned against it, state financial managers could derive makeshift estimates of whether a fund had been in surplus or deficit. Earlier deficits in specific funds, further depleted by current conditions (like wars) when expenses would be rising, signaled need for higher tax rates or new taxes.[113]

Governments went through such an exercise in forecasting and balancing for each of many autonomous accounts. As in modern government budgeting, the process of estimating receipts and spending in those days was incremental and serial. Estimates were based on small departures from the immediate past, and repeatedly connected. But there the relationship to modern budgeting stops. Early-modern government looked only at the parts of a budget. Without comprehensive, analytic accounts, it lacked useful information to consider the whole. Allocation within a total was not part of the expenditure process; information on aggregate receipts and expenses was unavailable. What is true today for today's expenditure entitlements was true yesterday for revenue accounts: the decentralized management that resulted from large numbers of autonomous accounts made it hard to know what had happened in each, let alone all together.

The process of relating anticipated resources to proposed expenditures derives, no doubt, from profit-and-loss accounting, then common in business and agricultural management. Shot through with errors and omissions as it was, early-modern governments' techniques for predicting income and balancing it against expenses nevertheless show that some men in government had started to think about state finance in modern ways. Consider, for example, the small Prussian state's procedures. By the late seventeenth century its methods of relating expected state income to likely expenditures began to embody elements of predictive budgeting. Each year the growing number of state agencies—traditional local bodies and new, specialized central agencies of a mercantilist state—prepared secret estimates of anticipated revenue. (Our sources do not say how Prussian officials arrived at the estimates, but we know that as early as the late sixteenth century Neapolitan fiscal officials derived revenue estimates by averaging receipts from any given tax for the three previous years.)[114] Prussian revenue estimates were checked by provincial officials and then submitted to the central government's financial agency. There ministers from each province verified local figures, then sent the estimates up to the king. Once the king had approved the estimates, ministers and their aides added up predicted tax receipts from all provinces to obtain an estimate of total central-government revenue. The entire task was completed before the new fiscal year started.

In this manner, the king and his ministers could determine whether more revenue was needed. The king's autocratic power would have permitted him unilaterally to levy new taxes to bring receipts and expense into balance, but, again, our sources do not say how such a gap was bridged. No doubt the king had to consider the feasibility of collection. We know, however, that Frederick William I tried repeatedly to attain a balanced budget. A new central accounting agency (established early in the eighteenth century, at the beginning of his reign) audited provincial agencies. Punitive enforcement compelled adherence to the budget; if an agency exceeded its estimated spending, officials paid fines. If the discrepancy was large, provincial administrators might even go to prison.[115]

Prussia's experiments in financial systemization, conducted at small scale, in secret, and under duress, did not last; nor did these experiments lead to later institutional development. For the source of modern financial procedures we must look at governments whose existing order was changed abruptly by early political revolution. Legislatures seized part of absolutist monarchs' power of fiscal decision-making in the Dutch Republic and in England after their seventeenth-century revolutions. Before administrators' proposals for new taxes could be implemented, these proposals were submitted to diverse constituencies within legislatures; whatever consensus they arrived at became law.

Documentation of a shift in decision-making power over financial matters from kings to legislatures is fullest in England. Hostility to Charles I's high-handed ways of raising money contributed substantially to the dissent that exploded into England's Puritan Revolution. Early in the Interregnum—faced with the immediate task of devising structures to support and govern a divided nation (at war both within itself and against its neighbors), Puritans, and those royalists in Parliament who voted with Cromwell, enacted new taxes on property and internal trade. When royal government was restored in 1660, Parliament continued to levy these new taxes, for the crown's traditional feudal dues were abolished as a condition of Charles II's restoration. In exchange for giving up claim to feudal privilege, Parliament agreed to grant Charles a sum of money (£1.2 million each year, secured by revenue from customs and excise taxes) for the duration of his life.[116]

Because kings remained personally responsible for all state expenditure, civil and military, and because the sum was not large (during his eleven years Cromwell had spent about £2 million annually),[117] Parliament aimed to control the young King's actions by limiting the amount he could spend. Evading Parliament's intentions, Charles II found ways to finance his wars and extravagance by borrowing. His successor, James II, presented a far greater threat to state stability: James's frugality at court stretched his annual parliamentary grant far enough to sustain a large standing army. So, it would seem, a king's behavior had a lot to do with whether his reign was marked by affluence or penury.

Having learned the danger of unrestricted grants of funds from James's bellicose behavior, Parliament acted to further limit the executive. When Parliament invited William III to take over English government in 1688, it granted him only enough money to maintain the civil establishment for a year at a time. A king who wished to wage war was forced to come back to the legislature to make his case for more money.

In fact, throughout the eighteenth century Parliament seldom denied a king's request for funds. By requiring the king's ministers to come before it to justify supplemental appropriations, however, the legislature maintained the principle of independence and guarded its autonomy against resurgence of royal absolutism.

PUBLIC GOVERNMENT, PUBLIC FINANCE, AND PUBLIC ADMINISTRATION

The most important idea related to the state and its finances formulated during this turbulent era was that of public government. Revolutionary rhetoric proclaimed a conception of the state as abstract entity, made of and responsible to a public collectivity. Men who administered such a state derived power from the nation as a whole, and hence owed it a different kind of service than if they were merely attending the king's personal interests, or serving their own. The sometimes simple, sometimes florid expositions of "public" enunciated by actors in seventeenth- and eighteenth-century governments reflected emerging theories of constitutional government. Such statements both supported and documented accumulating experience in legislative decision-making.

Toward the end of this era a number of other ideas, institutions, and technology related to state finance came together to create a climate favorable for administrative reform. Normative principles derived from Enlightenment theories—that order could be achieved through exercise of human reason—led men to consider, and some governments to adopt, new methods of financial management. Some governments could borrow directly from their people through central banks after the seventeenth century. Such governments no longer needed private administrators to serve as financial intermediaries in the capital market. When central banks operated to fund public debt, governments could give up tax farming.

To maintain a dependable flow of funds from the public, states acted to create and maintain confidence that loans would be repaid. Abortive speculative funding experiments led men to understand that it was not enough for a legislature to guarantee state debt if inadequate revenue received at uncertain times stood behind government borrowing.

Early British successes (and one spectacular failure not related to the government's management of the public debt) yielded normative and behavioral models for centralized debt management in other states. After the debacle of the South Sea Bubble* England administered its

---

*Conservative debt management by the Bank of England's early directors—issuance of long-term (forty-year) annuities when interest rates were declining—led an opposition faction to propose an alternative method of debt funding. In 1711 Robert Harley, newly appointed Tory Chancellor of the Exchequer, persuaded Queen Anne to charter a joint-stock company, the Company of the South Seas. As was customary with such joint-stock charters, the Queen granted the company a trading monopoly with South America and the Pacific Islands.

While the South Sea Company's manifest function was, in fact, trade, Harley and his supporters hoped to reduce interest costs of the public debt by consolidating the large volume of floating debt (about £9 billion) through a refunding operation managed by the company. The South Sea Company initially offered to exchange the current, outstanding debt (Bank of England notes) on favorable terms for shares of South Sea Company stock.

debt by earmarking—tying individual bond issues (as well as classes of expenditure) to receipts from specific taxes.

Chartered in 1693, the Bank of England spent nearly the entire first century of its existence funding war loans. By late eighteenth century, England's public debt had grown to enormous proportions by earlier standards—from £660,000 in 1688 to £246,000,000 in 1784.[118] Decade by decade between 1700 and 1800, combined spending for the military and debt service never fell below 82 percent of total spending. Both average and median expenditure for the army, the navy, and debt service were 88 to 89 percent of total spending throughout the century (see Table 6). Though interest rates fell steadily, debt service alone consumed from a quarter to half of each year's tax receipts throughout the eighteenth century. With continuous need for heavy borrowing, the Treasury could not wait years on end for autonomous administrators to send money in. It had to meet interest and amortization obligations on time to assure future credit.

PROFESSIONAL ADMINISTRATION REPLACES MARKET ADMINISTRATION

New technical-professional behavior norms for public officeholders had emerged during the Puritan Revolution. While many of the men Cromwell appointed to government offices still sought personal gain from their posts, technical ability (in addition to demonstrated godliness) also determined selection. Recommendation letters written to

---

(As with all joint-stock companies chartered by early-modern governments—capitalized with assets contributed by monarchs in their public capacity and supplemental funds from private investors—a distinction between public and private activities of such companies was not easily drawn.)

The South Sea Company's early trading ventures yielded regular annual dividends to stockholders who had exchanged treasury notes for stock, enhancing public confidence. By 1718 its directors (no longer Harley's faction but a new one) held such optimistic expectations that they proposed to underwrite England's entire outstanding public debt (this time the staggering sum of £51.3 billion). Again, they proposed to raise money by exchanging treasury annuities on favorable terms for company stock. Once more the company's debt-consolidation measure won out in policy competition over the Bank of England's conservative proposal for funding through sale of long-term Treasury annuities. Early in 1720, when South Sea stock was trading at £128.5 per share, more than half the holders of long-term Treasury annuities eagerly exchanged these assets for the South Sea shares.

Thus was initiated the world's first great speculative boom—and bust. No one with a surplus, however modest, could resist the frenzy to buy. By June 1720, South Sea shares were trading at £890 each; by July at over £1,000. But—except for a few company and Treasury officials who profited from insider trading, considered scandalous even for this freewheeling era—traders lost out when the bottom fell out of the market a few months later. By November 1720, South Sea stock traded at £135. (England was not the only nation stricken with a speculative fever; the affliction flourished in France and in other nations of Europe at the same time—with equally disastrous outcomes for investors.)

TABLE 6

AMOUNTS AND PURPOSES OF ENGLAND'S SPENDING DURING THE EIGHTEENTH CENTURY[119]

(given in millions of pounds, and as percentages of total spending)

Year	Civil Government £	%	Total Debt Charges £	%	Military Spending £	%	Debt Plus Military £	%	Total £	%
1700–09	0.7	12	1.3	21	4.0	66	5.3	87	6.1	100
1710–19	0.8	10	2.7	35	4.2	55	6.9	90	7.7	100
1720–29	1.0	17	2.8	47	2.1	36	4.9	83	5.9	100
1730–39	0.9	17	2.1	39	2.3	43	4.4	82	5.4	100
1740–49	0.9	9	2.4	25	6.2	65	8.6	90	9.5	100
1750–59	1.1	12	2.9	33	4.9	55	7.8	88	8.9	100
1760–69	1.1	8	4.5	33	8.1	59	12.6	92	13.7	100
1770–79	1.2	9	4.8	38	6.3	49	11.1	87	12.8	100
1780–89	1.4	7	8.4	39	11.5	53	19.9	92	21.6	100
1790–99	1.9	6	11.6	35	19.4	58	31.0	93	33.4	100

Cromwell for office-seekers stressed not only loyalty and reliability but also skill in writing, accounting, foreign languages, and management of men. During the eleven years of the Protectorate, some government officeholders were paid salaries; in some cases fees for services were reduced or abolished.[120]

Former Cromwellians somehow found their way into Charles II's Restoration government. Compared to the unqualified sinecurists who had managed state finance before the revolution, the king wanted "new blood . . . 'rougher hands,' 'ill natured men not to be moved with civilities,' "[121] but competent in financial administration.

To manage state finance Charles recruited (among others) George Downing, who had accumulated impressive professional credentials. Having served first as "scoutmaster-general" in Cromwell's field army, Downing went on to become teller at the Exchequer. Simultaneously with his Exchequer clerkship, Downing represented England as envoy to the United Provinces (Netherlands), leaving management at the Exchequer in young Pepys's hands for a time. Helped by capable assistants, Downing laid the groundwork for a funded debt by establishing systematic management methods at the newly created (1667) Treasury Commission. Although Downing's achievements soon dissipated, his record-keeping procedures provided an organizational format for the Bank of England to follow when it took over the state's debt funding. After 1688 the Treasury and the Bank of England installed double-entry bookkeeping.

By early eighteenth century, capacity for businesslike management became a hallmark of a breed of technically competent, professionalized managers who were sensitive to political issues. Besides such men as Lowndes, Godolphin, and Harley (all were Treasury managers), the Bank of England called in distinguished consultants. Locke, Newton, and Hobbes directed their formidable intelligence to state financial problems. Although market administrative methods dominated eighteenth-century English government, a strain of the organizational rationality introduced by Downing persisted as well.*

*After the state gave up tax farming, it had to recruit and train revenue officials. Writing in 1698, Charles Davenant, early economic theorist and Bank of England clerk, speculated about organizational problems and how state-run customs collection should be managed:

". . . the Men must be well Chosen, Young and Active. . . . They must be under an industrious, regular, skillful and steady management.

"In new Impositions, it will be difficult at first to put the collection into any tolerable Order and Method. The Officers will be Raw and Ignorant; and the People will have learned how to avoid Payment, long before the Collectors shall come to understand how

When legislatures played a part in determining financial policies, alliances among interest groups affected decision and outcome. At sporadic intervals, legislative commissions established by dissident factions looked into financial mismanagement. The inquiries of 1702, 1713, and 1741 (held more as political vendetta than for improving management) attested that finance was becoming politicized. Pointing at diversion of revenue and alleging corruption, backbenchers in Parliament attacked the party in power.

Concern for the high cost—both of debt service and of the Treasury's fragmented, decentralized revenue administration—produced growing pressure for reform in financial administration from midcentury on. Academics (Adam Smith, a former customs clerk; David Hume; James Postelthwaite, author of a *History of the Public Revenue*, become Treasury clerk) pointed the direction; public figures followed. Critical of the rising debt burden's cost to the nation, financial interests in Parliament pressed for changes that would limit need for new taxes by cutting administrative expense. Thus a gentleman from Norfolk in 1780 wrote to his friend in London:

> Reports are gone about of the immense profusion of the public Treasury; of the enormous emoluments of some places; of large sums not accounted for; of a vast expense in favouring contractors ... and providing for a useless set of men, in order to keep up an extravagant parliamentary influence under the direction of the crown.[123]

Corruption was the perceived cost. Edmund Burke, judging his nation's amateur and often self-serving financial administration, saw it as a fountain of

> corrupt influence ... the perennial spring of all prodigality, and ... disorder; [it] loads us more than millions of debt; [it] takes ... vigor from our arms, wisdom from our councils, and every shadow of authority and credit from the most venerable parts of our Constitution.[124]

Toward the end of the century even conservative country interests—seeing France's inability to abandon private methods of financial administration—favored some change. Centralized control of receipt and

---

they may reach the Duty. Tis not easy at first, to plant the under Officers in convenient stations and Districts. And the Principal Persons, whom the King instructs to Manage and Govern such a Branch, will themselves, in the beginning be puzzled ... whatever Skill and Dexterity they may pretend to."[122]

disbursement by a Treasury staffed with men trained in administration and skilled in finance, so reformers argued, would permit the state to retain more of its revenue. If costs were reduced, then taxes could be, too. That increased revenues would also mean increased spending, that there might be more efficient methods of lavish public spending, was not even considered; kings and corruption were the enemy.

REFORM AND REFORMERS

Changing perceptions of appropriate relationships between government, economy, and society generated widespread disaffection with government toward the end of the Ancien Régime. With the old ways in question, Enlightenment ideas provided a standard both for assessing the status quo and for modifying political and administrative structures to mitigate popular unrest. How, then, did ideas lead to action? How did Enlightenment ideas influence eighteenth-century reformers' perception of problems within government, and efforts to resolve such problems?

For these questions the French economist-administrator Turgot is our prototypical reformer.* His understanding of government and the economy, and his relationship to both, were shaped in the mid-eighteenth-century Paris salons, where intellectuals met to formulate and then to chew over ideas about how intelligence could be made to affect government. France was their prime example of how entrenched privilege, combined with administrative anachronisms, could sap a state's strength.

Turgot and his economist friends had pinpointed one root of France's difficulties—its chaotic fiscal system. After a period of peace, a series of costly wars once again had exacerbated the nation's perpetual problem of financing itself. Chronic deficits might be prevented, the économistes thought, by reforms that would tax wealth at its origin

*Turgot was not the first intellectual to put his ideas about public policy to test. Although the world was simpler then, creativity manifested in great works of science and philosophy could be turned to public-policy formulation (just as scientists advise modern governments). Soon after the English revolution of 1688, Locke, Hume, and Newton each gave the new King, William III, advice about the effect on the state's financial security of a proposed devaluation of currency. Adam Smith gained his understanding of the constraints market taxes exercise on the economy during the time he served as customs clerk. When the Scotsman John Law could find no receptive ears at home, he took his innovative theories of public banking to France, where they were implemented. In the late eighteenth century Joseph Priestley (English clergyman and chemist) and Jean Vauban (a French engineer) also gave financial advice to their governments. When Turgot left the Paris salons to enter government service, he followed a path trodden by all these illustrious men.

in the land so that owners, not poor tenant cultivators, would bear the burden. They believed tax yields would increase if the high cost of private administration of indirect taxes could be reduced.

Turgot's first role in government was to administer (as *intendant*) a distant, undeveloped province. There he put theory into practice by implementing changes in administrative methods. Gradually he reduced local nobles' power over local revenues and enhanced the state's. Delegating state agents to execute the tasks, Turgot reappraised property recorded in tax registers to improve fixed tax yields. Then, when men were asked to pay more than before, Turgot adjudicated disputes over amount and incidence to make the taxes more equitable. At a time when noble landowners were jealously protecting their traditional exemption from most direct taxes, these achievements alone were significant. Further, armed with an economist's understanding of comparative costs, Turgot conciliated the dissident peasant population by commuting the onerous road corvée into an optional tax. If a peasant's obligation for corvée came at harvest time, or if he preferred not to serve, he could pay a small fee, which the state allocated to remunerate other laborers. Because paid labor worked more effectively than conscripts under duress, France's road system improved.

Turgot's understanding of Enlightenment principles of economic and administrative rationality determined his policies as Louis XVI's finance minister. When Turgot assumed office France had deficits so huge that the state was near bankruptcy; he proposed to restore confidence in state credit (and hoped thus to forestall its collapse) by stringent economizing.

Turgot's situation interests us because of his financial strategies and also because it bears so many resemblances to the 1975 financial crisis in New York City. France in the eighteenth century—like New York City during the late 1960s and early 1970s—had been borrowing for years to finance ever growing deficits. When revenues were short, the standard procedure of previous finance ministers had been to borrow from some earmarked accounts (*caisses*) to pay obligations of others. Like New York, France deferred payment of interest on short-term paper, converted short-term notes into long-term bonds, and then postponed repayment of some long-term obligations.

When Turgot took office, France carried a debt burden of 235 million livres and faced an annual deficit of 37 million.[125] Outlining his policies in a letter to the King, Turgot wrote that henceforth the nation must tighten its belt. Under his ministry there would be "no bankruptcy, no increase of [taxes], no borrowing."[126] Turgot's proposed economies struck at the root of the French financial system's difficulties: he hoped to increase revenues by reducing the nobility's fiscal privileges, and to reduce costs by abandoning private administration of indirect taxes. Further, Turgot intended to control spending in all government departments by a process of administrative rationalization, something that had not been possible previously in any major European state. Of all the European nations in the eighteenth century, only the small, autocratically governed Prussian state briefly had managed to achieve financial accountability. "If these reforms fail," Turgot wrote prophetically to the King, "the first gunshot will drive the state to bankruptcy."[127]

As with recent efforts to cut costs by reducing the number of people deriving income from government (whether in New York City or elsewhere), Turgot's proposals were blocked immediately by those who would lose out. But, unlike the banks that held much of New York's debt, the French syndicate of farmers general had power to bring a great nation to its knees. As administrators of indirect taxes, the farmers general supplied the French government with essential operating capital through their advance payments on tax-farming contracts. By witholding advances and keeping monthly payments low, the tax farmers destroyed public confidence in state credit.[128] (Since tax farmers had much to gain from lending to government, they could tolerate high risks.) With the state's borrowing ability impaired, and forced to pay high interest to tax farmers and other wealthy financiers, the King had no choice but to dismiss Turgot after two years in office.

It is fashionable among some historians these days to ask "What if?" What if Turgot's policies had been implemented? Would the revolution in France nevertheless have occurred? Or might it have taken a different course? In the complex etiology of revolution, finance is but one contributing element. The only evidence we can draw on to answer this question is from states where Enlightenment ideas were partially implemented. In the Hapsburg empire, Prussia, and Russia, an enlightened monarch (Joseph II) and two absolutist despots (Frederick II and Catherine the Great) introduced some reforms proposed by Enlightenment theorists. In different ways, each taxed the nobility a nominal amount, abolished serfdom and tax farming, and tightened up administration of state finance. In these states no revolution occurred—not, at least, in the eighteenth century.

Not only should amateurs responsible for the nation's dire circumstances be removed from their posts, late-eighteenth-century reformers in England contended; as the central financial agency, the Treasury should take control of autonomous funds. England's great conservative statesman Edmund Burke argued for consolidation:

> How could the first lord of the Treasury . . . be responsible, if a variety of lesser treasuries . . . exist, each [of which] . . . would govern the branch of the public expenditure under its direction, just as it thought proper? It would be unfair [and] unjust, to expect a first lord of the Treasury to be responsible, unless the Treasury was the sole place for issuing public money, and governed the whole expenditure, as well in detail as in gross amount.[129]

Throughout the 1780s in England a series of commissions studied Treasury operations, suggesting procedural improvements; professionalization of management, consolidation of revenues and expenditures under Treasury control, and better auditing procedures (with its corollary, prompt payment of outstanding balances into the Treasury) were the main recommendations. Personnel should be rewarded for merit; only clerks "who have distinguished themselves most by their Diligence, Attention, and . . . Knowledge of Business"[130] should be promoted. Fees should be reduced or abolished and officials paid salaries commensurate with skill and responsibility. Public money should be closely controlled. An annual audit should be installed and enforced.

More was involved than administrative improvement. Proponents of reforms invoked the public ideology to justify their position. Summing up its objections to property-in-office, the Treasury Commission of 1783 articulated a broad conception of public interest. The state could abridge the sanctity of property if "the advantage of the public was the object":

> . . . The principle which gives existence to, and governs every public office is the Benefit of the State. . . . In every proposed official, the advantage or disadvantage of the officer can never properly be a subject of discussion. The only question is, whether the necessity or good of the State actually requires it? This decides the priority of the Regulation; and the determination of it belongs only to the Supreme power that watches over the public good, for its improvement as well as its protection.[131]

In the end, late-eighteenth-century English reforms accomplished much less than proponents had hoped. Legislative government, with its due process, commissions of inquiry, and respect for property, tends to dampen abrupt change. Proprietary rights in office and fee-taking could not be abolished without Parliament's consent. Life tenure was phased out gradually; as sinecurists died, the Treasury abolished their offices. Autonomous accounts were partially consolidated; the "sixty or seventy folios of accounts [whose] complexity beggars description and is hardly to be believed" (J.E.D. Binney's words) were reduced to about twelve.[132] Improved audits came later.

That reform was incomplete in late-eighteenth-century England should not surprise us. By then finance had become politics; its essence is compromise.

CONCLUSION: ACHIEVEMENTS OF AN ERA

Measured on the broad time scale of institutional evolution we have traced, this era links ancient, medieval and modern ways of thinking and acting about state finance. Therefore it is critical for understanding later events. Not only did European economy and society expand in scale and affluence beyond all precedent; governments altered their ways of coping in response to these changes. Both in and out of government, men invented new ways to deal with eternal problems of getting and spending money. Financial innovation was critical to economic and political change; methods of managing state finance were both cause and effect of all the other turmoil early modern states were embroiled in.

To list the permanent achievements of this era in state financial history is also to enumerate landmarks in the history of constitutional government; the idea of control of the purse emerged concurrently with legislative restriction of the sovereign. When legislatures seized the king's power to determine what taxes would be levied and granted him a limited financial stipend to manage his own affairs, state financial policies no longer could be formulated by fiat. Legislatures elected by the people of a nation, by affirming or denying proposed ways of raising and spending money, removed state finance from an authoritarian executive's personal prerogative and gave it to a wider, more representative constituency. The most important idea that emerged during this era was that state finance should be public finance.

The substantive innovations of this era followed and are subsidiary to the idea of legislative control. Central banking, the funded debt, administrative consolidation and simplification of accounts, specialization and professionalization of financial administration were all instruments of emerging legislative dominance in state finance.

By the late eighteenth century, constitutional foundations for modern state finance were firmer than were the technical instruments for executing the people's will. But those too had come a long way. Governments had learned how to borrow from the public, to fund debt in an orderly fashion, and were beginning to learn how to control state expenditures. As they have done ever since, financial reformers invoked cost and equity doctrine to justify policy proposals.

These achievements laid strong foundations for later development. When nineteenth-century governments enlarged the scale, and then the scope, of state activities, they were building on the legacy of constitutional ideas, economic doctrine, and administrative structures formulated by the many creative institution-builders of the early-modern era.

If we look at early-modern European financial history through the eyes of protagonists, it appears chaotic, haphazard, hand-to-mouth, a mélange of shifting expedients. And so it was. If we look back, as historians do, from the present vantage point of far more effective machinery for taxing and spending, the struggles against venality and corruption, and the replacement of market modes of finance, avowedly based on self-interest, appear heroic and public-spirited. It is all too easy to see the march of history as inevitable and to pronounce public virtue superior to private vice. But these inchoate events had a more diverse potential than has yet been realized. It is true that early-modern methods were inefficient and not a little corrupt. It is not true, however, that they were ineffective in raising revenue. Receipts rose continually in real terms. If the methods of the day did not squeeze out all they could have from taxpayers, some would count that an advantage. The coercive force of central government was limited by its financial inefficiencies. To coerce with enhanced equality would be more equitable but not necessarily more desirable. Early-modern governments may have begun poor, but they do not end that way. If their expenditures routinely exceeded their revenue, the deficit was incurred at higher and higher levels of affluence.

During the Middle Ages the various private governments could not control one another; relationships among them manifested the horizontal pluralism of interaction among near-equals. Within each government vertical relationships remained hierarchical, although traditions of reciprocal obligation modulated asymmetry in power. In early-modern Europe, governments became far more consolidated and centralized, yet more diverse than before. Within these larger governments, bureaucratization led to increasing hierarchy within horizontal relationships, but vertical relationships became more competitive. Growth of markets was not the only factor inducing competition; although change was halting and haphazard, the big difference between this age and its predecessor was growing competition among rival hierarchies. From the adjustment of relationships between church and state, competition spread to rival churches within the ecclesiastical realm, to rival estates in society, and then to factions and parties within the secular domain. A single fused religious and secular hierarchy gave way to dual and then to plural hierarchies. Of course the legislatures were not in any sense egalitarian, in their relationship either to the crown or to the citizenry, but the legislatures existed, and they mattered. Henceforth established authority would represent a coalition of hierarchical and market cultures. If elements of hierarchy still affected relationships in economic markets, competitive elements influenced political rule.

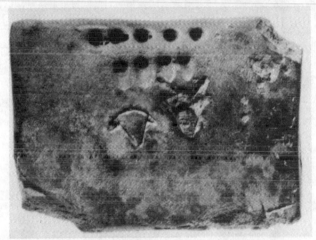

Ancient tax receipts. Impressed clay tablets from Sumer, about 3500 B.C., show taxes paid in kind. Each mark represents a unit: the top tablet may be for two small and three large measures of grain; the lower tablet for five oxen and four cows. (SEE CHAPTER 1.)

Corvée labor in Egypt. Top: Slaves moving a monument to be polished, about 2000 B.C. Bottom: Semites building the grand vizier's tomb, about 1400 B.C. (SEE CHAPTER 1.)

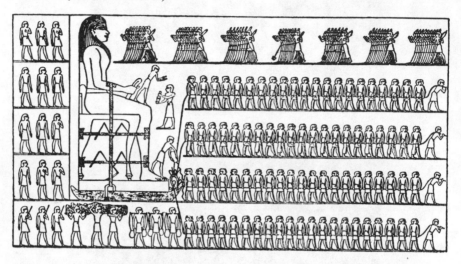

3

4

Nubians bringing tribute. Fragment of a wall painting from the tomb of a viceroy of Nubia under Tutankhamen, about 1360 B.C. The scene depicts royal offerings—oxen, a giraffe, gold rings, and seven enslaved warriors. (*SEE CHAPTER 2.*)

Tax collection by treasury officials. Scribes and fiscal officers record payments as deputies armed with sticks bring in reluctant taxpayers. The hieroglyphic caption reads: "Seizing the town rulers for a reckoning." (*SEE CHAPTER 2.*)

7

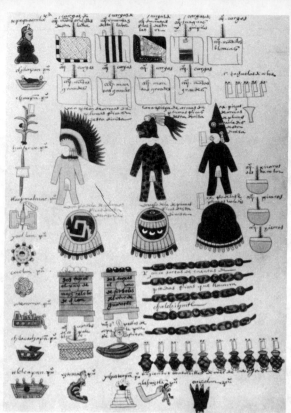

Aztec cadastral survey. A page from the Códice de Mendoza, *the cadastre of taxes owed the emperor Montezuma. Pictographs along the left and bottom sides represent villages; the remaining pictographs depict quantities and classes of taxes paid in kind. Annotations in Spanish by a friar named Mendoza interpret the pictographs and the Aztec symbols for numbers.* (SEE CHAPTER 2.)

8

Public tax register. Tablet from the Acropolis showing taxes paid by Athenian citizens in 454–453 B.C. (SEE CHAPTER 3.)

The Athenian treasury at Delphi.
Pilgrims from all city-states of
ancient Greece carried offerings to
the sacred temple of Apollo at
Delphi. Between the 6th and 4th
centuries B.C. the city-states
competed to build decorated
marble structures along the road
to the temple; visitors deposited
gifts for temple priests in the
treasury buildings. Athens paid
for its treasury, built between 490
and 485 B.C., with booty taken
from the Medes after its victory in
the Battle of Marathon.
(SEE CHAPTER 3.)

9

A late Roman bas-relief from Noviomagus in eastern Gaul showing payment
of taxes. (SEE CHAPTER 3.)

11

Chamberlain of the commune of Siena in 1264 making up the public accounts. (A painting on the cover of the public account book.) (SEE CHAPTER 4.)

12

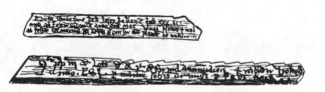

Exchequer tallies. Medieval tally sticks were seven or eight inches long, divided by a mark into two unequal parts. Specialized treasury clerks cut notches into both sides of the tally, thereby representing in standardized notation the amount each sheriff had paid into the treasury. When each sheriff's business with the treasury was concluded, the tally cutters severed the two parts. The larger piece of each tally (the countertally *or* counterfoil*) was stored at the treasury. The smaller part (the* foil*) was given to the sheriff as a receipt. Her Majesty's revenue officers continued to furnish the wooden tally until 1832. (SEE CHAPTER 4.)*

Late medieval monarchs couldn't keep up with the demand for money. A mint operated by the Holy Roman Emperor Maximilian I (1493–1519).
(SEE CHAPTER 4.)

13

14

Tax revolt in Amsterdam, 1748; rioters demolish the tax farmer's house.
(SEE CHAPTER 5.)

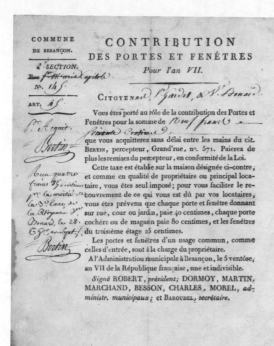

Contribution des Portes et Fenêtres Pour l'an VII. This receipt for door and window tax paid by a citizen of Besançon in France in 1796 reveals the revolutionary government's effort to collect taxes according to the subject's ability to pay. Citizen Bonnard paid 9 francs 89 centimes to the collector, Bertin (plus Bertin's fee). The printed form specifies tax incidence: the building's owner or its main renter must pay, but (to permit recovery from tenants) the tax is calculated as follows:

— each door to street, courtyard, or garden, 40 centimes
— every gate to carriage house or store, 80 centimes
— tax on doors and windows in common, such as hallway or entryway, must be paid by owner. (SEE CHAPTER 5.)

The South Sea Bubble. (SEE CHAPTER 5.)

The labors of Sisyphus: The finance minister struggles in vain to prevent the growth of the budget. (Lithograph by Honoré Daumier, 1869.) (SEE CHAPTER 6.)

17

18

John Bull and the tax demon, early nineteenth-century caricature by John Gillray. (SEE CHAPTER 6.)

19

20

A sectarian strain in U.S. political culture: Uncle Sam promises immigrants freedom—free education, free land, free speech, free ballot and a free lunch! (*SEE CHAPTER 7.*)

21

Post–Civil War anti-tax sentiment: "Put the shutters up" against the income tax, says Thomas Nast. It is nothing but a tax on virtue. (SEE CHAPTER 7.)

23

A British Conservative party poster for the 1929 election promises voters a rosy future. (SEE CHAPTER 8.)

22

The individualist strain in U.S. political culture. (SEE CHAPTER 7.)

Welfare spending during the 1930s conflicts with traditional U.S. preference for balanced budgets. (*SEE CHAPTER 8.*)

24

ONE PERSON OUT OF EVERY TEN
—*WPA Administrator Hopkins.*

25

The welfare state is expensive. Right: The Conscientious Taxpayer (Germany). Below: "Watch out for the Treasury!" (France). (SEE CHAPTER 8.)

26

27

(*SEE CHAPTER 9.*)

28

29

(*SEE CHAPTER 9.*)

THE MINI-AND-MAXI ERA

30

Von Riegen

Courtesy TRUE, The Man's Magazine

"I just wish they'd fight poverty with something beside taxes."

(*SEE CHAPTER 9.*)

31

"IDOL MUST HAVE HUMAN SACRIFICE."

(*SEE CHAPTER 10.*)

(*SEE CHAPTER 10.*)

32

33

(*SEE CHAPTER 10.*)

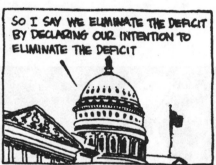

Chapter Six

THE WAYS AND MEANS OF PUBLIC GOVERNMENT: TAXING AND SPENDING IN REPRESENTATIVE STATES OF THE EARLY INDUSTRIAL AGE*

CHANGING PARADIGMS OF GOVERNMENT FINANCE

The rate of change in governments' financial institutions, barely perceptible for centuries on end, began to speed up during the last quarter of the eighteenth century. Having lagged behind, governments began to enter the modern world, sluffing off traditional modes of management that inhibited adaptation to broad shifts in economies and societies of Western nations during the nineteenth century. As an engine, moving from dead center, first overcomes inertia and then, developing momentum, runs ever faster, so governments changed at accelerating pace. Gradually in most states, but abruptly in some, governments developed institutions and structures of public finance.

Spreading through the nations of the Western world during the nineteenth century, a wave of democratic revolutions transferred the taxing power from kings to legislatures elected by gradually widening publics. Created in response to doctrine, without precedent or rules to guide their operation, these bodies gradually learned to function collectively in order to govern. As the play of interest groups created factions and parties, legislatures had to generate principles of decision and action congruent with ideas of democracy. During the nineteenth century the idea of legislative responsibility to the public came to be the core of democratic theory. Acting in response to public pressure,

*Work for this chapter was funded by a grant from the Alfred P. Sloan Foundation, Aaron Wildavsky, principal investigator.

late-nineteenth-century legislatures derived authority to enlarge governments' powers from this principle. Designing and implementing institutions for legislative oversight of public spending were but one expression of the principle of legislative responsibility.

The organizations that nineteenth-century governments created piece by piece to administer taxing and spending—each one an independent specialized structure—became complementary facets of a smoothly functioning whole. From the French Revolution to the First World War, mechanical metaphors characterized the financial administrations of Western nations. But between this period's beginning and its end, the connotation completely reversed. As they moved erratically from crisis to crisis during the seventeenth and eighteenth centuries, Western nations' financial administrations were often compared to broken-down machines. But, by the middle of the nineteenth century, commentators had begun to write of the mighty fiscal engines of government. As they developed into structures we can recognize and understand, financial administrations became powerful instruments for extracting revenue from the public, and then spending it for collective purposes that had no precedent in Western history. The wars of mass mobilization and the welfare state would not have been possible in the twentieth century without a vast increase in the ability to mobilize and allocate resources in the nineteenth century.

The metaphor of the benign machine came naturally in an age of industrialization. Growth in nations' fiscal capacity is, of course, inseparable from the Industrial Revolution that transformed economy and society in the West. The link between scientific thought, mechanical invention, and ways of organizing work, already apparent in the last quarter of the eighteenth century, strengthened as the nineteenth century unfolded. Dividing production into specialized tasks performed sequentially by individual workers, organizing labor into productive units of increasing scale, and enhancing human energy with mechanical power supplied by steam-driven machines combined to multiply productivity. In an environment gradually freed from governments' constraints, labor, productive capital, and entrepreneurship created a surplus. Parallel trends in agriculture had been providing rising yields since the late Middle Ages.

In industrializing nations of Europe and America during the nineteenth century, as in the modern developing world, economic growth gradually increased incomes. Underemployed agricultural laborers moved into towns, where some found work in factories. Freed from dependence on land, they gradually became integrated into monetized economies and urbanizing societies. With growing productivity, rising incomes, and better transport—a spreading railroad network linking city and countryside—the recurrent famine of the ancient and medieval worlds disappeared. Although most men were poor by contemporary measures, incomes and living standards rose slowly in real terms. And as diets and living conditions improved, as science found ways to cure or prevent the plagues of past ages, populations lived longer and increased in size.

While development bettered lives of most people over the long run, short-run dislocations created hardship. As each society shifted from an agricultural to an industrial base, patterns of personal interdependence that had provided a cushion against adversity in traditional societies were gradually attenuated. Development improved expectations, but in the early stages the gap between the mass of people who had nothing and no one to fall back on and the few who possessed property and security seemed to grow wider. The immiserization of wage laborers in Manchester noted by Engels—they lived in poverty and squalor, and were periodically thrown out of work by conditions beyond their control—is the dominant theme in social commentary about all industrial cities during the nineteenth century. Whether these conditions still might have been better than the "idiocy of rural life" is much debated today.

Eventually the benefits from development spread to all social levels, providing increasing returns to entrepreneurs and investors, and wages for workers. Government treasuries also benefited when rising incomes provided an expanding base for old and new kinds of taxes. As the changing thought and behavior that accompanied industrialization filtered slowly into government, gradually creating bureaucratic structures and administrative rules, it armed government with improved capacity to raise money and spend it.

The principal attributes of modern government finance—its generalized, widely accepted yet somewhat incompatible norms; its professionalized, centralized, *public* administration of taxing and spending; and its reliance on direct taxes on income for revenue—are a legacy from the nineteenth century. As the century unfolded, governments of Western democracies developed fiscal structures widely perceived to be efficient, productive, and, more than ever before, fair.

During the nineteenth century, too, public debate focused on issues related to taxing, spending, and financial administration that, lacking conclusive resolution, still dominate the public agenda. Foremost among them was the conflict implicit in attaining two general goals, both highly valued: raising revenue without inhibiting production, and, as the century progressed, improving societal welfare. Yet policymakers understood that it would not be possible to achieve either of these goals without interfering with attainment of the other. The orthodox economic theory that stood behind nineteenth-century fiscal policy specified that taxes should be low to create entrepreneurial incentive for production. Principles of debt management inherited from eighteenth-century innovations in public banking dictated that government budgets should be balanced to maintain a sound market for the public debt. By mid–nineteenth century the balanced-budget norm was so widely accepted that it had acquired moral overtones. The bad old days of no management or poor management, and spending in excess of governments' capacity to support it, were still within living memory. If they violated the taboo against unbalanced budgets, policymakers could be sure that their actions would undermine public confidence.

But since improving societal welfare entailed spending, governments could not balance budgets without improving fiscal productivity. Moreover, any change in patterns of taxing and spending would burden some groups while benefiting others. Although the context of the conflict between production and welfare has changed greatly between then and now, it substance is unchanged. In the language of modern welfare economics, it is a trade-off between norms of efficiency and equity.

This tension between productivity and welfare explains much of the history of the theory and practice of public finance in Western industrial nations between the beginning of the nineteenth century and today.[1] As public sympathy for limited government grows in all Western nations, it is useful to know where the ideas came from. Recent proposals for aggregating costs and trying to determine the incidence of benefits from government spending, and for reducing governments' size, cutting taxes, and setting expenditure limits, descend directly from the intellectual lineage we trace here.

Nineteenth-century ideas of public finance derived, in part, from an earlier intellectual revolution. Searching for general organizing principles for governments and economies, the natural-law philosophers of the seventeenth and eighteenth centuries had first propounded equity and efficiency rules for government finance. Adam Smith's synthesis, reflecting contemporary opinion, set forth four canons for judging a proposal for a new tax. It should be fair in its incidence, not falling more heavily on some groups than others. It should be simple to understand, convenient to assess, uniform in its application, and cheap to administer. Above all, it should produce adequate revenue.[2]

Emerging hand in hand, eighteenth-century ideas about equity, fiscal efficiency, and organizational rationality were codified during the nineteenth century into laws specifying nations' tax policies and limiting their capacities to borrow and spend. Gradually over the first half of the century a new rule-bound paradigm for taxing, spending, and financial administration replaced the opportunistic policies and practices of earlier ages.

Governments of European nations during the early-modern period had tried to raise revenue by taxing property and consumption. With the growing interest in individual rights during the seventeenth and eighteenth centuries, both kinds of taxes could be justified on equity grounds: property and purchases were tangible indices of ability to pay. But property and market taxes each entailed administrative difficulties no government had yet resolved. Pre-modern structures for taxing and spending, built up from a multiplicity of taxes—each one administered separately, often by private individuals for personal gain—consistently yielded meager returns. Traditional earmarking techniques did not measure up to Adam Smith's canons. Property and consumption taxes were hard to understand, complex to apply, and expensive to administer. They did not produce revenue commensurate with government effort. And if ability to pay consumption taxes were related to the limited resources of most taxpayers, these taxes did not conform to changing ideas about equity.

While nineteenth-century governments were riven by factions in all nations and shaken by sharp political discontinuity in some, nevertheless, during the first two-thirds of the century, most nations created modern financial administrations. Modeling them after factories organized according to the energy-conserving ideas of classical mechanics central to thought of that era, governments implemented a series of measures that centralized the levying and collecting of taxes, and the spending and auditing of the proceeds. In place of the many autonomous funds of earlier ages, nineteenth-century nations created a single organization for collecting taxes and a parallel organization for spending.

Trying to match fiscal means to desired expenditures while maintaining solvency, nineteenth-century legislatures and executives developed procedures for deciding ahead of time how all revenue flowing into the treasury would be spent. A budget of anticipated expenditures enacted each year to determine spending for the next year is a nineteenth-century innovation.

When rules designed to impose order on the spending process were implemented over time, repetition clothed procedures with authority. Instrumental rules then became ends; they acquired a life of their own. The great norms that provide a framework for budgeting in modern governments—unity, annuality, balance, comprehensiveness, and control—emerged during the nineteenth century. Professionalized public servants, agents of the executive with specialized knowledge of financial management, created these norms as they gradually endowed legislatively mandated rules with substantive content.

Organizations for taxing and budgeting embodied emerging ideas about separation of powers and joint oversight that became common as more governments developed effective centralized structures. Initiated by strong executives, after public debate, innovations in financial administration were enacted by legislatures. The executive implemented procedures, but the new organizations were accountable to legislatures. The ideal—of public mandate for taxes through legislative approval, and public control of spending by improved administration—was not universally attained, of course. Patterns of taxing and spending varied among nations and, within each one, from one decade to another. Even where a growing middle class supported ideas of public consent for taxation and government accountability for spending, opinion about tax incidence was far from unanimous. And as property qualifications for voting were gradually reduced and finally eliminated, public pressure on government reflected a wider spectrum of interests than ever before. By dividing authority, and insuring responsiveness to voters' demands, joint legislative/executive determination of taxes and control of spending were essential stabilizing elements in government.

Yet we must not go too far. Even as the franchise was extended, it was used to choose among competing elites, not to abolish them. During the early nineteenth century only a few isolated individuals crying out against establishment policies favored egalitarian ideas. Equality then meant only opportunity to share in society's decisions (by voting), and its wealth (by working). There was growing equality before the law, and more equality of opportunity than ever before, but the equality of condition sought by social critics remained an ephemeral goal.

Individual distress caused by mass poverty had been normal everywhere in the Western world before the Industrial Revolution. The private contributions to charity sanctioned by religious and public authorities were a rudimentary social mechanism for coping with misfortune. Because everyone faced the same life conditions, no doubt contributions were seen as social insurance, potentially available to one's own kin should need arise. Even if a family saved what it could, loss of providers could end its independence.

Humanitarian tradition justified charitable aid to the "deserving poor"—individuals confronted with abrupt, uncontrollable change in personal circumstances.[3] Through religious orders, private charities, and (after the fifteenth century) public funds generated by local taxes, European societies tried to provide food and shelter for persons suddenly made dependent by illness or death. Such philanthropies aimed to sustain widows, orphans, and old people without surviving children at some minimum level.

Since the Renaissance, societies have drawn a parallel distinction between poor persons worthy of assistance and the "rabble" whose poverty seemed to result from personal mismanagement. As judged by hierarchical authorities of that age, the army of homeless roaming across the land was counterpart to today's bag ladies or spare-change seekers—people out of synch with the established order. Like refugees in the Middle East or Africa today, early-modern vagrants were initially displaced by war or famine; their dependents became a permanent underclass. This growing mob of "undeserving poor" was all the more disturbing to supporters of hierarchy because it formed a potentially volatile social unit, one whose numbers (between a quarter and a third of Europe's population from the fifteenth century on) defied any effort at organized assistance.[4]

As it brought about a sharp break with the past, the Industrial Revolution created a host of new demands on governments. Changes in patterns of life and work during the nineteenth century converted individual problems of personal welfare into social issues for which public policy was to seek appropriate solutions: populations concentrated in large, densely inhabited cities; long-lasting cyclical fluctuations in production, employment, and income; the increased liability of factory workers to injury or death during long hours on the job. These problems grew too big too quickly to be resolved by private philanthropy.

The distinction between deserving and undeserving poor persisted; it influenced nineteenth-century social thought and public debate over poverty. When governments—first in Britain, then elsewhere—tried to mitigate distress caused by loss of family income from involuntary unemployment during trade recessions, anyone in need could claim public assistance. During the 1820s and 1830s "Tory Radicals" in England expressed their patriarchal concern by dispensing benefits to the less fortunate in order to preserve the existing social hierarchy. But helping the "laboring poor" (an open-ended segment of society) instead of the "poor" (widows, orphans, and old people in need, a circumscribed subset), converted an individual's moral obligation to give into the beneficiary's legal right to receive. Generalized public assistance attenuated the distinction between deserving and undeserving.[5] The small sums paid, and the personal constraints linked with receipt of public assistance in nineteenth-century workhouses, could hardly be construed as income by right. But critics of reforms granting public assistance to *any* able-bodied person in need understood that such policies could alter the traditional order.*

In an environment of widening franchise, governments no longer served only to protect the rights of the wealthy: they began to take action to improve the lives of the poor. Even as powerful interests, whose newfound political influence derived from wealth acquired in industry, urged governments to abandon constraints upon markets imposed during the mercantilist era, industrialization created contrary pressures. Social critics across the political spectrum—from the radical Thomas Paine to Bentham and his followers—promoted government regulation as a means of restraining self-serving actions. Unbridled individualism, they thought, would tend to produce effects that, although unintended, were harmful to the public. Critics viewed government as a neutral agent, with no interest of its own, and better qualified than any other organization to guard the public interest. Karl Marx's view, of course, was different. He maintained that governments controlled societies by defining progress in terms synonymous with capitalists' interests.

Pushed by continuing unrest associated with depression-induced unemployment, nineteenth-century legislatures slowly responded to reformers' demands. Enacting laws designed to correct the public's perception of the worst problems, governments began to regulate hours and work conditions in factories, at first for women and children, later

*Edmund Burke and Jeremy Bentham established the tone of a long-lasting argument against overly generous public assistance. When present-day individualists accuse welfare recipients of immorality, they sound a lot like Bentham, who thought the state should not reward the idle and negligent on the same terms as the diligent and industrious. Bentham, in turn, echoed Burke's belief: "Pity . . . tends to dissatisfy [the laboring poor] with their condition and to teach them to seek resources . . . in something else than their own industry, frugality, and sobriety." In a recent work, Charles Murray criticizes redistributive social programs of the 1960s and 1970s. The U.S. poverty program, he claims, transferred public resources "from workers to drones," "from the most capable poor (read "deserving"] to the least capable ["undeserving"], from the most law abiding to the least law abiding, and from the most responsible to the least responsible." Like Burke, Murray contends that these programs induced people to behave less responsibly than they might have, to their long-term detriment.[6] Egalitarian critics have challenged Murray's methods.

for all. Before germ theory linked sanitation and health, local governments acted to improve urban living conditions. By the last quarter of the century, large cities had built water mains and storm drains and sanitary sewers. They had paved roadways, provided street lighting and parks, and begun to regulate housing. By then, central and/or local governments guaranteed all children an education sufficient to provide basic literacy. Toward the end of the century, central governments (except in the United States) began providing insurance against loss of earning capacity—from the involuntary unemployment of old age, industrial accident, and economic decline—as a buffer against some of life's major risks in large-scale industrial society. Administering insurance funds contributed by employers and workers, governments would modify individualism by building a floor under incomes. The forced savings of good times would sustain later needs.[7] That is how late-nineteenth-century governments set out on a road that would lead to the welfare state.

For the first time in history, paying for government wasn't a serious problem in Western industrial nations. As long as spending increased slowly, rising productivity provided ample means to pay the bill. Once economies had taken off, nineteenth-century governments could finance state activities painlessly from the proceeds of growth. Tapping into expanding incomes and wealth, nations easily bore the cost of administration whose performance had been improved by internal reform. Growth also fueled the fires of nationalism. Although it was not always possible to do so, when kept within limits spending for armies and navies, and for colonial administration, yielded benefits in cheap resources for production and expanded markets for domestic products.

But *how* governments raised money *was* a serious matter. Nineteenth-century legislatures, representing a range of interests and opinions, subjected to a continuous barrage of criticism from vocal elements of societies whose composition they mirrored, argued over finance issues in the same ways legislatures do today. Two powerful new paradigms emerged from public debate about taxing and spending: market conservatism and interventionism. Both have survived to shape contemporary thinking.

If, for simplicity, we exclude measures designed to regulate economies, debate over fiscal policy in modern highly developed nations focuses on spending. Because of commitment to support a variety of government programs, formulation of fiscal policy starts from the premise that government will spend. Legislatures and publics then argue over how much government should spend, over the objects of spending, and over the best ways of raising whatever revenue is needed to pay for past and present spending. Until very recently the important questions have been *how* governments will spend, and *how much*.

For much of the nineteenth century such a conception of government's role would have been viewed as heresy. The ideas that circumscribed debate about taxing and spending dictated that government should be small. Policymakers and publics believed that the public interest would be best served if governments took the back seat, exercising minimal constraint on economies and societies. The machine metaphor, popular throughout the century, provided a model: government should act like the governor on an engine, a simple mechanical device that automatically maintains operation within tolerable limits, not too slow or too fast.

If there were no external disturbance, so the argument ran, there would be little need for government to spend. Requiring revenue only to pay for limited expenditure and to amortize debt, it could tax lightly. Taxes should be politically acceptable, yet interfere as little as possible with powerful market forces, which, if left unfettered, could by themselves regulate economies and societies. Less visible than direct taxes, indirect taxes on a few staple commodities could provide adequate revenue without arousing opposition from taxpayers.

A synthesis of eighteenth-century economic theory modified by nineteenth-century politics, this complex of ideas still exists in attenuated form. Known in Europe as economic liberalism (because it was first implemented by the Liberal Party in England between about 1853 and 1870) and in the U.S. as market conservatism, it reappears today as opposition to big government and to high taxes. Individualists cry out against what nineteenth-century political leaders called the spending mentality. In this they are joined by modern sectarians who continue to object, unless and until spending is devoted to specific government programs they favor.

The contrary paradigm of taxing and spending that emerged during the nineteenth century was interventionist, ameliorative, collectivist, and egalitarian. This new model expanded government's role, and supported spending from the proceeds of income taxes levied in accordance with ability to pay.

The ideas behind this paradigm derived from many different and incompatible sources, and from an incongruous assortment of revolutionaries and reactionaries, reformers and activists. Its centralizing, interventionist bias grew out of the utilitarianism of Jeremy Bentham and James Mill, reinforced by late-nineteenth-century empirical and theoretical social science. Its redistributive and collectivist components grew over many years. One common thread unites the ideas and policies of such disparate figures as the Levellers and the Diggers (radical sects of the seventeenth-century English Puritan Revolution), William Pitt the Younger, proposing reforms in England's Elizabethan poor laws, Thomas Paine, writing in response to the French Revolution, and assorted nineteenth-century figures ranging from William Cobbett, an early English sectarian, to the moderate English reformer Robert Owen, to Otto von Bismarck, archconservative prime minister of unified Germany, to the radicals Engels and Marx[8]: whether by direct confiscation of property, or by voluntary personal contribution, or by imposing taxes on the wealthy, each aimed to improve societal welfare by changing the distribution of income. Collectivism had moved ever so slightly toward egalitarianism.

While worker unrest and radical movements compelled governments to provide some security for ordinary people, nineteenth-century policymakers represented affluent interests for the most part. They took a dim view of expropriating property or its proceeds to help the poor. For much of the nineteenth century in most nations, the confiscatory ideas implicit in the income tax were acceptable only in emergencies, when receipts from all other revenue sources failed to cover rising current expenses and costs of past debt. Wars, which mobilized national consciousness while creating severe financial stress, gave nineteenth-century governments—coalitions of hierarchical and market regimes—sufficient reason to tax incomes to pay for defense, and to increase borrowing to secure the nation's credit.

Nineteenth-century governments preferred not to borrow. They tried to maintain balanced budgets by tying spending to tax receipts. But when they needed to raise money on the public capital market, policymakers knew that evidence of capacity to pay for past borrowing was needed for the investor confidence that would lead to successful sale of new debt. (Willingness to invest in British consols—nonmarketable debt instruments sold at a fixed rate, quarterly interest to be paid in perpetuity—was evidence of confidence in Britain's credit-worthiness.) Accommodating to discipline imposed by the market (and following the precedent of earlier war-induced taxes on the wealthy), nineteenth-century governments enacted income taxes to cover military costs.

England, however, at midcentury imposed an income tax in peacetime, reducing dependence on import and export duties in order to implement the Liberal Party's free-trade policies. Mercantile and manufacturing interests, believing that the many indirect taxes inhibited business, proposed to abolish most of them and reduce rates of the few that remained. England enacted its income tax as a temporary measure to provide revenue for a few years until receipts from indirect taxes increased enough to support government without other taxes. Like the makeshift structures put up on college campuses during wartime, temporary taxes have a tendency to become permanent, adding to rather than replacing the existing base.

With economic growth and improved administration, the income tax became an irreplaceable bastion of solvency, supporting rising expenditure by providing revenue to keep budgets balanced. It was too good to give up; from the early 1890s one nation after another (with America the usual exception) adopted various forms of income tax. As they do today, these taxes supported guns and butter—modest pensions for aged and incapacitated citizens, in some nations, and more for arms.

By the end of the nineteenth century most industrializing nations had found a way to pay the rising costs of government while taxing lightly and maintaining balanced budgets (most of the time). While spending was gaining momentum, with rising productivity and the new income taxes, revenue was keeping up.

Just before World War I, financial policies of most Western nations incorporated elements of the two paradigms of taxing and spending created during the nineteenth century: (1) minimal government supported by a few low but productive indirect taxes; and (2) small spending for welfare, defrayed from insurance funds and the proceeds of progressive income and inheritance taxes paid by the rich. Until World War I spending impelled governments to raise taxes and expand borrowing beyond all previous precedent, the ideas embodied in the two models maintained an uneasy balance. Collectivism was the mainstay of all regimes; usually it worked in tandem with individualism, but sometimes with tiny elements of egalitarianism. Governments began spending for welfare in an effort to mitigate the harsher aspects of individualism. But then, having been picked up by sectarians, redistributive ideas developed a life of their own. A synthesis of hierarchy, markets, and sects, the welfare state emerged as a larger and stronger entity than anyone originally intended.

THE CONTEXT FOR CHANGE

By all conventional indices, the nineteenth century marked a sharp break with the past, the beginning of a series of changes in the lives of entire populations. The democratic revolutions that spread from one nation to another did not immediately sweep away remnants of medieval ideas about government, economy, and society, as the first two revolutions (in the U.S. and France) tried to do by decree, but these vestiges lasted only a short time longer. The nineteenth century brought the end of the old political order, as most Western nations established constitutional governments. Although legislative government did not immediately transfer power from the few to the many, as the franchise gradually widened, nineteenth-century legislatures represented a broader spectrum of interests than did any earlier polity.

Division of long spans of time into manageable segments is an important conceptual problem in historical studies, involving ideas about the underlying forces that engender continuity and change. A period in history represents an intellectual synthesis, and a historian employs concepts and measures that may derive from his intellectual inheritance, or from his interests and values, in order to give unity to a stretch of time. In most instances the material conditions of life and ideas about them unfold along a continuum, with later developments building on the widely shared understanding that comprises the culture of a given period and place. Over the long history of governments and societies, changes have been gradual. Decisive events may mark boundaries between historical epochs, with shifts in artifacts and ideas—but the forces leading up to them were a long time in building and continue to operate long afterward. The seminal ideas and critical events influencing nineteenth-century developments came together throughout the last quarter of the eighteenth century, and even these were based on earlier changes.

For the entire early industrial age, populations throughout Europe and America grew larger and younger. People moved from country to city. Secondary and tertiary economic activities—manufacturing, marketing, and services—replaced farming as the main source of income. The rising productivity associated with machine technology and factory organization increased individual incomes. And, because there were no major armed conflicts between Napoleon's defeat and the beginning of World War I one hundred years later, governments could also benefit from productivity gains, retaining a small share of an increasing surplus.

Even though there were few wars to support it, nationalistic ideology grew throughout the nineteenth century. The electoral process fostered public consciousness of central government, giving meaning to the idea of a nation. New transport modes and improved communications, shrinking the time distance between places and overcoming isolation, reinforced the movements toward national unity. By raising the level of literacy, expanded education enabled citizens to understand abstractions like citizenship and public, and to make electoral choices. Reforms in central government administration simultaneously created professionalized public services. As public servants repeatedly demonstrated allegiance to the public interest, they provided concrete evidence of some abstractions implicit in democratic ideology.

Nations' policies reflected the relative strength of their dominant political cultures. Varying in rates of change and patterns of political and economic development, nations manifested different balances among hierarchy, competitive individualism, and nascent egalitarianism. As the century unfolded, diverse groups in each nation acquired power to enact laws favoring their special interests.

In Britain, where by the 1820s industrialization had created a vocal commercial middle class, business interests pressed the politically dominant landowning group to abolish some of the array of protective tariffs then in force. These tariffs, business interests maintained, raised costs of production, and inhibited British manufacturers' capacity to compete in world markets. Growing support for individualism during the 1830s and 1840s led Britain to break with precedent by cutting and then eliminating most tariffs to implement free trade.

A coalition of aristocratic elites and business interests shaped financial policy in France between Napoleon's defeat and the last quarter of the nineteenth century. Although France was the first nation to create comprehensive financial management structures, the procedural reforms enacted between 1817 and 1827 were not sustained long enough to become budgetary norms. Reforms were hierarchical in intention but not in execution, because France's tumultuous politics throughout the nineteenth century did not afford the stable climate needed to maintain a strong hierarchy capable of enforcing consistent financial policies. Through off-budget accounts and supplemental appropriations, its legislature evaded budgetary balance. By contrast, both before and after unification, the German states exemplified hierarchy: they sustained the autocratic financial management of the early-modern era. Since legislative consent was not mandatory, rulers and administrators imposed decisions about spending from the top. Tax structures consistently favored wealthy landowners over town interests. Likewise in Sweden: until the last quarter of the century the tax policies implemented by rulers maintained privileges for aristocratic rural residents at the expense of townspeople.

In a new nation of small farms and small business where many farmers were also businessmen, individualism served to set limits on central government and enhance market forces. The United States was founded in a tax revolt by people who believed that central government's power should be minimal; its citizens severely limited central government's capacity to tax and spend throughout the nineteenth century—except for a short time during the Civil War, revenue derived almost entirely from tariffs on imports.

Because change occurred quickly, the forces affecting government finance are more readily understood if we divide the early industrial age into two unequal parts. The first, overlapping the last part of the early-modern era, extends from 1776 to 1870; the second runs from 1871 to 1914.

Constitutionalism and rationality found firm footings in governments during the first period. It begins in 1776 because several events of at least symbolic importance occurred then: publication of Adam Smith's *Wealth of Nations;* invention of the steam engine; a recommendation to the Treasury by English Prime Minister Lord North that its personnel be selected on merit principles and paid fixed annual salaries according to skills and experience; a tax revolt in one of England's colonies on the American continent. For roughly the next one hundred years, central governments formulated, then gradually implemented modern ideas about taxation and methods of financial administration.

Encompassing a series of political revolutions as well as the first stages of the Industrial Revolution, these years were filled with all the stresses associated with shifts in political power and a major social transformation. Focusing on these strains, the mass of social commentary has fostered a largely negative image of nineteenth century life (until recently, when several revisionist historians have reinterpreted the evidence to refurbish its image[9]).

At least since the beginning of that century, social change gave rise to two opposing doctrines of public-policy formulation. The first, deriving from views about political rationality typical of the Anglo-Scottish Enlightenment, expresses a necessary relationship between intelligence and policymaking. The immediate source of this view was Bentham's proposal that legislation on any subject should be based on study by a citizens' commission. If laws are drafted and policies designed after study, they will reflect the best expert opinion filtered through politics. This way of thinking is constructive and interventionist. The tone is optimistic. Improvement in administrative structure that nineteenth-century governments introduced and most policies they designed follow this fact-finding approach, which is socially conservative in relying on experts, and financially liberal because of the tendency of experts to aggrandize their own areas of interest. From that day to this, experts have recommended that ever more money be taken from taxpayers—so government may spend according to their priorities.

During the first phase of the industrial age, eighteenth-century doctrines of economic individualism gradually changed. Ideas formulated in protest became reified in nineteenth-century public-policy debate, and then vulgarized. The paradigm of the free competitive market in equilibrium provided doctrinal rationale for free-trade policies, as concepts of rationality and efficiency did for administrative reorganization and efforts to maintain balanced budgets. The demand for results came from forces representing economic individualism; these demands assaulted and threatened social hierarchy. If results, rather than routines, were to be the criteria of effective government, the gates would be opened to other challenges to the established order.

Arguments about the beneficent effects of the market's invisible hand soon became a defensive ideology for the new economic and social order that industrialization was creating. Defense was needed, for, despite its success at raising output and wealth, as the nineteenth century progressed the new order stimulated vocal artistic and literary as well as political and economic critics. These anti-establishment forces inspired the second approach to policymaking, a Romantic reaction against the superrationality of the continental Enlightenment.

Celebrating intuition and emotion instead of cold reason, the Romantic movement was certainly antimarket; it condemned the "cash nexus" as an inappropriate basis for personal relationships. In the impersonal industrial system, leftists and rightists alike saw only dehumanized work under abhorrent conditions. Some Romantics idealized older patrimonial relationships governed by a hierarchy of affection. Others envisioned a rosy utopian future in which mankind, relieved from necessity—that is, from limited resources—could unite on a purely egalitarian basis. Failing that, Romantic views anticipate the contemporary sectarian critique of the establishment. Short of withdrawal from society into rural communes, or of violent political revolution, there was no way things could get better. If life was harsh for laborers in the new order, it was not only because businessmen were greedy, but because structural instability was built into the system. If, as Marx and Engels asserted, there was an inherent tendency in capitalism for profits to decline, there was no hope for improvement. Workers' lives could get only worse—unless they themselves seized the means of production, ending their alienation by making their own rules. Like the corruption of noble man by the evil institutions of hierarchy and markets, the industrial establishment's rape of unspoiled nature would lead inexorably toward disaster.

A lament for loss of rural virtue was the Romantic poets' response to industrialization; their metaphors rejected the present and idealized the past. Industry had created modern Babylon; rural villages, standing empty, symbolized the innocent simplicity of country life, forever lost. Before social science had developed empirical methods for analyzing social problems, but at a time when literacy was increasing and representative governments had reduced constraints on free expression, literature served as a powerful instrument of social criticism. Though not Romantics, the social novelists Dickens, Trollope, and Balzac conveyed the brutal quality of city life.[10] They created understandable working-class characters and then, with sympathy and compassion, compared them invidiously to members of the smug middle class and the shortsighted aristocracy that controlled business and government. They documented emergence of new, diffuse authority patterns that replaced traditional relationships founded in inherited status. Published in newspaper installments, the novels attracted a wide audience.

The political legacy of Romanticism was mixed: nineteenth-century welfare programs, as well as revolutionary socialism, both utopian and Marxian. As a remedy for poor living and working conditions, a few industrialists, impelled by humanitarian impulses, built planned settlements in the countryside integrating factories, housing for workers, and public facilities. John Stuart Mill, the leading theorist of political and economic liberalism, favored limited intervention by government to improve the lives of the poor. But rather than "issuing a command and enforcing it by penalties," Mill, like Bentham, thought governments could help workers by providing information and advice. Supporting measures permitting motivated individuals to improve their situations by voluntary effort, he favored public funding for education, and policies encouraging workers to emigrate to colonies overseas.[11]

Social and governmental problems during the first half of the nineteenth century in Europe and America, we realize with hindsight, were similar to those now confronting less developed nations. Converting a population of unsophisticated country folk into a disciplined labor force requires time and social learning. Ignorance and lack of skills isolate recent rural immigrants, forcing them to accept the least desirable living and working conditions. A life of rural or urban poverty may be equally squalid at early stages of development, but because city life is congested, problems are more visible.[12] During the first stage of the industrial age, knowledge of the relationship between sanitary conditions and public health was in its infancy. Nor had economic development created sufficient resources to support capital investment in public infrastructure—roads, lighting, water-supply networks, drains and sewers, and parks—which might have improved lives of large city populations. The promise of economic development lay in the future; its privations existed in the present.

If, after laboring long hours, working populations sometimes exploded into riots, it was not because city life lacked amenity, but because during repeated periods of depression (and even in intervals of recovery when prices rose but wages lagged behind) laborers' real incomes were declining.

Measured as per-capita consumption of all commodities, the gap between rich and poor appeared to be widening during the first part of the nineteenth century.[13] Up to 1850 in England, the most prosperous nation, working-class populations still spent more than two-thirds of household income for food. Compared to the gargantuan middle- and upper-class menus set down by Mrs. Beeton, their diets were limited in variety, high in carbohydrates, and low in protein.[14] Growth of national markets linked by improved transport networks had dispelled the age-old specter of mass famine, but, as in past eras, there was still a direct relationship between rising food prices in real terms, social unrest, and political instability.*

Unlike modern developing nations with access to technical assistance and financial aid from abroad, local and central governments at the beginning of the nineteenth century possessed very little administrative capacity to deal with small changes. Management of growth at the rate that was occurring was simply beyond them, and economic development and growth of cities occurred without much government intervention.

But gradually governments accepted knowledge accumulated in the private sector—about channels of authority and control; about organi-

---

*Tension was acute in the late 1840s, when a trade depression and mass unemployment compounded unrest caused by rising food prices. Having witnessed the riots in Paris during the early months of 1848 that led to the overthrow of monarchy, and government's savage reprisal against the rioters, Tocqueville appraised the social climate in France as a war of all against all. "I saw society split in two: those who possessed nothing united in a common greed; those who possessed something, in a common fear. No bonds, no sympathies existed between those two great classes, everywhere was the idea of an inevitable and approaching struggle."[15]

zation of work; about efficiency, cost cutting. and honest management of resources—and formulated it in new ways, making it useful in the larger scale and varying situations of public organizations. Creation of the legal, regulatory, and procedural bases for public administration (by and for the public) was the preeminent achievement of legislative governments during the first part of the nineteenth century, giving substantive content to abstract ideology.

In this context, rationality in government meant centralization. In spite of all their efforts, governments during the seventeenth and eighteenth centuries had not developed effective structures for central control. Critics inside and outside governments from the late seventeenth century on had found ample fault with mixed public/private systems. Acquisitive impulses motivated private individuals who provided administrative services to governments, which suffered as a result. At least so it seemed then, without considering the probable costs of an enlarged public bureaucracy.

By the early nineteenth century, adverse opinion about private administration in government had developed a critical mass. The reform-minded climate that followed political revolutions impelled governments to try out Enlightenment ideas of rationality, ideas put to practical use by business long before. Improved administration of public finance was high on nations' policy agenda, for the old private networks were very wasteful of public resources. Everyone knew that governments needed to speed up tax collection, and to insure that the entire proceeds would be sent in promptly to the treasury. Methods of managing spending were not adequate, either; earmarking fragmented authority. Since a foot-dragging mentality permeated all aspects of the taxing and spending process, governments were often left high and dry—short of revenue and without information about how much was forthcoming or when it would be available for disbursement. If governments were to meet their obligations to provide citizens with justice and security, better fiscal management was needed.

The movement toward rational financial administration entailed consolidating authority over taxing and spending within the treasury. Hierarchy would gain expertise. Moreover, developing rational methods entailed specialization—with one line of authority for revenue collection and a separate organization for spending. Since each of the departmental accounts and the many public and private revenue funds had operated with autonomy, procedures to insure that departments spent only the amounts appropriated, and only for the purposes that legislatures and executives designated, were essential. Coordination of departmental procedures to achieve uniformity—production of comparable information at regularly specified intervals—was vital. That all government agencies should maintain permanent records and follow the same format and observe the same rules has been such a universally accepted hallmark of good public administration that these practices seem timeless. But it was not until some time after the reforms of the early nineteenth century that rules specifying budgetary unity, comprehensiveness, annuality, and control of spending through post-audit became norms, followed by all branches of government without deviation.

Just as ideas about representative government spread rapidly from one nation to another during the first part of the nineteenth century, so, too, was there rapid diffusion of innovative thinking about financial administration. Between 1776, when a proposal for a consolidated Treasury fund administered by professional officials first surfaced in England, and about 1870, all the industrialized nations (except, of course, the United States) adopted modern financial-management procedures. Nineteenth-century executives and their administrative personnel—Baron Louis de Villèle in France between 1817 and 1822 and Louis Thiers around the turn of the century, Robert Peel and William Ewart Gladstone in England at midcentury, Ludolf Camphausen, a liberal elected in Prussia after the 1848 Revolution—transformed prescriptive rules, mere constraints against action, into affirmative behavioral norms. While few officials lower in the hierarchy are known, their contributions were equally important in implementing the untried ideas and rules set forth by nineteenth-century legislatures.

Professionalization was a corollary of this process of rationalization. By 1870 all the tasks of financial administration had been invested with legitimacy. Selected for competence, and paid salaries commensurate with responsibility and skill, the officials who performed these tasks owed loyalty and fidelity to the commonweal as it was embodied in the treasury's operation. Governed by emerging norms of efficiency, economy, and, above all, balance, the centralized finance structures built by public officials during the first part of the century served governments well after 1870 as public pressure for spending increased.

From our present perspective, the solutions to problems of taxing and spending devised by nineteenth-century legislatures and administrators seem simple enough. Once there was consensus that governments should try to attain economy in operations, unified management by a centralized treasury was seen by everyone as an obvious course. Yet in individualistic social orders, such as in England and the United

States, and even in hierarchical societies like Germany and France, consensus must have obscured a residual ambivalence. For, so it seemed, centralized structures hardly were operational before dissatisfaction began to emerge. Once the structures were established, the long and difficult development process seemed quickly to have been forgotten. People took them for granted, as if they had always existed. Thus the orthodoxy of one era gives rise to the dissent of the next.

It is fashionable now to censure the uniform rules of a centralized system. In large, complex governments that provide many different services to publics, so the argument goes, centralization creates rigidity. Tightly constrained by rules imposed from the center, large-scale organizations are incapable of responding to change (or, at least, slow to respond)—whether it is induced from within or from without. If a society wishes to foster innovation within government and to improve its responsiveness to publics, critics of centralization assert, hierarchy might conceivably retain generalized rules, but improve its performance by creating anew the decentralized structures and ideas characteristic of economic individualism. Yet, paradoxically, local authority unresponsive to the center, and market methods of administration and the autonomy (read corruption) that these entailed were what earlier generations of reformers had opposed. To curb just such excesses, nineteenth-century reformers had tried to devise rules and to create structures that would mandate a balance between government receipts and disbursements each year. Yet no sooner had budgetary balance become an accepted norm of behavior, than pressures began to build up to violate that norm. Faced with increasing demands from widening publics—to promote internal development and to improve societal equity—and in a climate of escalating nationalism, late-nineteenth-century governments were under constant pressure to spend more than they took in. The persistent tinkering with tax structures in all nations from 1880 until World War I reflects efforts—more successful in some nations than in others—to maintain balanced budgets while trying to modernize military forces and contain societal turbulence.

Change accelerated after 1870. Industrial economies raised productivity as manufacturing contributed steadily increasing proportions to each nation's output while agriculture declined. The trend was most pronounced in England. In 1900, one hundred years after the earliest phase of its Industrial Revolution, 40 percent of its gross national product derived from manufacturing. Imports had reduced the agricultural component to 6 percent. Although industrialization came later on the Continent, in some places it progressed more rapidly, for the conceptual, technological, and organizational groundwork had already been laid. Between 1860 and 1869, before Germany's unification, German industry had produced barely a fourth, and farming a third, of that nation's output. Rapid growth of large-scale, integrated industrial complexes using the latest technology to produce chemicals, steel, electrical products, and machine tools had raised the manufacturing component of GNP to 40 percent by 1905-14. Even though its eastern agricultural provinces retained preindustrial land ownership and authority patterns, by the same period output from farming had fallen to just under a fifth of GNP. Where farming continued to make a large contribution—in France, Italy, Scandinavia, Russia, and the United States—industrialization was well under way in the last quarter of the nineteenth century.[16]

Industrial production after 1870 reflects accumulating advance in science and technology. While textiles, the major product of late-eighteenth- and early-nineteenth-century factories, were still important, they were being supplanted by heavy industry. Blast furnaces turned out billets and plate for multiple uses: carriages and rails for trains, streetcars, and subways; steam engines and heavy machinery; steamships; structural members for bridges and skyscrapers; and armaments, bicycles, and cars. Electricity, mysterious before the nineteenth century but now understood, provided rapid communications links, enhanced motive power, and improved lighting for expanding populations. The material artifacts of life at the beginning of the twentieth century would be familiar to all of us.

For its beneficiaries—industrialists, financiers, investors, and the middle class—rapid technological progress generated boundless optimism for the future. It seemed warranted; as growth created an increasing surplus, living standards improved for all segments of society, even the poorest workers. Food consumption increased in amount and variety. With rising tax receipts, local governments could provide public facilities to mitigate some of the social costs of congestion. As publicly supported education up to secondary level gradually became mandatory in all Western nations, local and central governments allocated funds to support cultural facilities—libraries, theaters, and museums.

But although rapid growth improved expectations, it also had contrary consequences. The periodic fluctuations in economic activity that made their first appearance along with early-nineteenth-century factories seemed to become longer and more severe after 1870. Varying in duration and intensity from nation to nation, but extending roughly between 1873 and 1879, 1882 and 1886, 1890 and 1893, 1900 and 1903, and 1907 and 1909,[17] late-nineteenth- and early-twentieth-century depressions seemed to confirm Marx and Engels' dire predictions. Long periods without income radicalized workers. Violent conflicts—strikes and riots in all industrial nations—mobilized professionals and intellectuals into reform movements directed toward halting the strife and then trying to do away with its causes.

Conflict would slacken, reformers argued, if the material benefits of growth could be more widely distributed. Empirical research after 1880 provided statistical verification of the obvious: in spite of recent improvements in workers' living standards, the distribution of income, savings, and wealth in industrialized nations was still very uneven. A small proportion of their populations (less than 5 percent) held most of the wealth, and it was becoming more concentrated.[18] Though workers made modest gains during prosperous intervals, loss of income from unemployment during downturns seemed harder to bear. In this era, unlike earlier ages or the present, the destitute could not expect to receive aid from either public or private sources.

The popular ideology of economic individualism reinforced legal constraints against aid to the poor enacted during the nineteenth century. The secular gospel of work preached by Samuel Smiles and other apologists[19] stigmatized the need to accept charity as moral weakness. Workingmen should limit their families and then avoid all excess, especially alcohol. They should be frugal, in order to accumulate savings for a cushion against adversity. If workers practiced foresight, their misfortune could not be attributed, as labor unions and socialists were claiming, to a pervasive failure of the system.

Reformers pressed governments to mediate conflict between industrialists and the trade unions. Life insurance held by the middle and upper classes to protect their families against risk suggested a way to limit uncertainty in workers' lives also. If government, employers, and workers could jointly contribute to insure against loss of earnings from illness and old age, and if governments could create a fund for unemployed workers during prolonged economic decline, they would end workers' ever present fear of destitution.

The modest redistributive measures introduced by late-nineteenth- and early-twentieth-century governments were the establishment's response to inequality. These programs, it should be understood, were completely compatible with collectivism. Each group would contribute to the whole, and if some people contributed more than others, that was their place in the scheme of things. Cooptation of workers and trade unions (which were by then developing their own hierarchies) was the aim. In large measure these programs did succeed in mitigating conflict.

Relations among nations after 1870 also led to demands on treasuries. Specialization fostered interdependence among nations, but economic rivalry intensified nationalism. The minimum-tariff, free-trade policies of midcentury gradually fell out of favor as the international arms race built up momentum. The tariffs that one nation after another enacted after 1880 had several rationales. As they always had done before adopting free-trade policies, nations aimed to defend domestic producers against foreign competition. The demands of workers and trade unions for protection against the vicissitudes of economic life could be met not only by incipient social insurance, but also by trade barriers. Supporters also hoped that the new tariffs would yield sufficient revenue to pay for expensive military equipment—repeating rifles, cannon, and the fleet of steel-clad, steam-powered battleships that strategists of the age of Mahan and Mackinder viewed as the primary deterrent.

Changing public attitudes were enlarging the state's role, but, even with receipts from assorted new tariffs, spending for arms and welfare increasingly strained budgets. Except in Germany, whose massive investments in arms were paid mainly by borrowing, all the leading finance ministers before World War I believed that balanced budgets were essential for financial stability.[20] Because tariffs alone could not support rising spending, nations needed more productive taxes. Increasingly, late-nineteenth-century policymakers favored income taxes; their productivity when levied at nominal rates implied that higher rates would enhance the return.

Precedent existed for taxing the wealthy. Confiscation of royalist property during the French Revolution had convinced socialist critics that wealth not only should but could be heavily taxed; from 1848 on they had incited governments to tax the rich in order to give to the poor. Ever since the northern-Italian communes had levied the first income taxes during the Renaissance, the unequal burden at different income levels had prompted some governments to exclude people with the lowest incomes from paying these taxes.

Moderates in and out of government had not forgotten the tax revolts at the century's beginning. Nineteenth-century legislation broadened the equity principle through other means. In determining liable income, taxpayers could subtract a personal exemption for themselves and their dependents, equivalent to the amount needed to support a family above subsistence level.

Democratic governments in the late nineteenth century faced a difficult dilemma. Committed to principles of equity and equality derived from the French Enlightenment, yet holding to norms of minimal taxation and balanced budgets propounded by individualists (which had become fiscal orthodoxy, during the previous half century), policymakers hesitated to raise tax rates. Yet, when confronted with a growing discrepancy between receipts and expenditures, and given the massive concentration of wealth held by a few individuals, there was a measure of sympathy for the view that the protection the state offered the economy should be paid for by the main beneficiaries.

A new way of thinking about income, derived from neoclassical economic theory formulated after 1870, helped policymakers resolve the dilemma. Marginal theory presumes that, in a free market, an additional increment of anything has high marginal utility to someone who has none, while the utility diminishes in proportion to the amount of it he possesses.

As a universal principle, the diminishing-marginal-utility postulate is applicable to income as well as consumption. Thus, according to neoclassical theory, while an increment of income has high marginal utility to a poor person because he has so little to start with, it has smaller marginal utility to someone wealthier, simply because his income is higher. Ideas about progressive taxation, heretofore propounded only by rabble-rousers, suddenly became respectable, clad in scholarly garb. Taxing large incomes at higher rates than lower incomes was both justifiable and fair.

In addition to income taxes, marginal-utility theory provided rationale for inheritance taxes and for the progressive rate schedules on both that governments introduced to support social spending and arms. Between 1894, when England imposed the first progressive tax (on inherited property) to pay for battleships, and the beginning of World War I, socialist rhetoric lingered in the popular appraisal of income and inheritance taxes. How could anyone but the very wealthy object to them? Poor and middle-income people did not pay these taxes; they were designed to soak the rich.

EFFICIENCY, RATIONALITY, AND THE IDEA OF THE BALANCED BUDGET

Budgeting became a legitimate function in representative governments of the early industrial age. Its intellectual foundations fused ancient and medieval ideas of accountability within government and Enlightenment doctrines of rationality. Seventeenth- and eighteenth-century thought focused on the nature of order. Speculating about changing relationships between government and society, moral philosophers in England and Scotland derived a model for government from Newton's cosmology. Adam Ferguson and his pupil Adam Smith believed that government should manifest a balance among disparate elements. The synoptic model of human understanding developed by eighteenth-century continental thinkers implied that intelligence could find workable solutions to societal problems. Enlightenment theorists in France were searching for the best way to achieve order within government, and then to maintain it.

Financial matters especially demanded order. Critical to government's functioning, taxing and spending were still administered by the haphazard methods and outmoded structures of earlier ages. Long before the eighteenth century, repeated financial crises had demonstrated the inadequacy of budgetary devices for current conditions. Some innovation had occurred: public banks created a stable climate for debt-funding in the Netherlands and England. For the first time in the long history of government, nineteenth-century legislatures and executives developed improved management procedures that, along with steadily rising incomes, brought stability and predictability to government finance.

Sound finance was a by-product of adaptation to ideas that had governed decision and action in private endeavors since the late Middle Ages. Organized, goal-directed behavior has been the norm in all workaday activities of Western peoples ever since feudalism broke down. On manorial estates or agricultural smallholdings, in craft and industrial workshops, and in business, the linear conception of process that pervades Western thought typically prevailed. Productive activities are not ends in themselves but means to another end: organization of factors of production to enhance resources. Whether the goal was improved productivity on a manor or increased profit in an enterprise, the means were technical or managerial innovations to reduce waste, thereby cutting costs.[21] Cost-cutting was so common in private ventures that in the late Middle Ages bookkeeping and agricultural-management techniques evolved to facilitate it. Among modern practitioners, specialized terminology has emerged. The idiom of management—of public and private enterprises alike—characterizes cost-cutting to achieve economies as *rational* behavior, and the process itself as *rationality*. The classical economists are credited with inventing rationality, but it is fairer to say that they formalized what was happening all around them. Their creativity lay, rather, in isolating the components of rationality, then expressing them systematically. Their term for increasing returns through innovation that raises productivity is *economizing*, which is directed toward attaining *efficiency*—getting the most out of given resources or achieving a stipulated objective with the least input.

Eighteenth- and early-nineteenth-century physics and engineering based on efficiency, economizing, and rationality concepts also had roots in the revolutionary cosmology created by Newton in the late seventeenth century. In the Newtonian system, gravity's universal force creates a balanced universe. Because each action has its equilibrating counterpart, the system is parsimonious.* In Newton's world nothing happens by chance. All is organized, balanced, and predictable.

In short order, the simplicity of Newton's formulations rubbed off on those who thought about relationships among men. For philosophers of the Anglo-Scottish Enlightenment, Newton's cosmos created a model for government, economy, and society. If balance among opposing forces sustains order in the universe, might the balance principle also provide the means of maintaining order in society? Filtered through Locke, Newton's theories provided rationale for governance by representative legislators instead of absolute monarchy, for societal diversity rather than cultural uniformity.

In classical economics, Newtonian ideas suggested the automatically stabilizing, self-regulating competitive market in equilibrium, wherein norms of economic efficiency guide decision and action. Conceptions of efficiency in science, economics, and practical business and agricultural management came together during the late eighteenth and early nineteenth centuries, creating a hybrid idea with profound practical implications and even greater normative consequences for government: the unified, comprehensive, and *balanced* annual government budget.

Budgetary balance is the perfect compromise between individualism and collectivism. Hierarchies tend to spend too much as each level dignifies its place. Competitive individualists see nothing wrong with lavish private spending. But since they must pay the taxes to support public ostentation, market regimes favor minimal public spending. Both individualists and collectivists have a stake in the stability of the regime; one order contributes wealth, the other organization and rules. So hierarchy agrees to limit its appetite (or at least to pay its bill), and

*A religious man, Newton wanted his theory to be compatible with contemporary Protestant theology. In His infinite wisdom, God had created just what is needed, on earth and in the heavens, no more and no less. Until Darwin and Wallace conceived another way of looking at the world, no one comprehended the overwhelming scale of nature's prodigality.

individualism to pay more, provided the budget remains balanced.

The evolution of administration during the nineteenth century demonstrates attempts, common in recent years as well, to correct perceived institutional defects by contriving opposite arrangements. A conviction that change through competition would mitigate both confusion and corruption was the basis for early-nineteenth-century proposals for new administrative methods. (Today, under very different circumstances, public debate over taxing and spending policies takes place within the same conceptual framework. As deficits climb in rich and poor nations alike, there is a widespread belief that budgets are out of control.) Linking organization with economizing, the administrative structures that emerged for preparing annual consolidated central-government budgets marked a significant beginning of modern ideas about governmental rationality. Critical for the conduct of all other central-government functions, improved financial administration preceded rational management in other branches of government and, when central governments began to assume new functions late in the nineteenth century, served as a model for them.

The fourteen reports of a British parliamentary commission, created in 1780 in response to widespread public interest in "economical reform," contain policy prescriptions that might still appear in modern administrative-reform proposals; the efficiency-rationality principles they embody have become public-administration orthodoxy. The reports called for "simple and intelligible" financial administration whose regulations should promote economy—limiting or, better still, cutting off "every superfluous and redundant expense." There should be a single, consolidated expenditure budget instead of a profusion of revenue funds. To prepare that budget, summary estimates of departmental expenses should be drawn up a year in advance. To insure accuracy and comparability, all departmental expense records should be maintained in uniform format.[22]

The reports promoted budgetary unification and consolidation on several counts. Preparing annual expenditure budgets would save government money. Budgeting would therefore reduce need to levy taxes. It would impart flexibility, creating opportunities to transfer funds among services, impossible with existing methods of allocating the proceeds of specific taxes for particular expenditures. Simplification and unification of departmental accounting would discourage fraud by reducing the time lag in post-audit, then averaging between fifteen and twenty years.

Although the components of budgetary technology appear to have been formulated all at once, their implementation took over a century, varying in speed and in comprehensiveness from nation to nation. England began budgeting in the last quarter of the eighteenth century, but did not establish full treasury control of spending until 1866. In ten years, between 1817 and 1827, France enacted a series of laws establishing centralized management of taxing and spending, but during a century marked by revolutions in 1830, 1848, 1851 and 1870 its adherence to those laws was both sporadic and partial. Belgium, building its budgetary structures on the French model after its own revolution in 1830, soon developed segmented financial management. Its legislature voted taxes all at once before the fiscal year began, and then (as some Third World nations do today) reviewed spending proposals continuously throughout the year, trying to balance the budget in monthly installments. The Netherlands established centralized structures for legislative control of spending after 1848; Italy, in 1860; Sweden, after 1876; Norway, in 1905; Denmark, in 1915. In general, these changes occurred after radical changes in the structure of government. The United States trailed behind: the Bureau of the Budget was not created until 1921.

The making and enforcing of central-government budgets varied, but the procedures all rested on similar premises: departments should be subordinate to the treasury regarding expenditure; treasury taxing and spending policy should manifest legislative intent;* financial management should not be ad hoc; order should be maintained by planning ahead. The following general sequence of procedures emerged:

1. Each year departments submitted to the treasury detailed estimates of all spending anticipated in the next year.

2. Putting together departmental estimates, the treasury drew up *consolidated* estimates of anticipated spending.

3. The treasury prepared, then submitted to the legislature, a proposal for taxes and borrowing that was sufficient to cover spending anticipated in the coming year and debt-service obligations accumulated in earlier years.

4. The legislature debated the proposal. Because taxing and spending policies affect everyone, debate was passionate and often acrimonious; it reflected divisions among political, economic, sectional, and class interests. Accepting some measures, rejecting others, the legislature enacted the *budget*—a law specifying amounts and purposes of

---

*In Italy after 1860, and Germany (unified in 1871), however, budgeting still followed earlier patterns, controlled by an autocratic executive with power to override a weak legislature.

planned spending. In accordance with the economizing norms that governed the process, a *balanced* budget was mandatory. In all but the most unusual circumstances (involving extreme national emergencies), revenue should be at least equivalent to spending; preferably it should be greater. Taxes sufficient to support expenditures were therefore enacted either before or along with the spending plan. A corollary of spending, taxes were the balance-inducing element of the budgetary equation.

5. In due course taxes were collected; funds were allocated to departments and spent.

6. Finally, to determine whether actual spending corresponded with legislative mandate, all departmental receipts and expenditure records were examined retrospectively by the treasury. The audits occurred within nine months to a year after the end of the previous fiscal year.*

All in all, it would be hard to invent a budget process that better combined collectivism and individualism. It embodied hierarchy— from the top-down processes of formulation to the legislation and execution of budgets afterward. Following market principles meant checking on results—auditing to see that money was spent in accordance with the budget proposal—at least as well as was possible then.

As budgeting became established in nineteenth-century governments, all these stages were regularized and systematized in a process involving role specialization and division of labor between legislature and executive. Acting on advice of the treasury, the legislature authorized procurement and allocation of resources. Administration and control of spending was the executive's responsibility, carried out by the treasury.

Unlike covert, private management of state finance in earlier ages, financial policy was formulated and implemented in public in most states. Legislatures made decisions after open debate in which new interests tried to promote policies unacceptable to the old order.† Freed

---

*Upon Italy's unification in 1860 its audit bureau was granted formal authority not only to approve orders of payment before spending occurred, but also to rule on any other legislative action with financial implications. But, because its autocratic executive could always make decisions in secret, and enforce these decisions with legal decrees, restrictions on spending proved to be ineffective in practice. Like Germany, Italy practiced deficit financing before World War I; it sold debt to cover discrepancies between tax receipts and spending.[23]

†At midcentury Britain's Parliament adopted several rules specifically to block spending demands of working-class members: preventing MPs from initiating spending proposals (1852), and limiting debate on financial matters (1866).[24]

from threat of prosecution under libel laws, a vigorous press influenced public opinion. By the last quarter of the nineteenth century, though women lacked the franchise, most governments had abolished property qualifications for voting. Critics from all walks of life attacked legislatures; when voting on budgets their members had to pay attention to policy references of many different interests.

Attaining efficiency in government became the task of the treasury, which adapted old administrative structures for new purposes, and designed structures and procedures that had not existed before. Eventually there was so many changes in organization and behavior that they amounted to a managerial revolution.

Nineteenth-century treasuries tried to attain rationality by preparing useful estimates of spending in the short-run future and by improving the effectiveness and timeliness of audits of past spending. Good spending estimates required unified departmental procedures. Governments achieved better audits by constraining authority of individuals and departments.

Long before the nineteenth century, governments had tried to hold accountable the individuals who collected and spent funds. But with so many persons and so many organizations, each with independent authority, audit was difficult at best, more a symbol of superior–subordinate relationships among individuals than a deterrent to corruption or an incentive to better management.

Centuries of departmental autonomy had sustained a feudal mentality among administrators. Like high officials in some Third World nations today, late-eighteenth- and early-nineteenth-century administrators viewed appointment to office as a chance to get rich, and to help out friends and relatives by giving them jobs. In order to centralize control, treasuries had to develop better procedures for limiting individuals' authority over departmental funds. It took time to develop, implement, and enforce rules, but eventually the effort paid off. Comprehensive, synoptic accounting permitted post-audit soon enough to determine whether funds were disbursed as the legislature had mandated. A further step was prohibiting ministers and departmental subordinates from spending funds appropriated for one purpose on some other. And then, when they were forced to give back to the treasury the appropriations not spent by the end of the fiscal year, their authority was further reduced. Departments could no longer build up a private reserve fund to evade legislative intent.

At least it was not nearly so easy as before. Spending departments—as English Treasury officials call them, or ministries in continental terminology—still had ways of using up their unspent funds before the end of the fiscal year, in order to keep them from reverting to the treasury or, worse still, from providing a rationale for reducing funds the next year. Transfers between categories and unexpended balances still could be used to squirrel away money for use at departmental discretion. And then as now, spending by some departments had support from special constituencies, and departments could count on beneficiaries to defend their share of the budget. On the Continent, for example, business interests favored state spending for public works and railroad construction.

Making up a consolidated budget from departmental spending estimates was intrinsically difficult, for predicting the future, even for the short interval of a year in advance, has high probability of error in an uncertain world. But short-term prediction was not even possible when autonomous departments had few common procedures. Early reforms focused on seemingly simple matters—keeping uniform department records; using similar forms; observing the same fiscal period—all aimed at achieving comparability among departments' spending estimates. The core of the nineteenth century's administrative revolution, the procedural standardization and unification needed to make budgets, helped create modern bureaucracy. But nineteenth-century treasuries never developed sophisticated forecasting methods. They operated by a simple estimating rule: Take the amount of last year's spending as a base for next year's estimate. Whenever possible, reduce it, but if circumstances warrant, increase it, but only a little. Though they now forecast spending with sophisticated mathematical techniques, modern budget-makers still use this rule.

As budgeting became institutionalized, politics widened the focus of accountability. Structures and procedures for preparing annual consolidated expenditure budgets were developed concurrently with improved capacity to audit departmental accounts. By the time consolidated budgets had supplanted multiple revenue-expenditure funds, political and organizational accountability had displaced personal accountability.

Doctrinal and ideological differences divided nineteenth-century legislatures into factions and parties. Budgets were not merely technical devices for allocating resources and auditing spending, but potent weapons in continuing struggles for party dominance. As amounts spent grew steadily, a new kind of political technician replaced the aristocratic amateur and entrepreneur-administrator of earlier ages. If governments were to withstand opposition, officials responsible for finance had to present credible budgets. Capacity to generalize, to think in functional categories while understanding complexity, and ability to maintain high standards of personal and professional integrity became requisites for political leadership as well as for effective financial administration. Under party government, department officials were responsible for expenditure estimates, and liable if auditing exposed corruption or error. But as the new management methods took hold, their liability came to be political and organizational.

A single worthy purpose, saving money, shaped the auditing and estimating techniques, for economy was the principal goal of nineteenth-century governments' financial policies. Reformers initially viewed the balanced budget as technical means to an end: attaining economy. But nineteenth-century politics changed ideas about balanced budgets. Partisan debate over taxing and spending elevated the balanced budget from subordinate to primary importance. By the time the estimating and auditing procedures had become routine, the balanced budget became a norm of organizational behavior, and, finally, an ethical imperative. It became one element of prescriptive doctrine integrating ideas about efficiency, economy, organization, and the size and functions of government. Connoting balance among regimes as well as in finances, budget balance became a cultural ideal, with its own taboos. Representing stability, sound management, and absence of market constraints, the doctrine of the balanced budget defended important social relationships.

Its precepts are simple. First and foremost, always think small. Government should do only the minimum necessary to insure citizens' safety and welfare. Financial policies should be designed with that end in view. In the few activities it must undertake, government should cut down expenses whenever and wherever possible, to get the most for its money. Spending little, government then can tax lightly, spreading the tax burden over the entire society so resources can remain free for productive investment. Except to smooth cash flow, government should not borrow. It should aim to pay off existing debt by sequestering some revenue each year in a sinking fund earmarked for debt retirement.

How does the balanced budget fit into such a schema? The mandate of a balanced budget acts as a positive check against ever present tendencies to spend foolishly (or in any event to spend too much) or to permit unwarranted growth in government's size. Whenever the public demands new programs, then, equivalent economies elsewhere must offset the increased spending. If not, taxes must go up. The ultimate rule was that spending had to be matched by revenue.

The notion of balance formalized implicit social understandings about the acceptable levels of taxing and spending. While taxes might rise, they would not, because of opposition, go up very much. Spending might also grow, but it was limited by social expectations about limits and by the level of taxation considered tolerable.

With its consultation over estimates and public debate over alternative expenditures, the budgetary process ideally should approximate the allocative efficiency of a free competitive market in equilibrium. And yet, although balanced budget ideas were widely accepted, the bad old days of spending in excess of tax receipts did not disappear altogether. During the nineteenth century as well as today, political pressures often threatened budgetary unity and comprehensiveness, and when this happened budget balance also was sacrificed. External threat or internal instability led governments to violate these norms, in ways we might still recognize. In continental nations especially, the "extraordinary" budget and the "supplemental" appropriation were common features of financial management throughout the century. A Belgian commentator during the 1830s characterized the extraordinary budget as "the juggler's cup by which the Minister of Finance disposes of the deficit."[25] And when, as often happened, off-budget spending for special purposes was not paid out of tax receipts, but by borrowing, it added to the deficit. During the latter part of the century French legislatures repeatedly enacted supplemental appropriations to evade balance constraints.

The ideal, if not always the practice, of budget balance was made easier by rapid economic growth during the nineteenth century, which created a bonus for government, just as inflation did during the 1970s. Aggregate revenue increased steadily, but budgets remained a relatively constant proportion of GNP (between 3 and 5 percent). With rising incomes, governments could keep taxes low, spend gradually increasing amounts for traditional purposes and new ones, yet maintain balanced budgets most of the time without having to make serious efforts at reconciling differences.

Norms of balance were so widely accepted that when governments did begin to spend proportionately larger amounts for social programs and arms, they instituted new taxes in order to maintain balanced budgets. Though this was not originally envisaged, the balanced-budget norm could be construed (and was, by hierarchical regimes) as an invitation to raise taxes.

WAYS AND MEANS: TAXES

Taxation was a vital political issue in all nations throughout the nineteenth century. Widespread public reaction to the tax revolts at its inception established the tenor of subsequent discussion. While recognizing need for stable revenue, nineteenth-century men believed profoundly that government's taxing power should be limited. They thought taxes should be levied for revenue only, no more than was needed to cover the next year's expenses and the cost of servicing, refunding, and redeeming debt. Once norms of budgetary balance were established, interdependence of taxing and spending was the most important factor affecting formulation of financial policy.

As always before, taxation aroused passion. But now governments were obliged to justify tax proposals. When a larger public became involved in the policy debate, liable citizens provoked controversy when threatened with taxes. Antiquated traditional taxes modified by opportunism were unsuited to changing conditions and unacceptable to nineteenth-century publics. As widening franchise enlarged the political base and economic development gave powerful new interests representation in legislatures, capacity to produce revenue was not sufficient rationale for a tax. Those who argued in favor of one tax or another tried to formulate reasoned arguments: they invoked political theory, and mobilized support by citing axioms of political economists.

The taxes a government can impose are related to a nation's economy, its history, and the political climate at home and abroad. Citizens of Western nations will more readily support their government if its policies are seen by most people as benevolent, and if it makes moderate fiscal demands. In such circumstances governance approximates market exchange; taxes, as Justice Holmes said, are the price citizens pay for civilized government. A long history of punitive taxation, ended abruptly by revolution establishing legislative government, will have long-lasting effects on citizens' attitudes; in these places bias against central government persists for a long time. Such societies are slow to impose new taxes. When they do, remembering past injustice, reluctant taxpayers search for ways to evade.

A nation's economic development determines distribution of resources, income, and wealth; these factors, in turn, influence government's decisions about who should pay taxes, and how much. Possessing meager resources, agricultural societies can derive revenue only from taxes on primary production. Economic development through growth of commerce and industry creates complex markets and sophisticated financial institutions, and increases wealth; it enhances the resource base and creates institutional structures appropriate for more productive forms of taxation. Market taxes and income taxes become feasible.

History and economy leave their mark on the present in levies surviving from earlier stages of development, when governments had limited resources to support administration. Often now, the small fees paid for private transactions with government (import and export permits, visa, and passport fees) are merely symbolic of central authority. Representative governments tend to respond to social constituencies favoring one tax or another. Thus, excises on tobacco and alcoholic beverages, originally luxury-consumption taxes imposed opportunistically for revenue, persist for reasons of morality and health. For those who collect them, old taxes, as the maxim goes, are good taxes, and new rationales can always be found.

Commercial expansion during the eighteenth century had permitted most Western nations to derive significant revenue from indirect taxes on transactions, but sources of additional income varied. England, with a vigorous commercial economy and incipient industrialization, and the Netherlands relied much less on traditional direct taxes on land and personal property than did the other European powers. With limited manufacturing (of luxuries in state-subsidized workshops), large agricultural sectors, and slowly developing internal markets, the continental nations—France, Prussia, Russia, and the Hapsburg states—imposed direct taxes on persons, agricultural production, and property in the country districts, and a few transactions taxes in towns. A young nation on the American continent, born in a tax revolt, would allow its central government minimal taxing authority. Sale of confiscated royalist property supplanted taxation for a short time in France during the radical phase of its revolution against absolutism. Generated, in part, by oppressive direct taxes, that upheaval created a bias against direct taxation in France that persists to this day.

Resting on the Enlightenment principle of individual rights, the constitutions establishing representative governments during the early nineteenth century committed them to approach taxation with fairness. The arbitrary taxes of past ages no longer were acceptable. Fairness (or equity) became linked with economic efficiency, the major tenet of classical political economy. Together, these two principles established a normative framework for both individualists and emerging hierarchies in fiscal-policy debate. The best taxes should produce revenue without inhibiting production; and the tax burden should fall equally on each taxpayer, no matter how rich or poor. As balances in legislatures shifted over the course of the century, groups representing working people also mobilized efficiency and equity arguments to promote society's common interests.

Economic-efficiency concepts shaped public debate on taxation for the first two-thirds of the nineteenth century. (Because the effects of taxing and spending interact, efficiency ideas emerged concurrently with the ideas of organizational rationality that led to government budgeting.) Individualists argued that nations should not create artificial market barriers. If there were no import and export taxes to constrain trade, nations could profit from specialization. Each nation could produce and sell to all others the products for which its unique endowment of climate, resources, and skill yielded comparative advantage. Maximizing economic efficiency, unfettered markets could benefit everyone; sale of all nations' products at lowest cost would induce greater consumption.

In 1815, agricultural interests in England pushed through Parliament a tariff protecting domestic grain producers from foreign competition. High grain prices and need for self-sufficiency during the Napoleonic Wars had induced landowners to bring marginal land into cultivation. By permitting farms to maintain production on low-yielding acreage, the tariff effectively subsidized inefficiency. In many districts during the turbulent 1820s, the minimum wage in agriculture was tied to the price of grain. As rising food prices contributed to labor unrest in towns, it was obvious to individualists and to emerging egalitarians that the poorest people bore the major burden of the subsidy.

Sentiment built up to repeal the Corn Laws (as the grain tariffs were called), or at least to revise them to limit protection for agriculture. Viewing England's multitude of internal market taxes as another reason for its high costs of production, mercantile and manufacturing interests embarked on a reform campaign. Throughout the 1820s and 1830s a coalition of free-traders and anti-Corn Law activists speaking for labor pressed for reduction of excise taxes and tariffs. In spite of opposition by landed interests, the coalition managed to eliminate a few market taxes, and to lower rates on some others, by promising to cut spending. (Repeal of the paper excise—a "tax on knowledge," individualists claimed—was a major victory.)

Prompted by depression and reduced revenues, tariff reform was in the air on the Continent as well.[26] After the Napoleonic Wars, trade barriers were impeding sale abroad of Prussia's chief products: grains, timber, and linen. In 1818, aiming to promote domestic business and to increase exchange with neighboring German principalities, Prussia began to reduce internal market obstructions by abolishing sixty excise taxes on 2,800 different commodities. Barriers against imports also came down: raw materials could enter free of duty, and manufactured goods paid a tax (nominal for those days) of 10 percent of market price.[27]

Removing trade barriers improved the business climate in all the German states. Noting the advantage of collective action, these states organized into a customs union (called the Zöllverein) during the 1830s. Like the present European Common Market, it minimized internal trade barriers among member states; imposing moderate increases in import duties, it presented a common array of tariffs to nonmembers.

Continental reforms affected the policy climate in England, reinforcing individualists' claims. At hearings before a parliamentary committee on import duties in 1840, Board of Trade officials presented dramatic evidence corroborating free-traders' arguments about low rates of return from tariffs. In the previous year, 98 percent of the revenue obtained from duties on twelve hundred different items derived from taxes on eighty-nine items, and taxes on nine commodities had provided 83 percent of the revenue. Moreover, the import duties gave ample inducement to smugglers. Not only were most of these taxes an administrative headache and a societal burden, they produced very little revenue. The committee recommended abolishing all but the most productive duties.

Balanced-budget ideas played a central role in the politics of fiscal compromise. During the first third of the century governments acquired administrative capacity to forecast and control spending. Because accumulation of debt signaled need for higher taxes, all political and economic interests viewed borrowing as a threat to government's financial stability. Paying for spending out of current revenue without long-term loans was the principal goal of financial policy. Since the customs and excise taxes that produced two-thirds of England's revenue were immediately responsive to economic fluctuations, political leaders were reluctant to risk loss of *any* revenue source, fearing possible deficit. It was only by promising to cut spending that successive governments in the 1820s and 1830s eliminated a few indirect taxes and achieved modest rate reductions in duties on grain and several other commodities.

Creating a surplus above subsistence, growth in individual incomes among broader populations of industrializing nations made income taxes feasible for nineteenth-century governments. But the movement away from indirect taxes during the nineteenth and early twentieth centuries and the growing acceptability of income taxes were related to unique social forces. In France and Germany, where traditional hierarchies forged alliances with business interests to maintain control of government, and in the United States, where an alliance of market and sectarian regimes consistently withheld from central government all but minimal taxing authority, indirect taxes continued to yield the lion's share of revenue for most of the nineteenth century. In England and Holland, citizens' willingness to pay income taxes derived from the growing strength of balanced-budget ideas in their political cultures and from opportunism when confronted with large military and, later, social expenditures.

Wherever the income tax was acceptable, it permitted government to maintain balanced budgets while implementing policies to attain fiscal and economic efficiency. In a growth environment the income tax supplemented other revenues, providing resources for limited spending for rearmament and for wars without requiring massive borrowing. Simultaneously the income tax helped make taxes fair. As governments became representative of all groups in society, not merely propertied interests, fiscal equity became more important.

Precedents for an income tax derived from emergency. Mobilizing community consciousness, wars against neighboring states had made citizens of the northern-Italian communes during the Renaissance willing to tolerate income taxes.* In mid–seventeenth century, after the Stuart Restoration (1660), England levied an income tax for a short time to pay for its war against France. In the late seventeenth century, Jean Vauban, the engineer who advised Louis XIV of France, had tried, without success, to think of a way to tax incomes. During the Terror (1793), revolutionary forces in France imposed progressive taxes on wealthy individuals' incomes; about a third of France's revenue during the Napoleonic era (1797–1815) derived from a tax on types of property indicative of wealth, and from an income tax on trade and professions. Because it was obvious that market taxes alone could not produce sufficient revenue to support its campaign against Napoleon, England in 1798 enacted an income tax.† The year before, Holland had imposed an income tax to pay for its war expenses, and Austria did so the following year (as did the duchy of Baden in 1808, and Russia in 1812).

England's experience during the Napoleonic Wars has been well documented; with improved administration the income tax raised revenues with unparalleled effectiveness. Imposed at low rates (between 5

---

*See Chapter Four, pages 198–99.

†A tax on alcohol helped Napoleon pay for his wars. "He got five millions from the tax on brandy, and wished to know which of the virtues would have served him as well," an observer reported.[28]

and 10 percent of income) compared to modern income taxes, it produced about a fifth of total revenue for most of the war years. Collection was self-administering; taxpayers had to file oaths declaring their liability. But to insure at least minimum revenue, income tax on salaries of government servants and investors' income from government notes and bonds were withheld before payment.

Public debate over the income tax manifested modern attitudes of individualism. From the outset, legislators, policymakers, and the public argued over tax preferences. Business and agricultural interests raised questions about tax policy, and each group propounded measures favoring its respective interest. If income is taxable, how should income be defined? In computing taxable income, what costs of earning income may legitimately be deducted? Should not earned income, bearing as it does the cost of personal effort, be taxed at a lower rate than inherited income or the return from invested capital? What tax rates and what incidence would yield adequate revenue without penalizing entrepreneurial effort? To yield the highest return to government, at what point in its production should income be taxed? And how might the state raise revenue without burdening its poorest people? Each time England's income tax of 1798 came up for renewal—in 1802, 1806, and 1812—public and legislative debate focused on these issues.

Citizens tolerated the income tax only because it raised revenue to support the fight against Napoleon. Throughout the war, critics railed against the tax and all its associated procedures. The requirement that tax returns should disclose income from all sources was onerous enough; but having to swear an oath of truthfulness made things worse. (Believing that divine forces monitored their actions, taxpayers in those days feared the ultimate reckoning for understatement of income.) As always, people objected to government's fiscal hierarchy. Wealth and social position commanded deference in early-nineteenth-century England. Liable citizens looked upon administrators who might question their tax returns as tyrannical inquisitors. They regarded filing a return as an arbitrary invasion of privacy, degrading to gentlemen, and the tax itself "an outrage upon popular opinion," "unjust in principle." In 1815, a petitioner to Parliament characterized the income tax as "hostile to every sense of freedom, revolting to the feelings of Englishmen, and repugnant to the British constitution." Sharing his opinion, Parliament lost no time abolishing the hated tax as soon as the wars ended.[29] It met the same fate in continental nations.

Equity considerations also had shaped the war income tax in England. On grounds of hardship, the very poor were exempt. Incomes below £60 a year were not taxed; up to £150, people paid nominal amounts. A variety of measures aimed to equalize liabilities of taxpayers in different situations: deductions were permitted for family responsibility (dependents, life insurance) and for specific costs of earning income.

When the wars ended, equity arguments from an earlier era justified a return to indirect market taxes in all European nations. Political figures, more often than not, invoked the benefit rationale systematized during the eighteenth century by David Hume and Adam Smith and recently expanded by French political economists Frédéric Bastiat and J.-B. Say: market taxes did not favor one group over another. Since rich and poor derived equivalent benefit from the state's protection, requiring all citizens to pay the same taxes was justifiable and fair. Because luxuries were taxed at the highest rates, market taxes would bring forth revenue from the wealthiest taxpayers—those who could easily pay.

As long-run improvement in welfare was interrupted by short but violent episodes of depression-induced mass distress, destitution of unemployed workers during the 1820s and 1830s drew policymakers' attention to the regressive incidence of taxes on food and household staples. Well before embryonic social research had provided tangible evidence, sectarian critics like William Cobbett railed against the taxes levied by a corrupt establishment; he claimed that paying for subsistence exhausted working people's modest earnings. Taxes on sugar, bread, beer, candles, soap, and similar items consumed a larger proportion of workers' incomes than of rich people's.[30] Free-traders and anti–Corn Law activists in England reinforced their efficiency arguments for tariff reform by contending that market taxes were not really as even-handed as theorists had assumed. With liberals' support some market taxes were abolished during the 1820s and early 1830s, and other reduced.

Efficiency, equity, and balanced-budget ideas came together in 1842 when England restored the income tax. For the first time since the Napoleonic Wars, it had borrowed to cover budgetary deficits for several years in succession. Depression during the late 1830s had brought widespread unemployment in industrial centers. Private philanthropy, the churches, and contributions from local governments had supported poor relief in England since the Elizabethan era. But when relief demands in some places exceeded available resources, central government, fearing uncontrollable violence among the poor, hesitantly stepped in to supplement local contributions. Such action was in no sense a turning point in social policy; rather, it represented an extension of the upper orders' traditional paternalism. (This was, of course, long before anyone had conceived of countercyclical spending by government.) While depressed conditions pressured England's central government to spend money on poor relief, those very conditions were reducing its revenue from market taxes. When budget deficits appeared after 1837, policymakers in Parliament responded in the traditional way. Reviving protectionism, they imposed import duties on whiskey, raisins, sugar and tea, and levied an excise tax on domestically produced malt, an essential component of beer. Most of these products were mass-consumption items, recently added to the working-class standard of living.

By 1840 changes in England's economy during the previous half century had modified its social structure and politics. Using their new wealth to buy land, and arranging marriages between their offspring and those of older landed families, England's affluent businessmen and industrialists gradually merged with the nation's traditional landed elite. Abolition of the rotten-borough system during the late eighteenth century facilitated entry of businessmen into politics. As changing social and economic interests coalesced into political parties during the first three decades of the nineteenth century, members of Parliament with business backgrounds increasingly aligned with free-traders who opposed market taxes. A group of extreme individualists outside Parliament also mobilized: in 1841 Anti–Corn Law League members in Manchester threatened a tax strike if the hated laws were not repealed. A strike could "stop the wheels of government and convulse Threadneedle Street and Bond Street at any moment."[31] Middle-class professionals and young government administrators who aimed to increase participation in politics by reducing property qualifications for voting also supported free trade. The impetus for free trade thus stemmed from a coalition of business, liberal professionals, and young government administrators, representing regimes of market and hierarchy.

In 1842, after five years of economic distress marked by widespread unemployment and continuing budget deficits in spite of increased market taxes, the Whig Party (whose policies reflected agricultural interests for the most part) lost control of Parliament to the Tory Party. Convinced that removing trade barriers would restore the economy, a group of young reformers among the Tories encouraged party leader Sir Robert Peel to reduce tariffs. Like contemporary supply-side economists, these reformers were certain that in time tariff reform would generate sufficient revenue to maintain government services while paying off debt. But after five years of deficits the new government couldn't afford the luxury of waiting. It was politically imperative to balance the budget immediately.

Peel was no ideologue, but he could justify market taxes only if they either provided equivalent benefits to all groups or raised sufficient revenue. And they did neither. Before the election he had spoken out often about the market taxes' excessive burden on the poor. With protracted depression amplifying working people's hardship, it was clear to him that taxes on grain and other food imposed costs on all consumers while providing benefits only for domestic producers.

Remembering the income tax's earlier success at raising revenue, Peel decided to restore it temporarily. Once it was approved, import duties on grain, butter, and cheese were reduced immediately, and meat tariffs abolished. Eventually the first round of reform lowered tariffs on six hundred different commodities. When inadequate domestic production in 1846 led to rising prices, followed by food riots, the Tories responded by initiating another round of reductions more extensive than the first.

This joining of economic doctrine and political expediency, together with improved administration, had a fortuitous outcome. With expansion induced also by extensive private investment in railroads during the 1840s, business conditions improved, and England's revenue went up steadily during the 1840s and 1850s as its market taxes were reduced or abolished.

Among ordinary people, free-trade ideas were more popular in England than on the Continent. With manufacturing comprising a steadily increasing segment of England's economy, businessmen and workers there had greater incentive than their European counterparts to press for the reduced tariffs that they were sure would create new markets for their products. Egalitarian social forces also influenced tariffs. In the late 1840s, for example, as Liberals protested against the slavery still existing in some places, sugar was taxed at four different rates; slave-produced sugar paid the highest duty.

Although industrialization was just beginning on the Continent (partially subsidized by government investment in railroads in Germany and France), the efficiency ideas implicit in free-trade policy did have some impact. A retreat from protectionism had already occurred in Prussia; during the 1830s free-trade ideas spread to Switzerland and Saxony. After its liberal revolution (1830), Belgium entered into a tariff-reduction agreement with Prussia, and tried unsuccessfully to negotiate a similar agreement with France. Seeking to expand their market for fine wines and silk fabrics, French mercantile interests and agriculturalists also tried to reduce tariffs during the 1830s. Their efforts were blocked by spokesmen for infant coal, iron, and cotton textile industries who feared loss of markets if England's products were admitted free of duty. Emperor Louis Napoleon of France, an enthusiastic free-trader, did sign a commercial treaty with England in 1860. For the nineteen years it remained in effect, there was reciprocal reduction in trade barriers. An innovative provision in the treaty (the most-favored-nations clause) provided means to reduce the general level of tariffs. If either nation were to enter into a trade agreement with a third, its terms would automatically extend to the other. The Netherlands dropped nearly all tariffs between 1845 and 1875, and even Russia, with higher tariffs than any other nation in Europe, lowered a few barriers during the 1860s.[32]

The United States maintained protectionist policies throughout the nineteenth century. Except for two brief episodes when an income tax was enacted (in the North and the South during the Civil War, and in 1894, until the Supreme Court found it unconstitutional), customs duties and excises on tobacco and alcoholic beverages were the only taxes the federal government was authorized to collect.

Free-trade policy during the 1850s and '60s went hand in hand with an ideology of limited spending supported by minimal taxation. The English Liberal Party leader Gladstone's free-trade budgets of 1853, 1858, and 1862 rested on a presumption (by no means unanimous) of peace and internal stability requiring no action by government. As Chancellor of the Exchequer, and later as Prime Minister, Gladstone staunchly resisted spending proclivities within his own party, and among the opposition. A Treasury surplus, he believed, would merely endow government with money to spend on unnecessary enterprises. It was always best to keep taxes low, collecting just enough to support a bare-bones civil and military establishment.

Despite limited spending and steady revenue growth, the threat of budgetary deficits continued to haunt politicians. No political leader of the 1850s, '60s, and '70s could ever be certain that revenue would be adequate to balance the budget. Year after year at budget time, always offering profuse apologies to the public for failing to repeal the income tax as Peel had promised long ago, England's finance ministers deferred risk by retaining it a few years longer. Levied at nominal rates on incomes from rents, salaries, and capital, it supplemented tax receipts from other sources and assured financial security. Between 1843 and 1870 it contributed between 10 and 14 percent of annual revenue, while receipts from indirect taxes fell from 76 to about 62 percent during the same interval.[33] Thus, with a rationale of efficiency, the income tax became a permanent fixture of England's financial policy.

By the last quarter of the century, the demonstrated productivity of income taxes in England had created a movement for income taxes in other states as well. Enthusiastic advocates thought the income tax enabled governments to wring money from those who had it. And more was needed all the time—to support late-nineteenth-century nations' expansionist aspirations in world politics, and to pay for social-welfare programs at home.

There was a gradual shift in the climate of opinion after 1880: equity displaced efficiency as the chief rationale for taxation. As governments assumed responsibility for citizens' personal welfare by funding schools, public infrastructure (roads, water supply, sewers, parks), and public insurance against the risks of unemployment and old age, those who advised governments about taxes marshaled support from innovative fiscal theory formulated to be compatible with public-welfare ideas. According to the social theory of taxation emerging in Europe and America, in industrialized societies where large differences in wealth exist, a citizen's *ability to pay taxes,* not the *benefits* he receives from government, was the fairest criterion of how much he should contribute. Benefit theory fitted a mind-set favoring limited government: there must be a clearly articulated rationale for every proposed expenditure. With development of *faculty* theory (taxation according to ability to pay), ideas from a voluntaristic social order, suitable for a regime of equity, were challenging individualism and collectivism.

But if a direct tax on incomes was the road to fiscal justice, the route was neither certain nor direct. It was not easy to implement an income tax viewed by taxpayers as fair. As one nation after another adopted various types of income tax during the 1880s, 1890s, and the early years of this century (see Table 7), public debate focused on equity issues, posed in the technical idiom of the emerging academic specialty of public finance economics; the same questions were raised during the Napoleonic Wars, in 1843, and in each subsequent legislative debate over renewal of income tax. As it does today, mainstream public finance analysis dealt mainly with tax incidence; legislatures decided on the objects of spending.*

An important issue in the 1880s (as governments returned to protectionist policies) was whether market taxes are paid by the original tax-

---

*Toward the end of the century, theorists in Italy tried to analyze the productivity of public spending. The question of efficiency for what purpose had been ignored largely because consensus on governing institutions was assumed.[34]

TABLE 7

SOME NINETEENTH-CENTURY INCOME AND INHERITANCE TAXES[35]

Country	Income Tax		Inheritance Tax	
	Date Imposed	Percentage Rate	Date Imposed	Percentage Rate
England	1799	.01–10.0	—	—
"	1803	1.2–10.0	—	—
"	1842	1.5	—	—
"	1853	2.0– 2.5	—	—
"	1863	3.0– 3.5	—	—
"	1865	1.6	—	—
"	1875	1.3	—	—
"	1886	3.3	—	—
"	1894	1.3– 3.3	1894	1.0– 8.0
"	1907	5.0	1907	7.0–15.0
"	1910	5.5– 8.3	—	—
France	1909	3.0– 5.5	1901	1.0–20.5
Germany	1891	0.1– 4.0	1906	4.0–25.0
Holland	1892–3	2.0– 3.2	—	—
Denmark	1903	1.3– 2.5	—	—
Sweden	1897	1.0– 4.0	—	—
Norway	1905	2.0– 2.5	1905	1.0–10.0
Switzerland*	1840–on	1.5– 6.0	n.a.	0.1–75.0
Austria	1849	5.0	—	—
"	1896	1.5–10.0	—	—
Italy	1864	7.5–15.0	1902	0.1–22.0
"	1894	7.5–20.0	—	—
Australia*	1895	1.2– 3.0	—	—
New Zealand	1891	2.5– 5.0	—	—
U.S.A.	1862–71	3.0–10.0	—	—
"	1914	1.0– 6.0	—	—
Canada*	1892	1.5– 5.0	1892–4	1.5– 5.0
Cape of Good Hope	1904	2.5– 5.0	—	—
Japan	1887	1.0– 5.5	1905	1.2–10.0

* Provinces, cantons, and states imposed taxes at different times, and at varying rates. We give the lowest and highest rates for the date specified.

payer, or are passed on to others. In their academic work, and when they served on the boards and commissions being formed to provide tax policy advice for legislatures, public finance specialists tried to measure tax incidence to better determine who bears the ultimate burden. (Some writers, like F. Y. Edgeworth in England, were statisticians.) They wanted to find out how equality of sacrifice could be attained, and urged legislatures to consider how the tax burden might be equalized among citizens with similar incomes but different financial obligations. Objective analysis justified normative conclusions. Having determined that a tax bearing most heavily on high incomes best served equity, fiscal theorists tried to figure out how to levy it without interfering excessively with personal saving or inhibiting investment.

Nineteenth-century polities came no closer to resolving these questions than we are today. The difficulty is intrinsic to public-policy-making whenever absence of consensus produces many different specific measures for achieving generalized goals. One approach to equity, followed from the Napoleonic-Wars tax to the present day, involves classifying income. Whether income from different sources—wages and salaries, rent, returns from invested capital, profit or loss from business, income from legacies and gifts—should be taxed at the same rate was controversial from the start. Throughout the nineteenth century, business and professional interests in England contended that taxpayers who worked for a living incurred greater sacrifice by paying taxes than did recipients of "unearned" income. During debate over its 1799 income tax bill one member of Parliament spoke of the "glaring inequality of taxing [similarly] a man who had £1,000 a year arising from capital and the man who gained the same annual sum by profession or business." Such a tax would "strike with peculiar force at industry and the fruits of industry," he asserted. A Scottish landowner and industrialist thought the measure so unjust that it would "encourage a spirit of emigration."[36]

Individualists demanded lower tax rates on income from commerce and manufacturing, and generous deductions for the cost of doing business. But from the outset parliamentary leadership rejected selective rate reduction. They wanted to be fair, but they did not favor equality. Their aim in proposing an income tax was to raise revenue, not to redistribute income. Remembering with revulsion the way radicals had usurped property during the French Revolution, William Pitt the Younger, Prime Minister in the late eighteenth century, and his nineteenth-century successors opposed any measure granting tax exemptions or low rates to favored groups, which they believed would result in confiscation. Unequal tax rates "would amount to nothing more nor less than the introduction of a plan of equalizing fortunes." No matter what his source of income, every man gained the same benefits from the state, Pitt contended. "Is the industry of the artist, the manufacturer, the mechanic less [subject to] protection of law, less involved in the great contest in which we are engaged, less likely to be overthrown in any disaster of state than the income which arises from land?" Moreover, he asserted, a low tax on earned incomes would entail administrative complexity beyond government's capacity, for "without an investigation more oppressive, a disclosure more extensive than anything which the bill permits," differentiation of tax rates could not be achieved.[37] But the question of special treatment kept recurring. When England's income tax of 1843 came up for renewal, an MP from Ireland gave emotional testimony to the professional man's burden: "This tax is not only inquisitorial but most criminal[!]" In all fairness, governments should not impose "the same tax upon the income which is the product of a man's thought, and may be called the sweat of his mind, and upon [property] income which is as stable as the state."[38]

Promoters of the income tax did try to incorporate considerations of equity: by means of selective exemption of the lowest incomes, they aimed to write in norms of fairness. A minimum income is required for a family's subsistence, they reasoned, "and if from this income anything is taken away, the family is deprived of necessaries."[39] For the same reason the 1799 law permitted a deduction, scaled in relation to a taxpayer's income, for each of his children, and for the life-insurance premiums he paid. Not wanting to discourage enterprise, they tried to tax net income. Accordingly, taxpayers were entitled to deduct costs associated with its production. Property owners could subtract land tax, assessed taxes, and costs of drainage and improvements from gross income before calculating tax liability. Business could deduct production costs; salaried professionals, operating expenses.[40]

Increasing specificity in the tax code to attain efficiency or equity creates a public-policy dilemma. As specific measures are included to accommodate interest-group pressures, the code's increasing complexity, in turn, obscures general goals. Measures adopted to make taxes fairer for some taxpayers make them less fair for others. Revising a tax code to fit changing conditions over time by striking out some clauses and inserting others brings it closer to a polity's current ideals of fiscal justice. But as long as the law accommodates some taxpayers it will contain loopholes (special exemptions, deductions and rates we now call tax preferences) that others feel are not warranted.

Once ability to pay became an acceptable rationale for taxation, the way was opened to increased specificity as one group after another raised equity claims. The changing context after 1880 and the new fiscal theory together led to modification of mid-nineteenth-century ideas about limited taxation for revenue only. Marginal theory and the social theory of taxation enlarged the legitimate function of taxes. Besides providing revenue, taxes could be levied to provide incentives or deterrents to action. Operating as a surrogate market, the tax code became an instrument for achieving other goals valued by society. From Adam Smith and the Physiocrats through Henry George, for example, economists justified taxes on the so-called "unearned increment"—increases in land values and/or rents over time. Land was viewed both as the source of individual initiative and as the fountainhead of wealth in agricultural society, and it was widely believed that taxes on the unearned increment would weaken wealthy persons' incentives to buy land. Similarly, if governments permitted a deduction from taxable income for interest paid on loans taken out to buy land, the measure might stabilize society by widening the distribution of land ownership. In the late-nineteenth-century context of industrialization and urbanization, modest redistribution of income from the rich to the poor was a nonfinancial goal of taxation embraced by governments of Western industrialized nations.

With public spending rising, modest income redistribution through progressive taxation became acceptable to political leaders and the public. Progressive taxation was not a new idea. From the last quarter of the eighteenth century, minority opinion had favored taxing incomes of wealthy persons more heavily than those of poorer ones. Instead of relying on consumption of the rich to relate taxes to incomes (as did indirect taxes), proponents of progressive taxation suggested a direct tax on incomes levied at rates rising gradually with increasing income. Although he was by no means the earliest proponent, the English moral philosopher William Paley, writing in 1785, justified progressive taxation on equity grounds: ". . . I . . . believe that a tax . . . ought to rise upon the different classes of the community, in a much higher ratio than the simple proportion of their incomes. The point . . . is not what men have, but what they can spare." The French Declaration of the Rights of Man in 1789 echoed the same argument; it stipulated that taxes "ought to be equally divided among all citizens in proportion to their faculties [abilities]."[41] After publication of Thomas Paine's pamphlets *The Rights of Man* (1792) and *Agrarian Justice* (1797), radicals and reformers crusading for labor repeatedly demanded a graduated income tax. Whenever depression amplified normal hardship of workingmen, the outcry grew louder. Trying to reduce taxes on food and household goods in England during the 1820s and 1830s, workingmen's advocates such as William Cobbett supported a graduated income tax before aligning with free-trading business interests. On the Continent progressive income taxes are linked with socialism. Popular resistance to taxes on consumer goods was one cause of the Revolution of 1848. After 1848, especially where the revolution had aroused widespread sympathy, there were proposals to improve fiscal justice by taxing incomes instead of transactions. In 1849 Austria enacted a progressive tax on wages and salaries, and Prussia replaced some indirect taxes in towns with direct taxes. Several of the autonomous German principalities—Bavaria, Hesse-Darmstadt, Saxony, Baden—enacted income taxes with progressive rate schedules. Some of these taxes were never implemented. The political reaction after 1848 led to repeal of the others. Nevertheless, in these places, where change was coming about more slowly than in England, such actions indicated that the old order, with its reliance on royal-domain revenues, internal excise taxes, and external tariffs, was responding to forces of constitutionalism and egalitarianism.

All through the mid-Victorian era, income taxes in England were levied at flat rates, proportional to taxpayers' incomes. With the prevailing ideology of limited government, taxing income at low rates was barely tolerated. Prominent theorists like John Stuart Mill could not justify a progressive income tax, and progression was unacceptable to political leaders.

But toward the end of the century, opposition gradually weakened, again first in England, and again partly from fear of budgetary imbalance. Speaking before Parliament in the late 1880s, the Chancellor of the Exchequer alluded to recent spending increases. It is not because the state's business "has been conducted in a more costly manner," that expenditure has risen, he asserted, but because "new functions are constantly being forced upon the State, and . . . new services . . . being demanded of it . . . acting under pressure of public opinion, [Parliament] has been constantly imposing new duties upon the State, and compelling it to bear . . . the burden of work that has hitherto fallen on local authorities, or private individuals, or that . . . has not been performed at all."[42]

With rising expenses for arms and welfare, governments needed more revenue to maintain balanced budgets. Since renewed protectionism did not yield adequate returns, governments explored other alternatives. Social programs were justified by a redistributive ethic, and so were the graduated income taxes imposed specifically to pay for them.

In 1886 a backbencher in Parliament complained to the Chancellor about the excessive burden of income taxes on his middle-class constituents. He thought the wealthy were not paying their fair share.

> . . . The gentlemen of the Treasury bench . . . always have the
> remedy of screwing up Income-tax by a penny or two, in order to

meet deficiencies whether they are due to a declining revenue, to an increased expenditure, or to the relief of opulent landowners . . . I wonder whether Hon. members reflect on the . . . severity with which the Income-tax presses on such persons as work for their living, . . . who cannot in any way escape from the tax gatherer. I believe there is no class of persons . . . who contribute more to the Exchequer, in proportion to their resources, and with such serious sacrifices . . . I have always . . . attacked the theories of Socialism; but unless something is done, and . . . speedily . . . there will be a growing dissatisfaction [with] . . . escape of wealthy men from local contributions.[43]

That spokesman looked toward revised local property-tax rates to relieve the middle-class burden; others found the remedy to be heavier taxation of the wealthy. Since nothing but the accident of birth qualified recipients of legacies, a progressive tax on inherited income was one favored instrument.

In England during the early 1890s, rising spending was not being matched by equivalent revenue. Speaking before the House of Commons in 1894, the Chancellor conveyed the bad news: "Your expenditure has increased far more rapidly than your Revenue, and in these conditions, you must expect the consequences." The consequences were death duties with a graduated rate schedule. England adopted an inheritance tax specifically to pay for battleships. Estates valued between £100 and £500 paid the minimum tax of one percent; those worth more than £1 million paid the maximum rate of 8 percent. In spite of landowners' gloomy prediction that the tax presaged the end of the old order,[44] it was so successful that by 1898 (just before the Boer War) receipts had covered about half of increased spending since its passage.[45]

TAXATION AND WELFARE SPENDING

A theory of political culture can generate hypotheses about the origins of welfare policies. The programs implementing these policies are designed to accomplish one of two objectives: to increase security against adversity by forced saving, through contributing to social security; or by redistributing income: here the government collects taxes from the wealthiest people, then, by means of government programs, transfers funds or provides services to people who have less. Usually the security and egalitarian motives of welfare programs are mixed; from the beginning, most governments have mandated joint contributions to social security by workers and employers.

A cultural theory offers clues about who will prefer more welfare, and who will want less. For adherents of a market culture, for instance, risk entails opportunity for gain, and successful entrepreneurship inevitably leads to unequal reward. Market advocates thus oppose sizable welfare programs granting income or benefits by right. Because market regimes typically produce higher economic growth rates than the other regimes, growth alone can support welfare. Thus the theory predicts ("retrodicts" would be more accurate) that welfare schemes in regimes of competitive individualism are not initially supported by taxation according to ability to pay. Later on, if society's demands on welfare funding exceed the resources workers and employers have paid in, market regimes may accept modest redistributive taxation to maintain these programs.

Egalitarian regimes prefer redistributive programs without guaranteeing income security. Since the social leveling they seek remains to be accomplished no matter how much equality is achieved, egalitarians will always oppose efforts to stabilize an existing distribution of means.

Seeking to maximize societal security by stabilizing members' incomes, hierarchical regimes are most likely among the three primary cultures to originate and enhance welfare measures. Believing that the parts ought to (and do) sacrifice for the whole, hierarchies might also redistribute income in a modest way. The stronger the hierarchical element in a polity at a place and time (as opposed to its market elements), then, the greater is the likelihood that welfare programs will be introduced. Since social cohesion ranks higher than economic growth in hierarchical values, the cultural theory implies that slow-growing, hierarchically dominant societies should be the first to establish welfare programs.

Thanks to Jens Alber's major study of the origins of social-welfare programs in fifteen Western nations, these hypotheses can be tested. Undoubtedly, availability of resources opened the way for social programs. But neither the level of industrialization nor of urbanization (taken as measures of need to cope with the dislocations of economic growth) is associated with program origins. On the contrary, economically less developed nations initiated social insurance before nations with earlier industrialization. According to Alber, established authorities in less developed nations enacted welfare measures *specifically* to legitimate their authoritarian regimes "from above." In our terms, the nations with the weakest market forces and the strongest hierarchies took the first steps on the road to the welfare state.[46] This is a counterintuitive finding. Cultural analysis, it appears, *is* helpful in accounting for emergence of welfare programs.

How did this unlikely circumstance come about? In fact, establishment politics in the middle and late nineteenth century responded to egalitarian policy proposals of emerging socialist parties. In the German states, where aristocratic and autocratic influences were still strong, the redistributive doctrines espoused by socialist parties were attractive to laborers in expanding industrial establishments. After unification in 1871, Otto Bismarck, the conservative prime minister, watched with dismay as Germany's Social Democratic Party slowly but steadily increased its legislative representation: in 1870 it held one Reichstag seat, in 1873 seven seats, and by 1878 twelve seats. Having come out of Prussia, with its long tradition of centralized management, Bismarck had no real objection to expanding government's social and economic role. Seeking to weaken the Social Democratic Party by winning laborers over to the establishment, Bismarck deliberately promoted the socialists' programs. During the 1880s he proposed and then implemented several measures to enhance stability in working people's lives. Germany enacted compulsory sickness insurance, funded by joint contributions from workers and employers, in 1883, and accident insurance (funded the same way) in the following year. An old-age-and-disability-insurance fund was established in 1889; it was the world's first social security. While these programs failed to stem the Social Democratic Party's growth in membership or its legislative representation (in 1890 the party held thirty-five legislative seats), these earliest modern social programs quickly became the model for similar ventures in other industrialized states.[47]

As workingmen's parties gained strength elsewhere in Europe, members of the establishment began to see the state as an instrument of social justice and a counterweight against socialism. If the collectivity took responsibility for putting society "on a firmer and more solid basis," Arthur James Balfour, Conservative Party leader in England, told a Manchester audience in 1895, the working class would not be attracted to socialism.[48]

During the early 1900s David Lloyd George, England's flamboyant leader of the Liberal Party, wished to start an old-age-and-sickness-insurance scheme similar to Germany's, funded by joint contributions from employers and workers. But since he wanted to cover all citizens, including those never employed, supplemental funding was needed. During parliamentary debate on the Old Age Pensions Bill in June 1908, Lloyd George stated his intention to seek means to implement the new program: "I have got to rob somebody's hen roost next year. I am on the look-out which will be the easiest to get and where I shall be least punished, and where I shall get the most eggs."[49] Because he did not want to risk a deficit, Lloyd George set out to tax large incomes—those exceeding £2,000 a year—at higher rates than all others. England's Revenue Act of 1909 imposed a mildly progressive "super-tax"—a redistributive tax falling on the wealthiest citizens:

Annual Income	Tax (in Pence/Pound)	Rate (as Percent of Income)
up to £2,000	9	3.8
£2,000–3,000	12	5.0
above £3,000	14	5.8

Following nearly a decade-long decline in yields from domestic investments, the measure provoked outcry from individualists. Instead of creating long-term benefits, business and landed interests contended, the tax would weaken the nation: "Taxation would consume productive capital or frighten it abroad, would dampen enterprise and destroy the wealth-producing powers of the economy."[50] Since income earned in some of Britain's rapidly growing colonies was not subject to taxation, critics maintained, owners of large holdings in England had ample incentive to sell out at home. Reinvesting the proceeds in Canada or Africa could provide shelter from the progressive rates. Assessing the likely outcome of the new measure, a financial adviser to George V recommended that the monarch himself seek protection against eventual erosion of his patrimony: "No one who has watched the course of recent legislation in this country, both fiscal and social, can fail to see the wisdom of those who have capital to invest, taking advantage of the fields still open in Western Canada and certain parts of Africa."[51] Only about a million people paid income tax in 1909; about twelve thousand with the highest incomes were liable to the progressive rates.[52]

Even where the income tax had been well established for some time, it did not contribute as much to nations' revenue during the nineteenth century as it does today; it merely supplemented revenue from other sources. Each year, as policymakers searched for ways to balance budgets, it was always tempting to add on small percentages to existing indirect taxes, or to impose new ones. Free-trade policy at midcentury reduced the number and rates of indirect taxes, but even in England during the period of maximum commitment to free trade (between 1845 and 1870), indirect taxes contributed at least half of central-government revenue, and in some years brought in nearly two-thirds. (See Table 8.) After 1880 the proportion of indirect taxes to total revenue

did fall somewhat, but until progressive income-tax rates were imposed
in 1909, customs and excise still provided nearly half of England's annual tax receipts. Still, no European government during the late nineteenth century derived as much of its revenue from indirect taxes as
did Germany. Under its Constitution of 1871, power to impose direct
taxes was reserved for the states; central government possessed only
limited authority to levy indirect taxes. Between 1880 and the beginning of World War I, receipts from indirect taxes were never less than
80 percent of central-government revenues in Germany, and in most
years contributed nearly the entire amount (90 percent and up). France
was governed by a fluctuating coalition of individualists representing
middle-class business interests, and hierarchy—composed of factions

TABLE 8

CUSTOMS AND EXCISE TAXES AS PERCENTAGE OF TOTAL REVENUE,
ENGLAND, FRANCE, GERMANY, 1810-1916[53]

Year	England	France	Germany
1810	56		
1815	55		
1820	70		
1825	77		
1830	72		
1835	72		
1840	73		
1845	64		
1850	64		
1855	57		
1860	50		
1865	62		
1870	63	21	
1875	64	22	95
1880	53	29	97
1885	54	29	91
1890	50	29	94
1895	48	28	94
1900	46	28	90
1905	46	26	90
1910	35	35	80
1912	37	28	80
1913	36	28	80
1914	35	26	55
1915	35	36	53
1916			50

of the old aristocracy—during the late nineteenth century. The coalition repeatedly managed to stave off pressure from socialist groups to redistribute income through income taxes. The coalition enacted some new indirect taxes after 1880, but, because France still retained taxes on external manifestations of wealth adopted during the French Revolution,* indirect-tax receipts were only a quarter to a third of its total revenue during the four decades before the Great War. Likewise, Sweden's personal and corporate income taxes introduced by a coalition of workingmen and small farmers aimed more to penalize wealthy persons than to generate revenue.[54] In 1902 average Swedish income was 972 kroner; the first 1,000 kroner was exempt from the progressive income tax introduced that year—rates ranged between one and 4 percent of income. Together with local taxes and numerous indirect levies, wealthy persons paid a maximum of 10–12 percent of income before World War I.[55] In Italy after unification, profit from state monopolies in banking and industry, and direct personal taxes contributed more to total revenue than did indirect taxes.

Until the First World War, fiscal demands were very limited compared to the present: tax receipts were less than 10 percent of national income in most industrial nations. Shortly after the turn of the century an English public-finance specialist, summarizing informed opinion from several nations, predicted the probable impact of taxes in the near future. If a government commands 5 percent of national income in taxes, he said, that represents a minimal demand. From 5 to 10 percent is moderate and reasonable. Taking more than 10 percent is too heavy a burden for the people to bear, all his commentators agreed, and "when 15 or 16 percent is reached, it is impossible to increase it."[56] This was not the first time the undesirable was merged into the impossible. Even with expanded incidence and increased rates during World War I, no nation exceeded these predictions.

When a war of unprecedented scale broke out in 1914, resources existed for governments to fight it. Ideologies of national dominance, strengthened by material and political developments of the previous century, mobilized populations to support the war. Redirected to war production, technology accumulated during the nineteenth century combined with skilled industrial labor to provide instruments of battle. The growth in national incomes and the enhanced income equality in-

---

*The *quatre vieilles* (four old ones), unchanged since 1799, were taxes on (1) real property, (2) personal property based on rental value of lodging, (3) commercial and professional license fees, based on earned income, (4) window and door taxes.

duced by industrialization had created vast stores of capital that governments could borrow and tax. Massive war loans funded in stable financial markets, and progressive taxation of business incomes (supertaxes, excess-profits taxes) financed World War I. Having no choice, liable enterprises paid these taxes. A precedent for progressive taxation had become established before the war. In a time of emergency, these taxes were accepted as legitimate.

THE NINETEENTH-CENTURY LEGACY FOR MODERN TAXING AND SPENDING

A quest for peace, prosperity, and personal security is a recurring theme in Western thought. Throughout the nineteenth century a diverse assortment of reformers had searched for a humane alternative to emerging industrial capitalism. Most nineteenth-century utopias looked backward, resurrecting an idealized version of the medieval manorial economy. Although utopian proposals attracted a small following among intellectuals, they never caught on in the larger society. Both in private life and in formulation of public policy, the intellectual legacy of the Enlightenment, with its focus on progress through reason, was dominant.

When applied to government, the Enlightenment's legacy of rationality produced administrative structures for effective public management of taxing and spending. Two strains of Enlightenment thought, the Anglo-Scottish stressing individualism and spontaneity, and the French-Continental focusing on rationality and on control from the top as a way of maintaining collectivism, came together in proposals for balanced budgets. By the middle of the nineteenth century the balanced budget had not only become a reality, it had acquired overtones of moral compulsion. Parallel norms of budgetary annularity and comprehensiveness also governed the spending process. Executive submission of an annual budget to the legislature was mandatory in most governments. In most places, too, the budget enacted by the legislature was construed as an all-inclusive plan for spending. Hence spending came first in formulation of financial policies; raising taxes to cover spending was secondary.

Free-trade policies adopted in most European nations by midcentury rested on the presumption that a limited number of consumption taxes levied at nominal rates could provide sufficient revenue. When individualism was dominant, an ideology of minimum government reinforced balanced-budget constraints on spending. At the end of the century when collectivist tendencies strengthened, European societies responded to egalitarians' demands that government help redress the inequity of urban industrial life. Nations found resources by levying direct taxes on incomes, and progressive taxes on inherited property and wealth of their most affluent citizens. If they could not compel collectivists to reduce spending, individualists could at least try to avoid falling into debt.

Nearly all of the powerful ideas shaping nineteenth-century financial policies are still around in one form or another. Ideologies favoring liberalization of trade or protectionism, balanced budgets or deficit spending, minimal taxation to create investment incentive, or steep progressive taxation of income and inheritance to support programs with redistributive goals—all these are part of current controversy over taxing and spending in highly developed nations.

As we look back on their original context, it is apparent that history has a way of playing tricks with powerful ideas. Altered conditions often lead to their application in circumstances and for purposes that their original proponents never intended and could not possibly have foreseen. A stream of unintended consequences is as old as society itself. The movement toward rationalizing taxing and spending provides an example of means leading to ends quite different from those originally envisaged.

Reformers who supported the nineteenth-century movement for rationality in government could not have conceived of present-day large governments built on a base of high taxes. They would have abhorred them. Their immediate goals—increasing internal efficiency, eliminating venality and favoritism—aimed only to permit central governments to function in a better, preferably cheaper way.

There are many possibilities in any given idea, especially in such a powerful one as rationality, and it is not possible to limit them all.[57] Once means are created, they are available to anyone for any purpose. Implementation of ideas depends not only on their intrinsic content, but also on what happens to them over time.

By the time efficient resource allocation through budgeting and effective resource accumulation through income taxation had been achieved, capacity of governments to take action in new directions had also been legitimized. As the nineteenth century progressed, nationalism and patriotism fueled increased spending, supported by higher taxes. Governments could plausibly claim that spending for arms and welfare was sanctioned by popular demand through democratically controlled legislatures and executives.

In our own century a political climate increasingly supportive of large-scale government spending for warfare and welfare, coupled with improved technical capacity to mobilize and allocate resources, has led to a revolution in the size of government, as well as to its increased efficacy and legitimacy. If these outcomes were implicit in the rationality idea, they were certainly never intended. An old parliamentary aphorism decrees, "He who wills the ends must provide the means." It could well be modified to "He who improves *capacity* to provide the means can't be certain about the ends toward which they will be applied."

No one could claim, as the nineteenth century ended, that the millennium had arrived. There was still poverty and injustice. But if one wished to look backward, or at places that had not begun to develop, the previous century's progress supported an optimistic faith in man's capacity to further improve life on earth. By the beginning of this century representative governments were broadening the traditional conception of the public interest. In an age of industry it was no longer deemed sufficient for governments to keep the public peace and maintain the nation's defenses. Governments began to protect the interests of citizens who had little of the world's goods. Government's new role offered a promising alternative to socialism and an answer to utopian critics. For citizens who could anticipate further material progress, all these developments created confidence in the future.

Chapter Seven

BALANCED REGIMES, BALANCED BUDGETS: WHY AMERICA WAS SO DIFFERENT

A successful financial system will conform to the political ideas which for the time being control society, and adjust itself to the political structure of the particular society to which it applies.

—HENRY CARTER ADAMS[1]

From the middle of the seventeenth century to the second decade of the twentieth, the difference between American and European budgetary behavior is striking. It would be hard to invent a country so much at odds with European nations. Both revenue and expenditure per capita have been markedly lower in the United States than in Europe. America has awarded more financial power to the legislature, whereas all Europe has given the executive that authority, albeit in a legislative committee called the cabinet. European budgets have been unitary, with expenditures and revenue considered together. American budgets have been fragmentary: each agency submits spending proposals, and revenue is considered separately. Although a unitary device existed (the congressional Ways and Means Committee), after 1865 it was continually fragmented. Still, taken as a whole, American national budgets were more balanced over longer periods of time than their European counterparts. This most unideological of peoples practices more than it preaches. Why has America been so different?

Obvious explanations should not be ignored merely because of their familiarity. The United States of America was born in a revolution against a sovereign executive, the King of England. So no one need be surprised by American distrust of executive authority. Yet this is only part of the story of American exceptionalism, and it does not explain how it was translated into budgetary behavior. After all, the threat of Indian or foreign attack and the need for rudimentary social and economic order necessitated some sort of central government. The "Second American Revolution"—replacement of the Articles of Confederation by the Constitution—took place to establish a stronger cen-

358

tral authority. It was radical in its design for self-government, rather than for economic and social equality—or "leveling," as equality of condition was then called. The constitutional debates and the Federalist papers reflect both the founding fathers' distrust of the people and ultimate dependence upon their consent. The problem was to negotiate between too powerful government and its antithesis, "mobocracy."

The framers of the Constitution feared that elected officials would compete for popular support by taking measures against property—for example, by debasing currency, or by favoring debtors over creditors (under the Articles of Confederation both had occurred). They feared a recurrence of Roman bread and circuses. And politicians did compete for popular favor—but why, for the longest time, did they reject greater spending and taxation?

Writing near the end of the nineteenth century, Lord Bryce was one among many who said that Americans had been saved from financial follies (presumably, their failure to imitate Europeans) by their natural endowment.[2] (But how would he explain today why suddenly-oil-rich nations somehow manage to raise their spending, accommodating to a cornucopia of wealth?) Material abundance alone does not explain why American governments raised only a fraction of the public revenue that their nation's wealth would have permitted.

Perhaps it is not so much what America possessed but what it fortunately lacked—a hereditary hierarchy and a feudal tradition, as Louis Hartz maintains.[3] Then the question of how to correlate a weaker hierarchy with a different pattern of budgeting remains. In *Democracy in America*, the magisterial interpretation of American politics, Alexis de Tocqueville ties the general equality of condition to availability of land: dispersed settlement patterns in America promoted voluntary association;[4] the more Americans were involved in private groups, the less they would want government (especially central government) to do things for them. Tocqueville's law is that voluntary drives out involuntary (i.e., governmental, compulsory) association.

If one turns to the related, contemporary question of why the United States "lagged behind" European social democracies in expanding welfare, an answer comes from Anthony King: American values are opposed to large government.[5] American government does less because its people are opposed to its doing more. But surely there is more than one type of person in America; a fair number might like larger government.

The question underlies the perennial debate over why the United States, alone among Western industrial nations, does not have a strong socialist party.[6] Apparently America has sustained commercial values; juxtaposing free enterprise against governmental intervention, it has done well enough by its citizens for business to stem protest from the left. In the end, values seem to explain everything.

Yet such explanations all become new questions: Why are American values what they are? If they remain cohesive and consistent, what could account for the persistent political conflict in America—except disagreement over values, which brings us back to square one?

Assuming that there is only one political culture in a country at any time leads to tortuous efforts to explain diverse behavior in terms of a single value. By abandoning uniformity and postulating diversity in cultures—shared values and the social practices they support—we hope to explain the discrepancy between European and American behavior in mobilizing and allocating resources.

American exceptionalism, we contend, is a product of the relatively equal strength of three social orders, collectivism, individualism, and egalitarianism, whose corresponding political regimes we have named hierarchy, markets, and sects. In the special circumstances of American life, people favoring each of these regimes have been more evenly balanced than elsewhere. Americanism enables them to pursue not the same vision, but separate visions. The question of what would result in the abstract from conflict and cooperation among the different ways of life in America overwhelms the imagination. But if we can pinpoint the political manifestation of these cultures in the budget-making process, we will come closer to understanding America.

Collectivism, we know, has been weaker in America than elsewhere, partly because its elites have to compete for popular favor. Competitive individualism has been strong from the beginning. Egalitarianism has fluctuated in strength. More importantly, though maintaining the same objectives, it has radically altered its sense of the means best suited for egalitarian ends.

The tendency of contemporary egalitarians to support state welfare spending is misleading. Two hundred years ago, sectarians believed that the central government introduced unnatural inequality into society. Hence they restricted their support for egalitarian spending to state governments, which they favored as being closer to the people. They insisted on balanced budgets to curtail establishment spending.

Why did budget balance become almost a religion in America? Because it is the one thing that all three cultural tendencies could agree about.

Though individualists do not object to deficits in principle (as long as they benefit from the borrowing), they do not want to pay the tax bill. Thus market regimes offset the desire to gain from debt with the reluctance to pay higher taxes, and agree that revenues should ordinarily cover expenditures. The resulting balance limits the efforts of egalitarians to please the populace (common in state legislatures), and of hierarchies to aggrandize government in a manner inappropriate for a commercial people. Left to their own devices, hierarchies would run deficits at each level of the bureaucracy. But, in exchange for the ability to raise revenue, in an era in which revenues were more often promised than paid (during the Continental Congress and the Articles of Confederation), hierarchies agreed to limit spending. Since both markets and sects would limit central-government spending, hierarchies sought agreement at least on raising sufficient revenue. Hence the inability of any one regime to dominate the others led to consensus on the balanced budget. Violation of the boundaries of such agreement would lead (in the imagination, at least) to fearsome penalties—public immorality, private vice, inflation, unemployment, and collective ruin.

So much for speculation. Let us see how the hypothesis of cultural diversity is reflected in budgetary behavior.

THE COLONIAL PERIOD

In the fifty to a hundred years after the first settlers arrived (the late 1600s to early 1700s) there was no standard currency. The first colonists were poor. The only money in circulation was a mixture of Dutch, English, and, later, Spanish coins. Prices, particularly in New England, might be specified in guilders, pistoles, pieces of eight, doubloons, or rit-dollars as well as in pounds and shillings. Even worse, as in medieval Europe, each colony valued the separate coins differently; one kind of coin disappeared in one place, to be succeeded for a time by another.[7] Understandably, the shortage of ready cash was a constant theme in colonists' financial complaints.

When coins did not suffice, which was most of the time, trade was conducted by barter. As in the ancient monarchies, various staple commodities were declared legal currency—rice and tobacco in the South; cattle, corn, and furs (especially beaver) in New England. A college student's tuition fee might be a cow or a goat. Lacking anything better, Dutch settlers began to use Indian shell beads, or *wampampeake*—white beads from conch shells and the rarer, hence more valuable, black beads from mussel or clam shells. Taxes, labor costs, and court judgments were payable in wampum.[8] Inevitably, the ratio of two white to one black shell varied as much as did the value of the currency (and was depreciated even more when settlers or Indians charged that one or the other had dyed white shells black).[9]

In the absence of commercial banks—before the American Revolution there were none—credit was extended and commerce carried on by merchants, who minted silver "pine-tree shillings" deliberately made 22.5 times lighter than the English variety, so that they would be retained in the colonies rather than shipped abroad.[10] Other merchants acted as agents of exchange or issued letters of credit to Americans traveling abroad. Banking in those days was a hit-or-miss business. The Puritans who colonized New England believed that holding debt was immoral; indeed, the laws were so severe that an imprisoned debtor unable to raise cash for his release might languish there indefinitely. Experiments with paper money may well have sprung from colonists' understandable need to facilitate trade and to mitigate sanctions imposed on debtors.[11]

The colonists issued another form of currency: treasury bills, in anticipation of tax receipts, which paid for colonial wars or for general administration. As in medieval Europe, colonial governments discounted the notes to obtain ready cash; since they passed through so many hands and were of such uncertain value, they were finally abandoned in favor of floating loans in advance of tax collection.[12] Dependent as the colonists were on whatever credit they could muster internally, it is understandable that the English Bubble Act of 1719,[13] which prohibited issuance of bills of credit in the home country and then in America, led to considerable opposition by 1751.[14]

Shortage of specie (as the colonists designated metal coinage) was exacerbated by intermittent wars against the French between 1730 and 1760, when taxes rose as much as ten to twenty times their prewar rates.[15] Under the lash of necessity, several colonial legislatures issued "paper money" (bills of credit), which bore interest and required repayment in specie. So long as these bills were only a small portion of available currency, their value held up, but eventually they depreciated from half to a tenth of their former value.[16]

Under massive popular pressure, various colonies began to issue paper money, much of which not only fluctuated in value but also rapidly depreciated as the printing presses ran overtime. In response, moralistic tracts appeared, which suggested limiting the amount of circulating paper to prevent inflation. Benjamin Franklin issued one of his first broadsides on this subject, though his call for restraint was not so urgent in pacifist Pennsylvania, where, unlike the other colonists,

Pennsylvania's Quakers steadfastly refused to issue paper money to pay for war.[17] Nonetheless, Franklin's support of British restrictions on paper money led to his only electoral defeat.[18]

Though government in colonial times was simple and frugal, even rudimentary, it faced high start-up costs in relation to income, especially income in hard cash. The colonists needed to build forts and maintain courts, prisons, and roads. Added to these local needs for revenue were those of the mother country, which occasionally tried to rule in fact as well as name.

Mercantilism held sway in England; the major purpose of the trade and navigation laws and the mother country's customs and revenue service was to provide an outlet for British manufacturers. When the Seven Years' War (1756–63) ended, the Royal Navy established a "colonial squadron" to cut off unauthorized trade. Perhaps natural advantage would have won the trade for England anyway, but the prevailing economic doctrine was against putting it to the test.[19] Competing with the mother country was not considered a virtue. Having been designed to support the customs service rather than to raise funds,[20] the Navigation Acts actually produced only minimal revenue.

Within the colonies, taxes varied. The New England colonies favored a tax on personal property, such as cattle and slaves, as well as on houses and land assessed at current market value multiplied six times. Rates were a penny to the pound of assessed valuation and varied from a high of sixteen times assessed value during King Philip's War of 1676 to a low of eight. This tax weighed most heavily on farmers whose barns, cattle, and houses were hard to hide. To prevent farmers from bearing the entire burden, the colonies imposed a poll tax on persons; an individual was said to be worth twenty pounds sterling and was assessed at a rate of a penny per pound. The poll tax, which rose and fell with the property tax, was hard on the poor, and later was abandoned. There were exemptions, of course, for the governor of the colony, schoolteachers, ministers, invalids, and Harvard College students. Since property and poll taxes were not directly related to income, there was also a "faculty" (income or ability to earn) tax on those who made more than a given sum; it presumed, often without the best of evidence, that certain occupations would bring in an expected amount of money.[21]

With their wealth tied up in property, southern plantation owners preferred indirect taxes on all exports and imports rather than property or income taxes. The southern colonies also levied poll taxes, which often were paid in tobacco or some other commodity. The middle colonies, such as New York, New Jersey, and Maryland, used a combination of direct and indirect taxes. And they added refinements such as a graduated poll tax, which fell hardest on apparently unpopular segments of the community—wig wearers, rich bachelors, and lawyers. At one time or another, and despite Quaker opposition, all the colonies ran lotteries to finance education; Dartmouth, Princeton, Harvard, and Yale all gained. And, instead of forced labor on public projects, several colonies required contributions in kind, such as tobacco, for building a fort, or as a fine for failing to attend church.[22]

Viewed from a different era, colonial expenditures look as simple and bland as colonial taxation. As in the mother country, care of the poor, the insane, the sick or otherwise needy was a local responsibility. Limited resources inhibited construction of public works; highways were short and rough, and colonial courthouses were modest, though sometimes sporting handsome façades. There were few judges, and they did not require helpers. No colonial navy existed, and the army (except during the Indian wars or during the war with France for control of the North American continent) consisted of local militia. Legislatures met for short periods; members received nominal reimbursement if they were paid at all. According to prevailing practices, the few officials of the small executive departments collected fees-for-service, instead of salaries drawn from general revenue. The royal governors alone received substantial salaries.

It was not the actual expenditures but the power relations these signified that mattered in America. Why should the colonists pay to support governors whom they did not appoint and who might oppose the local will? And England was equally adamant. Why should the home country pay for distant colonial wars while the remnants of feudal dues, known as quitrents, paid to government in return for land, fattened colonial treasuries? By 1762, the King refused to supply garrisons to colonies that would not pay to maintain them.[23]

If the colonies belonged to England, and if the colonists were English subjects, then they owed support to royal governors. The colonists, however, who wanted British protection but not British rule, freely used the English tradition of denying supply in order to force compliance with the legislative will. The commonplace view so assiduously peddled by pre-revolutionary colonists, that if the English King were only reasonable they would love him, is not supported by financial fact.

Merely to say that royal governors were kept amenable to colonists' will does not do justice to "Yankee" ingenuity in devising financial restraints.[24] The extraordinary effort of colonial legislatures to control executives gives this period its peculiar stamp. Connecticut may have been extreme in making the salary of the governor and other important executives dependent upon semiannual appropriations, but it was common practice to vote salaries annually. It might be thought that indirect taxes, excises and import duties, would stand until changed, but often these were reenacted each year. The colonists did not willingly give royal governors permanent sources of revenue—that might make them "uppity."[25] But that was only the beginning. Appropriations specified both the object of spending and the amount to be spent. Extremely long appropriation clauses prescribed exactly what could and could not be done. The stipulation that all unexpended balances revert immediately to the treasury added insult to injury.

Even so, one might assume that once an appropriation was voted, the executive could spend the money. But no; several colonies elected treasurers independently, precluding governors from managing their own finances. Other colonial legislatures insisted that no payment be made except with government consent, thus giving legislatures control over disbursement of all public funds. And when some emergency justified a special appropriation, colonial assemblies might well appoint special commissioners to spend it; the commissioners were accountable to them rather than to the governor. If such measures proved too loose, there were yet others: revenues were segregated by voting taxes for exceedingly narrow purposes (such as the building of a fort or a lighthouse, or the salary of a governor), always with the added clause that once these purposes had been accomplished the money could be spent for "no other use or purpose whatsoever."[26] Colonial assemblies also reduced the salaries of royal officials; they stipulated the precise name of the person who was to do the work and was to be legally accountable for all funds expended without a direct and specific legislative act. If the character of a government be known by its finances, America was already "independent" in all but name.[27]

Everyone understood what was at stake: royal governors and their supporters desperately wanted a civil list of appointments and perquisites independent of legislative funding; colonists wanted to create uncertainty and parsimony, and to narrow the range of administrative action in order to bend royal governors to local will. To the English, it seemed only reasonable that colonists should support the royal government they acknowledged in name. To sectarian elements among the colonists, however, gubernatorial patronage smacked of the machinations of the king's placemen in Parliament who they believed subverted liberty by being beholden to the monarch rather than to the populace. The Stamp Acts, duties on tea, and other impositions on the colonists were a royal effort to provide independent sources of income for English officials in America. Power, not money, was the issue. The American Revolution was fought over a revolutionary issue: who should rule in America. As put by a contemporary, commenting on the colonial government of New York:

> It will be seen that the democratick branch of the colonial govern-
> ment had placed the governor, and almost every other office, in a
> state of dependence upon its votes and measures. Not a single shil-
> ling could be withdrawn from the treasury, but by legislative con-
> sent. This was particularly galling to the lieutenant governor. It
> had stripped him of that executive patronage and influence, which
> was deemed by him so essential to the support of his administra-
> tion. In truth, it was a great step towards that independence which
> was afterward obtained.[28]

Even this brief background should help modern readers appreciate the colonists' insistence on legislative direction of finance. That strategy for financing the Revolutionary War would not have been chosen by a contemporary European country, nor would it recommend itself to us today. But for the colonists it was entirely natural; indeed, from their perspective, a war for independence would be perverse if it merely replaced a distant English king with a new authority, all the more hateful for being closer to home.

THE FIRST AND SECOND AMERICAN REVOLUTIONS

The Continental Congress was hardly what its name implied; rather, it was a temporary association of colonial assemblies gathered to fight a "temporary" war. Executive bodies symbolized exactly the wrong kind of authority and suggested a permanence that no colonial assembly could imagine. Since what could be imagined was what colonial governments had been, colonists proceeded to behave in their new congressional home just as they had in their colonial legislatures. The Congress followed colonial assemblies in setting up committees to direct foreign affairs and other essential activities, including finance. These committees (the Board of Treasury and the Treasury Office of Accounts) were not to act directly but only, as seemed proper at the time, through colonial entities. The story is well known—a patchwork narrative of endless difficulties, embarrassments, ineptitudes and contradictions, with only the final victory justifying the plot. If we reiterate this well-worn story, it is not only to outline the weaknesses that the Constitutional Convention attempted to overcome, but also to better understand this noncentralized mode of operation.

Vastly understated, finances during the Revolutionary War were inadequate and chaotic. The colonies differed in their devotion to the war, in their capabilities and suffering, and in their ability to figure out what they were supposed to do, beyond paying more. It is true that colonial militia, paid and supplied by colonial assemblies, did part of the fighting, but this did not help the armies under General Washington.[29] As the Continental Congress began to demand ever larger contributions, colonial payments in kind and in coinage lagged ever farther behind. So the Continental Congress began to print paper. In a short time the currency depreciated to almost nothing, leaving as its only legacy a phrase that signifies to this day the epitome of worthlessness: "not worth a continental."[30] In the doggerel of the time:

> *A refugee captain lost two of his men;*
> *And ardently wishing to have them again,*
> *To the Major applied, on an exchange to fix,*
> *And requested to know if for two he'd take six?*
> *Major Adams agreed, nor said a word more,*
> *And Paddy was order'd to fetch them ashore;*
> *Who cried out in surprise: "By Ja--s, my honey,*
> *Our men now depreciate as fast as our money."*[31]

There were a couple of years of utter confusion in which ordinary soldiers received modest wages, often in arrears, while officers got even less, on the supposition that they had personal funds. Robert Morris, a signer of the Declaration of Independence, was called in to restore some semblance of financial order. At last a full-time executive rather than a part-time legislator was on the job. Despite his legendary ingenuity, however, Morris could not make something out of nothing. At the end of a lengthy correspondence, General George Washington wrote him:

I must entreat you, if possible, to procure one month's pay in specie for the detachment which I have under my command. Part of the troops have not been paid anything for a long time past, and have upon several occasions shown marks of great discontent. The service they are going upon is disagreeable to the northern regiments; but I make no doubt that a douceur of a little hard money would put them in proper temper. If the whole sum cannot be obtained, a part of it will be better than none, as it may be distributed in proportion to the respective wants and claims of the men.[32]

Morris replied:

I have already advised Your Excellency of the unhappy situation of money matters, and very much doubt if it will be possible to pay the detachment a month's pay, as you wish. Therefore it will be best not to raise in them any expectation of that kind. Should it come unexpectedly, so much the better.[33]

Pressed from all sides, and sometimes in danger of a thrashing from angry creditors or soldiers, Morris took the view that if he could not pay everyone he would pay no one.[34] As William Graham Sumner commented, "This reasoning shows that he had high qualifications for the Financier of the Revolution."[35] Under such circumstances, Morris' policy was to get money wherever he could, and worry later about payment. One of his tactics involved making a draft on Benjamin Franklin, who had gone to Paris to raise money. Morris cashed the draft, and sent the paper for collection through Cuba and thence to Madrid, knowing that his private communications would reach Franklin weeks before the paper. It was then "Poor Richard's" task to find some way to pay the bill when it actually arrived. Of course, Morris was not too tender about Franklin's feelings, but then, anyone with such scruples would not have been suitable for the task. No doubt, as Grayson put it, Morris "told some grand lies," but that, in another writer's opinion, did not justify criticism by little men, "none of whom would have been able to save a country when it was flat broke."[36] As more than one revolutionary hero did, Morris later received his grim reward: due to unfortunate speculation in land, he ended his days in debtors' prison in Philadelphia. His one recorded solace was that George Washington, upon hearing of the debacle, brought a good supper and spent the night with Morris in prison.[37]

The Continental Congress lasted from 1775 to 1781, when it was replaced by the Articles of Confederation. The Articles spoke of a common treasury but left taxing power in the hands of individual states. Financial difficulty had continued to plague revolutionary forces until the end. As debts multiplied during the war and in the following years, various states were called upon to print paper money. Yet debts remained unpaid, and were compounded by financial measures making it difficult for states to trade internally or abroad. Currency depreciated outside the issuing state, leaving the revolutionary elite wondering whether order could be maintained to keep the republic together.

Others saw things differently.[38] Far from condemning inflation, a writer in *The Pennsylvania Packet* gave his opinion that

> the natural unavoidable tax of depreciation is the most certain, expeditious, and equal tax that could be devised. Upon the scale which has lately existed, every possessor of money has paid a tax for it, in proportion to the time he held it. Like a hackney coach it must be paid for by the hour.[39]

Given time, a common market of currency and credit might have been created. No one will ever know, however, since ratification of the Constitution ended the experiment.

The framers of the Constitution realized that this trial in self-rule had little precedent. The common belief in those days was that governments evolved; they did not result from a willful act of self-creation. That men might live under rules of their own making without losing their liberties was exactly the radical experiment they thought it to be.

The Constitution outlined a central goverment sufficiently strong to levy taxes on its own, giving it the power to restore economic order.[40] Yet in 1789 the Constitution was only a piece of paper with which the people had yet to have a single day's experience. They had over two hundred years of being governed as colonists and governing themselves under colonial assemblies. It is not surprising, therefore, that the practices and habits of mind gained in those two centuries appeared in the rules created, amid controversy and consternation, as the chosen instruments of self-government.

The importance of the peculiar American practice of niggardly taxing and spending has been missed—first, because the lack of a hierarchical European structure has been taken to mean no structure; and, second, because the uniformity of practice suggested that there was no operating ideology, when it should have indicated the opposite. The new nation's commitment to budget balance is as significant for its history as its rejection of a centralized executive and preference for noncentralized, legislative forms of budgeting. America combined, extraordinarily, a lack of anything that could be called a central budget with a powerful, though informal, ability to coordinate expenditure and revenue. This phenomenon needs neither criticism nor praise, but understanding. The rise, at the beginning of the twentieth century, of a budgetary reform movement hostile toward past practices and structures (including the separation of powers in the Constitution), and favorable toward executive domination, has obscured the different budgetary process of the nation's early days.

PUBLIC DEBT AND BALANCED BUDGETS

In fine, taxation equal to the public expenditures is, in my opinion, the only method in nature by which our defence can be continued, our independence be preserved, a destructive increase of the public debt be avoided, our currency (hard or paper) be kept in a state of fixed value, the natural springs of industry be given to every profession of men, our supplies made plentiful, the public confidence be restored to the public counsels, the morality of our people be revived, and the blessings of heaven be secured to ourselves and our posterity.

—PELATIAH WEBSTER[41]

I wish it were possible to obtain a single amendment to our constitution. I would be willing to depend on that alone for the reduction of the administration of our government to the genuine principles of it's [sic] constitution; I mean an additional article, taking from the federal government the power of borrowing.

—THOMAS JEFFERSON[42]

The habits of private life are continued in public; and we ought carefully to distinguish that economy which depends upon their institutions from that which is a natural result of their manners and customs.

—ALEXIS DE TOCQUEVILLE[43]

The history of American attitudes toward public debt is apparent from a series of formulas relating revenues to expenditures, no less powerful for being simple. The first of these equations[44] is simplicity itself: revenues (essentially, the tariff) minus interest on the public debt equals allowable national-government spending. The new Constitution provided ample authority for all sorts of taxes, including direct levies on individuals and internal excise taxes. In the debate over ratification, however, the Constitution's advocates frequently insisted that revenue be raised mainly by customs duties and sale of public lands, with income and excise taxes reserved for emergencies. Despite Alexander Hamilton's effort to give the government a sound financial basis by authorizing internal taxes,[45] the Jeffersonians, like country interests in England, clung to their vision of a government financed mainly by tariffs. Given the widespread agreement on balanced budgets and parsimony in government, as well as the desire to pay off the public debt, the first equation prevailed most of the time.

In wartime, however, a second equation prevailed: revenues (this time including internal taxes) equaled ordinary civilian expenditures minus wartime debt. When surpluses appeared, or proposals for internal improvements proved irresistible, or both, a third equation operated: revenues in surplus minus ordinary spending, minus internal improvements, equaled central-government spending. The budget was still balanced, but at higher levels, as the surplus provided for roads, bridges, and what we would today call "infrastructure." It was only with the revolution in fiscal thought following the Great Depression of the 1930s that the fourth equation, sometimes called a full-employment surplus, established another budgetary norm: revenues plus a deficit sufficient to secure full employment equals spending. The idea was to balance not the budget but the economy at full employment. The formulation of a fifth equation, specifying, perhaps, how large a proportion of national product a deficit might be without being harmful, is under discussion today.

The Constitution reacted against the Articles of Confederation. The new government was designed to have sufficient powers to levy taxes without the states' direct concurrence, in order to provide a firm foundation for the national credit. In the first month after President George Washington took office (and before a treasury department existed), the Congress enacted laws establishing customs duties and administrative capacity to collect them.[46] In his reports on public credit in 1790 and 1795 as Secretary of the Treasury, Alexander Hamilton argued the importance of consolidating state debts, adding them to the national debt, and arranging to fund the total with revenues provided for this purpose. This was hard for his agrarian, Jeffersonian opponents to swallow. For one thing, much of the debt had been severely discounted and was now owned by speculators who stood to gain far more than the original holders if the debt was paid off at full value. Besides, as each side understood, the debt was a means of creating self-interest in the central government's stability. For proponents of a sectarian regime, Hamilton's proposal evoked anxiety; they thought corrupt legislators in Congress were trying to restore the monarchy. Yet the idea of public faith and sound credit proved as difficult to resist as the related idea that funding the debt strictly would help to balance the budget each year, thus encouraging each generation to pay its own costs.[47] In admitting defeat, John Taylor of Carolina spoke with eloquent hyperbole about the uneasiness Hamilton's arguments provoked in his agrarian opponents: "We moderns; we enlightened Americans; we who have abolished hierarchy and title; and we who are submitting to be taxed ... without being deluded or terrified by the promise of heaven, the denunciation of hell ... or superstition. A spell is put on our understandings by the words 'public faith and national credit' ..."[48]

Yet, as every schoolchild knows, Hamilton did manage to placate the Jeffersonians. In a classic case of bargaining, Hamilton arranged to transfer the nation's capital from New York to Washington, D.C. (which was closer to Virginia and the South), in exchange for enough votes to pass the debt-assumption bill.[49] Critical discussion of the compromise usually ends here, but it should continue. Without a general agreement on the virtue of a balanced budget, this political exchange would not have been feasible. Moreover, most historians do not mention the attack on executive powers by the Republicans (as the agrarian interests now called themselves). They did not merely agree (however reluctantly) to the assumption of state and national debt. With the same skill as those Federalists who sought to write institutional safeguards for solvency into the Constitution, the Jeffersonians filled in its interstices with severe limitations on the executive branch's use of all spending powers gained through assumption.

President Thomas Jefferson (1801–9) promoted a budgetary cause corresponding to his conviction that the soil of liberty had to be nurtured (with less hyperbole, fought for again) with the blood of martyrs in every generation. Thinking it wrong for one generation to bind the next, he believed that any debt should be paid off within twenty years. To this President, economy meant parsimony. Favoring the lowly style and the *lingua humis,* Jefferson viewed economy and repayment of debt as moral necessities. "I place economy among the first and most important of republican virtues," he wrote, "and public debt as the greatest of the dangers to be feared."[50] Jefferson preferred cutting spending to raising taxes. "I am for government rigorously frugal and simple, applying all the possible savings of the public revenue to the discharge of the national debt."[51]

As the quotation from Jefferson at the beginning of this section suggests, he thought a balanced budget was sufficiently important to propose enshrining the concept in the Constitution. Indeed, for him as for other antifederalists, republican government was at stake if balance precepts were violated. Harking back to the political philosopher James Harrington, and to the Whig "party of the country" in England, Jefferson viewed the debt, and especially its holders, as native counterparts of the king's placemen in Parliament, who corrupted government by promoting their personal financial interests.[52]

Jefferson's rejection of debt was not abstract, but depended on a particular historical context in which a central government, led by its executive power, was trying to introduce new inequalities. State governments, thought to be free from this corrupting temptation, presumably could incur as much debt as they liked.

Life was good to these early Americans. Despite the repeal of internal taxes in the first year of Jefferson's administration, and the $15 million spent to acquire the Louisiana Territory, growth in American commerce permitted substantial repayment of the debt and yielded increased Treasury reserves. Part of the impetus for Jefferson and Treasury Secretary Albert Gallatin to retire debt was surely to reduce this "moral cankerr"; but they also believed that wiping out the debt would free the remaining revenues for public purposes.

The expensive War of 1812 upset budgetary expectations; it disrupted commerce, thus reducing revenue. Initially, Congress expected to finance the war by issuing funded debt, but by 1813 expenses were so great that Congress had to vote millions in internal excise taxes, besides rate increases on tariffs. The urgency and proximity of war led citizens to pay these taxes willingly, but there was substantial misgiving about the debt incurred.[53] Following Jefferson's lead, President James Madison (1809–17) wanted his administration "to liberate the public resources by an honorable discharge of the public debt." Similarly, James Monroe (1817–25) and John Quincy Adams (1825–29) wanted to reduce debt, thus permitting use of customs revenues for the nation's development.[54] The ideal of a balanced budget took on moralistic overtones; John Quincy Adams considered its achievement "among the maxims of political economy," and his Secretary of the Treasury called debt reduction "amongst the highest duties of a nation," since it showed that a government is a prompt payer.[55] Debt reduction was a good thing either in itself or as a prelude to borrowing. Debt reduction could mean both less and more spending.

By the time Andrew Jackson became president (1829), debt reduction had become a patriotic duty. Realizing that the remaining debt might be retired during his administration, Jackson waxed lyric: "We shall then exhibit the rare example of a great nation, abounding in all the means of happiness and security, altogether free from debt." American exceptionalism was publicly proclaimed when Secretary of the Treasury Levi Woodbury heralded extinction of the debt as an "unprecedented spectacle . . . presented to the world."[56]

Give the devil his due. Out of the wellsprings of abundance surfaced the specter of a corresponding evil: "the unnecessary accumulation of public revenue," Andrew Jackson called it—more simply, a surplus. What would be wrong with that? As President Martin Van Buren (1837–41) argued in his last annual message, the surplus "would foster national extravagance." Too tempting to resist, it would start a vicious cycle of increasing expenditures leading soon enough to new deficits.[57]

For these presidents, as for the citizens they governed, both surplus and debt were anathema because they symbolized privilege. Either spending would lead to unearned advantage or debt would give special interests a hold over government. In either case, government would add to inequality in society.

Debt was also thought to sap national strength. As depression brought debt by depressing revenues, President John Tyler (1841–45) railed against owing money, maintaining (like his successor, James K. Polk, 1845–49) that debt reduction would strengthen America's relations with other nations. Recalling the errors of the War of 1812—in particular, excessive and unnecessary expenses—Polk argued that war was an additional reason for economy in all ordinary expenditure.[58]

These presidents did not believe government spending should redistribute the nation's wealth from the rich to the poor; to the contrary, they feared it would take from the ordinary man and give to the affluent. "Melancholy is the condition of the people," President Polk wrote, "whose government can be sustained only by a system which periodically transfers large amounts from the labors of the many to the coffers of the few."[59]

Between 1849 and 1860, when the Civil War began, every American national government pledged itself both to apply surpluses to retire its own debt and to reduce revenues to the level of spending (though the latter was not always accomplished). Beyond this minimum, President James Buchanan (1857–61) would allow only expenditures clearly warranted in the Constitution (such as increases in navy and coastal defenses).[60]

Faith in the balanced-budget ideal was strengthened by an economic theory that tied wages negatively to debt. As Secretary of the Treasury Robert J. Walker claimed in 1838: "Wages can only be increased in any nation, in the aggregate, by augmenting capital, the fund out of which wages are paid. . . . The destruction or diminution of capital, by destroying or reducing the fund from which labor is paid must reduce wages." This wage-fund argument had the added value of suggesting that wage earners would be hurt by any effort—either of individual employers or of national governments—to go into debt to improve their lot.[61] During the recession of 1837 and 1838, when Congress tried to increase federal spending in order to alleviate suffering, President Van Buren invoked the founding fathers' authority; they "wisely judged that the less government interferes with private pursuits the better for the general prosperity."[62] President Buchanan blamed the financial panic and recession of 1857 and 1858 on "the habit of extravagant expenditures."[63]

The Civil War of 1860–65 marked the first break in the consensus on debt reduction. Balanced budgets remained the norm, but enhanced executive power due to victory in war, and the beginning of industrialization, left the role of debt open to argument. Abraham Lincoln (1860–65) thought citizens "cannot be much oppressed by a debt which they owe to themselves." His idea, followed by President Rutherford B. Hayes a decade later (1877–81), was to secure a wider distribution of the debt among citizens. Considering that the debt might be paid over time, President Ulysses S. Grant (1869–77) asserted that the capacity to pay grew with the nation's wealth. Rather than raising taxes to pay the debt in a shorter time, he would, like the supply-siders of the 1980s, cut taxes to increase wealth, thus raising revenue in the long run.[64] During a time of territorial as well as economic expansion, providing the internal improvements needed to connect the nation seemed compatible with fiscal prudence.

Having inherited a Civil War debt of some $2.5 billion, President Andrew Johnson (1865–69) considered debt a burden on the economy that should be paid off within twenty years. Despite the considerable increase in population and wealth, Johnson was startled to learn that expenditures during his term would be around $1.6 billion—only slightly less than the entire amount for the seventy-year-plus period from 1789 to 1861. Grover Cleveland (1885–89) believed that withdrawing capital from the people and transferring it to government imperiled their prosperity. His words were a last stand against the spending boom that followed: "The public Treasury, which should only exist as a conduit conveying the people's tribute to its legitimate objects of expenditure, becomes a hoarding place for money needlessly withdrawn from trade and the people's use, thus crippling our national energies. . . ."[65]

The traditional view changed as the nation developed. By the late nineteenth century, as we have seen, segments of elite opinion came to view debt as something a people owes itself, not to be judged inherently evil, but relative to a country's ability to pay. This is not far from the idea that the size of the deficit matters less than the government's (and, through it, the people's) return on monies expended. The American people, Woodrow Wilson said as a harbinger of things to come, "are not jealous of the amount their Government costs if they are sure that they get what they need and desire for the outlay, that the money is being spent for objects of which they approve, and that it is being applied with good business sense and management."[66] Neverthe-less, Wilson, like McKinley, Theodore Roosevelt, and Taft before him, the presidents from 1898 to 1920, all spoke in opposition to deficits.[67]

A homiletic literature urging public thrift supported the emerging professional interest in efficiency (and the new civil-service move-ment's concomitant stress on neutral competence and expertise). Mr. Micawber's advice to David Copperfield in King's Bench Prison—spending just below income is happiness, while spending just above it is misery—was endlessly repeated. Frugality was synonymous with morality and success.

These vague rumblings of fiscal prudence—both against the growing debt and for a balanced budget—reappeared with a vengeance in the 1920s. There was public concern that profligate wartime habits would carry over into peacetime. The Liberty Loan Act of 1919 established a sinking fund to reduce the debt, which was cut by a third (from $24 to $16 billion) by the end of the decade. "We have demobilized many groups," observed David F. Huston, Secretary of the Treasury under President Harding (1921–23), "but we have not demobilized those whose gaze is concentrated on the Treasury."[68]

More than two thousand years before, Aristotle had contended that the government should be run like a well-managed house. During the 1920s the view that government should function like a business—that "our public household," like a successful private enterprise, should be operated under a "rigid and yet sane economy"—came into fashion. In earlier decades political leaders wanted to reduce the public debt in order to minimize the domestic influence of its foreign holders. Presi-dent Calvin Coolidge (1923–28) argued instead that low taxes and spending would give the American people "that contentment and peace of mind which will go far to render them immune from any envi-ous inclination toward other countries." Competition over markets would subside, leaders maintained, if Americans were prosperous at home.[69] Nor was retrenchment important only to governmental offi-cials; Coolidge contended that "economy reaches everywhere. It car-ries a blessing to everybody." Then came the market crash of 1929, followed by the Great Depression of the 1930s. The depression marked both an end to the primacy of the balanced budget and a beginning of variable expenditure as an instrument of economic stabilization. Em-phasis shifted from matching spending and revenue at the lowest pos-sible level to the creative use of expenditures. And there was another tradition, internal improvements, to which supporters of higher spend-ing could turn for historical justification of their position.

INTERNAL IMPROVEMENTS

The early and efficient aid of the Federal Government is recommended by still more important considerations. The inconveniences, complaints, and perhaps dangers . . . from a vast . . . territory, can not otherwise be radically removed or prevented than by opening . . . communications through all its parts. Good roads and canals will shorten distances, facilitate commercial and personal intercourse, and unite . . . the most remote quarters of the United States. No other single operation, within the power of Government, can more effectually . . . strengthen . . . that Union . . .

—ALBERT GALLATIN[70]

Canals . . . would bind a hundred millions of people in one inseparable compact—alike in habits, in language, and in interest; one homogeneous brotherhood, the most invulnerable, powerful, and respectable on earth.

—ROBERT FULTON[71]

Though the balanced-budget concept had its ups and downs, circumstantial evidence until the 1930s, and opinion polls thereafter, strongly indicate that most citizens supported it. In fact, the budget was in surplus (or less than 10 percent out of balance) for over three-quarters of the years from the republic's founding until 1960. Budget balance was a meeting place for American political cultures. But if one asks instead about the *purposes* for which revenues were raised and expenditures made, or who was to control their distribution, and how, there was more conflict in American history than consensus.

We may broadly characterize internal improvements (a cover term for spending that somebody thinks desirable) as including any government subsidy, not just the funds for roads and canals that were most often provided. According to our analysis, advocates of markets might generally wish low taxes and spending, but were always ready to accept subsidies for the purpose of spreading among all taxpayers the costs of sustaining commerce. Supporters of hierarchy generally are willing to spend to promote national unity, and to help maintain order. Egalitarians would be ambivalent. Social contact is vital for citizens' participation in the common cause, and a homogeneous body politic tends to reduce internal discord. Yet sectarians would not want to give advantages to members of central government. Nor would they want to help citizens already possessing more than their share of wealth and privilege. Americans who viewed internal improvement as a way of aiding small farmers scattered throughout the vast extent of the nation (much enlarged since the Louisiana Purchase) would be torn. They were to resolve this conflict by supporting a balanced budget; once it was attained, any surplus that accrued could be used to provide benefits for all citizens. Given this rough division of forces, it could be expected that over time the United States would have more rather than less subsidy. As the nation industrialized and market men had more to say about policy, opposition to spending for internal improvements dissipated.

George Washington and John Adams had resorted to long-term loans to cover current deficits. Until 1800, thirty percent of the federal budget went for interest payments on the national debt, and fifty-five percent for the Army and the Navy. Since the nation was still recovering from the Revolutionary War, it lacked capacity to fund internal improvements. The Republicans under Jefferson adopted a policy of retrenchment—nearly eliminating the Navy, slimming the Army, and reducing federal officeholders. They cut internal excise taxes also, but, wanting to create a surplus, continued to levy tariffs.[72] By 1805, with commerce improved and retirement of public debt in sight, Jefferson hoped that "the revenue thereby liberated may . . . be applied, *in time of peace,* to rivers, canals, roads, arts, manufacturers, education and the other great objects within each State." Undecided on the constitutional validity of such spending, Jefferson recommended that a constitutional amendment be adopted to dispel any uncertainty. Gallatin, his Secretary of the Treasury, had already started to build the Cumberland Road and the National Pike—funds came from the sale of public lands in Ohio, then still a territory.[73] At the end of Jefferson's administration, Gallatin prepared a major report on public works; it called for a $20 million program of canal and highway construction.[74]

Though Jefferson's abandonment of traditional Republican principles concerning internal improvements caused conflict within the party, a strict constitutionalism, concern for states' rights, and meticulous circumscription of the role of executive officials offset these departures from strict balance principles. Older Republicans, such as John Randolph and John Taylor, absolutely opposed these new federal commitments, while new Republicans, such as John Calhoun, John Quincy Adams, and, later, Henry Clay, favored liberal spending for canals and roads. But, even in the "Era of Good Feelings" (1817–24) during the presidency of Monroe, consensus did not extend to internal improvements.

Adopting Monroe's program, President John Quincy Adams avidly sought appropriations for rivers and harbors, lighthouses, beacons, piers, and, most of all, roads. According to his critics, Adams tried to use the surplus to provide "a permanent and regular system . . . of . . . internal improvements" so that "the surface of the whole Union would have been checkered with railroads and canals . . ."[75] Favoring development, his administration generated a House Committee on Roads and Canals and a Civil Engineer Corps within the Army Engineers. The federal government routinely granted public lands to new states to encourage construction of roads and canals. The second Adams presidency also initiated rivers-and-harbors appropriations; within the polity this soon became known as "pork-barrel" legislation. From that time on, it is alleged (with good reason), congressmen have dipped their hands into that barrel to benefit their districts—much as country folk in those days gathered for horse-trading around a barrel of salt pork in the local general store.[76]

What stopped this drive for internal improvements? President Andrew Jackson (1829–37) represented opposition forces in Congress. His supporters, frontiersmen from Ohio, West Virginia, and Kentucky, saw no need to spend money on projects mainly benefiting coastal states. Jackson maintained himself in office by dethroning "King Caucus" (the method of presidential nomination by senatorial caucus); he supported the more egalitarian and popular national nominating convention. The same sectarian impulses generated opposition to federal support or subsidy for internal improvements. Jacksonians believed that payment of interest on the national debt was reverse redistribution of income from poor to rich people, because the debt and interest upon it depleted the limited capital fund that wages were drawn from. If such capital were transferred from government into private hands, productivity would increase and wages would also go up. To Jackson's supporters, voting down internal improvements meant helping the ordinary citizen. Favoring the common man, in those days, meant promoting individual, not governmental, enterprise.[77]

It is essential to understand that the "progressive" opinion of the Jacksonian era believed that government took from—not gave to   the common man. Thus government-sponsored privileges—banks, charters, and monopolies—aroused violent antipathy among Jackson's frontier supporters. In their view, the economic freedom that political liberty depended on was best assured by eliminating the artificial privilege that government introduced into the natural equality among men.[78]

Among those who theorized about Jacksonian democracy in his

times, the widespread belief, apparently shared by the citizenry as well, was that equality of opportunity, meticulously pursued through the unimpeded operation of economic markets, would lead to approximate equality of result—as closely as innate differences in human ability permitted. At the very least, central government would not add artificial to natural inequality, thereby preserving representative government. It is this belief—not in equality undefined, or in just one kind of equality, but in *the mutual reinforcement of opportunity and result*—that made America truly exceptional. When and if that belief was shattered, as it was to be by emergence of corporate capitalism, the union of opposites that gave American life its distinctive cast also would be rent asunder.

The moral and legal sanctions that applied to the federal debt did not apply with equal force to the states. According to popular belief, state governments, controlled by their citizens, epitomized equality. Thus the states might be encouraged to help the citizenry by all manner of activities. (For example, Louis Hartz has shown that laissez-faire was hardly the prevailing practice in Pennsylvania before the Civil War[79]). When the states warmed up to this task, after the demise of the Second Bank of the United States, they borrowed more between 1835 and 1838 than the entire federal deficit from 1789 to 1838. The new state debt financed canal and railroad construction and provided capital for chartering state banks.[80]

Support for, and opposition to, internal improvements waxed and waned during the thirty years before the Civil War. Congressional spending advocates like Henry Clay produced one bill after another. What would stop "a disreputable scramble for public money," President Polk asked while vetoing a rivers-and-harbors bill, if congressional discretion were the only constraint? Why, internal improvements were "capable of indefinite enlargement and sufficient to swallow up as many millions annually as could be extracted from the foreign commerce of the country." Allied with a protective tariff that brought in ever larger sums, Polk believed that "the operation and necessary effect of the whole system would encourage large and extravagant expenditures, and thereby increase the public patronage, and maintain a rich and splendid government at the expense of a taxed and impoverished people."[81] Buying up Texas or another large territory was another matter, properly a part of the nation's "manifest destiny." Even so, many of the promises of federal largesse to get Texas into the Union remained unfulfilled.[82]

If money was what mattered to Polk, it was public morality that

Presidents Pierce and Buchanan cared about. They rejected federal spending on internal improvements as unconstitutional because it usurped state functions.[83] For other leaders—from Daniel Webster to John Calhoun and President Millard Fillmore—the great issue was, as it had been for Jefferson, growth of the nation. These men believed that a local improvement really contributed to the national welfare. While no one in the federal government would ever admit wanting to encroach on any state, a big brother should rightfully help a smaller one—to "strengthen the ties which bind us together as a people," as Fillmore put it.[84]

Needless to say, then as now, learned scribes lined up on both sides. It was neither Adam Smith's *Wealth of Nations* nor David Ricardo's *Principles of Political Economy and Taxation,* but rather Jean-Baptiste Say's *A Treatise on Political Economy* (which appeared in 1803) that became popular in the United States. Louis Kimmel, whose brilliant book on federal debt we have cited often, believes that "a factor in Say's favor was that he avoided Smith's distinction between 'productive' and 'unproductive' employment. Neither professors of moral philosophy nor the clergy had been quite willing to accept an exposition into the moral science of political economy that classified them as unproductive." Say did agree with Adam Smith, however, on the crucial consideration that consumption of wealth by government, while it might be necessary, was justified only to the extent that it produced economic returns of equivalent value. The doctrine of opportunity costs—that the value of an object is what has to be given up to acquire it—here finds an early statement. And so does a notion of cost–benefit analysis: "The whole skill of government," Say says, "consists in a continual and judicious comparison of the sacrifice about to be incurred, with the expected benefits to the community."[85] A native book, Henry Vethake's *The Principles of Political Economy,* objected to debt financing because if the funds expended did not derive from tax receipts, less care would be taken in spending public money. But so long as government funds went for productive purposes, Vethake thought, such spending was as good as if the money had been left in private hands.[86]

Compared to European behavior, spending in the United States stood practically still, barely keeping up with the population increase. Nevertheless, the federal government did take on a few new tasks. As early as 1796, revenue collectors helped enforce state quarantine laws. Medical care for disabled and sick seamen, instituted in 1798, eventually led to establishment of the United States Public Health Service.

Federal officials collected commercial and a few agricultural statistics; they distributed free seeds, and built lighthouses on the Atlantic coast. Moving on to larger matters, the goverment granted subsidies to carriers of ocean mail and to railroads.[87] Mail subsidies were justified by a parallel policy adopted in Great Britain, which encouraged acquisition of steamships that could be readily converted to naval use.[88] From the 1830s through the 1850s, despite presidential opposition, the federal government offered subsidies to railroads then being built. Sometimes it bought railroad stock outright. But more often, to reinforce entrepreneurial incentives for tying the nation together, the government deeded over to the railroads large amounts of public land—extending a mile wide on each side of the track. States' rights were preserved; cash subsidies were transferred from federal to state governments, which then passed the funds on to finance railroad construction.[89] Yet by European or even by absolute standards, there was only a minuscule outlay. Support for agriculture barely totaled $5,000 by 1860.[90]

In such a vast nation, unification entailed some regulation. *Niles' Weekly Register* reported in 1830 that fifteen hundred people had died from steamboat explosions. Boilers blew up with such regularity that the carnage eventually led to creation of a federal inspectorate. Mass importation of foreign drugs had the same result: questions about impurities led to investigation, followed by regulation.[91] (In Europe at the time, governments also began to set standards to protect citizens' health and safety.)

The Erie Canal in New York State was the first and most famous of the internal improvements built with combined public and private funding. Despite all predictions to the contrary, the canal returned handsome profits on its multimillion-dollar investment, starting a boom in canal-building in other states. In the 1820s and '30s the State of Virginia floated bonds to build a number of canals and railroads; though only one railroad survived the Civil War, Virginia continued retiring the debt (finally paid off in 1966).[92] A typical case was the Central Ohio Railroad, chartered in 1847, which had a hard time attracting subscribers. The vendors traveled throughout the territory making stump speeches, they published newspapers and pamphlets, and knocked on doors—all with indifferent success. Subscriptions from counties and towns, along with some state money, eventually made up the deficit. A more enterprising company went to London and borrowed, using State of Maryland bonds as security. Less savory, though equally enterprising, were the railroads issuing paper scrip to meet ongoing expenses; it was worth so little that workers sometimes rioted. Unsold stock might be used as collateral for still newer loans.[93] By the early 1840s things were so bad that seven states defaulted, failing to pay interest on their debt, though within a few years all states had made good on accrued interest. The specter of repudiation (as such default was called) led English bards to remonstrate in the manner of the Reverend Sidney Smith:

> *Yankee Doodle borrows cash,*
> *Yankee Doodle spends it,*
> *And then he snaps his fingers at*
> *The jolly flat who lends it.*
> *Ask him when he means to pay,*
> *He shows no hesitation,*
> *But says he'll take the shortest way*
> *And that's Repudiation!*
>
> *Yankee vows that every State*
> *Is free and independent:*
> *And if they paid each other's debts,*
> *There'd never be an end on't.*
> *They keep distinct till "settling" comes,*
> *And then throughout the nation*
> *They all become "United States"*
> *To preach Repudiation! . . .*
>
> *And what does freedom mean, if not*
> *To whip our slaves at pleasure*
> *And borrow money when you can,*
> *To pay it at your leisure?*[94]

Even so, federal government before the Civil War was tiny. Between 1800 and 1860, as the table below shows, federal expenditures rose from nearly $11 million to $63 million in total. More than half of this supported the Army and the Navy. The general category of "civil and miscellaneous" included a substantial amount for the postal deficit, thus covering everything except defense, pensions, Indians, and interest on the debt. Kimmel is correct in concluding "that federal expenditures made little or no contribution to the level of living. Only a minor portion of Civil and miscellaneous expenditures were for developmental purposes . . ."[95]

The Civil War changed all that. The government grew from tiny to small. It promoted the interests of businessmen and farmers, sometimes aiding railroads and at other times intervening to regulate railroads in the interests of farmers. Beginning with the Ordinance of 1787, which set aside sections of land for local schools, and the Morrill

TABLE 9

FEDERAL EXPENDITURES FISCAL YEARS **1800, 1825, 1850** AND **1860**[96]
(In millions of dollars)

	1800	1825	1850	1860
Civil and miscellaneous	1.3	2.7	14.0	28.0*
War Department	2.6	3.7	9.4	16.4
Navy Department	3.4	3.1	7.9	11.5
Indians	—	0.7	1.6	2.9
Pensions	0.1	1.3	1.9	1.1
Interest	3.4	4.4	3.8	3.2
	$10.8	$15.9	$39.5	$63.1*

* Includes postal deficit of $9.9 million.

Act of 1862, which gave huge land grants to states to establish agricultural and mechanical colleges, the federal government supported education in several different ways. Like Thomas Jefferson, post–Civil War presidents generally regarded education as an exception to whatever strictures they laid upon unnecessary expenditures. As the nation was settled, most of the vast public domain was transferred to private ownership; with the closing of the frontier in 1890, some pressure emerged to preserve for public use the few remaining choice sites in the wilderness. But it is not in such modest departures from the strict doctrine of the minimum state that one finds the sources of budgetary conflict or the seeds of future spending.

Soon enough the $3 billion Civil War debt became readily manageable as the nation industrialized and productivity increased; also, higher tariffs continued to produce substantial surpluses. Echoing litanies of former presidents, Grover Cleveland (1885–89) voiced the fear that growing surpluses "tempt extravagance" and, what was worse, public extravagance "begets extravagance among the people."[97] Budget balance and citizen morality were connected once more.

Money may not be the root of all evil, but the availability of substantial surpluses in the post–Civil War period proved a greater temptation than most private interests and public officials could resist. No one can say what mattered most in changing public perceptions: the change in national opinion following the swift pace of the Industrial Revolution; the acquisitiveness attributed to industrialists whose business scruples and public behavior were less than exemplary; the huge revenues generated by the protective tariff; or the attendant changes in the process of budgeting. Cleveland's predecessor, President Chester

A. Arthur (1881–85), also condemned surpluses on grounds that they corrupted public morality and inexorably contributed to rising expenditures.[98] Whether as cause or reflection of the temptations provided by these surpluses—which yielded money to spend without the need to raise taxes—changes in the congressional appropriations process facilitated expansion of internal improvements and increased the scale of federal spending.

For the first seventy-five years of the republic (from 1789 to 1864), revenue and expenditure matters in the House of Representatives were handled by its Committee on Ways and Means. In 1865, apparently as a reaction to the Civil War's accelerated spending, which produced an excessive work load for Ways and Means, a Committee on Appropriations was carved out of the old single committee; this dual committee system—one for taxes, the other for spending—lasted until 1885. By then, public business had multiplied to such an extent, congressmen maintained, that it was necessary to create new specialized appropriations committees to consider the various spending items in fine detail.[99]

"The source of House dissatisfaction in 1885," Richard Fenno concluded, "lay primarily in the image of an excessively independent Appropriations Committee, with an undercurrent of criticism of an excessive economy-mindedness." The vote in the House to establish a separate Appropriations Committee was overwhelming (227 to 70) and included substantial majorities of the members of other committees, including senior members. According to Joseph G. Cannon, then a member and later a powerful Speaker of the House, the change was largely prompted by hostility toward Appropriations Committee Chairman Samuel Randell, chief opponent of higher tariffs and higher spending.[100] The desire was to tax and spend more. In succeeding years, appropriations bills dealing with rivers and harbors, army, navy, diplomacy, post office, and Indian affairs were taken from the Appropriations Committees and given to the substantive legislative committees made up of spending advocates. By these acts, more than half of the total appropriations, including the most controversial items, were effectively removed from the Appropriations Committees' jurisdiction.[101] Soon enough Chairman Randell's prediction was confirmed: "the spending committees, having intimate and for the most part cordial relations each with a particular department," Lucius Wilmerding wrote, "launched out into an unrestrained competition for appropriations, the one striving to surpass the other in securing greater recognition and more money for its special charge."[102] The changes in the Appropriations Committee strengthened what is today called "the Iron

Triangle"—the special relationships between administrative bureaus, the interests affected by their activities, and the congressional committees concerned with bureau affairs.

The classic description of the activity spawned by breaking up the Appropriations Committee was Woodrow Wilson's:

> "Log-rolling" is an exchange of favors. Representative A. is very anxious to secure a grant for the clearing of a small watercourse in his district, and representative B. is equally solicitous about his plans for bringing money into the hands of the contractors of his own constituency, whilst representative C. comes from a sea-port town whose modest harbor is neglected because of the treacherous bar across its mouth, and representative D. has been blamed for not bestirring himself more in the interest of schemes of improvement afoot amongst the enterprising citizens of his native place; so it is perfectly feasible for these gentlemen to put their heads together and confirm a mutual understanding that each will vote in Committee of the Whole for the grants desired by the others, in consideration of the promise that they will cry "aye" when his item comes on to be considered. . . . Lobbying and log-rolling go hand in hand.[103]

Logrolling was the collective counterpart of the pork-barrel legislation introduced by individual congressmen.

The costs of logrolling were aptly described in 1916 by Representative Frear:

> The fact is notorious that after 20 years' improvement and an expenditure of over two and one-half million dollars on this 10 mile stretch of river not one ton of commercial freight has ever been hauled from St. Paul to Minneapolis or from Minneapolis to St. Paul by river, nor has a solitary lonesome passenger ever taken the trip on an excursion boat or otherwise in the recollection of the oldest inhabitant.[104]

A marked change in attitudes toward internal improvements came about during the Great Depression of the 1930s, when spending for public works became a positive means of increasing employment. The new perception did not spring from thin air; basing their recommendations on experience in Europe during the nineteenth century, the progressives before World War I favored government spending on public works to relieve unemployment. Compulsory labor on public works was a condition of destitute citizens' receipt of public assistance in Britain from the 1830s on. The earlier notion of internal improvements (to increase national harmony by extending communications) was replaced by an emphasis on putting people to work.

Beginning with the Civil War, high tariffs were the keystone of the new (founded in 1854) Republican Party's public policy. The tariff on manufactured goods, and the surpluses it generated, permitted Republican governments to do several things simultaneously.[105] Initially the surplus subsidized domestic manufacturing, and helped to pay off a substantial part of the Civil War debt. It also beat back sectarian efforts to introduce progressive income taxation; it cemented an alliance between hierarchy and markets, between advocates of a stronger central government and business interests. The tariff linked nationalism to capitalism.

In the twenty years before the Civil War, tariffs declined. Afterward, import duties on consumer goods rose. The surpluses produced by these tariffs (twenty-four years in a row following 1870) were used to pay off the Civil War debt. From 1894 to 1900, however, and with some frequency until the 1914 World War, there were deficits. What happened?

Congress responded to the Populist demand for greater equality in taxation by adding provision for an income tax to the tariff bill of 1893. The Supreme Court, in *Pollock v. Farmers Loan and Trust Company*, however, held that it was a direct tax that was unconstitutional because it was not apportioned equally among the states. To make up the revenue loss, Congress passed higher gift and estate taxes, but these proved insufficient.

By the mid-1890s the United States had become a net exporter rather than a net recipient of foreign capital. In order to protect the investments of its citizens abroad, according to Bennett Baack and John Ray, the United States began a major expansion of its navy, which cost a good deal. Veterans' pensions, the closest equivalent of welfare spending in the era, also rose rapidly. Hence the unaccustomed (though, by our standards, tiny) deficits.[106]

Political preferences for the tariff and against the income tax were rooted in the industrial states of the Northeast whose manufacturers benefited from the former and whose wealthier citizens paid the latter. Civil War experience showed not only that the income tax generated large revenues but that three states paid most of it—Massachusetts, New Jersey, and New York, with the last of these paying nearly a third. Baack and Ray contend that the placement of substantial military contracts in those three states made public officials there more willing to generate revenue through an income tax. Their position as exporters of goods also moderated the support for tariffs in the Northeast, thus increasing willingness to accept the income tax.[107]

A complementary explanation, offered by Douglas C. North, is that industrialization led to enhanced specialization that greatly lowered the cost of collecting income and sales taxes. What government could do, extract resources from the population at lower cost, it did do. The evidence lies in the decline of property taxes and the increase of income taxes as a proportion of the total tax take in the twentieth century.[108] Presumably, specialization proceeded apace in Europe as well as in the United States, leaving the later adoption of the income tax here still to be explained. On the grounds that fifty years more or less may not make all that much difference in the flow of history, the folk wisdom of tax historians, that every available tax is eventually used, may have merit. In any event, the growing specialization in society was also reflected in the increased attention paid to budgeting.

In the early years of this century, when the Progressive movement sought to regulate business, it justified governmental action by pointing to the federal government's need for efficiency, which a balanced budget, Progressives maintained, would assure. And even higher tariffs would support the increased expense of regulation. It is to this movement, with its advocacy of executive budgeting, that we turn next for an understanding of how a rival hierarchy within the Republican Party brought the United States into closer alignment with the European practices it so much admired, and so little understood.

THE AMERICAN MYSTERY: BUDGETING WITHOUT A BUDGET

The budget reformers were right; as W. F. Willoughby put it,

> No attempt is made to consider the whole problem of financing the government at one time. Expenditures are not considered in connection with revenues. Even the idea of balancing the budget does not exist. . . . Though the law requires all the estimates to be submitted by the Secretary of the Treasury, that officer acts as a mere compiling authority; he has no power to modify the proposals transmitted to him by the heads of the administrative departments. The estimates thus represent little more than the individual desires of the departmental heads.[109]

The reformers' rhetoric conveys the problematic aspect of American practice: how could budgeting be done without a budget? Obviously, revenue was collected and expenditures were made, but these actions were not part of predetermined plans. A person innocent of European experience might not question this relationship, but we must ask why, when most European nations had institutionalized expenditure budgeting by the late nineteenth century, no official within American government was given the explicit task of preparing a unified budget for its legislature to vote on? Unless an executive budget is part of the natural order of things, making contrary arrangements unnatural or perverse, American values and experiences may offer clues as to why its spending was managed differently from other nations'.

Which American past, the insurrection against the British crown or the revulsion against the impotent government under the Articles of Confederation, would prove decisive in designing the executive power? Though the Constitutional Convention was called by citizens opposed to the government of the Articles, both views were represented. Executive power, Roger Sherman of Connecticut said at the convention, was "nothing more than an institution for carrying the will of the legislature into effect; that the person or persons ought to be appointed by, and accountable to, the legislature only, which was the depository of the supreme will of the society." For Sherman, as for many others, an independent executive was "the very essence of tyranny." Edmond Randolph of Virginia went so far as to suggest choosing three executives—one from each of the major regions of the country. But a hierarchical view also existed. Confiding to his colleagues that the nature of the executive was "in truth the most difficult of all on which we have had to decide," James Wilson of New Jersey spoke for those who "preferred a single magistrate, as giving most energy, dispatch, and responsibility to the office."[110] Wilson's words echoed Alexander Hamilton's opinion in Number 78 of *The Federalist*: a single, energetic executive was to be the "leading character" in the centralizers' definition of good government. Not to be outdone, the second President of the United States, John Adams, wrote to his Secretary of State that "the worst evil that can happen in any government is a divided executive . . . incompatible with liberty."[111] George Washington agreed with Hamilton; anything that two or three men working at cross-purposes could accomplish, he maintained, thinking back to Revolutionary War days, would be done better by one.[112]

As they often characterized themselves, the Federalists were the party of order. Their Republican opponents feared executive power. Besides symbolizing abhorrent monarchy, a central executive could undermine popular rule, the Republicans believed. They therefore wanted to restrict executive power to the narrowest possible limits. The Federalists favored broad delegation of power.

Alexander Hamilton always saw political power behind financial power. The funding of the debt, for example, he believed necessary not only to establish strong credit, but to induce the rentier class receiving interest on the debt to support the new government's purposes.[113] From the outset of his term as Secretary of the Treasury, Hamilton tried to convince Congress that Americans had to learn "to distinguish between oppression and the necessary exercise of lawful authority."[114] Hamilton's interest in levying taxes other than tariffs, and in enforcing the federal government's power to levy an excise tax on whiskey, had as much to do with his desire to strengthen government as it did with the need to raise money.

The excise taxes, which supported most governments in those days, were not popular, either in England or in America. Samuel Johnson's *Dictionary of the English Language* captured the prevailing ethos; he defined an excise as "a hateful tax levied upon commodities." The colonists themselves, seeking support for their revolution from the people of Quebec, reminded them that the British had imposed an excise, which was "the horror of all free states."[115] In 1794, citizens in a frontier district of western Pennsylvania rejected a new federal excise tax on whiskey—the sole comfort, some said, in the frontiersman's rough existence. Up in arms, they resurrected the Revolutionary War practice of putting up Liberty Poles with banners proclaiming that the people might justly revolt against the distant rulers in Washington who had imposed the hated tax. Under George Washington, the government put down the Whiskey Rebellion by force, and made its point without collecting much more revenue.[116]

But the battle for a stronger central government, one with a single, potent chief executive, and with department heads serving as agents of executive power, was not yet ended. The quarrels at the convention continued afterward, and, in fact, have not ceased to this day. A few Federalists were disturbed at the thought of turning over the new government's financial activities to Hamilton, an extreme centralizer. They argued for a board of three commissioners, such as had served the Continental Congress and the government under the Articles of Confederation. But the experience of that time, together with the early Treasury Board's failures to make sense of its accounts, persuaded the majority to opt for a single executive.[117] Since pro- and anti-executive forces both believed that accounts had to be kept carefully and cash dispersed under rigorous safeguards, they rapidly agreed on a cumbersome method of multiple signatures for dispersing funds. A comptroller, a treasurer, a register, and an auditor—all appointed by the President—had to sign to approve major disbursements. With all these checks, spending the federal money was not so easy.

Though mentioning the President's power to remove the Secretary, the organic act establishing the Treasury Department did not specify the Treasury executive's fiscal responsibilities. Only in an act establishing salaries was the Treasury Secretary referred to as an executive officer; he was required to report annually to Congress, and to answer questions and provide information as Congress directed.[118] The question of executive power was still up in the air.

Immediately there arose a clamor, unfathomable outside the United States, that, by giving his opinion to Congress, a powerful Secretary of the Treasury might intimidate or otherwise influence the legislature. Why, Hamilton might become the real legislator in financial matters, and that would not do![119] "The secretary seemed to take the whole government upon his shoulders," William Findley of western Pennsylvania said in a speech, "and to consider all the great interests thereof to be committed to his providence." Findley's report spoke of Hamilton's using the "language of Frederick of Prussia, or some other despotic prince, who had all the political powers vesting in himself—not the language of a dependent Secretary, under a free and well-ordered government."[120] The arguments reflected polarized opinion; to a staunch Federalist like Representative Fisher Ames of Massachusetts, "Our proceedings smell of anarchy . . . The heads of departments are head clerks. Instead of being . . . the organs of the executive power . . . they are precluded of late even from communication with the House by reports." House practice had come to such a pass that departmental secretaries, like children, could speak only when spoken to by the legislature. The deliberative functions of the House were being undermined, in Ames's view, by its very own committees' monopoly over information. He complained bitterly about the inability of ministers to issue reports independently. Having ordained that ministers shall be dumb, Ames concluded, "we forbid them to explain themselves by signs."[121] The extraordinary character of these developments should not pass unnoticed.

Inevitably, informal mechanisms developed: Jefferson, particularly, made a high art out of personal persuasion of members of Congress.[122] The influence of both the Chief Executive and department heads had to depend on personal contacts with members of a congressional committee. Whatever the issue—were it personnel or finance—the question continuously arose of whether administrators were direct arms of the legislature or were subject to presidential direction. Or, if Congress was incapable and the President was denied the right, could department administrators act independently of either one?

Arguing that private wealth should not be used to make up for the defects of public contributions, President George Washington in 1796 asked for good salaries for public servants on grounds that would appeal to egalitarian principles: "it would be repugnant to the vital principles of our government, virtually to exclude from public trusts, talent and virtue, unless accompanied by wealth."[123] (From the late eighteenth century, merit principles increasingly governed selection of officials in European nations as well.) Upon taking office, Jeffersonian Republicans reduced the number of federal employees, and the amount of compensation. They insisted on what was then a new principle: making public the salaries and backgrounds of persons occupying official positions. By 1802, Congress had compiled a list of government officials. By 1806, department heads were required to provide lists of clerks, their pay, and the extent of their duties, including a statement as to whether these had increased or decreased.[124] Publicity served as a safeguard against multiplication of offices and excessive, ostentatious pay, but it was also a convenient starting point for congressmen who wished to reward supporters with government jobs.

Congressional patronage was easier to dispense after passage of the Tenure-of-Office Act of 1820; it specified that existing middle-level positions be subject to change every four years; any new offices required senatorial confirmation. Aside from enhancing the opportunity for senatorial patronage, the Tenure-of-Office Act created a new administrative principle, one that would become famous in President Andrew Jackson's administration as "rotation in office" (or, if one prefers the pejorative term, the "spoils system").

Even a government founded in equality needed some officials who were experts; the question was whether to have many or few such positions. Expertise entails specialized knowledge, and such knowledge implies differentiation. With a body of specialized administrators, knowledge is a basis of power, as some citizens make decisions affecting others. Expertise may be regarded as a form of inequality.[125]

The best vantage point for observing the struggle between adherents of executive versus legislative control of government is in the appropriations process. The nation's early history records innumerable efforts to make the Executive dependent on Congress (or at least its committees) and ingenious subterfuges adopted by administrators, either to escape congressional control or merely to do their jobs under regulations too specific and restrictive to cover changing circumstances. It took over a century before the concept of executive responsibility for budget preparation and execution was largely, though never entirely, accepted.

The law establishing the Treasury Department merely specified that the Secretary send annual departmental spending estimates to Congress; the law did not say that the Secretary was to revise these estimates or, if he did so, whether anybody had to pay attention. Over time, an informal understanding developed: though the Secretary might take an interest in the departments' estimates, his sole duty was to collect them, put them together in a package, and send them without comment to Congress. Sometimes a Secretary did question this or that estimate, and occasionally a President intervened in disputes. Settling a difference of opinion between his Secretaries of War and the Navy, for example, John Adams wrote:

> As it is an excellent principle for every man in public life to magnify his office, and make it honorable, I admire the dexterity with which you dignify yours, by representing an army, and means adequate to its support, as the first thing necessary to make the nation respected. Genius in a general is oftener an instrument of divine vengeance than a guardian angel.[126]

Congress generally voted appropriations without either the President's or the Secretary of the Treasury's formal participation.

Before it established a rudimentary division of labor, the House of Representatives (which originated money bills, according to the Constitution) considered spending as a committee of the whole. The House selected several members to write a bill expressing the prevailing view. Establishment in 1796 of a Committee on Ways and Means, whose jurisdiction included both revenue and expenditure, altered this ad-hoc procedure. Ways and Means became a permanent standing committee in 1802. By this time all formal communication between legislative and executive branches was carried on in writing. Relations between the branches in regard to spending centered on the question of how specific and detailed appropriations laws might become.

Since a strong executive was part of their platform, the Federalist Party favored lump sum appropriations, giving administrators as much leeway as possible. Favoring economy and distrusting the executive (the one reinforcing the other), the Republican Party sought specific appropriations to bind department heads to do *exactly* what Congress had commanded. Despite his position as Secretary of the Treasury under Jefferson, Albert Gallatin therefore worked hard to make sure that sums appropriated for one purpose would not be spent for another. "But I was specially jealous of Executive encroachment," Gallatin observed, "and to keep that branch within the strict limits of

Constitution and of law allowing no more discretion than what appeared strictly necessary, was my constant effort." Finding items intermingled in military appropriations, with funds voted for one purpose being spent on another (a matter that has not changed from that day to this), Gallatin strove to change the existing phraseology, "there be appropriated a sum not exceeding . . ." to his preferred language, namely, "the following sums be respectively appropriated."[127] Among nations, America's early effort to limit transfers was truly exceptional. France did not adopt legislation prohibiting *virement* (as such transfers were called) until its budget reforms of the early 1820s; and, in spite of Gladstone's constant exhortations for parsimony, England waited until 1866 to do so.

In America, no matter how appropriations bills were framed, whether in Gallatin's preferred language of specificity or its alternate, sometimes one view prevailed and sometimes the other. As always, it was mistakenly thought that legislation would resolve the dispute. An act of 1820 required unexpended balances to revert to the Treasury, forbade payment of contracts not authorized by law, and limited transfers from one category to another.[128]

The clarity of the instruction, however, was not a real deterrent to administrative officers closer to the scene who could always claim that deviation from the letter of the law was necessary in order to accomplish its spirit.

What could Congress do? As in England's medieval Exchequer, appropriations could be itemized in excruciating detail. Congress also could try to apportion agency funds periodically so that agencies did not run out of money before the year was over. (Deficiencies led agencies to ask for supplementary funds to carry out essential functions.) It could limit transfers, and recapture unexpended funds—or at least it could try. Congress could, and did, specify number of employees, exact remuneration, and sometimes their names. Appropriations bills listed supplies voted for each specific office, and contained detailed plans for forts and other public works. In 1859, for example, the superintendent of the Military Academy set aside $45,000 for "brooms, brushes, tubs, pails . . ."[129]

Departments had to give "minute and full explanations" of any deviation from prior estimates. One of the many budget reform acts, the Act of 1842, prohibited all departments except State from spending more than $100 a year on newspapers; denied funds for commissions of inquiry, except courts-martial; refused extra allowances and additional clerks; insisted upon detailed reporting about use of contingency funds; and prohibited purchase of engravings, pictures, books, or periodicals other than by written order of the head of the department. Whether it was known then that expert committees always recommend spending more on their specialization is not clear, but Congress did respond to President Tyler's appointment of three people to investigate public works in Washington, D.C., by denying them supplies.[130]

Despite continuous legislative effort to narrow administrative leeway, Congress could not control everything. The Army and the Navy, insisting that they could not be held to specific line items, had their way.[131] The legislated sanctions against executive offices for overspending, transfers, or other violations of the innumerable prohibitions were not invoked; no doubt enforcement was not possible.[132] Most departmental appropriations soon became regular and customary, as to both content and amount. Whether or not a new annual appropriations bill was mandated, Congress renewed allocations in more or less the same manner year after year. Social stability had produced agreement on a budgetary base.

An easy way around specific appropriations was to transfer sums from one purpose to another. The President was allowed by the Act of 1820 to make only certain transfers; all others were forbidden. But the logic of life intervened. Congress became overburdened with requests for change. Discovering it could not monitor even a small proportion of transactions, it tried to legalize prevailing practices. Funds for forts could be moved from one stockade to another, as could appropriations for naval forces from branch to branch, and postal funds from here to there. Departments kept appropriated funds from lapsing by finding ways to spend at the end of the fiscal year. When, in 1842, department heads received authority to transfer surplus funds from one item to some other (always excepting, of course, funds for newspapers, which in those days were party organs), the battle against transfers had been lost.[133]

Those who have the ability to redefine financial terms generally have the ability to get their way. What, for instance, was a surplus? In the 1850s, the Attorney General declared that the term "unexpended" actually meant an "unobligated" appropriation, thus reserving such a balance for future executive discretion. Congress did take away departments' power to transfer, but by then the Civil War had come and with it disinterest in expenditure control.[134]

When transfers failed to produce means to spend because funds were inadequate, departments could and did resort to the tactic of the coercive deficiency. What could Congress do if money for an essential

service ran out before the end of the fiscal year, other than pass a supplemental appropriation? There were doomsayers aplenty who could
claim that congressional control over spending had ended, as deficiencies before the Civil War rose to something like 10 percent of total
spending. It seemed easy enough to get around the latest Anti-Deficiency Act by merely running out of money and reporting this fact to
Congress. Congress did demand to be informed of an emergency leading to a waiver of required apportionments, but when the waiver was
reported it had no effective remedy.[135] Establishment of the Bureau of
the Budget in 1921 eventually limited the use of coercive deficiencies,
but they are still with us, though more likely now to take the form of
entitlements that must be paid. Congress has taken to meeting spending goals by voting appropriations for food stamps for only ten
months, for instance, unless the authorizing legislation is changed.

From time to time departments used unexpended balances for purposes not contemplated in congressional statutes. A department might
issue regulations stating that an activity was necessary, and expect
payment to follow. The year after 1868, when Congress reiterated that
funds should be spent only for authorized purposes, the Secretary of
the Navy began to rebuild the service with balances accumulated over
ten years.[136] It was not the first instance of administrative discretion. In
President Jackson's term, during the 1830s, the Congressional Committee on Public Expenditures expressed amazement at finding "a
Naval force springing up amongst us, controlled by the Secretary of
the Treasury, accountable to no one but him, expended at will by him,
supported by him out of the revenue before it gets to the Treasury, and
may cost the country whatever he shall direct."[137]

Congressional enactments still went into what was evidently stulti-
fying detail. Though Senator Lewis Cass wanted to authorize the Navy
to install the best condenser it could find for its ships, he protested
against the legislative requirement for a specific type of condenser.
Another Congress terminated one particular employee in the Corps of
Engineers and specified that his duties be performed by a different
person. Protesting the demoralizing effect of this on the Army, President Buchanan declared in 1850 that "officers might then be found . . .
besieging the halls of Congress for the purpose of obtaining special and
choice places by legislative enactment."[138] As late as the second decade
of the twentieth century, Representative Swagger Sherley (later chairman of the Committee on Appropriations) condemned the practice of
spending more and more time on matters of less and less importance.[139]

The written law exists side by side with the understood law of necessity. Believing an act essential, public officials may undertake it without legislative warrant, appealing to Congress to approve their conduct retrospectively. The strongest proponent of this view was undoubtedly Abraham Lincoln. As the nation divided into irreconcilable factions, Lincoln took the position that whatever was required for national defense had to be approved. On grounds that there was then "no adequate and effective organization for the public defense," he justified ordering the Treasury to advance $2 million to a variety of private agents to provide requisitions for the military:

> Congress had indefinitely adjourned. There was no time to convene them. It became necessary for me to choose, whether, using only the existing means, agencies, and processes which Congress had provided, I should let the Government fall at once into ruin or whether availing myself of the broader powers conferred by the Constitution in cases of insurrection, I would make an effort to save it, with all its blessings, for the present age and for posterity ... The several Departments of the Government at that time contained so large a number of disloyal persons that it would have been impossible to provide safely through official agents only for the performance of the duties thus confided to citizens favorably known for their ability, loyalty, and patriotism.[140]

The higher law was one thing and low down behavior another; investigations provided ample evidence of abuse of contract power during the war.[141]

Performance being more important than protocol during the war, Congress legally authorized all that it had been denying for the past century—lump-sum appropriations, spending in excess of authorizations and appropriations, transfers, revolving funds perpetuated by reimbursements, and more.[142] After the war Congress tried hard to take back these grants of authority.

So far as we know, there is no study of the appropriations process from the Civil War through the end of World War II. The vast literature on budgeting in those years was concerned solely with advocating one or another reform. What ought to be, overwhelmed what was. Without a monumental feat of historical reconstruction, the only way to get a glimmer of the actual practices involved in budgeting is to ask what the reformers most objected to, and assume that this was prevailing practice.

In his distinguished series on federal administration from its beginnings until 1900, Leonard White, referring to the Jacksonian years, concludes that "a large part of the annual appropriations . . . was fixed and well established, continuing by general consent year after year without much change."[143] Given the small size of government and the relative absence of new functions, it is not surprising that budgets of one year were much like those of another. Changes were incremental: the substance of allocations remained close to the past, and the amount varied up or down only a few percent from recent years. After the Civil War, the notable exception was veterans' pensions. Congress passed pension bills introduced under the "camel's nose" technique; expenditures were estimated far lower than they actually turned out to be.[144]

Earlier on we learned that the Ways and Means Committee was disaggregated in 1865; in the early 1890s, by Woodrow Wilson's count, five committees in the Senate and fifteen in the House then were concerned with spending. Frederick A. Cleveland, perhaps the leading budget reformer before World War I, excoriated the chairmen of these committees as "functionalized, bureaucratic, feudal lords [who] did not look to their titular superior, the leader chosen by and responsible to the nation, for powers and policies. They looked to irresponsible committees. And because of the independence that was thus given, each chief built around himself a bureaucratic wall that even the constitutional Chief Executive himself could not get over . . ." Cleveland's theme, bureaucratic feudalism, explicates the emergent pattern of budgeting. Close relationships developed between chiefs of governmental bureaus, and the chairmen and ranking members of the congressional appropriations committees that had vitually unrivalled jurisdiction over them.[145] Reading numerous other reformers complaining about lack of coordination,[146] we conclude that a norm of reciprocity existed. In voting on appropriations outside their area of specialization, members of each committee must have deferred to the judgment of all the others.

"The estimates are nearly always inflated by the officers who prepare them," wrote reformer Arthur Buck, "either intentionally or as a result of super-abundant enthusiasm for their work; . . . this, it seems, is to be expected."[147] To Buck, the bureau's role in budgeting was to advocate higher spending. The House Appropriations Committee was supposed to cut these estimates, but the Senate then acted as an appeals court to give the money back. "Appropriations bills generally provide for an expenditure considerably less than that called for by the estimate," Woodrow Wilson observed, "as returned from the Senate they usually propose grants of many additional millions, having been brought by that less sensitive body up almost, if not quite, to the figures of the estimate."[148]

The representative who said that the Appropriations Committee treats "every executive officer as if he were a suspicious character, and he treats us as if we were a lot of numbskulls who know nothing about the needs of the service"[149] was putting his finger on the slowly developing role of the overall Appropriations Committee as a "watchdog of the Treasury" or defender of the public purse. "You may think my business is to make appropriations," said Joseph Cannon, a powerful former Speaker of the House and chairman of the Appropriations Committee, "but it is not. It is to prevent their being made."[150] Presumably the committee performed the watchdog role by cutting the spending estimate, and it performed the advocacy role (as defenders of activities and bureaus under their care) by raising spending above the prior year.

Dragging its feet into the twentieth century, in 1921 the United States embraced a hybrid version of the centralized budgetary methods practiced by European governments since the first half of the nineteenth century. The Budget Reform Act of 1921 revived the Appropriations Committee without doing away with the substantive committees. Instead, a parallel system was created: substantive committees produced authorizations to spend; and what were formerly specialized spending committees became subcommittees of Appropriations that reported bills to do the actual spending. While U.S. budget reformers, writing between the turn of the century and 1920, proposed structures modeled on European nations' centralized spending agencies, congressional jurisdiction over spending was further fragmented.

With the Budget Reform Act of 1921 reassembling the Appropriations Committee, the pattern of roles and expectations that had developed in budgeting during the last half of the nineteenth century was carried over into the new structure. Bureaus, acting as advocates, padded spending estimates, knowing that these would be reduced. The House Appropriations Committee functioned as guardian of the public purse, reducing estimates, and the Senate as an appeals court,[151] increasing estimates above the House proposal but below the agency's own bid. Formalized by precedent, these roles lasted into the second half of the twentieth century.

From the practitioner's viewpoint, the absence of the executive budget in American national government is not anomalous. If the President and the Secretary of the Treasury do not review spending estimates, or if they do but their views are ignored, that is how it always was. Taking his own country's circumstances for granted, it did not matter to the American budget practitioner (both before and after

1921) that U.S. budget-making differed from other nations'. It took academics and intellectuals, men like Wilson and Buck, who preferred the European model, to argue that the United States was out of step.

The spectacle of the President and his subordinates arguing over expenditure, and of departments feuding within and among themselves, caused real dismay among scholars of budgeting, both during the Progressive era and afterward. With jurisdiction over spending so fragmented, they maintained, no single unit was responsible for making the orderly expenditure estimates that the sophisticated governments of western Europe were using in allocating funds. Moreover, around the turn of the century, as progressive reforms led to creation of new U.S. federal regulatory agencies—increasing both functional specialization within government and the amounts spent—there was yet no formal mechanism for relating expenditure to revenue.

While budget reformers lacked experience in making budgets, they did have ideas about how to improve the existing process—ideas derived from observation of hierarchical budget structures in western-European governments. As an example of the profound influence of ideas, then, the rationalizing, centralizing budget reform movement of the late nineteenth and early twentieth centuries in America was as unique a development for this nation as was the exceptionalism that movement sought to revive.

AN END TO BUDGETARY EXCEPTIONALISM? THE REEMERGENCE OF HIERARCHY

Generally speaking, students of administration have been hostile to the tripartite separation of powers. In this they have not been alone; their hostility must be viewed against the background of almost complete lack of sympathy for the principle by American reformism and political science. This lack of sympathy became more widespread decade by decade between the Civil War and the First Great War. It found its justification in the unhealthy condition of our government and politics; it was nourished by admiration for British practice and American business organization; and it found expression typically in proposals . . . to aggrandize the executive . . .

—DWIGHT WALDO[152]

The executive alone can and should do this work [prepare the budget]. Situated at the center of government, reaching through its hierarchical organization to the smallest unit, the executive more than anybody else is in a position to feel public needs and wishes, to appreciate their

comparative merits, and accordingly to calculate, in the budget, a just
appropriation which each of these needs and wishes deserves.
                                                    —RENÉ STOURM[153]

Reformers are not radicals; those who left their imprint upon
American budgeting between the turn of the century and 1920 were
not opposed to American social structure or to competitive markets,
nor were they proponents of income redistribution. A political force
unique in this most unusual of nations, they were the establishment's
anti-establishment—the anti-anti-hierarchy, critical of the way politicians did things, and the anti-anti-market, opposed to the trusts threatening to limit competition. Operating within a competitive political
system that legitimized opposition, progressive reformers sought to replace the existing establishment by altering its institutions. To lessen
the "irresponsible power" of party bosses and chairmen of congressional standing committees, the budgetary reformers wanted a visible
and democratically accountable Chief Executive served by experts
proclaiming their dedication to the public interest. These experts,
whose ideas and attitudes matched the reformers', would be the instruments of change.

Unlike the "muckrakers" who filled the press with charges of public
and private corruption (muckrakers saw politics and business as
equally debased), the progressive reformers had a positive program.
They wanted to tear down the establishment in order to replace it with
a better one. Some acted as guardians of the land, leading the movement for resource conservation and national parks. Others became
civil-service reformers, instituting some semblance of a merit system in
city, state, and national governments. Or they democratized party
structures by introducing party primaries in which candidates for nomination would compete for voter support. Following liberal tradition,
still others promoted useful education. In a nation populated by recent
immigrants, reformers established adult-education institutions designed both to acculturate and to educate, thus making immigrants
into more effective citizens. By infusing expertise into government and
by improving citizen competence, the progressives hoped government
would become open, honest, and efficient; it would be organized to intervene against special interests on citizens' behalf. An educated, artic-
ulate citizenry would in turn vote support for elites selected more for
expertise than for political allegiance.

Understandably, the reformers were ambivalent about the establishment; even in rejection, they embraced some of its ways. They excoriated "bossism," but then replaced it with executive leadership. "It is a strange fact that it was left to the 'boss,'" wrote Frederick A. Cleveland, "to impress upon the American people the idea that social and political ideals can be made real and practical only through organization; and that leadership is essential to both."[154] The boss was irresponsible; since he was not an elected official or part of the establishment, his motives and actions were hidden. The new executive of the progressives' vision would be out front, elected and accountable. From "the malefactors of wealth," as capitalists were called at a time of tumultuous economic development, the reformers absorbed business methods, especially the idea of industrial efficiency. (The new science of industrial engineering, with its cost-cutting through time-and-motion study, provided a model for government.) The argument against the old distrust of executive power was hierarchical: "Government is no longer a necessary evil; it is the needed servant of the people."[155] Contending that "the great American democratic electorate would not much longer continue to accept the domination of an irresponsible oligarchy,"[156] the progressives criticized the established political cultures (markets and hierarchies).

The reformers did not reject oligarchy per se; they wanted to replace the existing inefficient hierarchy with their own, more efficient hierarchy. We will better understand the reformers if we begin by trying to understand what they opposed, before looking at what they stood for.

The people of the United States had a deep attachment to the Constitution and the separation between executive and legislative branches it embodied. Yet it was precisely this separation (or at least the form it took in America) that the reformers opposed. Nicholas Murray Butler, the president of Columbia University, attributed to a defect in the principle of government the many "embarrassments and misfortunes" inflicted upon the country by its government (the use of the word "embarrassment" suggests an absence of good form), the "lack of coherence and of continuity in public policy," the concealment of information the people had a right to know, and the unfortunate absence of cooperation between the two branches. "The business of national government has become so huge and so complex," he wrote in 1918, "that the sharp separation of the executive and the legislative powers to which we have been accustomed for 140 years is distinctly disadvantageous."[157] And Woodrow Wilson, extending his criticism to the other great division of power, that between states and the federal government, had earlier concluded: "It is, therefore, manifestly a radical defect in our federal system that it parcels out power and confuses responsibility as it does."[158] Imagining (in the mode of the Germanic mental experiment) that it were possible to call together the "members of that wonderful [constitutional] convention ... in the light of the century that has tested it," Wilson was certain, "they would be the first to admit that the only fruit of dividing power has been to make it irresponsible."[159] Rejecting half measures, Frederick A. Cleveland suggested (without a shred of evidence) that the nation's hallowed framers actually had intended to set up something like British cabinet government, in which a vigorous executive was accountable to a legislature that made no pretense of running the government, but that the founding fathers' desires had somehow been frustrated by those lesser men who came after. Government by standing committees, the "irresponsible oligarchy" the reformers so often inveighed against, was no part of the original constitutional plan.[160]

The budgetary implication of this argument, according to W. F. Willoughby, was "that the legislative branch should be debarred from, or, if it possesses the Constitutional authority, should refrain from, using the right to initiate proposals for the expenditure of money. No appropriation of money should be made except upon the direct request of the executive."[161] By this budgetary sleight of hand, apparently, a pluralistic policy could be made unitary—congressional becoming parliamentary government.

Woodrow Wilson's principle (the clearest he claimed he knew) was that in government or business someone had to be trusted to act, providing he was held accountable.[162] Now, who might that be? Earlier, in an essay on college and state, Wilson had given his definitive response:

> If you would have the present error of our system in a word, it is this, that Congress is the motive power in the government and yet has in it nowhere any representative of the nation as a whole. Our Executive, on the other hand, is national; at any rate may be made so, and yet has no longer any place of guidance in our system. It represents no constituency, but the whole people; and yet, though it alone is national, it has no originative voice in domestic national policy. . . .
>
> We should have Presidents and Cabinets of a different calibre were we to make it their bounden duty to act as a committee for the whole nation to choose and formulate matters for the consideration of Congress in the name of a party and an Administration.[163]

Long before he ran for public office, Wilson thought government should be the result of an intentional design in which a single authority (the executive) states its position and is voted up or down. Thus the reformers did not think of a coherent budget as the mere sum of out-comes; coherence would derive from a budget's unitary input from a single sponsor of government policy.

The reformers' focus on *form* rather than *substance* came largely, we believe, from their effort to justify replacement of the existing hierar-chy by their preferred version. If we think of them as rationalizing a set of relationships in which educated people (as opposed, say, to party hacks or ignorant time-servers) governed without having to contend with the vulgarity of competitive politics, the reformers' interests be-come easier to understand.

Besides separation and fragmentation of power, the budgetary prac-tice the reformers most objected to was the timeworn one of itemiza-tion of spending, known today as the line-item budget. A line-item budget made government's top levels irresponsible, the reformers maintained. Moreover, with budgeting by line items, the experts—those with greatest knowledge and closest to the scene—could not do what they knew best.[164] Itemization was wasteful and it did not allow for executive discretion. President Taft's Commission on Economy and Efficiency argued that because government did not trust its officers, "judgments which can be made wisely only at the time that a specific thing is to be done are attempted to be made by a Congress composed of hundreds of Members from six months to a year and a half before-hand on the recommendation of a committee which at most can have but a limited experience or fund of information as a basis for their thinking."[165] The principle of deference to expertise was thus twice de-nied by Congress, once to the Chief Executive and again to his subor-dinates.

The piecemeal process by which budgets were put together—each committee recommending appropriations for the agencies and pur-poses under its control, and the houses of Congress acting on them one at a time—was singled out for special condemnation. "In the United States," as Charles Wallace Collins put it, "no one knows in advance of action, what the government proposes to spend for the coming year. This can be arrived at only at or near the close of the session by sum-ming up the various bills which have been acted on."[166] Reformers had no concept of informal coordination, nor did they ask whether all con-cerned might not have had a pretty good idea of where they were, and were likely to end up. It was chiefly the form of the budget, and what it represented, to which they objected: "no standard classifications . . . of expenditures according to their character and object . . . no uniform scheme of expenditure documents calling for the recording of expenditure data in accordance with any general information plan ... no budgetary message, no proper scheme of summary, analytical and comparative tables ..." In short, nothing in the United States appropriations process remotely resembled budgeting in Europe.[167]

In the same spirit, critics repeatedly asserted that Congress lacked a proper legislative audit. But since Congress had considerable control over the budget (and did in fact appoint auditors), one might wonder how they arrived at this appraisal. The system was undermined, reformers insisted, by the lack of an executive budget.

> The audit of accounts [Willoughby wrote], instead of being made by an officer of the body granting the funds, is made by an officer of the branch of the government whose operations are to be passed upon. Congress thus has no effective machinery for the exercise of supervision and control over the manner in which the executive performs its duties such as is possessed by the British parliament in its comptroller and auditor general and its standing committee on public accounts.[168]

For René Stourm, author of the definitive comparative study of budgeting at that time, any nation with budget practices different from Britain's departed from the best way of doing things. In fact, in the United States, independent tests were never made of the effectiveness of audits, one way or the other. Never mind. Since Congress refused to play its part in the ordained scheme of things, according to the reformers, it could not conceivably have an appropriate or effective audit. Yet we do not find any defense of traditional practice.

Actually, Congress did establish an executive post-audit when it first convened. From the beginning the Treasury Department had auditors who examined accounts and settled disputed cases. A comptroller of the Treasury gave opinions on the laws governing disbursement, and, on appeal, might decide who and what should be paid, revising the accounts of the Treasury auditors. No part of this procedure facilitated legislative control of spending.[169]

Instead of substituting the British principle, under which a parliamentary committee conducted the final audits of accounts, the Budget Reform Act of 1921 created an independent agency responsible to Congress, the General Accounting Office, headed by a comptroller general who, as Wilmerding states, "was expected to act simultaneously as administrative comptroller and as a congressional auditor ..."[170] The General Accounting Office, to some degree, replaced the old Treasury auditors and, in part, gave reports to Congress. The new agency's advocates do not appear to have been embarrassed by the arguments that it was a monstrous hybrid—neither legislative nor executive.

So much for what the reformers were against; what were they for? "Executive leadership" would appear to be the best short answer one can muster. Politics was to be purified by leadership. This was Woodrow Wilson's theory, and his practice as president.[171] Wilson was ready with the diagnosis and the remedy: "this feature of disintegration of leadership runs ... through all our legislation; but it is manifestly of much more serious consequence in financial administration than in the direction of other concerns of government." Budgets must be "under the management of a single body; only when all financial arrangements are based upon schemes prepared by a few men of trained minds and accordant principles, who can act with easy agreement and with perfect confidence in each other," will budgets make sense.[172] The major premise of executive leadership led also to its important corollary: executive discretion, by reliance on experts. It is important to understand that the reformers believed that their recommendations derived from scientific principles. Often they referred to "the science of budgetmaking,"[173] or said they were subjecting budgetary problems "to scientific analysis."[174]

The policy–administration dichotomy—in which political choices are made through general legislative enactments and administrative choices consist in technical implementation of these larger and prior decisions—was an essential postulate of budget reformers. For if administrators also made large, and therefore political, choices, the principle of neutral competence that justified civil-service reform, and the important role reformers wished to give to experts, would be undermined. Their text was Frank J. Goodnow's *Politics and Administration*. Goodnow believed that the two primary functions of government were to determine the will of the people and to execute that will. Though, as Dwight Waldo observes, Goodnow was far from making the distinction exclusive (seeing better than his followers the interpenetration of the two functions), when taken up by less sophisticated acolytes his ideas generated the doctrine of a strict separation between the two.[175] The reformers then tied this distinction to the requirement of democratic government through the doctrine of executive responsibility. "How is the schoolmaster, the nation," Woodrow Wilson asked, "to know which boy needs the whipping?"[176] The answer given by Cleveland and Buck and their peers was "leadership ... for achieving results," and "leadership for enabling the membership to determine ...

whether the results . . . are consistent with their determining will."[177] The distinction between politics and administration legitimizes taking power from the legislature and giving it to the executive and, ultimately, to the executive's expert administrators.

The reformers' recommendations to adopt business practices manifestly did not mean their approval of bidding and bargaining among legislature and executive. Rather, they took from big business its internal organization—i.e., its hierarchical structure—which, in a free government, served to solidify the distinction between policy and administration that the reformers wished to make. "Has Congress appreciated that its function as a board of directors is quite distinct from its function as a general lawgiver," Willoughby asked rhetorically, "and as such requires a different organization?" Answering in the negative, Willoughby came full circle, concluding that "Congress does its governing work so poorly" because it confuses policy with its administrative functions.[178] Congress had taken on the role of "running the government," Willoughby felt, without, unfortunately, at the same time establishing "an office of general administration corresponding to that of a general manager in a business corporation."[179]

The reformers' principle of principles is well known and is powerfully stated by René Stourm in the epigraph to this section. Its reiteration proceeds like a litany: "there must be established a national budget prepared and recommended by the Chief Executive."[180] And, to put it all in a nutshell, combining the main budgetary principle with the form of organization, W. F. Willoughby draws the logical conclusion—government by hierarchy:

> The Chief Executive can be put in this leading position only by the organization . . . of the government according to the principle of . . . an . . . hierarchical type of organization; that is, one where related services are grouped in departments under the . . . control of the Chief Executive and the line of administrative authority made to follow this gradation of units instead of running directly from the several services to the legislatures.[181]

If the proposals were adopted, how did the reformers picture themselves (or people like them) as participants in the budgetary process? As we shall see, they had already been instrumental in staffing commissions to recommend the proposed reforms. These same men aimed to become part of the expert staff of the executive—mayor, governor, or President—whose task would be formulating the budget. As A. E. Buck said so succinctly, "budget-making requires special staff assistance ... to ... assist the executive ..."[182] Once the Chief Executive becomes administrator-in-chief, as the reformers wished, "there must be," W. F. Willoughby maintained, "some [civil] service ... to prescribe the system of accounting and reporting ... analyze their contents ... prescribe the manner and form [of] estimates ... compile ... data and, finally, to take all steps needed to insure a proper standardization of personnel and administrative practices ..."[183] Prescription of budgetary methods, beginning with such detailed advice as "allotment forms should be prepared in triplicate by the spending department or agency, all three copies being sent to the Executive or his budget office," became a specialty in itself.[184] By extending this function to other governmental purposes, budget experts could easily become a general administrative staff supporting the Executive. When one recognizes that presidents of the United States up to Franklin D. Roosevelt's time were assisted at most by a few clerks, these were far-reaching proposals.

A simile, Be like Britain, justified recommendations for budget hierarchy in the United States. If British budgeting was not the reformers' ideal, it was close; it virtually epitomized hierarchy. The only way Parliament could alter the budget was to change the government. "If one looks for the secret of ... the English system," Willoughby comments, "it must be found in ... the clear distinction ... between legislative and administrative powers.... No proposals for ... expenditure... shall be made ... except ... by the cabinet acting as the custodian of the administrative powers of government ..."[185] Admiration for the British budget led reformers to recommend that the President and his department heads make budget speeches to Congress, and, as in Parliament, let congressmen question the Executive's budget-makers.[186]

Because the British Chancellor of the Exchequer and Department of the Treasury are responsible for both expenditure and revenue, the reformers believed that these would be taken up at the same time and that, therefore, comprehensive and simultaneous consideration would be given to the relative desirability of spending versus taxing.[187] Whether this would make any difference—either to the totals or to the division of expenditures among departments—was not a subject for discussion by reformers who already knew the answer. They did not think of the difficulties members of Parliament faced in deciding on expenditure issues when their choices were either to bring down the government or to object long after the fact when the expenditures were being audited. If the budgetary process followed the correct form, reformers maintained, the desired results were sure to follow.

The literature offers only a few examples of the hypothetical results expected from an altered form of budgeting. Replying to the charge that it would be difficult for agency heads to support estimates changed by the President, Cleveland and Buck claimed:

> This is a reason of no substance whatever. The heads of departments are and should be loyal to the Administration, and should . . . support the view which the President has adopted . . . in respect to the budget. They will have no difficulty in so doing. If any head of a department does, then his place is not in the Cabinet.[188]

If the President fires a dissident department head, the difficulty disappears. Apparently it never occurred to reformers that heads of spending departments might speak privately with legislators, or, if wide-ranging differences arose, that presidents might not be able to maintain dominance over the Cabinet. In those days Cabinet members represented party factions; asking a Cabinet member to step down therefore had significant political costs.

The new budget system was designed to nationalize public spending because every spending proposal, having gained executive approval, represents the national view. Reacting against late-nineteenth-century Darwinian social theories, the progressives viewed government with its expert administrators as a force competent to mediate societal turbulence. Defending the national view, Charles Wallace Collins insisted:

> After the budget is presented to the legislature there can be no "log-rolling" . . . to secure funds . . . A locality deserving a post office building would have to gain the sanction of the Post Office Department. After an examination of all of the facts the Department would come to a decision. Should it be favorable . . . the department would have further to gain the assent of the Treasury before the item . . . could be put into the annual estimates. . . . Both the Department and the Treasury would look at the matter from the national point of view.[189]

In Lewis Carroll's *Through the Looking Glass*, the Red Queen tells Alice, in the same manner, that anything she says three times is true.

At the time, the reformers' position was effectively criticized by Edward A. Fitzpatrick in his *Budget Making in a Democracy* (1918). Though we cannot say that they were well publicized, his views are interesting because they embody the stance of the expert administrator who does not aspire to be a staff assistant to the Chief Executive. It is as if one left the Ivy League and went to the state universities, where an experienced administrator (Fitzpatrick worked in Wisconsin state government) wondered what would become of him if he were besieged on one side by advocates of economy who took away his money, and on the other by advocates of executive control who took away his power. Generalist experts would rule over subject-matter specialists.

"Are we to have a one-man government? That," Fitzpatrick told his readers, "is the fundamental question back of the executive budget propaganda."[190] Behind the folderol about uniformity versus fragmentation, he saw transfer of power from the legislature to the executive. And dictatorship was not the American way. "Without the executive budget," in Fitzpatrick's jaundiced opinion, "the dominant Prussian military caste could never have permeated the German people . . . and made Germany synonymous with organized terror . . . Without control of the funds it could never have utilized the educational system [for] propagating a philosophy in support of its ends. . . . Without a Reichstag with real control over the purse strings, Germany could never have attained her present position as an outlaw among civilized nations."[191]

Executive budget-making was antidemocratic because it established a "vicarious government."[192] Fitzpatrick did not understand how the executive (even with enhanced powers to submit a unified budget) could operate successfully if it were unable to gain support in the legislature. The reformers said they favored popular control of spending, but reducing the legislature's power over budgets, he maintained, would in fact attenuate popular control.

When Fitzpatrick was less hyperbolic, he was more interesting. How could leadership follow from requiring the executive to initiate spending proposals? "Is it possible to create executive leadership by making leadership in the legislature impossible . . . ? A person with genuine qualities of leadership has under the existing laws all the opportunities for leadership that could be desired." Fitzpatrick goes on to say that the Constitution already requires the President to make recommendations—whether in the State of the Union Message or in designating departments' duties.[193]

As for the much vaunted British example, he said, cabinet government was not government by one man, but by a committee of the legislature, a parliament that has the ultimate right to dismiss its cabinet.[194] *"Do those who are proposing the executive budget also propose the legislative recall of the executive?"*[195] This is what the British Parliament does and that is what a business board of directors does when it loses confidence in management, but Fitzpatrick insisted such action is impossible under presidential government with its fixed terms.[196]

In a point-by-point refutation of the reformers, Fitzpatrick asked for actual evidence instead of presumption. Where were the executives who always thought about the business at hand and took a national instead of a local view? What is the nature of executive plans, and how had Congress frustrated them? Were the elected executives interested in administration, or even capable of it, or was executive capacity also a figment of the imagination? Reformers, Fitzpatrick contended acidly, should tell the people they want to make a fundamental change in the American form of government, and not camouflage the issue "under the name of 'executive budget.' "[197]

With but few exceptions, this writing on budget reform supported the recommendations of commissions appointed to study organizational problems within the federal government. In effect, budget reform theory armed the commissions for action.

THE EXECUTIVE BUDGET

The commissions appointed during the 1880s and 1890s to investigate the federal executive's operations aimed to keep the government as small as possible. Whether as a consequence of charges of corruption, or of perceived waste in government, the spirit of the times was not friendly to bureaucracy. The Cockrell Commission, named after a Democratic senator from Missouri who originated the idea, and who was known as the "watchdog of the Treasury," was concerned with work procedures such as legislative supervision of records kept by the executive branch. Aptly summed up by Oscar Kraines, its motto was, "The lowest going wages and disapproval of pensions." The business community favored its recommendations; an editorial in *The New York Times* summarized its views, warning "sensible people that the only safe way with all governmental work is to confine it in the closest practicable limits."[198] Its successor, the Dockery Cockrell Commission, officially the Joint Commission to Inquire into the Status of Laws Organizing the Executive Department, had both a broader and a narrower mandate. Inquiries into pension legislation were specifically ruled out, but the commission was to look into business methods, administrative rules, and laws surrounding executive departments' operations as well as employee efficiency. The latter question boiled down to whether there were too many employees, and whether they were paid too much. As always, no one wanted to cut essential services.[199] The Dockery-Cockrell Commission hired three experts on business accounting and organization (Joseph W. Reinhart, Charles W. Haskins, and Elijah W. Sells), who ushered in the first major reform in accounting procedures since 1817. In essence, federal accounts today still follow much the same form as the commission suggested. By reducing the number of times each account was examined, and otherwise limiting paperwork, the commission cut the cost of running the Treasury; the changes also eliminated need for nearly two hundred clerks.

Failing for the moment to create a climate for further change in federal budget practices, reformers campaigned for improvements in the cities and the states. When the National Municipal League drafted its model Municipal Corporation Act in 1899, the act included a budget directly supervised by the mayor. Many cities adopted the act. The New York Bureau of Municipal Research, founded by William H. Allen, Henry Bruere, and Frederick A. Cleveland (called the ABC Powers of Reform), greatly strengthened the municipal-budget movement. The bureau successfully initiated changes in New York City, then, acting with finesse and fervor, exported the new methods to cities around the country.[200] Under the catchwords "economy and efficiency" (using William H. Allen's slogan in his *Efficient Democracy* that "to be efficient is more difficult than to be good"), the efficiency movement, in Dwight Waldo's words, became a "veritable fetish."[201]

With support from business, numerous bureaus of administrative research sprang up all over the country.[202] Threatened by rising taxes, businessmen realized they should take an interest in local government; the business-reform movement generated yet another slogan—"More business in government." The haphazard patterns of municipal corruption, which made it difficult to anticipate events, or for outsiders to competently bid on projects, heightened businessmen's interest in reforming city government.[203]

As the Progressive movement (with which budget reform was identified) gained strength, pressure for improved budget methods reached the national government. Congress in 1907 asked the Secretary of the Treasury to prepare a comprehensive report on spending estimates and revenue projections. Should expenditures exceed revenues, Congress directed the President in 1909, he should recommend ways either to reduce spending or to increase taxes.[204]

The Keep Commission of 1909 wanted to build up the civil service; its members supported such unheard-of measures as raising pensions and wages of federal workers, and instituting lump-sum budgeting to enhance executive discretion.[205] Neither the President nor the Secretary of the Treasury acted on these directives. When the Secretary appointed a committee to look into the matter, once again he was told that what the government needed most was more businesslike methods.[206]

To promote the idea of a federal executive budget, President William Howard Taft set up a Commission on Economy and Efficiency. The commission's tone was set by its chairman, Frederick A. Cleveland, then director of the New York Bureau of Municipal Research, and by other noted budget reformers appointed with him—including Frank J. Goodnow and W. F. Willoughby.[207] The commission's basic idea, accepted by Taft in its entirety, was that the President would submit spending estimates to Congress and would assume responsibility for them.[208] The commission's major report, "The Need for a National Budget," completed in 1912, was followed by "A Budget for the Fiscal Year 1914," in which President Taft, at the Commission's instigation, submitted the kind of budget document he thought appropriate for the Chief Executive as top administrator.[209] It rejected the prevailing narrow view of economy—of merely spending the minimum. Instead, the President (like earlier advocates of internal improvements) stated that he wanted the government to operate with economy and efficiency in order to do more for the people with available resources.[210] In the White House, at least, budget reform finally found an advocate.

Congress was of a different mind altogether. Expressing fear of the Executive's usurpation of power (in language harking back to the early days of the republic), Congress passed a law requiring department heads charged with preparing estimates to do what they had always done: to send estimates directly to congressional appropriations committees.[211] How did department heads respond to these contradictory directives? They prepared one set as Congress specified, and another as directed by the President. The matter was less resolved than avoided by the election of 1912, in which President Taft was replaced by Woodrow Wilson. As business conditions improved and passage of the Sixteenth Amendment in 1913 permitted a graduated income tax, thus raising revenue, pressures for change in the budget system diminished. Nothing was done to establish an executive budget until after the First World War.[212]

The reformers were not entirely stymied; blocked at the national level, once again they turned to states and cities. Frederick Cleveland himself headed up a commission in 1915 to introduce an executive budget in New York State.[213] New York's proposed budget embodied every practice found in budget-making in the European nations Cleveland so admired: an expert staff to serve the governor; a provision that bills to carry out the chief executive's program should accompany the budget document; and a requirement that the governor appear before the legislature to defend his view.[214]

In 1916, chambers of commerce all over the country voted almost unanimously to introduce a national executive budget. The Republican Party platform that year criticized Democrats for their "shameless raids on the Treasury" and their opposition to President Taft's proposal for "a simple, business-like budget system." Not yet ready to adopt an entirely new budget system, the Democratic Party in its platform proposed, as a first step, a single committee in the House of Representatives to handle all appropriations bills.[215] In 1916 also, the experts created an Institute for Government Research. Directed by Willoughby and dedicated to "scientific investigation" of government administration, the institute focused mainly on the national budget.[216]

The end of World War I renewed interest in a national executive budget; between 1918 and 1921, the reformers presented proposals to congressional committees. Once again the reformers criticized the federal expenditure process: there was overlap among substantive committees, and hence duplication of effort; there was no comprehensive consideration of revenues and expenditures; and the consequence of bureaucratic rivalry was waste. In short, according to Representative Good of Iowa (chairman of the House Select Committee on the Budget System in 1919), "the estimates are a patchwork and not a structure." He thought "a great deal of the time of the committees of Congress is taken up in exploding the visionary schemes of bureau chiefs for which no administration would be willing to stand responsible."[217]

The Budget and Accounting Act of 1921 made the major changes that budget reformers had long supported. A single Appropriations Committee was established in both House and Senate. Departments sent spending estimates to the President through a new institution, the Bureau of the Budget, and the Chief Executive had total control over the Budget Bureau. Henceforth no appropriation could be made, or so it was supposed, unless first approved by the President and the two appropriations committees.

What remained to be decided was the function within the executive branch of the newly created Budget Bureau. Its first head, General Charles G. Dawes, a student and practitioner of administration, insisted that the offices not be in the Treasury Building, but outside it, near the White House (Dawes wanted to insulate the bureau from interdepartmental squabbles).[218] He insisted on his right to call department heads into conference; and President Warren Harding wisely suggested that such conferences be held in the White House Cabinet

Room instead of in the Budget Director's office—to emphasize the Chief Executive's commanding role in budget decisions.[219]

The 1920s witnessed a major assault on federal spending. Led by General Dawes, his successors, and businessmen whom Dawes brought into government (often working for "a dollar a year"), the bureau zealously pursued efficiency. Its accomplishments provoked panegyrics. Martin Madden, chairman of the House Committee on Appropriations, wrote as if the promised land had been reached: "One noticeable feature has been the . . . self-sacrificing of local interests in favor of the common good. When one recalls the former days when appropriations were sought with avidity for local projects, . . . it is appropriate to commend the change from local to national attitude."[220] While President Harding thought the bureau represented "the greatest reform in our financial history," according to Calvin Coolidge it simply meant "that the American Government is not a spendthrift and that it is not lacking in the force of disposition to administer its finances in a scientific way."[221]

Yet, remembering the difficulties governments in Europe faced for decades in forcing spending departments to conform to central controls, one wonders whether creation of the U.S. Budget Bureau actually did work instant wonders. True, the new budget procedures collected spending proposals into a single budget document that, when presented to Congress, symbolized presidential authority. Creation of a new executive layer in the budget process did not modify the separation of powers nor the federal system. After all, European parliaments and the cabinets that tried to control them, even when majorities were tied to party discipline, often did not limit spending. Passage of legislation alone does not instantly create the conditions legislators envision. Differences among social orders persist, giving historical meaning to contemporary political conflicts. So long as the desire to spend was small, and was moderated by unwillingness to raise taxes, legislators and bureaucrats both knew there were real, if informal, limits to achieving their desires. But if the belief in the desirability of budget balance were to decline and, with it, bounds on taxing (and, therefore, spending), more for one program and department would no longer mean less for others. What, then, would stop demands for spending from being piled, willy-nilly, on top of one another? Merely passing proposals through the Budget Bureau and the President (European prime ministers had, in effect, an item veto without noticeable effect) would not necessarily make a big difference.

Between 1870 and 1902 there was no growth in per-capita expenditures in federal government. Spending in absolute terms increased approximately 3.3 percent per year, but gross national product, adjusted for inflation, rose by more than 5 percent per year. The federal sector was growing continuously smaller in relation to the economy.[222] Using 1902 as a benchmark, federal spending constituted a mere 2.4 percent of GNP; by 1922 this proportion had more than doubled—to 5.1 percent. Nonfederal government spending had also grown, but not as quickly—from 4.4 to 7.5 percent of GNP.

By 1932 the budget reform had been in place for ten years. During that decade nonfederal spending almost doubled, to 14 percent of GNP; federal spending increased about 40 percent, to 7.3 percent. We present these comparisons to show that the increase in federal spending was about the same from 1913 to 1922 (2.4 to 5.1 percent) as from 1922 to 1932 (5.1 to 7.3 percent), and that, essentially, the reform was extraneous to the forces promoting increased spending. Or, the figures could be taken to mean that spending would have been still higher in the absence of reform; or that, in ways unmeasured by these brute numbers, the quality of spending improved. In the first third of the twentieth century, the larger trend showed that spending at all levels of government more than tripled, rising from 6.8 to 21.3 percent of national product.[223] An alternative explanation is that the constitutional amendment ratifying the income tax justified the minimum-government advocates' old concern: any revenue raised would be spent.[224] Whatever the explanation, inauguration of the executive budget ushered out the era of small government in the United States.

RAISING REVENUE IN THE AMERICAN FEDERAL SYSTEM: DIVISION OF LABOR

At least three rationales for taxation have existed from the beginning of the republic; they correspond closely with its dominant political cultures.

Raising revenue according to a citizen's ability to pay reflects the persisting strength of egalitarian forces. Favoring growth in individual and national wealth, market forces seek low levels of taxation. If revenue must be collected, however, market advocates maintain, taxes should accelerate capital accumulation. Elements of hierarchy in America consistently favor easily administered taxes and seek revenue sources that raise income painlessly as the population and the economy grow. For those who govern, an ideal tax should also be politically palatable, not stimulating too much resistance or requiring frequent increases. The easier a tax is to administer, the more likely it is that the people who are supposed to pay actually do pay.

Until the early decades of this century, property-tax receipts comprised over half of revenue collected from all levels of government, a distribution that reflects both the federal government's limited role up to that time and its nominal fiscal capacity.[225] Throughout the nineteenth century, as today, citizens railed against the property tax; since it was levied at the same rate on everyone, they claimed it was unfair to low-income citizens.[226]

Why, then, in a society placing high value on equality, was it the dominant revenue source? Given the initial preference for decentralized authority, the property tax conformed to the federal division of labor; moreover, variation in local assessment procedures created a flexible revenue base. Egalitarians favored the property levy because it taxed land, the dominant form of wealth in an agricultural society.[227] As commerce and industry expanded after the 1830s and citizens began to hold property in other forms, local governments tried to capture additional revenue by levying personal-property taxes.[228]

With industrialization, so massive and so evident in America by the last third of the nineteenth century, real-property taxes failed to capture revenue from the growing wealth in intangible property—bonds, stocks, credit, and other financial assets. Growth of cities during the same era created need to build urban infrastructure—schools, transit, and water and sewer systems. Because property taxes failed to tap existing sources of wealth, they did not keep pace with spending in local governments.

For a time there was a strategic interplay between levels of government: states tried to impose property taxes, and cities sought to escape state taxes by undervaluing local property.[229]

Whether a property tax was levied by state or local government, evasion was easy when personal declarations of assets established the tax base. Following procedures adopted in England during the Puritan Revolution, state and local governments asked taxpayers to render their property by listing such items as livestock (horses, mules, cattle, sheep, goats, hogs, dogs); conveyances (carriages, buggies, wagons); capital equipment (materials, tools, machinery, engines and boilers); money on hand, whether held by bank, broker, or stock jobber, in or out of the state; stocks and bonds; shares in private corporations; and status items such as organs, pianofortes, table silver, gold jewelry, and precious stones.

A citizen might sign such an oath, but since states and cities lacked capacity to investigate, nothing forced either individuals or enterprises to declare all their property. Under such circumstances, institutions like the national banks, with authority to operate only if assets were made public, paid these taxes in full while others could evade with impunity. In New York in 1881, for example, the national banks paid almost a third of the state government's receipts from property taxes.[230]

Between 1880 and 1920, nearly every state established commissions to study problems of state and municipal taxation. For that age of public parsimony, the commissions were generously funded, led by civic leaders and staffed by fiscal experts—university professors such as John Ely, Carl Plehn, and Charles Bullock, all leading authorities in fiscal economics. The first commissions in the 1880s proposed ways to improve property-tax receipts. By appointing boards of equalization (to equalize taxes among enterprises), searching out intangible property, improving assessment procedures, and developing skill in tracking down tax evaders, states tried to get at the real wealth. But such efforts met with limited success. The failure to derive adequate revenue from property taxes, together with depression during the 1890s, led later commissions to seek alternative solutions.

From the mid-1890s on, state fiscal commissions began to suggest that state governments abandon efforts to tax property, giving local governments exclusive jurisdiction over revenue from that source. Increasingly the state commissions saw direct and indirect taxes on business as a rich vein to tap; they proposed, and then states enacted, fixed-sum taxes on corporations, business franchises, and the railroads. Between 1910 and 1920, a few states imposed a corporate income tax, and taxes on collateral inheritance. Wisconsin, in 1911, passed the first income tax. In 1911 the new territory of Hawaii proposed a personal income tax. This was unusual because, in most states around the turn of the century, urban interests opposed the income tax. Spokesmen for business and labor maintained that because farmers had little cash income they would escape income taxes, leaving the burden to be passed on to city dwellers.

Both the Union government and the Confederacy had levied income taxes during the Civil War. (In North and South alike, only the financial emergency of high war expense permitted its passage.) The federal tax—a graduated tax of from one to 10 percent on income from wages, salaries, interest, and dividends—collected about $376 million at its peak (1866) and accounted for almost 25 percent of internal revenue collections. The six New England states, New York, and California contributed about 70 percent of its yield; New York alone generated about a third.[231]

Conflicts over equality, from that day to this, established a conceptual framework for public debate over the tax. In our nation "we make no distinction between the rich and the poor man," Senator Justin Morrill of Vermont contended during congressional revision of the tax in 1864. "The man of modest means is just as good as the man with more means, but our theory of government does not admit that he is better. . . . It [this tax] is seizing the property of men for the crime of having too much."[232] Morrill blamed representatives from the southern and western states for pushing the tax through Congress. Always seen as an emergency measure, it was abolished in 1871.

While the tariff raised adequate revenue during the prosperous 1880s (and in some years produced Treasury surpluses), it aroused opposition from citizens of agrarian states who felt they bore an undue share of the burden in high commodity prices generated by protection. Sporadically during the 1870s and 1880s, southern and western Democrats called for a new income tax to mitigate that burden. Growth of huge individual fortunes during the 1880s, moreover, stimulated egalitarian sentiment; Populists from the South and the West claimed it was not the American way to be as rich as Croesus. Their regions' backwardness with respect to the industrializing Northeast, Populists charged, derived in part from the machinations of trusts and monopolies. Thus both extremes of the political spectrum invoked idealized norms of equality to support political tactics.

A Treasury deficit after the depression of 1893 gave Democrats the opportunity they needed; they added a clause levying a 2 percent tax on incomes over $4,000 to the tariff-reduction bill of that year. Without a war emergency to justify imposition, the measure polarized opinion. Arguing against the proposal, an eastern senator protested that an income tax would cause more damage to the economy and inhibit individual initiative; it would reduce wages, and its administration would generate fraud and corruption. The tariff would produce adequate revenue as the economy revived, he maintained; there was no need to levy a tax that would place the whole burden on a specific region (the East) and the small number of citizens with incomes exceeding $4,000 a year. In a nation of equals, the income tax constituted class legislation, he contended; moreover, its passage would be the first step on the road to socialism![233] Another eastern congressman, without intended irony, argued that taxing wealthy citizens' incomes would deprive the majority of "their patriotic right . . . to support their government."[234]

Adopting a perennially favorite tactic of tax reformers, Populist Senator William V. Allen (Nebraska) claimed that the income tax burden would fall right where it belonged. Why, in New York alone there were 119 millionaires! Allen proceeded to read into the record the names of assorted Vanderbilts, Whitneys, and John D. Rockefeller, together with the tax each would pay if a 2 percent tax were imposed.[235] William Jennings Bryan of Nebraska clinched the Democrats' case in the House. Did the untaxable poor lack patriotism? Nonsense! "If taxation is a badge of freedom . . . the poor people of this country are covered all over with the insignia of freedom."[236] To a claim that wealthy citizens would move abroad if the income tax were imposed, he responded that the nation would be well rid of them: "If we have people who value free government so little that they prefer to live under monarchical institutions, even without an income tax, rather than live under the stars and stripes and pay a 2 percent tax, we can better afford to lose them and their fortunes than risk the contaminating influence of their presence."[237] Bryan apparently thought it better to forfeit a little revenue than to sacrifice ideological purity.

A relatively modest tax by today's standards, the 1893 tax set off an uproar that eventually brought on a constitutional debate and a negative ruling from the Supreme Court. Protagonists on both sides considered equality to be the critical issue. Advocates still claimed that the tax, falling only on the rich, was fair. Opponents argued that it was no better than the English law of 1641, which had imposed different rates on Jews, Protestants, and Catholics.[238] It was inequitable because it imposed a greater burden on a particular income group—the rich.

According to the Supreme Court's reasoning, the Constitution specified that direct taxes could be imposed only if assessed uniformly—that is, in direct proportion to state population. Since the 1893 income tax obviously did not, the Court ruled it unconstitutional in 1895.

Soon after this ruling, proponents of income taxes changed their arguments: like tax reformers elsewhere, they maintained that taxes should be levied according to "faculty," or ability to pay. But even with this new language the movement lost momentum. The issue dropped from both party agendas until 1909, when a coalition of midwestern Populists and liberal Republicans sought to reduce the burden of very high tariffs by imposing two new taxes on inheritance and incomes. Opposing both proposals, Republican leader Nelson Aldrich from New York appealed to President Taft to help devise a policy alternative acceptable to the party's conservative stalwarts. Revenue lost from modifying the tariff, Taft suggested, could be recaptured by imposing an excise tax of 4 percent on corporate profits; such a tax would be productive, and it would be wholly compatible with constitutional dicta. Reversing a policy stance of long duration, conservative Republicans supported the proposal; given the climate of antagonism to corporations, perhaps such a change seemed the better part of wisdom. After two months of debate, the tax passed both houses of Congress almost unanimously.[239] Thus, without much fanfare, the corporate income tax became law in America.

In 1909 Taft had also suggested drafting a constitutional amendment framed to bypass the Court's decision that the 1893 income tax constituted class legislation; Taft thought language of the proposed amendment should explicitly permit taxation of incomes *without* equal apportionment among the states. Populists played a large part in getting the Income Tax Amendment passed, largely for reasons of equality. They were joined by representatives of various regional industries who feared discrimination. Spokesmen for urban interests, who had generally opposed income taxation, gradually began to realize that the tariff hurt consumers more than an income tax might. Between Populists who wanted to punish corporations, progressives who wanted government to do more, and businessmen who preferred predictability, the movement for federal income tax gained strength.

The federal income tax, enacted soon after passage of the Sixteenth Amendment in 1913, levied a flat one percent rate on all incomes over $3,000 for a single person (over $4,000 for a married couple), whether derived from wages, rents, dividends, salaries, interest, entrepreneurial incomes, or capital gains. In addition, the 1913 law levied a surtax of 6 percent on very high incomes; thus the maximum effective rate was 7 percent. Average personal income that year was $621; only 2 percent of the U.S. population was liable to any income tax between 1913 and 1915.

As during England's Napoleonic War and in later income taxes, the tax built in specific exemptions and deductions to insure fairness in assessment and to preserve incentives to work, save, and invest. It encouraged saving by allowing liable citizens to deduct life-insurance premiums. Most business costs—interest paid on indebtedness, bad debts, casualty losses from fire, storm or shipwreck, and a depreciation allowance for replacement of business property—were also deductible. Citizens with modest amounts in stock dividends could deduct them to arrive at taxable income. In addition, the 1913 law contained provisions tailored to reflect the complex relationships of a federal system: taxes paid to any jurisdiction were deductible, and income earned from federal, state, and local debt instruments were exempt from taxation (as were salaries of federal judges, and those of priests, rabbis, and ministers). Most of these provisions survive today.

Between 1913 and 1915, ninety percent of federal revenue still came from customs and excise.[240] It was the First World War, with its large demands for revenue, that firmly established the income tax in America. After 1916 the revenue needs of a nation at war led to passage of the first federal inheritance tax (1916) and quickly pushed up income tax rates to a maximum of 15 percent in 1916, 67 percent in 1917, and 77 percent in 1918. The unprecedented use of excess-profits taxes contributed to these high rates.* As war expenses skyrocketed in 1917, the executive branch brought proposals before Congress to raise additional revenue by lowering exemption limits—to $1,000 for single persons and $2,000 for couples—effectively converting a limited soak-the-rich tax into a much more productive revenue instrument. But while the World War I income tax raised nearly 60 percent of all federal revenue at its peak, it still was not a mass tax; overall, its incidence was steeply progressive. One percent of the returns filed between 1917 and 1919 were for incomes over $20,000, yet this small number of taxpayers paid, on the average, over 70 percent of the income tax collected during those years.[241] The high rates imposed on large incomes remained in force until after World War I when the Republicans again gained control of the federal government, but the rates were maintained to facilitate debt reduction. Strong commitment to balanced-budget norms created pressure to pay off wartime debt quickly.

As a peacetime income tax became institutionalized during the 1920s, several tendencies characteristic of recent U.S. tax politics began to emerge. There was unanimous agreement among all political cultures that the high wartime rates were undesirable in peacetime, but when it came to cuts, differences arose. As with earlier controversy, disagreement over tax policies reflected the varying regional economies of a territorially vast and culturally diverse nation, rather than the more polarized class alignments of tax politics in Europe. As segments of the public liable to income taxes bargained to seek measures favoring specific interests, the original tax code underwent repeated revision—in 1921, '24, '26, '28, and '29. The code began to manifest an unintended complexity as each revision incorporated measures tailored to particular constituencies, thereby setting off a cascade of changes in related provisions. The 1924 act created a Board of Tax Appeals within the Internal Revenue Service, an action reflecting demands for adjudication of a tax process characterized by increasing specificity.

*An "excess" profit was a profit over a reasonable return on invested capital; more than an 8 percent return on investment triggered the tax, and liable enterprises paid 8 percent on such earnings.

Tax rates came down throughout the decade, largely by eliminating excess-profits levies and lowering exemption limits. Those whose incomes remained liable, however, sought ways to reduce the government's claims; in spite of the low interest rates paid on state and municipal bonds, these debt instruments were favored investments for high-income citizens throughout the 1920s (as they still are) because yields were exempt from federal taxation. During the twenties also, corporations began to retain earnings, raising market values of stocks while deflecting taxes on dividends.

Both a business-oriented Treasury Secretary and the Congress endeavored to mollify taxpayers by writing into the tax code provisions now known as tax preferences. Pittsburgh industrialist Andrew Mellon, who came to Washington as Secretary of the Treasury in 1920 and stayed on for twelve years to serve three Republican presidents, held a view of the tax process similar in some respects to Liberal party leaders' in nineteenth-century England. Mellon thought income taxes should be moderate and should create minimal interference with market incentives. "It seems difficult for some to understand," he wrote in 1924, anticipating modern supply-side arguments, "that high rates of taxation do not necessarily mean large revenue to the government, and that more revenue may often be obtained by lower rates."[242]

During Mellon's early years in Washington, the excess-profits tax was dismantled, and by 1925 personal income tax rates had been cut to a maximum of 25 percent.[243] In 1921 Congress passed the capital-gains exclusion recommended by Mellon. But this long-tenured and powerful Treasury Secretary was no diehard individualist. To maintain budget balance he favored raising corporate-income tax rates to compensate for revenue lost by cutting excess-profits taxes. Mellon argued also that investment income ought to be taxed at a higher rate than earned income, and he proposed a tax credit of 25 percent on earned income, which he thought would balance benefits among high-income and lower-income taxpayers. The reasoning—based on ability-to-pay premises—is that holders of property and savings can finance government's needs more easily than citizens who must rely only on earned income for subsistence. This point should not be overstated. The ability-to-pay rationale did, of course, have its opponents who argued that the rich perform a "special function" in society: providing investment funds to spur economic growth. Whereas the soak-the-rich proponents based their attacks on a puritanical image (the "idle rich"), the special-function argument for tax incidence held that invested wealth was busy and productive.

As prosperity during the mid-1920s raised Treasury receipts, Congress increasingly granted taxpayers more favors than even Mellon approved. Beginning with the 1921 revision, both parties competed by lowering tax rates and writing in preferences. Mellon campaigned throughout his term for repeal of the state- and municipal-bond exclusion, a measure he thought favored high-income taxpayers while distorting incentives; but no Congress—either during the twenties or afterward—would repeal this provision, seen as intrinsic to federalism. With a surplus of over a billion dollars in 1926, Congress cut estate tax rates also, and, intending to encourage exploration, it granted a favor to the oil industry. The 27.5 percent oil depletion allowance proved to be a focus of controversy for nearly fifty years. (It was repealed after the first round of oil price increases in 1973 had raised industry profits to huge, though temporary, levels as the value of oil increased manyfold overnight.)

The movement for scientific management peaked in the United States during the 1920s. Among elites with a fixation on all things scientific, the messy outcomes of congressional tax policy trade-offs generated cynicism; participants and observers of the tax process thought there must be a better way. Commenting on the 1921 revision, for example, Cordell Hull expressed his disillusionment with fiscal logrolling—it was wholly antithetical to the prevailing view of rational, i.e., scientific, management but apparently intrinsic to democracy. That process remains unchanged to this day.

> It was most unfortunate that the attempted revision legislation of 1921 degenerated measurably into a wrangle between champions of large income taxpayers and those of smaller taxpayers, each striving to see which could unload the largest amount of taxes first. The legislative situation thus became so confused and demoralized that but scant opportunity for consideration of comprehensive, scientific tax revision was afforded.[244]

Yet throughout the twenties, as in earlier U.S. history, balanced-budget norms were the ultimate influence on tax policy outcomes. Advocates of protection, for example, growing in strength, saw the income tax as a guarantor of sufficient revenue to maintain defense and other essential services so that the loss of revenue due to the extremely high tariffs enacted in 1929 would not cripple the government.[245] After 1929, when the depression reduced revenue to the point of incurring deficits considered substantial at the time, Mellon and all other tax experts favored increasing personal and corporate income taxes to restore budget balance. "These are not normal times," Mellon advised Congress in 1931 as deficits approached $2 billion.[246] With a rationale for countercyclical fiscal policy yet to be invented, Congress agreed; the only question was how the increases should be distributed, who should bear the burden. Besides raising tax levels, the outgoing Republican Congress somewhat increased progressivity.

Despite the Roosevelt administration's apparent fiscal conservatism, the soak-the-rich mentality resurfaced during the mid-1930s. Lashing out in 1935 and subsequent years against "economic royalists," Roosevelt found a scapegoat in wealthy taxpayers who, he claimed, were using trickery to avoid paying income tax.[247] The loophole-closing measures he proposed—taxing undistributed corporate profits, personal holding companies, incorporated yachts, and estates and family partnerships—aimed to recover revenue lost from tax-avoidance stratagems of high-income citizens. Until World War II, incidence of U.S. income tax focused on high incomes. In 1941, for example, when median income was about $1,200 a year, 82 percent of income tax returns filed were for annual incomes under $3,000; 12 percent more paid on incomes between $3,000 and $5,000. The revenue needs of World War II raised income tax rates to very high levels (at least for the rich), while withholding of taxes on wages and salaries converted it into a mass tax. Though the rates have fluctuated over time for all income brackets, they have never again dipped to the low levels of the 1920s.[248]

The end of the 1920s revealed emergence of a division of labor among the levels of government: cities specialized in property taxation, states began to levy sales taxes,[249] and the federal government collected income taxes. The clarity and distinctiveness in the sources of financing, one for each level of government, was to be blurred in the post–World War II period as the federal government sponsored a variety of programs for which it paid through outright grants, matching grants, proportional grants, and a host of new devices. During this time, also, the period of preponderant state and local spending (and, therefore, of revenue collection) passed, to be replaced by the dominance of the federal government.

THE END OF EXCEPTIONALISM

The simple structure of American revenue-raising opens up the question of whether America's exceptionalism in budgeting may be attributed to its federal form. One might reason that the division of labor, by keeping states large, kept the federal government smaller than it oth-

426   A History of Taxation and Expenditure in the Western World

erwise would have been in a unitary government. One could also argue just the opposite—namely, that deliberate decisions to keep the federal government small allowed more room for the states to expand. Actually, by contemporary standards, all levels of government were small in size and scope, and all, until the twentieth century, were characterized by legislative preponderance.

Might budgetary exceptionalism until the 1930s be explained by the relative ease with which the federal government financed itself through the tariff? It might. But that takes for granted what must be explained: relatively low levels of spending in the presence of abundant opportunities for raising revenues.

It is not the relative power of the executive and legislative branches, we submit, but the values that infused both that made America exceptional. Weak governments and strong societies stem from a balance among social orders. Where none overwhelms the others, compromise comes out in the form of limited government—low taxing, less spending, and a demonstration that the bargain has been kept by balancing the budget.

The balance among American political cultures was reinforced by a remarkable agreement: in the era of Jacksonian democracy, equality of opportunity (as in markets), it was broadly agreed, promoted equality of results (as desired by sects). The political culture most likely to challenge existing authority did so in a direct way: sectarians viewed large and intrusive central government as a bad thing. Since central government introduced inequality into society, it had to be limited. The supporters of hierarchy did not like this, but alone they were weak. So they forged an alliance with market forces to provide funds for internal improvements.

Growth of large industrial enterprises casts the old understandings into doubt. Big government was still considered bad, but so was big business. Populist challenges to the monopolies foundered on the Populists' reluctance to fund growth of government. The heroes of their past (Jefferson, Jackson) were against using big government to beat big business.

What role was there for the newly educated adherents of hierarchy who did not relish the practices of the corporate manager or the political boss of immigrant populations? They made a place for themselves as experts in the bureaucratic half of the policy–administration dichotomy. The executive budget was their creation; by promoting the city manager and establishing the federal Bureau of the Budget, the progressive reformers were creating their own jobs.

The rise of rival hierarchies based on service to the state, the progressive ideal, went part of the way toward promoting a positive conception of government. It took the depression of the late twenties and the thirties to create an American "left" that viewed bigger government as both a counter to big business and a force for good, reducing inequalities by spreading a more uniform national policy throughout the land. The nation, which had been made Republican by the Civil War, was turned Democratic by the depression. That is how the party of Jefferson became identified with uniform national domestic welfare policies, and the party of Hamilton with state diversity and a smaller federal government.

It took a quarter century past American entry into the Second World War for a revived sectarian regime to alter budgetary understandings, especially the norm of balance, in order to raise spending for redistributive purposes. American exceptionalism in budgeting would still exist—hierarchy, hence executive budgeting, would be weaker and spending, though growing, would be smaller than elsewhere—but it would no longer present so stark a contrast with European democracies. American exceptionalism had come to an end. From this time on, the United States would lag behind, but would not fundamentally differ from, the welfare states of western Europe.

Chapter Eight

STABILITY AMIDST TURBULENCE: THE HALF CENTURY AFTER 1914

Through our panoramic history of taxation and expenditure, we see a patchwork of expedients. Disorder is the dominant motif. Even our allusions to financial administration—for want of a better term for the improvisations, from antiquity through the Middle Ages and the early-modern periods—hardly do justice to the jumble of accounts and the confusions between the state and the kings' patrimony. Yet haltingly, then seemingly inexorably, order appears and feeds on itself, as the eighteenth century gives way to the nineteenth, and to the beginning of the twentieth century. Budgets became more than empty bags. They have some predictive value as proposals for spending and taxing, more likely than not to be fulfilled. And those who may be affected by them can adjust their behavior accordingly.

The great budgetary norms fought for with such fervor for more than two centuries—annualarity, balance, and comprehensiveness—are in place everywhere in the Western world. Among the major powers, promise is most often dignified by performance. Far more than before, budgets have become meaningful. Governments have control over budgets, therefore over themselves. It is almost as if they budget, therefore they are in control.

Yet before we slide over it too easily, here is an underlying assumption of budgeting so self-evident to all concerned, theorist and practitioner alike, that no one thinks to mention it: The size of the budget is determined by the total of the funds spent by the individual departments, with only small exceptions, perhaps a trust fund or two. Spending budgets are departmental budgets. Control of spending, therefore, means control of the governmental agencies that do the spending and their officials.

All traditional (i.e., dating from the mid– to late nineteenth century) spending controls are in some way based on this assumption. Were it challenged—so unthinkable a possibility that no one, so far as we know, has entertained it—traditional budgeting would collapse.

By contrast, everyone, whether proponent or opponent, has voiced the crucial assumption about taxation, especially income taxation: rates would be low. That, of course, went the way of all things.

But no one anticipated the First and Second World Wars, the depression of the 1930s, and the swift rise of the welfare state in Europe. The effect on the kinds and rates of taxation was immense, though mitigated in the 1950s and '60s by rapid economic growth. Taxes were different in 1960 or 1965—partly in kind, but mostly in quantity—from what they were after the First World War. Spending processes, however, were remarkably similar. Much more money was spent, of course, but anyone who was involved in requesting or allocating funds in the period between the world wars would have had little trouble in understanding what was happening in the early sixties. It seems strange to talk of budgetary stability for the half century beginning in 1914, given the cataclysmic events of the first half of the twentieth century, but, except in wartime, there was more continuity than change. Budgets went up a lot (after 1945) and down a little (in the 1930s) and some of each (in the 1920s by modest increments). But since the mid-1960s the norms and assumptions on which budgeting was based have become increasingly inapplicable. Facing forward, after 1960 or 1965, the immediate future, with its incessant discontinuity, looks more like most of the past than like the half century of stability.

In this chapter, which begins with the First World War, our interest is not so much with state finance during the war as with its postwar effects. (Later, we shall examine the Second World War in the same way.) It is true that war disrupts domestic routines, making possible new arrangements. But it is also true that war accelerates prior peacetime trends. By far the best predictors of what will emerge out of the caldron of war are the social ingredients poured in before the mixture began brewing.

The pent-up consequences of the 1920s and 1930s, decades concerned with the aftermath of war and with depression, do not show up until the immediate post–World War II period. Except for the United States, government expands, first in reconstruction, then in social policy, with economic growth raising revenues for a substantial defense buildup that is then overtaken by ever increasing expenditures for social welfare.

As spending rises absolutely and as a proportion of national product after World War II, new methods of control appear: performance budgeting, program budgeting, zero-base budgeting, volume budgeting. Yet one by one they are discarded. Spending continues as before. Why does the traditional budget last while these alternatives, though not without merit for certain purposes, are cast aside? Battles over budgetary methods—though they received much publicity—turned out to be sideshows. It is not the efficiency of spending and taxing but the amount that matters. To see why, we must exercise the prerogative of hindsight, before examining the revelations of the 1970s in the next chapter. Then the main show, growth of government, will come to center stage.

TWENTIETH-CENTURY FINANCE: AN OVERVIEW

Ranked against other centuries, ours is scarcely unique for its rapid social change. Two international wars, punctuated by prolonged severe depression, put the present century alongside the fourteenth, sixteenth, seventeenth, and eighteenth. The breakdown of feudalism in the fourteenth and fifteenth centuries, and the emergence of industrial capitalism in the nineteenth, brought equally significant changes in people's relationships to government. Yet in spite of and in some degree because of depression and war, and by any measure one chooses, the welfare of most people in Western nations has improved greatly. Not only has the link between technological innovation and economic growth created more for everyone, but governments, responsive to strong pressures within their polities, have also tried to distribute society's produce more equally than they might have otherwise. By taking on responsibility for income redistribution, though on a small scale, modern governments have assumed a role unprecedented in prior history. Like the righteous kings of ancient ages, they have set out to be benevolent.

Growth of government did not follow a preplanned course, but programs adopted hesitantly, and often temporarily, had a way of hanging on. Amidst the diversity of national histories, several trends are apparent: (1) Wars accelerated social mobilization. (2) Programs adopted initially to improve living standards for society's poorest members sooner or later expanded to include almost everyone. (3) Governmental expansion did not occur silently; everywhere a clash of ideas and interests accompanied the changes.

In European nations with long histories of hierarchy, this century's two great wars reinforced inherent tendencies toward centralization.

Not since the medieval Crusades had entire societies mobilized for a conflict presented by both sides as being in defense of a just cause. Total war fought with twentieth-century weapons commands all society's resources—its population, industry, agriculture, organizational capacity, creativity, and wealth. To support mobilization, all segments of these societies accepted significant governmental control of economies; some tolerated unprecedented levels of taxation and debt. Indeed, without modern means of resource mobilization and resource allocation, neither wars of mass mobilization nor the welfare state would have been possible.

Existing budgetary practices shaped finance during the First World War, and, once the crisis had passed, each nation's political culture influenced its pattern of taxing and spending during the 1920s. Germany and France displayed their usual reluctance to tax to pay for the war, preferring instead to rely upon sale of debt. The existence of huge unfunded debt in both nations accounts both for French negotiators' eagerness to exact reparations from Germany and Austria after the war and for inflation in all three countries from the war's end until the mid-twenties.

England and the United States discarded central controls and high taxes as soon as the war ended; both nations wanted a return to prewar individualism. Trying to turn back the world's clock to 1913, Britain in 1925 returned to the gold standard it had abandoned during the war. Its restored prewar currency/pound parities, now too high in relation to other nations' currency, kept Britain out of many of its prewar markets, and precipitated depression there earlier than elsewhere.

Government's rapid expansion during the present century has been accompanied by a conflict between new ideas facilitating growth of government (and, in turn, generated by that growth) with long-standing intellectual traditions of individualism. In other centuries, advocates of one public policy or another have been active in formulating or influencing financial policies, from the earliest mercantilist writers in the late Middle Ages until the present.* But it is much

---

*The recommendations of numerous mercantilist writers during the early-modern era led nations to impose import and export duties designed to protect economies against loss of scarce commodities—money, metals, and food. On the assumption that purchase of high-cost products abroad would drain away national wealth, seventeenth-century mercantilists such as Richelieu and Colbert advised Louis XIV of France to establish state-subsidized luxury industries; several German principalities followed his example. The classical economists formulated the earliest theories of national economic development, and some of them then tried to persuade legislatures to implement policies derived from these theories. Thus Thomas Malthus' prediction of national economic decline be-

more common now than ever before for governments to seek intellectuals' advice. As academics have moved into governments as members of the bureaucracy, or as advisers to politicians, debates over
public policy have taken place within an intellectual framework established by one theorist or another. The British economist John Maynard Keynes, the man who best described this process, was also perhaps
the intellectual most influential in shaping this century's fiscal-policy
debate.* Government finance during our lifetime, then, has a special history, colored by judgments of scholars of diverse theoretical
orientations, some of them still actively shaping the course of future
history.

Public policy during the depression in Europe and America reflected
tension among traditional balanced-budget ideology and innovative
ideas tying government deficits to the level of economic activity within
a nation. The massive failure of markets during the Great Depression
suggested the failure of unregulated individualism. In Europe, however, the traditional conservative view that government should be
small and supported by moderate taxes, with minimal borrowing and
with budgets balanced at a low level, remained strong in spite of substantial unemployment. Conventional economists, when called in as
advisers to governments, maintained that the best cure for depression
was to cut workers' wages. The resulting demands on insurance funds
proved too great, as unemployment persisted, and nations such as Brit-

---

cause of excessive population growth fueled a movement to abandon England's humanitarian poor-relief policies during the late eighteenth and early nineteenth centuries. David
Ricardo, the wealthy merchant trader who formulated the theory of comparative advantage in foreign trade, was elected to England's Parliament; there, in the early nineteenth
century, he tried without much success to reduce import and export taxes. During the
heyday of individualism in the middle and late nineteenth century, many academic advisers served on the boards and commissions established to investigate nations' social and
financial problems and recommend courses of action (or inaction). Professor Adolf
Wagner (who in the 1880s convinced Bismarck to introduce national social insurance as a
way of defusing radicalism among German workers) was one such figure, as was Edwin
Seligman, the German-trained fiscal economist whose work on taxation contributed to
the enactment of the U.S. income tax in 1916.

*In a much quoted passage Keynes wrote: "The ideas of economists and political philoso-
phers, both when they are right and when they are wrong, are more powerful than is
commonly understood. Indeed, the world is ruled by little else. Practical men who believe
themselves to be quite exempt from any intellectual influences are usually the slaves of
some defunct economist. Madmen in authority who hear voices in the air are distilling
their frenzy from some academic scribbler of a few years back. I am sure that the power of
vested interests is vastly exaggerated compared with the gradual encroachment of ideas.
Not, indeed, immediately, but after a certain interval . . . it is ideas, not vested interests,
which are dangerous for good or evil."[1]

ain with insurance against joblessness steadily reduced benefits to lower governments' costs.

As the depression deepened, economic theorists tried to find explanations. In spite of the century's achievements in science and technology, according to one school of thought—the secular-stagnation theory propounded by Harvard economist Alvin Hansen—the world economy's impaired productive capacity reflected the cumulative outcome of a lag in innovation.

Combining the rediscovered medieval revenue-flow metaphor with mechanical metaphors common during the eighteenth and nineteenth centuries, another group suggested that governments might ameliorate distress with a pump-priming policy. (This carefully crafted metaphor suggested that government need only initiate the flow of funds, not, as events proved, sustain it indefinitely.) If, as seemed to be true, an economy was stuck at dead center, a single infusion of government funds might be enough to get it going. In 1933, pump priming was the rationale for loans to business by the U.S. government's newly created Reconstruction Finance Corporation, and during the early 1930s for work relief funded by central government.

But as with a car of that vintage, which would stall repeatedly without an automatic choke, a single infusion of government money into the complex economy of that day still failed to make a difference. Searching for an explanation for continuing sluggishness in the world economy, one member of a student-and-faculty economics seminar at Cambridge University during the late 1920s and early 1930s invented the concept of the economic multiplier. Within an open economy, R. F. Kahn wrote,[2] any amount of money—whether created by expansion of bank credit in the private sector or by government expenditure financed through borrowing—can be spent more than one time. Funds paid in wages and for products and services will generate additional expenditure as recipients use them for other transactions. Yet from each cycle of exchange certain funds will be withheld—for savings, for goods made abroad, for taxes. Such uses constitute "leakage" from the social-income stream. So the economic benefits from a single infusion made by central government would soon become dissipated. As utilized by Keynes in his epoch-shaping work *The General Theory of Employment, Interest, and Money,* Kahn's multiplier principle justified continuing government spending, even if, in the process, it led to budgetary deficits.[3]

Keynes maintained that an economy could attain equilibrium at less than full employment, contrary to classical and neoclassical economic theory. Continuing depression convinced him that when considered in aggregate, decisions by individuals regarding wages, prices, output, consumption, and the like need not necessarily produce the best possible outcome for society. While individuals could govern the private economy, Keynes recommended that government take on the task of stabilizing economic aggregates.

The prescriptions stemming from Keynes's analysis shifted the focus from the individual to the collectivity, from supply to demand. (For the past hundred years or more, performance of most Western economies had been left to so-called self-regulating market forces.) While targeting programs to individuals might be acceptable for humanitarian reasons, he maintained, governments should be more concerned about an entire economy's deficit in demand.

"The New Economics" (as Keynes's theory was soon labeled) and traditional balanced-budget ideology clashed head-on. As newly convinced Keynesians began to propose deliberately *un*balanced budgets, even sympathetic observers who advocated government spending to revive economies and relieve human misery wondered whether it would really be possible to turn off the tap after citizens in democracies became accustomed to benefits provided by central government.[4] If an automatic budgetary equilibrium existed, what went up would have to come down. In times when unemployment was high, governments would pump money into their economies until the deficit was sufficient to bring the economy back to full employment. When times were good, governments should slow down spending. But would they?

As the debate over balance or imbalance grew hotter in the late 1930s, sober voices pointed to the likely outcome once the bastions of the balanced budget were breached. A *New York Times* editorial on December 27, 1938, maintained:

> There is one objective standard that everyone understands clearly—Federal budgets "annually balanced." Once we depart from that, except under the sheerest necessity, we are adrift on the seas of confusion, for all sorts of ingenious reasons are invented for not going back, and the vested interest in keeping the new situation is enormous. ...."To enable a legislator to vote for appropriation bills and at the same time avoid voting for increases in taxes is to provide him with the politician's paradise."[5]

Extrapolating from the depressed economies of the late 1930s, a doomsayer contended, "There is a real and very great danger that a democracy may spend itself to death, as it were, once it departs from a balanced budget."[6] The critics were right in one respect: there was to be no law of budgetary gravity; spending proved to be an escalator that went only one way—up. Whether imbalanced budgets would prove fatal was another matter.

Massive arms spending during World War II seemed to validate Keynes's prescription (just as rapid wartime innovation showed how unfounded the secular-stagnation hypothesis was). As government spending rose, consuming from a third to nearly half of GNP in England and the United States, their economies revived, restoring incomes. Mass military mobilization and production for war brought about labor shortages. Through its control of wages, prices, and allocation of resources to maximize war production, an expanded governmental hierarchy circumscribed free-market forces. In the United States and Britain taxes on incomes of individuals and businesses and on luxuries went up sharply, providing resources to finance the war while controlling inflation. Employer withholding of income taxes on wages, adopted by the U.S. in 1943, converted the income tax into the mass tax it has been ever since.

Fear of depression after the war remained strong; manifestos published during the mid-1940s called for expanded spending on social welfare and public infrastructure.* Only after World War II did scholars set out to untangle the intellectual lineage of recent public policy regarding taxing, spending, and debt—a chain of thought and events that represented a significant shift in government financial management. By the end of World War II, the taxing and spending process acquired a broader economic as well as a narrower financial function. No longer was it sufficient to maintain a reasonable balance between amounts raised in taxes and amount spent. As macroeconomic fiscal policy became superimposed on the process of budget-balancing, taxing, spending, and borrowing became an inseparable trinity of tools for economic management. The restorative effects of wartime government spending legitimized this new social technology.

There is a sense in which governmental growth in Europe and America since 1930 reflects optimism about government's capacity to favorably influence society, an optimism comparable to the collective

---

*Published in the same year (1943) in both England and the U.S., two policy documents outlined the shape of things to come. William Beveridge's *Full Employment in a Free Society* (known as The Beveridge Report) laid the groundwork for welfare-state social-insurance measures adopted by England's Labour Party after its victory in 1945. A report by the National Resources Planning Board, a U.S. depression agency, received less attention. But in their own untidy ways, American policymaking interests—ranging from the National Association of Manufacturers to the California industrialist Henry Kaiser to congressional committees—began to publish statements about how to reconvert to a peacetime economy with minimal social friction. Soon this resulted in the landmark legislation, the Employment Act of 1946.

intellectual euphoria of the eighteenth-century English and French Enlightenments. Echoing Diderot and Voltaire, in tone if not in substance, pro-government activists maintained that market forces alone should not determine the circumstances people lived in. In nations tolerant of strong hierarchies, the influence of the French Enlightenment provided a conceptual basis for planning—to reconstruct war-damaged industry, to build infrastructure (like parks, housing, and highways), and to provide social insurance. Remembering the pockets of severe regional distress during the depression (in northwest England, the U.S. cotton belt, Germany's Ruhr), policymakers for the postwar world merged Enlightenment doctrines of egalitarianism with Anglo-Scottish ideas of individualism. By channeling public and private investment into depressed areas, and through subsidies, tax incentives, and job retraining programs, government and the private sector together could promote social justice and a better life for all. This, at least, was the ideal.

Spurred by latent demand accumulated during depression and war, rapid postwar economic growth in Western democracies brought prosperity beyond anyone's expectations. In view of the immediate results, Gunnar Myrdal's *A Warning Against Peace Optimism* was disregarded.[7] But, unlike the aftermath of World War I, in the post–World War II decade governments did not contract absolutely. Rapid economic growth obscured governments' growth in size as taxes brought in increasing shares of nations' expanding GNP. Persistent international tension during the late 1940s and 1950s, moreover, sustained support for military spending. Nations fought small wars, so they thought, to minimize the grim possibility of large wars. Scientific research funded by central governments, initiated just before World War II and carried on afterward, was an essential weapon in the competition for national strength. Spending went up in aggregate, and in some nations as a proportion of GNP, but, because of rapid growth, budgets remained balanced. More accurately, imbalance was small. Even then, however, by the mid-1960s, the high rates of economic growth were insufficient to fund the built-in increases in pension, health, and other social-welfare programs. The future was inherent in the past. It is to that past, beginning with the First World War, that we now turn.

TAXING AND SPENDING IN THREE WESTERN DEMOCRACIES DURING WORLD WAR I

War was an almost continuous condition in past ages; in the modern world, war disrupts society's normal functioning, leading to total mobilization of the economy, which greatly affects taxing and spending.

Does war provide momentum for drastic postwar changes? Higher levels of taxation—or greater spending, or spending for new purposes—may become acceptable afterward. Even if taxing and spending levels have receded from wartime highs, some policy changes hang on, with long-term effects. We will trace the impact of World War I on the budgets of three Western democracies—the United States, the United Kingdom, and France; victorious in the war, these nations maintained political continuity. Even in emergency, each nation's political culture, developed in past ages, influenced the way its government approached war finance; the institutions embodying these cultures also structured the lessons they drew from their experiences.

From the late Middle Ages, governments in France had approached finance incrementally, relying on ad hoc taxes to bring in needed revenue, and improvising methods to borrow and spend. Despite the massive mobilization needed to fight World War I, French fiscal behavior changed little during the war.

According to rules for budgeting that France adopted during the nineteenth century, its parliament, rather than the Finance Ministry, maintained control of the budget. The minister of finance presented budget proposals to the Chamber of Deputies, which reserved the right to initiate money bills and propose increases in the original estimates. Such an arrangement encouraged legislators to expand spending by horse-trading; and, in the process, to weaken what in those days was called the equilibrium of the budget. Long before the war began, revenue normally lagged behind expenditures, because, given the multiplicity of parties, no political leader was strong enough to assume the risk of proposing higher taxes.[8] Thus when war broke out, the Chamber of Deputies gave the government a carte blanche, a lump-sum credit for spending, without distinguishing between civil and military use. According to a wartime Minister of Finance, in such circumstances, "one is led to think that there are no limits and that one may spend without reckoning."[9]

The war did provoke a tremendous expansion of spending. While expenditure in the prewar decade (1903–13) went up by 56 percent, total spending increased 10.4 times between 1913 and 1920, doubling every year between 1913 and 1916. More than 70 percent of increased spending paid for arms and equipment (see Table 10).

World War I was the first war of total industrial mobilization; France, a nation of small merchants and farmers, needed substantial government intervention in the economy in order to fight. To achieve "continuous and unlimited output of munitions and war materials,"

TABLE 10

DISPROPORTIONATE INCREASE IN EXPENDITURE VS. TAXES INDICATES
HEAVY FRENCH BORROWING DURING WORLD WAR I ERA[10]

Year	Expenditure as a percentage of GNP	Defense Expenditure as a percentage of Total Expenditure	Tax Receipts as a percentage of GNP
1905	9.4	27.8	8.1
1913	9.7	35.7	7.9
1914	19.8	66.3	7.0
1915	35.0	79.3	5.6
1916	36.6	79.8	5.5
1917	33.8	75.8	5.1
1918	32.6	72.2	4.5
1919	30.6	43.9	7.5
1920	25.5	17.7	7.5
1924	19.0	13.1	11.0

the government imposed wage and price controls and offered subsidies
to producers of critical commodities. Unlike Britain and the United
States (or even Germany and Austria-Hungary), France's government
itself also acted as entrepreneur, buying raw materials, paying workers'
wages, and advancing funds to producers.[11] To maintain social cohesion it did not make much effort to limit consumption.

In 1913 France had followed other nations by adopting an income
tax, but when war broke out implementation was postponed. Since
politicians anticipated rapid victory, relying on a kind of negative consensus, they planned to pay for the war with reparations exacted from
a defeated Germany. (Loss of the Franco–Prussian War in 1870 still
rankled; perhaps French politicians hoped to recoup indemnities paid
to Germany at that time.) Without additional war taxes, the nation
limped along by relying on assorted antiquated market taxes (some
had been adopted after the revolution of 1789).

Lacking adequate revenue as the war dragged on, France's government had to borrow. Between 1914 and 1919, tax receipts covered only
16.5 percent of spending, while the remainder was defrayed by loans.
Much of France's war debt was not even funded, but was issued for
short term at above-market interest rates as need for cash arose. By
1918, tax revenues could not cover debt-service charges, so the printing
presses ran overtime.

The outcome of all this was inflation; well before the war ended, rapid price increases raised both public and private budgets, and, as the French government continued to run deficits, inflation persisted into the 1920s. When Germany failed to meet scheduled reparations payments, France faced continuing insolvency. Moreover, since much of the war debt was held by foreigners, fluctuating postwar exchange rates increased the absolute amount the nation needed to pay off, just as recent currency fluctuations have increased Third World nations' debt burdens.

Another significant outcome was expansion of France's social-insurance programs, minimally developed before the war. The fighting in France created an urgent need for social services, and an important component of war spending was for direct relief to its own citizens. The government gave financial aid to families of war victims, provided funds to care for orphans and wounded soldiers, and established retraining facilities for disabled veterans.

Relief efforts led to an "inspection" of the nation's social situation that revealed greater deprivation than had hitherto been recognized. As a result, citizens and political leaders pressed for expanded social insurance following the war. In 1928, after ten years of intensive public debate, France enacted a social insurance program (quite different from the joint worker-employer contributory schemes operating in Germany and Britain). The government assumed sole responsibility for funding and administering comprehensive programs for old-age and sickness insurance, and, given the loss of population during the war, for child allowances.[12]

With a political culture very different from France's, Britain approached war finance with societal discipline created by entrenched balanced-budget norms in a mature, stable democracy. Well accustomed to paying taxes on income and purchases, Britain's citizens supported the wartime coalition government's plan to pay for the war through taxation, avoiding both excessive debt and its inflationary consequences. Acceptance of high wartime tax levels by all political parties—Labour, Liberal, and Conservative—tangibly expressed British society's cohesiveness in response to challenge. Unlike the French Chamber of Deputies, Great Britain's Parliament was not disposed to provide unlimited authorization for ministerial expenditures. (Since the revolution of 1688, it had in fact been illegal to do so.)

For ten years before the war, spending and taxes in Britain had increased only slightly—about 1.3 times, although if we went back to 1895, thus eliminating the effects of the Boer War, the rise would be larger. Between 1914 and 1918 (see Table 11), the war increased England's expenses eightfold. When war broke out, political leaders set out to pay for it with the proceeds of steeply progressive income taxes. David Lloyd George, Prime Minister for the first two years of the war, was criticized for not raising taxes soon enough. At war's end, receipts from the income tax produced about four-fifths (83 percent) of total revenue. Having collected income taxes since the mid–nineteenth century, the government knew well how to bring in more revenue. The government's economic advisers also understood that high taxes would control inflation by reducing disposable income. Despite Britain's determination not to borrow heavily, however, debt service did consume about a fifth of wartime budgets. A policy of "pay as you go" covered about a third of war expenditure, far more than in France, but far less than necessary to minimize inflation and future costs of debt service. Inflation fueled immediate postwar increases in spending.

Britain had established unemployment and old-age insurance before the war, and social service costs were its largest expenditure (33 percent of the budget in 1913). While social programs consumed smaller proportions of expanded wartime budgets, the absolute amounts spent for welfare went up, especially toward the end.

For the first two years the government had tried to conduct business as usual. The war did affect society's perception of social needs, however, creating a climate favorable to previously unacceptable changes. Although the prewar suffrage movement had encountered widespread resistance, women's participation in the war eventually led to the passage of legislation giving women the vote. Trade union membership and the Labour Party's representation in Parliament went up, spurred

TABLE 11

BRITAIN DEVOTES HALF OF NATIONAL INCOME TO WAR EFFORT[13]

Year	Expenditure as a percentage of GNP	Defense Expenditure as a percentage of Total Expenditure
1905	6.7	42.3
1913	7.1	40.2
1914	20.4	78.3
1915	47.2	89.7
1916	58.0	89.8
1917	57.0	89.1
1918	47.6	85.2
1919	29.0	41.5
1920	19.1	24.6
1924	16.3	15.3

on by national unity, which made them seem more desirable and respectable. (The Second World War had a similar effect on the more egalitarian party, as Winston Churchill was to discover.) As pressure groups, both women and labor favored expansion of social programs.

The wartime coalition government created a new, centralized Ministry of Health, and in 1916 the government established a Ministry of Reconstruction to explore postwar problems. The ministry's "scope was far reaching . . . dealing with almost every aspect of the society."[14] Most of what it proposed was ignored.[15] Nevertheless, consensus about the value of social programs led to expansion in their coverage and cost. By 1920 enhanced unemployment and health insurance coverage, and a new program of housing subsidies, raised social welfare spending to four times the prewar level. By 1924, with a depression limiting output and with expanded welfare spending, the public sector consumed about 20 percent of GNP, or approximately twice the proportion in 1913.

Although the United States's late entry into World War I limited claims on its fisc, compared to costs incurred by Britain and France, the war modified Americans' traditional niggardliness toward central government. Central-government spending in 1913 (see Table 12) was only about 2 percent of GNP. By 1917 war expenses raised government's share of GNP to nearly 21 percent. Once the war ended, however, spending declined, almost but not quite as rapidly as it had started.

TABLE 12

U.S. DEVIATES BRIEFLY FROM BUDGET PATTERN FOR WAR EFFORT[16]

Year	Total Expenditure as a percentage of GNP	Tax as a Percentage of GNP	Defense Expenditure as Percentage of Total Expenditure
1905	2.3	2.2	43.3
1913	1.8	1.7	41.1
1914	1.9	1.6	39.8
1915	1.8	1.8	42.8
1916	4.0	2.1	30.9
1917	21.0	5.6	56.2
1918	24.1	5.9	73.4
1919	7.6	6.8	62.8
1920	5.5	5.4	51.0
1924	3.4	3.7	20.5

At the beginning of this century, the U.S. government had neither a productive source of revenue beyond the tariff nor a centralized spending agency for expenditure budgeting. By the second decade, the federal government had everything it had been missing except, of course, the always elusive secret of perpetual prosperity.

The federal tax on corporate income enacted in 1909 was a start. After a constitutional amendment in 1913 permitted it, Congress again enacted personal-income-tax legislation. The burden of the new tax, originally intended to fall only on the very wealthy, was neither excessive by present standards nor widely distributed. People with personal incomes below $3,000 ($4,000 if married) per year paid no tax (average annual per-capita earnings in 1913 were $621 per year).[17] Generous personal exemptions, deductions, low rates, and wide income brackets minimized the impact on all but the very wealthy.

As the struggle over whether the United States should enter the war continued, policymakers, looking back to the Civil War (paid for almost entirely by borrowing), agreed that sale of debt should be avoided. In 1914 Congress enacted a supplemental tax on luxuries. To expand revenue further after the declaration of war, Congress raised taxes on corporate incomes and levied an income tax on personal income exceeding $2,000 per year. The exponential increase in federal revenue after 1917 demonstrates the extraordinary productivity of a broadly based income tax when the domestic economy grows rapidly. The federal government had collected $735 million in 1914. In 1917 revenue receipts were $1.118 billion, and in 1920 $6.698 billion.

Nevertheless, given America's entrenched individualism, expansion of taxing and spending during the war did create trauma. Expanding federal revenues (which raised taxes per capita from $23 in 1913 to $75 in 1919) could not cover war expenses. In spite of determination not to do so, the government had to pay for most of its war expenses (about 70 percent) by borrowing. Two Liberty Loan Acts passed in 1917 authorized the Secretary of the Treasury to borrow "such ... sums [as] ... may be necessary to meet public expenditures, and to issue therefore certificates of indebtedness."[18] There was no fiscal improvisation; Congress and the recently established Federal Reserve Board maintained tight control over the Treasury by limiting amounts borrowed and permissible interest rates.*

---

*In this regard, J. Fitzgerald, chairman of the House Committee on Appropriations, said: "More than $840,000,000 requested by the administration was refused ... because the purposes ... proposed were not essential for the conduct of the war..."[19]

During and immediately after the war, political elites feared that wartime deficits would weaken balanced-budget norms. According to wartime Secretary of the Treasury Carter Glass, "... there appears to be grave danger that the extraordinary success of the Treasury in financing the stupendous war expenditure may lead to a riot of public expenditure after the war."[20] Like Gladstone, Britain's zealous nineteenth-century guardian of the public purse, Glass believed that a surplus would lead to unnecessary spending. While debt retirement was a prime concern of policymakers right after the war, highest priority went to reducing the size of central government. When he became president in 1920, Warren G. Harding enunciated mainstream opinion: "War is not wholly responsible for staggering costs, it has merely accentuated the menace which lies in mounting costs of government and excesses in expenditures which a successful private businessman would not tolerate."[21] Touching on a theme often heard today, elites who supported a market regime contended that a high level of peacetime public spending would stunt economic growth.[22] If the American people wanted a small government, they should, as in the past, levy minimal taxes and maintain a balanced budget. By 1923–24, as a consequence, federal expenditures had fallen from a wartime high of 24 percent of GNP to 3.4 percent (up from 2 percent in 1913). With interest payments on the national debt absorbing 40 percent of public spending in that year, the public sector was necessarily limited.

America inherited the English tradition of voluntarism and localism for providing aid to the poor. The rapid industrialization and urbanization during the last quarter of the nineteenth century left that tradition intact when the war started; veterans' pensions were the only federal assistance citizens could claim. As in England before the social-reform legislation of 1908, an American citizen had to be deemed deserving as well as destitute to obtain public relief from local sources. In those days, the deserving poor were mainly widows and orphans without personal resources or familial support.

Although death and injury from work-related accidents were far greater in the United States than in Europe in the early 1900s,[23] until 1912 neither federal nor state governments adopted mandatory compensation for death or injury on the job. But the war did modify individualism; reform ideas latent in peacetime gained support as the society mobilized. By 1920 forty-one states and the federal government had adopted workmen's compensation.[24]

The Progressive movement did not align itself with the emerging

labor movement in the United States as did the Fabians with Labour in late-nineteenth-century Britain. Though the progressives wanted no part of socialism, they believed both in a caring collective and in the ability of educated elites, like themselves, to help those less fortunate.*
During World War I the Progressive Party generated pressure for child-welfare and maternal-health legislation, slum clearance and urban housing programs, as well as social insurance. That so many potential draftees were disqualified on the grounds of poor health led to demands for health insurance. But preference for small government, both during the war and afterward, meant that little action was taken.

The war enhanced preexisting tendencies. Social programs initiated before the war in Britain and France were expanded afterward, and new programs were added. While the military received by far the largest component of war spending, aggregate spending by governments of these three nations never did return to prewar levels.

The administrative significance of the war was immense. The bureaucracy grew by a factor of two or more, and its competence in extracting resources and managing large projects rose still further, with long-lasting consequences. There was a lot of learning about how to raise money and allocate it. Fear of the consequences—a bureaucracy out of control, especially in spending on social welfare—led to reinvigorated central-expenditure control. The system of spending allotments became formalized. The boundaries around the civil service were strengthened as outside experts, much in favor by advocates of social spending, were denied entry to the civil service. Treasuries and finance ministries blossomed. In the political climate of the 1920s and early 1930s, the heads of those units (Sir Horace Wilson, Sir Wallace Fisher, General Dawes) became famous to some insiders and

---

*In a minority report prepared for the federal government's Industrial Commission (appointed in 1914 to investigate the Ludlow Massacre and to suggest ways of improving relations between labor and capital), John Commons, professor of economics at the University of Wisconsin and an old Progressive, suggested labor policies similar to those adopted during the New Deal. William M. Leiserson, an economist on the commission staff, recommended setting up a "state fund for public improvement which would be a sort of insurance fund for industrial depressions." To be administered by state boards and funded also with state matching grants, this fund would be used to relieve unemployment by building public infrastructure and undertaking land reclamation and reforestation projects. A considerable part of the New Deal labor and social-insurance legislation was written by Commons' students, by then also University of Wisconsin professors, who whenever possible emulated what they had previously wrought at the state level in Wisconsin. Indeed, the peculiar federal-state combinations (e.g., in public assistance) of New Deal legislation was in part the result of their conviction that the states were the right level for all kinds of social programs.[25]

infamous to others. But they fought a losing cause. When the political tides turned in the 1930s, and swelled in the 1950s and 1960s, however, these administrative skills were turned to increasing state spending.

Peacock and Wiseman, who have made a major study of growth in governmental spending, contend that social disturbances displace public attitudes toward taxes.[26] During wars people become used to paying high taxes; even though the taxes are reduced when wars end (though not to prewar levels), citizens are accustomed to wartime taxes and prepared to finance greater postwar spending. This hypothesis has merit, but it neglects intentional choice. How social forces respond to upheaval also influences the extent of displacement. Displacement is a two-way process.

For example, postwar spending fell off more sharply in the United States than elsewhere. The key factor was elite consensus on budget balance. Prewar ideological orientation toward competitive individualism in the United States did not change; indeed, reaction against wartime expansion of central government enhanced postwar public pressure to cut it down to size.

DEBT AND IMMOBILITY IN THE 1920s: A STUDY OF FRANCE, GERMANY, BRITAIN, SWEDEN, AND THE UNITED STATES[27]

Debt management and debt reduction were the most important budgetary issues of the 1920s. Following the First World War, the United States and countries in western Europe were burdened with huge debts; interest payments dominated public budgets. How each nation managed its debt tells us something about its political as well as its financial life.

There are a number of ways of measuring trends in public debt; none is perfect, but all reveal something. The most obvious measure, level of debt in current terms, indicates whether debt is being retired or increased, but gives no indication of its importance in the total economy, or of inflationary effects. Debt expressed as a percentage of GNP does stress the importance of debt in the economy, but does not provide information about why changes have occurred (e.g., the proportion of debt to GNP can be the same if debt remains constant while GNP rises, or declines while GNP is stable). Since interest payments on public debt are a continuing burden, moreover, their rates and amounts are as important as the gross size of debt in measuring the effects of borrowing on an economy. Ignoring the difficulty of repaying principal, a $4 billion debt at 2 percent is no worse than $2 billion at 4 percent. Understanding changes in the debt position of a country, therefore, requires a variety of analytic approaches.

Britain and America did not inflate their currency after World War I. Germany—defeated, unable to reschedule massive debt accumulated by deficit financing before and during the war—suffered rampant post-war inflation because its citizens lacked confidence in its capacity to pay back loans. France, by contrast, was able to avoid massive inflation because its citizens were willing to buy their government's debt. In Germany and France, there was a lot to buy: for the years 1920–23, German government revenue was less than 30 percent of expenditures; over the same period, French revenues were 40 percent of expenditure—better than Weimar, but still less than a model of responsible government finance. When the German government could borrow no more, it began printing. The outcome was rapidly accelerating inflation, which climaxed in 1923.[28]

Each of these countries dealt with its indebtedness in a very different way. In 1919 the U.S. gross domestic debt was $25 billion, on which it paid nearly $1 billion in interest. Never before having experienced such a deficit, American leadership wished to reduce it. By 1930 the debt had been reduced about a third—to $15.9 billion—because the economy grew throughout the decade, bringing in ample revenue.

With its legacy of individualism, the United States was the only country we studied that actually paid off any substantial portion of its national debt during the 1920s. But it was not the only country to reduce its burden. Germany paid off its war debt in full, and in a remarkably short time, because the inflation of the early 1920s had so reduced the value of the Reichsmark. In 1924, when the currency was stabilized, the Germans were left with the smallest debt of any nation—2.9 percent of GNP. Germany's debt repayment was in no sense comparable to America's, however, since there was only a slight deflation in the United States over the decade: U.S. debt was paid off at full value. Belief in a balanced budget over the long term did make a difference. In spite of a few years of budget surplus, the French actually added to their national debt during the 1920s. Inflation, however, left debt payments lower at the close of the decade than at its beginning.

It is extraordinary to think that a country with an enormous domestic debt would pursue a deflationary policy—since par value of outstanding debt rises inversely with interest rates, the present market value of outstanding debt rises as the economy and interest rates decline. But that is indeed what Britain did in the decade following World War I. The British mostly balanced their budgets, so the level of the debt did not rise—but they were unable to reduce it. Throughout the twenties, interest comprised nearly 40 percent of public spending (slightly more than 6 percent of GNP). Debt did not decline in gross amount or as a share of GNP; Britain was left at the end of the decade with the same huge war debt, a costly obligation to finance it, and the concomitant high rates of taxation, said to be "bleeding the country to death." The United States and Sweden also experienced some deflation, but neither had as large a debt as Britain's.

A different strategy, a one-time, heavy tax on capital gains, was unsuccessfully supported by the British Labour Party, with its socialist leanings. The idea was to wipe out the debt in one fell swoop, to accomplish in a straightforward manner what the German inflation did indirectly—in effect eliminating existing debt without having to pay it off. The capital levy presumably would have been paid by debt holders, so that the tax would have been tantamount to canceling the debt.

In the years immediately following the war, France and Germany both ran phenomenally large deficits but reacted differently, the Germans by borrowing and printing money and the French by cutting spending and raising taxes. The French budget for 1922 eliminated funding for 42,000 government servants, and the 1923 budget provided for still further reductions.[29] By 1925 the French budget was in surplus. Balanced budgets with a small surplus were the rule until the onset of the depression—remarkable considering the magnitude of the deficit in 1920. The French Third Republic is generally described as "immobile," a characterization that the balanced budgets, tax increases, and spending cuts, when things got bad enough, would tend to disconfirm.

It is not what was done about the debt but how it was done that mattered most. John Maynard Keynes observed the irony in the differences between French and British debt policy:

> In Great Britain our authorities have never talked such rubbish as their French colleagues or offended so grossly against all principles of sound finance. But Great Britain has come out of the transitional period with her debt aggravated, her obligations to the United States unabated, and with deflationary finance still appropriate to the former and a million unemployed as the outcome of the latter. France, on the other hand, has written down her internal war debt by four-fifths, and has persuaded her Allies to let her off more than half of her external debt; and now she is avoiding the sacrifices of Deflation. Yet she has contrived to do this without the slightest loss of reputation for conservative finance and capi-

talist principles. The Bank of France emerges much stronger than the Bank of England; and everyone still feels that France is the last stronghold of tenacious saving and the rentier mentality. Assuredly it does not pay to be good.[30]

Whether Britain's better performance in climbing out of the depression of the 1930s may be attributed to its facing up to its debt, as opposed to France's evasion of it, cannot be established with any certainty.

SPENDING IN THE 1920s

Spending in the 1920s was higher everywhere than before the war. But, except for Germany, spending did not increase over the course of the decade, and often went down. England's unemployment insurance, adopted in the first decade of this century, was broadened somewhat in the twenties, but expenditures in money did not rise at all until 1929. (During the 1930s the old patchwork fell apart under greater strain than it was meant to handle; payments to the unemployed merged imperceptibly with support for the poor.) France adopted a voluntary plan in 1905, though unemployment insurance did not become compulsory until 1931. Germany, having established social insurance early, enacted unemployment insurance in 1927.[31] Sweden did not adopt unemployment insurance in any form until the thirties.*

Why didn't social spending increase more in the 1920s than between 1900 and 1910? Many countries were in the midst of a boom, a fact that may explain a lot; the United States, France, and Sweden—all countries where social spending was moderate—enjoyed healthy GNP growth throughout the decade. When the capitalist economy is humming along, the urge and the need to correct for its failings diminishes. Britain experienced little growth in social spending; even with one million unemployed, the British, feeling the constraints of a large public debt and already high taxes, thought it prudent to restrain spending. A major debate on the British budget revolved around whether it was

*Jan-Erik Lane has informed us that there was help of a kind. Beginning in 1914 a state commission was responsible for the arrangement of public works all over Sweden. No doubt many were helped, but there was conflict over the conditions on which those unemployed should be enrolled for public works. As in nineteenth-century Britain, recipients of public assistance lost personal autonomy. The conservative majority in parliament maintained that (1) salaries should be lower than market wages, and that (2) it should be possible to send unemployed people to factories where there was a strike. If the unemployed refused such work, then they should be cut off from further assistance. In 1933 the Social Democratic government changed these rules so as to improve labor relations and fight against the depression. As war preparations increased the market for Swedish goods, economic conditions improved.

preferable to cut taxes or to amortize debt. Conservatives favored tax cuts and Labourites debt reduction; but neither party seems to have thought of keeping taxes high and refunding wartime debt to finance more public spending. Cabinet minutes reveal that deflationary economics—lower wage rates and lower spending seen as essential to recovery—were a powerful influence on both parties.

The situation in Britain is indicative of a more general characteristic of politics in the twenties, the weakness of labor and socialist parties, which can account for stability in spending. Dankwart Rustow explains that in Sweden from 1920 to 1932 "governments of right, left, and center formed in quick succession, yet no group could rule without Liberal support. Time after time, therefore, demands for a strong army by the Conservatives and for an active welfare policy by the Socialists were whittled down until they met the Liberals' criteria of economy."[32]

Why, then, when spending remained constant or declined everywhere else, did public spending increase in Germany? In what way was Germany different? Power was fragmented among parties, but it was elsewhere, too. Perhaps the crucial difference is that Germany was more threatened by social unrest than were Britain, France, Sweden, and the United States, and greater spending was seen as a means of buying calm. In 1913 social insurance in Germany was nearly 12 percent of government expenditure; it rose to over 15 percent in 1925. During the next five years, spending on social insurance increased nearly 10 percent more, so that in 1930 it comprised just over 25 percent of government expenditures.[33]

Thanks to the depression of the 1930s, programs initially intended as social *insurance* became social *security*. In 1911 Britain initiated a program of unemployment relief that was very limited in scope and not based on employee contributions. Every subsequent unemployment program was designed as an insurance scheme. Employed workers and their employers paid into an insurance fund; accumulated contributions provided compensation during layoffs. Welfare schemes were devised with contributory funding, a Twentieth Century Fund study reported in 1937, because "many countries, faced with the acute problem of finding new sources of revenue, found it politically more feasible to collect the needed revenues under the name of 'contributions' than in the form of increased general taxes. This is the basic cause of the trend toward contributory pensions."[34] Contributory and noncontributory elements are mingled, because nowhere have contributions alone been adequate—as England found in the 1920s, when employment entered a nearly twenty-year slump, almost immediately after benefits had been extended to most workers. A premier student of social policy, T. H. Marshall, explains:

> Insurance benefits were soon exhausted and the choice had to be made between abandoning the relationship between contributions and benefits altogether [and] passing the burden on to the Poor Law, that is to say on the local rates. This was impossible, so the compromise was adopted of abandoning the principle of insurance but retaining the apparatus and as much of the terminology as possible. . . . Social insurance was originally contractual in character, in that it conferred a right that was conditional on the payment of contributions. Now the obligation to pay the contributions was lapsed, but the right to the benefit was still acknowledged.[35]

Gradually, through the twenties and thirties, the proportion of contribution to government subsidy shifted in both Britain and Germany.[36] And, characteristically, when the United States adopted old-age and unemployment insurance in 1936, both programs were designed to be paid solely from a trust fund supported by joint contributions from workers and employers.

The nations with large debts in the 1920s were the highest spenders, but debt explains only a portion of this variation. In Britain and France, with very large debts, government spending in 1920 was 19.8 and 27.8 percent of GNP, respectively. The United States and Sweden, with smaller debts, both devoted considerably less of national product to public spending—5.5 and 7.1 percent in 1920. When interest payments are subtracted, Britain still was spending much more than the U.S., and somewhat more than Sweden. (Lack of data does not permit comparisons with France and Germany.) With the exception of Germany, the high-spending states remained high over the decade, and the low ones low. The same forces that impelled Sweden and the United States to work at paying off debt also led them to spend less.

Not only do the indebted nations spend more of their GNP than do the nations relatively free of debt, but Table 13 shows that, except for Germany, government spending as a percentage of GNP decreased steadily during the decade. As nations continued to pay off interest on their debt and retire some of the obligations, expenditure relative to GNP went down, since most other allocations, such as defense and social spending, remained constant. France achieved the largest reductions in relative spending, so that, by the end of the decade, its total expenditure accounted for about 15 percent of GNP, similar to Britain. The United States and Sweden also managed to lower this ratio: from 5.5 to 4 percent for the U.S., and from 11.3 to 7 percent for Sweden.

TABLE 13
GOVERNMENT SPENDING DECREASES OVER THE 1920s[37]

Year	Government spending as a percentage of GNP				
	France	U.K.	U.S.	Sweden	Germany
1920	25.5	19.1	5.5	7.2	*
1921	22.5	20.1	4.7	11.3	*
1922	27.9	17.1	4.2	12.4	*
1923	21.1	16.3	3.4	9.3	*
1924	19.0	16.3	3.4	8.5	7.2
1925	15.1	15.9	3.1	9.0	8.1
1926	13.8	16.9	2.9	8.5	9.0
1927	14.1	15.9	3.1	8.2	8.7
1928	12.8	15.5	3.2	8.7	9.7
1929	14.9	15.7	3.2	7.4	9.3
1930	14.3	16.6	4.0	7.7	10.2

* GNP unavailable.

Only Germany's government steadily increased government spending as a proportion of total national product, reaching 10 percent by 1930.

What is most impressive about the composition of public spending in the twenties is its static quality. British and American budgets (available in greater detail than are the others) fail to show important changes. The German budgets for 1926, 1927, and 1928 (the only years for which we have comparable data) show no changes in shares allotted to different functions, though the size of the budget was increasing. No such comparison can be made for France. Comparison in Sweden is not easy, but over the twenties the budget share for defense remains constant at 20 percent. All evidence points to budgetary immobility. Perhaps, when one considers the proliferation of "caretaker" governments, the rigidity of the twenties is not altogether surprising. Bold action, which inevitably hurts some groups as it benefits others, is exactly the kind of policy that a government based on a weak coalition is incapable of implementing; offending even a small group of supporters could cause the government to fall. Such a structural analysis, however, presumes support for higher spending and taxing by some part of the coalition. So far as we can tell, such support was minimal. Holding such coalitions together through "side payments" from ever higher public spending was a discovery of the second half of the century.

TAXATION IN THE TWENTIES

The tax structures of France, Germany, Sweden, Great Britain, and the United States were remarkably similar in the 1920s; all relied more or less heavily on the income tax, assorted excise taxes, and customs duties. The proportion of direct to indirect taxation among these countries was also roughly the same. For each, income tax was the most productive single tax; in the United States, given the substantial reductions from wartime levels, it had not yet become the dominant tax. An array of indirect taxes levied before the income tax was imposed still brought in a large proportion of revenue.

Prior to the war, a substantial portion of Britain's indirect-tax receipts came from the so-called "breakfast-table duties" on tea, sugar, coffee, cocoa, and preserves; after the war, "sin taxes" on tobacco and alcohol replaced these regressive consumption levies. Britain enacted new excise taxes during World War I and added still others in the interwar period. While Winston Churchill served as Chancellor of the Exchequer (1924–29), the trend toward reduced taxes on consumption was halted, but not reversed. Throughout the twenties, indirect taxation provided about 35 percent of tax revenue.

More important on the Continent than in the English-speaking countries, indirect taxation comprised 50–60 percent of revenues in France and Germany, and 70 percent in Sweden, an extension of nineteenth-century fiscal policies. Continental governments collected excise taxes on a number of similar, common consumption items, such as sugar. With enhanced protectionism during the twenties, customs duties also contributed a significant share of tax revenues—10 percent or so in France, Germany and Britain, and close to 20 percent in Sweden and the United States.

There was a progressive income tax in Germany and the United States, but not in Sweden, Britain, and France. In Germany, the base rate was 10 percent, rising to 40 percent on income above 80,000 marks. Compared to Germany's high tax rate, the United States's was modest, and only slightly progressive. In 1926, the rate was lowered to 1.5 percent on the first $4,000, rising to 5 percent on amounts over $8,000. Britain, France, and Sweden had flat rates, although France, hoping to increase the birth rate after the carnage of war, charged higher rates for bachelors and childless couples. The French flat rate was 30 percent in 1926 (lowered in that year from 60 percent), and the British rate varied from six shillings in the pound, or 30 percent (1920–21), to four shillings, 20 percent, in 1929–30. During the 1920s, in sum, there was little or no innovation in taxation, only the effort to exploit the same old taxes in order to pay for the war.

THE DEPRESSION AND THE WELFARE STATE IN WESTERN EUROPE AND THE UNITED STATES[38]

The economic, political, and social history of the 1930s is necessarily a history of the Great Depression. One cannot discuss the taxation or public-expenditure policies of Western nations without frequent reference to their attempts to cope with the most severe and prolonged economic downturn in over sixty years. (The depression of 1872–79 was greater in its impact and magnitude.) How and in what ways did the Great Depression contribute to public policies deliberately designed to modify market forces—to guarantee individuals and families a minimum income, and to offer all citizens a range of social services?[39] In many nations social policies now categorized as welfare state began or were expanded during the Great Depression.

The 1930s brought a major shift in economic thinking, although differences over the legitimacy of state intervention had long existed among countries. Before World War II, none of the Western countries could be termed Keynesian, but by 1948 all of them to varying degrees were pursuing policies of demand management. Not only did the depression bring about an eclipse of classical liberal doctrines, it also led to the common acceptance of and, indeed, demand for an expanded role for government in the economy. Changes in power also brought into office public officials who favored these demands. Initially, the welfare state arose in an ad-hoc manner, but policies of the thirties set up the institutional bases upon which was grafted a fundamental change in public perception; what had begun as a mere expedient was reinforced and built upon a systematic way.

The New Deal in the United States never was a coherent set of measures. Rather it comprised ad-hoc answers to immediate crises.[40] Franklin D. Roosevelt was an old progressive, and his ameliorative approach to the depression embodied some of the same measures he proposed as governor of New York State from 1929 to 1933—spending for resources conservation and antitrust, policies that concentrated on the internal economy. He campaigned for president on the platform that the cause of the depression lay within the American economy and hence could be cured only through domestic action. Accordingly, Roosevelt's program (presented to Congress in the famous first Hundred Days) aimed at relief, recovery, and reform. Barely established in Washington, Roosevelt offered proposals to reestablish public confidence in the banking system; to achieve a balanced budget by cutting government spending; to revive agriculture through an increase in farm incomes; to assist industry by creating a system of price codes; and to institute a program of public works. Specifically, Roosevelt sought to bring output into line with consumer demand by limiting production and reducing government spending. Clearly, he was no believer in the desirability of deficits. Indeed, when Keynes conferred with Roosevelt in Washington in 1935, the two apparently did not agree. Roosevelt maintained his balanced-budget preferences; throughout the 1930s he viewed current spending as pump priming. After his overwhelming victory in the 1936 election, he tried to cut spending in 1937 to balance the budget, but a sharp upturn in unemployment in 1938 forced him to abandon this effort.[41]

During those first Hundred Days the House of Representatives passed the Economy Bill, which halved the pensions of disabled war veterans, reduced congressional salaries as well as those of all federal employees, and curtailed other federal expenditures. The Economy Bill was designed to balance spending with revenue, which, as two-thirds of it was based on individual and corporate income taxes, had declined by nearly a half between 1930 and 1933. This bill increased hardships among pensioners and, by curtailing government expenditure, reduced individual purchasing power.

Aside from attempts to balance the budget, the most significant areas of government intervention in the U.S. economy were in regulating industrial prices through government-business collaboration, and in inaugurating a public works program designed to reduce unemployment. Here began the merger of market individualism and hierarchical collectivism, which we now call, familiarly, the establishment. The National Industrial Recovery Act created a new agency, the National Recovery Administration (NRA), embodying three main proposals: (1) a set of price-fixing codes designed to promote "fair competition"—in effect, promises to avoid undercutting a competitor's selling price, and (it was hoped) thereby to reduce unemployment; (2) a Public Works Administration with a sizable appropriation to promote heavy construction projects (most of them focused on managing natural resources in the western states); and (3) measures to deal with labor relations. The New Deal was most immediately concerned with the serious decline in farm incomes due to falling agricultural prices. The intention of the first Agricultural Adjustment Act was to raise prices by reducing the surplus through deliberate restriction of crops.

To limit production, the government established an Agricultural Adjustment Administration empowered to decide on an "acreage allotment" for each basic crop to be planted in the next season. Initially the scheme applied to wheat, cotton, field corn, hogs, rice, tobacco, and daily products; in 1934 it was expanded. The cost of agricultural subsidies was to be paid out of a new processing tax levied on food manufacturers, not out of general revenues. Roosevelt and his advisers chose this off-budget device in an effort to maintain some semblance of budget balance. Congress also passed a bill establishing the Farm Credit Administration to consolidate all existing rural credit agencies.

In trying to pull the United States out of the depression, Roosevelt was as concerned with unemployment as with sectoral output. Accordingly he proposed to Congress three additional activities: "the provision of direct relief to provide food and clothing by means of federal grants to the states; job creation through the employment by the federal government of workers on immediate projects which would not interfere with private industry; a longer-term public works program."[42]

The first of these proposals was embodied in the Federal Emergency Relief Administration (FERA), the second in the Civilian Conservation Corps (CCC), and the third through formation of the Civil Works Administration (CWA) and the Works Progress Administration (WPA) These agencies represented an unprecedented intervention in the economy by central government to put unemployed citizens to work.

In 1935 WPA became concerned solely with providing work, whereas direct relief was handed back to the states and to local government. The Securities and Exchange Commission was established in 1934; unsavory business practices during the securities boom of the 1920s were widely viewed as one source of the depression. The National Labor Relations Act, which, among other things, "legalized" trade unions, became law in 1935, as did the Social Security Act; for the first time in American history it involved the federal government directly in providing welfare. Social Security resembled Britain's unemployment-insurance and old-age benefits: joint contributions from employers and workers went into a government trust fund earmarked to dispense old-age pensions. In 1937 the U.S. Housing Authority began to operate; it was empowered to make loans and give federal aid to clear slums and build low-rent houses. Additional legislation governing agricultural policy was embodied in the second Agricultural Adjustment Act of 1938, which created the Commodity Credit Corporation, designed to stabilize farm incomes through the accumulation of buffer stocks.[43]

A look at federal income and expenditure between 1929 and 1939 gives some sense of government's growth and its expanded role in the economy. In 1929, federal expenditure was $3.3 billion; in 1939, $8.9 billion. While federal spending increased by 270 percent, there was only a 125 percent increase in federal revenues (from $4.0 billion in 1929 to $5.0 billion in 1939). Federal expenditure as a percentage of GNP, moreover, tripled (from 3.2 percent in 1929 to 9.7 percent in 1939), whereas federal revenue as a percentage of GNP during the same period did not even double (from 3.9 to 5.5 percent).

Although military expenditures began to go up in 1938, with passage of the Naval Construction Act, they did not significantly increase until 1940, when Roosevelt submitted an $8.4 billion budget, $1.8 billion for national defense. Aid to agriculture, relief and work relief, and public works made up approximately 25 percent of total expenditure in 1933, nearly 50 percent in 1936, and over 50 percent in 1939 (about 54 percent). As Jim Potter has pointed out, "Until the sharp cut-back in expenditure between 1937 and 1938, seen in considerably reduced deficit in 1938 (and reflected in the sharp recession of that year), the effects of federal fiscal actions were expansionary through the mid-1930s."[44] This expansion was not part of the original theory, but it soon became standard practice.

After several increases during the First World War, income taxes, impelled by what today would be called "supply-side" economics, fell rather sharply in the twenties, reaching their lowest point between 1927 and 1932. In 1935, Roosevelt sent Congress a proposal to raise taxes on inheritances, impose gift taxes, make the income tax more progressive, and increase the corporate income tax. By the time Congress passed the Wealth Tax Act of 1935, however, the basic thrust of Roosevelt's proposals had been blunted. The legislation did little to redistribute wealth, and still less to raise revenue, but it did increase estate, gift, and capital-stock taxes, and levied an excess-profits tax. Apparently, in those depression days, few profits were in excess.[45]

The enduring legacy of the New Deal was acceptance by the American public of the doctrine that the federal government has ultimate responsibility for the economy. Belief in collective responsibility grew. There might be arguments about how large government should grow, but the era of small government was over.

Britain, having suffered high unemployment through the 1920s, devalued its overvalued pound in 1931. As its products became more competitive in world markets, modest recovery came about. Except for Scandinavia, Britain was the least hard hit of the European countries during the 1930s. David Landes states that the dip experienced by the British economy, as contrasted with the plunge elsewhere, reflected in part the previous decade of persistent unemployment and quasi-depression. . . . Britain did not sink as far because she was already half submerged. The fact remains that the British economy did stand up better to the crisis; that it began to recover earlier than those of the other western European countries; and that its upswing was both longer and stronger—again, with the exception of the Scandinavian economies.

Britain better withstood the depression, according to Landes, for two reasons: the beneficent effects of government policy, specifically devaluation of the pound and provision of cheap money through the very low discount rate of the Bank of England; and the housing boom and the new industries—electrical, automobiles, and chemicals.[46]

British expenditure on social services expanded significantly. Although payments for war pensions had declined markedly by the onset of the depression, expenditures on old-age pensions rose sharply; unemployment and poor-relief benefits increased in the early thirties and grew throughout the period. Between 1920 and 1934, aggregate expenditure for old-age pensions more than doubled and unemployment insurance rose by a third, though war pensions declined by half.[47] Housing and education also drew a noticeable portion of central-government expenditure.[48]

Such an increase in government spending meant major changes in the methods of raising revenue to balance the budget. Income and capital taxes expanded significantly.[49] To these sources of revenue were added new market taxes on gasoline and motorcars, and, after the Ottawa Conference of 1932, revenue derived from a new "imperial preference" tariff.

British taxation in the thirties was not as progressive as some have argued. Rather, the tax structure was steeply progressive at the upper end, largely as a result of the income tax and surtax, and steeply regressive at the lower end, due to its traditional taxes on tea, sugar, tobacco, and alcohol.[50] Those with medium incomes enjoyed the lowest percentage burden of taxation.

Not until the early years of World War II was Keynesianism (interpreted crudely here as higher spending when unemployment was extensive, and lower spending when inflation threatened) accepted as valid economic doctrine. Before then, the prevalent economic position was that government borrowing and spending created only a little extra temporary employment, and no additional permanent employment, for market forces would adjust to and wipe out uneconomic activity. Rather, government's role was to assure a stable currency through "orthodox" finance, i.e., balancing the budget. Accordingly, the 1930–32 budgets show decreased tax receipts due to falling incomes, with commensurate reduction in expenditure. Significantly, until rearmament began, the budgets of 1933–36 show small surpluses. Expansion of government's role in the economy developed through incremental growth rather than any sudden or rapid change in economic doctrine or economic practice.

The British government's primary effort in industrial planning was its Special Areas Policy, introduced in 1934. Unemployment rates of up to 70 percent of able-bodied workers, lasting in some districts for five years or more, sustained the belief that local industries in old regions could never again expand to employ their former numbers without some help from central government. To planners, the solution was to introduce new industries into the Special Areas (Scottish Special Area, South Wales and Monmouth, West Cumberland and Tyneside). George Orwell's descriptions of the desolate life in a Welsh mining town (*The Road to Wigan Pier*) and in London's East End (*Down and Out in Paris and London*) aroused widespread empathy, even among nonsocialists. Despite some notable successes, the Special Areas Acts (like their successors after the Second World War, or the recently proposed "enterprise zones") did not significantly reduce unemployment in those regions.

Massive government intervention in the agricultural sector reversed a century-long policy of laissez-faire. Between 1931 and 1933, the British government turned agriculture into a highly protected, organized, and subsidized sector of the economy, primarily through the Wheat Act of 1932, the Import Duties Act of 1932, and the Agricultural Marketing Acts of 1931 and 1933. The Wheat Act provided direct subsidy, whereas the Import Duties Act protected domestic producers of all horticultural products as well as oats and barley against foreign competition. The Agricultural Marketing Acts gave farmers power to establish organized marketing schemes, and authorized them to control output and to set the prices of their commodities. On the whole, these measures met with limited success.

Given rapidly rising unemployment and loss of business in the early thirties, the government was compelled to expand its activities. The direction of this expansion, however, was not predetermined. As Landes puts it, "The state, in short, preferred to help business help itself."[51]

The French were much more comfortable with government intervention. The French state had long been active in offering tariff protection, subsidies, and preferential tax treatment for selected sectors of the economy; and of course its bureaucracy was already highly centralized. Landes says that, to some Frenchmen, "the shift to increased government participation in the economy, the proliferation after the war of state or mixed enterprises in banking, transport, electricity, and manufacturing, seem a perfectly natural response to new economic circumstances."[52] To others, however, the economic role of the state became a seriously divisive issue.

The depression hit the French relatively late: for almost two years following the collapse of the New York stock market, France avoided any serious economic trouble. But when it did arrive, it persisted far longer than in any other Western country. Once decline and stagnation set in in 1931, it did not stop. Other countries began to recover in 1933 or 1934, but France showed no signs of upturn till late 1935; even then, there was little improvement until 1938.

The most interesting period in France during the depression was the "Blum Experiment" of 1936–37, historically important because Popular Front policies broke with the deflationary policies of the previous years.[53] Premier Léon Blum believed that the root cause of the depression was a lack of purchasing power in the hands of the people, and that by giving them more money government could reverse economic stagnation. Blum neither offered detailed proposals for a planned economy nor proposed nationalization of basic industries and big industrial firms. Aside from making good on policies long desired by labor the paid vacation and the eight-hour day—he did what he could by modestly expanding existing benefits. Pushed by political events, however, and the wave of strikes and factory occupations, Blum intervened in economic affairs far more than he had planned or promised.

Against the threat of potential revolution, the Blum government induced the parliament to pass several pieces of social legislation, including legalized collective bargaining. Moreover, Blum devalued the franc, nationalized the Bank of France (though the rest of the banking system remained in private hands), created a minister of national economy, nationalized a portion of the armaments industry, and took control of all dealings in wheat.

According to Kuisel, six factors explain Blum's reluctance to act as a radical socialist: (1) He understood his mandate as a call for renewed order, security, and welfare within the capitalist framework, never as a call for socialism. (2) Disagreement within the Popular Front circumscribed his maneuverability—the Radicals insisted on restraint, and the Communists wanted to insure the coalition's cohesion. (3) The government wanted to placate the working class without losing the confidence of business and its middle-class allies. (4) Blum inherited problems restricting his ability to maneuver—budgetary deficits, a troubled treasury, and a negative trade balance. (5) Blum did not want to impose controls, which he viewed as fascistic, nor did he want to cut France off from the economies of democratic Western countries. (6) He was also constrained by unforeseen events—the Spanish Civil War, German rearmament, and serious labor disorders at home.[54]

There are different views. Kemp, for instance, considers the ultimate failure of the Popular Front as political: "the relationship of forces in French society, the position of the parties which made up the Popular Front, and the role played by the Communist Party in restraining the working class in and after the strikes of 1936," in order to maintain unity against Nazism, precluded any attempt either to satisfy demands within a capitalist framework or to move successfully toward a revolutionary solution.[55] Kindleberger contends that the Popular Front program collapsed because none of the conditions of success were present, i.e., "a strong responsible labor movement, employer acceptance of limitations on authority, continuity of governmental policy, or international security."[56]

The experiment ended in June 1937 when Blum resigned because the parliament refused to grant him decree powers to deal with the mounting trade deficit. Camille Chautemps, a Radical (read "conservative" or "moderate"), followed Blum as premier; within a short time Chautemps had reversed many of Blum's policies and halted further structural reforms. The Popular Front broke up in the spring of 1938 as Daladier assumed the premiership with a program based on rearmament. Through decree laws, the Daladier government tried to regain business confidence by offering incentives for investment in new plants yielding higher output, as well as by pointing out ways business could circumvent the forty-hour week. The government returned to a "liberal plan"; it curtailed consumption and tried to lengthen the work week.

Yet this return to nineteenth-century liberal principles did not signal a complete restoration of free-market state-capital relations. Rather, a mixed economy had taken root, with the state acting as chief promoter of economic expansion. One member of the Daladier government described government economic policy as "a guided economy within the framework of liberty,"[57] a phrase that might well characterize the indicative planning in France since World War II. "On the eve of the

Second World War," Kuisel concludes, "many Frenchmen including certain government officials had come to accept the neo-liberal hybrid as the shape of the nation's future political economy."[58]

Obviously, policy depends in part on which of the major political tendencies is in power.

In contrast to the French, who were seriously divided over the issue of state intervention, and the British, who viewed it with considerable reluctance, for instance, the Germans "took to it without any difficulty."[59] Historically, the German state had shown itself ready and able to impose price and output controls on selected industries. Before World War I, the German economy had been organized into cartels, syndicates, and employer associations, and its government hierarchy dated back to the early nineteenth century, if not earlier. By the thirties, government was already a major producer of coal, lignite, and potash; and, at the same time, various government agencies had been granted extensive power over economic activity. The thirties brought a substantial increase in state intervention in the German economy.

Beginning in 1931, as a result of the financial crisis (collapse of Austria's Credit-Anstalt bank led to large-scale flight of capital from Germany), the government established institutional controls in the banking sector, imposed strict limits on food imports, and subsidized certain grain growers. These measures proved insufficient to stem unrest caused by deflationary policies (high taxes, reduced unemployment benefits), with more than 30 percent of the labor force unemployed. Hitler came to power in January 1933, promising to reestablish German prosperity.

Hitler's program of state capitalism combined tax rebates to private industry to create subsidized employment. It encouraged consumer spending and, after 1935, stimulated the economy with massive expenditures for rearmament. In its first two years, the Nazi regime spent about 4 percent of the annual GNP to promote employment.[60] It initiated a large public-works program to build waterways, railroads, public buildings, and superhighways, stipulating that when possible work was to be done by hand rather than machine, and that new employees were to be hired from relief rolls. Furthermore, the government significantly enlarged the state and party bureaucracy, pressed employers to expand their personnel by hiring part-time workers, and promoted housing projects. Unemployment was down by one-third at the end of 1933.

In order to further reduce unemployment, the government introduced universal compulsory military service. It established the obligatory Reich Labor Service (similar in conception to the Civilian Conservation Corps) and discouraged employment of women, except in certain positions.[61] These additional measures were also successful; by 1936 unemployment had been cut virtually to zero, and during the last two years before the war there were more jobs than available workers. The price of success was the abolition of a free labor market. By 1937 a worker could change jobs only after receiving a labor book, which detailed his employment record; by 1939, comprehensive labor conscription was introduced to meet shortages in certain sectors.

In the industrial sector, the Nazi government introduced the Four-Year Plan of 1936. It would either entice business in the desired direction with subsidies and sales guarantees or order firms to form compulsory partnerships to meet government aims. The plan represented a codification and extension of a technocratic strain of thought common in Germany at least since the end of the First World War (some of its elements were attractive to intellectuals in Britain's Labour Party and to Roosevelt's academic advisers as well). It entailed raising the scale of manufacturing and marketing operations from the level of the industrial enterprise to the organization of an entire industry or group of industries. The rationale was improved technical efficiency in manufacturing and heightened control of markets at a time when German enterprise sought to recover from the cumulative effects of war and inflation. Such organization was well suited to direction by governmental bureaucracy, and as the economy revived and then rearmed, the alliance among political cultures of hierarchy, fatalism, and markets which we call a regime of state capitalism sustained German political life.[62] The sectarian challenge to authority that was rife during the last years of the Weimar Republic was forcibly suppressed. The cacophony of criticism directed at democratic governments—*das System,* allegedly responsible for every evil—was replaced by the Nazi dictatorship.

Striving to attain self-sufficiency in the agricultural sector, the government regulated food production and distribution by establishing a variety of commodity boards empowered to control farming, processing, shipping, storing, wholesaling, and retailing. The government also enacted laws designed to curtail rural migration.

Arms expenditures increased from 4 percent of national income in 1933 to 20 percent in 1938.[63] Yet rearmament did not induce serious inflation.[64] The Nazis controlled consumption by slightly increasing the already high taxes of the Weimar period. While in 1932 tax receipts represented 25.4 percent of national income, by 1938 they were 29.5 percent.[65] After 1934 the government also fixed rigid wage controls, and maintained stable prices by allocating imported and home-produced raw materials and controlling trade margins by regulating profits.

The government controlled investment by reserving to itself the capital market for long-term borrowing—restricting the private sector either to self-financing or to short-term borrowing. Furthermore, the government regulated establishment of new firms through government licensing. A business reluctant to comply with government preferences could be quickly brought in line through cuts in imported raw materials and reduced labor allocations.

Government-operated labor exchanges in effect dictated to workers where, for whom, and how long they would work. A year of national service became compulsory for young women, and men of retirement age were encouraged to continue working. Between 1933 and 1939, as Hardach says, "The Nazis were slowly but surely creating a governmentally guided economy where state directives instead of the laws of the market determined production and consumption, helped by the availability of well-trained and generally loyal civil servants and the existence of a dense system of industrial federations and economic associations."[66] On the one hand, the government increased the sphere of private ownership by denationalizing some banks, and by leaving entrepreneurial enterprise to private individuals. On the other hand, a huge state bureaucracy empowered to restrict and redirect economic activity could restrain pursuit of private interests. Confiscated Jewish property was turned over to favored individuals.

Although the German government poured much money into the rearmanent program, nonmilitary public expenditure also increased. "Little consideration was given to an increase in taxation as an alternative to deficit spending," as Hardach points out, "because the Nazis had promised 'guns and butter'."[67]

The figures on government expenditure as a percentage of national income register a steady increase between 1933 and 1939, with defense, as expected, showing a huge increase (3.7 percent of government expenditure in 1930 as opposed to 24.3 percent in 1935). Social and health services decreased significantly (30.1 percent in 1930; 21.2 percent in 1935), as did education (15.2 percent in 1930; 10.7 percent in 1935), and communal services and housing (9.0 percent in 1930; 5.0 percent in 1935), while economic services went up slightly (9.1 percent in 1930; 12.2 percent in 1935).[68] The numbers suggest that although expenditure on nonmilitary items and civilian consumption between 1933 and 1939 rose substantially, the government was less concerned with providing social services and more with enhancing its ability to wage war.

Germany's economic performance during the thirties indicates that among nations it was best at curing the economic ills of the depression. This was in part due to the use of deficit financing on a large scale. Germany was the only country to pursue a policy of public borrowing to revive the economy. The French took a Malthusian approach: reducing output to the current consumption levels, rather than trying to increase consumption, meant deflationary monetary policies and decreased government spending. Britain achieved a limited recovery: its policies transferred 5–6 percent of national income to the poor, and raised the real income of the working class between 8 and 14 percent over the decade. By 1937, Britain had increased industrial output by 30 percent (over the 1933 level) and had cut its large unemployment in half. British industrial policy resembled the American NRA.

Under the New Deal in the United States, relief initially granted as an expedient became "relief granted as a principle; embodied in the Social Security Act of 1935 which formed the basis of all subsequent welfare legislation in the United States."[69] Correspondingly, the New Deal changed people's attitudes about the proper role of government vis-à-vis the economy. After that period, government intervention in the economy, albeit circumscribed, was seen as legitimate. In terms of recovery, however, the aggregate data reveal the limited extent of New Deal success: unemployment never fell below 14 percent. Total annual investment never approximated the $16.2 billion figure of 1929.

MILITARY EXPENDITURES BETWEEN THE FIRST AND SECOND WORLD WARS[70]

Military spending (or the lack thereof) in the 1920s and 1930s rehearsed the debates over defense in the 1980s. Should there be lower spending and greater emphasis on disarmament (or, at least, disarmament conferences), or the reverse? Does higher military spending on the part of a potential aggressor signify insecurity, which can be modified by reducing one's own efforts, or intention to attack, which can be deterred only by greater preparedness? Is the source of war mainly at home in economic depression and inequality, or mainly abroad in the desire for conquest? The answers of the pre–World War I and II periods are known. Unfortunately, they point in opposite directions for

Western democracies: to doing less for defense in the earlier period, and more in the latter. No prior period is a sure guide to what happens afterward—history has lessons, of course, but they are often contradictory.

BRITAIN IN THE 1920s AND 1930s
(WITH COMPARISONS TO NAZI GERMANY)

There is a common belief among historians of British rearmament that Britain's initial military performance in World War II would have been much better if the Treasury had not continued to control defense expenditures.[71] In the words of one historian, the Treasury's influence had been "excessive, dominating the arguments of the Chiefs of Staff and the Foreign Office."[72] Of course, it is quite possible that more money might have been spent on the wrong things, or could have weakened the nation economically.

Peace in 1919 marked the beginning of a period of intense political pressure on successive British governments to reduce the country's armed forces. Conscription, adopted as a wartime expedient, was abandoned and not renewed until the spring of 1939; the size of the armed forces was thus limited to the results of voluntary recruitment. The Royal Navy and Air Force were, on the whole, successful in attracting recruits, but the British Army was much less so and for most of the interwar years stayed below planned (called "establishment") levels. A more important restriction after 1919 was the popular demand for the government to reduce what were then considered to be high rates of taxation (the standard rate of income tax in 1919, six shillings on the pound, was about five times the prewar level),[73] and also to balance the budget to prevent inflation (prices had risen rapidly during the war, and continued to do so during a brief postwar boom).

Defense expenditure and interest payments on the war-swollen national debt made up the greater part of the budget during the 1920s; men of all political persuasions, therefore—were they Conservative businessmen seeking reductions in taxation, or left-wing pacifists opposed in principle to arms—could agree on the need for lower defense spending.

How far defense spending should be reduced depended on the dangers of the international situation. In 1919 the Cabinet decided to assume, for the purpose of drawing up service estimates, "that the British Empire will not be engaged in any great war during the next ten years, and that no Expeditionary Force is required for this purpose."[74] The Treasury used this "Ten-Year Rule" to compel defense departments to accept lower estimates, reduced from a total of £604 million for the three services in 1919 to £111 million in 1922. Subsequently further defense economies were made, but these, though painful to the services, did not succeed in bringing the estimates below £103 million in 1932, the interwar nadir of defense expenditure.

Britain began to reduce its defense services without waiting for any international agreement on arms limitation, with the important exception of those imposed on Germany by the Allies in 1919. A major problem of British foreign policy in the interwar period, therefore, was how to persuade other powers to limit their armed forces to levels that would afford Britain and her empire reasonable security. Consequently, in 1921 the British government eagerly accepted the invitation of President Warren Harding to participate in a disarmament conference in Washington. Because the British naval staff was alarmed at the prospect of completing no new capital ships for ten years, a compromise was reached permitting the Allied Powers to build only a limited number. Not until 1930, however, was the first London Naval Treaty (limiting cruisers, destroyers, and submarines) signed by Britain, the United States, and Japan, though not by France or Italy (who would not agree on limits).

THE DOMESTIC IMPACT ON BRITAIN

Restrictions on the Royal Navy accepted at the Washington and London Conferences have often been criticized, but it was not really the principle of parity with the United States which hampered British sea power. The underlying cause was parsimony on the part of both Conservative and Labour governments; the constraints of the annual estimates made it impossible for the Admiralty to build ships up to the limits specified in the treaty. In November 1924, Winston Churchill, then Chancellor of the Exchequer, made a determined attempt to reduce future military expenditure so as to expand (slightly) social expenditure within balanced budgets. The Treasury believed borrowing for government expenditure to be impossible, given the need to reduce the national debt and to keep foreign confidence in sterling—without which the gold standard, soon to be reestablished, could not be maintained. Given the desire for balanced budgets, and—on the part of Churchill and other ministers—for lower taxation, the Cabinet preferred domestic over defense spending.

The Cabinet was guided in its choice by the Foreign Office's view that war with Japan was unlikely so long as existing conditions prevailed in Europe. The Ten-Year Rule, extended indefinitely in 1928, was canceled only in March 1932, after Japan had invaded Manchuria the previous September.

There can be little doubt that Treasury advisers had considerable impact on the military spending cuts. Nonetheless, financial orthodoxy at home and optimism about foreign affairs were hardly the sole prerogatives of the Treasury, being shared by every British government of the period and, so far as is known, by a majority of the electorate.

From 1933 to 1938, Britain's military capacity fell behind that of Germany, which spent, it has been estimated, about three times as much for military purposes.[75] Since Germany had a greater national product than Britain, some disparity was to be expected; a fairer comparison of the military effort in the two countries is the proportion of GNP devoted to military expenditure. When the Ten-Year-Rule was canceled, the then Chancellor of the Exchequer, Neville Chamberlain (1931–37), insisted, and the Cabinet agreed, that this action alone should not be taken to justify an expansion of defense expenditure without regard to current economic difficulties.

Events in 1935 compelled the Cabinet to review the situation. German rearmament, openly proclaimed in defiance of the Versailles Treaty, was going ahead rapidly, particularly for the Luftwaffe. The British government responded by accelerating expansion of the Royal Air Force. Further increases in all three services were already under consideration when Mussolini's attack on Ethiopia emphasized the growing dangers to Britain's far-flung empire, which already faced possible threats from Germany and Japan. Attempts to halt the growing arms race had almost no success. Hitler's offer to limit the German Navy to 35 percent of the Royal Navy was accepted in the Anglo–German Naval Treaty of 1935, but Japan made it clear that it would not renew the Washington and London Naval Treaties when these ran out at the end of 1936. A second London Naval Conference in 1936 failed to replace these treaties, since Britain and the United States would not concede Japan's claim that all three powers should have a common upper limit to the size of their navies, and Japan would not settle for anything less. Disarmament treaties are not only often violated, they are frequently canceled.

At the end of 1935 Whitehall estimated that Germany was spending the equivalent of £500 million a year on rearmament outside its budget, and it was thought that this figure might double in a peak year. In the same year, British defense expenditure was £137 million, and the government did not intend to spend more than £225 million in what was anticipated would be the peak year (1938). Adoption of this rearmament program was followed almost immediately by Hitler's occupation of the Rhineland in March 1936, which represented a further sharp increase in the dangers facing Britain.

As other nations expanded their armaments, and as new weapons were developed, Chamberlain, now prime minister, and his Cabinet decided to give first priority to the defense of Britain and its trade routes, and to economize at the expense of the British Army's expeditionary force, which was no longer to be manned at levels necessary to support potential European allies at the outbreak of a war. Although the defense department's "ration" of finance was eased somewhat in February 1938, policy remained unchanged until the spring of 1939. Then British defense expenditure rose rapidly; the War Office's peacetime spending estimates doubled over the previous year's, and by the outbreak of war Britain's arms production had caught up with or exceeded Germany's, though its total armaments, a cumulative product of years of niggardly reduced spending, were still behind.

Had Britain rearmed at that rate in earlier years, inflation might have resulted—which Keynes warned was a risk in 1937—or the government might have had to impose heavier taxation, or greater controls over investment than its supporters would have tolerated, except in direct danger.[76] Inflation was an unattractive alternative. It would have increased balance-of-payments difficulties, aroused fears in financial and business circles, and exacerbated social tensions by placing the burden of rearmament upon Britain's middle- and low-income population. The Labour Party opposed government borrowing for rearmament on grounds that it would be inflationary. The Treasury did not accept this view, but a balanced budget continued to be a Treasury ideal. The alternative to greater borrowing was higher taxation. One of the main reasons Germany could spend larger sums on armaments than could Britain was the relative product of taxation. Whereas British industrialists insisted on no more than a 5 percent tax on profits, their German counterparts paid a 40 percent tax on profits, in addition to income tax. British industry's unwillingness to sacrifice discouraged the trade unions from reforming industrial practices. Neither found it convenient, given the uncertainties about Hitler's motives, to accept Winston Churchill's cries of alarm, for that would have meant abandoning business as usual.

Treasury officials had to take society and prevailing economic beliefs as they found them and give advice accordingly. Even had society been more ready to substitute guns for butter, the limits set by geography, and Britain's need to earn a living by trade, would have remained.

Hitler could escape balance-of-payments problems by seizing resources of neighboring countries; unless the British government was prepared to make a preemptive strike against Germany, British defense had to be planned on the basis (at least up to 1939) of long-term deterrence. In this context, Treasury concerns over the financial and economic limits of the arms burden played a major role.

Critics assumed that Britain ought to have been as well armed as Nazi Germany and that Britain had the means of making itself so. But industrial capacity set narrow limits on British rearmament in the short term, and comparative figures of output in key industries suggest that in the longer term Britain's capacity was inferior to Germany's.[77] In the period 1936–39, paper pounds alone could not remove industrial bottlenecks and permit Britain's rearmament to match Germany's.

The difference between proposed and actual expenditure indicates the Treasury's influence, combined with the Cabinet's own preferences. Air Ministry expenditure overtook that of the War Office in 1937 and of the Admiralty in 1938. Of course, more could have been produced for all services if the government had exerted greater control over finance and industry before the war, but it had felt unable to take such action. Had it conveyed a far greater sense of urgency about rearmament, as Churchill wished, the Chamberlain government might have persuaded public opinion. We shall never know. Whether this downplaying of perceived threat was based on a different reading of the signs or a desire to maintain a different domestic policy, or some combination of both, is also unknowable. The choice was between different services pursuing their own policies (regardless of overall policy laid down by the Cabinet), or establishing priorities in light of spending restrictions. The Treasury's use of the power of the purse forced ministers and military men to come to decisions about priorities and thereby insured that essential elements in Britain's defenses were completed first.

The United States and Germany spent one percent (or less) of their GNP for military purposes in 1929 (see Table 10), while Britain slightly exceeded this level (2 percent). America maintained the level of one percent throughout the 1930s. Britain's military expenditures rose from 3 percent of GNP in 1933 (see Table 14) to 7 percent in 1938. In Germany, however, military expenditures went up steeply in the same years, from 3 percent of GNP in 1933 to 17 percent in 1938. It may be noted that the sharpest rise in German military spending took place between 1935 and 1936 (a huge increase of 4 percent of GNP in one year), and that in 1938, for the first time, German military spend-

TABLE 14

MILITARY EXPENDITURE AS A PERCENTAGE OF GNP

GROSS NATIONAL PRODUCT AND MILITARY EXPENDITURE IN GERMANY, THE UNITED STATES, AND BRITAIN, 1929–45[78]

Year	Germany			United States			Britain		
	GNP*	Military Expenditures (Billions, Reichsmarks)	Percent	GNP†	Military Expenditures (Billions, Dollars)	Percent	National Income‡	Military Expenditures (Billions, Pounds)	Percent
1929	89	.8	1%	104	.7	1%	4.2	.1	2%
1932	58	.8	1	59	.6	1	–	.1	–
1933	59	1.9	3	56	.5	1	3.7	.1	3
1934	67	4.1	6	65	.7	1	3.9	.1	3
1935	74	6.0	8	73	.9	1	4.1	.1	2
1936	83	10.8	13	83	.9	1	4.4	.2	5
1937	93	11.7	13	91	1.0	1	4.6	.3	7
1938	105	17.2	17	85	1.0	1	4.8	.4	8
1939	130	30.0	23	91	1.3	1	5.0	1.1	22
1940	141	53.0	38	101	2.2	2	6.0	3.2	53
1941	152	71.0	47	126	13.8	11	6.8	4.1	60
1942	165	91.0	55	159	49.6	31	7.5	4.8	64
1943	184	112.0	61	193	80.4	42	8.0	5.0	63
1944				211	88.6	42	8.2	5.1	62
1945				214	75.9	36	8.3	4.4	53

* For the years 1939–43, including Austria and the Sudetenland, figures are rounded to the nearest billion.

† Figures rounded to the nearest billion.

‡ Britain's GNP may be estimated at about £1 billion above national income, resulting in a slight downward revision of the percentages calculated here. For example, military expenditures calculated against GNP would give 7% in 1938, 18% in 1939, and a peak of 57% in 1942.

ing exceeded 10 percent of GNP (a level not reached by England until after 1938, nor by the United States until 1941).

The assumption of power by the Nazis in 1933 reversed the relationship between Germany's and Britain's defense spending. The economy of Germany was still "peace oriented" in 1932. Beginning in 1936,[79] in its investments and its government expenditures, armaments dominated Germany's economy, but still this should not be called a "war economy." From 1938 on, however, that designation can legitimately be used.

THE UNITED STATES

Military expenditure in the United States did not exceed one percent of the GNP until the eve of World War II. All the armed forces were minimal in size; such personnel as remained had obsolescent equipment and little training in new modes of warfare.[80] After 1918 Americans were war-weary; a well-prepared Army was not regarded as normal. It would also be expensive. Presidents, as well as Congresses and publics, were prepared only for a very limited investment in national defense in the years between the two World Wars.

Many voices said that "the war to end all wars" had made an effective Army an unnecessary luxury. The country hoped that the United States would never again go to war. Americans aimed to gain what security was necessary not by defense but by disarmament, and through diplomatic agreements such as the Washington Naval Treaty of 1922 and the London Naval Conference of 1930. Government economy was one of the keynotes of the Harding-Coolidge administration; the armed forces were an inviting target for a reduction in expenditures. The depression of 1929 accelerated demands for curtailing military appropriations and reflected the views coming out of congressional investigations—wars were the result of a desire for profit by munitions makers. The source of aggression was presumably at home rather than abroad. Only under the spur of the dangerous international situation did the administration take important steps toward rearmament beginning in 1936 and increasingly in 1938.

FRANCE

During most of the period after World War I, France (as it does to this day) devoted a greater share of government expenditures to national defense than did the United Kingdom and the United States. Though its elites were divided on ideological grounds, French governments acted on different perceptions of disarmament. Geographically isolated from their neighbors, the British and the Americans believed that disarmament would produce security; the French, sharing a fragile boundary with traditionally hostile powers, thought that security should precede disarmament. As against the British—who aspired to base European peace on a community of relatively disarmed states, mutually confident about the intentions of all—the French wished to guarantee peace by arming themselves and their allies.[81] There was, however, no domestic consensus in France regarding the proper approach. Until 1936 rearmament was mainly advocated by the right, whereas the left called for conciliation and reliance on the League of Nations for French security.[82] These ideological-political pressures against military spending, bolstered by the sustained economic decline in the 1930s, which reduced the absolute size of the national economy,[83] limited France's capacity to equip and support an effective military establishment, and generated widespread disillusionment with the Third Republic itself.

Against the claims that Léon Blum's government (after 1936) had insured the subsequent defeat by hindering rearmament, Parker[84] contends that a serious French effort to rearm began only when the Popular Front government came to power. Whereas in the early 1930s a major proportion of French resources was devoted to fortification (the Maginot Line), the Blum administration began reequipping the Army, though French industrial capacity limited the arms buildup. In 1939 there were real weaknesses in French armed forces, especially in the Air Force. Consequently, a heated debate has emerged over whether it was relative lack of arms or collapse of will that led to the rout of the French Army. As students of political culture, however, we are inclined to place greater emphasis on morale. The terrible losses and disruption caused by fighting on French territory were within living memory.

EFFECTS OF WORLD WAR II
IN THE UNITED STATES AND BRITAIN

The disruption caused by past relationships has future effects.[85] During World War II, some nations, like France, were occupied; others, Japan and Germany, were defeated. To assess the effects of that war on subsequent spending and taxing, we must focus on the United States and Britain, which alone maintained political continuity.

Requiring mobilization on a scale without precedent, the war brought a massive increase in expenditure. Spending in the United

States during 1940–46 reached $391.1 billion—ten times the amount spent in World War I. Wartime expenditure was about nine times higher than during the interwar period, and in the first three post–World War II years the average was about five times higher than just before the war.

The biggest items in U.S. spending in 1940 were social welfare (37.3 percent), economic development (22.0 percent), military spending (17.0 percent), and interest (11.5 percent). This pre–World War II pattern shows some difference from spending before World War I: the proportion of social spending in the federal budget had increased during the 1930s.

The magnitude of postwar military spending reflects not only America's vast involvement in World War II, but also its changing role in world politics. Along with foreign aid, eruption of the Cold War with the Soviet Union in the late forties caused military spending to be sustained, and then expanded in the fifties during and after the war in Korea. The lesson learned from the First World War was that the United States had to assume an international role, especially by becoming part of the United Nations, in order to secure collective security. The lesson learned from the Second World War was that a strong defense and early intervention were the best safeguards. These were not the only possible "lessons," but they combined to secure a much higher level of arms spending after World War II than after the first war.

The Great Depression transformed federal finance; as it created demand for government to help the economy recover, deficit spending was recognized as an instrument of economic stabilization. The justification for increased spending lay in doctrines of compensatory fiscal policy. However, in no way was high spending over the long run seen as normal activity of central government. As late as 1938 and 1939, some political figures and economists spoke of paying off debt and balancing the budget.

Table 15 displays U.S. defense spending after World War II in order to show that the U.S. did not return to isolationism as it did after World War I. The military's share of total government spending looks relatively high after World War I only because there was very little social spending. After World War II, the United States still had to pay for the social programs started up during the depression. Thus, the increase of the defense portion of the budget after World War II, compared to World War I, is all the more significant evidence of the United States's intention to maintain a prepared military. The large

TABLE 15

U.S. ALLOCATES MORE EXPENDITURE TO DEFENSE AFTER WWII[86]

DEFENSE EXPENDITURES AS A PERCENTAGE OF TOTAL
GOVERNMENT EXPENDITURE

Number of years After last year of war	Post-WWI	Post-WWII
0	73.4%	72.5%
1	62.9	35.4
2	51.0	35.8
3	28.3	32.3
4	21.7	31.1
5	22.4	49.2
6	20.5	64.8

increases in the fifth and sixth years are due to the Korean War of 1950 to 1952.

The character of the budget changed as budget-balancing policies broadened to include economic management. The assumption of a flexible and automatic relationship between the budget and the economy meant betting that present deficit spending would mean future economic recovery.

Keynesian theory, which justified increased spending as a means of creating demand, made it difficult for politicians to face the loss of services available for constituents if spending were to be cut.

World War II also produced an unprecedentedly high level of taxation in the United States. Exclusive of the Federal Old Age and Survivors Insurance Trust Fund, revenues were $5.3 billion in 1940; during the war they increased eight times up to $40 billion. (By contrast, from 1931 to 1940, receipts had increased only 1.6 times.)[87] These revenues covered 45 percent of the total war expenditure, compared to the World War I record of 30 percent. The rest was financed by borrowing. (This portion, 55 percent, was lower by far than the 70 percent of expenditure borrowed during World War I.) Sale of war debt to wage earners aimed to control inflation by reducing disposable income, besides raising money to pay for the war.

The war brought a permanent change in the structure and incidence of the individual income tax. Need to raise revenue to pay for the war, together with efforts to control inflation, led to deliberate expansion of the tax base—by lowering the level of earned income liable to tax, by raising rates significantly, especially at high income levels, and by instituting mandatory withholding by employers of taxes on earned income. (Before withholding was adopted in 1942, those liable to income tax made voluntary declarations of taxes due and paid quarterly installments.) In 1939 progressive rates ranged from 4 percent in the lowest bracket (between $1,500 and $4,000 of earned income, depending on marital status) to 79 percent in the highest (over $1 million). During the peak tax years, 1944–45, the lowest bracket, now reduced to between $750 and $2,000, paid 23 percent of earned income. The highest bracket, cut sharply from prewar levels to $200,000, paid at maximum rates of 94 percent of adjusted gross income (earned income minus exemptions and deductions).[88] After the war, rates declined somewhat, but never again to prewar levels. The income tax became a mass tax, the fiscal bastion of an expanding federal establishment. Highly productive in the rapid growth years following the war, the income tax permitted central government to increase its spending.

There was learning from history. Compared to World War I and its aftermath, lower borrowing and higher taxes during the second war did limit the inflation rate.[89] Interest payments, therefore, were not so large a proportion in budgets as after World War I. In 1923 interest payments represented 40 percent of total spending, while in 1948 they came to only 13.5 percent.

In Britain, the war caused expenditure (most of which, 70–80 percent, was military) to grow to four times the prior level.[90] The general pattern of British spending before and after the war was roughly the same, although social-service expenditure increased considerably after labor's victory in 1946, and defense declined.[91]

With overwhelming support for the war against Nazi Germany, it became easier to justify taxation. The only question was one of technique. Theory and elite consensus led to higher income taxes levied at progressive rates for financing Britain's war. In contrast to the 30–35 percent of tax-supported financing during the First World War, 52 percent of total World War II expenditure was financed by taxation.[92] This meant a tax level 3.4 times higher in 1946 than in 1939.

World War II intensified the "inspection process"—whereby the nation took a good look at its human services—and social spending grew. As Titmus says:

> This [expanding medical service] would not have come about but for the second World War and the Labor government. The first supplied the decisive motive power, the second the will. One of the lessons of the war, as a citizens' war, was the popular demand for the abolition of the poor law; of ineligible citizens; of personally

merited disease; of inequality before the best ascertained laws of health.[93]

The disruption of war, including the evacuation of children from London to rural areas, led to a far greater intermingling of economic classes and thus a far more personal awareness of the condition of the poor.

The Assumptions of Post–World War II Budgeting

After World War II, ministers of finance, whose interests and expertise were concentrated in economic policy, became almost exclusively concerned with managing the economy; controlling spending was a secondary purpose of government budgets. This change in roles was itself a product of a more momentous transformation: everywhere, though more so in Europe than in the United States, government had become preoccupied with changing society, not with controlling itself. Though government faced outward toward society, its budgetary procedures continued to reflect its older orientation toward internal control. Within these older forms, however, central budgetary procedures were becoming more concerned with relating spending to economic management than with the substance of spending itself.

In stable times, assumptions taken for granted are as important as (or more important than) those explicitly recognized. In most of Europe and the United States, after the initial fear of postwar depression proved unfounded, rapid economic growth in stable economies was expected to continue indefinitely. Keynesian doctrine of economic stabilization by means of countercyclical spending triumphed everywhere. Its precepts dictated that when unemployment and output indices indicated the economy was beginning to slow down, governments should borrow, incurring deficits if necessary, and should spend the proceeds to stimulate the economy. Manipulation of discount rates and tax cuts targeted to specific sectors were part of overall strategy to promote economic revival. Once recovery set in and an economy began to heat up, government should retire debt, raise discount rates, and repeal recent tax incentives.

So powerful was the faith in the feasibility of economic fine-tuning and of its potential for sustaining economic stability, that few if any mainstream advisers to governments in those days considered the possibility of having to make cuts in spending. Although the political difficulty of cutting was still recognized, expecting the expansion to go on indefinitely, no one worried much about how to implement reductions.

Under Keynesian doctrine as understood and practiced at the time, the idea was to balance the economy at full employment (between 3 and 5 percent of "frictional" unemployment), not necessarily to balance the budget. To the extent, therefore, that budgetary calculations depended upon a known relationship between revenue and expenditure, the pillars of stability on which the relationships rested were severely shaken. If (or rather when, in view of historical experience) economic growth declined, clearly the assumed sources of budgetary predictability would decline with it.

In an uncertain world, stability is elusive; in this respect, governments' situation between the end of World War II and the early 1960s was not too different from what it had always been. In view of the doctrinal differences among present-day advocates of macroeconomic management and proponents of old and less direct monetary strategies for modulating oscillation in levels of economic activity, a counterfactual historian might ask what could or would have happened during the two decades following World War II if governments had not intervened. Comparing fluctuations in output and employment levels in the United States between 1854 and 1980, studies by the National Bureau of Economic Research and the Commerce Department reveal that during the post–World War II period of active effort to stabilize the U.S. economy, both the amplitude and the duration of fluctuations in GNP were smaller than for earlier business cycles. Before World War I, for example, downturns lasted on the average twenty-two months and expansions twenty-four months. Between the wars (counting the Great Depression) expansions averaged twenty six months and contractions twenty months. After 1945 (and up to 1973) expansions lasted more than three times as long as contractions. Added to the high overall growth rates after 1945, demand management through the 1960s did seem to make a difference. During the 1974–75 recession (the worst in the previous thirty years), real output fell by 20 percent compared to about 50 percent in 1907, 33 percent in 1920, and 60 percent in 1929.[94] Eventually, "stagflation," an insidious combination of inflation and unemployment, undermined easy confidence in Keynesian demand management. Whether stagflation was a direct consequence of Keynesian policy or of failure to follow it is still subject to dispute.

With no threat of constrained resources, conflict management proved to be the main theme of post–World War II budgeting. The aim was to keep things quiet, whether by interpersonal trust, as in Britain, or by stronger hierarchical control, as in France, or by social norms stressing harmony, as in Japan.[95] Now, conflict reduction may not be everyone's idea of the good life. In view of the inequities some citizens perceived in social relations, they may well have believed there was too little conflict. Our observation is that budgeting does not go against the grain of contemporary forces. On the contrary, it overidentifies with them. However great societal stability may have seemed in the 1950s and early 1960s, budgetary processes reinforced prevailing tendencies. Budgeting was like the rest of social life, only more so.

The process of budgeting became introspective rather than critical. The question of "How much?" was transmuted into "What for?"—as if there would always be enough. How best to spend was the question; so the search for the best method of budgeting got under way. None of the new budgeting methods attempted to limit total spending, except for what might follow from greater efficiency in attaining desired objectives. Either totals were considered to be under control or they were thought not to matter. The belief that control had been achieved turned out to be a delusion; the conviction that it didn't matter was revealing of the temper of the times.

COORDINATION BY ROLE

The most powerful coordinating mechanisms in budgeting undoubtedly stem from the roles adopted by the major participants. Roles—the expectations of behavior attached to institutional positions—are calculating mechanisms. In American national government during this era, the administrative agencies acted as advocates of increased expenditure; the Bureau of the Budget (later, in 1965, to be the Office of Management and Budget) acted as presidential servant with a cutting bias; the House Appropriations Committee functioned as a guardian of the Treasury; and the Senate Appropriations Committee served as an appeals court to which agencies carried their disagreements with House action. The roles meshed, and set up a stable pattern of mutual expectations, which markedly reduced the burden of calculation for participants. The agencies did not have to worry about how their requests affected the President's overall program; they knew that such criteria would be introduced by the Budget Bureau. Since the agencies could be depended upon to advance all the programs for which there was prospect of support, the Budget Bureau and the appropriations committees could concentrate on fitting them into the President's overall plan, or paring them down.[96]

A writer on Canadian budgeting refers to the tendency for an administrator to become "an enthusiastic advocate" of increased funds for his policies.[97] When disagreements over departmental budgets arose, as they frequently do in private firms, the controller and the departmental representatives came to a meeting armed to the teeth to defend their respective positions.[98] The same interministerial battles went on in Great Britain,[99] the Netherlands,[100] and the Soviet Union; "serious clashes" arose when ministries and republics wanted greater funding for their plans.[101] Indeed, in Britain, ministers were judged by the ability to defend their "corner," i.e., to get more money for their departments.[102]

Civil servants are expected to support the programs entrusted to them. What would we think of a state forester who loved to see wilderness converted into highways or welfare workers who wanted to cut programs for the poor or soldiers who favored unilateral disarmament? Indeed, just the opposite accusation—bureaucrats refusing to go along with redistributive programs rather than welcoming them—has often been made. As our cultural analysis of the growth of government in the final chapter should make clear, it is the people and the politicians who want these programs, not bureaucrats who somehow impose higher spending on an innocent and unwilling populace. Caught up in the rules of program and agency advocacy, of course, bureaucrats play their part. They do participate in raising spending. Were the political process organized so as to make it worthwhile for them to ask for less, there is good reason to believe that as faithful servants they would do that too. If today some of us see these experts as the problem, whereas Jeremy Bentham and the reformers of an earlier age saw them as the solution, that is not because bureaucrats have let us down but rather because they have done their job, a job much bigger than anyone in earlier times envisaged, only too well.[103]

Agency heads, W. Drees[104] points out, can defend the interests of their sectors because, since it is so hard to relate their modest portion of total spending to the overall budgetary situation, anything they might save through a spirit of forbearance would be too small to make the sacrifice worthwhile. From their point of view, total expenditures are irrelevant. It follows that those who would make serious efforts to limit spending must confront such advocates with a fixed total for the entire budget so that it is clear that more for one agency and program means less for others. This was the significance of the doctrine of budget balance. The absence of limits is a good indicator of the desire to increase spending.

The role of guardian or defender of the public treasury did not come naturally. In all nations during the early days, as our history shows, government finance served private purposes. Without much restraint, the private financiers governments relied on to provide loans and collect taxes appropriated the spoils of the nation and used for their own profit funds intended for the treasury. The only restraint lay in the understanding that when their plundering exceeded the measure of tolerance, they might be thrown into jail or even executed. For governments, such action was a summary procedure of control *a posteriori*.[105] It took centuries to develop a finance minister such as Louis Thiers, whose definition of his role specified that "ferocity" was "needed to defend the Treasury."[106]

Until the mid-1960s, members of the U.S. House Appropriations Committee considered themselves guardians of the Treasury; they took pride in how often they could reduce spending estimates.[107] They reconciled this role with the defense of constituency interests by cutting estimates to satisfy one role, and generally increasing amounts spent over the previous year's total to satisfy the other.

Among legislatures of the world, generally, acceptance of the guardianship role appears to be quite rare. During the mid-1950s, for example, legislative specialists concerned with finance in the Netherlands were defending policy areas over which they had jurisdiction by advocating higher appropriations—an advocacy that transcended party lines.[108] Much the same thing happened in France during the Fourth Republic.[109] It may be that guardianship depends, first, on appropriations committees with continuing power to affect outcomes—a rare phenomenon in the modern world—and, second, on the development of cultural values and legislative mores that support an insistent financial check on the bureaucracy. Legislative committees in such nations as Mexico (where virtually complete budgetary power is in the hands of the President, who heads the single party[110]), or Great Britain (where party responsibility overwhelms parliamentary initiative[111]), are hardly in a position to develop a role of guardianship.

WHY THE LINE-ITEM BUDGET LASTED, AND SOME RECENT COMPETITORS FOR ORGANIZING BUDGETS

The main concern of governmental budgeting during most of the period after the end of the Second World War, both before and after 1960, was to find proper methods for resource allocation. By itself, this concentration on form tells us a good deal. Concern over rising expenditures was sublimated into a search for the right technique. Presumably, during this era of stability, the ends of government spending were less in question than were the best ways to achieve them. This was no-where more evident than in social security, which, despite its immense size, was often contained in a separate account outside the formal budget. Only later, under less favorable economic conditions, were so-cial entitlements to become subjects of significant debate.

Whatever the differences among Western democracies, these nations retained one thing in common in the way they budgeted: line-item budgeting was nearly universal. Yet, many competitive methods had arisen. Why, then, did this oldest of all budgetary methods survive?

Over the last century, the line-item budget has been condemned as mindless, because its lines do not match programs; irrational, because the items deal with inputs instead of outputs; shortsighted, because budgets cover one year instead of many; fragmented, because, as a rule, only changes are reviewed; conservative, because these changes tend to be small.[112] Despite these faults, real and alleged, the line-item budget reigns supreme virtually everywhere, in practice if not in the-ory. Why?

Having grown out of nineteenth-century reforms in financial man-agement within governments, the line-item budget is a product of his-tory, not of logic. It was not so much created as evolved. Its procedures and purposes represent accretions over time rather than propositions postulated at any single moment in time.

Attaining control over public money, and accountability of spenders to public authority, were among the earliest purposes of budgeters. Ability to plan by knowing what will be available to spend over time enhanced financial stability. Relating expenditure to revenue was of prime importance from the beginning. In our day, spending is varied to suit the economy. After World War II the need for money came to be used as a lever to enhance the efficiency or effectiveness of policies. He who pays the piper hopes to call the tune. Here we have it: budgeting is supposed simultaneously to contribute to continuity (for planning), to change (for policy analysis), to flexibility (for the economy), and to ri-gidity (for limited spending).

These different and (to some extent) opposed purposes contain a clue to the perennial dissatisfaction with expenditure budgeting. Ob-viously no process can simultaneously provide stability and change, ri-gidity and flexibility. And no one should be surprised that those who concentrate on one purpose or the other should find budgeting unsat-isfactory; or that, as purposes change, these criticisms should become perpetual. The real surprise is that line-item budgeting has not been replaced in recent years by any of its outstanding competitors. Perhaps the complaints are the clue: just what is it that is inferior for most purposes and yet superior over all?

The ability of a process to score high on one criterion may increase the likelihood of its scoring low on another. Planning requires predictability and economic management requires reversibility. There may well be no ideal mode of budgeting.

Traditional budgeting is annual (repeated yearly); it is incremental (departing marginally from the year before); it is conducted on a cash basis (in current currency); and its content comes in the form of line items (such as personnel or maintenance). Alternatives to all these characteristics have been developed and tried, though never, as far as we know, with success. Why this should be so, despite the obvious and admitted defects of tradition, will emerge as we consider the criteria each type of budgetary process has to meet.

UNIT OF MEASUREMENT: CASH OR VOLUME

Budgeting can be done not only in cash but by volume. Instead of promising to pay so much in the next year or years, the commitment can be made in terms of operations performed or services provided. Why might anyone want to budget in this way? One reason is to aid planning. If public agencies know they can count not only on variable currency but on what the currency can buy—that is, on a volume of activity—they can plan ahead as far as the budget runs. Indeed, if, to help assure consistency over time, one wished to make decisions now that would otherwise be made at future periods, then stability in the unit of effort—so many applications processed—is the very consideration to be desired.

So long as purchasing power remains constant, budgeting in cash or by volume remains a distinction without difference. However, should the value of money fluctuate (and, in our time, this means inflation), the public budget must absorb additional amounts so as to provide the designated volume of activity. Given large and unexpected changes in prices, the size of the budget in cash terms can fluctuate wildly. Budgeters can lose control of money because they have to supply whatever is needed. Evidently, no government could permit itself to be so far out of control. Hence, the very stability that budgeting by volume is designed to achieve turns out to be its major unarticulated premise.

What budgeting by volume says, in effect, is that the public sector will be protected against inflation by getting its agreed level of services before other needs are met. Who pays the price of budgeting by volume? The private sector and the central controller. Budgeting by volume is an effort by elements of the public sector to invade the private sector. In the clash between individualism and collectivism, volume budgeting loads the dice in favor of the latter. The real resources necessary to close the gap between projected and current prices must come from the private sector in the form of taxation or interest paid for borrowing. In other words, for the public sector, volume budgeting is a form of indexing against inflation.

Given an irreducible amount of uncertainty in the system, not every element can be stabilized at one and the same time. Who, then, will be kept stable and who will have to bear the costs of change? Within government the obvious answer, until the late 1940s, was that the treasury would be protected; afterward, it was decided that spending by agencies would be kept whole. The central budget office (the Treasury, the Ministry of Finance, or the Office of Management and Budget, as it is variously called)—i.e., the instrument of hierarchy—bears the brunt of covering larger expenditures, and it takes the blame when the budget goes out of control by rising faster and in different directions than predicted. In Britain, where budgeting by volume in the 1960s went under the name of the Public Expenditure Survey, the Treasury finally responded to years of severe inflation by imposing cash spending limits in the 1970s. Of course, departmental cash limits do include an amount for price changes, but this is not necessarily what the Treasury expects, but rather the amount it desires. Spending departments must make up deficits caused by inflation. Instead of the Treasury forking over the money automatically, as in the volume budget, departments will have to ask for more and may be denied. Departmental spenders, not central controllers, have to pay the price of monetary instability.[113]

TIME SPAN: MONTHS, ONE YEAR, MANY YEARS

Multiyear budgeting has long been proposed as a reform: advocates maintain that it can enhance rational choice by presenting problems of resource allocation in a long-term perspective. Considering only one year, it has been argued, leads to shortsightedness because only the next year's expenditures are reviewed: One-year budgets foster overspending because huge disbursements in future years cannot be foreseen. And because incremental changes cannot take account of larger future vistas, one-year budgets foster conservatism. Also, because problems tend to be viewed in isolation rather than against future costs in relation to expected revenue, one-year budgets contribute to parochialism. Extending the time span of budgeting to three or five years, it

is argued, would permit long-range planning to overtake short-term reaction and would substitute financial control for merely muddling
through. The practice of stepping up spending to use up resources before the end of the budgetary year, moreover, would decline.

The longer the term of the budget, the more significant inflation becomes. To the extent that price changes are automatically absorbed
into budgets, a certain volume of activity is guaranteed. But to the extent that agencies have to absorb inflation over time, their real level of
activity declines. Budgeting in cash terms diminishes the relative size
of the public sector, leaving the private sector larger. This is precisely
why the Thatcher government in Britain has adopted it. Behind discussions of the span of the budget, the real debate is over the relative
shares of public and private sectors—which will be asked to absorb inflation, and which will be allowed to expand into the other. Individualism and collectivism are in contention.

A similar issue of relative shares is created within government by
proposals to budget in *some* sectors for several years, and in others for
only one year. This poses the question of which sectors of policy are to
be exposed to the vicissitudes of life in the short term, and which are to
be protected from stress. Like any other device, multiyear budgeting is
not neutral, but distributes indulgences differently among the affected
interests.

Of course, multiyear budgeting has its positive aspects. If control of
expenditure is the goal, for instance, a multiyear budget makes it necessary to estimate spending far into the future. The old camel's-nose
tactic—beginning with small expenditures while hiding larger ones to
come later—becomes more difficult to execute. Still, hard in, as the
British learned, often implies harder out. Once an expenditure gets
into a multiyear projection, it is likely to stay in because it has become
part of an interrelated set of proposals that could be expensive to dis-
rupt. British experience shows that reductions in future years (which
are always iffy) are easily traded for maintenance of spending in the
all-important present.

Suppose, however, that it were deemed desirable to reduce some expenditures significantly in order to increase others. Due to the built-in
pressure of continuing commitments, what can be done in a single year
is extremely limited. Making arrangements over a three- to five-year
period would permit larger changes in amount in a more orderly way.
With constant prices, 5 percent a year for five years compounded
would bring about a one-third change in the budget. But other things
seldom remain equal. In the 1960s, when the British were working

under a five-year budget projection, prices and production could barely be predicted for five months at a time.

Given economic volatility and theoretical poverty, the ability to outguess the future is extremely limited. Responsiveness to changing economic conditions, therefore, if that were the main purpose of budgeting, would be facilitated with a budget calculated in months or weeks rather than in years. Under the volatile conditions beginning in the mid-1970s, a budget whose premises could be accepted for a whole year would have been quite an accomplishment. Such short-term budgets do exist in poor and uncertain countries. Caiden and Wildavsky have called the process "repetitive budgeting" to signify that the budget may be made and remade several times during one year.[114] Because finance ministries often do not know how much is actually in the nation's treasury or what they will have to spend, they hold off making decisions until the last possible moment. The repetitive budget is not a reliable guide to proposed expenditure, but an invitation to agencies to "get it if they can." When economic or political conditions change, as so often happens, the budget is renegotiated. Adaptiveness is maximized, but predictability is minimized.

CALCULATION: INCREMENTAL OR COMPREHENSIVE

The main modern alternatives to the line-item approach are planning, programming, and budgeting (PPB), and zero-base budgeting (ZBB). With its cross-hatch of columns and numbers specifying who can do how much, the line-item method that exemplifies hierarchy has been challenged by the market methods of PPB and by the sectarian rejection of the immediate past that is exemplified by ZBB.

Program budgeting requires a structure in which all policies related to common objectives can be compared for cost and effectiveness. Based on analogies to economic markets, PPB has the focus on competition and result common to a culture of individualism. Any combination of resources is all right if it produces a good result. According to David Novick, perhaps the leading exponent of PPB in its early days in the U.S. Department of Defense (the mid-1960s), the idea was generated during World War II. Military performance (in areas like bombing, and antisubmarine warfare) was improved by using simple, quantitative models that, in some instances, proved better than existing "seat-of-the-pants" methods of search.[115] Activity bundles replaced military targets in this civilian version of modeling.

As its designation implies, zero-base budgeting (ZBB) suggests that each year each item expenditure will be considered anew, from the ground up, as if there had been no yesterday. ZBB was intended as a method of cost control.[116] In concept, however, ZBB belongs to the culture of sectarianism, whose leitmotif is rejection of established orders of society. Deliberately abandoning past patterns of decision, as ZBB is supposed to do, gives a concrete cast to the views of those who would build the world (a world that must be horribly flawed) anew each year. Following its political mentor, President Jimmy Carter, ZBB is a born-again budget doctrine.

Let us think of PPB as embodying *horizontal* comprehensiveness—comparing alternative expenditure packages to decide which best contributes to larger programmatic objectives. ZBB, by contrast, might be thought of as manifesting *vertical* comprehensiveness: Every year alternative expenditures from base zero are considered for all governmental activities or objectives treated as discrete entities. In brief, PPB compares alternative programs, ZBB compares alternative fundings.

ZBB is an ahistorical information system. The past, as reflected in the budgetary base (common expectations as to amounts and types of funding), is explicitly rejected: there is no yesterday; nothing is to be taken for granted. At every period everything is subject to searching scrutiny. Consequently, calculations become unmanageable. To say that a budgetary process is ahistorical is to say that nothing can be settled. Old quarrels resurface. Doing without history is a little like abolishing memory—momentarily convenient, perhaps, but ultimately embarrassing.

Insofar as financial control is concerned, ZBB and PPB raise the question, "Control over what?" Is it control over the content of programs, or the efficiency of a given program, or the total costs of government, or just the legality of expenditures? How far control extends, however, depends on the form of financing, a matter to which we now turn.

APPROPRIATIONS VERSUS TREASURY BUDGETING

A traditional budget depends on traditional practice—authorization and appropriation to departments followed by departmental expenditures that are post-audited by external authorities. Yet in many countries traditional budgeting is not, in fact, the main form of public spending. More than half of public spending in the United States, and even more in Europe, does not take the form of appropriations budgeting, but of budgeting by the treasury. We find this nomenclature useful in avoiding the pejorative connotations of what would otherwise be called "backdoor" spending—that is, spending that bypasses the appropriations process through automatic disbursement of funds by the treasury.

For present discussion, the three forms of treasury budgeting that constitute alternatives to traditional appropriations are: loan guarantees, tax expenditures, and entitlements. Providing a guaranteed loan lowers interest rates and is therefore equivalent to a cash subsidy. Guarantees are worth money. Concessions granted to individuals—in the form of tax reductions for home ownership, or college tuition, or medical expenses—are equivalent to budgetary expenditures, except that the money is deflected at the source.

Entitlements, our third category of treasury budgeting, mandate that anyone eligible for certain benefits must be paid, whether or not enough has been budgeted. Until the legislation is changed or a "cap" limits total expenditure, entitlements constitute obligations of the state through direct drafts on the treasury.

Obviously, treasury budgeting leaves a great deal to be desired in controlling costs of programs, which depend on such variables as benefit level set in prior years and rate of application by potential beneficiaries. The most significant outcome of such practice is that departments are mere conduits for spending, not controllers. The premise of traditional budgetary control, that if you control the departments you control spending, is no longer helpful because the money is not being spent by departments.

For purposes of economic management, treasury budgeting is a mixed bag. It is useful in providing what are called automatic stabilizers. When it is deemed desirable not to make new decisions every time conditions change, an entitlement enables funds to flow according to the size of the problem. The difficulty is that not all entitlements are countercyclical (child benefits, for example, may rise independently of economic conditions), and the loss in financial flexibility generated by entitlements may hurt if the time ever comes to do less. Indeed, if budgeting means resource allocation, while entitlement signifies resource addition, budgeting and entitlement may be incompatible.

WHY THE TRADITIONAL BUDGET LASTS

Every criticism of line-item budgeting is undoubtedly correct. It is incremental rather than comprehensive; it does fragment decisions; it is heavily historical, looking backward more than forward; it is indifferent about objectives. Why, then, has traditional budgeting lasted so long? Because it has the virtue of its defects.

Line-item budgeting makes calculations easy precisely because it is not comprehensive. History provides a strong basis on which to rest a case. The present is related to the past, which may be known, instead of the future, which cannot be comprehended. Choices that might cause conflict are fragmented, so that not all difficulties need be faced at one time. Budgeters may have objectives, but the budget itself is organized around activities or functions. One can change objectives, then, without challenging organizational survival. Line-item budgeting does not demand analysis of policy, but neither does it inhibit it. Because it is neutral in regard to policy, traditional budgeting is compatible with a variety of policies, all of which can be converted into line items.

Budgeting several times a year can aid economic adjustment, but also creates chaos in departments, disorders calculations, and exacerbates conflict. Multiyear budgeting enhances planning at the expense of adjustment, accountability, and, possibly, price volatility. Budgeting by volume and entitlement also aids planning in government at the cost of control. Budgeting becomes spending. Traditional budgeting lasts, then, because it is simpler, easier, more controllable, more flexible than modern alternatives like PPB, ZBB, and treasury budgeting, such as indexed entitlements.

A final criterion has not been mentioned, because it is inherent in the multiplicity of others—namely, adaptability. To be useful a budgetary process should perform tolerably well under all conditions. It must perform under the unexpected—deficits and surpluses, inflation and deflation, economic growth and economic stagnation. Because budgets are supposed to be contracts within government signifying agreed understandings, and signals to the world outside government—so that others will know how to adapt to what government is likely to do—budgets must be good (though not necessarily great) for all seasons. Traditional budgeting has lasted long not because it succeeds brilliantly on every criterion, but because it does not entirely fail on any one.

"Fool's gold," which Irwin Gillespie aptly calls "the Quest for a [he might have written, "the one and only best"] Method of Evaluating Government Spending,"[117] underlines not only the limited knowledge applied to budgeting but also its cultural components. Far from being neutral, each method favors a different culture: markets (PPB), sects (ZBB), and hierarchies (line item). Each has different distributional consequences. The "who gets how much" of budgeting matters, not only its efficiency. These methods are political as well as analytical.[118] The way they operate depends on how the larger political system structures choice. The presence or absence of global spending limits, for instance, makes a big difference, as the varying experiences and methods used by President Elsenhower and Secretary of Defense McNamara will reveal in the next chapter. When attention changes from how much to how best to spend, a revolution in budgeting is in the making.

If everyone badly wants to do something, one would think that someone, somewhere, actually would do it. While dealing with differences among budgetary procedures, we have failed to see that what they shared was far more important: there was no longer an understood, though informal, limit on rates of taxation or levels of expenditure. Hence increases for one agency or program do not detract from another. Why, then, should any agency (or interest) restrain its spending demands?

Chapter Nine

THE GROWTH OF THE WELFARE AND TAX STATES: FROM THE 1960s UNTIL TODAY

BUDGETING IN TURBULENT TIMES

It is often tempting to regard one's own times as unique, but the financial crisis of the Western world in the 1980s *is* different in some respects from anything that went on before. The level of public spending is much, much higher than it ever has been. Besides requiring far larger revenues and more extensive spending controls, the sheer size of the task of getting and spending creates not only quantitative but qualitative differences. Relationships among participants in the process are harder to change, because there are so many of them and they are so highly interconnected. It is not just that taxes are high and therefore pressure to lower them (or to keep them from growing higher) is intense; in a densely packed policy environment, taxes tend to conflict—an increase here leads to lower yield there, a phenomenon called "fiscal cannibalism." It is well and good to impose some form of national sales tax, for example, but, by restraining consumption, it may inhibit economic activity, which will raise unemployment, which in turn reduces receipts from income and payroll taxes. When wage negotiations are tied to the level of welfare benefits—through negotiations on income policies between government and unions—the difficulty of changing either one is multiplied.

The changing and expanding role of government itself is a—perhaps the—major force influencing policy change. No longer limited to its traditional role—provider of national defense, justice, and a few other narrowly defined and widely agreed-upon services—government has branched out. It helps manage the economy, redistributes income, provides social welfare, and otherwise affects citizens' behavior. And the more opportunities government provides, the more outside interests are motivated to put pressure on government.

During the 1950s, '60s, and early '70s, paying for new programs and enhanced spending on old ones were not serious problems for governments of nations whose productivity produced steadily rising revenue, adequate to cover most spending. (When deficits occurred, as happened after 1960, borrowing could be and was rationalized as a countercyclical measure.) After the late 1960s, it is apparent in retrospect, inflation masked declines in productivity. As rising incomes pushed taxpayers into higher income tax brackets and as they spent more, government revenues went up, producing what Richard Rose calls fiscal buoyancy. For each percentage increase in individual income, government revenues went up 11.6 percent.[1] Thus legislators and tax policymakers did not have to take actions (raising taxes) sure to be unpopular with constituents. When taxpayers new to the highest brackets complained they paid too much, government moved toward indexing—tying tax brackets and rates (as well as benefit levels of some government programs) to changing price levels. As indexing became hierarchy's settled policy, policymakers were further insulated from liability for change—either up or down.[2] The trouble was that indexing expenditures led to increases in spending, while indexing tax brackets leads to a decrease in revenues.

But by the late 1970s and early 1980s, budgeting in most Western nations became so overwhelming a task that it had to be done several times a year, for no budget lasted more than a few months. In nations whose programs were indexed against many things, departments watched the budget being invalidated automatically. They were on an escalator, and it went in only one direction—up. Resource allocation became resource addition. The central budget unit had to find funds to finance price changes, higher interest rates, wage settlements, and all the rest. When the budget office clamped down, unprotected programs bore the brunt of turbulence. They were kept on a short string, by preauditing, monthly apportionments, and hiring and travel freezes, for example—not necessarily because these maneuvers were desirable in themselves, but because they saved money in the short run. Naturally, the beneficiaries of these programs protested. They wanted to move into the protected category, or to move out of the budget altogether by being funded from earmarked taxes. Consequently, as its room for maneuver decreased while its proportion of the national product increased, the central budget unit, compelled by circumstances, frequently tried to ratchet the budget down.

But repetitive budgeting was only the beginning. Because the budget was never really fixed for the year, spending departments acted accordingly. Afraid that their funds would be taken away, departments kept up legislative pressure all year long, instead of just at the beginning. The budget thus became a starting point for negotiations instead of a commitment. Not only were there more claimants for government funds, they made claims more often, and with greater tenacity, than before. With no distinction between the "off" and "on" budget season, the central budget unit led a chaotic existence.

Spending departments also experienced difficulties. Client demands for additional benefits had increased after every past commitment. Thus, to their constituents, departments' inability to meet new demands connoted failure. Departments could be responsive—by transferring their problems to the central budget office. To make their position impregnable, departments sought funding through the panoply of modern devices—entitlements, loans and guarantees, and off-budget corporations.

Trying to accommodate to new conditions, government officials were forced to take actions whose results they could not control. Higher taxes not only lowered the government's popularity, but caused higher prices (reflected in the cost of living), and indexing of government benefits led to increased spending as well. Inflation served as a major policy instrument. What the government could not do directly— lower the cost of its debt, reduce the real value of wage increases, and redistribute income—it tried to do indirectly, all the while relying on what it understood very well were temporary expedients.

In earlier decades, conditions had helped cushion the financial impact of big government. Increased spending was supported both by accumulated productivity and by economic growth. In addition, during the 1960s and most of the 1970s there were significant transfers in real spending from defense to social welfare. With a surplus in social-security funds, benefits could be raised significantly with small increases in payroll taxes. When inflation took hold, taxes automatically provided more money without need to legislate change; thus inflation was good business for government. Where all else failed, governments could borrow to finance deficits that at first were small in relation to national product.

All that has changed. Financing government from growth is possible only if there is growth. Defense has been used up as a source of transfer for domestic spending; indeed, defense spending is rising. Social-security funds are being depleted. That fewer people are working to support an ever growing pool of beneficiaries is not merely a vague threat to solvency but an imminent problem.

Big government breeds bigger pressures. Each new program creates interests who organize around it. More people make demands on politicians. Decisions must be made to satisfy them and to cope with the consequences of prior policies. Politicians find themselves busier than before but with less room to maneuver.

External turbulence and internal incoherence radically foreshorten time horizons. In the good old days, politicians could play the spending tune today and pay the piper tomorrow (or, better still, in the distant future, when someone else would have to cough up the cash). Nowadays the consequences of policies follow so swiftly on their appearance that the day of reckoning cannot be postponed. The long term is gone, the middle term appears beyond grasp; the short term—measured in months or within political terms of office—is all there is. The undeniable truth dawns: no longer can politicians pass on the consequences of their policies to their successors. What Tarschys calls the "scissors crisis,"[3] spending rising faster than revenues, has created a structural budgetary fault in the West, with demands that cannot be reduced and supplies of revenue that cannot be raised sufficiently to satisfy them. We have seen the budgetary future and it is here now.

The era of industrial maturity—the 1960s, the 1970s, and the early 1980s—has exhibited three budgetary trends: increased spending on social programs, decreased relative but increased absolute military expenditure, and the inability of a vast increase in revenue to keep pace with both. In this chapter we will survey trends in welfare and defense spending and in taxation in a number of Western nations. We shall also review the so far unsuccessful efforts to control spending. Knowing more about what has happened will enable us to tackle the great question, why government grows, in the next and final chapter.

GROWTH OF THE WELFARE STATE[4]

The essence of the social-welfare state is provision of transfer payments and helping services through a bureaucratic mechanism. Authority over that mechanism is ultimately vested in citizens, who exercise it, at some distance, through elections. Income transfers and helping services might otherwise be provided by private bureaucracies, by an exchange relationship, or within collectivities (such as the family) in which neither bureaucracy nor exchange describes the social process.

According to two sympathetic commentators, the welfare state has expanded greatly in recent years because industrial workers lack "accumulated savings in the form of economic capital."[5] Nor, when confronted with misfortune, can workers count on sufficient support either from families or from voluntary social groups. Whether government is an adequate substitute, or whether people are in fact unable to care for themselves, these factors nonetheless stand as the conventional rationale for social spending.

There is general consensus about a core of helping services: care of young and old, the sick and the disabled.[6] But beyond this consensus, polities clearly differ as to how much of these services to provide, or what other services might be provided. Not only have nations followed different policies at given times, but expenditure in each welfare state has grown at different times and at different rates. Therefore the data cannot show that political developments result directly from the economic context. Yet neither can we safely regard the welfare state—here considered as income transfers and social services—as a pure product of political circumstances.

In growth of welfare spending, government has served more as a clearinghouse for funds than as a direct provider of services. When it transfers funds among taxpayers, government is adjusting inputs into a market. Modern governments have learned rather well how to move money from taxpayers to beneficiaries.[7] Sometimes transfers comprise the only politically feasible activity. Since publicly supported health care for everyone has not been acceptable in the United States, for instance, the government has created programs (Medicare, Medicaid) to subsidize medical costs for the poor and the elderly. Political barriers against public medicine in the United States may be traced either to interest-group power or to political culture (American dislike of collectivism). But, as Table 16 shows, the move to income transfers is so ubiquitous as to suggest that all governments find it advantageous.*

* Expenditure as a proportion of GNP is the indicator of government share of societal product most commonly used. In Table 16, gross domestic product (GDP), instead of gross national product, is used (to eliminate transfers to and from abroad). There are several conceptual problems implicit in this measure, however, and the reader should be aware of them:

1. The government can require spending (by regulations) or encourage it (with loan guarantees)—thereby replacing markets with public decision-making—but these changes will not alter the spending/GDP ratio.

2. Public consumption counts in the GDP denominator, but transfers do not. What should count is a matter of judgment, but the effects of what is included are large.

3. GDP fluctuates for numerous short-term reasons, being produced in a less regular manner than government spending. Thus year-to-year figures may fluctuate in ways that

TABLE 16

TRENDS IN PUBLIC EXPENDITURE BY ECONOMIC CATEGORY[8]
percent of gross domestic product at current prices—3-year average

	1955–1957			1974–1976		
	Final Consumption	Transfers	Total expenditure	Final Consumption	Transfers	Total expenditure
Australia	9.7	5.6	21.7	15.9	9.3	32.8
Austria	12.6	11.8	29.0	16.2	15.8	39.9
Belgium	11.5	10.5	—	16.2	19.3	43.0
Canada	13.2	6.2	25.1	19.7	11.8	39.4
Denmark	12.6	7.4	25.5	24.0	15.8	46.4
Finland	12.1	9.1	29.2	18.6	13.4	37.3
France	14.1	15.0	33.5	14.4	21.9	41.6
Germany	12.5	12.4	30.2	20.3	16.9	44.0
Greece	10.9	9.3	—	17.8	6.2	—
Ireland	12.5	12.5	—	20.4	19.7	49.4
Italy	11.9	10.9	28.1	13.7	21.5	43.1
Japan	9.7	4.0	—	10.7	8.4	25.1
Netherlands	15.1	9.5	31.1	18.0	27.3	53.9
New Zealand	12.9	7.6	—	17.8	9.1	—
Norway	11.3	11.1	27.0	16.7	22.3	—
Spain	9.2	2.9	—	9.9	11.1	25.3
Sweden	15.6	8.2	—	24.8	19.3	51.7
Switzerland	9.4	6.0	—	12.1	13.6	(33.5)
United Kingdom	16.6	7.9	32.3	21.5	14.7	44.5
United States	16.7	4.5	25.9	18.8	11.2	35.1
OECD* Average (unweighted)	13.0	8.8	28.5	18.0	16.1	41.4

* Organisation for Economic Cooperation and Development

Between the middle 1950s and the middle 1970s, Table 16 reveals, government expenditure in the average OECD (Organisation for Economic Cooperation and Development) country increased from just under 30 percent to just over 40 percent of gross domestic product. Of this 12 percent increase, 5 percent resulted from government purchases of goods and services—its final consumption—while 7 percent came from growth of transfers and subsidies. Thus transfers rose from 30.9 percent to 38.9 percent of government spending.

The relative growth of transfers is more pronounced if one adjusts public consumption for price differentials between the public and private sectors. "Because the government sector is largely a service industry with relatively low capital-labor intensities," some analysts maintain, its "productivity . . . would likely be small when compared to . . . the manufacturing and primary [commodity] sectors."[9] Therefore, even if productivity of services could be adequately measured, prices for a given amount of product would increase more rapidly in the public than in the private sector, changing the ratio of *costs* without changing the ratio of *outputs*.[10]

Since we cannot measure public-sector productivity, the fundamental problem lies in evaluating outcomes of increased spending. Who is to say whether higher education costs reflect better education? In limited fields, calculation may be possible. Between 1949 and 1963, for example, a study of teachers' salaries in France found that wages increased at a mean rate of 9.2 percent annually. This was in line with pay increases in metallurgy, averaging 9.4 percent. But productivity in metalwork was increasing at somewhere around 5.3 percent per year. Could teachers' productivity have been going up, too? The curriculum had not changed, the school year's length had not changed, teachers were still trained the same way, and all attempts to demonstrate a better relationship between teacher and student failed.[11] While such calculations are suggestive when trying to determine public-sector productivity changes over time, the only feasible alternative is to adjust spending totals for price changes during the period considered. After the effect of inflation is eliminated from data on growth of government

confuse trends. For that reason, the OECD figures cited here are based on trend GDP over a period of years, and the work tables analyzed later do not represent actual data, but a "smoothing-out" series.

4. GDP is calculated differently by different countries at different times. Even international attempts to standardize confuse matters by creating changes in the middle of series. Since spending categories are also idiosyncratic, different sources provide different results. Moreover, as with the United Nations National Accounts compilations for Sweden in 1965, different editions of a different source may provide inconsistent data.

spending as a proportion of GDP since 1960, productivity growth is still far lower in government than in the private sector.

If something like 4 percent of the 13 percent increase in government spending as a proportion of GDP between the midfifties and the mid-sixties can be associated with inflation, we still need to explain the rest. Where, we ask, did spending increase the most? A substantial proportion of the increased social spending (see Table 17) was for health, education, and income-maintenance programs. The growth of each holds different political meanings. Expanded social spending might simply be related to demographic shifts—as when the baby boom produced more schoolchildren, and an aging population raised the pension burden. Or inputs per service recipient might have gone up—with more being spent to educate each student, and with larger pensions and improved medical care supported by more elaborate technology. Finally, services could have been extended to an expanded population. School enrollment ratios could rise; government could encourage pensions for the self-employed, and could implement subsidies that en-

TABLE 17

PUBLIC WELFARE EXPENDITURE IN OECD COUNTRIES (1974)[12]
(PERCENT OF GDP IN CURRENT PRICES)

	Income maintenance expenditure	Education	Health	Total welfare expenditure elasticity GDP*
Japan	2.8	2.6	3.5	1.28
Australia	4.0	3.0	5.0	1.33
New Zealand	6.5	4.4	4.2	1.10
Canada	7.3	6.5	5.1	1.66
United States	7.4	5.3	3.0	1.52
United Kingdom	7.7	4.4	4.6	1.33
Sweden	9.3	5.9	6.7	1.61
Norway	9.8	4.9	5.3	1.72
Denmark	9.9	(7.0)	6.5	1.65
Italy	10.4	4.0	5.2	1.44
France	12.4	3.0	5.2	1.25
Germany	12.4	3.0	5.2	1.25
Belgium	14.1	4.9	4.2	1.25
Austria	15.3	4.0	3.7	1.17
Netherlands	19.1	5.9	5.1	2.04
OECD average (unweighted)	9.5	4.9	4.9	1.42

* Elasticity is the percentage increase in welfare spending for each percentage increase in gross domestic product.

courage the poor to consume more health service. Public policy is not responsible for demographic causes of increased welfare spending. But, in reaching out to the poor, growth in welfare services may reflect more egalitarian goals, or it might represent a political tendency to build a coalition by giving something to everyone.

Extending services to more citizens is often justified in terms of establishing a "social-minimum" standard of living. Risk is socialized. Dennis Guest writes about

> the growing recognition that because of the nature of social organisation in an urban-industrial society, the risks to an individual's social security are part of the social costs of operating a society which has provided higher standards of living for more people than ever before in our history ... There is a duty on the part of a civilized society to see that the costs and benefits of industrial progress are shared by all and that the protection of the most vulnerable members of the community—the aged, children, disabled, workers who have been made redundant by rapid social change—are first priorities in policy and programming.[13]

This fairly standard example of the social-work advocate's mind reveals a not quite egalitarian collectivism. A more explicit concern with equality is shown by T. H. Marshall:

> The extension of the social services is not primarily a means of equalising incomes ... What matters is that there is a general enrichment of the concrete substance of civilised life, a general reduction of risk and insecurity, an equalisation between the more and less fortunate at all levels—between the healthy and the sick, the employed and the unemployed, the old and the active, the bachelor and the father of a large family ... *Equality of status is more important than equality of income* [emphasis added].[14]

The OECD working party on public-expenditure trends in expenditure for health, education, and income maintenance[15] reported that the main cause of increased spending was enhanced program coverage. Most of the people in many countries were eligible for health benefits, a fifth were supported in higher education, and a tenth received old-age benefits. In a daring leap for a committee, the working party concluded that

> society, over the last decade, has more or less suceeded in fulfilling what might be called its "democratic" objectives—the extension of coverage to as large a share of the relevant population as possible. Only slow progress, however, has been made towards fulfilling its

more "egalitarian" aims involving selective help to the economically vulnerable and socially disadvantaged. Indeed insofar as the
effort to achieve generalised coverage has restricted the increase of
benefits, these two objectives may even have been in conflict.[16]

The idea of a social floor has been vastly extended, but equality of income or service is far from being realized.

Widely distributed, automatically vested benefits are politically useful, for they make it harder to attack unpopular recipients. At the same
time, however, by extending coverage to the better off they diminish
the redistributive effects. Despite the popularity of income transfers
within OECD countries, these programs have grown at different rates.
It is necessary for us, therefore, to calculate the changing pattern of income-maintenance expenditures.

In the mid-1970s (see Table 17), income-maintenance expenditures
were low in America, Britain, Canada, Australia, New Zealand, and
Japan, and high in the Netherlands, Italy, France, Germany, Austria,
and Belgium. Denmark and Sweden had high health service costs, but
these were moderate in America, Austria, New Zealand, and Japan.
Education expenditures were highest in the Scandinavian countries
and Canada. The United States is actually an above-average spender
for education, while non-Scandinavian countries that are high on income maintenance (Germany, France, Italy, Austria) are laggards.
Britain was a below-average spender on pensions in the early 1960s,
and by the mid-1970s was below average in all three categories—not
exactly our image of the British welfare state!

The welfare leaders are thus the small European states—the Scandinavian countries as a group, Austria, Belgium, and the Netherlands.
The Netherlands, Denmark, Norway, and Sweden also show high
welfare growth in relation to the GDP (see the "elasticity" column).
The other rapidly rising country is Canada. From a low base, its
spending is particularly high in education and health (the latter from
adoption of national health insurance). Low growth, from a high base,
characterizes France, Germany, Austria, and Belgium.

Pensions grew everywhere but Australia. The size of the individual
pension (expressed, roughly, by the transfer ratio—the share of expenditure paid for by the public sector) has increased most in the
Scandinavian countries and France. On the whole, rising pension costs
are due more to demographic structure and changes in eligibility than
to improved benefits, but benefits have increased as well.

By contrast, child allowances fell nearly everywhere. Eligibility was
not restricted, but only in Belgium and Denmark did the public-sector

share of spending increase, and there only slightly. In most of the old welfare leaders—Germany, France, Italy, Austria—child subsidies were reduced substantially. (Having no system, the United States saw neither increase nor decrease. Deductions for children available to taxpayers in the United States do not alter its low ranking as a subsidizer of childbearing, especially since deductions have not been indexed to inflation.[17])

Generally, increases in unemployment benefits reflect rising unemployment and looser eligibility requirements. (Only in Canada and Britain did real benefits improve.) Eligibility for unemployment benefits, and payment levels have both risen since the fourfold oil price increases of 1973 and the concomitant unemployment. In 1974 the Emergency Jobs and Unemployment Assistance Act in the United States extended coverage to twelve million workers. Other legislation extended the benefits period when the national unemployment rate exceeds 4 percent (as it has ever since), and established a massive public employment and training program (CETA), since repealed and reestablished with emphasis on training. The Canadian system vastly expanded in 1971. The French created a supplementary-assistance plan in 1974, and the Italians enlarged their system in 1975. The Japanese, enjoying high employment during the early seventies, and the Germans, having indexed benefits previously, did less; but both governments nevertheless implemented measures to create jobs.[18] Since unemployment, still high during the seventies, rose sharply in the early eighties, there is reason to believe that benefits have continued to increase as a proportion of GNP. Unemployment benefits thus reflect not simply society's wish to be generous, but also fluctuations in the economy, and government's attempts to manipulate the economy by maintaining demand. The benefits are automatically countercyclical.

Cash benefits for illness or disability are the fourth major category of income-maintenance expenditure; again, growth was largely due to broadened eligibility. Data here are extremely unreliable, since programs vary widely in definition of eligible population, while sickness benefits and unemployment schemes may overlap. Benefits were particularly high in 1972 in the Netherlands (1.91 percent of GDP), Sweden, Belgium, and Norway. This grouping is beginning to look familiar.[19] In Holland, at least, the system seems to encourage "sickness": 15 percent of the labor force (600,000 workers) were receiving payments in early 1982.[20] Those nations with generous systems apparently have adopted the rule that "when in doubt, overpayment is preferable to underpayment."[21]

The baby boom of the 1950s raised spending for elementary education during the decade, and by the late 1960s institutions of higher learning were spending more to accommodate the bulge in student populations. Governmental action to meet the demand created by differentials between wages of college graduates and others, and by changing social aspirations, meant that universities and their students everywhere in the developed world benefited. By creating more flexible paths through the school system toward the university, governments also expanded demand for university places.[22] If parents could manage without children's earnings, governments could and did provide modest stipends for eligible students. Central-government funding of basic research in science further supplemented university budgets.

Cost changes are the major source of growth in spending for education, and of national differences in growth. Canada stands out for exceptional dedication to educational improvement at all levels, while the United States, Australia, Sweden, and Norway expanded real resources devoted to primary and secondary education. There may even have been economies of scale in the "multiversity"; it is at least suggestive that real growth (relative to GDP increase) seems to have been lowest in France, where students revolted in 1968 and again in 1983. As with spending on pensions during these years, the Netherlands stands out for its increased educational costs.

Health is the prototype of an area for which government has become responsible without attaining control of services. Generated case by case, demand is seemingly limitless; and people do seem to value health care highly. Thus costs keep rising; except for rationing resources by means of ceilings on expenditures, and by limiting access to hospitals, there seems no way to halt the increase. Determining the value of inputs to health care systems is a problem that has so far baffled researchers.* We do know, however, that no nation supplies all the care its citizens would like.[24]

While welfare spending has risen in all nations, data on the structure of social spending suggest three groupings:

1. *Welfare state leaders*—Denmark, Norway, Sweden, and the Netherlands—spent increasing amounts for all welfare functions.

---

* The OECD working party tried to spell out the effects of spending on health, but ended up punting: "Almost certainly the increase in costs attributed to increased inputs is understated and the increase in relative prices overstated; but because of various weaknesses in the data and deficiencies in deflating procedures it is difficult to say by how much."[23]

2. *High spending, weighted disproportionately toward pensions,* occurred in the old European powers—Germany, Italy, France, and Britain, still the major economies of Europe. Social spending got its start in
these nations, but Britain, once the exemplar of the welfare state, now
is falling behind the others.

3. *Medium spenders, with more on education,* are former British colonies: the United States, Canada, Australia, and New Zealand. Relative
to the second group, these nations spend more for education and less
on employment security. Because economic growth permitted large
absolute-spending increase without affecting the ratio of spending to
GDP, Japan appears as a very low spender from 1960 through the
mid-1970s.

What can explain these groupings? One possibility is different political and economic circumstances. Let us begin by looking at raw (and
perhaps indigestible) data on year-by-year growth of spending in each
nation.[25]

Sweden is the prototypical welfare state; its growth in spending took
place between 1951 and 1978. Relative to GDP, government's consumption grew 4 percent during the fifties, more than 5 percent during
the sixties, and more than 7 percent during the seventies. Transfers increased by 3 percent during the fifties and sixties, and by 8 percent
during the seventies. Throughout this period the Social Democrats
dominated the government, until a coalition led by the Center (formerly Farmers') Party took office in 1976. If anything, the result was
greater spending; confounding everyone, it leaped to 55.5 percent of
GDP in 1977. With oil price increases and declining productivity during the seventies, central government became incapable of financing
expenditures out of revenue. Debt went from 1.5 percent of GNP in
1970–71 to 4 percent in 1974–75 to 10 percent in 1979–80. Taxes having been "adjusted," i.e., reduced, annually in the seventies, while
spending increased "automatically," the national government got into
financial trouble. Swedish budget authorities believed that taxes could
not be raised, therefore transfers must be cut in order to reduce the deficit by one percent of GNP per year.[26] But consensus as to the need for
cuts has been more easily achieved than agreement over who will get
the ax. Consequently, the deficit-reduction target was not met.

Growth of government expenditure in Italy has been confined
largely to transfers, debt, and investment, rather than public consumption. Transfers grew unevenly, but may be related to the formation of
the center-left coalition of Christian Democrats and Socialists in 1964
and the costs of its maintenance after the 1968 election. A wave of

strikes in autumn of 1969 created a new alignment of labor and subsequent pressure to appease the workers with social programs.[27] Italy's economic crisis of 1975 brought a far more substantial leap in transfers, possibly associated with earlier reforms of unemployment compensation. The jumpy pattern of growth suggests that spending went up with ad-hoc reactions to political and economic pressures.

Britain's government, by cutting military expenditure during the 1950s, reduced spending a little from earlier levels. In light of all the controversy about British "stop-go" policies, its variation in spending throughout the late fifties and early sixties seems trivial. In fact, a weak and struggling Labour government raised spending during 1965–67, especially in 1967 (reinforced by an election triumph in 1966). Efforts to protect the value of sterling after the 1967 devaluation, however, inhibited further growth until 1972, when the Conservative Heath government's labor-relations policy collapsed. The oil shocks of 1973 were reflected in a sharp increase (nearly 5 percent) in the government share of GDP in 1974. Expenditure grew again in 1975, then declined slightly as a share of GDP in the next three years. Conservative governments apparently were not interested in repealing Labour's welfare state enactments. Under a Tory Prime Minister, Harold Macmillan, who had during the thirties written a book calling for national planning, there was moderate growth in welfare spending. His term was followed by alternating governments that favored (Labour, 1964–70 and 1974–79) and disfavored (Conservative, 1970–74) welfare expansion, but neither party altered the system significantly, perhaps because of continued economic decline. Although both parties accepted government's responsibility for the health of the economy, neither was able to do much about it. The Conservative Party government of Margaret Thatcher, while selling off some nationalized industry, did little to alter the pattern of social spending. Indeed, she campaigned in 1983 on the grounds that her government had done more than its Labour Party predecessors.

Germany's economy, rebuilt after wartime devastation, boomed during the 1950s and the 1960s. Because of rapidly rising productivity, a high absolute level of social spending increased very little as a proportion of GDP between 1951 and 1966. An unexpected recession in 1967 accounted for the 2 percent growth in spending as a proportion of GDP, but that increase was nearly erased during the next three years. Formation of the alliance between Social Democrats and Free Democrats in 1969 led to expanded social spending. The oil shock of 1973 led to the appearance of accelerated social spending; while the GNP went down, pensions and health insurance continued their normal rate of growth. Increased spending in the early seventies was mainly government consumption—an expanding bureaucracy—while the jump after 1975 was largely for transfer payments. These developments suggest that, as in other countries, German expenditure as a proportion of GDP was sensitive to recession, but, unlike either Italy or Britain, the changes reflect moderation on both sides. A government slightly to the left of center was able to establish a stable spending pattern different from that of its somewhat conservative political rival. The return of the Christian Democrats to power in 1982 has not altered the level of spending.

In France, for which data are especially poor, expenditure appears to have increased substantially—in the range of 5–6 percent of GDP from 1951 through 1956. While the defense proportion of total spending fell slightly to just over 25 percent during the late 1950s,[28] total spending as a proportion of GNP rose during the 1960s and '70s. Between 1959 and 1974, government spending in France at all levels consumed about 40 percent of national product. Between 1975 and 1980, and adjusted for price changes, the public sector consumed about 46 percent of GNP.[29]

Though some of this increase must have been military, a large proportion was social transfers. Growth was halted by the debacle over Algeria that ended the Fourth and created the Fifth Republic. Under President de Gaulle increased spending was supported entirely by the earmarked social-security budget, which is separate from that of the state. The student uprisings in May 1968 seem not to have disturbed the pattern of a slow but steady increase in social security's share of GDP (about one percent every four years), and a slight rise in government consumption. Accession in 1974 of the "liberal" Giscard d'Estaing, an alleged opponent of statism, instead heralded rapid growth in spending. Again, the economic crisis is one cause, but continued expansion since 1974, whether under capitalist or socialist auspices, suggests that more is involved than a short-term reaction.

In Canada, government spending as a share of GDP spurted at the beginning of the fifties, then stabilized. In the second half of the sixties, Canadian provincial governments substantially expanded social services, especially education and health.[30] During the same period, the federal government rediscovered poverty, enacting such programs as youth allowances, adult occupational training, and the Guaranteed Income Supplement Program.[31] Growth after 1970 consisted mainly of transfers through "demogrant" programs—pensions and family allowances. During the seventies persistent unemployment led to much higher pension payments.[32] After a small rise resulting from adjustments in oil prices, public expenditure in Canada since 1975 has been expanding at a modest rate of about one percent of GDP every four years.[33] Growth in the public share of product is the outcome of a series of government decisions. The climate supporting those decisions has passed, yet a substantially broadened welfare state does exist there now. Benefits are less heavily means-tested in Canada than in the United States, are more uniform across localities, and are subject to less public criticism.[34] Unlike European governments since 1974, Canada's seems better able to deflect whatever pressures have continued to raise public-sector spending.

In the United States, lagging behind Europe, government spending increased by about 2.5 percent as a proportion of GDP from the end of the Korean War to the finish of Eisenhower's term. Growth occurred largely at the federal level—in higher Social Security payments (as the system matured), rising unemployment compensation, and infrastructure investment—housing, highways, and water development projects.[35] From 1961 through 1966 expenditure as a proportion of GDP was fairly steady; transfers did not increase, but civilian consumption rose about 1.5 percent, while defense spending fell by the same amount. The last three years of the Johnson administration—with the War on Poverty, the war in Vietnam, and violence at home—produced a jump of about 5 percent in government share of GDP. Of this, 2 percent seems to have been war-related, one percent general federal social programs, and .5 percent targeted federal social programs; the rest occurred at state and local levels, largely as a result of federal initiatives. During the Nixon-Ford years, the Vietnam War wound down; defense spending fell from around 9.4 percent to 5.4 percent of GDP. But nevertheless total spending rose by about 3.5 percent of GDP. Thus during those years government's civilian expenditures grew by about 7.5 percent of GDP. Expanded access to existing programs and increased funding for federal programs targeted to the disadvantaged accounted for the change. During the Carter administration (1977–81), government spending did not rise much as a proportion of GDP. While the government may have adopted "end runs" to secure its objectives seemingly without spending money (e.g., huge increases in loan guarantees and regulations imposing costs on the private sector), direct federal spending did not rise rapidly, perhaps because it was passed on to state and local governments, whose spending accelerated throughout this period.

As for Republican President Ronald Reagan, he succeeded in sub-stantially raising defense spending and cutting general government and means-tested social spending. Since universal entitlements contin-ued to grow at a fast clip and revenues declined due to recession and tax cuts, government overall grew larger in relation to GNP.

In Australia, government-consumption expenditure (largely health and education) expanded by about 3.5 percent of GDP from the end of the Korean War through 1973; transfers, by about 1.5 percent. The only really clear pattern is a rapid increase in spending between 1974 and 1977—about 6 percent of GNP—half of it for consumption, half for transfers. The Liberal-Country Party coalition that took office in 1975 was unable to cut spending, but did succeed in reducing the bud-get deficit, apparently by raising taxes.[36] Between 1972 and 1975 a La-bour government expanded both old-age pensions and health coverage; it was soundly defeated due to the state of the economy and political scandals.[37] Since then Liberal and Labour governments have watched expenditure increase moderately but without let or hindrance.

Once enacted, no polity finds it easy to take benefits away from its people. Before 1981 there were no significant program reductions in either Canada, Australia, the United States or the other nations dis-cussed here. Between 1965 and 1975 all these governments elected to increase benefits. Significantly, even in the United States, where sup-porters of market relationships are stronger than in Europe, govern-ment continues to grow.

In sum, expenditures on income maintenance swamp all others in distinguishing the larger from the smaller spenders.

MILITARY SPENDING FROM THE END OF WORLD WAR II THROUGH THE MID-1960s

As the only Allied Power with an intact economy when the war ended, and with large domestic balances of foreign exchange earned from sale of war materials early in World War II, the United States unwittingly fell heir to Britain's former role as stabilizer of the world's economy. However, as the dollar became the postwar world's trade medium, and as the U.S. spent more to shore up defense against the Soviet Union and Communist China than did nations in Europe with domestic economies to rebuild, defense-spending policies during the late 1940s and the 1950s reflected the United States's ambivalence about its changed role. Pressure from the U.S.S.R.—at first political, then military, and finally technologic—eroded its long-entrenched preference for moderate spending and balanced budgets.

More than the distribution of political and economic power had changed during World War II. Development of nuclear weapons with awesome destructive capacity profoundly altered the context for international politics. As polities came to understand their long-term consequences, consensus emerged that future use of such weapons was insupportable. Yet once the U.S.S.R. got the bomb, strategists contended that only a superior or at least equivalent stockpile of nuclear weapons could effectively inhibit the other side from striking first.

National-defense spending in the United States reached its World War II peak–annual rate of $90.9 billion in the first quarter of 1945.[38] A few months later, military spending began to decline. In the second quarter of 1947, defense expenditure reached its postwar low—an annual rate of $10.3 billion. During this pause between the immediate aftermath of World War II and the first military stimuli of the Cold War, contribution to European recovery loomed as the major claim on U.S. spending for foreign aid.

The Czechoslovakia coup and the first Soviet moves against Berlin in the spring of 1948 provoked fear of imminent war, prompting the administration to secure from Congress new Selective Service legislation and supplemental defense appropriations. These were reflected in the steady increase in defense spending from the summer of 1948 to a peak of $14.1 billion in summer 1949. Almost immediately, however, government policy shifted and a major economy wave got under way. An easing of the Berlin crisis was in part responsible. When an unprecedented commitment to contribute funds for rebuilding Europe's economy, together with domestic spending proposed in the administration's Fair Deal, threatened to produce deficits, defense seemed the obvious place to cut. (A tax reduction in 1948 led to lower revenue in 1949.) Even so, altered policy did not produce a turnabout in military spending until the end of 1949, by which time State Department officials and administration advisers were again concluding that the defense effort should be expanded.

The Korean War produced a sustained three-year increase in defense expenditures (from $12 billion in the second quarter of 1950 to $50.5 billion in the second quarter of 1953). While holding federal domestic spending relatively constant, Congress raised taxes to support expenses for national security. The end of the Korean War and proposals for a "New Look" in military strategy brought spending cuts for the armed forces. (The defense budget was $38.4 billion at the end of

1954.) With increased emphasis on nuclear weapons and cutbacks in conventional forces, the New Look permitted major tax reductions in 1954.

The cuts initiated a long period of relative stability in defense spending. It reflected an equilibrium between New Look cutbacks in personnel and conventional forces, on the one hand, and rising prices and increased expenditure for missiles and other weapons on the other. If Vietnam War expenses are excluded, defense spending in constant dollars (see Table 18) did not change between 1954 and 1979.

But within a year, between mid-1956 and 1957, defense spending rose almost 15 percent (to $44.9 billion in the summer of 1957). This increase was not the outcome of planned expansion; missile expenditures did go up during the year, but more significant were rapidly rising missile prices, accelerated payments to contractors, and faster deliveries than had been anticipated. The rapid rise threatened to force an increase in the federal debt ceiling. To avoid this, a vigorous (if short-lived) economy drive got under way in the summer of 1957; the severe restrictions imposed on military spending forced drastic cuts in force levels and personnel. By deliberate planning for contraction, accelerating spending was reined in.

TABLE 18

GROSS NATIONAL PRODUCT AND NATIONAL-DEFENSE SPENDING, 1944–60[39]

Calendar Year	Gross National Product ($ billion)	National Defense Spending ($ billion)	Defense as Percent of Total
1944	211.4	88.6	41.9
1945	213.6	75.9	35.5
1946	210.7	18.8	8.9
1947	234.3	11.4	4.9
1948	259.4	11.6	4.5
1949	258.1	13.6	5.3
1950	284.6	14.3	5.0
1951	329.0	33.9	10.3
1952	347.0	46.4	13.4
1953	365.4	49.3	13.5
1954	363.1	41.2	11.3
1955	397.5	39.1	9.8
1956	419.2	40.3	9.6
1957	442.8	44.4	10.0
1958	444.2	44.8	10.1
1959	482.1	46.0	9.5
1960	503.2	45.1	9.0

Countercyclical spending to combat the recession of 1957 produced yet another policy turnabout. Then, undoing the best-laid plans, launching of the Soviet sputnik in 1957 created a national crisis of confidence. Once again Congress lifted expenditure restrictions. The start-up of costly new programs to close the alleged missile gap raised military spending by over $2 billion (from $44 billion to $46.2 billion) by mid-1959.

Despite frequent shifts in policy and its direction, the Eisenhower administration did succeed in achieving a reasonably stable absolute level of defense spending, which it bequeathed to its successors. For five years—from the third quarter of 1954 to the third quarter of 1959—the quarterly rate of defense spending stayed between $36.3 billion and $39.7 billion.

U.S. defense efforts differed markedly before, during, and after the Korean War. At the peak of World War II almost 42 percent of the GNP supported the war effort. After demobilization, but before the Korean War, about 5 percent of GNP went for national security. In 1953, during the Korean War, military spending rose to a peak of 13.5 percent of GNP. From 1955 through 1959 (see Table 19), it remained stable—at about 10 percent.

TABLE 19

TOTAL BUDGET EXPENDITURES AND MAJOR NATIONAL-SECURITY
EXPENDITURES, FY 1946–FY 1961[40]

Fiscal Year	Total Expenditures ($ million)	Major National Security Expenditures ($ million)	National Security as Percent of Total
1946	60,448	43,507	72.0
1947	39,033	14,392	36.9
1948	33,068	11,675	35.3
1949	39,507	12,902	32.7
1950	39,606	13,009	32.8
1951	44,058	22,306	50.6
1952	65,408	43,976	67.2
1953	74,274	50,363	67.8
1954	67,772	46,904	69.2
1955	64,570	40,626	62.9
1956	66,540	40,641	61.1
1957	69,433	43,270	62.3
1958	71,936	44,142	61.4
1959	80,697	46,426	57.5
1960	77,233	45,627	59.1
1961	81,500	47,389	57.8

Similarly, before the Korean War, national security accounted for roughly one-third of federal spending. Rearmament increased this to a peak of 69.2 percent in 1954. For the remainder of the 1950s, the ratio of national-security spending to total federal-budget expenditures hovered around 60 percent.[41]

President John F. Kennedy entered office determined to correct what he and his advisers believed to be the two fundamental flaws in the United States's military posture:[42] inadequacy of its strategic deterrent of missiles and nuclear warheads, and of armed forces equipped with conventional weapons. Administration leaders argued that greater reliance on conventional armies, combined with more powerful strategic weapons, would minimize the risk of inadvertent nuclear war, retard proliferation of nuclear weapons, and provide a foundation for negotiating arms control treaties.

By the end of its first year, the Kennedy administration had made substantial progress toward improving conventional armed forces. Stimulated in part by the threat in Berlin in 1961, administration officials requested, then received, additional funds for the military. Aiming to increase military personnel, the government bought nonnuclear ordnance and equipment for expanded ground and air forces, as well as ships and planes for transporting them. Total military manpower increased by 200,000 before the Vietnam expansion in 1965. Having attained superiority in numbers of warheads and deliverable megatons and conventional fighting force by the mid-1960s, the Johnson administration cut back military spending. Ironically, Eisenhower's New Look defense strategy differed little in total costs and manpower levels from the conventional defense posture developed under Presidents Kennedy and Johnson. Measured in real dollars, annual defense budgets in the mid-1960s averaged only $3 billion higher than those of the late 1950s; and total military manpower during these years was only slightly above the 2.5 million reached in Eisenhower's second term.[43]

Between 1970 and 1975 the size and composition of the total defense budget reflected the Nixon administration's interest in supporting conventional options. If Vietnam War expenses are not counted, allocations approached and then surpassed allocations of the mid-1960s for conventional armies; over 90 percent of funding supported nonnuclear uses. Between 1969 and 1973 strategic nuclear forces consumed slightly more than 20 percent of the total defense budget on the average. Measured in constant dollars to account for inflation, the Nixon administration's average annual strategic budget of $18 billion for this period was lower than typical budgets under the Kennedy and Johnson administrations.[44] The bulge in defense spending was due to the war.

In many respects the Nixon administration's defense policy was similar to the "flexible-response" strategy of the Kennedy-Johnson years. But the role of nuclear power in Nixon's defense policy was somewhat different from that of previous administrations. For one thing, comparisons of budget levels, without taking inflation into account, can be misleading. Because actual equipment costs during the early 1970s were substantially higher than in the previous decade, U.S. conventional forces under Nixon cost as much as forces mobilized by Kennedy and Johnson, yet were not equivalent in effectiveness. Furthermore, because of the Nixon doctrine's redefinition of America's overseas commitments, and congressional insistence on keeping defense spending in check, administration officials concluded that the general-purpose forces (particularly ground forces for Asia) could be reduced below target levels developed under Johnson. In theory, these forces had been designed to handle a so-called two-and-a-half-war contingency—that is, to fight the initial stages of simultaneous major wars in Europe and Asia as well as a smaller conflict elsewhere. The Nixon strategy assumed the unlikelihood of simultaneous conventional attacks against Europe and Asia. Recognizing China, it postulated that long-term U.S. interests lay in northeast Asia. Asian allies (especially Japan), the administration believed, could and would improve their conventional defenses. Hence U.S. air and sea power should be concentrated in the western Pacific.

THE DEFENSE BUDGET-MAKING PROCESS

As part of its effort to revise U.S. military policy, the Kennedy administration made important changes in defense planning. Defense Secretary Robert McNamara replaced Eisenhower's fixed-budget-ceiling approach with an attempt to evaluate defense needs on the basis of overall requirements, using cost-effectiveness criteria and systems-analysis techniques. The symbol and the procedural core of the "McNamara Revolution" was the Planning-Programming-Budgeting System (PPBS),[45] a new method for resource planning and budgeting.

The rhetoric of decision-makers in the 1960s implied dramatic contrasts between their predecessors and themselves in using budget process as a policy instrument. However, Kanter demonstrates that budget data from the two periods reveal striking similarities, if not essentially indistinguishable behavior.[46] (Abrupt change, as we have seen from the past, is not easily accomplished.)

By establishing a fixed ceiling, Eisenhower compelled the services to compete, coming to him for final decision when they could not agree on weapons programs. For Eisenhower, as for McNamara, the budget was the blueprint of the administration's defense policy, and the budget process was the mechanism for monitoring compliance. Eisenhower used his bargaining advantages to dominate internal allocation of the defense budget among the services.

Under McNamara's leadership, there were to be no predetermined budget limits. Decisions were to be made about defense programs rather than totals, and the budget season was to be a technical-review exercise rather than a crash effort to reduce spending. As a matter of fact, McNamara's program decisions had to be postponed until his review of budget estimates was completed. The annual defense budget was not calculated simply by adding up the costs of activities required for national security. McNamara did not have a blank check, and he did work hard (if not openly) to keep his spending within predetermined limits.

Political leadership of the Kennedy and Johnson administrations yielded to the same pressures for fiscal balance that figured so prominently in the Eisenhower years. As a result, civilians in the Kennedy and Johnson administrations found themselves in a position with respect to the services that was not as different "from that of their predecessors as they might have wished."[47] Their behavior and choices were limited by many of the same constraints operating under Eisenhower. Neither public disclaimers of unavoidable resource limits nor new management techniques insensitive to organizational dilemmas and participants' incentives produced the consequences sought by their proponents. If the "McNamara Revolution" failed to achieve dramatic improvements in defense management and organizational control, however, it did leave a legacy of explicit analysis that has continued to shape national-security policies and civil–military interactions.

BRITAIN, FRANCE, AND GERMANY AFTER WORLD WAR II

During World War II, defense needs held overriding priority in the competition for scarce national resources in Britain. Security priorities, in turn, were determined by the Allies' grand strategy. After the war, the resources-allocation problem assumed its more familiar form: how much for military purposes as opposed to other things? The legacy of war and depression complicated the calculation. There were insistent and inescapable claims for "other things"—reconstruction, rehabilitation, and the elusive promise of a secure life for all. At the same time there were new military purposes to be considered, in a context that the war itself had significantly altered. Consequently, defense won a place among national priorities unprecedented by twentieth-century peacetime standards. Still, security goals in the immediate postwar years were assigned as low a priority as prudence would allow.[48] Until the urgent tasks of economic restoration had been completed and headway made toward social-policy goals, British policymakers believed, only parsimonious provision for defense would be possible, just enough to give credibility to the nation's external policies.

The war in Korea led to a shift in Britain's minimalist approach. It was not principally the demands of the fighting that prompted urgent revision of defense plans and programs. Rather, the outbreak of war in itself seemed a signal that an open power struggle between the "free world" and Communism had got under way. Any idea of simultaneous contraction in defense spending and political withdrawal from empire hence had to be revised. Nearer home, NATO would acquire more military muscle to match Soviet armed strength deployed in eastern Europe.

Plans were made to increase arms spending despite anxieties about inflation, chronic payments problems, and continuing difficulty with industrial capacity. In 1951 defense expenditures were granted the first claim on national output; it would be financed by massive tax increases and cuts in nonmilitary spending. Not until 1952, as the burden on metal-using industries became apparent, was the defense program drastically modified. Moreover, even at this juncture the new Conservative government insisted that the adjustment was not meant to downgrade defense in national priorities. Contending that "any further substantial diversion from civil to military production would gravely impair our economic foundations and, with them, our ability to continue with the programme,"[49] the Tories stretched out procurement plans; nevertheless, actual spending on arms continued rising, and defense's share of GNP stayed high.[50]

In the spring of 1952—that is, some months before the first British nuclear device was exploded—Churchill directed the Chiefs of Staff to incorporate nuclear weapons into a new strategic policy. One of the reasons was the recent rearmament effort. With the economy still convalescent, supporting large, balanced, well-equipped conventional forces was incompatible with maintaining internal and external economic stability. Thus, the Global Strategy Paper of 1952 advocated nuclear weapons as the central element in Britain's defenses.

Because of the failure in 1954 to establish an integrated European force that would include Germany, the United States threatened western Europeans with "agonizing reappraisal" of America's commitment to their defense if some alternative framework for cooperation (and German participation) was not found. In order to create that framework, the British government assumed a binding obligation to maintain four divisions and a tactical air force on the Continent; it was the one really substantial, firm contractual commitment in Britain's postwar defense experience. Meanwhile, the question of how much was complicated by the fact that British perspectives and responsibilities stretched beyond Europe.

No clear defense priorities emerged.[51] From 1952 on, there was an underlying tension between British doctrine, which advocated strategic air power, reliance on nuclear weapons, and a smaller army, and its practice, which demanded battalions, airlifts, and conventional naval forces. The significant thing about the data on spending in real terms from 1955 to 1974 is its stability. There are only small year-to-year fluctuations. Close inspection reveals that the average level for each successive five-year period from 1960 on is fractionally above the preceding year's.[52]

All the quantitative indicators—strength, units, hardware, and infrastructure—show a clear downward trend. Expenditure in real terms stayed more or less the same. Resources must therefore have gone heavily into qualitative improvements or rising costs. Economic growth was not rapid and sustained in Britain, but some growth did occur. Allotment to defense of a near-constant absolute amount of output, then, meant that its share of GNP edged downward over time. Until the early 1970s the defense/GNP ratio fell steadily. The effect of the government's allocative choices was to stabilize the absolute level of resources devoted to defense, allowing civilian uses (i.e., private investment, private consumption, and public-sector domestic programs) to benefit from such economic growth as did occur.

Approaching their resources-allocation problem free from the special demands of postwar adjustment and the abnormalities of the Korean episode, Britain's governments markedly altered the pattern of public spending and the balance between the private and public sectors. After an initial preference for personal consumption and industrial investment, the growth dividend accrued primarily to social welfare. Ranking second and third among total expenditures up to 1958, social security benefits and education afterward commanded increased budget shares.

Over time, defense accounted for a diminishing share of total spending (see Table 20). While commitment of real resources to na-

TABLE 20

COMPOSITION OF BRITISH PUBLIC EXPENDITURE (AT CURRENT MARKET PRICES—SELECTED YEARS)[53]
(MILLIONS OF POUNDS)

	1958 £m	1958 %	1963 £m	1963 %	1968 £m	1968 %	1972 £m	1972 %
Military defense	1,543	18.6	1,892	16.2	2,443	12.8	3,097	11.4
Social-security benefits	1,345	16.2	1,988	17.0	3,340	17.5	5,119	18.9
Education	785	9.4	1,282	11.0	2,182	11.4	3,508	12.9
National Health Service	728	8.8	1,035	8.9	1,688	8.8	2,644	9.7
Industry and trade, including employment services	543	6.5	791	6.8	2,016	10.5	2,322	8.5
Roads, transport and communications	531	6.4	832	7.1	1,497	7.8	1,950	7.2
Housing	419	5.0	592	5.1	1,129	5.9	1,449	5.3
Environmental services	286	3.4	475	4.1	837	4.4	1,321	4.9
All others	1,082	13.1	1,493	12.8	2,099	10.9	3,314	12.3
Debt interest	1,046	12.6	1,236	11.0	1,907	10.0	2,420	8.9
Total public expenditure	8,308	100.0	11,666	100.0	19,138	100.0	27,144	100.0
Public expenditure as percentage of Gross Domestic Product	36.0		37.8		43.8		43.3	

tional security was relatively stable, defense efforts did undergo significant reshaping. Coinciding as it did with decline in the United Kingdom's overseas empire, and hence with relative erosion of influence, this process has been perceived as absolute diminution and contraction. In one sense, this is misleading. Real defense spending was higher in 1974 than in 1955. If more money were spent without equivalent increases in quality, however, then Britain might have been falling behind while marching ahead.

To the Labour administration which took office in 1964, the scale of the defense effort envisaged by Conservatives was unacceptable. Labour had pledged to restore spending on social programs without raising taxes; reduction of the proportion of national resources allotted to defense was thus obligatory. Forced by a newly adopted budget ceiling to contemplate exactly what they would retain in their predecessors' plans, Labour's ministers were inescapably driven to decide how security would be provided. They chose to let force levels east of Suez run down and to reduce strength elsewhere, but not to withdraw battle corps stationed in Germany. The Suez crisis, in which the United States compelled Britain to retreat, led it to reduce its commitments.

In 1968 the die was cast decisively. The rundown schedule was accelerated and extended to include withdrawal from the Persian Gulf. Moreover, the Labour government declared that henceforth British defense efforts would be concentrated in Europe and the North Atlantic. The strategic nuclear force was retained, for functional and symbolic reasons, at its annually declining costs.[54]

That this synoptic view of the changes in the defense effort emanating from Labour's decisions can be read across a nine-year time scale, from 1965 to 1974, illustrates a major point: military spending requires long lead times. Defense decisions (like other major public investments) are not and usually cannot be effectuated immediately. Today's posture reflects past choices. Today's priorities prescribe tomorrow's programs.

Before the Korean War it seemed unlikely that France (as well as the other western-European nations) would have rearmed. The focus on economic recovery reinforced French citizens' abhorrence of yet another war in Europe. Frenchmen were momentarily as shocked by the North Korean attack as were the Americans and the British; it was tangible confirmation of the beginning of an open power struggle. Reluctantly, then, policymakers concluded that containment of expansion by Moscow and Peking would require a large military effort. This view produced an expanded arms program.[55]

The escalating colonial war in Indochina, and by 1956 in Algeria, also enhanced French military spending. The level of hostility in the colonies (and hence French military expense) tapered off in the late 1950s and the early 1960s after de Gaulle assumed power, but expenditure rose again in the mid-sixties as France began to build an independent nuclear force. (This reflected de Gaulle's perception of France's unique role as a world power independent of NATO.) Increased defense spending was relatively modest, no more than 6 or 7 percent of GNP.

Despite the nuclear buildup, French social-services expenditures exceeded defense spending, and this pattern has been maintained. Aspiration for self-sufficiency in arms production generated capacity to fund part of the French defense budget by selling weapons to Third World nations. Income from arms exports permitted accumulation of a nuclear arsenal without jeopardizing domestic living standards.

The Second World War, like the First, created strong opposition to German rearmament—not only abroad, as might be expected, but at home as well (especially during the first decade after the war). The Berlin crisis of 1961 posed a threat sufficient to weaken German pacifism. Pressed by the United States to pay its share of European defense costs or have American troops withdrawn from West Germany, the Reichstag raised its defense budget from DM10 billion in 1960 to 18.36 billion in 1963. With that funding its defense force was increased by one-third (from 350,000 to 500,000 men) and the term of armed service was extended from twelve to eighteen months.

Germany's conventional rearmament corresponded to U.S. strategic policy in Europe at that time, reflecting political orientation to the West (by contrast with de Gaulle's antipathy toward the Atlantic Alliance). German citizens' expressed preference for consumer goods reduced defense spending in the midsixties; it went up slightly in the late sixties and the early seventies as Willy Brandt's policy of Ostpolitik led to diplomatic rapprochement with the Eastern Bloc while simultaneously maintaining cooperative relationships with Washington and NATO.

A NOTE ON TECHNOLOGY

Technological advances in equipment and commitment to technological superiority led to dramatic increases in defense spending. Military support for science and technology absorbed less than one percent of the major powers' budgets between the two World Wars. By the mid-1950s between 10 and 15 percent of military budgets went for research and development; R-and-D expenses have been sustained at that level ever since. The threefold increase in world military expenditure since World War II[56] has not been due to increases in either the number of men under arms or the quantity of weapons deployed, but to qualitative improvement in weapons. Each successive "generation" of weapons costs more to develop, manufacture, operate, and maintain.

Technological changes have produced an average annual increase in real costs of about 5.5 percent in the postwar period.[57] On the average, the real cost of major weapons systems doubled every thirteen years (see Table 21). Arms spending has become a more or less permanent commitment; allocation of large quantities of nations' resources to maintenance of the armed forces and continuous modernization of military equipment is now a normal state of affairs.

TABLE 21

COST GROWTH IN SELECTED CATEGORIES OF U.S. WEAPONS SYSTEMS[58]

Type of system	Period	Average annual increase in real cost Percent
1. Main battle tank	1940–1980	4.8
2. Attack/utility helicopters	1950–1980	4.3
3. Solid-fuel ballistic missiles	1960–1979	4.8
4. Tactical aircraft:		
High mix	1960–1975	9.2
High, low mix	1960–1985	5.3
5. Major ships/submarines/aircraft carriers	1945–1975	4.5
6. Average, all major weapons systems	1940–1985	5.5

Cost per man has been going up faster in most developed countries than has total military spending,[59] largely because of the changing attitude toward conscription. If a nation abandons conscription for an all-volunteer force, expenditure per man will inevitably rise because pay and allowances are higher for professional soldiers than for draftees. England and the United States made this transition in 1965 and 1973 respectively. Spending for personnel has increased relatively little, however, largely because the number of men under arms was declining in Britain, and in the United States as well after the war in Vietnam. Most western-European nations have changed their approach to the draft in another way: no longer are conscripts paid the bare minimum; they earn more while serving shorter terms. In turn, reduced length of service raises personnel costs. Requiring lengthy training periods for optimal use, the complex equipment of modern military forces is incompatible with short terms of service.

DEFENSE AS A FUNCTION OF REGIME

Decisions about the pattern and the size of military expenditures result to some extent from struggles within the military, and between the military and civil branches of government; within any nation these internal decisions are only loosely related to what other countries do. Legislators and officials may make decisions about whether or not to support a particular weapons system by appraising its anticipated effect on employment. The level of spending and the geographic distribution of defense production influence both economic stability and regional development patterns. Coupled with doubts about the gravity of external threats, such factors must affect defense policies.

Residual uncertainty about foreign danger cannot be resolved by anything short of experience, by which time is may too late. When we say the external threat is real and apparent, we mean there is widespread agreement. Lacking such consensus, elite and mass alike must use whatever preconceptions they have—call it theory or ideology—connecting how they would like to live (their values) with how they think the world works (the facts). The most general theories held by citizens, we have argued, are their political cultures. The more citizens support an existing regime, the more they will be prepared to pay for its defense. Contrariwise, if they see their regime as unworthy, citizens are more likely to believe that it is a producer rather than an alleviator of danger to national security, and hence will not favor spending on defense.

Among our several political cultures, which would interpret events to support more defense spending, and which less? Hierarchies believe in defense of the collective—recall World War I. In such a culture, public doubt about military spending would suggest attenuation of hierarchical principles. The experts—the military and the civilian leadership are not trusted to appraise the situation or competent enough to know what to do about foreign dangers.

The antimilitary culture is sectarian. Opposed to authority, seeing their own society as the cause of corruption, fearing subjugation by established institutions, sectarians favor only a small volunteer army. They respond to such unifying slogans as "The War to End All Wars" or "The War to Make the World Safe for Democracy" or "Unconditional Surrender!" because they can justify even minimal subordination to authority only by sustaining a belief that their cause is entirely just and their opponent's entirely evil.

Since democracies are hybrid regimes, we are interested in how combinations of political cultures react to defense spending. Where strong hierarchies join with moderately strong sects (as in social democracies), defense spending will be held down by sectarian objections to resultant curtailment of funds to the government programs they favor. The stronger the sectarian element, then, the larger will be the size of the welfare-state program, and the smaller will be the proportion of its budget devoted to defense. The largest relative military effort comes from a combination of hierarchy and fatalism. Spending in the Soviet Union is by far the largest proportion of national product (though its national product is less than in western-European nations and the United States). The greatest absolute amounts are spent by regimes with dominant hierarchies and sufficiently rich markets to provide the means, e.g., France. Weak hierarchies and sectarian regimes, e.g., the United States, support only modest efforts at preparedness, but rapidly reach a huge output when under fire, providing there is consensus that the cause is just. These composite regimes are poor in anticipation, but rich in resilience.

Cultural analysis does a good job of explaining the lack of military preparedness in the United States before and after the First and Second World Wars. It is not, by itself, adequate to explain why the Korean War buildup was sustained for the next two decades, or why the Reagan administration has been successful in raising defense spending, even though it is still a much smaller proportion of the budget than it was in the 1950s or the 1960s.

What has been left out is the international system of nation states in an era of nuclear weapons. By taking its place as one of the bipolar powers after the Second World War, the United States committed itself to a position as "leader of the free world," responsible for nuclear deterrence and for containing Communist expansion in various parts of the world. Given its military dominance but its formal equality in relation to allies, the United States has had to cope with "free rider" problems in which the small members contribute less than their share (while the big member pays more) because they get the benefits whether they pay enough or not. Placed in this international position, the United States does more than its domestic political complexion would warrant.

Behavior has to be interpreted in context. Whether the United States devotes too few or too many resources to defense depends not only on an appraisal of the degree of external threat but also on whether it is considered alone or as the leading member of an international alliance. If the cultural explanation has merit, the United States should seek to meet its international responsibilities by a greater sharing of burdens, so as to bring its foreign policy into line with its domestic political cultures, rather than seeking dominance within the Western alliance by expanding its commitments.

In conclusion, it is important to understand that throughout the Western world since 1955, defense has dropped drastically as a proportion of national product and of the budget itself. Sects, we conclude, have been growing at the expense of hierarchies.

The Political Culture of Taxation[60]

Revenues have grown since 1945 along with Gross National Product. Since World War II, in only two OECD democracies did revenues actually decline as a percentage of GNP for any extended period. In both of these countries, Italy and New Zealand, revenues increased sharply between 1955 and 1960 but then declined markedly over the next five years. Both were still below their 1960 tax levels in 1975. In all other nations there has been a slow to rapid increase of the total tax bite. On the average, the tax share of national product rose between five and ten percent in most democracies. Where it stood in 1955 seems to be a fair indicator of where it ended up in 1975. The northern-European social democracies, however, increased their take significantly more than other OECD countries. Though many started as relatively small spenders in 1955, Norway, Sweden, the Netherlands, Belgium, and Luxembourg all had climbed to the uppermost ranks by 1975.

There is little correlation between heavy taxers and countries relying on progressive taxation for revenue. This is a curious finding; many analysts think high government levels of spending are associated with redistribution of income. Based on these beliefs, we would have predicted that countries with the strongest commitment to redistributive policies would finance large public sectors with receipts from personal income taxes levied at progressive rates. Instead, social-security taxes and value-added tax (VAT) have helped support welfare spending.

The waters are even further muddied if we look at corporate and personal income taxes together.* Norway, Belgium, and the Nether-

---

* While lumping these two taxes together may be questionable on economic grounds— it is far from clear where the actual incidence of corporate taxes lies—on political grounds it certainly makes sense to put them together. Both taxes have the political appeal of at

lands—all very high taxing countries—collect relatively little of either tax. With regard to corporate tax receipts, on the other hand, Denmark and Sweden are in the company of the United States, New Zealand, Australia, and Canada, all relative tax laggards. Taking corporation taxes alone, Luxembourg is the only OECD social democracy that collects more than 10 percent of total tax receipts from corporate profits.

Reviewing the relative share contributed to a treasury by various types of taxes reveals very little about how these taxes are used, and how they have been manipulated over the years by various governments. It comes as no surprise, of course, that taxes are used to pursue a variety of public-policy goals other than raising revenue. In implementing macroeconomic policy, investment and savings policy, employment policy, pollution policy, industrial-adjustment policy, etc., taxes have been used to influence private actors' economic decisions. More and more during the past thirty years, taxes have been used to attain purposes unrelated to raising revenue. All governments have come to intervene purposefully in the economy through the tax system. Who gets exemptions from tax payments and how these are to be applied are among the most important decisions facing public-policymakers today.

Taxes are used for different purposes in different nations. Although tax incidence (who pays how much) is a focus of intense controversy in the economic class warfare of British politics, it is largely left to administrative discretion in France. While German authorities use taxes principally to promote economic growth, Sweden uses them to promote economic stability. Clearly, growth, stability, and incidence motivate policymakers in each of these countries, but the concerns are not equally important in each. Certainly, issues of equity cannot forever be ignored by those who formulate tax policy, but in Germany tax policymakers can and do subordinate this goal to attain prosperity through economic growth. Issues of economic growth cannot be ignored in designing tax policies in the United States, even though equity is the principal objective and, indeed, the main point of contention.

In the past one hundred years there has been a decided trend for central governments to collect an increasingly greater proportion of total revenues. As we might expect, however, within this overall relationship central governments in federal systems, such as the United States and West Germany, collect a considerably lesser proportion than do those in unitary systems.[61]

---

least appearing to redistribute wealth by taxing high incomes more heavily than low incomes.

TABLE 22

BELOW THE NATIONAL LEVEL IN FEDERAL AND UNITARY
GOVERNMENTS, PERCENT OF TOTAL REVENUES, 1880–1980[62]*

Country	Year			
	1880	1920	1935	1980
Austria	—	—	28	28
France	3	3	3	3
Germany	50	60	37	50
Italy	25	16	15	1
Netherlands	20	50	2	1
Norway	40	40	35	30
United Kingdom	30	23	9	12
United States	(62†)	57	30	40

* All social-security revenues are excluded.

† This entry refers to 1902.

That different objectives are sought in different countries bespeaks differences in political cultures, which in turn are reflected in a nation's political structure. It is the very openness of the American decision-making process to public pressure that insures policymakers' dedication to equity. Similarly, the insulation of German tax policymakers contributes to their ability to make growth-oriented—and not equity-oriented—decisions. In order to make our inquiry into the political culture of taxation manageable, we will concentrate on trends in diverse Western democracies—the United States, France, Germany, Britain, and Sweden.

CORPORATE TAXATION AND TAX PREFERENCES

The corporate income tax in the United States was imposed in 1909—four years before the personal income tax. To avoid a constitutional issue, Congress levied the tax as an excise on the privilege of doing business as a corporation.[63] This one percent tax on corporate income has grown into one of the heaviest corporation taxes in the Western world. Until the Reagan presidency, the tax rate stood at 48 percent of earned income (with a 26 percent exemption on the first $25,000). Though 1981 law reduced effective yields, corporate taxation accounted for approximately 11 percent of total tax yield—4 percent higher than the average yield from corporate taxes in countries surveyed by OECD.[64] Since Reagan's advent, effective tax rates have declined, though they are still higher than in the other democratic countries.

Since World War II the tax has fluctuated very little either in its structure or in its effective rates.* Still, it has been a major political issue. Major battles have been fought over whether corporations were "getting away with" paying less than they should, as well as over what the proper rates ought to be. Pechman and Okner claim that "there is no evidence in figures that the supply of corporate funds has been impaired by the corporate income tax."[65] But business interests have argued that they—as a group—pay too much in taxes and that this has had a negative influence on their (and hence the country's) potential for economic growth.

Much of the debate is over issues much more subtle than the elusive concepts of what the maximum growth environment is or what the premium tax yield might be. According to Irving Kristol,

> The hidden agenda behind the more extreme attacks upon the inequities of our tax system . . . is nowhere more obvious than in the case of corporate taxation. Many ardent reformers insist that corporations, by one devious means or another, slyly escape their "fair share" of the tax burden.[66]

William Vickery declares that our corporate, property, and income taxes "make the U.S. the most anti-capitalist nation in the free world."[67] This view is not the average taxpayer's. On the contrary, reflecting a legacy of Populism, there seems to be widespread agreement that corporations ought to pay high taxes. What upsets most taxpayers is that because corporations can afford high-priced tax accountants they therefore get away with paying significantly less than their "fair share." (There are over 200,000 tax preparers in the United States.) Tax concessions to particular groups are resented in the United States precisely because citizens feel that these violate the principle of equal opportunity. If the rich are getting special breaks, other citizens should be able to share the largesse.

The argument that some tax breaks go to the privileged is true. The argument that the best off receive most tax preferences is false.[68] In the United States, for instance, some 16 percent of the dollar value of tax preferences are a product of its federal structure—the national govern-

---

* During World War I, World War II, and the Korean War an extra "excess profits" surcharge was added to insure that no corporation was reaping special rewards for a war that everyone else was paying for.

ment does not tax interest from local and state bonds. Rich people do benefit more from this provision than poor, but, because the general purpose is deeply grounded in the country's constitutional history, repeal of the tax exemption for lower-level government bond interest would be tantamount to denial of the states' independence within the federal system.

Approximately 9 percent of "tax breaks" go to recipients of Social Security and other income-security programs because the federal government does not wish to tax its own transfers. With trust-fund deficits looming, a strong case was made for taxing high-income individuals' receipts from income-security programs. Today, one-half of income from Social Security is taxable. Roughly 20 percent of tax expenditures derive from employment fringe benefits—education, insurance for life and health, pensions, stock options, and the rest. Even subsidized meals provided by employers may be construed as income subject to tax. Approximately 17 percent of the dollar value of tax preferences derives from consumer benefits—largely the mortgage-interest deduction. Of course, that deduction is worth more to people with high incomes, but in a nation of homeowners it still is worth a good deal to tens of millions of others. And those of us who now pay tuition for college-age students may ponder whether they are in the privileged classes because they can continue to claim their children as dependents or to deduct interest paid on student loans.

The largest category of tax expenditures (about 26 percent) and the one calling forth the most opprobrium in the United States derives from efforts to increase business investment. It is easy to imagine that these tax breaks are larger in capitalist America than in social-democratic Europe. That conclusion is unwarranted, however; the truth is closer to the opposite.

All Western nations use tax incentives to aid business; most provide more extensive inducements than does the United States. The Japanese and Israeli governments, for instance, devote over half of their tax preferences to help for business and to stimulate savings to aid investment; the Dutch and the West Germans devote a third to this purpose and a third to subsidizing employment and pensions. Tax reductions for such purposes as promoting exports or lowering the bill for imported oil comprise just over 6 percent of federal revenue lost from U.S. tax collections; and depletion allowances that result in lower taxes on income produced from mining coal and iron ore, together with rapid amortization (in seven years) for expenditures on reforestation, comprise just under 6 percent of lost revenue. Perhaps these provisions have acquired such a bad name because the investment inducements have served also as entrepreneurial stimulus for syndicators of tax-shelter partnerships.

Tax benefits for individuals in special circumstances—often granted to improve horizontal equity—account for another 6 percent of lost revenue. These include such disparate measures as deductions for the blind and the disabled, double exemptions for the elderly, the one-time exemption from capital-gains tax if old people sell their homes, medical-expense deductions, and charitable contributions. In sum, about half of tax expenditures serve some limited interest, while the other half are more widely distributed.

In terms that fit well with our cultural theory of budgeting, Ronald King argues essentially that tax preferences vary with the relative strength of market (he says "liberal") and hierarchical regimes. He expects the leakage of revenues to be most used "by conservative administrations in office during periods of expanded federal activity," and to be least practiced in areas such as defense and justice, widely acknowledged to be appropriate for government. Most of all, King expects that "selective tax erosions should be greatest in those countries with a strong heritage of liberal individualism, protective of private rights against the ambitious power of central authority, and least in those countries, whether feudal or collectivist in orientation, that perceive social realms to be more highly integrated."[69] And so it is.

Up to a point. Tax preferences are neutral mechanisms that can be used for diverse, even opposed, purposes. Strong market regimes, as King argues, may use them to reduce effective tax rates. But strong hierarchies can also employ preferences to direct the activities of private companies without experiencing the grave difficulties of nationalization. And so, we shall see, they do. If market forces were indeed dominant, in the sense that they need please only (or mainly) themselves, if they really exercised hegemonic power, there would be no need for tax preferences, because rates would be much lower than they are now.

FOR BETTER OR FOR WORSE: INCOME TAXATION AS A MIRROR OF DEMOCRACY

As a system of relationships for replacing existing governmental leaders with another set through competitive elections, democratic procedures have little to do with what governments do in office but a great deal to say about how they ought to leave office. Viewed in this way,

THE GROWTH OF THE WELFARE AND TAX STATES

democracy is about the detection and correction of errors—errors about the personnel and policies of the party or parties in power. The essence of democratic relationships, therefore, is the ability of citizens to switch their support from the current occupants of the highest public offices. By testing the null hypothesis, as it were, that the people in power are farther from the preferences of the voting public than an alternative set of leaders, democratic procedures bring public policy and citizen views into line.

Opposed to this view of how governmental personnel and policy are made responsive to the popular will is a well-known array of arguments. Whether citizens are ill informed because they are denied data or because of disinterest or the complexity of the subject matter, they are alleged to be unable to form preferences or to organize to put those they do have into effect. Special interests—whether conceived of as a class of capitalists or merely the well-to-do, or disaggregated by a particular material stake in public policy—overwhelm the general mass of citizens, so this thesis runs. These special interests are better organized, have more money, hire talented lobbyists, and otherwise gain decisive advantage. Policies to aid poorer people or the broad middle of the population are argued away as sops or illusions or as a small price to pay for even greater elite privilege.

Fortunately for us, political scientist John Witte's comprehensive book on the history of the income tax in the United States, replete with blow-by-blow descriptions of the major battles as well as ample use of public-opinion surveys in more recent times, provides an opportunity to test these rival conceptions of democratic theory in an area of policy that all would agree is important, complex, and controversial. If democracy works on the income tax, it ought to work anywhere. Conversely, if the major tax in national government does not reflect the popular will, then there would be good reason to criticize the American national political system as unresponsive, at least in one vital area of policy.

The criteria we will employ to assess the democratic character (especially the responsiveness) of decision-making on taxation are related to our views of democracy as a system for testing hypotheses and correcting policy errors. Our major criterion is this: Given any set of alternative provisions, far more people prefer the existing tax code; what exists, provision by provision, is preferable to what has been proposed. The null hypothesis, demonstrating an unresponsive government, would be that different provisions are preferred to those in the tax code. Moreover, our second criterion goes, changes over time work toward rather than away from the preponderant public preference. At any one time, of course, there are errors—provisions that could be replaced by others with greater public support. Over time, however, old errors are corrected faster than new ones creep in.

By all accounts, the progressive income tax, modified by numerous tax preferences, is mildly redistributive. And the expenditures it supports are also, on balance, moderately redistributive, especially if services in kind are cashed out, because tax money goes from people who have more to those who have less. There is no conflict, we would say, between mild redistribution and popular preference because, when asked, most people prefer only a little income redistribution. Indeed, rather than relying further on the income tax (painfully evident in every wage or salary check), most of us say we would prefer a sales tax. Numerous surveys reveal that substantial income redistribution does not have anywhere near majority support in the United States.

Is the income tax properly conceived as a progressive system with all too numerous and regrettable lapses, we may ask, or are the exceptions part of the rule, the proper system being one that is both progressive and yet modified by numerous exceptions? As we will see when asking how policies and preferences are brought so close together, the exceptions are part of the price for the general rule. Which is only to say that more people prefer the rule and its exceptions together, i.e., existing tax policy, than they do alternatives like steeply progressive income tax rates with few or no exceptions.

What citizens get a chance to decide about, the actual structure of alternatives, as distinguished from survey questions, depends on the possibilities offered by the political leadership. As yet there is no evidence that people would prefer anything substantially different from the current income tax, though majorities would pay more or add a sales tax to reduce the deficit. But virtually everyone—citizen and expert alike—believes that the tax code is too complicated and unfair in its offering of selective benefits. When the very people who prefer all or most of the provisions that make up the tax code say they do not like the code as a whole, this conflict between the parts and the whole deserves further analysis. How is it to be resolved?

Presumably, the answer to the complexity of the code is a flat-rate income tax without any "gimmicks." On grounds of simplicity, it has widespread appeal. Immediately, however, objections come crowding in. A flat-rate tax is not progressive. A conflict ensues over making it progressive. Certain tax preferences have widespread popularity. So the home mortgage deduction, the charitable deduction, the exemption from taxation of fringe benefits such as retirement and health, are put back in. Right before our eyes, the old discredited income tax rises from the ashes of the new. Nevertheless, a majority or plurality of citizens might prefer a progressive, low-rate income tax with fewer (but not zero) tax preferences to what exists.[70] The passage of time, however, which provides opportunities to test numerous small hypotheses about whether some deserving group—working mothers, infants from poor families, working people who wish to supplement Social Security for retirement, industries that employ people in distressed areas— might be included without too great a departure from principle, may well manifest a return to something like the existing complex code. Why? The selfsame features of the tax process that have generated the most criticism—its complexity, its resistance to radical change, its reliance on trading favors and on tit-for-tat retaliation (you threaten my preference, I'll threaten yours), its lack of consistent principle, in sum its incremental character—have also made it sensitive to fine gradations of public opinion.

The income tax, we contend, is a paradigm of a responsive democracy. How can that be, the informed reader may ask, when everyone knows that tax legislation is rife with the influence of special interests, extending even to helping a single firm or individual? In this case, "what everyone knows" is perfectly true but, in context, insignificant. When revenues amount to hundreds of billions, hundreds of millions (which is all these very special interests add up to) do not matter much. They do matter, to be sure, because public morality must be seen to be observed, blatant privilege gives the entire process a bad name. But they are a trivial part of the whole.* Were this not so, were tax preferences reserved for the few and not the many, the democratic character of the tax process would be in doubt.

Trying to explain why the tax code runs counter to public preferences, or how various villains (by class, race, or position) impose their nasty special interests on the wholesome general interest of the citizenry, is to falsify the content and the spirit of the tax process. No, it is the hypersensitivity of the process of making decisions on taxation that is responsible for both its best and worst features—for its satisfaction of innumerable desires on individual provisions and for the general disenchantment with certain of its summary characteristics, such as

---

* Except for one thing: Regulations to rule out "very special" interests might make it more difficult to accommodate others when public opinion favors them. Like the discussions of "waste" in spending, there is little doubt that a few percent is wasted. The problem is to figure out which few percent fit the description.

complexity and selective benefits. This gap between individual and collective rationality, between what we do case by case and the total consequences of all individual actions, a gap observed also on the spending side, is at the root of our tax dilemmas. Let us (condensing Witte's summary of a rich body of tax data) ask why what really happens, supersensitivity to public preferences, does take place.

The responsiveness of the political system is not the only criterion used to appraise the tax process; operating side by side, heard more in common discourse than in scholarly discussion, is the criterion of responsibility. When political leaders are not manifesting the popular will, they should oppose it; i.e., they should guard the populace, in the language of the Federalist, against its passions. Applied to taxes, this protection of the people against themselves insures that their desire to pay less is balanced against the nation's need to maintain revenue. Politicians in power would prefer to have revenues maintained by silent processes while reductions are loudly proclaimed. These apparently contradictory requirements—responsiveness and responsibility, visible tax cuts and invisible revenue increases—are met by a number of conditions and practices.

The ubiquitous effect of war, to which we have referred before, assures a high progressivity in income taxation that is politically acceptable. This spirit of sacrifice, as Peacock and Wiseman argue, leads to acceptance of a higher rate at the end than at the beginning of major wars.[71] There are tax cuts every few years for which the party in power takes credit. Because rates are high, revenues follow suit in this most elastic of taxes. Economic growth hopefully offsets rate reduction. So does "bracket creep," the tendency of increases in the price level to push people into upper categories where they pay a higher rate. As always, inflation is the "silent tax," as are the revenue-enhancing effects of economic growth. When all else fails, the guardians of the Treasury in Congress, especially the chairmen of the House Ways and Means Committee and the Senate Finance Committee, acting in conjunction with the "Troika" (the Chairman of the Council of Economic Advisers, the Secretary of the Treasury, and the Director of the Budget), hold down revenue reductions to low levels. Most of the postwar period (roughly from 1945 to 1975) can be characterized in this way: quiet increases and loud cuts.

What happened to alter the postwar pattern of the tax process? Almost everything. Economic growth slowed down in the 1970s. "Stagflation," the combination of unemployment and inflation, decreased the revenue base while increasing mandatory spending. The rate of increase in spending (the "scissors crisis") substantially exceeded even the best rates of economic growth. Inflation rose so sharply as to call attention to bracket creep, leading eventually to a successful proposal to index tax brackets against inflation. Nor was this all. A combination of misadventure (personal problems experienced by Wilbur Mills, the once formidable chairman of the House Ways and Means Committee) and institutional change (the end of the seniority system for choosing chairmen, the further fragmentation of committees, the increasing desire of legislators for individual expressiveness) conspired to weaken the sense of responsibility in Congress for raising revenues. Consequently, the institutional barriers against excessive loss were weak when two of the most evident tendencies of the tax process became apparent in 1981. The longer the legislative debate lasted, the more the various sides offered "sweeteners" to attract support for their views. Opening up the proceedings to public scrutiny, moreover, led to cumulative reduction of revenues.[72]

The process also varies with the taxpayers' economic circumstances, but not, as Witte demonstrates, in the direction expected by economic determinists. His study of the frequency of changes in the tax code reveals that provisions favoring poorer people, once enacted, are seldom changed. Provisions affecting middle-income groups, where most of the money is, are changed most frequently, especially in the direction of expanding benefits. Upper-income groups find themselves mired in controversy: do provisions favoring "the rich" aid economic growth, thus providing benefits to the less fortunate, or are they examples of unconscionable favoritism? Hence, over time, there is a balance between deprivation and advantage.[73]

"Indeed," as Witte says so cogently, "if tax expenditures were the exclusive privilege of the wealthy, containing the system would be much easier."[74] The income tax system is so difficult to change because it confers benefits so broadly. Otherwise, it would be much easier to single out the few wealthy beneficiaries for removal of their special treatment. The truth is out: As Pogo might have put it, we—the broad middle and lower classes—have met the special interests, and "they is us." In view of the need for politicians to get elected, and reelected, doing something for large numbers of constituents is exactly what we would expect.

Once the false cynicism surrounding the tax code (the view that it provides advantages only for a few organized wealthy) is consigned to the oblivion it deserves, the conclusions of public-opinion polls become much more understandable. The truth is that tax preferences are widely distributed. Despite the talk about "loopholes," substantial majorities support existing tax preferences as reasonable dispensations. And when citizens were asked to compare radical change—such as a broad-based tax with few preferences—and the existing system, they chose the status quo by large margins.[75]

Now the fact that, provision by provision, citizens favor the present code does not mean they have no complaints. Again we-the-people like the parts, but not necessarily the whole to which our partial preferences add up.[76] How can we explain this apparent anomaly?

It exists because there is no alternative to the present system that, item for item, is superior. Decisions are not normally made on rival systems but on marginal changes in individual provisions that someone thinks need fixing. This serial, remedial process, as Charles E. Lindblom described it in a brilliant paper, works by repeated, successive, limited comparisons.[77] It fairly well guarantees that each provision of interest to an active public is compared to a series of alternatives that differ from it only in small ways. Eventually, what is left in the tax code, each provision considered separately, is the refined product of public preferences tested and retested at the margins.

None of the above, however, necessarily signifies that the collective consequences of these choices are "correct" according to different perspectives, or that the people involved like what happens, or even that they would regard the results as tolerable.

On the contrary, there could well be a radical change. Just as scientific theories may last until a sufficient number of anomalies arise to call them into question, or a rival theory appears to provide a choice (a theory that may have to wait until the old generation of scientists dies out and is replaced by a new one), so public feelings about the existing income tax may have to get a lot worse in a democracy before, by trying a new hypothesis (a different tax system), it has a chance to get better.

Another reason tax anomalies continue is that they reflect a perennial conflict of objectives. Think, for a moment, of the progressive income tax as an ideal. One reason "the poor pay more" than some think they should is that the personal exemption and the standard deduction have not kept up with inflation. Given a steeply progressive tax, the higher up the income scale one goes, the more the exemption and the itemized deductions are worth. Helping the "masses," it turns out, helps the "classes" even more.

For most low-income people, the Social Security tax is by far the biggest tax they pay. Isn't that regressive? That depends on whether you think Social Security is based on contributions or is an income transfer. If the latter, why not take the money from general revenues? When Denmark did this, the resulting income tax increases were so great they led to a tax revolt. Supporters of the social-welfare state are in the uncomfortable position of choosing a progressive income tax, which they probably cannot raise sufficiently to pay for what they want, or regressive Social Security and sales taxes. That helps explain why the status quo is preferred to seemingly more desirable tax policies.

Stimulating economic growth conflicts with high tax rates. If a polity were to decide that narrowing income differences is of paramount importance, even if some people are made worse off, the choice would be easier to make. Then it would have to give up on growth. Until now, however, the American people have rejected redistribution on these grounds.

A third reason tax anomalies continue is that the good things we want often lead to the bad things we complain about. The legendary complexity of the tax code (its sheer length as well as the number of its provisions has multiplied many times over) is a case in point. The desire to equalize incomes, or to tax based on ability to pay, has at times led to very high marginal rates. The higher the rates, however, the greater the force of arguments for exceptions. And the more deductions there are, the more complex the code becomes. The existence of special provisions, moreover, violates the principle of horizontal equity. Deciding who or what should be treated equally takes up a lot of space. Comparability, moreover, requires extending changes in one area to many others that are or may be related to it. Multiplying horizontal times vertical equity, times types of individuals and businesses, times variations in conditions, times efforts to control abuses by stretching these provisions, produces sufficient complexity for everyone—except, perhaps, for those who make a living out of interpreting or manipulating the tax code.

The view that decision-making in small, sometimes tiny steps, eschewing radical change, going over the same problem again and again, does not add up to anything is plain wrong. In the beginning, except in wartime, there was a flat-rate income tax; the tax was applied only to the wealthy, leaving government with the limited task of devising ways to tax the already affluent. The tax code was only a few pages long. Today most of us pay many taxes, and the code is immense. But, compared to earlier eras, the hundreds of billions raised now dwarf earlier revenue collections.

The florid rhetoric of radical change surrounding the subject of tax reform (meaning substantially steeper progressivity) is both misleading and significant. It is misleading in opposite directions, suggesting, on the one hand, that the battle is over fundamentals, and on the other that it is trivial because any given change fails to transform the tax system. Denigration of ideology would be even more misleading, however, because it suggests that the status quo is not ideological, while those who wish to replace it are proposing ideological policies. Ideology, which is the rationalizing part of any political culture, establishes the context within which debate is conducted and decisions are made. In regard to the income tax, the reigning ideology favors a moderately progressive tax with major exceptions. This ideology is based on compromise among hierarchical and market regimes. Not until sectarianism becomes strong enough to propose a more egalitarian alternative will there be a serious challenge to the ideology embodied in the tax code.

Accusation has become a fine art. It was Vice-President George Bush, we believe, who, when running against Ronald Reagan for the Republican presidential nomination, suggested that his opponent, who maintained that tax cuts would produce more revenue, was engaging in "voodoo economics." Actually, Bush was borrowing from former Speaker of the House Joseph W. Martin. Speaking in a climate of opinion within which Democratic President Harry Truman was described as surrounded by "hard-core Socialist planners," Martin insisted, "The Administration's contention that this tax bill is needed to control inflation is economic voodoo talk. No set of controls and no pyramid of taxes ever devised by man will stop inflation in America when the root of the evil is government spending."[78] Far more accurate was the astute Senator Russell Long, the experienced Democratic chairman of the Senate Finance Committee, who advised that "once you get into tax legislation there is always a majority for 'reform' but very seldom a majority—after the special interests have done their work—for any particular reform."[79] Long was also right, Democratic Senator Edmund S. Muskie of Maine opined, when the chairman of the Finance Committee observed that it was easier to cut taxes than to abolish preferences. Long did not directly say what should now be obvious—namely, that the difficulty exists because the tax process is such an accurate reflection of public opinion. Investment in adjustment to the existing tax code is great, and uncertainty about the effects of alternatives so substantial that, even if the tax code in its entirety were not supported by a single individual, the odds are against radical change.

GERMANY: THE POLITICS OF GROWTH

Germany's history of political fragmentation is reflected in its tax code: different levels of government share responsibility for sixty different taxes,[80] and the codes have been changed a multitude of times. Between 1951 and 1956, according to some estimates, an average of 615 sections of its tax law were amended each year.[81] Within this diversity, several outstanding tendencies permit us to discuss the German tax system as a whole.

More than in any other country (except, possibly, Japan), tax policy formulated by the German Ministry of Finance after World War II was explicitly directed toward stimulating and then sustaining economic growth. Although other issues have influenced its fiscal policy throughout the postwar period, these have been less urgent than maintaining high growth rates. The Finance Ministry, moreover, possesses greater power to formulate tax policy and more discretionary authority to administer it than do comparable bodies in any other Western industrialized nation.

The Finance Ministry's clout is only partly a result of Germany's circumstances after World War II; it is also founded in German administrative tradition. Since Frederick Wilhelm II of Prussia created an elite administrative corps during the mercantilist era, German administrators have been highly trained specialists with considerable authority in their jurisdictions. After World War II, its political elites agreed that the nation's many urgent needs could be dealt with most effectively if the Finance Ministry once again possessed unconstrained authority to formulate and implement tax policy—unthinkable in less hierarchical countries such as the United States. These manipulations were immensely effective in fostering Germany's economic growth, but would certainly have been impossible in a more politicized atmosphere. As Andrew Shonfield informs us, "Subsidies, cheap loans provided by the state and, above all, discriminating tax allowances which support favored activities, were used with abandon that could only be acceptable in a society where the average citizen expects the state to choose its favorites and intervene on their behalf."[82]

Yet in keeping with its tradition of hierarchy, Germany's fiscal bureaucracy has retained close administrative control of whatever policies have been imposed. German tax bureaucrats look closely at individual returns, and taxpayer audits are far more frequent than elsewhere. If an audit reveals underpayment, evaders are brought to trial and forced to pay up. As a consequence of stringent enforcement, administrative costs of Germany's income tax are four to six times higher as a proportion of revenue than in the United States.[83]

Tax policy in Germany can be conveniently divided into two quite distinct periods: reconstruction (1948–60) and stabilization (1960–present). Maintaining high rates of economic growth by promoting savings and investment seemed to have been the tax authorities' only goal during the post–World War II reconstruction period; other issues became important during the late 1950s and early 1960s.

The Allied Control Council imposed extremely heavy taxes on West Germany after World War II. Its income taxes were set at rates that were then the most progressive in the world—top-bracket taxpayers paid 95 percent of income. Two goals influenced the design of this tax policy: bringing in the maximum revenue for repatriation, and further weakening of the German economy.

The Germans "had only a limited possibility of influencing tax policy effectively."[84] By 1948 they were able to exert more control.

> Incentive devices were proposed by the German government not as an ingenious fiscal device to stimulate recovery but as an instrument for evasion of tax policies imposed by the Occupation powers. The incentive devices simply made utterly ineffectual the steeply graduated income tax rates of the Allied Control Council of 1946.[85]

It is important to note that "it was this 'excessive' taxation which contributed in a decisive way to Germany's economic growth."[86] Tax rates were so high that the wealthy were forced to choose either to invest their income in certain ways or to lose it to the government. Realizing that Germany would need significantly more private capital than was forthcoming at the time, the Ministry of Finance created a variety of tax "preferences" (or loopholes) to help wealthy individuals and corporations avoid taxes, while generating substantial national wealth.[87]

These tax incentives came in many forms. The most important were tax exemptions for income from savings or investment, and highly favorable depreciation allowances for targeted industries—iron, steel, coal, gas, shipyards, shipbuilding, and construction.[88] These incentives were deliberately designed to appeal to the wealthy; the effect on fiscal equity was, at best, a minor consideration.[89] "These changes transformed this tax," Tanzi writes, "in the relatively short period of a decade, from probably the most progressive income tax in the world to the least."[90]

Turning to the problems of less wealthy citizens, the government enacted the "Equalization of Burdens" law. It gave generous tax breaks to persons disadvantaged by the war, especially the ten million or more immigrants from East Germany.

With all these tax incentives, German industry did quite well. Annual gross investment went up from DM 20 billion in 1950 to 50 billion in 1955—or from 20 percent to 30 percent of GNP.[91] By the late 1950s, reconstruction clearly had been accomplished. At this point several new policy issues arose involving industrial concentration and fiscal equity.

Convinced that domestic capital was no longer in short supply by the middle to late 1950s, tax authorities withdrew many tax incentives for investment in specific industries, retaining only those for shipbuilding and construction on grounds that such concessions would promote the "common interest." Wanting to promote social equity, the authorities began to give tax advantages to lower-income groups during the early 1960s so as to increase their savings capacities; a larger share of revenue was collected in income tax rather than in the regressive turnover tax (a form of sales tax).

The next major change occurred in 1967, when Germany passed the "Law Promoting Stability and Growth of the Economy." This statute allows the government to use tax and other fiscal policies to stabilize business cycles, to control bank deposits during boom periods by altering interest rates and discount rates, and to establish wage guidelines during recessions. Though some parts of these programs failed along with the Grand Coalition between the Christian Democrats and the Social Democrats of 1966–69, others continue to this day. Central government still must prepare five-year investment programs, and scheduled investments are ranked according to a priority scale that local authorities must consult. The federal government may offer "assistance to individual enterprises or industries to preserve them, to facilitate their adaptation to new economic conditions or to promote their growth, particularly through new production methods."[92] In sum, the Ministry of Finance has moved from promoting industrial growth to specific regions to much more fine-grained intervention into selected industries and even individual enterprises.

With all that has been said of the German tax system's complexity, one might reasonably confuse it with the American system. But this would constitute a serious misunderstanding, though it is true that both are complex. The U.S. Tax Code—more than six thousand pages of law and amendments—has not changed fundamentally since World War II. Its multitudinous amendments and clauses represent concessions favoring specific taxpayers. The German Tax Code has undergone significant reorganization several times in the past three decades; it also includes a large number of particularistic rulings, but they can be and are removed when their economic function has been served. Repeal of preferences is hard to accomplish in the United States.

How each of these countries makes tax policy explains the differences. As Joseph Pechman notes:

> Congress has always guarded this power [to legislate taxes] jealously. Presidents can recommend changes, but only Congress has the power to translate these recommendations into law. Practically every major presidential tax proposal is thoroughly revised by Congress, and not a few are rejected outright. This system allows interst groups access to, and indeed power within, the tax policy process far beyond interest groups' power in any other Western European nation.[93]

In Germany the situation is quite different: the Federal Ministry of Finance enacts tax statutes and submits them to the Bundestag and the Bundesrat. This tradition reaches back into German history. The basic income tax law was written by one man, Enno Brecker, the Minister of Finance in 1919.[94]

Taxing authority in America is the explicit domain of political elites more vulnerable to public pressure than are administrative elites. Where such elites are relatively well insulated from the public (as are the tax authorities in Germany), tax exemptions and investment credits can be more readily used for economic purposes than they can in the United States. Whether tax incentives prove to be effective is a different matter.

Another major difference between the German and American systems is the large amount of discretion held by the Finance Ministry as compared to the United States Internal Revenue Service. Administrative ordinances in Germany have the force of law and provide clear delineations of ministerial discretion. The states, which implement much of the tax code, must abide by these ordinances, though they have never been legislated. Such administrative autonomy would be anathema in the United States. Indeed, the U.S. federal code's intricacy is in part related to the public's desire to constrain discretion in the IRS with the aim of protecting "fairness" and "equity."

Perhaps Germany "needed" a tax system focused on reconstruction and economic growth after World War II. In the immediate postwar years a national consensus existed, permitting fiscal measures that would not have been politically feasible in nonhierarchical countries like the United States. Yet these factors do not explain the German system's single-minded focus on economic growth.

In Germany (as well as in France and Japan) the bureaucratic elites who populate the Ministry of Finance believe that they represent (or must calculate) the "national interest,"[95] and believe they must filter demands made by particular groups. Insulated as they are from politics, these administrators can focus single-minded attention on such "apolitical" issues as growth.

SWEDEN: THE POLITICS OF STABILITY

Policymakers in Sweden have designed their tax structure to accommodate at least three basic goals: redistributing wealth, insuring that revenue will appease the voracious appetite of the welfare state, and stabilizing fluctuations in the business cycle. Among most Swedish citizens a large degree of redistribution is a settled policy. Whenever these goals have conflicted, however, redistribution has yielded to stabilization.

Considering the socialist origins, tradition, and rhetoric of the Social Democratic Party, which has governed most of the time since World War II, it may seem a bit surprising that redistribution is not the primary goal. Ironically, Rose and Peters observe, "taxes are the least progressive in Sweden [of all the OECD democracies], because of the high level of tax paid by ordinary workers. . . . In Sweden, persons earning half the average income and with normal family deductions pay as much as 31 percent of their income in tax."[96] Since most of the people have most of the money, financing the welfare state requires dipping heavily into almost every purse. By taxing everyone, Sweden's welfare state has improved living standards at the lowest levels without unduly penalizing the wealthy.

It seems, rather, that the Swedish authorities have decided to redistribute wealth through government spending.* This feature of the Swedish tax system is surprising only if we focus on the socialist rhetoric of the Social Democratic Party. If we instead look at its corporate decision-making process, such surprising features of the tax system are more easily understood.

Sweden's citizens have the dubious distinction of paying more taxes,

---

* One could argue that the Swedish income tax structure is in fact progressive (due to high maximum rates). The system is much more regressive when we include the flat-rate local tax as well as social-security payments and the value-added tax.[97]

as a percentage of GNP, than any other people in the world. Although Sweden was a relatively high taxing country at the end of World War II, its tax take has grown in the past three decades, and voters have tolerated this increase.[98] Perhaps, since Sweden's citizens favor the welfare state, they accept higher taxes to support it. Still, tax policymakers in Sweden have been conscious of the visibility of new taxes or of tax increases.[99] Though local and national income taxes are still slightly larger, this perception has increasingly moved policymakers to rely for revenue on social security (which is solely a payroll tax in Sweden), VAT (a value-added tax, essentially a sales tax on stages of production, hence a regressive tax), and excise taxes on specific goods.

The Social Democrats were without question the dominant force in Swedish politics by the end of World War II. Overwhelming public support permitted the party to set the political agenda for the next several decades. By 1945 it had already imposed a steeply progressive national income tax and by international standards had created a substantial wealth tax. Thus the political battles over taxes were in large measure different in Sweden than in other countries.

During the 1950s distributive issues influenced the fiscal policy debate. In what Nils Elvander calls "one of the fiercest political battles which has ever occurred in Sweden," the bourgeois parties (as nonsocialist but welfare-statist parties are called there) fought for and won reductions in income tax rates for all income groups.[100] Sweden's tax structure was modified in 1970; yet the Social Democratic Party's long tenure in office (over thirty years) had permitted periodic reforms to restore progressivity.[101] It permitted new accounting methods to accommodate two-income families; this reform made the system more progressive.

In short, the major political battles over the intended progressivity of the income tax system in Sweden seem to have been settled by 1945. While there was a major debate during the 1950s on the overall size of the income tax (ultimately reflecting differences about government's optimal size), most of the actual reforms of this era resulted in lower effective rates. According to Elvander, "Tax policy was, therefore, to some degree, depoliticized."[102] But we think this judgment is premature. There is agreement on greatly reducing income disparities, but not by how much.

Sweden has been called a pioneer of fiscal economic management, and tax changes have served as its principal weapon in this endeavor. Sweden possesses an "arsenal of revenue devices, probably unmatched elsewhere in the world,"[103] including the "mobile income tax," the "investment reserve system," investment taxes, and occasionally a sales tax.

First imposed in 1917, the mobile tax designates the legislated tax rate as a base rate. Thus it is readily utilized for management of the economy according to Keynesian principles. With this tool the government can raise or lower effective rates, depending on its desire to stimulate growth or dampen inflation.[104] The investment reserve system has a similar purpose. It was designed "to allow corporations to iron out economic fluctuations by encouraging private corporate savings in years of high profits, and private capital expenditure in years when the government wishes to stimulate investment."[105] To this end corporations are able to set aside 40 percent of a year's profit into a tax-exempt investment reserve that may be drawn upon during an economic slump. These reserves, interestingly, can be put to use only when a central administrative agency (the Labor Market Review Board—a telling name) releases them, and only to finance new investment.[106] In effect, the government finances countercyclical investment from what enterprises would otherwise have paid in taxes.[107]

Another innovative stabilization measure is the investment tax, instituted in 1951–53 and again in 1955–57. In simplified form, this tax levies a 12 percent charge on investments in agriculture, property, and business. Within these sectors it exempted a very specific set of investments,[108] again to direct funds to governmentally designated areas and purposes.

The sales tax has been used from time to time for economic stabilization. To promote spending, the wartime sales tax was abolished in 1947, but in 1959 it was imposed again to curb inflationary pressures. (It must be added, however, that renewal was also motivated by the need to generate revenue.) By then tax policymakers were well aware of resistance to direct taxes. The Social Democrats had to overrule other parties' objections to impose this blatantly regressive tax.

Through use of such stabilization measures, generous depreciation schemes, and liberal tax accounting methods for companies, Swedish corporations have been able to avoid heavy taxation of corporate profits. High corporate tax rates do not result in high returns in revenue. Though the rates have remained high by international standards, fluctuating around 56 to 58 percent, the amounts actually collected have remained low and are consistently decreasing. The reason for this discrepancy between intention and outcome is found in the variety of tax-avoidance mechanisms offered to corporations. "An essential feature of these devices is the degree of control they give business taxpayers over the amount of profit to be reported for tax purposes."[109]

Sweden's policymakers have also been admired by tax experts around the world for the country's depreciation schemes. Between 1938 and 1955 corporations could use the "free depreciation system," permitting them to write off costs of investment in machinery at whatever rate they preferred, even in one year. In 1955 free depreciation was replaced by "book" depreciation, a method allowing somewhat less generous rates. It was introduced not because the old system was seen as a corporate giveaway; rather, it was because policymakers believed that the free depreciation system contributed to inflation by encouraging too much self-financing by profitable firms during boom periods.

Paradoxically, all these measures were adopted by an avowedly socialist government to aid large capitalist enterprises. Although economic stabilization was Sweden's original justification, there can be little doubt that the direct beneficiaries of these incentives are large (by Swedish standards) corporations. Because of these policies large private corporations in Sweden are considered more socialistic than small family-held firms. In the short run, instead of promoting redistribution of wealth, the nation's corporate tax policies have exactly the opposite effect: facilitating its concentration.[110]

We do not mean to imply that Swedish tax authorities do not tax the rich. Quite the contrary. Sweden has the steepest wealth tax of any country. We must again note, however, that corporations are exempt from this 2.5 percent tax on net wealth and/or assets. Although Sweden's property tax was abolished in 1955, it was replaced by a new system, *garentibelopp,* which imputes a 2.5 percent annual income on real-property holdings, added to the individual's actual income for computing local income taxes.

Sweden's tax system has often been criticized on grounds that it is too progressive. Ingmar Bergman's widely publicized emigration is but one example of a disgruntled wealthy taxpayer fleeing the heavy burden. Apparently income derived from filmmaking—an activity not deemed by tax authorities as contributing either to national wealth or to economic stability—is not protected by exemptions and subsidies. Unless "properly" invested, such income is taxed heavily. Critics claim that the system promotes flight of capital; in fact, some wealthy owners of family businesses have transferred assets abroad to escape wealth and inheritance taxes, but no one knows how much. Yet wealthy industrialists—steel manufacturers, say, or shipbuilders—often receive special dispensations. According to a prominent student, "In Sweden, tax expenditures are important in making tolerable otherwise extremely high rates of taxation. Thanks to government investment and depreciation allowances, a company may be able to avoid paying any tax on a gross profit of up to $100 million. Swedes earning a million or more kroner a year may avoid taxes on much of that income by invoking tax loopholes."[111]

This same logic can be found in the extremely high taxes on liquor, tobacco, and especially automobiles. These commodities can be taxed so heavily because, being luxuries (at least to some economists who call them, with their usual felicity, "nonmerit goods"), they do not contribute to Sweden's "national interest."

Sweden's tax system avoids taxing economic sectors or individuals seen as contributing to economic stability and, to a lesser extent, to growth; but it places a very heavy burden on virtually everything else.

Corporatism—a designation given to a particular style of public-policy decision-making—has received much attention in the past decade.[112] Major interest groups are brought into the policymaking process when the government decides issues that affect them. Students of corporatism generally focus on issues of wage bargaining, and occasionally on social policy. As a major concern of both business and labor, tax policy is a likely topic for joint decision.[113]

Operating within rules specified by the party in power, selected representatives of interest groups (most often peak associations bringing together all veterans, or industries, or unions) are brought into the decision-making process, an exchange aptly described by Rostow as "the politics of compromise." Since policy recommendations usually require near-unanimous consent, one would expect a tax to emerge that taxes wealth—in keeping with political pledges made by the Social Democratic Party—but is very careful not to tax away corporate capacity to invest.

Given the fact that major producing interests already belong to the governing coalition, stability has to be a major goal (perhaps ultimately the major goal) of fiscal-policy management. Businesses are always interested in reducing uncertainty, and labor unions (and therefore the Social Democratic Party) consistently seek lower unemployment. Interests that participate in decisions, then, have little to gain, and a lot to lose, from sharp fluctuations in the nation's economy.

In sum, Swedish corporatism involves socialization rather than nationalization of industry. As long as private resources are invested in socially acceptable ways, money is left in industrial hands. Though this compromise—capitalist survival in return for state direction—does result in egalitarian measures for taxing and spending, elements of inequality inherent in corporate capitalism nevertheless remain.

The Swedish experience appears to refute the alleged conflict between high income taxes and low economic growth. It may be, instead, that the structure of taxes—lower capital gains and effective corporate rates—rather than their total may be important.

CLASS POLITICS IN BRITAIN

In Britain, tax politics is class politics. The British have not been able to settle the issue of what taxes should do. The left aims to use taxes to promote labor's interests; the right, to induce capital formation. As each party takes its turn in controlling the government, it implements policies favoring its respective constituency; the institutional legacy of the preceding program, however, invariably mitigates each policy's effects. As Kay and King write,

> Anyone who came to it [the British tax system] for the first time would regard the present system with some incredulity. There is a maze of taxes on different kinds of income, each tax with its own rules for determining taxable income and liability. The interaction between these taxes is difficult to comprehend and, because of this, is rarely brought out into the open when tax changes are discussed. No one would design such a system on purpose, and nobody did. Only a historical explanation of how it came about can be offered.[114]

The result is that "one of the most noticeable characteristics of the British tax system is that it is under continual change. Writing about it is very much like trying to hit a moving target."[115]

Taxes are consistently used to regulate the economy. Rates are lowered to heat up the economy in economic downturns, then, after the recession has slackened, raised to help pay for the debt so incurred. The Treasury periodically creates, revamps, restructures, or totally removes old taxes. The "stop-go" politics of postwar Britain are a product of this oscillation.

Over the past three decades, taxes on savings, pension incomes, and investments have been manipulated in order to maintain employment and increase economic growth. Incoming governments altered rates and exemptions on income from savings and, in 1965, capital gains.[116] Under Britain's "free depreciation system," companies can manipulate depreciation of capital investments, in many cases permitting write-offs of 100 percent of amounts spent in any given year. As in the United States, income from capital gains is subject to a different rate (30 percent) than taxes on ordinary income.[117] Wage earners have benefited from special provisions targeted to recipients of low incomes: small-income relief, child relief, earned-income credit, personal relief, and old-age relief.[118]

Analysts of British taxation are adamant in lambasting the system, though awareness of a problem, willingness to do something about it, and the insulation needed to accomplish reforms (in the German style) do exist in Britain. As a tax authority writes, Britain's slow economic growth "does not appear to have been the result either of failure to recognize the problem or unwillingness to try to do something about it."[119] Yet, "a look through the major book on the Chancellor's postwar economic management, Samuel Brittan's *Steering the Economy*, suggests that in retrospect Chancellors rarely do the right things and, if they do, it is often done for the wrong reasons."[120]

The left in England favors high income taxes largely because of a belief that income should be redistributed. From the early years of this century labor has contended that income taxes should be paid mostly by the rich. Trying to protect capital without arousing antipathy, the Tories have manipulated rates for high- and low-income taxpayers.[121] So rates go up and down. The redistributive elements in the present tax structure rely heavily on high tax rates on salary income. Since high earnings are not an important source of wealth inequality in the United Kingdom, these taxes fall heavily on people working in productive sectors of the economy, without achieving much in the way of redistribution.[122]

The corporate income tax also has had its ups and downs. Not only have rates changed many times since Labour introduced this tax in 1947, but definitions of corporate income or profit have undergone multiple revisions.

If a set of rules guides political actors' intervention into Great Britain's economy, in effect they specify using arm's-length policies. Rather than intervening directly, the Labour Party tries to manipulate the economy by using general-purpose tools (such as the level of expenditures or types of taxation). In doing so, Labour legislates measures that inhibit operation of a relatively free market economy. When the Tories return to power, they expend much of their political energy trying to undo "damage" done by the preceding government, but are only marginally successful. Normally the Tories devise a few market-stimulating policies; these are layered onto the labor-oriented strategies of previous governments. Viewing these market strategies as attempts to harm their class interests, Labour Party activists, in turn, push through opposing legislation when they return to power. Generally tax receipts have increased during years of Labour government (1956–61, 1966, 1974) and fallen off during Conservative rule (1953, 1959, 1963, 1970).

The Selective Employment tax (initiated 1966, removed 1973) is a good example of a tax levied by a Labour government, only to be abolished by the Conservatives. This tax was an explicit attempt to aid low-profit companies with large numbers of employees. Although the measure granted a tax preference to the liable companies, a need to protect specific working-class interests was sufficient justification for this policy. As intended, it encouraged labor-intensive rather than capital-intensive industry.[123]

British administrators are reluctant to engage in "hands on" manipulation of the business sector.[124] "By contrast [to Germany]," Heidenheimer, Heclo, and Adams write, "the British tax system was found to treat businessmen and professionals with great caution, dispensing with most administrative auditing, offering a rich reservoir of 'loopholes' and imposing fewer obligatory accounting procedures than are required in Germany."[125]

Despite Labour's dedication to creating a progressive personal and corporate tax structure, Conservatives have been able to manipulate these taxes in ways that mitigate their redistributive effect. According to OECD, the extent of slippage in Britain is second only to that found in the United States.[126]

> But modifications and special provisions in the application of these taxes have been made in such a way that it is difficult to consider them any longer as straightforward income-based taxes. Many of these modifications have moved this part of the tax structure from an income base towards what is in effect a consumption-expenditure base.[127]

As a result of this slippage, income taxes cannot generate sufficient resources to support the British welfare state. Before Britain adopted the VAT system in 1973, excise taxes on tobacco, petrol, and alcohol were major revenue producers, and they still are. (As anyone who has tried to buy a bottle of scotch at the distillery can tell you, it's cheaper at the corner liquor store in the United States.)

Politics in Britain may be changing, but public policy is not. The split in the Labour Party, between adherents of a mixed economy and those favoring drastic redistribution of wealth and income, has been settled, in a manner of speaking, by exodus. Under Prime Minister Thatcher's government the cleavage within the Conservative Party between the "wets" and the "drys"—the hierarchical heirs of Tory radicalism, and proponents of competitive individualism—has temporarily been decided in favor of the latter. The coalition of Social Democrats and Liberals has offered sharper choices, yet the voters have elected to continue past policies. As for progressivity, the current Tory government is taking about the same amount in taxes, with lower rates at the very top and bottom, and making up the difference with selective additions to the value-added tax. Elements of nationalized industry will continue to be sold off but the pattern of spending and taxing seems fairly well fixed.

TAXATION IN POSTWAR FRANCE

Ever since the revolution of 1789, French politicians have hesitated to impose direct taxes. Long after the overthrow of France's Ancien Régime direct taxes still epitomized its inequitable fiscal system. Throughout the nineteenth century and up to the present, indirect taxes on commodities and services—appropriate for a nation of small farmers and small businesses—have supported the government. A fiscal structure based on indirect taxes reflects the continuing influence in French politics of the petite bourgeoisie.

Crisis accounts for French citizens' willingness to tolerate such major reforms of direct taxes as have occurred—during World War I, after World War II (1948), and in 1959 when de Gaulle assumed power. Overall, however, tax receipts do contribute an increasing proportion of public resources, having gone up from about 75 percent of money spent in 1900 to 80 percent between the wars, to about 90 percent in 1960.[128]

The value-added tax (VAT) is the mainstay of the modern French tax system. Unlike other Western industrialized nations, in France the personal income tax is not the most important revenue source. Because the conservative governments of the past two decades depended for support on interests still adamantly opposed to direct taxes, they have instead relied for revenue on turnover and value-added taxes.

First imposed in 1954, VAT replaced assorted turnover and sales taxes. To prevent evasion, VAT is collected at each stage of the production process; hence it is more productive than a simple indirect tax on final consumption.* Rates range from 7 percent on necessities to 33.3 percent on luxuries. Intermediate products pay 17.6 percent of invoiced value, while commodities produced for export are exempt. To meet the European Economic Community's tax harmonization requirements, VAT's coverage was extended in 1979 to encompass agricultural commodities. By 1963 the tax produced about a third of France's revenue; today it brings in almost half (48 percent).[131]

Besides VAT, the government derives some revenue from modest local sales taxes (levied at 2.75 percent of sales price). Seeking to improve fiscal efficiency, the government has several times tried to replace these taxes with an expanded VAT, but local authorities, and ultimately the parliament, have rejected the measure each time it was introduced.[132] A tax on petroleum yields about 8 percent of total revenue.

While France does have an income tax, strong popular resistance—expressed in the Poujadist rebellion of the mid-1950s—has made it hard to enforce. Trying to create a tax structure similar to those of Britain, Germany, and the United States, the Gaullists modernized France's existing income tax in 1958. In spite of a progressive rate structure (collecting 65 percent of income in the highest bracket), it yields only moderate amounts—20 percent of total revenue in 1979.[133] Payroll taxes (equivalent to U.S. Social Security), introduced in 1948 and made permanent in 1952, however, do tap wage workers' incomes.

France's first postwar revision of income tax in 1948 also added a tax on corporate incomes. Taking 50 percent of corporate profits (whether distributed or not), it produces about 10 percent of French revenue. A declining-balance depreciation system, introduced in 1959,[134] moderates the high rates; and deductions for costs of doing business normal in the other Western nations are available in France as well.

An effective tax system includes the loopholes as well as the rates. Since the late 1940s several governments have tried to tighten deductions for businessmen's travel and entertainment expenses, but each time the tax proposals "fail of passage or are rejected or amended beyond recognition."[135]

---

* The costs of compliance are a major consideration in the choice of instruments of taxation. One reason for the great popularity of the value-added tax in western Europe (soon we expect it to be a major item of contention in the United States)[129] is the incentives it provides for self-policing. Though each business in every stage of production is liable for taxes on its sales, this liability is reduced by the amount the firm pays in taxes to its suppliers. "Those in the middle of a production process," therefore, as James Alt observes, "have an incentive to turn in complete returns of purchases, thereby policing those who sold to them."[130]

A political culture characterized by exceptionally strong hierarchy and markets fosters enmity between individualism and collectivism. This mutual enmity produces tolerance for tax evasion; faced by a hostile public, the tax authorities take what they can get. According to Rose and Peters,

> The Romance pattern of taxation in France and Italy is based on mutual distrust between citizen and state. Both countries believe that individuals will deceive the government when making tax declarations, and history justifies this belief. Income taxes contribute less than one-sixth of tax revenue in France and Italy. To collect income taxes, officials estimate what they think an individual earns, and wait for the person to accept the figure or bargain for a lower assessment. Like buyers and sellers in a used car transaction, tax collectors try to get as much as possible, and citizens try to pay as little as possible. For this reason, one-third or more of total individual income is not reported for tax purposes.[136]

With such widespread evasion, tax inspectors try to ferret out delinquency; each inspector may look at three hundred personal and four hundred corporate returns, with uncertain outcome.[137] Vito Tanzi attempts to explain evasion in terms of Latin nations' "individualist" character.[138] Others have accused the Catholic Church of condoning tax evasion.* Still others say the French and the Italians have "low civic consciousness."[139] These are not explanations but reiterations, in other forms, of the same question. The fact, for instance, that the major local tax, the *taxe professionielle*, is basically a tax on salaries constitutes a disincentive to hire workers; especially when combined with the high social-security taxes paid by business, its evasion is more than a matter of temperament.[140]

The French fiscal bureaucracy's use of administrative discretion resembles, and in fact surpasses, the Germans'! This may be why tax politics seems to have a low profile in France, so long, to be sure, as governments do not impose higher income taxes. Requisite revenue is generated through VAT and social security, while economic goals are met by granting tax concessions to industry. For example, "the French Fourth Plan enumerates eight major categories of tax relief. Economic planners invoke any or all of these measures to induce cooperation by individual private enterprises."[141] Tax concessions are a very impor-

---

* Specifically, the official Vatican newspaper, *Osservatore Romano*, declared that tax evasion was not a sin.

tant part of the French system of indicative planning, itself a merger of markets and hierarchy.

A CULTURAL EXPLANATION OF TAX DIFFERENCES

What accounts for the distinctive patterns of taxation that persist in each country—patterns that emerge even after the vicissitudes of life, which may cause temporary departures, have been accounted for? Why, we ask, has the fiscal system of the United States remained fixated on equality, Germany's on economic growth, and Sweden's on dampening economic fluctuations?

Equality is viewed differently in the various cultures. Equality before the law emerges from hierarchy; there the concept serves to adjudicate status, delineating who has the obligation to collect and to pay how much in taxes. To competitive individualists, equity connotes access to opportunity, permitting those who perform best in markets to retain most of their gain. Favoring taxation to support the state, hierarchies emphasize tax collection. Individualists, who prefer private to public spending, want to reduce tax rates. Since sectarians believe that all people's share in the social order should be equal, equality entails changing the distribution of wealth—taxing the wealthy to give to the poor.

Members of hierarchies and market regimes are interested in economic growth to pay off collective or individual obligations. Sectarians focus exclusively on the danger of new wealth; it threatens to increase the inequalities they dislike.

The United States is culturally pluralistic. While its hierarchies are weak compared to the European social democracies, its political culture does favor markets, and it also possesses powerful sectarian tendencies. Resistance to high income taxes, and in general to state power, may be explained by the strength of competitive individualism and the weakness of hierarchical collectivism in U.S. political culture. The continuing strength of sectarianism accounts for its pervasive concern for equity in taxation.

If sufficient funds are to be raised for the modern state, there must be an income tax; it is the fiscal instrument most productive of revenue. Since income is broadly if unequally shared, this tax must cast its net widely. Sectarians prefer high progressivity; market forces want progressiveness to be minimal. The inevitable compromise falls somewhere between. Depending on the balance among the three cultures in any place at any given time, therefore, the different conceptions of equality—equal shares, equal opportunity, equal treatment before the law—result in continuous changes in the tax code, changes that operate within the fundamental compromise of moderate progressivity.

Where hierarchy is definitely dominant (as it has been in Germany) but market forces have moderate strength, the tax system serves the establishment. Hierarchy and markets agree on economic growth. Hierarchy manipulates the tax system to increase wealth, holding on to a substantial proportion to fulfill its obligation to poorer members of the collectivity. The new Green Party in Germany is opposed to economic growth and national defense, and its views are echoed among some Social Democrats.

How can insistent demands for redistribution—characteristics of the alliance between hierarchies and sects that is called social democracy—be handled without damaging the productivity required to maintain and enhance high standards of living? (When and where productivity is increasing—as it did everywhere in the Western world between the end of World War II and the early 1970s—this problem does not arise.) In the Swedish compromise, private markets are permitted to operate if the actors in these markets will pass through substantial income to the state. Government then redirects the receipts into investments preferred by its planners, and into social services. In this process, hierarchy is enhanced and the state brings about significant redistribution of income while retaining markets. Maintenance of the governmental hierarchy permits consistent use of tax preferences favoring markets. Rather than being a departure from equity, the preferences are converted into an aid to state planning.

Should this tripartite compromise be replaced by an alliance of hierarchies and sects without markets (as union ownership of industry might produce), the bargaining would be much different. Were the new economic forces from labor to pursue sectarian aims, they might well insist on more redistribution without being willing to tax union members for the purpose. The state's authority would come into question. Sweden would be faced with hyperpluralism—an excess of demands over capability to achieve them, and inadequate authority to lay down limits.

In Britain, class cleavages are so pervasive that they run within as well as across parties. The Labour Party is divided between hierarchic and sectarian elements the constituencies being more sectlike, and the unions more hierarchic. The Conservatives are split between adherents of hierarchy and of markets. Compromises within parties mean that the distance between the parties is reduced. Though there are only occasional interparty compromises, hierarchical elements in each party maintain continuity. Should hierarchic components in both parties weaken, and the Social Democratic/Liberal coalition fail to catch on, the ensuing struggle between a sectarian Labour Party and a market-oriented Conservative Party might make class conflicts of the past pale in comparison.

WHY PROGRESSIVE STATES TAX CORPORATE INCOME LOW, AND LOW AND MIDDLE INCOMES HIGH

It is not easy—but not impossible—to decipher national tax codes or to relate them in their diversity and detail to one another. Let us tackle them forward and backward, first considering their similarities to and then their differences from practices in America, which, after all, borrowed many of them from European countries.

Ths history of the United States—its long dependence on the tariff; the division of labor in which cities used the property tax, states adopted sales taxes, and the federal government the income tax—is not duplicated elsewhere. Every nation has some tax that came first. Are they acceptable, fruitful, and easy to implement? The adage of the revenue department, "An old tax is a good tax," speaks volumes. This signifies not only easier compliance, because people are accustomed to paying, but also that the economy has adjusted to the alteration of activity produced by the tax. Each nation's tax history, therefore, has to be traced separately in order to understand its selection and rejection of various provisions. Where it is now—the proportion of the various revenue sources that make up the total tax take—is determined in part by where it has been.[142] To put the point backward, all tax systems are alike in their historically related differences.

They are also alike in their complexity. Considerations similar to those operating in America make tax systems in social democracies complex. In all, there is the "domino effect" of changes in a few provisions. Likewise, affected interests try to secure beneficial changes, and tax officials try to keep revenues secure. Conflict among objectives is common.

The desire for revenue is a constant surrounded by a variable. All nations wish to collect enough, but how much is enough varies. In general, the stronger the market culture, the lower the revenue demanded. Given whatever level of revenue is deemed desirable, all seek to collect (though all are not equally successful in collecting) enough. The postulate of revenue maximization is not a good guide, because no Western nation collects all the revenue it might, and only those at the very top in spending try to come close.

Just as revenue is a function not only of economic capacity but of political preference, mobilizing resources is far from the only objective of taxation. Varying the level and composition of taxation is, as everyone knows, a major mode of economic regulation. Without going into the efficacy of these measures, it should be evident that consistency in taxation must, to some extent, be sacrificed for economic stability. Varying taxation means deliberately destabilizing the economy. Here we have an explanation for both the volatility and the complexity of tax systems.

Beyond economic management (and the fine-tuning that leads to constant tinkering with taxes), which is ubiquitous, taxation has objectives in the modern welfare state that are well known but are yet to be recognized in the literature on revenue. Taxation has become an instrument for regulating individual behavior. Of course, the taxation of "luxuries" or of commodities deemed to be bad for you, like tobacco and liquor, is very old indeed. Incentives for behavior deemed desirable—low or no taxes on churches, universities, and charitable bodies—go back a long way. In amount and extent, however, there has been a quantitative change in favor of inducing this or that behavior—from not planting to selling crops, from adopting costly safety measures to reducing the price of labor through rebates, on and on in great and bewildering profusion. Yet all this and more is insufficient to indicate the qualitative change that has taken place in making taxation a primary instrument for regulating individual behavior.

Were the purpose of taxation solely to redistribute income, tax systems would be much simpler than they are today. A steeply progressive, broad-based income tax, without tax preferences, would do. Why, then, has this all-too-obvious choice not been adopted by any single country? Why are there a multiplicity of taxes instead of a single income (or even, as Henry George urged, a land) tax? Why are many of these taxes regressive or only mildly progressive instead of taking from the better for the worse off? Why are people with relatively low or middle incomes taxed so heavily, especially in the nations most dedicated to equality of condition? To make the anomaly complete, why do the most progressive nations place low taxes on corporations and high taxes on people with low and middle incomes?

Tax systems are the way they are because there are prudential considerations linked to the ease of generating large amounts of revenue.

A multiplicity of tax sources provides a far-reaching redundancy into the nooks and crannies of income otherwise hard to reach. Where income may be hidden it is found by multiple probes from different vantage points.

There is also the problem of how to maintain the revenue base for future revenue mobilization. Nationalizing industry makes government responsible for losses as well as gains. It bogs government down in administration instead of in redistribution. Goals become displaced; the focus shifts to making government rather than society more equal. And there is the question of consent. The social democracies require consent, but are not necessarily antagonistic to industry, provided it supports egalitarian measures. Relationships among political, administrative, and business elites are still good. Led by complex hierarchies whose collective concerns include a regard for industrial elites, social democracies have evolved a better way to make their policy preferences effective.

If workers held on to their newly equalized wages, there is no telling what they would do with it. Far better for elites to collect income at the center and then redistribute it in ways designed to secure egalitarian objectives. After all, it is not the money, as the saying goes, but what it can buy that matters. Recycling worker income into a set series of services enables governing elites to determine what will be done with income. Should equalizing life chances among men and women call for more equalized income, for instance, central allocation can provide for child care and whatever other services the government decides are desirable.

In regard to corporate income, a similar purpose leads to a different method. Rather than taxing directly, thus raising questions about international competitiveness and domestic economic growth, money may be left in the hands of employers, providing they agree to use it for a long list of socially approved purposes. Whether employee income is recycled through the state (a term applied to government when it becomes conscious of itself) or redirected from employers, governing elites use the tax process to regulate behavior.

So far as we can see, absent tax revolts or indications of massive discontent in opinion polls, citizens in social democracies approve of high levels of total taxation and of the regulatory purposes to which the revenues are put. Though they agree with the general rationale of government taxing and spending, many people still try to escape as much of the tax bite as they can. They may engage in barter. Work may be performed at a lower price, providing the artisan is paid in cash with no record kept. And so on. When this phenomenon is carried to an extreme (estimates are that the "gray economy" in Italy amounts to a fourth or a third of its national product), the scope for redistribution is limited. But, in most countries, most of the time, not by very much. Despite complaints about excessive and complex taxation, the modern industrial state remains a mighty financial engine.

So long as expenditure keeps growing faster than revenue, however, this engine will be increasingly unable to pull its load. Hence it is understandable that efforts to slow down spending are ubiquitous. And so are failures to achieve that result.

THE EMERGENCE OF SPENDING LIMITS

All over the Western world, not merely in the United States, serious efforts to control public spending are now under way. Nowhere have these succeeded. With defense spending rising in the United States, and universal entitlements going up automatically, recent spending cuts in the United States and Britain (though substantial by historical and comparative standards) do not alter the basic trends.

Only in the United States is there significant elite and citizen support for reducing government's size. Selling off parts of nationalized industry in Britain, as we reported earlier, does not affect the size of income transfers or social services, or, in the last instance, the total size of government. Nevertheless, faced with what is, in some respects, a similar problem, how to bring revenues and expenditures into concordance, various Western nations have adopted quite similar strategies.

In the most comprehensive study of efforts to limit government spending, Daniel Tarschys reports that "governments in many countries now seem to be groping for some artificial norm to replace the dethroned ideal of equilibrium between revenue and expenditure."[143] The idea is "to commit the government apparatus itself to budgetary stringency" by "imposing strong restraints on all actors involved."[144] The type of control varies from one country to another, depending on national vulnerabilities and traditions. A nation that has had trouble borrowing in international markets may try to limit the total amount of borrowing. Where inflation is rampant, efforts are made to limit the size of the deficit. The most common control, however, is a limit on total public spending, either in absolute terms or at some proportion of Gross National Product. Indeed, the targets may be combined. In Sweden, for example, current budget policy prescribes that the central government's deficits should be reduced to correspond with changes in the nation's external accounts balance. Table 23 from Tarschys illustrates the range of purposes encompassed in spending limits.

TABLE 23

MEDIUM-TERM BUDGETARY OBJECTIVES[145]

Country	Time Scale	Objective
United States	1981–1984	Achievement of Federal budget balance via expenditure cuts; amended to objective of a fiscal 1985 federal deficit/GNP ratio below the average for 1970s.
Japan	1979/80–1984/5	Reduction of public sector deficit from 11.25 percent of GDP in 1978 to 3.3 percent, implying the elimination of "exceptional bonds" to finance public consumption.
Germany	1981–1985	Reduction of Federal deficit from DM34 bill to DM17.5 bill.
France	1976–1980	Reduction of central government deficit from 3 percent of GDP in 1975 to .3 percent. No current target.
United Kingdom	1980/1–1984/5	Reduction of PSBR (Public Sector Borrowing Requirement) from 5.7 percent of GDP to 2 percent; total expenditure growth fixed at 37 percent in cash terms, implying a fall from 45 percent of GDP in 1982/3 to 41 percent.
Italy	1981–1983	Freezing of PSBR at 1980 level.
Canada	1981/2–1985/6	Reduction in Federal deficit to 1.9 percent of GDP from peak of 5.3 percent in 1978–9, via reduction in government expenditures from 20.5 to 19 percent of GDP (without debt charges expenditures rise in line with GDP).
Australia	1975/6 onwards	General objective to reduce the central government deficit and size of public sector.
Austria	1978–1981	Reduction of central government deficit to 2½ percent of GDP, via expenditure restraint.
Belgium	1979–1982	Reduce government borrowing to 5 percent of GDP, with zero volume growth of current spending (excluding unemployment benefits and debt interest).
Denmark	1980–1993	Medium-term action program; general objective to reduce the central government deficit and restrict growth of public spending to achieve external balance.
Finland	1976–1982	Growth in the volume of public consumption to be restricted to 1 percent per annum below the annual average growth rate of GDP; tax burden to be stabilized.
Netherlands	1978–1982	Reduction in public sector deficit from 5.25 percent to structural norm of 4–4.5 percent of GDP, via expenditure restraint.

TABLE 23   Continued
MEDIUM-TERM BUDGETARY OBJECTIVES[145]

Country	Time Scale	Objective
Norway	1982–1985	"Long-term program" to contain public expenditure growth and stabilize gross tax level.
Portugal	1981–1984	Stabilize or reduce the central government deficit.
Spain	1979 onwards	Medium-term objective to control public sector deficit and curtail current expenditures.
Sweden	1980–1990	Reduction of central government deficit in line with the achievement of external current account balance.
Switzerland	1980–1983	Establish federal government budget balance by 1984, by restricting the growth of spending.

Another ubiquitous practice involves trying to take advantage of inflation by altering the rules for indexing. Linking government expenditures to price indices (as distinguished from wages) drives spending up, while indexing tax brackets reduces future tax collections. To reduce deficits, it is desirable to "un-index" both taxes and spending. This increases the government's certainty—at the expense of also increasing uncertainty for individuals who expect transfer payments with constant purchasing power. Apparently there is no way to simultaneously increase the sense of certainty within government, in economic enterprise, and among citizens. Policymakers try to chip away at government's difficulties by such tactics as eliminating energy prices from the cost-of-living index (as in Denmark and Sweden) or deleting government subsidies from the food price index (as in Ireland). Who can say whether the programs of certain agencies need extra funding because they are so labor intensive, or whether others need more because they are so technology intensive? While government can grant compensation for this or that inflationary increase on grounds of equity or efficiency, indexing everything only restates the difficulty.

Why, the reader may well ask, is there so much fiddling with indexing when the results are often so mixed? One answer is that big money accrues to those programs that are granted cost-of-living increases. Another, perhaps more fundamental, reason is that as government stretches its resources close to the limits, more people, in and out of government, begin to wonder whether it is possible to protect everyone simultaneously against adversity, and whether one generation will remain committed to supporting another.

The third major trend in expenditure limitation is to package to-gether disparate items of spending in order to consider them all at the same time. Whether called "reconciliation," as in the United States or the "well-balanced package," as in Europe and Japan, debates over these composites are really another way of setting overall spending limits. The difference is that the packages are considered at one time, rather than over a period of years, and cover only a few major spend-ing items. The rationale for the technique is to provide incentives for program reductions by aggregating the totals. Departments may think it is worthwhile to make some sacrifices if other departments face cuts, too, so that the total reductions are meaningful. The aggregation tech-nique also creates interdependence, so that any given department will have reason to oppose "excessive" increases in others.

This packaging strategy has interesting side effects already emerg-ing. If how much is spent matters more than what it is spent on, gov-ernments may try to bargain with spending units, offering greater discretion in spending in exchange for staying within spending limits; this seems to be happening throughout Europe. Canada and New Zea-land have pioneered in use of trade-offs—agencies and programs may reallocate for their own purposes whatever is saved beneath the totals. If reductions were the only possible outcome of the spending package, agencies and programs would lose their incentives to participate in the process.[146]

Spending reforms during the 1950s and 1960s focused on improving the process of budgetary calculation, not on limiting total spending. A broad-brush review of taxation shows that the major emphasis was on developing methods to better manage the economy or (as with the value-added tax) to raise revenue without stirring up political protest. Starting in the mid-1970s, financial turbulence generated a different budget strategy, one beginning to set limits on total spending. From 1979 on, for example, liberal and conservative Canadian cabinets have sought to keep spending within the total spent in the prior year plus the percentage increase in national product during that year. More than this small percentage increase for one department or program would mean less for another.[147] In the United States, a similar strategy un-derlies the proposed balanced-budget amendment to the Constitu-tion.[148] Were the amendment to be adopted, growth of expenditures would be held to the rate of economic growth—last year's spending times the percentage increase in national product. Imposition of "cash limits" in Britain works the same way: departments must stay within these limits despite unfavorable price changes. If the Gramm-Rudman-

Hollings Balanced Budget Act of 1985 survives, its mandated cuts to achieve balance in five years (see the final chapter) would represent the most severe attack on spending in the Western world.

So far these experiments have occurred only in the English-speaking democracies where market forces are stronger than elsewhere. So far these limits have not been tested—either in years of budgetary stringency or in better times with higher revenues. Whether the 1980s usher in an era of resource limits or not, however, the movement to impose ceilings on the growth of government is bound to recur if the public sector keeps growing faster than the private.

No one can say whether or to what extent these measures will succeed. Past history is against them. And it may be that renewal of economic vigor will save the day, at least for nations (the vast majority) that would prefer to maintain government spending at high proportions of national product. But we know also that spending cannot keep rising far faster than revenue indefinitely. There will be changes because there must be. What will these changes be about? Tarschys sums up a continuing debate:

> The real value of consumer price-indexed benefits relative to non-indexed wages has risen in many OECD countries. Simultaneously there have been considerable cost increases in many income maintenance programs because of soaring unemployment, pension age reductions, and other extensions of the coverage. This has given birth to many questions about the construction of various national support systems. One point frequently raised is whether the liberal pension pledges given at a time when there was no end in sight to stable material growth can be upheld in an age of economic stand-still. Another query is whether one should not make a distinction between "micro-risks" and "macro-risks." The first category includes such uncertain yet foreseeable events against which the insurance system provides a rational technique for risk-sharing; the latter concept, on the other hand, stands for perils against which there can be no compensation by collective redistribution since everybody is hurt, e.g., wars and changes in the terms of trade. If the coverage of our social insurance system were confined to the insurance "micro-risks," considerable savings might accrue.[149]

We expect the question of "Who shall bear the costs of change, different categories of citizens or government itself?" to recur with increasing force and frequency.

Chapter Ten

A CULTURAL THEORY OF GOVERNMENTAL GROWTH AND (UN)BALANCED BUDGETS

If we consider the shortness of human life, and our limited knowledge, even of what passes in our own time, we must be sensible that we should be forever children in understanding, were it not for this invention, which extends our experience to all past ages, and to the most distant nations; making them contribute as much to our improvement in wisdom, as if they had actually lain under our observation. A man acquainted with history may, in some respect, be said to have lived from the beginning of the world, and to have been making continual additions to his stock of knowledge in every century.

—DAVID HUME[1]

The themes which appeal to historians may have no more real relationship to the facts they are supposed to organize than the obsessions of a madman. A friend of mine once heard some lectures on Greek myths and became so ensnared by the myth of Sisyphus that all stories for him became as one—the myth of Sisyphus seemed to him the sole plot for all human enterprises.

—HASKELL FAIN[2]

In a practical age one may wonder about the utility of historical study. There is nothing to be done about the past. We can't change it. Would it not, then, be more sensible to give our time and attention to present emergencies or to future hopes?

—JOHN WILLIAM MILLER[3]

When Rehoboam sought to succeed his father, Solomon, as king of Israel, spokesmen for the various tribes came to him asking that he lighten the grievous tax burdens his father had imposed on them. Rehoboam consulted the old men who had advised Solomon; they counseled conciliation. But he listened to the young men he had grown up with; they counseled confrontation. "My father made your yoke heavy," Rehoboam told the assembled congregation of Israel, "and I will add to your yoke; my father also chastized you with whips, but I will chastize you with scorpions." Uttering the famous call for dis-

560

establishment, "To your tents, O Israel," leaders of ten of the twelve tribes departed, leaving Rehoboam with only the tribes of Judah and Benjamin to govern. As the Bible says, with its solemn air of finality, "So Israel rebelled against the house of David to this day."[4]

The disintegration in Rehoboam's time of the centralized state, pieced together so craftfully by David and consolidated by Solomon, appears to be as clear an instance as one could wish of a government that lost the allegiance of a substantial portion of its people through heavy taxation. Basing sermons on this text, specialists might support a thesis that all history is the history of public finance. But is it?

We have maintained that what matters most to people is how they live with others. Protecting a way of life, modifying it, or rejecting it in favor of another, are the global objectives of political regimes. Taxing and spending are adjuncts to these objectives, not the objectives themselves. Limits on resources may constrain what is possible to do, finances may reduce alternatives that can be considered, but they cannot determine, even by reducing the possibilities to one, what must be done. Though rulers may govern to tax (and spend the proceeds, of course) rather than tax to govern, this says as much or more about the social order embodied in political institutions than it does about budgetary practices.

Had Rehoboam and his advisers merely been foolish, we might criticize their personal shortcomings. How shortsighted not to see that they had sacrificed their kingdom forever for temporary gain! But Rehoboam's actions represent an intensification of his father's policies; and Solomon's reign offers a paradigmatic example of the institutionalization of hierarchy. Bureaucracy, through a minute division of labor, greatly expanded the royal household. Despite the microscale of polities in those days, the state's grandeur (even apart from the great Temple in Jerusalem) was visible everywhere. Wars of conquest provided forced labor, in addition to the labor of Solomon's own people—in lieu of taxes, or as part of compulsory labor service (the corvée). The classic abuses of hierarchy appear: public opulence and private squalor; spending commitments requiring ever increasing revenues; entangling foreign alliances. Indeed, Solomon became so self-important that he began to worship his own wisdom, committing the sin of idolatry. The asymmetry in power between him and his subjects led Solomon to forget them and their burdens, even as he forgot his God in favor of foreign deities.[5] Rehoboam's scorpions are the counterpart of Solomon's doing "evil in the sight of the Lord";[6] if worshiping foreign gods is immoral, it is equivalent to neglecting the needs of one's own people. We learn more about the breakup of the kingdom of Israel by seeing it as part of a syndrome associated with a hierarchical regime than we do by attending only to the punitive taxation that was the precipitating event.

PROBLEM SUCCESSION

Grandly conceived, political life may be thought of as an ongoing referendum on the existing regime. The various political cultures compete for shares of victory in that referendum. Hence budgeting matters most when it is centrally implicated in a web of explanation strengthening one culture and weakening another. Established authority may be held to account for evil consequences, for instance, and a contrary set of policies legitimating rule by a different combination of cultures may take its place. The depression of the 1930s originally was perceived as the outcome of failure to stick to the precepts of neoclassical economics: however low, wage rates still remained too high to clear employment markets, i.e., to provide full employment. Whatever the merits of this theory, and however talented its expositors, elite Western opinion turned a deaf ear. With more unemployed than markets could absorb at existing wages, such a theory would, at any wage, have encouraged employers to further reduce remuneration. If economic disaster had actually been attributed to the failure to follow the good old ways, market capitalism would have emerged from the depression stronger than ever. Instead, there appeared within the framework of neoclassical economics a new doctrine that belied earlier orthodoxy: advocacy of governmental intervention through varying rates of taxation and, especially, by varying expenditure to manage the economy. Waxing triumphant by the end of the Second World War, Keynesian economics captured virtually all Western capitals. The new economics strengthened governmental hierarchy by increasing its capacity to affect market forces so as to protect the populace against adversity. In this way, budgeting—in the past largely concerned with achieving balance at relatively low spending levels, even when this precept was violated under the whiplash of events—became associated with securing a therapeutic imbalance. The rise of egalitarian forces, together with the ordinary operations of interest-group politics, prevented the accumulation of surpluses in boom years, so that, in application, Keynesian budget theory was practiced only halfway. Nevertheless, as the world emerged from depression and war, Keynesianism was part of the social change that gave budgeting greater significance, and fundamentally altered its direction by infusing with moral legitimacy high spending for social purposes. It is not that Keynes discovered welfare spending—antecedent forces include Catholicism, socialism, and Tory "radicalism" or paternalism, forces imbued with the sacrificial ethic of hierarchy—but that the interpretation of his doctrines reinforced pre-existing desires by giving them a hitherto lacking economic rationale.

Today the phenomenon of stagflation has led many to reconsider Keynesian economics. But it is not yet clear how the problem (and hence the solution) will be defined. Is the difficulty insufficient revenue, which can be made up by "soaking the rich"? Has there been too little spending to secure greater equality, so that workers understandably are unwilling to make sacrifices, the solution being a negotiated "incomes policy"? Are spending and taxation too high, leading to less economic growth than would otherwise occur, an explanation suggesting that governments reduce both taxing and spending to let economic nature take its course? There are rationales for policies increasing or decreasing economic equality, raising or lowering taxes and/or spending. Government budgeting remains at center stage of the contemporary political economy, but it is not the stage itself. Ultimately, though we cannot spend more than we have, at least not more than we can borrow, there is a lot of leeway. Vast inflations or deflations, or gross reductions in the standards of living, may force change. But even then the direction of change is not prefigured. We still make our own history by choosing to uphold, modify, or reject existing authority.

Nothing is forever. In recorded history, the city-states of Greece and the republic and empire of Rome, though long vanished, nevertheless lasted far longer than the democracies of the West—including the United States, whose constitutional government is still less than two hundred years old. So far as we know, the very idea of government by consent emerged in the Greek city-states. Humility in appraising the past is especially appropriate for people who, however much they benefit from technical advance, cannot claim yet to have resolved those same problems of getting and spending that beset the polities of classical times.

No matter where governments have tried to raise revenue, there has seldom been enough. Fiscal insufficiency is as old as government itself. The causes of fiscal pressure range from a society's deficient production, creating universal scarcity, to its real reluctance to support government. Or, a society can possess adequate resources, but ineffective or corrupt internal organization may siphon off revenues and dissipate assets. Governments may manifest willingness to tax, and may choose to spend heavily, eventually exceeding their capacity to generate sufficient wealth to sustain desired spending levels. During most of history, correspondence between receipts and expenditures has been an aberrant condition. Only within the past hundred years or so—perhaps a century and a quarter—have societies achieved the technical-organizational capacity, if they so wished, to sustain that correspondence.

No matter what a society's patterns of taxing and spending are, supporting government has always been problematic. In this respect, at least, past and present merge.

Virtually every aspect of modern budgetary behavior that we regard as especially distinctive has its analogue in ancient practices. Governments, from the Mauryan kings of ancient India to early Roman emperors to the feudal monarchies of medieval Europe and the new nation-states of the early-modern era, have tried to maintain accounts of tax receipts, and sometimes (but never successfully) to keep records of spending for different purposes. Though the technology differs, the results are often the same: as with the off-budget trust funds in modern governments, detailed line-item accounts of spending did not help much if receipts in a given fund were insufficient to cover mandated spending. If, to end where we began, the king is the state and his body the treasury, there is not all that much, except our pride and our technology, to differentiate our problems of getting and spending from his. It was difficult then; it is difficult now.

It is a long time since kings' personal territorial control was limited to the distance a man could walk in a day. Poor transportation meant, among other things, that food supplies might be plentiful in one place, while not far away (by modern standards) there was famine. Without mechanisms for orderly funding of deficits or even for transferring funds easily, medieval and early-modern governments found themselves shipping substantial quantities of coin throughout their domains. The need for kings to rely on untrained administrators, and the absence of convenient accounts for checking up, generated corruption with attendant loss of revenue. All these difficulties and many others eventually were overcome by improved technology. So technology does make a difference. But there is nothing to stop governments with the most modern technology from developing similar problems. The same administrative capacity that enhances revenue collection also facilitates spending.

Ancient, medieval, and early-modern governments certainly lacked effective technical and administrative instruments, but they did use expedients to help stay afloat. They taxed the land and necessities; they debased currency and confiscated as much as possible; they sold offices, crown lands, and sometimes the king's jewels; they conquered and pillaged. When officials could not get inside houses, they taxed columns, windows, and doors. They levied hundreds of taxes on the production and sale of commodities and services. In doing this, governments alienated their subjects, debased public morality, and wrought havoc with trade. But, for the most part, they got by. And when, after centuries of reform, such venal and inefficient practices were abolished, governments still faced financial crises. The big difference today is that crises take place at much higher levels of expenditure and revenue.

What stands out in the ebb and flow of financial tides is problem succession: old solutions give rise to new problems that are in their turn superseded.[7] No policy instrument is good for all seasons. Tax farming and administration for fees enhanced the certainty of revenue, but these marketlike methods in turn led to extortionate collection, which alienated the people from their government. Eventually—and here "eventually" is a long time, counted in centuries—the governing council of the king's household turned into something like a civil service. For a time, the costs of collection might have been reduced and a more responsive bureaucracy established. But over time those too went the way of all things. Corruption reappeared in other guises; and extortionate practices, never entirely suppressed, again became common as government demands on the people grew, or as the appetite of its functionaries increased with the eating. A bureaucracy may create pension obligations in perpetuity; such commitments can be canceled only by defeat in war, disintegration of government, or the forceful breaking of public promises. No way is without flaw.

If the history of budgeting (along with many other histories) teaches us anything, it is that problems never stop. The one thing there cannot be—our impossibility theorem—is a millennium, a time when old problems fade away and no new ones arise.

It may well appear to students and practitioners of budgeting today that everything changes except the inability to cope. Here we do observe a difference between past and present. Only in the past fifty years of taxing and spending have governments been willing to move quickly. It took hundreds of years to develop reliable accounts, to end the sale of offices, to establish a civil service, to unify sources of revenue. As slowly as we think we move, the pace of change today—the rise of macroeconomic management and varieties of devices to increase efficiency; discussions of radically different tax systems, like the flat rate or consumption taxes (radical in our time, though not in historical perspective)—is far faster than in past ages. Our guess is that two factors are involved: the ever larger proportions of national product consumed by governments, and the increasing interrelatedness of the world economy, mean that the consequences of actions rebound on decision-makers more swiftly than before. Budgets matter more to more people, and their consequences are more immediately felt. Nor is delay as helpful as it once was. Passing problems on to one's successors makes less political sense when one is the successor and has to face the same difficulty in more aggravated form.[8]

Whether or not governments stay solvent, at the very least our lengthy chronicle of the difficulties continuously associated with efforts by governments at diverse times and places to raise and spend revenue should convey the message that taxing and spending are never a straightforward matter.

For the pragmatists who seek lessons in history, we offer this caveat: While it is always tempting for actors within government to promise a painless quick-fix acceptable to everyone, we conclude—knowing the long and tortuous route to modern fiscal management—that simplicity is always illusory. Since the Renaissance, when Western governments began to develop capacity to vary ways of taxing and spending to fit changing circumstances, the new fiscal instruments often complicated affairs within governments as well as life for taxpayers. From the mercantilist policies of early-modern governments to the ill-fated program budgets of the 1960s or the zero-base budget of the 1970s, to the value-added tax once touted as a substitute for the income tax—as circumstances vary over time, any change in budget policy generates new problems not previously anticipated.

Knowing this, the public in modern, welfare-oriented democracies rightfully should be as skeptical of facile promises from government's hierarchy as it is of the criticism by advocates of market-oriented policies that economic growth will dissolve all difficulties, or by egalitarians who would have government give to everyone. Even Iceland, which came close to balancing its budget, has high inflation, suggesting, as Jesse Burkhead wrote us, that "balancing the budget does not solve all problems."[9] More now than in the old days (when even poor kings sometimes had their way about taxing and spending), we know that any change acceptable to some regimes inevitably will antagonize others.

Unanticipated consequences must be older than recorded history itself. It is not so much that no anticipated consequences occur—decentralization of financial management, for instance, often does reduce the burden of calculation at the center—but that new circumstances attach themselves to old reforms, thus creating unexpected results, such as a bid for independence from a now more experienced and wealthier periphery. Enhanced ability to control allocation of resources does not guarantee that government, seeing what can be done, will not spend a good deal more than before. Similarly, there is nothing necessarily incompatible between government's raising more revenues and its going further into debt.

The slow conversion of subjects into citizens able to hold rulers to account, for example, was incompatible with early-modern governments' draconian politics of raising taxes for wars and for monarchical splendor. That liberty turned out to be expensive (though the cost was barely foreseen) is perhaps understandable. That methods for curbing venality and increasing neutral competence (such as establishing professional civil services in the nineteenth and early twentieth centuries) should prove indispensable for conducting wars of mass mobilization and administering the welfare state, so far as we have been able to discover, was entirely unforeseen.

Like history, budgeting is about trouble, partly because that is what historians write about, but mostly because it is true to life. But troubles come in different sizes and shapes. Lest we overwhelm our readers with a catalogue of the Western world's budgetary ills, past and present (which is, more or less, what this book already has done), we shall limit ourselves here to the three most critical questions: Why does government grow? Why are budgets so seldom balanced? Why has expenditure control collapsed in the West? Our thesis, like that of the volume as a whole, is that when people choose how to construct their institutions, they also create different kinds of budgetary dilemmas.

WHY GOVERNMENT GROWS

The question of why government grows may usefully be decomposed into several smaller queries:

1. Why does government spending in Western democracies grow in small steps or large leaps but hardly ever decline as a proportion of Gross National Product? Why, when the costs of some programs increase, are others not reduced to keep spending as a proportion of GNP constant? Why, in short, are there no global spending limits? The purpose of putting the question in this way is to avoid the usual air of inevitability by asking why a decision not to do the opposite, i.e., not to

limit the growth of government, fails to be taken. One of the few obvious aspects of the situation is that if moves to drive spending up are sometimes halted but seldom reversed, the end result over time must be a continuous increase in government's relative share of the national product. Nor, in spite of recent efforts to reverse direction, is there any evident stopping place. The growth of government has to be explained not only by the impetus upward, but also by the resistance to downward movement.

2. Why do governments in some nations grow faster than others? Why does the United States "lag behind" yet also gradually increase the size of government? Why do the other "Anglo-Saxon" democracies, such as Canada and Australia, fit the general trend of growth but still spend less than the western-European nations? If there is a "logic of industrialization," why does it not operate equally on all industrial nations or proportionately to the size of their economies?

3. Why, when political parties pledged to reduce spending get into office, do they maintain or even increase the general level of prior commitments rather than reduce them? If there is a consensus among all important parties and political elites that existing programs will either expand or remain stable, then it must be the underlying consensus, rather than the surface flux of political events, that requires explanation.

4. Why is most of the growth of government attributable to programs—pensions, health, education—that contain a significant redistributive component? Demographic change, especially the aging of the population, is evidently important. But why do programs for youth, especially education, not decline proportionately, or are programs for the elderly not altered to reduce their rate of increase?

5. Why do the Western nations and the Soviet Union spend approximately the same proportion of GNP on social-welfare programs? What does the Soviet Union, despite the evident differences, have in common with the Western nations that would account for their likeness in this respect?

The rising proportion of national product spent through governments in the twentieth century, we contend, cannot primarily be explained by growing wealth or industrialization. Nor can it be attributed, as recent authors do, to the political changes that follow from modernization. Except in the tautological sense that citizens in a democracy must in some way approve of rising expenditure, these explanations do not tell us why government grows even when the party in power opposes such an outcome. On the contrary, the very wealth and technological capacity of these countries would make it possible, were they so inclined, to diminish the proportion of state activity in national economies.

Over time, every democratic, industrial, rich nation has spent proportionately more than it did before on social welfare, and on government as a whole. Equations that try out a number of variables on government spending as a proportion of national product and conclude that wealth is by far the most important factor influencing spending are valid—as far as they go. But we do not believe that the correspondence between wealth and growth of government is predetermined, existing apart from and despite human will.

Conceive, by contrast, of a world in which competitive individualism is the dominant culture. An upswing in the economy would be attributed to the automatic, self-regulating operation of markets. If periodic depressions occurred, the cause would be attributed to violations of market principles—too-high subsidies, excessive income transfers, or unduly restrictive trade practices. As the nation became wealthier, it would indeed be easier to spend more absolutely. Spending to mitigate some of the worst effects of poverty might well increase, but not necessarily faster than economic growth.

We shall try to show that while the prevailing economic and political explanations do have a measure of truth in them, they are not the whole truth. We argue that a cultural theory of governmental growth fits the facts better than alternative explanations. Asking the cultural question "Which political cultures—shared values legitimating social practices—would reject ever greater governmental growth, and which ones would perpetuate it?," we hypothesize that the size of government in any given society is a function (consequence, if you prefer) of its combination of political cultures. Finally, we shall extend the theory to account for the tendencies of political regimes to balance or unbalance their budgets.

WAGNER'S LAW

The first and still the most important effort to explain why public expenditures grow faster than the economy was Adolf Wagner's "law of increasing state activity."[10] He did not claim that richer nations will spend more proportionately than their less affluent neighbors. He maintained that as per-capita real income increases in particular nations, their governments will spend a higher proportion of national product than before.

In Wagner's work, as in much of the literature on governmental growth, there is a teleological element. These explanations assume that there exists an unspecified yet ever present and powerful logic of industrialization that pushes the development process in only one direction.

Wagner believed that the density of urban living would exacerbate social frictions. As in all industrializing nations during the nineteenth century, government eventually would step in to ameliorate dissension, either by exercising its police power or by adjudicating differences. No one, it appears, has countered Wagner's argument with its opposite: that density also provides opportunities for economies of scale. Here is a counterexample from public health (one of the earliest activities entered into by governments): Although city dwellers face higher risk from spread of epidemic diseases than do rural residents, the per-capita cost of mass immunization (say against smallpox when it was prevalent, or polio) is lower in cities. So also is the cost per person of publicly provided transportation service, communications networks, sewers, and an adequate and safe water supply. Of course, there may also be diseconomies of scale; the point is that one should not be able to have it both ways.

Reflecting upon public support given for railroads in France and Germany during the nineteenth century, Wagner maintained that some investments require public funding because more capital is needed than private enterprise can or will provide. Like most of the arguments of Wagner and his innumerable successors, this thesis has merit; public intervention may be justified for "public goods," services for which no market exists or is likely to emerge. For every past and present example, however, other places either have done without it or have financed it with user charges, thus shifting the support burden from general revenues to direct beneficiaries. Tolls have paid for highway networks in some places, for example, as have gasoline taxes earmarked for highway construction and maintenance. Private capital built canals and railroads in the United States and England. Markets for parcel post exist in some countries; indeed, by removal of the government monopoly on first-class mail, postal service could once again be provided by private enterprises. The irony is that the rationale for shifting postal services from private to public management in the past was often to raise revenue. If the explanation for growth is not what the state ought to do but whether it faces inexorable demands that cannot be resisted, the evidence is against the deterministic hypothesis.

Education, for instance, constitutes a major component of government spending. A literate population, one with capacity for abstract thinking, is indeed a requirement of an industrial society. Yet in some industrial nations some education is privately provided; in Japan and Korea, for example, industry itself provides technical training for its employees. Among Western industrial nations, the proportion of secondary-school graduates going on to college varies from something like 8 to 45 percent; though some nations provide full public subsidy for college students, others furnish little or none. Nations evidently do vary in their perception of education as a universal public good.

Or consider the rationales most often given for the state's increasing role in poorer countries. Since private entrepreneurship is weak, some authors say, government must step in to accumulate resources for investment. But why, then, does government intervene in richer nations that have substantial private resources? For example, since vital data would not otherwise be collected, governments in poor countries must do it. Yet, in richer nations with all sorts of private data collection, government still is actively involved. Though reducing poor nations' exposure to international economic fluctuations is a motive frequently cited as a source of their governments' protectionism, the relative security enjoyed by richer nations should (and sometimes does) enable them to engage in freer trade. Minimal political legitimacy in poorer nations, combined with intense internal conflict over limited resources, does sometimes encourage governments to mitigate disruption by subsidizing consumption. Why, then, do richer nations often act in the same way? Why is it that the one thing poor and rich nations share is a propensity to increase state activity? Comparing the literature on poor countries[11] with the explanations offered for rich countries, we find that the same reasons cited for larger government in poor nations these days are applied to governments operating under opposite conditions.

WILENSKY'S LAW

The strongest contemporary statement of economic determinism in government growth comes from Harold Wilensky; after doing a cross-sectional analysis of some sixty-four poor and rich nations, he concludes that "alternative explanations collapse under the weight of such brittle categories as 'socialist' versus 'capitalist' economies, 'collectivistic' versus 'individualistic' ideologies, or even 'democratic' versus 'totalitarian' political systems. . . . These categories are almost useless in explaining the origins and general development of the welfare state."[12] As with Wagner, there is no doubt about the conclusion, but only about the theory on which it is based.

In a wide-ranging argument, Wilensky is well aware that differences between such diverse countries as Nepal and Sweden might well not explain more subtle relationships among the world's twenty or so richest nations. He knows as well that ideology in parties out of power is something else again compared to ideology enforced by parties with mass support in power. Nevertheless, his emphasis on economic resources—they remain the root cause of indifferences—is unmistakable. Wilensky goes on to say that "social security programs simply do not appear without sufficient national surplus to make them a policy option, or if, as in many poor countries, these programs are enacted, they remain weak paper programs or are severely restricted in coverage until such surplus is produced."[13] If one were to imagine a different set of values guiding decision-making, however, one could argue that the economy was rich enough to permit most people to invest for their own retirement. Why, the question is, should wealth compel nations to spend proportionately more rather than proportionately less?

If only because it has slowed down in the 1970s and 1980s, economic growth cannot be invoked as a recent cause of rising spending. At a quarter of GNP, with a spending increase of 8 percent, as Guy Peters shows,[14] government can be supported by a 2 percent expansion of the economy. At half of GNP, with an 8 percent annual spending increase, however, a 4 percent increase in growth is required to service government with nothing left over for additional private consumption or investment. Yet many European governments are spending nearly or more than 50 percent of GNP, while their economic growth is less than 4 percent. The decline in take-home pay during the 1970s revealed the difficulties of supporting governmental growth at an average of 131 percent of economic growth. Concern with "ungovernability" in Western democracies proceeds directly from the gap between growth of government and of the economy. If, as Wilensky says, "over the long pull, economic level is the root cause of welfare-state development,"[15] does that mean that state spending will decline proportionately? Apparently not.

In posing the grand question, Harley Hinrichs' formulation is helpful—except that today his upper bound might well be doubled:

> From all these positions, one can find enough "whys" for a growing government share of national income in the course of social mobilization. One thing, however, should be clear. Two elements are involved: one is the structural change in the economy during the process of social mobilization, involving industrialization, urbanization, specialization, democratization, secularization, productivity, and income changes, producing a greater government

share of national income irrespective of the ideologies of government. The second is the ideological change both in theme (the last hundred years) and in the process of social mobilization itself. A complex democratic industrialized state could function with a public sector, say, between 20 and 40 percent. The point where it settles within (or above) this range is most likely to be determined not by structural needs (which would demand, say, only 20 percent) but by ideological commitments, toward a "welfare state" and/or toward the "security and defense" of an existing ideological system.[16]

Since, up to the present time, "welfare" continues to dominate "warfare" spending in the democracies by more than two to one, it is to their "ideological systems," their values and practices, that we would look for explanations of the growth of government.

Economic growth, so long as it lasts, provides a facilitating condition; without money to spend, aspirations are limited by resources. Once these resources are available, however, the question is whether they will be used to expand the private sector (thus increasing state spending absolutely but not relatively) or to expand the public sector at the expense of the private. Sustained economic growth makes the choice unnecessary. When it does become necessary—either in times of adversity or because government grows faster than the economy—spending does not decline, we think, because the commitment to equality, which comes from culture, requires even greater governmental effort to maintain social-welfare programs.

Assar Lindbeck, a Swedish economist, raises a pertinent question:

It is often believed that conflicts over the distribution of income are likely to fall when the size distribution is equalized, as unfairness and envy would be expected to recede. . . . Those who regard distributional conflicts as a result of inequality in general, or of income differentials . . . would . . . probably argue that the drive for further equalization would fall. For instance, in the context of the median-voter theorem . . . it is often hypothesized that the drive for further equalization, and then also distributional conflicts, will fall when the difference between mean and medium income goes down. . . .

However, this is certainly not the only possibility. Indeed, a case can be made for the opposite view. Firstly, conscious attempts by public authorities to redistribute income focus political discussion and conflicts on distributional issues, rather than on other issues. Secondly, the possibilities of individuals to raise their incomes by way of productive effort tend to go down due to higher marginal

tax rates. Both factors would be expected to stimulate income re-
distributions via the political process. Moreover—though this is a
more speculative point: people may feel envy mainly towards
those who have only *slightly* higher incomes than themselves, because such incomes would be regarded as within their own reach,
in contrast to the incomes of the very rich. On the basis of that hypothesis the more equal the distribution of income is made, the
more pronounced would be the conflicts over the remaining inequalities, as most people then have more individuals than before
to make relevant comparisons with. . . .[17]

His speculation would be a prediction of our cultural theory.

MARXIST THEORIES

Perhaps economic explanations are faulty or perhaps they have not
been carried far enough. To explore the latter alternative, large-scale
economic determinism, we consider Marxist theories.

So long as Marxist theorists maintained that the state was merely
and only the repressive arm of the capitalist class, they did not have to
confront growth of welfare programs. Welfare programs could be conceived as disguised forms of oppression, buying off discontent by getting people used to living on the dole. Eventually, however, the
expansion of welfare programs became anomalous. For if welfare programs helped those people worst off, the government could not be
called entirely exploitative; and if workers approved of the programs,
as they evidently did, then the demise of capitalism might not necessarily be inherent in its operations. If the state was paying people off but
couldn't keep these bribes up, however, it would be doing good for bad
reasons, reasons that would eventually catch up with it. This is how
deficit spending and governmental growth became signs of capitalist
contradiction for Marxists as well as for conservatives.

Capitalist contradictions, James O'Connor holds, arise as the state
simultaneously seeks to increase the profits of capitalists (including big
union labor) by rigging markets, and to dampen discontent through
welfare services. Social welfare and economic investment compete for
the same resources, resulting in decline on both sides.[18]

Put another way, as Alan Wolfe does, the welfare state sets authority
and democracy at odds. He attributes democratic (called liberal) political structures to the ideology of the marketplace. Government seeks to
facilitate accumulation of capital, reducing impediments to labor mobility along the way. As alternatives from prior eras are used up (that

is, as welfare spending increases faster than economic growth), government gets exhausted (Wolfe's term for overload). Bureaucracy, he believes, is good at distribution but not at accumulation.[19] Previously this criticism was raised only by opponents of the welfare state who thought that welfare spending undermined the incentive to produce. According to Marxist doctrine, capitalism depends on exploitation, i.e., surplus value or profit. Thus Picciotto and Holloway describe how the state does different things at different times, according to whether capitalist accumulation is strong or, as they think today, the rate of profit starts to slow down.[20] But has it? Evidence is inconclusive.[21]

Can government expand to take up slack in the private economy, or will this very expansion threaten private production? Ian Gough's efforts to forge a synthesis of Marxist thought on this question is worth quoting:

> By securing an overall agreement on wages, prices, taxes and social benefits, the state may be able to ensure a growing level of welfare expenditure without generating excessive inflationary pressures or harming profitability.... This could dampen down some of the conflicts over financing welfare expenditure that have proved harmful to the stability of capitalist economies in recent years. At the same time, by combining [negotiation between business, union leaders and the state] with policies to restructure industry, aid the private sector and channel funds to stimulate investment, this could lay the basis for a renewal of capital accumulation and growth, without encountering some of the risks and adverse consequences of the alternative, right-wing strategy.[22]

Capitalism saves itself through corporatism.

Since relationships between the state and society are no longer predetermined, detailed empirical study is required to assess what is happening. What, then, is the difference between Wilensky and Gough—that is, between an empirical analysis by a Marxist of the relationship of government policy to interest-group activity and one by any other social scientist?

We agree with Guy Peters:

> What is perhaps most remarkable about these discussions of the fiscal crisis of the state is the degree of similarity between the market and radical reformers (i.e., Marxists). They both see a direct connection between the political and economic factors in determining the current condition of the welfare state. The downward spiral which both sets of analysts conceive of as almost inherent in these systems is the result of the need of the systems to legitimate

themselves. For the "radicals," this need is inherent in the capitalist system and its structural deficiencies, while for the market reformers the need is based more upon specific political considerations and commitments such as the pledge to full employment, or the fear of the political consequences of high unemployment.[23]

The growth of welfare programs bothers both capitalists and Marxists, because the former dislike the development, and the latter approve only of welfare programs run by a socialist state.

Less use of welfare policies, as Herbert Tingsten said long ago, signifies willingness to accept inequality of results. It is not—as Offe and Wolfe maintain, along with a host of reactionaries—that state planning is incompatible with capitalism. Hierarchy and markets have coexisted for a long time. Intervening to guarantee everyone against loss so as to maintain equality of result, however, would be incompatible with capitalism because it would destroy the rationale for competition.

TAX HYPOTHESES

Turning from the demand for public spending to the supply of public revenues, Peacock and Wiseman[24] have proposed their "displacement-effect hypothesis": Spending, in their view, is limited by available revenues. Casting about for an explanation of substantial increases in revenue in recent times, they observed that after the First and Second World Wars the level of taxation, though it receded from the enormously high wartime levels, did not quite fall back to the old level. In general form, their hypothesis is that major crises expand public tolerance for higher levels of taxation, after which spending floods in to make up the difference between older and newer levels of revenue. In finer detail, Peacock and Wiseman believe that spending expands to use up available revenues. The question they do not answer is, Why? Even if the displacement effect makes it easier to retain higher taxes, one must still explain why this option is preferred to lowering tax rates. Missing in this argument is an explanation of why no great surge of spending occurred after the First World War but did after the Second, or, for that matter, why elites did not demand even greater tax reduction after World War II.

Rudolf Goldscheid, who wrote late in the nineteenth century, did not explain why government grows, because he thought it was too small. Recall the "poor" kings of the late Middle Ages and the early-modern era. Sometimes, but just barely, they could live off their own without requiring much financial support from subjects. Alas, capitalism changed all that. It created the "tax state," in which government's income depended on taxes raised through the private sector. Unfortunately, the private sector liked its private income, and was reluctant to give it up. Hence, in an inversion of both capitalist and Marxist claims, the private sector exploited the public, which had to work for it.[25] This unfortunate separation of capital from government should be reconstituted, Goldscheid contended, by once more giving government its own property. Then there could really be a mixed society. Instead of sacrificing the present to an unreal future classless society, as if there need be no government, or sacrificing public authority to benefit private property, Goldscheid would resolve the contradictions of capitalism by overcoming the state's alienation from property.[26] No doubt he had in mind nationalizing "winners," i.e., profitable concerns, rather than "losers," as has been done since World War II.

Do not sell Goldscheid short. The distinction between public and private accepted by all governments today could not have come about if the lord and ruler owned everything. In the modern era a form of government came into being that had to raise revenue not from slaves but from citizens whom the government did not control absolutely. If the power to spend other people's money is the hallmark of modern government, this estrangement between ownership and control of productive resources—widely acknowledged to be a hallmark of corporate capitalism—has a more significant predecessor near the turn of the century in the postfeudal split between state and society. Knut Wicksell and his followers developed a counterargument to hierarchical theories; in democracies, he contended, taxes reflect a balance among political factions. An emerging school of neoclassical theorists in Vienna were attracted to his views.

"The crisis of the tax state," according to Joseph Schumpeter, the Vienna school's most illustrious member, is that capitalism sets the stage for its own destruction—not, as Marxists would have it, because it has failed, but rather because it is too successful. At the center of his analysis, Schumpeter placed alienated intellectuals. Affluence supported a bevy of social critics who wanted government to do more but would not support it. Our term for this critical culture is *sectarianism*. Affluence also leads to downgrading the profit motive on which productivity depends. As revenues increased, Schumpeter predicted, so would social sympathies, and government would improve welfare by spending richer people's money. Eventually, taxation would become so excessive that the economy would decline and with it the "tax state."[27] Here also, as in the literature on governmental overload, the defects of capitalism are inherent in its political organization: affluence leads to moral collapse as the bourgeoisie ceases to believe that capitalism is worth defending.

Perhaps, in view of the diversity of tax sources, people do not realize how much they are paying. Known as "fiscal illusion" (named, possibly, after the [in]famous "money illusion" in which it is face amount and not purchasing power that people perceive), this doctrine contends that since indirect taxes hide the total amount paid, citizens are misled into paying more than they otherwise would pay.[28] Maybe. A close connection between tax revolts and a high proportion of revenue from direct taxes has been noted by Wilensky.[29] Perhaps it is possible to fool some of the people some of the time; but is it really possible today to fool all of the people all of the time? How might we explain decades, if not of foolishness, then at least, according to the doctrine of fiscal illusion, of being fooled? Could it be that citizens are so easily "duped" into taxing themselves more because they *want* government to spend more?

OLSON'S LAW AND OTHER POLITICAL HYPOTHESES

Mancur Olson seeks to explain the growth of government not for its own sake, but as part of a larger theory accounting for the rise of nations to economic prominence and their fall from that lofty estate. Japan and Germany reached record levels of growth after the Second World War, while Britain and the United States, among others, did not, Olson contends, because losing the war destroyed the complex of interests that by gaining excessive benefits slowed down growth. He sees a gradual but pervasive cause of economic decline in the political organizational mechanisms of modern democracies—especially the desire of broad spectrums of the population for goods available to all, without the necessity of paying for them.[30] (This thesis is an extension of his seminal *Logic of Collective Action*.) Though it had facetiously been suggested before that nations might be better off to lose than to win wars, this is the first time a general law has been made out of such aspersions.

Olson's law of the inadvertent decay of capitalism would be entirely plausible if there were not significant elements in these communities who make a point out of pressing for what Olson considers disastrous as national policy. At least since the Second World War, proponents of welfare programs have used Keynesian analysis to defend the position that government spending is good for the private economy. Other proponents have defended social-welfare programs as a mechanism for maintaining political systems which otherwise, in their view, would have collapsed or at least had greater difficulty maintaining consent. And there are still others in contemporary societies who rail against economic growth as being undesirable or who prefer distribution to accumulation. Olson's latent functions, to use the language of sociology, are the manifest functions of capitalism's critics. From their point of view, the only thing wrong with the current situation is that government has not grown enough.

There is hot debate over the question of whether socialist parties in power actually undertake measures that increase economic equality. Hewitt and Higgs say they do,[31] while Jackman and Parkin argue they do not.[32] To restate the difficulty: Why do the electoral opponents of socialist parties spend as much as or more than the socialists do, thus obscuring the differences among them?

In general, as both Pryor and Wilensky argue, economic capacity is more powerful than political leftism in correlations with state spending.[33] Always, of course, the United States remains anomalous, being wealthier and spending less proportionately. Nevertheless, Wilensky argues that such broad national political ideologies as individualism versus collectivism have virtually no effect on spending.[34] But he also contends that Catholic parties do matter in determining rates of spending. The power of a Catholic party within a nation, according to Wilensky, is more important than the power of a leftist party as a determinant of its welfare effort.[35] Francis Castles contends that both Social Democratic power and right-party power (the latter negatively) correlate strongly with welfare effort, but right power (or its absence) is more important.[36] Could they have discovered the same phenomenon?[37]

What is important in determining national differences is not whether the "right" or the "left" of a particular country's spectrum is winning, but the range of attitudes represented on that spectrum, especially whether there is a strong anti-statist party.[38] Wilensky's analysis defines the American Democratic Party and the Swedish Social Democratic Party as similarly "left." Yet in Sweden none of the "right" parties is similar to (that is, as "right" as) American Republicans. Therefore we must restate the question to ask why in some countries there is no important anti-statist party. And why does what is "left" and what is "right," insofar as they involve the growth of government, differ so markedly from one country to another? The range of the political spectrum minimizes economic and technological factors and instead focuses on different ways of life; that is what we mean by political culture. And a concern with culture is reinforced if one interprets Catholic parties not only in terms of hierarchical religious practice but also as invoking a particularly strong version of the sacrificial ethic in which the richer parts have a duty, reinforced by a concern for large families, to aid the poorer in the interests of the collective.

There may be no need for grand theories when straightforward interest-group politics, meshed with government's desire for support, will explain what is happening. It is said, for instance, that the median voter will vote for government's expansion unless and until his income is reduced. As Herbert Kaufman wrote:

> When a group of activists grows dissatisfied with what the market provides in some specific respect, they turn to public authorities to intervene. Each such effort meets with resistance, but there are so many of them that even a modest success rate will expand governmental functions. Moreover, each success becomes a precedent for new interventions.
>
> The result is a multicentered system of government composed of many islands of decision dominated by promoters of those activities. Eventually, even former opponents in each area become accustomed to, if not dependent on, the new arrangements. The beneficiaries of the status quo increase. The foes "capture"and are captured by the system. Proposals to expand activities within the island prevail more easily. People pay close attention to their own island, little to others. The occupants of each island in effect concede spheres of interest to other groups if the others will respect theirs. If someone tries to abandon a function around which interests are mobilized, the occupants, no matter how much they have been squabbling with each other over details, get together to block effort.
>
> If the opponents of a function try to enter the island and change or reverse policy from the inside, they find it difficult to break the monopoly of the collected insiders. They must therefore mobilize collections of disparate interests in general organs of government—principally the legislatures—to override individual islands. This is not easy to do; it takes time and money and persistence. Many vetoes must be overcome. An alternative is to start a new island dominated by interests you favor (e.g., an environmental island or a consumer island to offset producer and distributor islands). You add to government in order to pit the part you control against the parts you oppose. All of the foregoing explains why rolling things back is difficult—why all change from the status quo is hard.[39]

Interest-group activity under democratic conditions is a better explanation of why spending does not decline once it has reached a certain level, in our opinion, than of why it goes up in the first place. The group explanation does not demand that new programs be financed on top of old ones. After all, if new expenditures did not exceed the rate of economic growth, sooner or later government would decline in relative size even while growing absolutely. Were there global limits on spending, the budgeting-by-addition that Kaufman implies could not operate. We must ask why programs are added instead of subtracted from one another.

And the same is true of incremental growth, which uses time as a variable. If one wishes to explain why certain programs are larger than others, incrementalism points to a truth: The earlier a program was established, the longer it has had the opportunity to build up increments, the larger it will be in relation to comparable programs that began later. Henry Aaron says that the best explanation of the relative size of twenty-two large social-security programs was the time they had to develop.[40] "Once a program is launched," Wilensky concludes, "precedent is the major determinant of who gets what the government has to give, and how much goes to the program or agency depends on what it got the last time around."[41]

What is it that makes incrementalism a one-way street? Nothing in budgetary theory requires positive rather than negative increments.[42] And there is something—the suggestion of adaptation via successive small steps—that suggests that decremental changes might, on occasion, be desirable also. Were that so, if increments and decrements offset each other, there would be no law of increasing state activity. What factors operating in the government environment lead to a polity's selection of increases, and its rejection of decreases?

Demographic changes have been proposed as an explanation for the growth of government. Since pensions and medical care are the largest items of welfare-state expenditure, the aging of the population does indeed contribute to higher levels of spending. Yet an increase in certain items cannot explain why other items are not reduced to maintain a desired proportion of spending to the size of the economy. People might be required to retire later, for example, or to save toward their retirement. When advocates argue that other programs cannot be reduced—defense is life and death, and education is sacrosanct—they merely restate the problem.

Expansion of government, Hugh Heclo believes, is a product of special historical circumstances. Heclo divides the growth of the welfare state quite reasonably into three stages. The first, beginning at the end of the nineteenth century and running to the First World War, he calls the era of "experimentation": governments tried out a variety of proposals for social insurance, especially pensions. No one was certain whether all people should have the same pension, or if pensions should be income related, or if only the poor should receive them or whether everyone should have them as a matter of right. During the period of consolidation, lasting through the 1950s, new programs on housing, education, health, and unemployment were established and old ones became politically inviolate. In a series of elections, politicians who opposed these programs were uniformly defeated; the programs became part of what every government was pledged to defend. Government, it was everywhere believed, had to be intimately involved in public welfare. During the third period, which Heclo classifies as "expansion," "government tax extractions grew faster than economic resources, and total expenditures grew faster still. In every country the result has been a gradually increasing share of national economic product absorbed by the public sector."[43] The substantial economic growth that occurred after the Second World War was largely unexpected, as Heclo rightly reminds us. He believes that this bounty reduced the perceived need to maintain political support for welfare spending. "Instead of shared risks and vulnerability, its ethic was based on piecemeal compensation for anyone who lagged behind others' gains ... Virtually everyone could claim to be entitled to one or another kind of compensation." The "unsettling rediscovery of inequality" in the Western world at the end of the 1960s, Heclo concludes, together with decline in economic growth, led to disillusionment with the welfare state.[44] As the adverse aspects of this growth become evident, Heclo suggests, policies will change. Were the "rediscovery of inequality" not merely a passing fancy but an indicator of deeply rooted and broadly powerful political forces, however, the special circumstances of yesterday might become tomorrow's growth of government.

Why was inequality of condition so suddenly discovered during the sixties and seventies? There seems to be nothing inherent in the situation, indeed a great deal running in the opposite direction. People were better off than ever before. Welfare spending had been growing, not declining. Why, in the face of this improvement, would there be still greater demand for equality of results? Economic and political explanations either fail empirically or assume the very thing that needs to be explained, namely, the increased value given to equality of condition.

Observing that a particular conception of equality grows in importance as a rationale for public policy is only the beginning of analysis. What we want to know is, what sort of people believe in and attempt to attain equality of condition as a solution to their own problems? Few nations approximate income equality, though there is an effort to move in that direction. Opposition as well as support exists. Let us reformulate: What political culture (or combination of cultures) desires to move toward, though it does not necessarily achieve, equality of results?[45] This is equivalent to asking about the origins of political preferences.

Hierarchy justifies inequality on grounds that specialization and division of labor enable people to live together with greater harmony and effectiveness than do alternative arrangements. Hence hierarchies are animated by a sacrificial ethic: the parts are supposed to sacrifice for the whole. This behavior explains the mildly redistributive policies of governments in societies with strong hierarchies. Why, then, have such societies recently gone further?

Committed to a life of purely voluntary association, sectarian cultures can live a life without coercion or authority only if complete equality of condition exists. Translated into budgetary terms, reducing human differences means transferring income from richer to poorer people. Generalized into a desire to do good for the less fortunate, the principle of narrowing differences leads to ever larger spending programs. It is the rise of sectarian political cultures, with their passion for equality of condition, that best explains the continuous increase in the size of government.

There are good reasons why it is difficult to disentangle the influence of ideas and of institutions. Assar Lindbeck raises the right question:

> What is the reason why government spending in Sweden (in 1984), largely designed to redistribute income, is about 70 percent of GDP, while the corresponding figure for Switzerland is less than half of that (about 30 percent)? Is it because voter preferences concerning public consumption, income insurance and distribution of income differ drastically between the two countries, for instance due to a higher fear of inflation, a greater aversion to left-wing ideology and perhaps also a more important role of "individualistic ideology" in Switzerland than in Sweden? Or is the main explanation instead, as I personally believe, differences in political institutions, such as the rules of decision-making and party competition? More specifically, is an important reason behind the difference that Switzerland, by contrast to Sweden, is

characterized by (1) permanent, broad coalition governments (where no party gets the entire political benefits of giving specific favors to various population groups), (2) referenda (where benefits and costs tend to be tied together), and (3) a federal system (which tends to concentrate both costs and benefits to smaller groups of citizens than in more centralized nations)? If the answers are "yes," it is unavoidable that the attitudes towards various political constitutions partly have to be based on considerations to the likely consequences of the choice of constitution for the *content* of policy, including redistribution policies and the size and rate of expansion of the public sector.[46]

There is no doubt that the rules of representation do affect the content of policies. Preferences, as cultural theory asserts, emerge from the process of decision-making in institutions. It is also true, however, that choice of political culture influences the kinds of institutions that give them expression. That is why we would expect what Lindbeck calls the "individualist ideology" of the Swiss, in our terms a strong market culture, as opposed to the hierarchical-collectivist culture of the Swedes, to lead not only to different policy preferences but to a different array of institutions for expressing these tendencies. The mutual reinforcement of institution and ideology is another way of referring to culture.

   Does cultural theory, then, imply that institutions do not matter? On the contrary, cultural theory seeks to unite ideas and the organized means for their expression.

TESTING CULTURAL THEORY

How does one judge cultural theory? By the same standards—coherence, persuasiveness, comparison to others—as any other theory. Cultural theory applied to budgeting, we claim, answers the initial five questions about the growth of government better than do the alternative explanations here reviewed. How might such a claim be tested? How, most importantly, would we know whether and to what extent cultural theory is wrong?

   In the present instance, cultural theory asserts that different regimes cause different budgetary behaviors. To have a theory at all, we must be able to separate out different combinations of political cultures (the regimes) in various countries and relate them to patterns of expenditure. These patterns are taken from the common empirical literature on which we all draw. The regimes we have specified are based on a combination of reading (mostly) and observation (some) for the nations discussed. For formulating hypotheses, this casual empiricism will do; for testing them, it leaves a lot to be desired. Here we wish to argue only that, in principle, it would be entirely feasible to develop indicators of types of regimes so that they could be classified appropriately with a high degree of intersubjective reliability. Indeed, Gross and Raynor have developed a codebook to do just this.[47]

Evidently, we are not about to take on this task. Nor can we, in this book, justify the deep assumption underlying the theory, namely, that there are only a limited number of viable ways of life. We will do three things: supply evidence that cultural theory is compatible with other knowledge; argue that it can usefully be extended beyond the growth of spending per se to account for inability to deal effectively with perennial deficits; and demonstrate that the norms underlying budgetary practices have been transformed so as to increase rather than decrease public spending.

APPLYING CULTURAL THEORY

It is time to apply the theory. America has historically marched to its own drummers, a combination of weak hierarchy, strong markets, and variable sects. Before the Civil War, this unusual combination of social forces opposed strong central government. Since Americans believed that government would introduce unnecessary inequality into society, there was little demand for welfare spending. That was then; today hierarchy is still weak, but sectarian forces, which now view government as a force for sustaining equality against the inegalitarian outcomes wrought by markets, has impelled the United States to move toward large government. European nations, which share strong hierarchies and moderate to strong sectarianism, all have stepped up spending; and some, being more egalitarian, spend more than others. Canada and Australia are in between because, while hierarchy remains strong there, so do market relationships. Let us briefly consider Canadian experience. Canada is recognizably in the mold of the European welfare state, and the United States is not. Thus there is no "welfare backlash" in Canada nor any disposition to dismantle any part of the panoply of welfare programs. Why not?

"Canada," as Robert Kudrle and Theodore Marmor tell us (echoing, as they say, existing literature), "was originally settled by people with a different structure of values from the Americans, and the distinctions persisted."[48] In Canada there were criminals but not, as in the United States, outlaws. Desperadoes who rode outside the law in the

American West might be pursued by vigilantes or local sheriff's posses. Their neighbor to the north would dispatch the Royal Canadian Mounted Police, a centralized organization serving a central hierarchy. Whether French or English in origin, Canadians came from established hierarchies and were joined by American Tories who, having defended the English king, fled north when Britain lost the Revolutionary War. Although, for evident historical and geographic reasons, a federal structure did evolve, there is, as all observers agree, "great centralization of power within the federal and provincial levels of government in Canada."[49]

The cultural difference is that the United States has had strong markets and weak hierarchies while both hierarchies and markets have been strong in Canada,[50] though hierarchical norms do weaken as one travels west. ("The larger the percent of the labor force who have had a taste of self-employment," Wilensky argues, "the greater the economic individualism and concomitant resistance to the welfare state.")[51] The consequences for legislation have been that Canadian public policy has been more egalitarian and redistributive than in the United States, while manifesting greater concern (due to market influence) for limiting total spending than is found in Europe.

After observing that the trade union movement in Canada has been much more socialist than in the United States, Kudrle and Marmor go on to make this point in different words: "In sum, the ideological difference ... between Canada and the United States appears to have made a considerable difference in welfare state development."[52] If, instead of a disembodied concept of ideology as pure thought, one substitutes the meatier cultural expression, shared values legitimating desired social practices, differences in policy may be seen to stem naturally from differences in ways of life.

If there are cultural influences affecting budgetary outcomes, and if there is cultural variegation among countries, then it should follow that their patterns of expenditure will differ despite the fact that they face similar economic conditions and apply similar methods of budgetary control. This is exactly what C. Stephen Wolfe and Jesse Burkhead find when they study budgetary responses to the recession of the late 1970s and the early 1980s in France, Germany, Italy, Sweden, Britain, and the United States. Though all these governments grew, they conclude, "Resource allocation patterns continue to differ substantially even when economic conditions and central government budget procedures are very much alike."[53]

Whatever might be said about the nations of eastern and western

Europe, strong hierarchies exist on both sides of the border. If welfare-spending patterns in western-European social democracies and Soviet Bloc governments are similar, as they are, that must be because they share such factors as a history of authoritarian monarchy, rather than because they differ in such matters as democratic decision-making. They also increasingly differ in another dimension—sectarian groups (destroyed in the Soviet Union after the Bolshevik Revolution)[54] are growing stronger in the West. Therefore we expect that by the twenty-first century it will become clear that equality of condition has been more nearly achieved in western rather than eastern Europe.

PELTZMAN'S LAW, OR CULTURE RECONSIDERED

An empirical test of this cultural theory we have been propounding would have to include the reverse causal sequences to that postulated by the numerous camp followers of Wagner's law: increased equality would have to *precede* growth in proportion of public expenditure to national product. The rise of sectarian political cultures would lead to an increased desire for redistribution through government. Soon (say, in a generation) government spending on welfare and in total would rise significantly. Fortunately, Peltzman has provided exactly the kind of test we require. His findings pose a direct challenge to those who maintain that economic development is the main reason for growth in government spending.

Peltzman's law, as we call it, states that "reduced inequality of income stimulates growth of government."[55] His contribution lies in showing more precisely than others how equality affects spending. The greater the inequality between taxpayers in a prior period, Peltzman contends (generalizing from much empirical data here omitted), the less inclined they are to support redistributive spending in a later period. If wealth and income are unequally distributed, the "winners," so to speak, will want to maintain their advantage. Or, contrariwise, if substantial equality already exists, then citizens will want still more of it. Equality, it seems, is a self-generating condition.* Whether it is also

* Using wage (in)equality as a surrogate for general economic trends, Peltzman summarizes the data and relates it to his theory:
"The broad outlines of the British, American, and Canadian twentieth-century experience hold almost everywhere in the developed world. Some time around World War I, wage and salary inequality began to decline and some time around 1950, the decline flattened or stopped. ... Around World War I the top 5 percent of income recipients in the typical developed country account for around 30 percent of the national income. ...

self-limiting, with a reduction in economic equality leading to a decrease in state spending, remains to be seen.

Mancur Olson's historical, developmental theory reinforces Peltzman's. Olson believes groups seek special advantage by limiting competition. It follows that (with special force after the early 1960s) "the
longer a state has been settled and the longer the time it has had to accumulate special-interest groups, the slower its rate of growth."[57]
Lower growth rates, combined with efforts to redistribute income, lead
to a larger-size government.

Following the public-choice literature, Peltzman's general argument
is that "the size of government responds to the articulated interests of
those who tend to gain or lose from politicization of the allocation of
resources."[58] Once we agree that it is impossible for people to live as
isolated individuals, we can refer to the "interests" of public-choice
theory in two ways. One would be "local advantage" or, as psycholo-
gists call it, "secondary gain," as when a person's income is directly
determined by a governmental action. The other sense of interest, explicitly recognizing the social character of interaction, refers to shared
values legitimating various ways of life. This is political culture. So
Peltzman's law may be broadened to say that cultural change precedes
and dominates budgetary change: The size of the state today is a function of its political culture yesterday.

EGALITARIAN PROGRAMS GROW FASTEST

If the cultural theory explains change, moreover, expenditure should
not merely have increased as a proportion of national product; its most
egalitarian components should have gone up far faster, and the least

---

However, by about 1950 this share falls to just under 20 percent. . . . In broad outline, the
growth of government follows a similar path. . . . For many countries a major part of the
growth of government has occurred in the last twenty-five years, or after the main force of
the trend toward equality had been spent. If equality is indeed a major determinant of the
equilibrium size of government, a lagged-adjustment process has been dominating recent
experience. Thus recent growth of government would be more closely related to the level
of inequality than absolute size.

"Size of government and inequality were essentially uncorrelated in the late 1950s. But
there is a very strong negative correlation between inequality then and subsequent
growth."

Testing the theory on a set of data for countries outside Europe, Peltzman concludes:
"The international data seem to say something even stronger. Nothing much besides income inequality is needed to explain the growth of government. We are able to pretty
much write the history of government growth in the next fifteen years from what we know
about income inequality in 1960."[56]

egalitarian (say, military spending) much slower. This too has happened.

Looking at the programs that dominate budgets in Western nations from 1954 to 1980, Richard Rose finds that though the overall increase in the share of national product taken by government was 22 percent, the growth rates of major programs differed substantially from one another, and only economic infrastructure (i.e., roads and housing) increased at the average rate. Everywhere spending on defense fell as a proportion of national product, whereas income maintenance, education, health, and interest on the debt greatly increased. In the United States, for instance, spending on health rose 213 percent, whereas defense declined by 59 percent.[59] From this we conclude that among major programs the rates of change in spending do indeed differ. Leaving out debt interest (which is a product of increasing deficits), programs concerned with income transfers, health (another form of equalizing income), and education (which tends, though not so strongly, in the same direction) have risen sharply.[60]

Evidently, comparing the growth of major programs among and within countries, as Rose recommends, is a must for the serious student of spending. But this comparison of programs by itself is insufficient without considering whether governments also set limits on total spending.

Spending could have increased absolutely by following the trend rate of increase in national product. Some programs could have gone beyond that rate if others were reduced by a similar amount. But that did not happen. More for one major program did not signify less for another. More for all programs is possible only if economic growth rises at the same rate, which did not happen, or if an implicit choice is made, not merely once but repeatedly, to increase the share government takes of national product, i.e., to increase taxes. When movement toward equality of result is at stake—as in income maintenance, health, and education—one major program may be favored more than another, but all rise absolutely and relatively in regard to proportion of national income. It is this trend toward equalization—a steady increase in spending for redistributive programs—that we hypothesize is best explained by a cultural hypothesis.

Why has budgetary control in the West collapsed? The obvious answer, because governments and their constituents want to spend more, should not be ignored. On what do they want to spend? Largely, on egalitarian measures. We have come full circle to explaining the consequences of the rise of regimes favoring that budgetary outcome.

IS THE DEFICIT IN THE BUDGET OR IN SOCIETY?

If there is a continuous and substantial deficit in the budgets of every Western nation, with the exception of Iceland, there is a surplus of irony. The Socialist government of France is trying to cut the spending that benefits its major voting blocs, while calling its major objective tax reduction. The Conservative government of Britain, reelected partially on a platform of maintaining social and health services, sought legislation reducing the autonomy of local governments to raise property tax rates—thus diminishing the decentralized character of decision-making that Conservatives are pledged to enhance. In the United States the Democratic Party, long used to denying the desirability of balanced budgets, makes achieving them a central issue in the presidential election. A Republican President, who had formerly backed his party's decades-long condemnation of unbalanced budgets, now raises deficits to unprecedented levels.

In each instance, knowledge of national circumstances—the ability of local councils, dominated by the British Labour Party, to raise rates on businesses who lack voting power; President Reagan's preference for forcing spending cuts rather than tax increases; the grip of international economic forces on the alternatives available to French President Mitterrand's Socialist government—helps make sense out of these apparent and (to some) amusing anomalies. But such insights do not explain the general budgetary trends that produce these discordant events: perennially unbalanced budgets, the growing size of government, and the ineffectiveness of governments that try to reduce spending. Does the history of budgeting, we may ask, help us understand what, if anything, might be done to alter these trends? For when we speak of learning from history, it is generally not to alter the past, as Miller reminds us, but to do something positive in the present that will affect the future. Before going back to the ancient practices recorded in these pages, it might be wiser to interrogate the recent past so as to specify with greater precision what we wish to know.

Except for our regular exceptions (the United States and Iceland), no Western nations set great store on attaining rough budget balance. Not seeking this goal, it is perhaps not so surprising that they do not achieve it. On the contrary, budget imbalance is regarded as a positive good for managing the economy or redistributing income. Nevertheless, there is general agreement that deficits of the current magnitude are unwise, either because some nations are having trouble borrowing, or others confront excessive interest rates, or because interest on the debt is growing as a fixed charge. Why, then, have deficits grown so large so fast, and why, with virtually everyone calling this state of affairs undesirable, is there evident and painful inability to get together on a remedy? And, since the remedy has to mean tax increases and expenditure reductions, and since everyone knows where the "big bucks" go to (social welfare and defense) and come from (income and corporate taxes), the difficulty cannot be that the solution remains unknown. It turns out that the debate over budget balance is also a surrogate for other issues, no less interesting for being more mundane—issues to which the historical record may be made to speak more directly, though hardly conclusively.

Size of government is an issue. At what size should the budget be balanced? Balance, however, is only a relationship; by itself it does not determine whether government should be larger or smaller in relation to the rest of society. One also can ask whether the budget would be balanced better by upping taxes or by lowering expenditure. Raising revenues increases government size, while reducing expenditure decreases its relative size. The balance at stake is between the public and private sectors.

Equity is an issue. If taxes go up, how should the burden be distributed among segments of the population—richer or poorer, this industry or region or that? If spending is cut, who will feel the pain of reductions? Here defense competes against domestic programs, and universal against means-tested entitlements. To answer these questions is also to say a good deal about what sort of foreign and domestic policies a government will undertake.

Effectiveness is also an issue. It is one thing to raise taxes and another to collect them. Virtually all governments have tried to cut spending, but, in recent times, none has succeeded. More and more, governmental ability in the West not merely to formulate but also to implement budget policy has come into question.

Now we know what the discussions concerning deficits are really about: size (or the role and extent of government), equity (or who shall pay and benefit), and effectiveness (or whether and to what extent governments can govern). When we understand the larger question raised by deficits and budget imbalance, What sort of society and government shall there be?, we see the magnitude of the answer required.

If, as Hume says, a "man acquainted with history may, in some respects, be said to have lived from the beginning of the world, and to have been making continual additions to his stock of knowledge in every century," what would history have to offer about the reduction of deficits? Even if a few readers were inclined to put in a capital "H," History could hardly tell us how we ought to live in our time. Yet that—just that, and not merely how different societies and their governments have been organized in the past—is the kind of answer the mega-issue of the composition of budgets requires.

The subject of budget balance as a rough equivalence between revenue and expenditure in total could hardly have arisen in modern form before the last 125 years or so, because methods of accounting were too imprecise. Nowadays, presumably, we know how far from this norm we have wandered. Or do we? No matter whether necessity or social preference has mothered these inventions, new budgetary devices dominate modern governmental spending. In magnitude, sophistication, and opaqueness, such widespread devices are without recent historical precedent. They encompass varieties of loan guarantees, tax preferences, capital budgets, off-budget entities, and the like. These new budget instruments either do not show up in the budget or, by much reducing the formal budget's size, serve to confuse the calculation of balances. Whether it is better not to be able to know, as in days of old, or to obfuscate what can be known, as at the present time, readers will have to decide for themselves.

Continuity can be maintained by decomposing the question of balance into its component parts; some awareness of revenues and of expenditures has always existed. All governments have had to pay the bills, and, as with debts of Third World nations today, inability to meet financial commitments leads to embarrassment, if not outright catastrophe. Has there ever been a time and a place, we may ask, where there were continual surpluses? Yes: the United States of America from the founding of the republic until the 1930s. How was this achieved? Part of the answer lies in the capacity of the tariff (chief revenue source until the First World War) to raise considerable revenues in an expanding economy. Yet other countries also had a substantial revenue base. What the United States had, and the European nations did not have, was internal opposition to national executive power. Hierarchy was weak in America while market forces were strong, and sectarians in the early years looked upon central government as a source of inequality. Americans were able to agree on and enforce a balanced-budget ideology because their political cultures were balanced in favor of it as well.

Unlike procedures in the European nations, the peculiar American financial practices are a product as well as a proximate cause of budget balance within a context of low to very low spending. One might think that a strong central executive would be better able to achieve balance than a fragmented government without a mechanism for simultaneously relating revenue to expenditure and enforcing its will; but the American exception reveals the power of a sustained balance among social forces to maintain equilibrium between getting and spending.

What does our history of spending and taxing tell us about budget balance? From the earliest time we know anything about, through the seventeenth and eighteenth centuries (depending on the country involved), revenues and expenditures were not considered together because there was no way to do so. No comprehensive accounts of receipts or of spending existed. Except for sporadic and ineffective efforts to enforce a post-audit of revenue collectors (to limit corruption), earmarking taxes into funds for special purposes was the dominant means of allocation. Budgeting mostly meant ad-hoc expedients in taxing to cover emerging spending, which, except for efforts to cut down here or there—say by trying to enforce sumptuary regulations—continued as part of past patterns. Expenditure could not be allocated within a total because there was no way to establish one. Nor was it clear how much was in the various accounts or precisely how much was being spent for what. The budget did not exist except as a patchwork.

Whether governments were rich or poor, or different social strata were taxed too much or too little, depended on the actor's perspective. Early-modern kings rarely had enough for what they wanted; and the middle and lower ranks of society, who paid because they could not escape paying, thought all government was exorbitant. Certainly, governments spent all they could lay their hands on, and more, a tendency exacerbated after the seventeenth century by the emerging availability of loans from public capital markets. If governments had too little, it was because their economies were not wealthy enough, and they had not learned either to tap society's assets more effectively or to create institutional arrangements for increasing consent.

Beginning in the seventeenth century and extending all the way into the first decades of the twentieth century, the doctrine of budget balance evolved from the interpenetration of economic individualism and social hierarchy. Budget balance connoted a combination of parsimony and efficiency well suited to industrial societies seeking to maximize investment. With accepted limits on taxation, reinforced by the belief that terrible things would happen if spending continuously exceeded annual revenue plus short-term borrowing, something like balance was obtained in most Western countries. But not for long. When the technology that permitted balance to be conceived and, to a lesser but real exent, achieved was joined to an egalitarian social premise—as we quoted Kautilya from his *Arthasastra,* "finance is the chief means of performing virtuous acts"—balance gave way to imbalance, including the modulation of economic swings for the benefit of the entire society. As saving souls in religion yielded to redistributive measures to achieve social justice, saving money by budgeting gave way to protecting citizens against adversity.

The great unanswered contemporary questions—Who will protect government against budgetary adversity if most resources go to protecting the bulk of its population? Who will protect people in Western democracies if government cannot protect itself?—are with us now. It is easy to imagine that the combination of growing wealth and the enormously enhanced technical capability of mobilizing and allocating these resources would make achieving budget balance so much easier now than before. It might, but it does not. Such simplistic reasoning— it can be, therefore it will—leaves the purposes of people outside the equation. During the all-too-brief era of the balanced budget, no one would have thought that government spending, whether on war or on welfare, would come to be so highly valued; or, for that matter, that the very same technical capabilities giving governments capacity to limit spending might also be used to increase it. That today it is possible to conceive of handling revenue and expenditure together, with sets of accounts backing up each, does not mean that governments will necessarily wish to do so; a conception of deficits as desirable was dominant between the mid-1950s and the mid-1970s. Or, as happened from the mid-1970s through the mid-1980s, if governments decide that balancing the budget would be a good idea, mere existence of accounts and procedures does not mean that they will be able to do so. It is hard to find a Western government that not only was or is able to arrive at a preferred policy of relating revenue and expenditure, but is also able to implement it. There is, to be sure, a difference: modern technical capacity to achieve balance makes failure to do so even more problematic.

Why has budget balance not been achieved? By connecting budgetary to political (im)balances among regimes, we also hope to improve understanding of what it would take to achieve a rough congruence between revenue and expenditure.

BUDGETARY BALANCE AS A FUNCTION OF REGIME

The Micawber principle, that it is not the level of income and outgo but their relationship that matters, is essential to budgeting. It is important, therefore, to ask how expenditure and revenue are related in each political regime. Which regimes run deficits? Which run surpluses? Which spend more than they take in, or take in more than they spend? Which regimes are likely to have what kind of problems—too low revenues, too high expenditure, or inability to vary either one?[61]

The number of ways in which governments can manage spending in relation to their management of resources is quite limited. The following possibilities exist:

1. Governments can manage neither their expenditures nor their revenues.
2. Governments can manage their expenditures but not their revenues.
3. Governments can manage their revenues but not their expenditures.
4. Governments can manage both their expenditures and their revenues.

These logical possibilities, of course, are not all-or-nothing conditions; government may be able to manage a little or a lot. The significance of these all-or-nothing conditions is that they map out the extremes. Governments may have two options: they can act in one way if they have sufficient leeway to manage spending; or they can make different kinds of choices if they have scope to manage their resources. If governments can manage both, they can also manage the overlap. Depending upon how they simultaneously mix increases or decreases in revenue and expenditures, governments can vary the size of the balance or imbalance.

There are five strategies for relating revenues and expenditures so that these are kept within hailing distance:

1. Do nothing.
2. Decrease spending.
3. Increase revenues.
4. Increase revenue and increase spending.
5. Decrease revenue and decrease spending.

Our hypothesis is that the five alternative strategies generated by the ability or inability of governments to manage income and outgo are related to culture. Translated into political terms, this means that the essential relationships between revenue and expenditure vary with type of regime. Slaves, to begin with the easiest example, will vary neither revenue nor expenditure; by themselves, their life is beyond control.

To understand budgeting by competitive individualists in market

TABLE 24

BUDGETARY STRATEGIES UNDER POLITICAL REGIMES

Regime: *Slavery* Slaves cannot manage expenditure or revenue. Strategy: (1) Do nothing. Balance: Spending equals revenue by imposition from above.	Regime: *Hierarchy* Can manage revenues but not expenditures. Strategy: (3) Maximize revenue. Balance: Spending marginally exceeds revenue with both at high levels.
Regime: *Market* Can manage both expenditure and revenue at low levels. Strategy: (5) Minimize expenditure and revenue. Balance: Deficit varies at low levels.	Regime: *Sect* Can manage expenditure but not revenue. Strategy: (2) Redistribute resources at high levels of expenditure and low levels of revenue. Balance: High expenditure greatly exceeds low revenue.

regimes, we must compare private and public budgeting. In the private sphere, each member competes with the others for goods, for credit, and for followers. Competition for resources increases spending. If investments bear fruit, individualists are able to pay off; if not, competitors take their place. At the governmental level, however, there is little motivation to legislate spending that does not directly benefit particular entrepreneurs. The state is kept poor; only wealthy persons in the private sector have resources for ostentatious display. While market regimes spend as little as possible for public purposes, they are even more averse to taxing. Hence there are deficits at low levels.

The egalitarian collectives we call sects try to hold down personal consumption. Wealth is regarded as both a sign of inequality and a temptation to give up an ascetic life. By abjuring wealth, egalitarians implicitly criticize the individualists whom they oppose, and whose wealth egalitarians cannot, in any event, match, for they find accumulation difficult. Lacking internal authority, they cannot make large revenue demands on members. Because capital accumulation is a source of inequality, it is rejected. Whatever wealth exists in society is soon redistributed. This regime eschews the private conspicuous consumption of market regimes or the public display that goes with hierarchical authority. Budgets are imbalanced by the combination of low revenues and high expenditures.

A hierarchical regime is able to expand its revenues. Collective investment through forced saving enables past commitments to be made good in the future. Taxes, like other rules, are imposed from the top and punctiliously collected. But spending is less easily controlled. Each role within the hierarchy has its prescribed duties, including the kinds of display that are required. New rules limiting display are hard to formulate or accept because they upset prevailing distinctions. Hierarchies can raise money far more successfully than reduce spending. Hence their budgets are unbalanced, with high revenues being exceeded by even higher expenditures.

The careful reader will observe that one of the available budgetary strategies, (4) increasing both revenue and expenditure, has not been attributed to any of the four regimes. Perhaps this strategy represents a logical possibility though not an empirical actuality. But we think not. The reason for the omission is that heretofore we have considered only basic types (primary colors, if you will) and not the hybrid regimes that may be formed among them. In a social democracy composed of hierarchies and sects, for instance, the impulse toward equality of result is strengthened, thus leading to greater redistribution of income by the state. Social democracies, therefore, both tax and spend at maximal levels, thus fitting the fourth budgetary strategy.

All Western nations are pluralist democracies. That means they have elements of the three primary political cultures; they differ in the proportions of each, and it is the differing shapes of these hybrid regimes that create the kinds of imbalance experienced in recent decades. As hierarchy becomes even weaker in the United States than it was, the ever strong market elements combine with a renascent egalitarianism to produce deficits fueled from rising social entitlements (the sectarian contribution) and lower tax rates (a product of the market mentality). With stronger hierarchical and equitable political cultures—think of Sweden and the Netherlands—and weaker market forces, we find a combination of very high taxation and still higher expenditure. Where market forces are stronger and sectarian elements weaker, but hierarchy is still dominant (as in Germany, England, France, and Japan), spending, though still high, diminishes, and deficits are not quite so large.

Why, we may well ask, has the debt risen so sharply in the United States and much less so in Britain when President Reagan and Prime Minister Thatcher are both committed to pro-market policies? No doubt economic conditions in the two countries differ. More important by far, however, since many in Reagan's Republican Party advocated higher taxes and lower deficits, is the cultural context. Hierarchy is far stronger and markets are far weaker in Britain than in America. Consequently, the hierarchical desire for stability triumphed in Britain while the preference of the market culture for smaller government, impelled by lower taxes, was victorious in the United States.

What, if anything, can we predict about budget imbalance in the future from this analysis? First, we would have to know what the future balance of power among political cultures will be. Since this would be tantamount to understanding the sources and operation of social change in the world, we make no such claim. Rather ours is a "when/as/if" theory: when, as, or if various combinations of political cultures appear in the world, we predict patterns of expenditures, revenues, and deficits (rarely surpluses) that will be associated with them. We do expect history to do one thing for us: show if and in what ways we have been wrong.

Suppose that some of us place a high value on balance—provided, however, that the size of the budget is low, amounting to no more than a third of national product. Without a strong market regime, we can say, this objective is unlikely to be realized. The combined presence of strong sectarian and weak hierarchical regimes, moreover, would likely lead to imbalance as the redistributional desires of sects worked side by side with disinclination to raise taxes.

Perhaps others also value budget balance but only if it amounts to as much as two-thirds of national product. The combination of strong hierarchy with substantial sectarianism, as in social democracy, would probably achieve such a result. Depending on the level sought, our precept is that balance in budgets depends on balance in society—a proposition in its general import at least as old as Aristotle. The types of budgets we get depend on the kinds of people we are. We-the-people in the Western world would not be experiencing unbalanced budgets unless we preferred political regimes that, acting together, produce that outcome. Now you see it, now you don't. If once we had something like balanced budgets and now we do not, this is not due to the conjurer's art but to the fact that the balance among our ways of life has changed.

THE TRANSFORMATION OF BUDGETARY NORMS

What effects on the budgetary process would we expect from cultural change, that is, assuming it has taken place? In order to facilitate steadily increasing spending, the norms guiding budgetary behavior would have to be transformed. Since the norms of balance, annularity and comprehensiveness that emerged in the eighteenth and nineteenth centuries (as the epitome of rational budgeting) evolved in order to balance budgets at what would today be low levels of spending, they stand in the way of steadily increasing expenditure. From the perspective of governmental growth, it is far better to justify budgets that are unbalanced, noncomprehensive (i.e., that allow spending from many more sources) and continuous, like entitlements, rather than subject to frequent scrutiny.

Developed by accretion, installed by revolution, the basic budgetary norms which the nineteenth century bequeathed to the twentieth, were it entirely possible to trace their origins, go back at least five hundred years—more, perhaps, if we allow for numerology and auditing. Change was measured on a time scale calibrated in centuries instead of decades. Over all this time most new methods were adopted piecemeal, not to plan spending, but to improve financial control. The rate of innovation was not constant, but, as better methods and attitudes about public government emerged, the pace of change in government financial institutions did speed up. Equipped to capture the fiscal dividend produced by growing economies, improved administration had made the budgetary process manageable in most nations by the mid-nineteenth century. Improvement did begin to slow down, but only because the basic budgetary norms established by the early years of this century—norms of annularity, comprehensiveness, and balance—proved adequate to administrative demands made by governments at that time.

Nowadays one hears much less than before about *norms* of budgeting. Embedded in common understanding, the norms seem timeless; they have retreated to the background. One by one these norms have been undermined while the expectations which rest on them continue as if nothing had happened. Yet it is these silent norms that provided the common understanding on which budgetary control, until this very day, is based.

Is attrition of budgetary norms a concomitant of rapid growth of government in our time, and is that attrition an abrupt change, discontinuous with the recent past? Perhaps growth of government and attrition of budget norms represent a reversion (but at a greatly magnified scale) to tendencies held by governments before the nineteenth century to spend without limit, and without means.

Since the Second World War, the norm of the balanced budget has been discarded almost everywhere. Occasional moments of concern were blotted out by the prevailing consensus, rationalized by Keynesian economic theory, that spending for purposes mandated by a public was a source of economic stability.

It would be helpful to find peoples who still adhered to the norm of budget balance and to compare their taxing and spending patterns with those that do not. With the United States in the throes of struggle over whether it will adhere to this norm, the Western world can offer the investigator only Iceland. Though not large in area or population, it is a nation and it is all we have. Among all Western countries, Iceland's central government has grown least (from 27.3 percent of national product to 29.3) from 1972 to 1980.[62] It has also maintained the strongest attachment to the balanced budget. Bringing in an unbalanced budget, as distinguished from emerging with a small one, is unacceptable in Iceland's political life. In a phrase, revenue limits expenditure. Tolerable tax increases, in the context of a balanced budget, serve to limit spending. A law passed in 1968 brought virtually all off-budget spending within the scope of central accounts. Most important, the idea of the balanced budget is interpreted to mean the absence of surpluses as well as deficits. As a former Director of the Budget in Iceland, Gisli Blöndal, put it, "A surplus, it is feared, would quickly be eliminated by further expenditure appropriations in the Parliamentary Process."[63] Maintaining balance without a deficit or a surplus implies, as Blöndal affirms, "a *de facto* rejection of Keynesian doctrine."[64] A single decision rule, "Balance the budget!," while it gives up a Keynesian counterfiscal capacity (surpluses when there is inflation, deficits with deflation or unemployment) is powerful in limiting spending.

Loss of comprehensiveness in budgeting has provoked even less attention. As with state finance in the old days before consolidated budgets existed, fragmentation of jurisdiction over spending into special funds inhibits accounting for the total amount spent. Modern policymakers' ingenuity, moreover, has created mechanisms for spending unknown in past ages; and extensive use of such devices has made modern budgets into things of shreds and patches. Indeed, we doubt whether in any Western nation the traditional budgetary process—estimation, authorization, appropriation, execution—is followed for as much as one-third the total funds. However weak one might judge the controls exercised in that process, these controls evidently have been considered far too strong. Everywhere in the West concerted (and successful) efforts have been made to get around them.

Instead of having the government spend its revenues directly for particular purposes as comprehensive budgeting principles decree, money may be left in the hands of taxpayers, providing such funds are used for governmentally approved purposes. Home ownership may be encouraged by allowing mortgage interest to be deductible for tax purposes, for example, or industry to locate in certain places by deducting part of the cost incurred. These tax preferences or "tax expenditures" (so named because they are a substitute for ordinary spending) may be estimated, but are not a formal part of the budget, nor are the amounts involved counted toward total spending or the size of the deficit. Thus the revenues forgone do not appear in the budget.

Neither do loan guarantees. Government may loan money directly or may pledge its credit, thereby guaranteeing payment of loans. During the past two decades huge volumes of loan guarantees (over a trillion in the United States alone) have been issued. Guarantees appear in the budget only if there should be a default so that the government has to pay, but not otherwise. The difference between the market rate of interest and the lower guaranteed rate times the sums outstanding may amount to many billions. As potential borrowers change places, some crowding out others, capital markets are affected and interest rates may rise. Yet the interested person would be fortunate to find as much as an appendix to the budget document indicating the scope of direct and guaranteed government credit.

Another avenue of escape from comprehensiveness is variously called "entitlement," "backdoor financing," or "mandatory items." Without requiring a specific appropriation, legislation authorizes payment to people who qualify for unemployment compensation, say, or for child benefits. The monies spent appear in the budget as estimated outlays, but are not subject to review in the legislative process unless the enabling legislation is revised. Governments learn how much they have spent retrospectively by adding up the checks sent to individuals in a given year.

With loans, loan guarantees, and tax expenditures outside the budget, and entitlements (often involving income transfers) within the budget but not subject to annual control under budgetary procedures, little remains of the norm of comprehensiveness. In recent years, moreover, a large number of "off budget" corporations have been chartered. Generally engaged in activities (such as housing) which could otherwise be in private hands, such corporations, and the work they accomplish, may be mentioned in the budget, but their expenditures are neither listed nor included in budgetary totals. When all these developments are looked at together, the movement away from comprehensiveness is seen as a stampede.

The norm of comprehensiveness was established bit by bit between the sixteenth and nineteenth centuries. Instead of coping with the multiplicity of public and private revenue funds then existing, reformers wanted to channel all money spent by government through a single budget instrument. By the late nineteenth century, when the norms had become well established, a comprehensive budget in most nations included *all* agency spending. But while comprehensiveness is still taken for granted in some circles, a truly comprehensive budget is seldom found these days. Most government money is spent by means of income transfers from government to citizens, by national grants to local governments, and by off-budget entities. The doctrine of comprehensiveness once assumed a small, self-contained public sector supported by tax revenue, but the reality since 1960 is that most government payments go directly to individuals and groups outside government, and are financed by borrowing. We can no longer look to the government budget to provide for a monetary measure of the public use of financial resources.

From the late nineteenth century to 1960, the main escapes from comprehensiveness were earmarked revenues (or, as the British called them, hypothecated funds); separate capital funds for development projects; and special-purpose accounts sequestered from treasury funds. Often the difference in purpose between capital budgets, investment budgets, extraordinary spending, and the spending in the regular budget proved to be illusory. Nevertheless, by adding these other budgets to the regular budget, the expert reader had a pretty good idea of how much was being spent, by whom, and for what purpose. With transfers, government-guaranteed credit arrangements, regulations imposing costs on private parties, varieties of government industries—fully owned, partially owned, or only regulated, all excluded from the budget—any assessment of the cost of government is bound to be both suspect and incomplete. The result is a creeping, but invisible and nameless, revolution in budgeting.

While comprehensiveness and balance have been attenuated, the norm of annularity still seems to be with us. With each passing year, however, appearances become more deceiving. Pervasive uncertainties regarding expenditures and revenues have led to repetitive budgeting—that is, the budget is continuously reformulated. When the six-month economic forecast is out of date after six weeks, the resort to "midcourse" corrections, including mini–spending budgets, make an annual budget almost a relic of a bygone era. Ironically, just as electronic data processing was introduced during the 1950s as a tool for budgetary control, and as near-universal satisfaction was expressed over its achievement, government began to have difficulty estimating the size of the annual budget, let alone choosing its contents.[65]

When you control departments, the understanding used to be, you control spending. Now, with departmental disbursements for goods and services accounting only for 15 to 30 percent of spending in industrial democracies, the inescapable conclusion is that the vast body of expenditure is no longer covered by traditional budgetary norms. Most money is spent to affect citizen behavior rather than for direct government action. Since most spending is by individuals who receive payments or loans, and by subnational governments, the traditional way of controlling spending by establishing departmental budgets is no longer effective.[66]

In an effort to control private behavior, Allen Schick says, the public sector has lost grip on itself:

> The growth of off-budget expenditure produces . . . "the paradox of control." . . . Off-budget expenditures have resulted from the transformation of the public sector from one in which spending was done within government to one in which spending largely occurs outside government. Not the least of the reasons for this transformation has been the striving of government to strengthen its control of the economy, the distribution of income, investment policy, and the supply of goods and services. The paradox is that in its effort to extend its control over the private sector, government has surrendered a good deal of its control over the public sector.[67]

Control of spending has declined along with the norm of comprehensiveness because one cannot maximize simultaneously in opposing directions. Varying the level of spending to help modulate swings in the economy, or to redistribute income, or to strengthen family finances is not wholly compatible with controlling departmental behavior. The more government tries to affect citizen behavior, it appears, the less able it is to keep its own house in order. This new relationship between government and citizen may have many advantages, but control over spending is not one of them.

Nor can it be said, in appraising the norm of comprehensiveness, that there is a house of budgeting whose conceptual rooms are comparable. Accounting is in a shambles. Money borrowed one way ends up entirely in the budget, money borrowed another way partially within it, and if borrowed still a third way it may not appear in the budget at all. Reallocating nontraditional resources—including guaranteed loans, tax preferences, entitlements, and spending by government corporations—along with department spending is not possible (not, in the sense of being intended) because there is no common conversion factor.

Since the nineteenth century, an annual budget has been equivalent to insuring fiscal predictability. That norm has denoted that an annual budget is not only desirable but feasible—the budget will last a year. Certainty motivates agencies to cooperate with central controllers. Though not spelled out, this is the mutual understanding: because the treasury promises to pay the amount passed in the budget, agencies will both exercise restraint in requests and try to stay within the allotted amounts.

Once that implied contract is broken, a number of consequences ensue. Because the treasury cannot guarantee the allotted amount, agency political activity increases, not merely to get what it asked for, but to keep it. If the budget signals to "get it if you can," early accommodation is unwise, resulting in delayed decisions and enhanced uncertainty. Agencies that find this uncertainty intolerable will try to escape from prior restraints by demanding even more (so that more will be left when cuts come). Thus initial bids become even less reliable as a gauge of agency expectations.

Rather than accepting the appropriations process with its considerable uncertainty, agencies might try to escape from it by making direct drafts on the treasury (called "backdoor spending" or entitlements). Or they may seek loans or loan guarantees, or try to shift functions to off-budget organizations within government funded by earmarked taxes. Agencies may also try to impose regulations so that private parties have to bear the cost (say, of medical care or reducing pollution); funding for such activities then can be deleted from the agency budget.

Inevitably, as funds available to the central treasury dry up, representing a smaller proportion of total expenditure, and as the treasury grows less able to calculate how much is being spent (since it lacks direct control over loan guarantees, entitlements and the rest), the treasury seeks to impose a harsher regime on the agencies it does control; this tempts agencies and program advocates to engage in further escape measures.

We see where we are: the decline of predictability, which used to be based on the norm of annularity, lessens the treasury's ability to maintain comprehensiveness. Revenues are diverted through increasing use of tax preferences and special funds. Because of the numerous devices just mentioned for getting around the appropriations process, expenditures cannot be compared one with another. No one can say how much an appropriation is worth compared to a direct loan, a guarantee, or any of a number of other spending devices.

Loss of comprehensiveness weakens control. Not knowing how much is being spent, central budget offices are in a weaker position to say that any amount (In which account, please?) is too much. Looking good, as opposed to doing well, becomes tempting. Treasurers, who tend to be judged by the degree of budget imbalance, can improve their position by shifting spending to accounts such as loan guarantees that, except for a small amount for defaults, do not show up in the budget. Or they can trade lower spending outlays in one year for larger authorization in future years. Without rules that equate all major forms of spending, accounting sleight of hand substitutes for spending control.

Advocates of setting limits on expenditure and/or taxation say that such a measure might make things different. Those bidding for spending would perhaps be restrained by knowing that more for them would mean less for others. Forcing agencies to practice self-discipline might alter recent trends. But if the social understandings necessary to make restraint effective are weak, there are many strategies—regulation to impose costs on the private sector, tax expenditures, loan guarantees, etc.—to get around formal spending limits.[68]

As things now stand, without widespread agreement on either taxing or spending, the inner discipline that kept the budget battle within tolerable limits gives way. With interdependence eroded—because the effects of spending here do not necessarily implicate others elsewhere—budgetary control has deteriorated into a free-for-all.

No longer can governments control spending by controlling departments; most spending is outside departments. No longer is it possible to control departments by controlling spending; most spending in which departments are interested is subject neither to annual review nor to central control. No longer are the participants clear about whether control is desirable or feasible. Thus it appears that when the authority of one norm becomes attenuated it will soon happen to the others.

There is a supportive relationship among the classical budgetary norms: if one declines, the others are weakened also. Once predictability diminishes, spending advocates are encouraged to sidestep the appropriations process. The new forms of financing they develop upset any notion of a single set of accounts. And, as comprehensiveness withers away, predictability in expenditure decreases accordingly. In sum, it was the achievement of budgetary comprehensiveness that made predictability possible; and it was the delivery of a budget that could be counted on that permitted movement of funds across revenue and expenditure categories.

A revolution in behavior has accompanied the transformation of budgetary norms. Restating what has been said in terms of social relations, the old norms placed the participants in budgeting in the same boat. Their actions were interdependent: if a program or a department got a great deal more, other programs and departments had to do with less. Each department or agency restrained its bid partly because other spending interests who suffered were prepared to impose similar sanctions on it. And if spending units played by the rule of limiting aspirations for spending, they got into the budget and stayed there. Mostly, however, *expenditure was controlled, as it has to be in so complex a system, not by sanctions but by inhibiting demands at the source.* As soon as every bid grows large, that is, as the spending process becomes normless, with every participant out for himself, no central controller—who cannot possibly know as much as each department does about its own affairs—can cope.

To describe the loss of confidence in expenditure control as "normlessness," however, while it does convey the sense that every participant is in it for himself, leaves us with an explanation in terms of what was missing from budgetary relationships, rather than of something actively causing the consequences for control we observe and wish to explain. If budgetary norms have been altered, into what (staying with the current terms of discourse) have they been transformed? If it is "off with the old and on with the new," what exactly are the new norms?

Having funds authorized and appropriated every year is an obstacle to smooth spending. Why not five-year authorizations and appropriations or, better still, "no-year" appropriations? Indeed, why not permanent authorizations and appropriations by vesting spending in a class of recipients, rather than in the taxpayers who provide the funds, or the government that collects and apportions them? Thus allocation gives way to entitlement.

Entitlement is the enemy of annularity; the latter term prescribes a periodicity to the budgetary process, and the former the legal right to receive government funds. Annularity is designed to enable government to control itself, while entitlements are created to enable beneficiaries to make claims on government. Annularity encourages restriction, and entitlement expansion of spending.

The opposite of the norm of budgetary comprehensiveness, multiplication of spending spigots, is easier to explain. To reiterate the flow metaphor of finance going back to the late Middle Ages, the more modes of spending there are, the easier it is to turn one on when others are off. The larger and more diverse the number of spigots (loans, guarantees, preferences, entitlements, etc.), the harder it is to know exactly how much is being spent, for which purpose, by whom, with what result. The more restricted the focus becomes, the easier it is to justify each program in isolation as something desirable to do. For all programs do some good for somebody. Whatever disadvantages spending might entail are to be found in its aggregate consequences for taxation, borrowing, interest rates, inflation, economic growth, and so on. Emphasizing the "disaggregates," encourages a focus on increasing items of expenditure, and discourages attention to reducing total spending.

Disaggregative and continuous budgeting both contribute toward and fit in with unbalanced budgets. Operating under these norms serves to disguise amounts of total spending. The uncomfortable question of the desirable relationship between expenditure and revenue, i.e., the size of the deficit, need not be faced. In the traditional budget process, limited, not unlimited, spending is normative. Budgets that are unbalanced, continuous, and disaggregated are meant to be larger than budgets that are balanced, annual, and comprehensive.

BALANCED BUDGETS AND UNBALANCED REGIMES

Is the "dead hand of the past" visible today in budgeting? With our usual force and conviction, we answer, "Yes and no."

Going back to the last half of the nineteenth century, when formal budgeting became widespread, we face discontinuity: though outer appearances have remained relatively constant, in recent years budgetary forms have been emptied of meaning. As the levels of taxing, spending, and borrowing have grown, the stable structure of understandings providing a foundation for budgetary control have been undermined—from its very desirability to its accomplishment by central control of departments. Today budgeting is more continuous than annual, disaggregative rather than comprehensive, unbalanced, not balanced.

Perhaps, in considering the relationship between past and present, the reader has in mind a more direct causal nexus. Is the past dead, as J. H. Plumb told us, in that its power to cause us to act differently than we otherwise would has waned?[69] All ways of life rest on a past that is prologue to the present people wish to maintain, or tear down, in favor of a different social order. To what extent, we may ask, does the ghost of budgets past still hold portent?

In one respect the past is as present as today's headlines. Major spending programs—pensions, education, health, the armed forces, and the like—are the cumulative result of decades of incremental change. Agreements entered into in an earlier age still affect the amount and feasibility of change. In other respects, however, the ideas that animated past taxing, spending, and borrowing, like that of the balanced budget, appear out of synch with contemporary conditions.

If a regime strives to be rational by supporting its way of life, that does not mean each one will be successful in maintaining or enhancing it, or in weakening others. For intention and outcome to coincide requires perfect foresight; but our own experiences, as well as whatever we know of history, precludes such possibility. Again, we shall draw upon budget balance as an idea and an outcome to illustrate our reading of history.

How shall we characterize the brief period in Western history when some governments balanced their budgets some of the time and none unbalanced them all the time? Were the elements of a finely wrought equilibrium manifest then? From hierarchy's perspective, budget balance would mean that all was well with the world. In Enlightenment language, as mankind's material progress matched its spiritual growth each class of citizens would get roughly what it deserved and needed. Or, as sectarians might put it, was the balanced budget a repressive ideology, doubly vicious because it ignored social needs and justified domination by the economically rich and socially powerful? During its heyday, the last quarter of the nineteenth century and the first of the twentieth, market regimes dominated the still-strong hierarchies. The "establishment" that emerged made a virtue of balance at low levels. But budgeting was by no means all that was happening. After the male youth of the West annihilated one another in vast numbers during the First World War, and the Great Depression occurred, neither market nor hierarchical regimes recovered their former force. Needless to say, these catastrophes were not intended nor supposed to influence budgeting, but they did.

The reorientation of hierarchical regimes in the West toward modestly redistributive policies—together with stronger sectarian and weaker market forces—exemplified the post–World War II welfare state. No one foresaw the "scissors crisis" in which expenditure outruns revenue, but it is here nonetheless, a product of a strengthened egalitarianism and a weaker individualism.

Current discourse focuses on the deficit as a structural problem. The term "structure" means that built-in spending is expected to exceed built-in revenue. The very term "structure" (like "system" in Newtonian mechanics) suggests a significant change in budgeting. Unlike the term it has replaced (the Keynesian full-employment budget), calling the deficit structural suggests that government is out of (instead of in) control. The budget's focus on social purposes, especially full employment, is challenged by a return to the old-time religion of budget balance. After all, if there is a structural defect, indeed a structural imbalance, then it must be eliminated by restoring balance.

But how? Sectarians seek balance by taxing the rich and giving to the poor, market regimes by reducing taxes and spending, and hierarchies by doing some of both. Unless hierarchy and markets grow stronger or sects weaker, there will be no balance, for balance in budgets requires a corresponding balance among regimes. For the time being, European governments, mostly social democracies, can blame the United States for high interest rates allegedly stemming from huge deficits. But if deficits are bad in the New World, why are they good in the Old? Either these social-democratic regimes will move toward defacto socialism, as government spending swells to 70 or 80 percent of national product, or they will have to act to keep spending from growing much higher. Though budget balance per se may not emerge as a significant issue, therefore, the balance between public and private sectors surely will.

The expenditure-limit, balanced-budget amendment is advocated by American adherents of a market regime. By limiting spending to the prior year plus the increase in GNP, the public sector is to be kept from growing faster than the private. Elsewhere among Western nations, as we saw in the previous chapter, there are efforts under other names to establish global limits within which all spending must fit. In Canada this is done by Cabinet decision to try to limit spending to the trend rate of growth of national product.[70] These spending-limit proposals are efforts to introduce the norms of comprehensiveness and balance by law rather than by custom. So far, none of these efforts has been successful. It may finally dawn upon observers that the peoples involved must not want to succeed all that much if they keep failing.

The U.S. Gramm-Rudman-Hollings law (GRH for short), the Balanced Budget Act, is the most recent effort to attain a budget balance through legal means. To achieve the stated goal of wiping out the deficit in five years, all expenditures except interest on the debt and a number of social welfare entitlements, such as Social Security and Aid to Dependent Children, are subject to inexorable, across-the-board cuts.* The mutual hostage-taking associated with passage of the act may be viewed either as a manifestation of balance among market and sectarian regimes, or as negation of that balance.

By passing this law, liberal Democrats and Republicans meant to hold defense hostage—to compel a market-oriented president to go back on his promise not to raise taxes, while conservative Republicans aimed to threaten domestic social programs most affected by the cuts. In this game of budgetary chicken, one side assumes that as automatic defense spending cuts are triggered, the president will become willing to raise taxes, while the other hopes that as meat-ax cuts in domestic spending approach, Democrats will accept the policy decisions needed for domestic program reductions. Each side hopes to prevail by making the budgetary process unworkable. This political Ludditism does not bode well for the ability to govern.

Agreement on GRH itself obscures the built-in disagreement it embodies. Polarization among political regimes has produced agreement on extremism—the measure mandates that Congress should make fundamental choices on *total spending and revenue every year*. But these self-same regimes continue to wrangle over what spending and tax levels should be, or how burdens and benefits should be divided. There is agreement over budget resolutions—these should by all means be passed—but profound disagreement over their contents.

So how did this happen? Year after year in recent times, Congress has taken longer and longer to bring in a budget. Tired of budgeting to no purpose, its members despaired sufficiently of accommodation to wish to cover over their disputes with a formula—all the while expecting, even hoping, that the balancing mechanism would prove so onerous that it would collapse of its own weight. This is no way to run a ship, especially the ship of state, unless, of course, one regards destruction a lesser evil than giving in to the other side.

What Robert Reischauer has called "the fiscalization of the public policy debate" is a sign of polarization. Few programs are considered solely on their substantive or political merit, but, instead, on their contribution to the deficit. The substantive question of what the money will buy is increasingly shunted aside as Congress asks "How much?" Manifesting widespread polarization among regimes, quantity serves

---

* The extraordinary events leading up to the Gramm-Rudman-Hollings Act are described and analyzed in Joseph White and Aaron Wildavsky, *The Battle of the Budget* (book manuscript).

as surrogate for quality. Each appropriation becomes subject to test: Does a program fit within the latest congressional budget resolution, or the president's budget? And, how fast would spending for defense or welfare grow?

Fiscalization of the policy debate is a crude but effective way of accounting for wins, losses, and ties. To the extent that bigger is deemed better for some regimes and worse for others, allocating more for welfare or less to defense, or imposing higher or lower tax rates, intensifies the political struggle. It was once believed that restricting conflict to amounts spent would help to reconcile differences (a little more here means less there), but fiscalization has had the opposite outcome. By aggregating totals and converting them into symbols of which regime is ahead or behind, this way of budgeting highlights conflict, making differences increasingly difficult to resolve. The decision maker is forced to choose between a market regime's preference for equality of opportunity, by reducing taxes, or sectarian efforts to attain equality of condition, by increasing spending on welfare, or a hierarchical regime's desire to spend more on defense.

Ronald Reagan, a conservative determined to reduce the size, and with it the influence, of the domestic government, has been the commanding general in this war of symbols. Unlike his Republican predecessors whose tolerance of hierarchy matched their market preference, Reagan was determined to starve his opponents of revenue. Like budget balancers in nineteenth-century governments, he believed that revenue encouraged spending. His across-the-board tax cuts reduced revenues with one blow, while large increases in defense spending (rationalized as defense of existing authority) stepped up the pressure on domestic programs. Then, as economic decline compounded loss of revenue caused by the tax cuts, this market oriented president, rather than raising taxes, chose to let the deficit rise to maintain his first priority—limiting central government. Soon enough, everyone discovered that a large and growing deficit exerted immense downward pressure on total spending. Indeed, the deficit became, if not the only, then undoubtedly the most effective tool for controlling spending since the expansion initiated in the 1930s by the New Deal.

Following precepts of Keynesian economics, liberal Democrats had favored modest deficits since the late 1940s; in this way they could simultaneously help manage the economy and support the social programs which manifested the utility of an active central government. Inflation during the 1970s did create doubt about the benefit of therapeutic imbalance, but it was not until deficits began to expand exponentially during the early 1980s that the Democrats, led by presidential candidate Walter Mondale in 1984, became advocates of budget balance.

Perhaps anger at the president for opposing their policy preferences, amid consternation that his promised balance had turned into the largest deficit ever, made mainline Democrats so angry that they abandoned long-held beliefs in order to punish him. (Meanwhile, the president kept blaming Democratic programs, instead of his tax cuts, for the deficits.) But both sides also appeared to be making a rational political calculation: in effect, they invoked a rule of compound interest.

Where deficits rise quickly and become high enough, the rule of compound interest applies: rising debt drives out new spending. If interest on the public debt rises faster than revenues, so that new debt compounds on old, government spending is severely squeezed. This has not always been true, of course; during the early modern era, before governments possessed capacity to relate expenditures to revenue, debt-service was the largest single item of expenditure. In modern third world nations, and in European social democracies, moreover, the rate of increase in costs of debt-service already has become larger than rates of revenue growth. Concerned more with ability to borrow than with maintaining budget balance, European social democracies accept the situation.

But in the U.S. a strong market culture keeps the tax take down; hence Democrats are confronted with a difficult choice: either they must recommend large, unpopular tax increases, or, year by year, reduce spending for their preferred government programs. With a rising deficit, compound interest is a budgetary sword of Damocles. The Democratic Party's advocacy of the Keynesian "full employment surplus," a doctrine rationalizing therapeutic deficits to balance the budget at full employment, has been abandoned. Future historians of budgeting, we believe, will appraise this turn of events as a historic change.

A formula has been substituted for thought because political polarization has prevented successful direct annual bargaining on the budget. Only moderate Republicans and Democrats, who see their hierarchical devotion to compromise threatened by unbalanced budgets as well as extremism, prefer workability to adherence to doctrine. But they are not in the majority.

The budgetary process is not a substitute for power. It cannot, by itself, create regime majorities and enforce their will. While the rules for voting on spending and taxing may make agreement marginally easier or more difficult, rules alone cannot close unbridgeable gaps. In short, budgeting does not determine political alignments; rather, because budgeting is a subsystem of politics, political cultures shape budgeting.

Does this causal connection between regimes and budgets signify that people must change their ways of life before they can alter budgetary outcomes? In the short run, no, but in the long run, yes. Americans, for instance, might choose an oil tax. Perhaps efforts to limit entitlements will be more effective than heretofore. Other nations might discover a new tax or better methods of enforcing old ones until they too use up that bonus. Perhaps the cries of alarm will be discovered to have been overdone as nations live reasonably well with historically high deficits. However, all these "solutions" to budget imbalance depend on increasing the size of government.

The advent of big government has been accompanied by doomsaying. If government grows past 25 percent or 50 percent, or some such proportion, of national product, the sky will fall in. Presumably, democracy will die or the economy will collapse if political pluralism or economic growth is undermined by governmental control. Now that all Western nations have passed the 25 percent mark and many, especially the Netherlands and the Scandinavian nations, have exceeded or approached 50 percent, it is not so evident that the wolf is at the door. It could be that nations with the largest public sectors are special in their degree of homogeneity or in their devotion to democracy so that they escape from the predicted disasters (but other, less fortunate nations will suffer them). Or it could be that democracy and economic growth are compatible with very large government. What there cannot be is strong or even moderate strength in competitive individualism when government takes well over 80 or 90 percent of national product.

Eventually (and by that we mean no longer than the first quarter of the twenty-first century, now just forty years away—as far in the future as World War II was in the past), at current rates of governmental growth, market regimes will be exceedingly weak or have essentially disappeared. The alliance between hierarchical and market regimes would disappear with them. Established authority would be under attack as sectarian forces seek simultaneously to expand the size and to deny the legitimacy of government. The real test of whether democracy could exist without substantial market forces would be under way.

Now, none of this need happen. The peoples of the West may want larger but not the largest-size government. And they may act through their politicians to achieve that result. But how? Accommodation between sectarian and hierarchical regimes would lead to a greater degree of balance at much higher levels of taxing and spending. The hierarchical desire to fund defense, coupled with belief in balance as a political good, would encourage its adherents to accede to higher taxes. The sectarian desire to redistribute income may lead its supporters to accept higher defense spending and perhaps a big moneymaker such as a value added tax. Alternatively, markets and hierarchical regimes, the established authorities, may agree to achieve balance at much lower levels of taxing and spending. Whatever the immediate outcome, we can be sure that the method adopted will generate new problems of which we are as yet unaware.

No choice, as usual, is choice for the status quo under which Wagner's law of increasing state activity has had near-universal applicability. Inexorably, quantitative will lead to qualitative change. Either this law will be broken, resulting in the stabilization of government spending, or it will continue to apply, leading to the absorption of the private into the public sector. Exactly that—what sort of government the nations of the West ought to have—is what the budgetary struggles of today and yesterday are about.

What about budget balance? A struggle between sectarian and hierarchical regimes would lead to higher imbalances as they compete for credit over who has provided the most benefits. Ultimately, if history is any guide at all, the cohesive will beat the divided; hierarchies will defeat sects and, without challenge, impose greater balance at a cost of reducing liberty. Should the size of government be stabilized, meaning that market regimes will grow somewhat stronger while sectarian regimes decline, budgets will come closer into balance as economic growth catches up with government spending. By then, to be sure, these solutions will generate new problems of which we are as yet unaware.

NOTES

CHAPTER ONE

1. Denise Schmandt-Besserat, "Decipherment of the Earliest Tablets," *Science,* Vol. 211, No. 16 (Jan. 16, 1981), pp. 283–85, and "The Envelopes that Bear the First Writing," *Technology and Culture,* Vol. 21, No. 3 (July 1980), pp. 357–85.
2. See Mary Douglas, "Environments at Risk," in *Implicit Meanings* (London: Routledge & Kegan Paul, 1975), p. 230.
3. "Speech of Edmund Burke on American Taxation," in Thomas Michael Kettle, *Irish Orators and Oratory* (Dublin: Talbot Press, 1916), pp. 1–24.
4. Robert W. Tucker and Robert E. Good, *Force, Order, and Justice* (Baltimore: Johns Hopkins Univ., 1967).
5. The categories we use are freely adapted from "Cultural Bias," in Mary Douglas, *In the Active Voice* (London: Routledge & Kegan Paul, 1982). See also Mary Douglas and Aaron Wildavsky, *Risk and Culture* (Berkeley and Los Angeles: Univ. of California, 1982).
6. See Aaron Wildavsky, *The Politics of the Budgetary Process,* 4th ed. (Boston: Little, Brown, 1984), pp. 16–18 and 108–26, for discussion of the budgetary base.
7. Margaret Levi, "Rule and Revenue Production," paper prepared for presentation at the Western Political Science Association meetings, Sacramento, Calif., April 1984.
8. See Douglas C. North, *Structure and Change in Economic History* (New York: Norton, 1981).

CHAPTER TWO

1. U. N. Ghoshal, *Contributions to the History of the Hindu Revenue System* (Calcutta: Univ. of Calcutta, 1929), p. 15.
2. *Ibid.*
3. M. H. Gopal, *Mauryan Public Finance* (London: Allen & Unwin, 1935), pp. 19–20.
4. For a discussion of evidence available to scholars of ancient civilizations, see Hermann Bengston, *An Introduction to Ancient History* (Berkeley: Univ. of California, 1970), Ch. IV and V.
5. F. Heichelheim, *An Ancient Economic History* (Leyden: A. W. Sijthoff, 1965), pp. 26–29, 96–97, 100–103; Eduard Meyer, "Wirtschaftliche Entwicklung des Altertums," and "The Development of Individuality in Ancient History," in his *Kleine Schriften* (Halle A. S., 1910), pp. 88–91, 217; Robert McC. Adams, *Heartland of Cities: Surveys of Ancient Settlement and Land Use on the Central Flood Plain of the Euphrates* (Chicago: Univ. of Chicago, 1981), pp. 21, 134, and *passim.*
6. Sources: *Encyclopaedia Britannica,* 1969 ed., Vol. 2, "Egypt"; Vol. 5, "Babylonia and Assyria," "China"; Vol. 12, "India." John A. Garraty and Peter Gay, eds., *The Columbia History of the World* (New York: Harper & Row, 1981). William H. McNeill, *The Rise of the West: A History of the Human Community* (New York/Toronto: New American Library, 1963).
7. Hartmut Schmoekel, "Mesopotamien," in *Kulturgeschichte des Alten Orient* (Stuttgart: Alfred Kroener, 1961), p. 46.
8. *Ibid.,* p. 25.
9. See Gordon Childe, *What Happened in History* (Baltimore: Penguin, 1964), p. 102; Jacquetta Hawkes and Sir Leonard Wooley, *The Beginnings of Civilization* (*History of Mankind,* Vol. 1) (New York: Mentor, 1965), Part 2, p. 125.
10. For a discussion of the connection between the development of irrigation systems and the emergence of governments, see Max Weber, "Agrarverhältnisse im Altertum," in *Gesammelte Aufsätze zur Sozial- und Wirtschaftsgeschichte* (Tübingen: J. C. B. Mohr, 1924), pp. 10–11, 17, 46, 63. Karl Wittfogel, *Oriental Despotism: A Comparative Study of Total Power* (New Haven: Yale Univ., 1957). Hawkes and Wooley, *The Beginnings of Civilization,* pp. 112–15. Childe, *What Happened in History,* pp. 78–81. W. H. McNeill, *The Rise of the West* (Chicago: Mentor, 1963), pp. 45–49, 61, 80–82, 86–87n.
11. James H. Breasted, *A History of Egypt from the Earliest Times to the Persian Conquest* (New York: Scribners, 1916), p. 161.
12. A. Burn, "Hic Breve Vivitur: A Study of the Expectation of Life in the Roman Empire," *Past and Present,* Vol. 4 (1953), pp. 1–31; A. H. M. Jones, "The Social Structure of Athens in the 4th Century B.C.," *Economic History Review,* 2nd Series, Vol. VIII, No. 2 (December 1955), p. 146; *Encyclopaedia Britannica,* 1969 ed., Vol. 8, p. 41.
13. Wolfram Eberhard, *A History of China* (Berkeley: Univ. of California, 1960), p. 65.
14. Heichelheim, *Ancient Economic History,* Vol. I, pp. 104–6, 39–40, 52–56.
15. Schmoekel, *Das Land Sumer: Die Wiederentdeckung der ersten Hochkultur der Menschheit,* 2nd ed. (Stuttgart: W. Kohlhammer, 1956), p. 82.
16. Heichelheim, *Ancient Economic History,* pp. 175, 178.

17. E. Fournier de Flaix, *L' Impôt dans les diverses civilisations,* Vol. I (Paris: Guillaumin & Cie., 1897), pp. xix, 7; and Seton Lloyd, *Archeology of Mesopotamia, from the Old Stone Age to the Persian Conquest* (London: Thames & Hudson, 1978), p. 44.

18. Kurt Heinig, *Das Budget,* Vol. 1 (Tübingen: J. C. B. Mohr, 1948); Bruno Meissner, *Babylonien und Assyrien* (Heidelberg: C. Winter, 1920–25), Vol. 1, p. 117; Alfons Dopsch, *Naturalwirtschaft und Geldwirtschaft in der Weltgeschichte* (Natural Economy and Money Economy in World History) (Vienna: L. W. Seidel, 1930), p. 41.

19. Eberhard, *History of China,* p. 65.

20. Ernest O. Reischauer and John K. Fairbank, *East Asia: The Great Tradition,* Vol. 1 (Boston: Houghton Mifflin, 1960), p. 161; Heichelheim, *Ancient Economic History,* p. 11; Childe, *What Happened in History,* p. 119.

21. Karl A. Wittfogel and Feng Chia Sheng, *History of Chinese Society: Liao (907–1125)* (Philadelphia: Transactions of the American Philosophical Society, 1949), pp. 312–13; Ghoshal, *Contributions to the History of the Hindu Revenue System,* p. 129; Wittfogel, *Oriental Despotism,* pp. 333–34; Breasted, *History of Egypt from the Earliest Times,* p. 162; Heichelheim, *Ancient Economic History,* Vol. 1, p. 172.

22. Heichelheim, p. 173.

23. For a variation on this theme see Henri Frankfort, *Ancient Egyptian Religion* (New York: Harper, 1961), pp. 6–7, 31–2 and *passim;* Eberhard Otto, *Wesen und Wandel der ägyptischen Kultur* (Essence and Transitions of Egyptian Civilization) (Stuttgart: W. Kohlhammer [Urban], 1969), pp. 32–39 Childe, *What Happened in History,* pp. 121, 129. On the Mesopotamian priest-kings see Schmoekel, *Kulturgeschichte des Alten Orient,* pp. 47ff., 85–88, and *Das Land Sumer,* pp. 61–62, 85–86; Georges Roux, *Ancient Iraq* (Harmondsworth: Pelican, 1966), pp. 125–28; Childe, *What Happened in History,* pp. 108, 116, 172; Hawkes and Wooley, *Beginnings of Civilization,* pp. 352–53. For China, see Henri Maspéro and Étienne Balasz, *Histoire et institutions de la Chine ancienne des origines au XIIè siècle après J. C.* (Paris: Press Universitaires de France, 1967), pp. 7–13; Wen-Ching Yin, *Le Système fiscal de la Chine* (Paris: Éditions et Publications Contemporaines, Pierre Bossuet, 1930); Robert Boutruche, *Seigneurie et féodalité: Le Premier Age des liens d'homme à homme* (Paris: Éditions Montaigne, 1968), p. 252; Adams, *Heartland of Cities,* p. 81; A. Leo Oppenheim, *Ancient Mesopotamia: Portrait of a Dead Civilization* (Chicago: Univ. of Chicago, 1977), pp. 97–98; and Lloyd, *Archeology of Mesopotamia,* pp. 57, 135.

24. Bruno Meissner, *Babylonien und Assyrien,* Vol. I, pp. 20, 48–49, 80; E. Otto, *Ägypten: Der Weg des Pharaonenreiches,* 3rd ed. (Stuttgart: W. Kohlhammer, 1958), pp. 151–56; A. Scharff and A. Moortgat, *Ägypten und Vorderasien im Altertum,* 3rd ed. (Munich: F. Bruckmann, 1962), pp. 133–34. See also M. Weber, "Agrarverhältnisse," *loc. cit.,* p. 63; Heichelheim, *Ancient Economic History,* p. 170.

25. Meissner, *Babylonien und Assyrien,* Vol. I, pp. 148, 153; Frankfort, *Ancient Egyptian Religion,* pp. 42–45, 53–57; Hawkes and Wooley, *Beginnings of Civilization,* pp. 193–94.

26. Hawkes and Wooley, pp. 204, 206–207.

27. Dopsch, *Naturalwirtschaft*, p. 53; Heichelheim, *Ancient Economic History*, pp. 169–70; Adams, *Heartland of Cities*, pp. 59, 66; and Seton Lloyd, *Foundations in the Dust* (New York: AMS Press, 1978), pp. 176–77.

28. Raymond Bogaert, *Les Origines antiques de la banque de dépôt* (Leyden: A. W. Sijthoff, 1966), pp. 141–43.

29. Chester Starr, *A History of the Ancient World* (New York: Oxford, 1983), p. 35; Lloyd, *Archeology of Mesopotamia*, p. 89.

30. Bogaert, pp. 48–49; and Lloyd, *Archeology of Mesopotamia*, p. 122.

31. Schmoekel, "Mesopotamien," *loc. cit.*, pp. 49, 55–57; Schmoekel, *Das Land Sumer*, pp. 56–65; Meissner, *Babylonien und Assyrien*, Vol. I, pp. 24, 56; Hawkes and Wooley, *Beginnings of Civilization*, pp. 626–27; Roux, *Ancient Iraq*, p. 159; McNeill, *Rise of the West*, p. 61; Samuel Noah Kramer, *History Begins at Sumer* (Philadelphia: Univ. of Pennsylvania, 1981), pp. 46–49.

32. Oppenheim, *Ancient Mesopotamia*, pp. 121–24.

33. E. Otto, *Ägypten*, pp. 87–89, 160–162; Luigi Pareti, Paolo Brezzi, and Luciano Petech, *The Ancient World, 1200 B.C. to A.D. 500* (New York: Harper & Row, 1965), pp. 178–79.

34. E. Otto, *Ägypten*, p. 122.

35. Hawkes and Wooley, *Beginnings of Civilization*, p. 624.

36. John Hicks, *A Theory of Economic History* (Oxford: Clarendon Press, 1969), pp. 13–14.

37. *Ibid.*, pp. 14–15.

38. For a description of a similar animistic ritual in an Indonesian village, see James P. Sterba, "A Report from the Majority of the World," *New York Times Magazine*, Sept. 4, 1971. See also Reynier, *De l'Économie publique et rurale des Arabes et des Juifs* (Geneva: J. J. Paschaud, Imprimeur-Libraires, 1820), pp. 307–11; Lloyd, *Archeology of Mesopotamia*, p. 44.

39. McNeill, *Rise of the West*, pp. 69–70.

40. Childe, *What Happened in History*, pp. 182–83.

41. McNeill, *Rise of the West*, p. 63.

42. Max Weber, "Agrarverhältnisse," *loc. cit.*, p. 66.

43. Adams, *Heartland of Cities*, p. 21.

44. McNeill, *Rise of the West*, pp. 48–52; A. L. Oppenheim, "A Bird's Eye View of Mesopotamian Economic History," in Karl Polanyi et al., *Trade and Markets in the Early Empires* (Glencoe: Free Press, 1957), pp. 31–34; M. Weber, "Agrarverhältnisse," *loc. cit.*, pp. 11, 46, 63; Adams, *Heartland of Cities*, p. 134.

45. Meissner, *Babylonien und Assyrien*, Vol. I, pp. 7, 49.

46. McNeill, *Rise of the West*, pp. 51–52.

47. *Ibid.*, pp. 48–52.

48. Schmoekel, *Das Land Sumer*, p. 86.

49. Arthur L. Stinchcombe, "Social Structure and Organizations," in James G. March, ed., *Handbook of Organizations* (Chicago: Rand-McNally, 1965), pp. 150–51.

50. Wolfgang Helck, *Untersuchungen zu den Beamtentiteln des Ägyptischen Alten Reiches* (Hamburg: J. J. Augustin, 1954), pp. 12–17, 55–56; E. Otto, *Ägypten*, p. 64.

51. McNeill, *Rise of the West*, pp. 64, 68; Childe, *What Happened in History*, p. 151.

52. Roux, *Ancient Iraq*, p. 156.

53. Helck, *Untersuchungen zu den Beamtentiteln,* pp. 22–23; E. Otto, *Wesen,* pp. 39–42; *Ägypten Weg,* p. 64; McNeill, *Rise of the West,* p. 93; E. Fournier de Flaix, *L'Impôt dans les diverses civilisations,* Vol. I, p. 23.

54. A. Scharff and A. Moortgat, *Ägypten und Vorderasien im Altertum,* p. 66; Frankfort, *Ancient Egyptian Religion,* pp. 35–36; E. Otto, *Ägypten Weg,* pp. 64, 81–87; Otto, *Wesen,* pp. 40–42; Helck, *Untersuchungen zu den Beamtentiteln,* pp. 13–16, 132–33.

55. Quoted from the Kahien Papyrus in Breasted, *History of Egypt from the Earliest Times,* p. 166.

56. McNeill, *Rise of the West,* p. 93.

57. Scharf and Moortgat, *Ägypten und Vorderasien,* p. 66; Frankfort, *Ancient Egyptian Religion,* pp. 35–36; E. Otto, *Ägypten Weg,* pp. 64, 81–87; Otto, *Wesen,* pp. 40–42; Helck, *Untersuchungen zu den Beamtentiteln,* pp. 13–16, 132–33; Childe, *What Happened in History,* p. 129.

58. Breasted, *History of Egypt from the Earliest Times,* pp. 79–80; E. Otto, *Ägypten Weg,* pp. 121–23.

59. E. Otto, *Ägypten Weg,* p. 155–56; Scharff and Moortgat, *Ägypten und Vorderasien,* p. 133.

60. Breasted, *History of Egypt from the Earliest Times,* pp. 98–99.

61. *Encyclopaedia Britannica,* 1969 ed., Vol. 8, p. 45.

62. Breasted, *History of Egypt from the Earliest Times,* p. 64.

63. Helck, *Untersuchungen zu den Beamtentiteln,* pp 61–63. See also Heichelheim, *Ancient Economic History,* pp. 178–179.

64. Fournier de Flaix, *L'Impôt dan les diverses civilisations,* quoted in full from Maspéro, *Histoire ancienne de l'Orient,* p. 284.

65. Breasted, *History of Egypt from the Earliest Times,* p. 64.

66. A. H. M. Jones, "Taxation in Antiquity," in his *The Roman Economy* (Oxford: Basil Blackwell, 1974), pp. 156–57.

67. McNeill, *Rise of the West,* p. 65; Schmoekel, *Das Land Sumer,* p. 86.

68. Roux, *Ancient Iraq,* pp. 157–58.

69. *Ibid.,* p. 183.

70. McNeill, *Rise of the West,* pp. 69–70.

71. A. L. Oppenheim, "Mesopotamia, Land of Many Cities," in Ira M. Lapidus, ed., *Middle Eastern Cities* (Berkeley: Univ. of California, 1969), pp. 9–11.

72. Meissner, *Babylonien und Assyrien,* Vol. I, pp. 124–25; Schmoekel, "Mesopotamien," *loc. cit.,* p. 107; Hawkes and Wooley, *Beginnings of Civilization,* p. 358; Dopsch, *Naturalwirtschaft,* p. 53; Roux, *Ancient Iraq,* p. 183.

73. Hawkes and Wooley, *Beginnings of Civilization,* p. 358.

74. Meissner, *Babylonien und Assyrien,* Vol. I, pp. 119–26; Hawkes and Wooley, *Beginnings of Civilization,* p. 358.

75. Meissner, *Babylonien und Assyrien,* Vol. I, pp. 127–28; Schmoekel, "Mesopotamien," *loc. cit.,* pp. 49, 69, 76, 103–7.

76. McNeill, *Rise of the West,* pp. 246–48.

77. *Ibid.,* p. 248.

78. Henri Maspéro, *China in Antiquity* (Chatham: Univ. of Massachusetts, 1978), p. 46.

79. Henri Maspéro and Étienne Balasz, *Histoire et institutions de la Chine ancienne,* pp. 71–76.

80. Wolfram Eberhard, *A History of China,* pp. 74, 81, 82–85; Michael Loewe, *Imperial China, the Historical Background to the Modern Age* (New York: Praeger, 1966), pp. 152–59.
81. K. C. Wu, *The Chinese Heritage* (New York: Crown, 1982), p. 417.
82. Maspéro and Balasz, *Histoire et institutions de la Chine,* pp. 175–76.
83. Wu, *The Chinese Heritage,* pp. 417–18.
84. The philosopher Han Fei is quoted in Maspéro, *China in Antiquity,* p. 325.
85. Kautilya, *The Arthasastra,* transl. R. Shamasastry (Mysore: Mysore Printing & Publishing House, 1961), p. 352.
86. For a discussion of early Hindu government and literature, see McNeill, *Rise of the West,* pp. 327–32.
87. *Ibid.,* pp. 331–32.
88. *Ibid.*
89. Kautilya, *Arthasastra,* pp. 55–57.
90. Ghoshal, *History of the Hindu Revenue System,* pp. 46–47.
91. *Ibid.,* pp. 202–4.
92. Kautilya, *Arthasastra,* p. 63; Gopal, *Mauryan Public Finance,* p. 204.
93. Lloyd, *Archeology of Mesopotamia,* p. 188.
94. Heichelheim, *Ancient Economic History,* pp. 170–71.
95. Kautilya, *Arthasastra,* p. 12; Gopal, *Mauryan Public Finance,* p. 20; Ghoshal, *History of the Hindu Revenue System,* p. 24.
96. Quoted in Roux, *Ancient Iraq,* p. 188, taken from the Epilogue to the Code of Hammurabi, transl. T. J. Meek.
97. Meissner, *Babylonien und Assyrien,* Vol. I, p. 56.
98. Frankfort, *Ancient Egyptian Religion,* pp. 44–46, 62–73.
99. Kautilya, *Arthasastra,* p. 12.
100. Hicks, *Theory of Economic History,* p. 22; Heichelheim, *Ancient Economic History,* p. 180.
101. Heichelheim, p. 180; Wittfogel, *Oriental Despotism,* pp. 36–41.
102. Maspéro and Balasz, *Histoire et institutions de la Chine,* p. 95. See also Wittfogel, *Oriental Despotism,* pp. 48–49.
103. *Encyclopaedia Britannica,* 1969 ed., Vol. 5, p. 579. Wittfogel, *Oriental Despotism,* pp. 39–40; Eberhard, *History of China,* p. 65; Starr, *History of the Ancient World,* p. 637; Arthur Cotterell, *The First Emperor of China* (London: Macmillan, 1981), pp. 77–78, 150–51, 174; Michelle Pirazzoli-t'Serstevens, *The Han Dynasty* (New York: Rizzoli, 1982), pp. 13–17, 24.
104. Hawkes and Wooley, *Beginnings of Civilization,* p. 582.
105. *Encyclopaedia Britannica,* 1969 ed., Vol. 5, p. 579; Wittfogel, *Oriental Despotism,* p. 33.
106. Hawkes and Wooley, *Beginnings of Civilization,* p. 115.
107. McNeill, *Rise of the West,* p. 68.
108. Roux, *Ancient Iraq,* p. 187.
109. Breasted, *History of Egypt from the Earliest Times,* p. 161.
110. *Ibid.*
111. Heichelheim, *Ancient Economic History,* p. 180; Hawkes and Wooley, *Beginnings of Civilization,* p. 324; E. Otto, *Ägypten Weg,* pp. 87–88.
112. Gopal, *Mauryan Public Finance,* p. 20.
113. Dopsch, *Naturalwirtschaft,* p. 44.
114. Ghoshal, *History of the Hindu Revenue System,* p. 157.

115. Kautilya, *Arthasastra*, p. 278.
116. Ghoshal, *History of the Hindu Revenue System*, pp. 158–59.
117. *Ibid.*, p. 160.
118. *Ibid.*, p. 162.
119. *Encyclopaedia Britannica*, 1969 ed., Vol. 6, p. 570.
120. Childe, *What Happened in History*, p. 125; *Encyclopaedia Britannica*, 1969 ed., Vol. 6, p. 560.
121. Wittfogel, *Oriental Despotism*, pp. 40, 363–66.
122. *Ibid.*, pp. 39, 363–66.
123. Wittfogel, *Oriental Despotism*, p. 39.
124. Hawkes and Wooley, *Beginnings of Civilization*, p. 357.
125. Childe, *What Happened in History*, p. 131.
126. Heichelheim, *Ancient Economic History*, p. 176; Hawkes and Wooley, *Beginnings of Civilization*, p. 357.
127. Meissner, *Babylonien und Assyrien*, Vol. I, pp. 144–45.
128. Étienne Balasz, *Le Traité économique de "Souëi-Chou"* (Leiden: E. J. Brill, 1953), pp. 135–36; 189–90.
129. Pirazzoli-t'Serstevens, *Han Dynasty*, pp. 27–28.
130. Balasz, *Traité économique de "Souëi-Chou,"* pp. 135–36; 189–90.
131. Wen-Ching Yin, *Le Système fiscal de la Chine*, pp. 30–31. See also Reischauer and Fairbanks, *East Asia, The Great Tradition*, p. 161.
132. Wittfogel, *Oriental Despotism*, p. 30.
133. Kautilya, *Arthasastra*, p. 100–1.
134. E. Otto, *Wesen*, pp. 41–42.
135. Breasted, *History of Egypt from the Earliest Times*, p. 238; Genesis 41:25; Starr, *History of the Ancient World*, p. 59.
136. Kautilya, *Arthasastra*, p. 99; Gopal, *Mauryan Public Finance*, p. 65.
137. Wittfogel, *Oriental Despotism*, p. 72.
138. Henri Maspéro, *La Chine antique* (Paris: E. de Boccard, 1927), pp. 92–93.
139. Michael Loewe, *Imperial China*, p. 203.
140. Kwang-Chih Chang, *Shang Civilization* (New Haven: Yale Univ., 1980), p. 238. Poem translated by Arthur Waley.
141. Meissner, *Babylonien und Assyrien*, Vol. I, pp. 125–26; Hawkes and Wooley, *Beginnings of Civilization*, pp. 358–59; Schmoekel, "Mesopotamien," *loc. cit.*, pp. 106–7.
142. Breasted, *History of Egypt from the Earliest Times*, pp. 238–39.
143. Kautilya, *Arthasastra*, pp. 100–1.
144. Maspéro, *La Chine antique*, pp. 92–93; Maspéro and Balasz, *Histoire et institutions de la Chine*, p. 213; Yin, *Système fiscal de la Chine*, p. 22.
145. Maspéro, *La Chine antique*, pp. 92–93.
146. Chang, *Shang Civilization*, pp. 236–37.
147. Kautilya, *Arthasastra*, pp. 271–72.
148. Gopal, *Mauryan Public Finance*, p. 26; Heichelheim, *Ancient Economic History*, Vol. I, pp. 171–74; Meissner, *Babylonien und Assyrien*, Vol. I, pp. 121–22; Schmoekel, "Mesopotamien," *loc. cit.*, pp. 56, 79; *Cambridge Economic History of Europe*, Vol. II (Cambridge: Cambridge Univ., 1952), p. 30.
149. Kautilya, *Arthasastra*, p. 99; Schmoekel, "Mesopotamien," *loc. cit.*, p. 51.
150. Heichelheim, *Ancient Economic History*, p. 175.
151. *Ibid.*, p. 178.

152. *Encyclopaedia Britannica*, 1969 ed., Vol. 1, pp. 890–91.
153. T. R. Glover, *The Ancient World* (Baltimore: Penguin, 1935), pp. 58–59, 65.
154. Breasted, *History of Egypt from the Earliest Times*, p. 79.
155. Wittfogel, *Oriental Despotism*, p. 331.
156. Kautilya, *Arthasastra*, p. 271.
157. *Ibid.*
158. K. Asakawa, *The Early Institutional Life of Japan: A Study in the Reform of 645 A.D.* (New York: Paragon Book Reprint Corp., 1963), p. 109.
159. E. Otto, *Ägypten Weg*, pp. 192–94.
160. *Ibid.*
161. Kautilya, *Arthasastra*, p. 69; Gopal, *Mauryan Public Finance*, p. 25.
162. Breasted, *History of Egypt from the Earliest Times*, p. 404; Childe, *What Happened in History*, p. 167.
163. Schmoekel, "Mesopotamien," *loc. cit.*, pp. 106–7; Meissner, *Babylonien und Assyrien*, Vol. I, p. 3, 127.
164. S. N. Kramer, *History Begins at Sumer*, p. 49.
165. Kautilya, *Arthasastra*, p. 273–75.
166. *Encyclopaedia Britannica*, 1969 ed., Vol. 16, pp. 757–60; Vol. 1, pp. 6–7.
167. Kautilya, *Arthasastra*, p. 56.
168. Ghoshal, *History of the Hindu Revenue System*, p. 49; Gopal, *Mauryan Public Finance*, p. 202.
169. *Encyclopaedia Britannica*, 1969 ed., Vol. 1, p. 45.
170. Ghoshal, *History of the Hindu Revenue System*, pp. 34–35; Kautilya, *Arthasastra*, p. 158.
171. Ghoshal, pp. 50–51; Gopal, *Mauryan Public Finance*, p. 64; Kautilya, *Arthasastra*, p. 159.
172. Scharff and Moortgat, *Ägypten und Vorderasien*, p. 68.
173. Heichelheim, *Ancient Economic History*, p. 179.
174. Wittfogel, *Oriental Despotism*, p. 51.
175. Breasted, *History of Egypt from the Earliest Times*, p. 239.
176. *Ibid.*, p. 235.
177. Kautilya, *Arthasastra*, p. 36.
178. *Ibid.*, p. 37.
179. *Ibid.*, p. 57.
180. Gopal, *Mauryan Public Finance*, pp. 158–59; Ghoshal, *History of the Hindu Revenue System*, p. 153.
181. Ghoshal, p. 161; Gopal, pp. 155–56; Kautilya, *Arthasastra*, pp. 58–59.
182. Maspéro and Balasz, *Histoire et institutions de la Chine*, p. 74.
183. *Ibid.*, pp. 239–41.
184. Kautilya, *Arthasastra*, p. 101.
185. *Ibid.*, p. 61.
186. *Ibid.*, p. 60.
187. *Ibid.*, pp. 276–77.
188. *Ibid.*, pp. 102–3.
189. *Ibid.*, p. 15.
190. *Ibid.*
191. *Ibid.*, p. 16.
192. Gopal, *Mauryan Public Finance*, p. 67.

193. Asakawa, *Early Institutional Life of Japan*, pp. 271–72.

194. *Ibid.*, pp. 218–19.

195. Breasted, *History of Egypt from the Earliest Times*, p. 162.

196. Loewe, *Imperial China*, pp. 171–74.

197. Ghoshal, *History of the Hindu Revenue System*, p. 147.

198. Loewe, *Imperial China*, p. 170.

199. Breasted, *History of Egypt from the Earliest Times*, p. 406.

200. Otto, *Ägypten Weg*, p. 171.

201. Gopal, *Mauryan Public Finance*, p. 204; Kautilya, *Arthasastra*, p. 63.

202. Kautilya, *Arthasastra*, p. 62.

203. *Ibid.*

204. *Ibid.*, p. 64.

205. *Ibid.*, pp. 66–67.

206. *Ibid.*, p. 66.

207. *Ibid.*, p. 68.

208. *Ibid.*, p. 70.

209. Gopal, *Mauryan Public Finance*, pp. 203–4.

210. Kautilya, *Arthasastra*, pp. 61–65; Gopal, p. 205.

211. Kautilya, *Arthasastra*, p. 17.

212. *Ibid.*, pp. 17–20; Gopal, pp. 203–4.

213. Gopal, pp. 159–60.

214. Kautilya, *Arthasastra*, p. 21.

215. Loewe, *Imperial China*, p. 202.

216. Maspéro, *China in Antiquity*, p. 57.

217. Jones, "Taxation in Antiquity," *loc. cit.*, pp. 157–58.

218. See Michael Thompson, *Rubbish Theory* (Oxford: Oxford Univ., 1979); Fredrik Barth, *Political Leadership Among Swat Pathans* (London: Athlone Press, 1959); and E. E. Evans-Pritchard, *The Nuer* (Oxford: Oxford Univ., 1940).

219. Louis Dumont, *Homo Hierarchicus*, English ed. (London: Weidenfeld & Nicolson, 1966).

220. Deuteronomy 14:24–26.

CHAPTER THREE

1. Keith Hopkins, "On the Probable Age Structure of the Roman Population," *Population Studies*, Vol. XX, No. 2 (November 1966), pp. 245, 250, 253–54; A. H. M. Jones, *Athenian Democracy* (Oxford: Basil Blackwell, 1966), p. 82; Jones, "The Social Structure of Athens in the 4th Century B.C.," *Economic History Review*, Vol. VIII, No. 2 (December 1955), p. 146; Mikhail Rostovtseff, *Social and Economic History of the Hellenistic World* (Oxford: Clarendon, 1941), p. 95; A. R. Hands, *Charities and Social Aid in Greece and Rome* (Ithaca: Cornell Univ., 1968), p. 71; Donald Engels, "The Use of Historical Demography in Ancient History," *Classical Quarterly*, Vol. XXXIV (1984), No. 2, pp. 386–93; Ansley Coale, "A History of the Human Population," *Scientific American*, September 1974, pp. 43–44.

2. Victor Ehrenberg, *The Greek State* (Oxford: Basil Blackwell, 1960), p. 84; Fritz Heichelheim, *An Ancient Economic History*, Vol. II (Leyden: A. W. Sijthoff, 1965), p. 137; Augustus Boeckh, *The Public Economy of the Athenians*, Vol. II

(London: John Murray, 1828), pp. 196–97, 379; Albert E. Trever, *History of Ancient Civilization,* Vol. I, *The Ancient Near East and Greece* (New York: Harcourt, Brace, 1936), p. 288; Raymond Bogaert, *Les Origines antiques de la banque de dépôt* (Leyden: A. W. Sijthoff, 1966), pp. 151–52; A. C. Littleton and B. S. Yamey, *Studies in the History of Accounting* (Homewood, Ill.: Irwin, 1956), pp. 26–27.

3. Augustus Boeckh, *Public Economy,* Vol. II, pp. 280–81.

4. A. French, *The Growth of the Athenian Economy* (London: Routledge & Kegan Paul, 1964), p. 146; A. H. M. Jones, "The Social Structure of Athens in the 4th Century B.C.," *Economic History Review,* 2nd Series, Vol. VIII, No. 2 (December 1955), p. 143.

5. Rostovtseff, *Social and Economic History of the Hellenistic World,* pp. 91–92.

6. Frank W. Walbank, "Trade and Industry Under the Roman Empire in the West," in *Cambridge Economic History of Europe,* Vol. II (Cambridge: Cambridge Univ., 1952), pp. 46–47; Tenney Frank, *An Economic Survey of Ancient Rome,* Vol. 1, *Rome and Italy of the Republic* (Baltimore: Johns Hopkins, 1933), pp. 89–93; Mikhail Rostovtseff, *The Social and Economic History of the Roman Empire* (Oxford: Clarendon, 1926), pp. 138–39.

7. Heichelheim, *Ancient Economic History,* Vol. II, pp. 72–74; A. H. M. Jones, *The Greek City from Alexander to Justinian* (Oxford: Clarendon, 1966), p. 140; Hermann Bengston, *Griechische Geschichte von den Anfängen bis in die römische Kaiserzeit,* 3rd ed. (Munich: C. H. Beck, 1965), p. 106; C. Hignett, *A History of the Athenian Constitution to the End of the 5th Century B.C.* (Oxford: Clarendon, 1952), p. 88.

8. Heichelheim, *Ancient Economic History,* Vol. II, p. 140; Rostovtseff, *Social and Economic History of the Hellenistic World,* p. 135; M. Abel, *Histoire de la Palestine depuis la conquète d'Alexandre jusq'à l'invasion arabe,* Vol. I (Paris: Librairie Lecoffre, J. Gabelda & Cie., 1952), pp. 17–18; Hignett, *History of the Athenian Constitution,* pp. 235–39.

9. M. I. Finley, *Politics in the Ancient World* (Cambridge: Cambridge Univ., 1983), p. 15.

10. Constantin D. Sterghiopolous, *Les Finances grèques au VIè siècle* (Athens: Collection de l'Institut Français d'Athènes, 1949), pp. 30–31; Hignett, *History of the Athenian Constitution,* pp. 80–92, 308, 311.

11. Boeckh, *Public Economy,* Vol. I, pp. 268–74, 279–80, 289, 323, 329.

12. Hignett, *History of the Athenian Constitution,* pp. 145–49, 191–95, 202–3, 235–38; N. G. L. Hammond, *A History of Greece to 322 B.C.* (Oxford: Clarendon, 1967), pp. 330–31; Heichelheim, *Ancient Economic History,* Vol. II, pp. 142–43.

13. A. French, *The Growth of the Athenian Economy* (London: Routledge & Kegan Paul, 1964), pp. 91, 105; Finley, *Politics in the Ancient World,* p. 17.

14. See H. H. Scullard, *From the Gracchi to Nero: A History of Rome from 133 B.C. to A.D. 68* (London: Methuen, 1965), p. 6. For further discussion of this oligarchical nucleus among the patrician senatorial families, see Ronald Syme, *The Roman Revolution* (Oxford: Clarendon, 1960), pp. 10–13 and *passim.*

15. Scullard, *From the Gracchi to Nero,* pp. 7–8, 19–40, 115–17, and *passim;* P. A. Brunt, *Social Conflicts in the Roman Republic* (London: Chatto & Windus, 1971), pp. 92–95 and *passim.*

16. Brunt, *Social Conflicts in the Roman Republic,* pp. 99, 110, 148–49. See also pp. 169–70ff.

17. Scullard, *From the Gracchi to Nero,* pp. 217, 233; Richard A. Talbert, "Augustus and the Senate," *Greece and Rome,* Vol. XXXI, No. 1 (April 1984), p. 56.

18. P. A. Brunt, "Princeps and Equites," *Journal of Roman Studies,* Vol. LXXIII (1983), p. 44.

19. Finley, *Politics in the Ancient World,* p. 32.

20. Ehrenberg, *The Greek State,* p. 85; Karl A. Wittfogel, *Oriental Despotism: A Comparative Study of Total Power* (New Haven: Yale Univ., 1957), p. 71; Boeckh, *Public Economy,* Vol. II, p. 9; Finley, *Politics in the Ancient World,* p. 32.

21. Boeckh, *Public Economy,* Vol. II, p. 200.

22. Finley, *Politics in the Ancient World,* pp. 36–37; Finley, *The Ancient Economy* (Berkeley: Univ. of California, 1973), pp. 150–51.

23. Ehrenberg, *The Greek State,* p. 87; Heichelheim, *Ancient Economic History,* Vol. II, pp. 135, 137; Boeckh, *Public Economy,* Vol. II, p. 202; A. H. M. Jones, "Liturgy," in *Oxford Classical Dictionary* (Oxford: Clarendon, 1957), pp. 508–9; Jones, *The Greek City from Alexander to Justinian,* pp. 167–68, 247–48; Jones, *Athenian Democracy,* pp. 55–57, 100–1; Hands, *Charities and Social Aids in Greece and Rome,* pp. 37–38, 40–41, 52.

24. Frank F. Abbott and Allen Chester Johnson, *Municipal Administration in the Roman Empire* (Princeton: Princeton Univ., 1926), pp. 94–95.

25. Heichelheim, *Ancient Economic History,* Vol. II, p. 135; Ehrenberg, *The Greek State,* p. 83; Boeckh, *Public Economy,* Vol. II, pp. 200–3, 212, 217–18; Rostovtseff, *Social and Economic History of the Roman Empire,* p. 140.

26. E. Fournier de Flaix, *L'Impôt dans les diverses civilisations,* Vol. I (Paris: Guillaumin Cie., 1897), pp. 115–18; Boeckh, *Public Economy,* Vol. II, pp. 206, 320–22; Ehrenberg, *The Greek State,* p. 83; Bengston, *Griechische Geschichte,* pp. 161–62.

27. G. L. Cawkwell, "Athenian Naval Power in the Fourth Century," *Classical Quarterly,* New Series, Vol. XXXIV, No. 2 (1984), p. 327.

28. Boeckh, *Public Economy,* Vol. II, pp. 202, 327; Ehrenberg, *The Greek State,* p. 87; Hammond, *A History of Greece to 322 B.C.,* p. 527; Cawkwell, "Athenian Naval Power," *loc. cit.,* pp. 340–41.

29. Fournier de Flaix, *L'Impôt dans les diverses civilisations,* pp. 115–18.

30. Rostovtseff, *Social and Economic History of the Roman Empire,* pp. 140–41, 333–35.

31. Tenney Frank, *An Economic History of Rome* (New York: Cooper Square Publishers, 1962), pp. 493–94; Tenney Frank, *An Economic Survey of Ancient Rome,* Vol. 5, *Rome and Italy of the Empire* (Baltimore: Johns Hopkins, 1940), pp. 95–101; Abbott and Johnson, *Municipal Administration in the Roman Empire,* pp. 142–45; Rostovtseff, *Social and Economic History of the Roman Empire,* pp. 140–41; Finley, *Ancient Economy,* p. 153.

32. Rostovtseff, *Social and Economic History of the Roman Empire,* p. 141. See also Frank, *Economic History of Rome,* p. 141; Hands, *Charities and Social Aids,* p. 73.

33. Nicolas Hohlwein, *L'Égypt romaine; Recueil des termes techniques relatifs aux institutions politiques et administratives de l'Égypt romaine suivi d'un choix de*

textes papyrologiques (Brussels: Hayez, 1912), pp. 312–30; Abbott and Johnson, *Municipal Administration*, pp. 98–100, 321–31; Rostovtseff, *Social and Economic History of the Roman Empire*, pp. 334–35; Frank, *Economic History of Rome*, p. 392; Hands, *Charities and Social Aids*, pp. 58–60, 144–45.

34. Boeckh, *Public Economy*, Vol. II, pp. 201–2, 206, 322.

35. *Ibid.*, pp. 320–22; Fournier de Flaix, *L'Impôt dans les diverses civilisations*, pp. 115–18; Ehrenberg, *The Greek State*, p. 87.

36. Fergus Millar, "Empire and City, Augustus to Julian: Obligations, Excuses and Status," *Journal of Roman Studies*, Vol. LXXIII (1983), p. 80.

37. Rostovtseff, *Social and Economic History of the Roman Empire*, p. 341; Albert E. Trever, *History of Ancient Civilization*, Vol. II, *The Roman World* (New York: Harcourt, Brace, 1939), p. 516; J. B. Bury, *History of the Later Roman Empire*, Vol. II (New York: Dover, 1959), p. 59.

38. Peter Garnsey, "Aspects of the Decline of the Urban Aristocracy," *Aufsteig und Niedergang*, Vol. 2, No. 1, p. 240, quoted in Peter Brown, *The Making of Late Antiquity* (Cambridge, Mass.: Harvard Univ., 1978), p. 35.

39. Brown, *Making of Late Antiquity*, pp. 36–37.

40. *Ibid.*, p. 48.

41. Frank, *Economic History of Rome*, p. 494; Rostovtseff, *Social and Economic History of the Roman Empire*, pp. 340–41; Abbott and Johnson, *Municipal Administration*, pp. 94–96; Bury, *History of the Later Roman Empire*, Vol. II, pp. 519, 544; Trever, *History of Ancient Civilization*, Vol. II, pp. 519, 544; A. H. M. Jones, *Ancient Economic History* (London: H. K. Lewis, 1948), pp. 19–20; P. A. Brunt, "The Revenues of Rome," *Journal of Roman Studies*, Vol. LXXI (1981), pp. 169–70.

42. Bury, *History of the Later Roman Empire*, p. 59; Abbott and Johnson, *Municipal Administration*, pp. 96, 115; A. H. M. Jones, *The Later Roman Empire*, Vol. I (Oxford: Basil Blackwell, 1964), Ch. XIX, pp. 724–29, 732–57, and *passim*.

43. Rostovtseff, *Social and Economic History of the Roman Empire*, p. 462; Frank, *Economic History of Rome*, pp. 493–95; Bury, *History of the Later Roman Empire*, p. 59; Jones, *Ancient Economic History*, pp. 19–20; Brunt, "Revenues of Rome," *loc. cit.*, p. 169.

44. Abbott and Johnson, *Municipal Administration*, pp. 102–11; Millar, "Empire and City," *loc. cit.*, pp. 94–95.

45. Abbott and Johnson, *Municipal Administration*, p. 106; Jones, *Later Roman Empire*, Vol. II, pp. 543–52.

46. Abbott and Johnson, *Municipal Administration*, p. 103; Hohlwein, *L'Égypt romaine*, pp. 313–16.

47. Brown, *Making of Late Antiquity*, pp. 85–87.

48. Abbott and Johnson, *Municipal Administration*, p. 111.

49. *Ibid.*, pp. 96–97.

50. *Ibid.*, pp. 104–5, 113, 131–32; Rostovtseff, *Social and Economic History of the Roman Empire*, pp. 468–69; Frank, *Economic History of Rome*, p. 496; Bury, *History of the Later Roman Empire*, Vol. I, p. 60; Frank W. Walbank, "Trade and Industry Under the Roman Empire in the West," *loc. cit.*, p. 63; Jones, *Later Roman Empire*, Vol. I, pp. 739–40.

51. Abbott and Johnson, *Municipal Administration*, pp. 103–5.

52. Hammond, *History of Greece to 322 B.C.*, p. 528; French, *Growth of the Athe-*

nian Economy, p. 126; Boeckh, *Public Economy,* Vol. II, pp. 24, 44; Bury, *History of the Later Roman Empire,* Vol. I, p. 45.

53. Abbott and Johnson, *Municipal Administration,* pp. 97, 115; A. H. M. Jones, *A History of Rome through the 5th Century,* Vol. I, *The Republic* (New York: Walker & Co., 1968), pp. 255–56.

54. Boeckh, *Public Economy,* Vol. II, pp. 380–81.

55. Heichelheim, *Ancient Economic History,* Vol. II, p. 133; Sterghiopolous, *Les Finances grèques,* pp. 43–44; Joachim Marquardt, *Römische Statsverwaltung,* Vol. 2 (Leipzig, 1876), also cited as Vol. 5 of *Handbuch der römischen Alterthümer,* by J. Marquardt and T. Mommsen, pp. 145–47; French, *Growth of the Athenian Economy,* p. 51; Boeckh, *Public Economy,* Vol. II, pp. 9–11; Brunt, "Revenues of Rome," *loc. cit.,* p. 161.

56. Ehrenberg, *The Greek State,* p. 86; Boeckh, *Public Economy,* Vol. II, pp. 23–26; John Ferguson, *The Heritage of Hellenism* (New York: Science History Publications, 1973), p. 56.

57. Heichelheim, *Ancient Economic History,* Vol. II, p. 134; French, *Growth of the Athenian Economy,* pp. 125–27; Hammond, *History of Greece to 322 B.C.,* p. 529.

58. Heichelheim, *Ancient Economic History,* Vol. II, p. 134; Boeckh, *Public Economy,* Vol. II, pp. 49, 228.

59. Jones, *Athenian Democracy,* pp. 23, 28–29, 55–56; Hammond, *History of Greece to 322 B.C.,* pp. 489–90, 525; Ehrenberg, *The Greek State,* p. 86; Heichelheim, *Ancient Economic History,* Vol. II, p. 138; Boeckh, *Public Economy,* Vol. II, p. 271; Finley, *The Ancient Economy,* p. 95; A. H. M. Jones, "Taxation in Antiquity," in his *The Roman Economy* (Oxford: Basil Blackwell, 1974), p. 154.

60. Marquardt, *Römische Statsverwaltung,* p. 160; Wittfogel, *Oriental Despotism,* p. 71; Jones, "Taxation in Antiquity," *loc. cit.,* p. 161.

61. Marquardt, *Römische Statsverwaltung,* pp. 166–67; Frank, *Economic Survey of Ancient Rome,* Vol. I, pp. 121–22.

62. Frank, *Economic History of Rome,* p. 149; Marquardt, *Römische Statsverwaltung,* p. 175; Allen Chester Johnson, *Egypt and the Roman Empire* (Ann Arbor: Univ. of Michigan, 1951), p. 177; Abbott and Johnson, *Municipal Administration,* pp. 117–18; Trever, *History of Ancient Civilization,* Vol. II, p. 128.

63. Jones, *History of Rome Through the 5th Century,* Vol. I, pp. 267–68; Abbott and Johnson, *Municipal Administration,* p. 119; M. Dureau de La Malle, *Économie politique des Romains,* Vol. 2 (Paris: Chez L. Hachette, 1840), pp. 356–57; Brunt, "Revenues of Rome," *loc. cit.,* pp. 161–63.

64. Jones, *History of Rome through the 5th Century,* Vol. I, pp. 282, 285, 323–24; Frank, *Economic History of Rome,* p. 383; Ehrenberg, *The Greek State,* p. 235.

65. Marquardt, *Römische Statsverwaltung,* p. 181; Frank, *Economic History of Rome,* p. 383.

66. J. S. Richardson, "The Spanish Mines and the Development of Provincial Taxation in the Second Century B.C.," *Journal of Roman Studies,* Vol. LXVI (1976), pp. 139–52.

67. Frank, *Economic History of Rome,* pp. 171–73.

68. Jones, *History of Rome Through the 5th Century,* Vol. I, p. 300.

69. *Ibid.,* p. 277.

70. Keith Hopkins elaborates this argument in his "Taxes and Trade in the Roman

Empire (200 B.C.–400 A.D.)," *Journal of Roman Studies,* Vol. LXX (1980), pp. 101–25. See also his introduction to Peter Garnsey, Keith Hopkins, and C. R. Whittaker, *Trade in the Ancient Economy* (London: Chatto & Windus, 1983), pp. xix–xxi.

71. A. N. Sherwin-White, "Procurator Augusti," *Papers of the British School at Rome,* Vol. 15 (1939), pp. 11–19; P. A. Brunt, "The 'Fiscus' and Its Development," *Journal of Roman Studies,* Vol. 56 (1966), pp. 87–88; Scullard, *From the Gracchi to Nero,* pp. 228–29, 233–35; Fergus Millar, "The Emperor, the Senate, and the Provinces," *Journal of Roman Studies,* Vol. LVI (1966), pp. 156–66.

72. Abbott and Johnson, *Municipal Administration,* pp. 123–24; Trever, *History of Ancient Civilization,* Vol. II, pp. 329–30; Richard Duncan-Jones, *The Economy of the Roman Empire* (Cambridge: Cambridge Univ., 1974), p. 5, note 3.

73. P. A. Brunt, "The Role of the Senate in the Augustan Regime," *Classical Quarterly,* Vol. 34 (1984), No. 2, pp. 435–37.

74. Trever, *History of Ancient Civilization,* Vol. II, p. 125; M. Abel, *Histoire de la Palestine,* Vol. I, pp. 429–30.

75. Jones, "Taxation in Antiquity," p. 168.

76. Duncan-Jones, *Economy of the Roman Empire,* p. 8. Duncan-Jones urges caution in interpreting his price comparison; because of uncertainty about the base price, his calculations of inflation in wheat prices may be too high. See his note 2, p. 8.

77. Hopkins, "Taxes and Trade in the Roman Empire," *loc. cit.,* pp. 120–21.

78. Frank, *Economic Survey of Ancient Rome,* Vol. 5, p. 18.

79. Jones, *Later Roman Empire,* Vol. I, pp. 23–24.

80. Frank, *Economic History of Rome,* p. 492.

81. *Ibid.,* p. 394.

82. *Ibid.,* p. 492; Rostovtseff, *Social and Economic History of the Roman Empire,* pp. 462–63; Bury, *History of the Later Roman Empire,* Vol. I, pp. 46–47; Walbank, "Trade and Industry Under the Roman Empire in the West," *loc. cit.,* p. 66.

83. A. H. M. Jones, "The Roman Civil Service, Clerical and Subclerical Grades," reprinted from *Journal of Roman Studies,* Vol. XXXIX (1949), in Jones, *Studies in Roman Government and Law* (Oxford: Basil Blackwell, 1960), pp. 162–67.

84. R. E. Lammert, in Frank, *Economic Survey of Ancient Rome,* Vol. 5, p. 86; Johnson, *Egypt and the Roman Empire,* p. 48; Walbank, "Trade and Industry Under the Roman Empire in the West," *loc. cit.,* p. 57; G. R. Watson, *The Roman Soldier* (Ithaca: Cornell Univ., 1969), pp. 13–25; Hopkins, "Taxes and Trade in the Roman Empire," *loc. cit.,* p. 123.

85. A. H. M. Jones, "Inflation Under the Roman Empire," *Economic History Review,* 2nd Series, Vol. V (1953), No. 3, p. 317; Johnson, *Egypt and the Roman Empire,* pp. 46–47; Frank, *Economic History of Rome,* pp. 492–93.

86. Rostovtseff, *Social and Economic History of the Roman Empire,* pp. 463–64; Frank, *Economic Survey of Ancient Rome,* Vol. 5, pp. 302–3.

87. Abbott and Johnson, *Municipal Administration,* pp. 127–29; Rostovtseff, *Social and Economic History of the Roman Empire,* p. 464; W. Eusslin, "The Reforms of Diocletian," in *Cambridge Ancient History,* Vol. 12 (Cambridge: Cambridge Univ., 1939), pp. 399–400.

88. Bury, *History of the Later Roman Empire,* Vol. I, pp. 46–47; Abbott and John-

son, *Municipal Administration*, p. 130; Rostovtseff, *Social and Economic History of the Roman Empire*, pp. 465–66; Eusslin, "Reforms of Diocletian," *loc. cit.*, p. 403; Walbank, "Trade and Industry Under the Roman Empire in the West," *loc. cit.*, p. 64; R. P. Duncan-Jones, review of Walter Goffart, *Caput and Colonate: Toward a History of Late Roman Taxation* (Toronto and Buffalo: Univ. of Toronto, 1974), in *Journal of Roman Studies*, Vol. LXVII (1977), pp. 202–4.

89. Rostovtseff, *Social and Economic History of the Roman Empire*, p. 467; Frank, *Economic History of Rome*, pp. 501–2; A. Woolf, *A Short History of Accountants and Accountancy* (London: Gee & Co., 1912), p. 51; Walbank, "Trade and Industry Under the Roman Empire in the West," *loc. cit.*, pp. 64–66.

90. Walbank, p. 273.

91. Frank, *Economic History of Rome*, p. 491.

92. Hopkins, "Taxes and Trade in the Roman Empire," *loc. cit.*, pp. 123 24.

93. Sterghiopolous, *Les Finances grèques au VIè siècle*, pp. 33–34.

94. Paul Millett, "Maritime Loans and the Structure of Credit in 4th Century Athens," in Hopkins, Garnsey, and Whittaker, *Trade in the Ancient Economy*, p. 48.

95. Boeckh, *Public Economy*, Vol. II, p. 28; Hammond, *History of Greece to 322 B.C.*, p. 326.

96. Boeckh, *Public Economy*, Vol. I, pp. 208 9.

97. Oskar Seyffert and Walther Schwann, "Telonai," in *Real-Encyclopädie der Classischen Altertümswissenschaft*, by Pauly-Wissowa, Vol. 5A, No. 1 (Stuttgart: Metzler, 1934), pp. 418–25.

98. Tenney Frank, "The Financial Activities of the Equestrian Corporations," *Classical Philology*, Vol. 28, January 1933, p. 3; Jones, "Taxation in Antiquity," *loc. cit.*, pp. 154–55.

99. Hammond, *History of Greece to 322 B.C.*, p. 52.

100. *Ibid.*, p. 55; Hignett, *Athenian Constitution*, pp. 201–2, 235–36.

101. Rostovtseff, *Social and Economic History of the Roman Empire*, pp. 273, 328–30, 338, 345.

102. Boeckh, *Public Economy*, Vol. II, pp. 27–28.

103. Seyffert and Schwann, "Telonai," *loc. cit.*

104. Boeckh, *Public Economy*, Vol. II, p. 51.

105. Rostovtseff, *Social and Economic History of the Hellenistic World*, Vol. I, pp. 243–44.

106. Frank, "Financial Activities of the Equestrian Corporations," *loc. cit.*, p. 3; Garnsey, "Grain for Rome," in Garnsey, Hopkins and Whittaker, *Trade in the Ancient Economy*, p. 122; E. Badian, *Publicans and Sinners* (Oxford: Basil Blackwell, 1972), p. 62.

107. Giacomo Lombroso, *Recherches sur l'économie politique de l'Égypte sous les Lagides* (Turin: Imprimerie Royale, Bocca Frères, 1870), pp. 320–22; Hohlwein, *L'Égypte romaine*, pp. 128, 133 37, 245, 355, 403; Henri Maspéro, *Les Finances de l'Égypte sous les Lagides* (Paris: Presented to the Faculty of Letters, 1905), pp. 157–73; Heichelheim, *Ancient Economic History*, Vol. I, p. 181, Vol. II, p. 72; Rostovtseff, *Social and Economic History of the Hellenistic World*, Vol. I, pp. 328–31; Rostovtseff, *Social and Economic History of the Roman Empire*, pp. 340–41; Frank, *Economic History of Rome*, pp. 382–85.

108. Jones, *History of Rome Through the 5th Century*, Vol. I, pp. 265–66, 271–73;

Jones, "The Aerarium and the Fiscus," in his *Studies in Roman Government and Law,* p. 102; A. C. Littleton and B. S. Yamey, *Studies in the History of Accounting* (Homewood, Ill.: Richard Irwin, 1956), pp. 45–46; Badian, *Publicans and Sinners,* pp. 107–8.

109. Garnsey, "Grain for Rome," *loc. cit.,* p. 121.
110. Frank, *Economic Survey of Ancient Rome,* Vol. I, pp. 84–86; Frank, "The Financial Activities of the Equestrian Corporations," *loc. cit.,* p. 2; Badian, *Publicans and Sinners,* p. 17.
111. M. P. Charlesworth, *Trade Routes and Commerce in the Roman Empire* (Cambridge: Cambridge Univ., 1926), pp. 86–87.
112. M. Dureau de La Malle, *Économie politique des Romains,* Vol. 2, pp. 387–90.
113. Badian, *Publicans and Sinners,* p. 76.
114. Woolf, *Short History of Accountants and Accountancy,* p. 41; Badian, *Publicans and Sinners,* p. 69.
115. Badian, p. 77.
116. Jones, "Aerarium and the Fiscus," *loc. cit.,* pp. 102–3; Littleton and Yamey, *Studies in the History of Accounting,* pp. 49–50.
117. Jones, *History of Rome Through the 5th Century,* Vol. I, pp. 312–13.
118. *Ibid.,* pp. 27–73, 285–87, 291, 308–310; Frank, *Economic History of Rome,* pp. 151–54, 280–82.
119. Jones, *History of Rome Through the 5th Century,* Vol. I, pp. 291, 309–10; M. Dureau de La Malle, *Économie politique des Romains,* pp. 387–90; Trever, *History of Ancient Civilization,* Vol. II, p. 128; Frank, *Economic History of Rome,* pp. 152–53.
120. Badian, *Publicans and Sinners,* p. 114.
121. Jones, *History of Rome through the 5th Century,* Vol. I, pp. 290–91, 299–300, 311–12.
122. Badian, *Publicans and Sinners,* pp. 102–3.
123. J. P. Matthews, "The Tax Law of Palmyra: Evidence for Economic History in a City of the Roman East," *Journal of Roman Studies,* Vol. LXXIV (1984), pp. 174–77.
124. Garnsey, "Grain for Rome," *loc. cit.,* p. 116.
125. For a description of the prosperity in Periclean Athens, see Hammond, *History of Athens to 322 B.C.,* pp. 328–29, 523–24.
126. Aristotle, *The Art of Rhetoric,* trans. John Henry Freese (London: Heinemann, 1926), pp. 41–42.
127. Johnson, *Egypt and the Roman Empire,* p. 47.
128. Jones, "Inflation under the Roman Empire," *loc. cit.,* p. 296.
129. Trever, *History of Ancient Civilization,* Vol. II, p. 267; Rostovtseff, *Social and Economic History of the Roman Empire,* p. 462.
130. Boeckh, *Public Economy,* Vol. II, p. 191.
131. Max Weber, *General Economic History* (Glencoe: Free Press, 1927), p. 242.
132. Heichelheim, *Ancient Economic History,* Vol. II, p. 144; Boeckh, *Public Economy,* Vol. I, pp. 214–15.
133. Boeckh, p. 274.
134. Hammond, *History of Greece to 322 B.C.,* p. 532; Boeckh, *Public Economy,* Vol. I, pp. 246–47, 299; E. M. Walker, "The Periclean Democracy," in *Cambridge Ancient History,* Vol. 5 (Cambridge: Cambridge Univ., 1940), pp. 103–4; A. W.

Pickard-Cambridge, "The Rise of Macedonia," in *Cambridge Ancient History,* Vol. 6 (1953), pp. 222–23; Charles J. Bullock, *Politics, Finance, and Consequences* (Cambridge, Mass.: Harvard Univ., 1939), pp. 142–44.

135. Boeckh, *Public Economy,* Vol. I, pp. 272, 277, 291.

136. Michael Crawford, *The Roman Republic* (Hassocks, N.J.: Harvester Press, 1978), p. 78.

137. *Ibid.,* p. 78; Badian, *Publicans and Sinners,* pp. 31–32.

138. Frank, *Economic Survey of Ancient Rome,* Vol. V, pp. 19, 25, 72–73; Trever, *History of Ancient Civilization,* Vol. II, pp. 329, 513–14; P. A. Brunt, "Free Labour and Public Works at Rome," *Journal of Roman Studies,* Vol. LXX (1980), pp. 93–98.

139. Frank, *Economic History of Rome,* p. 481; Wittfogel, *Oriental Despotism,* pp. 210–11; Johnson, *Egypt and the Roman Empire,* pp. 148–49; Trever, *History of Ancient Civilization,* Vol. II, p. 515.

140. Brunt, "The Fiscus and Its Development," *loc. cit.,* pp. 75, 78, 90–91; Millar, "The Aerarium and Its Officials Under the Empire," *loc. cit.,* pp. 33–34, 40; Scullard, *From the Gracchi to Nero,* p. 303.

141. Scullard, p. 229.

142. Brunt, "The Fiscus and Its Development," *loc. cit.,* p. 88; F. Millar, "The Fiscus in the First Two Centuries," *Journal of Roman Studies,* Vol. LIII (1963), p. 42.

143. Brunt, "The Fiscus and Its Development, *loc. cit.,* p. 88; A. H. M. Jones, "Procurators and Prefects," in his *Studies in Roman Government and Law,* pp. 123–24.

144. Millar, "The Fiscus in the First Two Centuries," *loc. cit.,* p. 42.

145. Jones, "The Aerarium and the Fiscus," *loc. cit.,* p. 110.

146. Bernard d'Orgeval, *L'Empereur Hadrien: Ouevre législative et administrative* (Paris: Éditions Domat Montchrestien, 1950), pp. 256–57; Gustave Humbert, *Essai sur les finances et la comptabilité publique chez les Romains* (Paris: Ernest Thorin, 1886), pp. 207–8; Bernard W. Henderson, *The Life and Principate of the Emperor Hadrian* (New York: Brentano, 1923), p. 63.

147. Rostovtseff, *Social and Economic History of the Roman Empire,* p. 172.

148. Frank, *Economic Survey of Ancient Rome,* Vol. V, pp. 82, 231–32.

149. Graham Webster, *The Roman Imperial Army of the First and Second Century A.D.* (London: Black, 1969), pp. 256–58.

150. Watson, *The Roman Soldier,* pp. 13–25; Webster, *Roman Imperial Army,* pp. 22, 113–15; Hopkins, "Taxes and Trade in the Roman Empire," p. 125.

151. Duncan-Jones, *Economy of the Roman Empire,* p. 10.

152. Webster, *Roman Imperial Army,* pp. 118, 256–69; Watson, *The Roman Soldier,* pp. 89–99; Walbank, "Trade and Industry," *loc. cit.,* p. 57.

153. Walbank, pp. 38–39n.

154. Frank, *Economic Survey of Ancient Rome,* Vol. V, pp. 492–93.

155. Jones, "Taxation in Antiquity," *loc. cit.,* p. 169.

156. Humbert, *Essai sur les finances,* p. 200; Frank, *Economic Survey of the Roman Empire,* Vol. V, p. 79; Trever, *History of Ancient Civilization,* Vol. II, p. 633; Wittfogel, *Oriental Despotism,* p. 73.

157. Frank, *Economic Survey of Ancient Rome,* Vol. V, pp. 79–83.

158. Bury, *History of the Later Roman Empire,* Vol. I, p. 52; Jones, "The Aerarium and the Fiscus," *loc. cit.,* pp. 112–14.

159. Boeckh, *Public Economy,* Vol. I, p. 54.

160. *Ibid.,* pp. 291, 320.

161. *Ibid.,* pp. 214–15; Woolf, *Short History of Accountants and Accountancy,* pp. 28–30; Hignett, *History of the Athenian Constitution,* p. 146.

162. Boeckh, *Public Economy,* Vol. I, p. 253, Vol. II, pp. 325–26.

163. Littleton and Yamey, *Studies in the History of Accounting,* pp. 23–26.

164. Hignett, *History of the Athenian Constitution,* pp. 201–4, 238.

165. Boeckh, *Public Economy,* Vol. II, pp. 325–26.

166. *Ibid.,* Vol. I, p. 260; Littleton and Yamey, *Studies in the History of Accounting,* pp. 24–26; H. Burford, "Heavy Transport in Classical Antiquity," *Economic History Review,* 2nd Series, Vol. XIII, No. 1 (August 1960), pp. 5–6; *Cambridge Ancient History,* Vol. 5 (1940), p. 2.

167. Boeckh, *Public Economy,* Vol. I, pp. 257–60.

168. *Ibid.,* p. 248.

169. Hignett, *History of the Athenian Constitution,* pp. 205–6.

170. Boeckh, *Public Economy,* Vol. I, p. 261.

171. *Ibid.*

172. *Ibid.,* Vol. II, pp. 183–87, 266; Woolf, *Short History of Accountants and Accountancy,* p. 33; Heichelheim, *Ancient Economic History,* Vol. II, p. 145.

173. Crawford, *The Roman Republic,* p. 78.

174. Trever, *History of Ancient Civilization,* Vol. II, pp. 140–41.

175. Woolf, *Short History of Accountants and Accountancy,* pp. 38–39; Jones, "Aerarium and the Fiscus," *loc. cit.,* pp. 101–3.

176. Jones, *History of Rome Through the 5th Century,* p. 101.

177. Jones, "The Aerarium and the Fiscus," *loc. cit.,* pp. 101–2; Frank, *Economic History of Rome,* p. 150.

178. Jones, "Roman Civil Service, Clerical and Subclerical Grades," *loc. cit.,* pp. 156–57, 170–71.

179. Crawford, *The Roman Republic,* p. 79.

180. *Ibid.,* pp. 136–37.

181. P. A. Brunt, "The Administration of Roman Egypt," *Journal of Roman Studies,* Vol. LXV (1975), p. 125.

182. *Ibid.,* pp. 140–41.

183. Quoted in translation in A. M. Duff, *Freedmen in the Early Roman Empire* (Cambridge: W. Heffer, 1958), pp. 155–56.

184. Abbott and Johnson, *Municipal Administration,* p. 121; Sherwin-White, "Procurator Augusti," *loc. cit.,* pp. 11–19; Brunt, "The Fiscus and Its Development," pp. 87–88; Brunt, "The *Equites* in the Late Republic," in Robin Seager, ed., *The Crisis of the Roman Republic* (Cambridge and New York: Heffer/ Barnes & Noble, 1969), p. 101; Scullard, *From the Gracchi to Nero,* pp. 228–29, 233–35; Millar, "The Emperor, the Senate and the Provinces," *loc. cit.,* pp. 156–66.

185. Boeckh, *Public Economy,* Vol. I, pp. 224–25; Trever, *History of Ancient Civilization,* Vol. II, pp. 140–41; Marcus N. Top, "The Economic Background of the 5th Century," in *Cambridge Ancient History,* Vol. 5 (1940), p. 18.

186. See Fergus Millar's review of H. G.-Pflaum, *Les Carrières procuratoriennes équestres sous le haut-Empire Romain, Journal of Roman Studies,* Vol. LIII (1963), pp. 195–97. See also Sherwin-White, "Procurator Augusti," *loc. cit.,* pp. 20–25; Brunt, "The 'Fiscus' and Its Development," *loc. cit.,* pp. 86–88; Scullard, *From the Gracchi to Nero,* pp. 301–3.

187. Abbott and Johnson, *Municipal Administration*, p. 150.
188. d'Orgeval, *L'Empereur Hadrien*, pp. 256–57.
189. Abbott and Johnson, *Municipal Administration*, pp. 149–51; Trever, *History of Ancient Civilization*, Vol. II, p. 529; Rostovtseff, *Social and Economic History of the Roman Empire*, p. 467.
190. Frank, *Economic Survey of Ancient Rome*, Vol. V, pp. 69–70; R. H. Rogers, "What the Sibyl Said: Frontinus AQ, 7.5," *Classical Quarterly*, Vol. 32 (1982), No. 1, pp. 174–77.
191. See Chapter Two, "Finance Without Money," pp. 77–78.
192. Trever, *History of Ancient Civilization*, Vol. II, pp. 337–38; G. H. Stevenson, "The Imperial Administration," in *Cambridge Ancient History*, Vol. 10 (Cambridge Univ., 1971), pp. 192ff.; G. F. M. de Ste.-Croix, "Greek and Roman Accounting," in Littleton and Yamey, eds., *Studies in the History of Accounting*, for general background on ancient accounting.
193. Millar, "The Fiscus in the First Two Centuries," *loc. cit.,* pp. 37–40; Millar, "The Aerarium and Its Officials Under the Empire," *loc. cit.,* pp. 33 35, 40; Brunt, "The Fiscus and Its Development," *loc. cit.,* pp. 75–91.
194. Jones, *The Later Roman Empire*, Vol. II, p. 544.
195. Bury, *History of the Later Roman Empire*, Vol. II, p. 273.
196. Jones, *The Later Roman Empire*, Vol. I, pp. 566–69.
197. Frank, *Economic History of Rome*, p. 501.
198. Heichelheim, *Ancient Economic History*, Vol. II, p. 139; Jones, "Inflation Under the Roman Empire," *loc. cit.,* p. 296; Boeckh, *Public Economy*, Vol. II, pp. 381–83; Walbank, "Trade and Industry Under the Roman Empire in the West," *loc. cit.,* pp. 54–58.
199. Hopkins, "Taxes and Trade in the Roman Empire," *loc. cit.,* p. 123.
200. Abbott and Johnson, *Municipal Administration*, p. 115; Walbank, "Trade and Industry," *loc. cit.,* pp. 56–58. For a more detailed analysis of the problem of currency devaluation, see Chapter Four, "Finance in the Private Government of Medieval Europe," especially the section "Revenue Strategies of Late-Medieval Governments."
201. Johnson, *Egypt and the Roman Empire*, p. 48; Hopkins, "Taxes and Trade in the Roman Empire," *loc. cit.,* pp. 116–17.
202. Trever, *History of Ancient Civilization*, Vol. II, p. 267.
203. *Ibid.,* p. 268.
204. *Ibid.;* Boeckh, *Public Economy*, Vol. II, p. 381.
205. Boeckh, *Public Economy*, Vol. II, pp. 378–79.
206. Trever, *History of Ancient Civilization*, Vol. II, pp. 378–79.
207. Fergus Millar, "The Political Character of the Classical Roman Republic, 200–151 B.C.," *Journal of Roman Studies*, Vol. LXXIV (1984), p. 9.
208. Crawford, *The Roman Republic*, p. 80.
209. Trever, *History of Ancient Civilization*, Vol. II, p. 141.
210. Frank, *Economic Survey of Ancient Rome*, Vol. V, pp. 79–80; Wittfogel, *Oriental Despotism*, p. 73.
211. Woolf, *Short History of Accountants and Accountancy*, p. 48; Trever, *History of Ancient Civilization*, Vol. II, p. 328, 515; Jones, "The Aerarium and the Fiscus," *loc. cit.,* pp. 107, 109–110.
212. Frank, *Economic Survey of Ancient Rome*, Vol. V, p. 77.
213. Trever, *History of Ancient Civilization*, Vol. II, pp. 267–68.

214. Frank, *Economic History of Rome,* p. 501; Rostovtseff, *Social and Economic History of the Roman Empire,* pp. 466–67.
215. See Hopkins, "Taxes and Trade in the Roman Empire." *loc. cit.*
216 Bury, *History of the Later Roman Empire,* p. 54.
217. Abbott and Johnson, *Municipal Administration,* pp. 107–8; Fergus Millar, "Empire and City, Augustus to Julian: Obligations, Excuses and Status," *loc. cit.,* p. 83.
218. Bury, *History of the Later Roman Empire,* p. 59.
219. *Ibid.,* p. 60; Walbank, "Trade and Industry," *loc. cit.,* pp. 48, 63.
220. A. H. M. Jones, "Overtaxation: The Roman Empire in Decline," in Jones, *The Roman Economy,* pp. 88–89.
221. J. F. O'Sullivan, trans., *The Writings of Salvian the Presbyter* (Catholic University of America, 1947), quoted in Brian Tierney, Donald Kagan, and L. Pierce Williams, eds., *Great Issues in Western Civilization,* Vol. I (New York: Random House, 1968), pp. 172–73.
222. Abbott and Johnson, *Municipal Administration,* pp. 136–37.
223. Peter Brown, *The World of Late Antiquity from Marcus Aurelius to Muhammad* (London: Thames & Hudson, 1971), pp. 44–45.

CHAPTER FOUR

1. Most historians since the eighteenth century, in analyzing medieval feudal government, have focused on its *private* aspects. See, for example, Joseph R. Strayer, "The Two Levels of Feudalism," in his *Medieval Statecraft and the Perspectives of History* (Princeton: Princeton Univ., 1971), pp. 63–65. We are aware that many medieval historians have given a specialized meaning to the term "feudalism." Carl Stephenson, for one, would limit its use to the complex of personal clientage relationships and their associated rituals that developed after the ninth century in western Europe for mutual defense against Nordic invaders. Because we are more concerned with institutions of civil government than with military organization (although during the feudal period in western Europe it is indeed difficult to separate the two) we prefer the broader conception of feudalism—extreme government decentralization—enunciated by the political scientist James W. Fesler and others. For Stephenson's opinion, see his *Medieval Feudalism* (Ithaca: Cornell Paperbacks, 1969, especially Chapters I, II, and V. For Fesler's writing on decentralization see his article on Centralization–Decentralization in *New International Encyclopedia of the Social Sciences* (Macmillan and Free Press, 1968), Vol. 2, pp. 370–77; "The Political Role of Field Administration," in *Papers in Comparative Public Administration* (Ann Arbor: Univ. of Michigan Institute of Public Administration, 1962), pp. 117–43; "French Field Administration," *Comparative Studies in Society and History,* Vol. 5, No. 1, pp. 76–111; and "The Presence of the Administrative Past," in Fesler, ed., *American Public Administration Patterns of the Past* (Washington: American Society for Public Administration, 1982), pp. 1–27. See also Lynn T. White, Jr., *Medieval Technology and Social Change* (London: Oxford Univ., 1967, pp. 3–7, 135–36 (note 2, p. 3).
2. Henri Pirenne, *Economic and Social History of Medieval Europe* (New York: Harcourt, Brace, 1933), pp. 164–65; *Cambridge Economic History of Europe,* Vol. III (Cambridge, Eng.: Cambridge Univ., 1965), pp. 198–99; Carlo Cipolla,

Clocks and Culture (London: Collins, 1967), pp. 47, 125 note 2; David S. Landes, *Revolution in Time: Clocks and the Making of the Modern World* (Cambridge, Mass.: Harvard Univ., 1983), pp. 77–82.

3. Ernst Kantorowicz, "Kingship Under the Impact of Scientific Jurisprudence," in his *Selected Studies* (Locust Valley, N.Y.: J. J. Augustin, 1965), p. 153.

4. Arnold Meltsner, *The Politics of City Revenue* (Berkeley and Los Angeles: Univ. of California, 1971), Ch. 1; Richard Netzer, *The Property Tax* (Washington: Brookings Institution, 1966), Chs. I and VII. The fiscal problems of late imperial Rome are described in A. H. M. Jones, *The Later Roman Empire* (Oxford: Basil Blackwell, 1964); see especially Vol. II, pp. 695–705, 708–11. See also Terry Nichols Clark and Lorne Crawley Ferguson, *City Money: Political Processes, Fiscal Strain, and Retrenchment* (New York: Columbia Univ., 1983); and Henry J. Raimondo, "State Limitations on Local Taxing and Spending: Theory and Practice," *Public Budgeting and Finance*, Vol. 3, No. 7 (Autumn 1983), pp. 32–42.

5. J. A. G. Pocock, *The Political Works of James Harrington* (Cambridge, Eng.: Cambridge Univ., 1977), p. 48.

6. Bryce Lyon's analysis of the extensive literature on the transition from ancient to medieval society has helped us to find our way through it and to decide what we think. See his *The Origins of the Middle Ages: Pirenne's Challenge to Gibbon* (New York: Norton, 1972). Other sources we have used include A. H. M. Jones, *The Later Roman Empire;* Oxford: Basil Blackwell, 1964; R. H. C. Davis, *A History of Medieval Europe* (London: Longmans Green, 1957), Chs. 2 and 3; *Cambridge Economic History of Europe,* Vol. I (Cambridge, Eng.: Cambridge Univ., 1966), Chs. 1–4; Margaret Deanesly, *A History of Early Medieval Europe* (London: Methuen, 1956), pp. 476ff.; P. Boissionnade, *Life and Work in Medieval Europe* (New York: Harper Torchbooks, 1964); Carl Stephenson and Bryce Lyon, *Medieval History* (New York: Harper & Row, 1964), Chs. 2 and 3; Aurelio Bernardi, "The Economic Problems of the Roman Empire at the Time of Its Decline," reprinted from *Studia et documenta historie et juris,* Vol. 31 (1965), in Carlo Cipolla, ed., *The Economic Decline of Empires* (Oxford: Clarendon, 1965); Frank W. Walbank, "Trade and Industry Under the Roman Empire in the West," in *Cambridge Economic History of Europe,* Vol. II (Cambridge, Eng.: Cambridge Univ., 1952), Ch. II.

7. Peter Brown, *The World of Late Antiquity* (London: Thames & Hudson, 1971), pp. 29, 115–16.

8. *Ibid.,* pp. 123–24.

9. Davis, p. 26; *Cambridge Economic History,* Vol. II, p. 51.

10. Brown, pp. 34–35.

11. Jones, *The Later Roman Empire,* Vol. 1, pp. 402–3; Brown, p. 126.

12. Brown, p. 126.

13. Boissionnade, pp. 18–19; Walbank, "Trade and Industry Under the Roman Empire in the West," *loc. cit.,* p. 52; Jones, *The Later Roman Empire,* Vol. 1, pp. 248–55.

14. Jones, *Later Roman Empire,* Vol. 2, pp. 1028–32, 1066–67.

15. Boissionnade, p. 20; Heinrich Fichtenau, *The Carolingian Empire* (Oxford: Basil Blackwell, 1957), pp. 6–8.

16. Ewart Lewis, *Medieval Political Ideas,* Vol. I (New York: Knopf, 1954), pp. 88–90.

17. Boissionnade, p. 159; Marc Bloch, *Feudal Society* (Chicago: Univ. of Chicago, 1961), pp. 62–63, 66–67; Pirenne, *Economic and Social History of Medieval Europe*, pp. 78–79.

18. Georges Duby, *The Early Growth of the European Economy: Warriors and Peasants from the Seventh to the Twelfth Century* (Ithaca: Cornell Univ., 1974), p. 19.

19. *Cambridge Economic History*, Vol. III, pp. 10–15, 119–26. Marc Bloch, *Feudal Society*, pp. 64–66.

20. Charles Parain, "The Evolution of Agricultural Technique," in *Cambridge Economic History of Europe*, Vol. I, pp. 138–39. Courtenay Edward Stevens, "Agriculture and Rural Life in the Later Roman Empire," *Cambridge Economic History*, Vol. I, pp. 92–119.

21. Boissionnade, p. 226.

22. White, Ch. II.

23. Lyon, *Origins of the Middle Ages*, pp. 36–38.

24. M. Keith Hopkins, "On the Probable Age Structure of the Roman Population," *Population Studies*, Vol. 20, No. 2 (November 1966), pp. 245–64.

25. Jones, *Later Roman Empire*, Vol. II, pp. 1040–45; Duby, *Early Growth of the European Economy*, p. 13.

26. Boissionnade, pp. 90–93: Georges M. Duby, "Manorial Economy," in Vol. 9 of *The New International Encyclopedia of The Social Sciences* (Macmillan and The Free Press, 1968), pp. 562–65; Marc Bloch, "The Rise of Dependent Cultivation and Seignorial Institutions," in *Cambridge Economic History of Europe*, Vol. I, Ch. IV; Philip Jones, "Medieval Society in Its Prime," *Cambridge Economic History*, Vol. I, pp. 398–99; White, Ch. II.

27. Joshua Prawer and S. N. Eisenstadt, "Feudalism," in *New International Encyclopedia of the Social Sciences*, Vol. 5 (1968), p. 396.

28. White, Ch. II; W. H. McNeill, *The Rise of the West* (New York: Mentor, 1963), pp. 499–500. Jean Gimpel, *The Medieval Machine* (New York: Holt, Rinehart and Winston, 1976), pp. 33–44.

29. White, pp. 69–70; Robert S. Lopez, *The Birth of Europe* (London: J. M. Dent, 1967), plate facing p. 176; Warren S. Ilchman, "New Time in Old Clocks: Productivity, Development and Comparative Public Administration," in Dwight Waldo, ed., *Temporal Dimensions of Development Administration* (Durham, N.C.: Duke Univ., 1970), esp. pp. 137–46.

30. Lopez, pp. 125–26; Richard Koebner, "The Settlement and Colonization of Europe," in *Cambridge Economic History of Europe*, Vol. I, Ch. I, esp. pp. 50–91; *Cambridge Economic History*, Vol. III, p. 287; Gimpel, p. 47.

31. Duby, *Early Growth of the European Economy*, pp. 91, 95–96, 126, 149–50.

32. Pirenne, *Economic and Social History*, p. 83.

33. White, pp. 67–68; Duby, *Early Growth of the European Economy*, pp. 131, 134–35, 137–39.

34. Lopez, p. 172; Bruce Lyon, *The High Middle Ages* (Glencoe, Ill.: The Free Press, 1964), p. 11.

35. Stephenson and Lyon, *Medieval History*, pp. 270–71.

36. Daniel Waley, *The Italian City Republics* (New York: McGraw-Hill, 1969), p. 35.

37. For further comparisons between Venice and Japan, see Chalmers Johnson, "La Serenissima of the East," *Asian and African Studies,* Vol. 18, No. 1 (March 1984), pp. 57–61.

38. Hilmar C. Krueger, "Economic Aspects of Expanding Europe," in Marshall Clagett, Gaines Post, and Robert C. Reynolds, eds., *Twelfth Century Europe and the Foundations of Modern Society* (Madison: Univ. of Wisconsin, 1961), pp. 71–75; Duby, *Early Growth of the European Economy,* pp. 144–48.

39. William Langer, *Western Civilization* (New York: Harper, 1968), pp. 441–52; Lopez, pp. 126–32; Boissionnade, pp. 162–63, 168–69; Pirenne, *Economic and Social History,* pp. 78–79, 82–83; White, p. 66; Brian Tierney and Sidney Painter, *Western Europe in the Middle Ages* (New York: Knopf, 1970), pp. 216–17; *Cambridge Economic History of Europe,* Vol. III; James W. Thompson, *Economic and Social History of Europe in the Later Middle Ages* (New York: Frederick Ungar, 1931), pp. 467–70.

40. Lopez, pp. 141–42; *Cambridge Economic History,* Vol. II, pp. 267–68; Waley, p. 47.

41. Raymond de Roover, "The *Cambium Maritimum* Contract According to the Genoese Notarial Records of the Twelfth and Thirteenth Centuries," in David Herlihy, Robert S. Lopez, and Vsevolod Slessarev, eds., *Economy, Society and Government in Medieval Italy* (Kent, Ohio: Kent State Univ., 1969), pp. 22–23.

42. See, for example, A. C. Littleton and B. S. Yamey, *Studies in the History of Accounting* (Homewood, Ill.: Irwin, 1956), *passim;* R. Emmett Taylor, *No Royal Road: Luca Pacioli and His Times* (Chapel Hill: Univ. of North Carolina, 1942), pp. 61–77; Arthur H. Woolf, *A Short History of Accountants and Accountancy* (London: Gee & Co., 1912), pp. 105–7, 111–17; *Cambridge Economic History,* Vol. III, pp. 91–92; Alfred E. Lieber, "Eastern Business Practices and Medieval Commerce," *Economic History Review,* 2nd Series, Vol. XXI, No. 2 (August 1968), pp. 230–43.

43. From *The Annals of Xanten,* pp. 849–51, quoted in Brian Tierney, Donald Kagan, and L. Pearce Williams, *Great Issues in Western Civilization,* Vol. I (New York: Random House, 1967), p. 259.

44. Georges Duby, *Rural Economy and Country Life in the Medieval West* (London: Edward Arnold, 1968), p. 61.

45. Charles Homer Haskins, *The Normans in European History* (Boston: Houghton Mifflin, 1915), pp. 60–61.

46. Bryce Lyon, *The High Middle Ages* (Glencoe: The Free Press, 1964), p. 7.

47. James W. Fesler, "The Presence of the Administrative Past," *loc. cit.,* pp. 3, 5.

48. Dorothy Whitlock, *The Beginnings of English Society* (Penguin, 1952), pp. 95–96; Georges Duby, *The Early Growth of the European Economy,* pp. 54–57, 69–70.

49. Tierney and Painter, *Western Europe in the Middle Ages,* p. 73; *Cambridge Medieval History,* Vol. III, p. 140.

50. Duby, *Early Growth of the European Economy,* p. 43.

51. Bloch, *Feudal Society,* p. 131. *Cambridge Economic History,* Vol. III, pp. 292–93, 443; *Cambridge Medieval History,* Vol. III (New York: Macmillan, 1913), pp. 480–83.

52. Tierney and Painter, p. 73; *Cambridge Medieval History,* Vol. III, pp. 480–83.

53. Bloch, *Feudal Society*, p. 62; *Cambridge Medieval History*, Vol. III, pp. 139, 650; Tierney and Painter, p. 152; Lyon, *High Middle Ages*, p. 4.

54. Calculated from a map in Maurice Powicke, *The Thirteenth Century* (Oxford: Clarendon, 1970), p. 512.

55. Lucien Fèbvre, *Life in Renaissance France* (Cambridge, Mass.: Harvard Univ., 1977), pp. 12–19, quote on p. 18; Mark Girouard, *Life in the English Country House: A Social and Architectural History* (New Haven: Yale Univ., 1978), p. 110. James W. Fesler called our attention to this source.

56. Georges Duby, *Rural Economy and Country Life*, pp. 38–39.

57. *Ibid.*, pp. 40–41; Pirenne, *Economic and Social History*, pp. 64–65; Bloch, *Feudal Society*, p. 250; *Cambridge Medieval History*, Vol. III, pp. 480–83; Fichtenau, pp. 145–49; Whitlock, pp. 64–65, 72–75, 100–1; Bruce Lyon and Adriaan Verhulst, *Medieval Finance: A Comparison of Financial Institutions in Western Europe* (Brussels: Univ. of Ghent, 1967), p. 18; Thomas N. Bisson, *Fiscal Accounts of Catalonia under the Early Count-Kings (1151–1213)* (Berkeley: Univ. of California, 1984), pp. 38, 42–46.

58. Boissionnade, p. 126.

59. Bloch, *Feudal Society*, pp. 114–15, 206; *Cambridge Medieval History*, Vol. III, p. 140.

60. *Cambridge Medieval History*, Vol. III, p. 404.

61. Bloch, *Feudal Society*, p. 251; Boissionnade, pp. 139–40; Pirenne, *Economic and Social History*, p. 65; Duby, *Rural Economy and Country Life*, p. 39.

62. Pirenne, *Economic and Social History*, p. 65.

63. Geoffrey Vickers, "Institutional and Personal Roles," *Human Relations*, Vol. XXIV, No. 5 (October 1971), p. 444.

64. Tierney and Painter, p. 223; Frank E. and Fritzi P. Manuel, "Sketch for a Natural History of Paradise," *Daedalus*, Winter 1972, pp. 83–128, especially 97–104, 110–13.

65. White, pp. 29–30, 32; *Bloch, Feudal Society*, pp. 152–62; *Cambridge Medieval History*, Vol. III, pp. 23–26.

66. *Cambridge Medieval History*, Vol. III, p. 47.

67. Bloch, *Feudal Society*, pp. 167–69, 221; White, p. 29.

68. Stephenson, pp. 9–14; *Cambridge Medieval History*, Vol. III, p. 47; Bloch, *Feudal Society*, pp. 158–59.

69. Thompson, pp. 305–6; Bloch, *Feudal Society*, p. 220; White, p. 31; Strayer, "Feudalism," in his *Medieval Statecraft*, p. 66.

70. Duby, *Early Growth of the European Economy*, p. 171.

71. Georges Duby, *The Knight, the Lady and the Priest: The Making of Modern Marriage in Medieval France* (New York: Pantheon, 1983), pp. 199–200.

72. Bloch, *Feudal Society*, p. 224; Thompson, p. 304.

73. Robert Fawtier, *The Capetian Kings of France* (New York and London: Macmillan, 1962, pp. 64–67.

74. For limits on this generalization, see Strayer, "Feudalism," in his *Medieval Statecraft*, p. 83.

75. G. O. Sayles, *The Medieval Foundations of England* (London: Methuen, 1964), p. 418.

76. René Stourm, *The Budget*, transl. Thaddeus Plazinski from the 13th ed., Paris, 1931 (New York: D. Appleton, 1917), pp. 26–35.

77. Tierney and Painter, p. 317; Sayles, pp. 396–97.
78. From "Establishment of the King's Household" (*Constitutio Domus Regis*), in David C. Douglas and George W. Greenaway, eds., *English Historical Documents*, Vol. II (New York: Oxford Univ., 1953), p. 422.
79. *Ibid.*
80. Charles Petit-Dutaillis, *The Feudal Monarchy in France and England* (New York: Barnes & Noble, 1966), p. 62.
81. Lopez, p. 332.
82. Conversation with Thomas N. Bisson; Bloch, *Feudal Society*, p. 206; Duby, *Rural Economy and Country Life*, pp. 181, 207–8, 214–5; Lyon and Verhulst, pp. 48, 58, 94–95.
83. Strayer, "Normandy and Languedoc," in his *Medieval Statecraft*, p. 18; see also his "Italian Bankers and Philip the Fair," in *Medieval Statecraft*, pp. 241–42; Bloch, *Feudal Society*, p. 207.
84. Bisson, *Fiscal Accounts of Catalonia*, pp. 110–11.
85. Strayer, "Feudalism," in *Medieval Statecraft*, pp. 81–82; Bloch, *Feudal Society*, p. 223.
86. *Cambridge Economic History*, Vol. II, p. 332.
87. Petit-Dutaillis, pp. 187–88; Strayer, "The Crusades of Louis IX," in *Medieval Statecraft*, p. 165.
88. H. Bibicou, "Une page d'histoire diplomatique de Byzance au IXe siècle: Michael VII Doukas, Robert Guiscard et la pension des dignitaires," *Byzantion*, Vol. XXIX, pp. 44–45, 74–75, 94.
89. Lemerle, " 'Roga' et rente d'état aux Xe XIe siècles," *Revue des Études Byzantines*, Vol. 25 (1967), p. 97.
90. Duby, *The Knight, the Lady and the Priest*, p. 105.
91. Strayer, "The Crusades of Louis IX" and "The Laicization of French and English Society in the Thirteenth Century," in his *Medieval Statecraft*, pp. 177, 183, 185, 256–57; Petit-Dutaillis, pp. 256 57.
92. Girouard, p. 20.
93. Tierney, Kagan, and Williams, Vol. 1, p. 300. See also Sayles, p. 438.
94. Powicke, pp. 33, 549–52; May McKisack, *The Fourteenth Century* (Oxford: Clarendon, 1959), pp. 238–39; A. R. Myers, *England in the Late Middle Ages* (Penguin, 1952), p. 52.
95. Bloch, *Feudal Society*, pp. 220–21.
96. *Ibid.*
97. Powicke, pp. 542–58; Myers, pp. 27–28.
98. Petit-Dutaillis, pp. 248, 252, 304–5.
99. Joseph R. Strayer, *The Reign of Philip the Fair* (Princeton: Princeton Univ., 1980), p. 82.
100. Thomas N. Bisson, *Conservation of Coinage, Monetary Exploitation and Its Restraint in France, Catalonia, and Aragon* (*c. A.D. 1000–c. 1255*) (Oxford: Clarendon, 1979), Ch. III.
101. George Holmes, *The Later Middle Ages* (Edinburgh: Norton, 1962), p. 75.
102. Sayles, p. 420; Tierney and Painter, p. 422.
103. Lewis, pp. 89–92.
104. Gaines Post, "Patria Potestas, Regia Potestas and Rex Imperator," in Herlihy et al., p. 185; Sayles, pp. 419–20.

105. Strayer, "Problems of State Building in the Middle Ages," in his *Medieval Statecraft,* p. 260.
106. *Ibid.,* pp. 261, 296; see also his "The Two Levels of Feudalism," in *Medieval Statecraft,* p. 81; Powicke, pp. 527–28.
107. Quoted in Thompson, p. 586. For other town charters, see also Duby, *Rural Economy and Country Life in the Medieval West,* pp. 242–45, 410–13; *Cambridge Economic History,* Vol. III, pp. 29, 189–91, 301–2; Lyon, *High Middle Ages,* p. 11; Petit-Dutaillis, p. 196; Sayles, pp. 440–42; Powicke, pp. 308–10; Tierney and Painter, p. 220; Boissonnade, pp. 248–51, 198–99; Pirenne, *Economic and Social History of Medieval Europe,* pp. 70–73.
108. We owe this insight to James W. Fesler.
109. Powicke, pp. 529–35; Joseph R. Strayer and Charles H. Taylor, *Studies in Early French Taxation* (Cambridge, Mass.: Harvard Univ., 1939), pp. 51–52, 67–68, 72, 77, 83, 90, 151–54; Tierney and Painter, p. 326; Lopez, pp. 334–36; Sayles, pp. 441–42; *Cambridge Economic History,* Vol. III, pp. 29, 189–91; Bisson, *Conservation of Coinage,* pp. 13–14, 50–51.
110. Richard W. Kaeuper, *Bankers to the Crown: The Riccardi of Lucca and Edward I* (Princeton: Princeton Univ., 1973), p. 188.
111. Powicke, pp. 505–6, 527–28; Strayer and Taylor, p. 66.
112. Bloch, *Feudal Society,* pp. 348–51, 402–3; Tierney and Painter, pp. 173–74; *Cambridge Medieval History,* Vol. III, p. 144; Margaret Howell, *Regalian Right in Medieval England* (London: Athelone Press, 1962), pp. 9–12.
113. Fawtier, pp. 72–73; Petit-Dutaillis, pp. 187, 251.
114. Sidney Painter, *The Rise of the Feudal Monarchies* (Ithaca: Cornell Univ., 1969), p. 49; Howell, pp. 186, 206.
115. See Strayer, *Reign of Philip the Fair,* p. 241.
116. Howell, pp. 35, 72; Duby, *Early Growth of the European Economy,* pp. 215–21.
117. Howell, p. 167.
118. *Ibid.,* pp. 2–3.
119. *Ibid.,* pp. 40–41; J. E. A. Jolliffe, "The Chamber and the Castle Treasures Under King John," in R. W. Hunt, W. A. Pantin, and R. W. Southern, eds., *Studies in Medieval History* (Oxford: Clarendon, 1969), p. 131.
120. Jolliffe, *loc. cit.,* pp. 43, 53, 124–34; *Cambridge Economic History,* Vol. III, pp. 302–6; Fawtier, pp. 90–91; Thompson, pp. 494–96; Lopez, pp. 343–35; Holmes, pp. 76–77; Sayles, p. 396; Powicke, pp. 498–500.
121. Kaeuper, p. 78.
122. *Cambridge Economic History,* Vol. II, p. 238.
123. *Ibid.,* Vol. III, p. 480.
124. Tierney and Painter, pp. 486–87; Powicke, pp. 221–24.
125. "The Dialogue of the Exchequer" (*Dialogus de Scaccario*), by Richard FitzNigel, reproduced in Douglas and Greenaway, pp. 491–92. See also Petit-Dutaillis, pp. 254–55, for the variety of French royal expenses.
126. Holmes, p. 77; Howell, pp. 154–63.
127. Holmes, pp. 163–64.
128. *Ibid.,* pp. 90–91.
129. *Ibid.,* pp. 150–51.
130. Bruce Lyon, *A Constitutional and Legal History of Medieval England* (New York: Harper & Brothers, 1960), pp. 394–95.

131. *Cambridge Economic History,* Vol. III, pp. 313–14, 456; Myers, pp. 29–30; McKisack, pp. 242–44.
132. See Lyon and Verhulst, pp. 17, 37, 39; Littleton and Yamey, pp. 79–80; Paul Einzig, *The Control of the Purse: Progress and Decline of Parliament's Financial Control* (London: Secker & Warburg, 1959), p. 95.
133. G. L. Harris, "Fictitious Loans," *Economic History Review,* 2nd series, Vol. VIII, No. 2 (December 1955), pp. 187–99.
134. *Cambridge Economic History,* Vol. II, p. 322.
135. For a sophisticated discussion of currency manipulation as a financial strategy of medieval and early-modern governments, see John Hicks, *A Theory of Economic History* (Oxford: Clarendon, 1969), pp. 88–92. Bisson's *Conservation of Coinage* provides fine-grained evidence both for debasements and for rulers' efforts to increase revenue by promising subjects to refrain from altering currency values.
136. Bisson, *Conservation of Coinage,* pp. 5, 7.
137. Tierney and Painter, p. 432; *Cambridge Economic History,* Vol. III, p. 483, Petit-Dutaillis, pp. 253–54; Lopez, p. 333.
138. See Carlo M. Cipolla, "Currency Depreciation in Medieval Europe," *Economic History Review,* 2nd Series, Vol. XV, No. 3 (April 1963), p. 419; and Harry A. Miskimin, *The Economy of Later Renaissance Europe, 1460–1600* (Cambridge, Eng.: Cambridge Univ., 1977), pp. 155–56.
139. Bisson, *Conservation of Coinage,* p. 7.
140. Miskimin, pp. 159–61.
141. *Cambridge Economic History,* Vol. III, pp. 305, 482.
142. Tierney and Painter, p. 431; Boissonnade, p. 283.
143. *Cambridge Economic History,* Vol. III, p. 453; Miskimin, p. 163.
144. *Cambridge Economic History,* Vol. III, p. 456; Pirenne, p. 134; Carlo Cipolla, *Money, Prices and Civilization in the Mediterranean World* (Princeton: Princeton Univ., 1956), p. 64.
145. Kaeuper, pp. 80–81, 96.
146. Powicke, pp. 637–40; *Cambridge Economic History,* Vol. III, p. 475, and Vol. II, pp. 236–38; Glenn Olsen, "Italian Merchants and the Performance of Papal Banking Functions in the Early Thirteenth Century" in Herlihy et al., pp. 43–64; Tierney and Painter, p. 423, A. R. Myers, *England in the Late Middle Ages* (Penguin, 1952), p. 35; Kaeuper, pp. 46–47.
147. McKisack, p. 353.
148. Kaeuper, pp. 121–22, 150.
149. *Cambridge Economic History,* Vol. III, p. 455.
150. *Ibid.,* pp. 455, 457, 458, and Vol. II, pp. 241–42; Powicke, pp. 304–6; Kaeuper, p. 123.
151. *Cambridge Economic History,* Vol. III, p 484.
152. Kaeuper, p. 78, Chapter V.
153. *Cambridge Economic History,* Vol. III, p. 452; Sayles, p. 396.
154. A. J. Forey, *The Templars in the Corona de Aragón* (London: Oxford Univ., 1973), pp. 344–52.
155. Bisson, *Fiscal Accounts of Catalonia,* pp. 82, 153.
156. *Cambridge Economic History,* Vol. III, pp. 305, 473–74, 477–79; Pirenne, pp. 134–35; Petit-Dutaillis, p. 250; Lopez, p. 334; Strayer, *Reign of Philip the Fair,* pp. 285–92.

157. *Cambridge Economic History,* Vol. III, pp. 457, 473–74, 477–80; Strayer, "Italian Bankers and Philip the Fair," in his *Medieval Statecraft,* pp. 239–50.
158. Quoted in Powicke, p. 640. See also Myers, p. 52, and Einzig, pp. 96–97.
159. *Cambridge Economic History,* Vol. III, pp. 466–68, 471, and Vol. II, pp. 238–41; Myers, p. 52.
160. McKisack, pp. 469, 479, 481–84; *Cambridge Economic History,* Vol. III, p. 479.
161. Bisson, *Fiscal Accounts of Catalonia,* pp. 56–59, 66, 132, 149.
162. *Cambridge Economic History,* Vol. III, pp. 469, 485–86; McKisack, pp. 403–4; Einzig, p. 95.
163. Bloch, *Feudal Society,* pp. 174, 324.
164. Holmes, pp. 77–78; *Cambridge Economic History,* Vol. II, pp. 236–38, 241, and Vol. III, pp. 304, 317–18; John Hicks, p. 82; Powicke, pp. 628–33.
165. *Cambridge Economic History,* Vol. III, p. 305.
166. *Ibid.,* Vol. II, pp. 76–77, and Vol. III, pp. 317, 459; Powicke, pp. 523–25.
167. *Cambridge Economic History,* Vol. III, pp. 318–19; Duby, *Rural Economy and Country Life,* p. 251.
168. William M. Bowsky, *The Finance of the Commune of Sienna, 1287–1355* (Oxford: Clarendon, 1970), pp. 110–12; Bowsky, "Medieval Citizenship: The Individual and the State in the Commune of Sienna, 1287–1355," in his *Studies in Medieval and Renaissance History,* Vol. IV (Lincoln: Univ. of Nebraska, 1967), pp. 226–27; Bowsky, "Direct Taxation in a Medieval Commune: The Dazio in Sienna," in Herlihy et al., pp. 212–13; *Cambridge Economic History,* Vol. III, p. 197; Henri Pirenne, *Medieval Cities: Their Origins and the Revival of Trade* (Princeton: Princeton Univ., 1948), p. 207.
169. See Joel T. Rosenthal, *The Purchase of Paradise: Gift Giving and the Aristocracy, 1307–1485* (London: Routledge & Kegan Paul, 1972), *passim;* Forey, pp. 48–49; and Gertrude Himmelfarb, *The Idea of Poverty: England in the Early Industrial Age* (New York: Knopf, 1984), pp. 3–4.
170. Bowsky, *Finance of the Commune of Sienna,* p. 108.
171. David Herlihy, "Direct and Indirect Taxation in Tuscan Urban Finance," *Finances et comptabilité urbaines du XIIe et XIVe siècles,* International Colloquium at Blankenberge, Sept. 6–9, 1962 (Brussels: pro Civitate, 1964), p. 396.
172. Bowsky, *Finance of the Commune of Sienna,* pp. 101–6, 108.
173. Herlihy, "Direct and Indirect Taxation in Tuscan Urban Finance," *loc. cit.,* pp. 393–94.
174. Daniel Waley, *The Italian City-Republics,* pp. 78–79.
175. David Herlihy, *Medieval and Renaissance Pistoia: The Social History of an Italian Town, 1200–1430* (New Haven: Yale Univ., 1967), p. 185.
176. *Cambridge Economic History,* Vol. III, p. 92.
177. Bowsky, *Finance of the Commune of Sienna,* p. 80.
178. *Cambridge Economic History,* Vol. II, p. 92.
179. Herlihy, "Direct and Indirect Taxation in Tuscan Urban Finance," *loc. cit.,* pp. 293–94.
180. Bowsky, *Finance of the Commune of Sienna,* p. 116.
181. Thompson, pp. 235–37; Gino Luzzatto, *Il debito pubblico della Repubblica di Venezia* (Milan: Istituto Editoriale Cisalpino, 1963), p. 9; Charles M. de La Roncière, "Indirect Taxes or 'Gabelles' at Florence in the Fourteenth Century: The Evolution of Tariffs and Problems of Collection," in Nicolai Rubenstein,

ed., *Florentine Studies: Politics and Society in Renaissance Florence* (London: Faber & Faber, 1968), pp.146–47.

182. La Roncière, "Indirect Taxes," *loc. cit.*, pp. 144–45.

183. *Ibid.*

184. Luzzatto, p. 9.

185. La Roncière, pp. 144–45.

186. *Ibid.*, pp. 181–82.

187. McKisack, pp. 357–58; Boissionnade, pp. 284–85; *Cambridge Economic History*, Vol. II, pp. 191–95.

188. *Cambridge Economic History*, Vol. III, p. 203, and Vol. II, pp. 338–42; McKisack, pp. 336, 406, 423; La Roncière, "Indirect Taxes," *loc. cit.*, pp. 186, 188–89; A. R. Myers, ed., *English Historical Documents*, Vol. IV (New York: Oxford Univ., 1969), pp. 126–40; Boissionnade, pp. 328–29, 218–19; Pirenne, *Economic and Social History*, pp. 200–1; James W. Thompson and Edgar N. Johnson, *An Introduction to Medieval Europe* (New York: Norton, 1937), p. 869.

189. Quoted in McKisack, p. 407.

190. *Cambridge Economic History*, Vol. III, p. 470.

191. Waley, p. 80; Bowsky, *Finance of the Commune of Sienna*, p. 177; M. B. Becker, "Economic Change and the Emerging Florentine Territorial State," *Studies in the Renaissance*, Vol. XIII (New York: Renaissance Society of America, 1968), pp. 11–12; Emilio Cristiani, *Nobilità e Popolo, nel comune di Pisa* (Naples: Istituto Italiano per gli Studii Storici, 1962), pp. 306–7; Tierney and Painter, p. 453; Luzzatto, pp. 5–6, 14–16.

192. William M. Bowsky, "The Impact of the Black Death Upon Sienese Government and Society," *Speculum*, Vol. XXXIV (1964), pp. 11–12; Bowsky, *Finance of the Commune of Sienna*, p. 218.

193. Pirenne, *Economic and Social History*, pp. 136–37.

194. Littleton and Yamey, pp. 131, 135.

195. Pirenne, *Economic and Social History*, p. 136.

196. Luzzatto, p. 16.

197. John of Salisbury, selected passages from the *Polycraticus*, in Douglas and Greenaway, *English Historical Documents*, Vol. II, p. 785

198. FitzNigel, quoted in Reginald L. Poole, *The Exchequer in the Twelfth Century* (Oxford: Clarendon, 1912), p 36

199. Lyon and Verhulst, pp. 56–58.

200. *Ibid.*, pp. 42–47.

201. Quoted in Petit-Dutaillis, p. 133.

202. Lopez, pp. 328–29; Joseph R. Strayer, "The Promise of the Fourteenth Century," in his *Medieval Statecraft*, pp. 318–19.

203. Bloch, *Feudal Society*, pp. 337–38; Boissionnade, pp. 180–81.

204. James W. Fesler, "French Field Administration," *loc. cit.*, pp. 81–82; Bloch, *Feudal Society*, p. 337.

205. Whitlock, p. 79.

206. Petit-Dutaillis, p. 184; Bloch, *Feudal Society*, pp. 338–39.

207. Bloch, *Feudal Society*, p. 339.

208. Fesler, "French Field Administration," *loc. cit.*, p. 93; Petit-Dutaillis, p. 185.

209. Strayer, "Normandy and Languedoc" in his *Medieval Statecraft*, pp. 49–52; "Problems of State Building in the Middle Ages," *idem*, p. 318; "The Develop-

ment of Feudal Institutions," *idem,* pp. 85–87; "Viscounts and Viguiers under Philip the Fair," *idem,* pp. 213–31.

210. Esther Moir, *The Justice of the Peace* (Harmondsworth, Eng.: Penguin, 1969), pp. 16–24; Helen M. Jewell, *English Local Administration in the Middle Ages* (Newton Abbot: David & Charles, 1972), pp. 92–97.

211. Petit-Dutaillis, p. 131.

212. Thompson, p. 477.

213. Kautilya, *The Arthasastra,* Shamasastry translation (Mysore: Raghuveer, 1956), p. 18.

214. A. Andreades, "Le Montant du budget de l'empire byzantine," *Revue des études grècques,* Vol. XXXIV, pp. 49–50.

215. Lemerle, p. 81.

216. See Strayer, "Normandy and Languedoc," in his *Medieval Statecraft,* p. 51; Lyon and Verhulst, *passim;* Petit-Dutaillis, pp. 132–34, 344ff.; Bisson, *Fiscal Accounts of Catalonia;* and James Fesler, "French Field Administration," *loc. cit.,* p. 402.

217. Jewell, pp. 88–90, 92–97.

218. Lyon and Verhulst, p. 59.

219. D. C. Twitchett, *Financial Administration Under the T'ang Dynasty* (Cambridge, Eng.: Cambridge Univ., 1963), p. 101.

220. Lyon and Verhulst, p. 59.

221. Published in Douglas and Greenaway, Vol. II, pp. 490–569; a partial collection of manorial accounts from the royal demesne from the twelfth century on (known as the Pipe Rolls), greatly abridged, is reproduced in that volume on pp. 469–583. Secondary sources cited often are: Poole, *The Exchequer in the Twelfth Century;* Hubert Hall, *Antiquities and Curiosities of the Exchequer* (London: Elliot Stock, 1891); and Lyon and Verhulst. Bisson's *Fiscal Accounts of Catalonia* reproduces Catalonian documents.

222. Poole, *The Exchequer,* pp. 132–34.

223. Powicke, pp. 63–64.

224. *Ibid.,* pp. 144–46.

225. *Ibid.,* p. 360.

226. *Ibid.,* p. 366.

227. See Bisson, *Fiscal Accounts of Catalonia,* pp. 47, 109–10.

228. Littleton and Yamey, p. 64.

229. Lyon and Verhulst, p. 65.

230. "The Dialogue of the Exchequer," in Douglas and Greenaway, Vol. II, p. 545.

231. Powicke, p. 365.

232. Quoted from Pipe Roll of 1181–82 in Poole, *The Exchequer,* pp. 70–71.

233. Jolliffe, pp. 120–21.

234. *Ibid.,* pp. 124–25.

235. Dorothy M. Broome, "Exchequer Migration to York in the Thirteenth and Fourteenth Centuries," in A. G. Little and F. M. Powicke, *Essays in Medieval History* (Freeport: Books for Libraries Press, 1967), p. 295.

236. *Ibid.,* p. 294.

237. Florence M. G. Higham, "A Note on the Pre-Tudor Secretary," in Little and Powicke, pp. 364–65.

238. *Cambridge Economic History,* Vol. III, pp. 478–79, 482–84.

239. *Ibid.*, pp. 488–89.
240. Powicke, pp. 523–24.
241. *Ibid.*, p. 525.
242. *Cambridge Economic History*, Vol. III, pp. 469–84.
243. Douglas C. North and Robert Paul Thomas, "An Economic Theory of the Growth of the Western World," *Economic History Review*, Vol. XXIII (1970), No. 1, pp. 11, 12, 16.

CHAPTER FIVE

1. Fernand Braudel, *Capitalism and Material Life, 1400–1800* (New York: Harper & Row, 1973), p. 37.
2. Walter Minchinton, "Patterns and Structure of Demand, 1500–1750," in Carlo Cipolla, ed., *The Fontana Economic History of Europe*, Vol. II, *The Sixteenth and Seventeenth Centuries* (London and Glasgow: Collins/Fontana, 1974), pp. 96–97; Domenico Sella, "European Industries," in Cipolla, Vol. II, p. 357. See also Robert Darnton, *The Great Cat Massacre and Other Episodes in French Cultural History* (New York: Basic Books, 1984), p. 27; and Emmanuel L. Ladurie, "The Rouergue Through the Lens," in his *The Mind and Method of the Historian* (Chicago: Univ. of Chicago, 1981), pp. 200–3.
3. Ernest H. Phelps-Brown and Sheila V. Hopkins, "Seven Centuries of the Price of Consumables Compared with Builders' Wage Rates," *Economica*, New Series, Vol. XXIII (1956), p. 297; *ibid.*, "Wage Rates and Prices: Evidence for Population Pressure in the Sixteenth Century," *Economica*, New Series, Vol. XXIV (1957), p. 293.
4. Ladurie, p. 187. Robert Darnton finds evidence for the life conditions of the poor of this era in the folk tales passed from generation to generation in European peasant societies; themes of poverty and brutality, of peasant fatalism tempered by sharp dealing, run through the folk tales he cites. See his "Peasants Tell Tales: The Meaning of Mother Goose," in his *Great Cat Massacre*, pp. 9–74.
5. Braudel, *Capitalism and Material Life*, p. 42.
6. *Ibid.*, p. 11; Roger Mols, "Population in Europe," in Cipolla, ed., *Fontana Economic History*, Vol. II, p. 39.
7. Braudel, pp. 74 78.
8. Mols, *loc. cit.*, p. 40.
9. Walter Minchinton, "Patterns and Structure of Demand, 1500–1750," in Cipolla, ed., *Fontana Economic History*, Vol. II, p. 98; Christopher Hill, *Society and Puritanism in Pre-Revolutionary England* (New York: Schocken, 1972), pp. 145 49.
10. Mols, *loc. cit.*, p. 40
11. *Ibid.*, pp. 42–43
12. *Ibid.*, p. 40.
13. Peter Mathias, *The First Industrial Nation* (New York: Scribners, 1969), p. 25.
14. Clifford Geertz, *Peddlers and Princes: Social Change and Economic Modernization in Two Indonesian Towns* (New York and Chicago: Univ. of Chicago, 1968), pp. 12–14, 28–47; "Social Change and Economic Modernization in Two Indonesian Towns: A Case in Point," in E. Hagen, ed., *On the Theory of Social Change* (Homewood, Ill.: Dorsey Press, 1962), pp. 390–93.

15. For analysis of the evolution of markets, see Fernand Braudel, *The Wheels of Commerce: Civilization and Capitalism, 15th–18th Century,* Vol. II (New York: Harper & Row, 1982), pp. 26–49, 67–75.
16. Robert Darnton, "A Bourgeois Puts His World in Order," in his *Great Cat Massacre,* pp. 136–38.
17. Braudel, *Capitalism and Material Life,* p. 204. See also Darnton, pp. 23–29.
18. See Darnton, "Peasants Tell Tales," *loc. cit.,* p. 26; Braudel, *Wheels of Commerce,* Vol. II, pp. 506–12; Ladourie, "The Rouergue Through the Lens," *loc. cit.,* pp. 183–85, 200–2.
19. In his essay "Food Supply and Public Order in Modern Europe," Tilly has analyzed data on the relationship between food supply and political change. See Charles Tilly, ed., *The Formation of National States in Western Europe* (Princeton: Princeton Univ., 1975), pp. 380–455. For analysis of one food riot in a small town in France during the late sixteenth century, see Emmanuel LeRoy Ladurie, *Carnival in Romans* (New York: George Braziller, 1979).
20. Minchinton, *loc. cit.,* p. 111.
21. *Ibid.,* p. 159.
22. Tilly, "Food Supply and Public Order," in his *Formation of National States,* p. 410.
23. *Ibid.,* p. 111; Samuel E. Finer, "State- and Nation-Building in Europe: The Role of the Military," Ch. 2 of Tilly, ed., p. 122.
24. Finer, *loc. cit.,* p. 134.
25. *Ibid.,* pp. 122, 130, 134, 140.
26. F. C. S. Northrop, *The Meeting of East & West* (New York: Macmillan, 1960; see esp. Ch. III, pp. 74–84.
27. Hill, *Society and Puritanism,* Ch. 4.
28. Adam Smith, *The Wealth of Nations* (New York: Modern Library), p. 423.
29. Geoffrey Parker, "The Emergence of Modern Finance in Europe," in Cipolla, ed., *Fontana Economic History,* Vol. II, p. 538.
30. Violet Barbour, *Capitalism in Amsterdam in the Seventeenth Century* (Ann Arbor: Univ. of Michigan, 1963), pp. 104–29 *passim.*
31. Robert Ashton, *The Crown and the Money Market, 1603–1640* (Oxford: Clarendon, 1960), p. 10.
32. Alfred B. Kerr, *Jacques Coeur, Merchant Prince of the Middle Ages* (New York: Scribners, 1927), Chs. 24–27, pp. 213–50.
33. J. F. Bosher, " 'Chambres de Justice' in the French Monarchy," in Bosher, ed., *French Government and Society, 1500–1850* (London: Athelone Press, 1973), p. 20.
34. *Ibid.,* pp. 20–40, esp. 27–29.
35. Fernand Braudel, *The Mediterranean and the Mediterranean World in the Age of Philip II,* Vol. I (New York: Harper & Row, 1966), pp. 501–2.
36. Richard Ehrenberg, *Capital and Finance in the Age of the Renaissance* (New York: Augustus M. Kelley, 1963), esp. pp. 21–63; Ashton, pp. 35–36, 40–46, 56, 61–62, 157–60, 169, 183, 190.
37. See Naomi Caiden and Aaron Wildavsky, *Planning and Budgeting in Poor Countries* (New York: John Wiley, 1974).
38. Parker, *loc. cit.,* p. 563.
39. Ashton, pp. 165–67, 175.

40. *Ibid.,* p. 183.
41. Parker, p. 535.
42. Ashton, pp. 26–27.
43. Parker, pp. 568, 570.
44. Braudel, *The Mediterranean,* Vol. I, p. 695.
45. Charles Wilson, *The Dutch Republic and the Civilization of the Seventeenth Century* (New York: McGraw-Hill, 1968), p. 25.
46. Barbour, p. 81.
47. *Ibid.,* p. 83. ˙
48. *Ibid.*
49. *Ibid.,* p. 81. See also Sir William Temple, "Observations on the United Provinces," in his *Collected Works,* Vol. I (New York: Greenwood Press, 1968), p. 188.
50. Quoted in P. G. M. Dickson, *The Financial Revolution in England: A Study in the Development of Public Credit, 1688–1756* (London: Macmillan, 1967), p. 5.
51. *Ibid.*
52. *Ibid.,* frontispiece.
53. Quoted in Dickson, p. 16, from a parliamentary debate of March 28, 1737.
54. Quoted in A. H. M. Jones, *A History of Rome Through the 5th Century,* Vol. I, *The Republic* (New York: Walker & Co., 1968), p. 277.
55. Rudolf Braun, "Taxation, Sociopolitical Structure and State-Building: Great Britain and Brandenburg-Prussia," in Charles Tilly, ed., p. 243, citing the sociologist of taxation Fritz Karl Mann, whose work, "Steurpolitische Ideale: Vergleichende Studien zur Geschichte der ökonomischen und politischen Ideen und ihres Wirkens in der öffentlichen Meinung 1600–1935," *Finanzwissenschaftliche Forschung,* 5, quotes Bodin's work of 1583 (L, VI, Ch. II, p. 855, pp. 5ff.).
56. Braudel, *The Mediterranean,* Vol. I, pp. 421–22.
57. Quoted in Ehrenberg, p. 22.
58. Goethe's *Faust,* transl. Sir Theodore Martin (New York and London: Everyman, 1971), Part II, Act I, p. 182.
59. *Ibid.,* p. 181.
60. Gustav Schmoller, *Umrisse und Untersuchungen zur Verfassungs- Verwaltungs- und Wirtschaftsgeschichte besonders des Preussischen Staates im 17. und 18. Jahrhundert* (Leipzig: Duncker & Humblot, 1898), p. 139.
61. K. W. Swart, *Sale of Offices in the Seventeenth Century* (Rotterdam: Martinus Nijhoff, 1949), p. 39.
62. Roland Mousnier, "Variations on the Main Theme," in Arthur J. Slavin, ed., *The "New Monarchies" and Representative Assemblies* (Boston: D. C. Heath, 1964), p. 12.
63. William R. Scott, *The Constitution and Finance of the English, Irish and Scottish Joint-Stock Companies to 1720,* Vol. I (Cambridge, Eng.: Cambridge Univ., 1912), pp. 171–72.
64. Douglas Dakin, *Turgot and the Ancien Régime in France* (New York: Octagon Books, 1965), p. 61.
65. See Ladurie, *Carnival in Romans,* pp. 36–39, and his "The Rouergue through the Lens," *loc. cit.,* p. 189.
66. Ian Gentiles, "Sale of Crown Lands During the English Revolution," *Eco-

nomic History Review, 2nd Series, Vol. XXVI, No. 4 (November 1973), pp. 614–35.

67. Lionel Rothkrug, *Opposition to Louis XIV: The Political and Social Origins of the French Enlightenment* (Princeton: Princeton Univ., 1965), pp. 424–25.

68. Braudel, *Capitalism and Material Life,* p. 355; Parker, *loc. cit.,* pp. 527–28.

69. Quoted in Braudel, *The Mediterranean,* Vol. I, p. 521.

70. Lawrence Stone has documented this process for England in his books and articles. See his *The Crisis of the Aristocracy, 1558–1641* (London: Oxford Univ., 1965), and *Family and Fortune* (London: Oxford, 1973); for the continental absolutisms, see Stuart Woolf, "The Aristocracy in Transition: A Continental Comparison," *Economic History Review,* 2nd Series, Vol. XXIII, No. 3 (December 1970), pp. 520–31.

71. Hugh Trevor-Roper, "The General Crisis of the Seventeenth Century," in Trevor Aston, ed., *Crisis in Europe, 1550–1650* (New York: Basic Books, 1965), p. 86.

72. Braudel, *The Mediterranean,* Vol. I, pp. 690–91.

73. Martin Wolfe, *The Fiscal System of Renaissance France* (New Haven: Yale Univ., 1972), pp. 262–63.

74. Swart, p. 26.

75. Quoted by Wolfe, p. 292.

76. *Ibid.,* p. 131; Julian Dent, *Crisis in Finance: Crown Financiers and Society in Seventeenth Century France* (Newton Abbot: David & Charles, 1973), p. 59: A. D. Lublinskaya, *French Absolutism: The Crucial Phase, 1620–29* (Cambridge, Eng.: Cambridge Univ., 1968), p. 230.

77. Eleanor C. Lodge, *Sully, Colbert and Turgot: A Chapter in French Economic History* (Port Washington, N.Y.: Kennikat Press, 1931, 1970), p. 97; Max Beloff, *The Age of Absolutism* (London: Hutchinson University Library, 1967), p. 73.

78. E. J. Coornaert, "European Economic Institutions and the New World: The Chartered Companies," in. *Cambridge Economic History of Europe,* Vol. IV (Cambridge, Eng.: Cambridge Univ., 1967), p. 227.

79. Betty Behrens, "Nobles, Privileges and Taxes in France at the End of the Ancien Régime," *Economic History Review,* 2nd Series, Vol. XV (1963), No. 3, p. 451.

80. Joseph Schumpeter, *History of Economic Analysis* (New York: Oxford Univ., 1955), p. 162.

81. C. H. Wilson, "Trade, Society, and the State," in *Cambridge Economic History,* Vol. IV, pp. 487–575 *passim.*

82. R. W. Harris, *Absolutism and the Enlightenment* (New York: Humanities Press, 1966), pp. 37–38; Wolfe, p. 351.

83. Ian Hacking, *The Emergence of Probability: A Philosophical Study of Early Ideas about Probability, Induction and Statistical Inference* (Cambridge, Eng.: Cambridge Univ., 1975), pp. 102, 105, 109.

84. Christopher Hill, *The Century of Revolution, 1603–1714* (New York: Norton, 1966), p. 218.

85. Gabriel Ardant, "Financial Policy and Infrastructure of Modern States and Nations," in Tilly, ed., pp. 164–242; Rudolf Braun, "Taxation, Sociopolitical Structure and State Building: Great Britain and Brandenburg-Prussia," in

Tilly, ed., pp. 243–327; James Vincent Vives, "The Decline of Spain in the Seventeenth Century," in Carlo Cipolla, ed., *The Economic Decline of Empires* (Oxford: Clarendon Press, 1970), pp. 123–92; Braudel, *The Mediterranean,* Vol. I, pp. 534–35; Cipolla, "The Economic Decline of Italy," in his *Economic Decline,* pp. 207–8; Doris Gill, "The Treasury, 1660–1714," *English Historical Review,* Vol. XLVI, No. 184 (October 1931), pp. 600–22.

86. Aston, p. 200.
87. A. E. Bland, P. A. Brown, and R. H. Tawney, *English Economic History: Select Documents* (London: Bell, 1915), p. 679.
88. *Ibid.,* p. 679.
89. Charles Tilly, "Food Supply and Public Order in Modern Europe," in Tilly, ed., pp. 380–455. For a detailed analysis of one food riot in France soon after the revolution, see his *The Vendée* (Cambridge, Mass.: Harvard Univ., 1976).
90. Bland, Brown, and Tawney, p. 679.
91. Dakin, p. 20.
92. Eugene Rotwein, ed., *David Hume: Writings on Economics* (Madison: Univ. of Wisconsin, 1955), p. lxxxii.
93. Robert Latham and William Matthew, eds., *The Diary of Samuel Pepys: A New and Complete Transcription* (London: Bell, 1971), Vol. I, pp. 222–23.
94. *Ibid.,* Vol. V, p. 134.
95. O. A. Ranum, *Richelieu and the Councillors of Louis XIII: A Study of the Secretaries of State and Superintendents of Finance in the Ministry of Richelieu, 1635–1642* (Oxford: Clarendon, 1963), p. 20.
96. Wolfram Fischer and Peter Lundgren, "The Recruitment and Training of Technical Personnel," in Tilly, ed., p. 461.
97. G. R. R. Treasure, *Cardinal Richelieu and the Development of Absolutism* (London: Black, 1972), pp. 143–46.
98. Compiled from data presented by Julian Dent in *Crisis in Finance,* pp. 35–40.
99. Joseph A. Pechman, *Federal Tax Policy* (Washington: Brookings Inst., 1973), p. 53.
100. From D. B. Horn and Mary Ransome, eds., *English Historical Documents, 1714–1783* (New York: Oxford Univ., 1957), pp. 328–29.
101. Julian Dent, "An Aspect of the Crisis of the Seventeenth Century: The Collapse of the Financial Administration of the French Monarchy, 1653–61," *Economic History Review,* 2nd Series, Vol. XX, No. 2 (August 1967), p. 252; Dent, *Crisis in Finance,* p. 98.
102. "Extracts of the Report of the Commissioners of Public Accounts, 1780–82," in Horn and Ransome, eds., p. 332; Ranum, pp. 125–26.
103. Martin Wolfe, pp. 279–80.
104. Braudel, *The Mediterranean,* Vol. I, p. 484 and note 142.
105. Report of the Commissioners of Public Accounts, in Horn and Ransome, eds., p. 331.
106. J. E. D. Binney, *British Public Finance and Administration, 1774–1792* (Oxford: Clarendon, 1958, pp. 54–55.
107. Report of the Commissioners of Public Accounts, in Horn and Ransome, eds., p. 331.
108. G. E. Aylmer, *The King's Servants: The Civil Service of Charles I, 1625–1642* (London: Routledge & Kegan Paul, 1974), Ch. 3.

109. Wolfe, p. 321.
110. Bosher, in Bosher, ed., pp. 20–40.
111. *Ibid.,* pp. 26–27.
112. Samuel Pepys, *Diary and Correspondence,* ed. Richard Braybrooke and M. Bright, Vols. V–VI (April 1665–Jan. 31, 1667) (New York: Dodd, Mead, 1887), p. 249.
113. Ranum, pp. 125–26; Dent, "An Aspect of the Crisis," p. 254; Wolfe, pp. 281–83; A. Neymarck, *Colbert et son temps* (Geneva: Slarkine Reprints, 1970), pp. 48–52.
114. Antonio Calabria, "Taxes and Budgets: The Neapolitan Fiscal System in the Sixteenth and Seventeenth Centuries" (mimeo), p. 59, note 3.
115. Otto Hinze, "Die Behoardanorganisation und die allgemeine Staatsverwaltung Preussens im 18. Jahrhundert Regierungsantritt," *Acta Borussia, Die Behoardanorganisation* 6/1 (Berlin: Paul Parey, 1901), pp. 189–97; Reinhold Dorwart, *The Administrative Reforms of Frederick William I of Prussia* (Cambridge, Mass.: Harvard Univ., 1953), pp. 152–79.
116. Paul Einzig, *The Control of the Purse: Progress and Decline of Parliament's Financial Control* (London: Secker & Warburg, 1959), pp. 141–42.
117. Alex Radian, "Budgeting in England from the Restoration to the Beginning of the Napoleonic Wars: Impoverished Kings, Affluent Kings and Wasteful Ministers" (mimeo) (Berkeley, 1972), p. 22.
118. John Sinclair, *A History of the Public Revenues of the British Empire* (London: Strahan, 1790), p. 93.
119. Adapted from Peter Mathias, Appendix, Table 13 (Net Public Expenditure 1700–1939), p. 463; Mathias took his data from B. R. Mitchell and P. Deane, *Abstract of British Historical Statistics* (1962), pp. 389–91, 396–99, 401–3.
120. Aylmer, pp. 113–20, 314.
121. Henry Roseveare, *The Treasury: The Evolution of a British Institution* (New York: Columbia Univ., 1969), p. 58.
122. Charles Davenant, *Discourses on the Public Revenues and the Trade of England* (London: Charles Knapton, 1698), pp. 114–15, 125.
123. Quoted in Binney, p. 8.
124. Speech before Parliament on economical reform, 1780, quoted in *The Oxford Dictionary of Quotations,* 2nd ed. (London: Oxford Univ., 1966), p. 101.
125. Dakin, pp. 155–56.
126. Quoted in Dakin, p. 131.
127. *Ibid.*
128. *Ibid.,* p. 167.
129. Quoted in Roseveare, p. 121.
130. *Ibid.,* p. 122.
131. From the Reports of the Commissioners appointed to examine, take and state the Public Accounts of the Kingdom, reproduced in Henry Roseveare, *The Treasury, 1660–1870: The Foundations of Control* (London and New York: George Allen & Unwin/Barnes & Noble, 1973), p. 149.
132. Binney, p. 110.

CHAPTER SIX

1. Arthur M. Okun, *Equality and Efficiency: The Big Tradeoff* (Washington: Brookings Inst., 1975).

2. Arthur D. Lynn, Jr., "Adam Smith's Fiscal Ideas: An Eclectic Revisited," *National Tax Journal,* December 1976, pp. 369–78; Adam Smith, *An Inquiry into the Nature and Causes of the Wealth of Nations,* ed. Cannon (New York: Modern Library, 1937), Book V, pp. 777–78.

3. Gertrude Himmelfarb, *The Idea of Poverty: England in the Early Industrial Age* (New York: Knopf, 1983), pp. 3–5.

4. Fernand Braudel, *The Wheels of Commerce: Civilization and Capitalism, 15th–18th Century,* Vol. 2 (New York: Harper & Row, 1979), pp. 507–8; Himmelfarb, pp. 27, 77.

5. Himmelfarb, pp. 39, 41, 68–69, 75–78, 149–52, 159–63, 167–68.

6. Charles Murray, *Losing Ground: American Social Policy, 1950–1980* (New York: Basic Books, 1984), pp. 201–3; Himmelfarb, pp. 69, 75.

7. Jack Wiseman, "Genesis, Aims and Goals of Social Policy," paper delivered at the 39th Congress of the International Institute of Public Finance, Budapest, Aug. 22–26, 1983 (mimeo), p. 17.

8. Himmelfarb, pp. 86–99, 209–15, 239–42, 285–87.

9. Thomas S. Ashton, "The Standard of Life of the Workers of England, 1790–1830," *Journal of Economic History,* Vol. IX (1949), Supplement, pp. 19–38. R. M. Hartwell, *The Industrial Revolution and Economic Growth* (London: Methuen, 1971), *passim;* E. J. Hobsbawm, "The British Standard of Living, 1790–1850, *Economic History Review,* 2nd Series, Vol. X (1957), No. 1, pp. 46–61.

10. Asa Briggs, *Victorian People* (Chicago: Univ. of Chicago, 1970), Ch. 4, *passim;* Himmelfarb, pp. 153–88.

11. John Stuart Mill, *Principles of Political Economy* (Boston: Little, Brown, 1848, Vol. II, Ch. XI, *passim.*

12. Peter Mathias, *The First Industrial Nation: An Economic History of Britain, 1700–1914* (New York: Scribners, 1983, p. 199; Himmelfarb, pp. 135–38, 142–43.

13. Walter Minchinton, "Patterns of Demand, 1750–1914," in Carlo Cipolla, ed., *The Fontana Economic History of Europe,* Vol. III, *The Industrial Revolution* (London and Glasgow: Collins/Fontana, 1973), pp. 115–19. J. F. Bergeier, "The Industrial Bourgeoisie and the Rise of the Working Class, 1700–1914," in Cipolla, ed., pp. 428–29.

14. Cipolla, ed., p. 123.

15. Quoted in Guy Routh, *The Origin of Economic Ideas* (New York: Vintage, 1977), p. 206. See also Roger Price, ed., *1848 in France* (Ithaca: Cornell Univ., 1975), pp. 20–42; and Charles Tilly, "Food Supply and Public Order in Modern Europe," in Tilly, ed., *The Formation of National States in Western Europe* (Princeton: Princeton Univ., 1977), pp. 449–50.

16. Minchinton, *loc. cit.,* p. 156, based on data from Simon Kuznets, *Modern Economic Growth-Rate, Structures and Spread* (New Haven: Yale Univ., 1966), pp. 88–93.

17. Maurice Flamant and Jeanne Singer-Kerel, *Modern Economic Crises and Recessions* (New York and Evanston: Harper Colophon, 1970), pp. 13–52 *passim.*

18. Kuznets, pp. 208–9; Mark Abrams, *The Condition of the British People, 1911–1945* (London: Gollancz, 1946), p. 110, quoted in Minchinton, *loc. cit.,* p. 114.

19. Briggs, pp. 116–39; Routh, pp. 181–97; Theodore S. Hamerow, *The Birth of a*

New Europe: State and Society in the Nineteenth Century (Chapel Hill and London: Univ. of North Carolina, 1983), pp. 267, 278.

20. Joseph A. Schumpeter, *History of Economic Analysis* (New York: Oxford Univ., 1954), pp. 769–70.

21. Sidney Pollard, *The Genesis of Modern Management* (London: Edward Arnold, 1965), pp. 209–72 *passim.*

22. Henry Roseveare, *The Treasury: Evolution of a British Institution* (New York: Columbia Univ., 1969), pp. 150–53.

23. René Stourm, *The Budget,* transl. Thaddeus Plazinski (New York: Appleton, 1917), p. 511.

24. Frances E. Gillespie, *Labour and Politics in England, 1850–1867* (Durham, N.C.: Duke Univ., 1927), p. 41.

25. Stourm, p. 259.

26. W. O. Henderson, *The State and Industrial Revolution in Prussia, 1480–1870* (Liverpool: Univ. of Liverpool, 1958), p. 124.

27. L. C. A. Knowles, *Economic Development in the Nineteenth Century* (London: Routledge & Sons, 1932), p. 257.

28. James E. Alt, "The Evolution of Tax Structures, *Public Choice,* Vol. 41 (1983), p. 200.

29. B. E. V. Sabine, *A History of Income Tax* (London: George Allen & Unwin, 1966), pp. 26–43 *passim.*

30. E. P. Thompson, *The Making of the English Working Class* (New York: Vintage, 1963, pp. 303–5, 470, 603–4, 621, 757; Himmelfarb, p. 209.

31. Alexander Llewellyn, *The Decade of Reform: The 1830s* (New York: St. Martin's Press, 1971), p. 158.

32. Hamerow, p. 273.

33. Sabine, p. 96.

34. See James Buchanan, "The Pure Theory of Public Finance," in his *Fiscal Theory and Political Economy* (Chapel Hill: Univ. of North Carolina, 1960), pp. 8–23, and "The Italian Tradition in Fiscal Theory," *loc. cit.,* pp. 31, 35–36; Aaron Wildavsky, "The Political Economy of Efficiency," *Public Administration Review,* Vol. 26, December 1966, pp. 7–14.

35. Edwin Seligman, *Progressive Taxation in Theory and Practice* (Princeton: Princeton Univ., 1908); Seligman, *The Income Tax* (New York: Macmillan, 1914); Joseph Pechman, *Federal Tax Policy* (Washington: Brookings Inst., 1971, pp. 247–48.

36. Sabine, pp. 27–28.

37. F. Shehab, *Progressive Taxation: A Study in the Development of the Progressive Principle in the British Income Tax* (Oxford: Clarendon, 1953), pp. 48–50.

38. Sabine, p. 63.

39. Shehab, p. 50.

40. *Ibid.,* p. 52.

41. *Ibid.,* pp. 39–42.

42. *Ibid.,* pp. 210–211, notes.

43. James E. Thorold Rogers, "Local Taxation, Especially in English Cities and Towns," a speech delivered before Parliament March 23, 1886 (London: Cassell & Co., 1886), pp. 12, 19.

44. Hamerow, p. 310.

45. Shehab, p. 213n.
46. Jens Alber, *Von Armenhaus zum Wohlfahrtsstaat: Analysen zur Entwicklung der Sozialversicherung in Westeuropa* (Frankfurt: Campus Verlag, 1982).
47. Peter Gay and R. K. Webb, *Modern Europe* (New York: Harper and Row, 1973), p. 798.
48. Hamerow, pp. 278–79.
49. Avner Offner, "Empire and Social Reform: British Overseas Investment and Domestic Politics, 1908–1914," *The Historical Journal,* Vol. 26 (1983), No. 1, pp. 120–21.
50. *Ibid.,* p. 123.
51. *Ibid.,* pp. 123–24.
52. John Grigg, *Lloyd George: The People's Champion, 1902–1911* (Berkeley: Univ. of California, 1978), p. 179.
53. Derived from B. R. Mitchell, *European Historical Statistics, 1750–1970* (New York: Columbia Univ., 1975).
54. Sven Steinmo, "Taxation as an Instrument of Public Policy: Sweden—the Carrot and the Stick," paper presented to the European Consortium of Political Research, Salzburg, Austria, April 13–18, 1984 (mimeo), p. 6.
55. Daniel Tarschys, "Government Growth: The Case of Sweden, 1523–1983," Glasgow: University of Strathclyde, Center for the Study of Public Policy, Studies in Public Policy #121, 1983, p. 12.
56. C. F. Bastable, *Public Finance* (London: Macmillan, 1903), p. 136.
57. Giandomenico Majone and Aaron Wildavsky, "Implementation as Evolution," in their *Implementation,* 2nd ed. (Berkeley, Los Angeles, London: Univ. of California, 1979), pp. 177–94, and the citation therein (n. 8, p. 184); John Henry Newman, *An Essay on the Development of Christian Doctrine* (New York: Longmans, Green, 1949), pp. 98–99.

CHAPTER SEVEN

1. Henry Carter Adams, *The Science of Finance: An Investigation of Public Expenditures and Public Revenues* (New York: Henry Holt, 1899), p. 8.
2. James "Lord" Bryce, *The American Commonwealth* (London: Macmillan, 1891), p. 188.
3. Louis Hartz, *The Liberal Tradition in America* (New York: Harcourt, Brace, 1955).
4. Alexis de Tocqueville, *Democracy in America* (New York: Knopf, 1945).
5. Anthony King, "Ideas, Institutions and the Policies of Governments: A comparative analysis: Part III," *British Journal of Political Science,* Vol. 3, No. 4 (October 1973), pp. 409–23.
6. Seymour Martin Lipset, "Why No Socialism in the United States?", in Seweryn Bialer and Sophia Sluzar, eds., *Sources of Contemporary Radicalism* (Boulder, Colo.: Westview Press, 1977).
7. William J. Shultz and M. R. Caine, *Financial Development of the United States* (New York: Prentice-Hall, 1937), pp. 7–9.
8. *Ibid.,* p. 10.
9. Margaret G. Myers, *A Financial History of the United States* (New York: Columbia Univ., 1970), p. 3; and Davis R. Dewey, *Financial History of the United States* (New York: Longmans, Green, 1939), pp. 18–19.

10. Shultz and Caine, *Financial Development of the United States,* p. 9.
11. Dewey, p. 8.
12. Charles Bullock, "The Finances of the United States from 1775–1789 With Special Reference to the Budget," *Bulletin of the University of Wisconsin,* Vol. 1 (1894–1896), p. 225.
13. The act prohibited issuance of bills of credit in England and then in America.
14. Myers, *A Financial History of the U.S.,* p. 11.
15. Gary B. Nash, *The Urban Crucible: Social Change, Political Consciousness and the Origins of the American Revolution* (Cambridge, Mass.: Harvard Univ., 1979), pp. 60–70.
16. *Ibid.,* pp. 225–53.
17. Myers, *A Financial History of the U.S.,* p. 10. Franklin's argument was so effective his printing company got the contract for putting out the paper money. The money Franklin left in his will to aid industrious and honest mechanics reflected in large part his recognition of the difficulty ordinary people faced in amassing any amount of capital in the absence of a plentiful sound currency.
18. Dewey, *Financial History of the U.S.,* pp. 23–30.
19. Shultz and Caine, *Financial Development of the U.S.,* p. 23.
20. Dewey, pp. 9–10.
21. Myers, pp. 15–16; and Dewey, pp. 11–12.
22. Myers, pp. 17–18; and Dewey, p. 17.
23. Shultz and Caine, p. 15.
24. See Robert C. Tucker and David C. Hendrickson, *The Fall of the First British Empire: Origins of the War of American Independence* (Baltimore and London: Johns Hopkins, 1982), pp. 152–59, 174–75, 406–10.
25. Bullock, "Finances of the United States from 1775–1789," *loc. cit.,* pp. 217, 225.
26. *Ibid.,* pp. 216–19.
27. *Ibid.,* pp. 219–21.
28. *Ibid,* p. 218.
29. Shultz and Caine, pp. 60–61.
30. Myers, pp. 30–31; and Bullock, pp. 214–15.
31. Shultz and Caine, p. 69.
32. William Graham Sumner, *The Financier and the Finances of the American Revolution* (New York: Dodd, Mead, 1891), pp. 301–2.
33. *Ibid.,* pp. 302–3.
34. Theodore J. Grayson, *Leaders and Periods of American Finance* (New York: Wiley, 1932), pp. 36–37.
35. Sumner, p. 301.
36. Grayson, p. 34.
37. *Ibid.,* pp. 44–45.
38. See Shultz and Caine, pp. 37–38.
39. Albert S. Bolles, *The Financial History of the United States, 1774–89* (New York: Appleton, 1879), p. 201. For a persuasive argument that colonial finance under the Articles was not nearly so bad as claimed, see E. James Ferguson, *The Power of the Purse: A History of American Public Finance, 1776–1790* (Chapel Hill: Univ. of North Carolina, 1961).
40. Bullock, "Finances of the United States from 1775–1789," *loc. cit.,* pp. 115–20.
41. Pelatiah Webster, *Political Essays on the Nature and Operation of Money, Public*

Finances, and Other Subjects (Philadelphia: Joseph Crukshank, 1791), p. 145.
42. Thomas Jefferson to John Taylor, Nov. 26, 1798, in *Works,* ed. Paul Leicester
    Ford, Vol. VIII (New York: G. P. Putnam's Sons, Knickerbocker Press, 1904),
    p. 481.
43. Alexis de Tocqueville, *Democracy in America,* Vol. 1, p. 222.
44. See Samuel P. Huntington's *The Common Defense* (New York: Columbia
    Univ., 1969); and Patrick Crecine et al., "Presidential Management of Budge-
    tary and Fiscal Policymaking," *Political Science Quarterly,* Vol. 95, No. 3 (Fall
    1980), pp. 395–425, for contemporary versions during the administrations of
    Harry S. Truman and Dwight D. Eisenhower.
45. Dall W. Forsythe, *Taxation and Political Change in the Young Nation,
    1781–1833* (New York: Columbia Univ., 1977), p. 38.
46. Lewis H. Kimmel, *Federal Budget and Fiscal Policy, 1789–1958* (Washington:
    Brookings Inst., 1959), p. 8.
47. *Ibid.,* p. 9.
48. Forsythe, *Taxation and Political Change,* p. 31.
49. *Ibid.,* pp. 28–29.
50. Kimmel, *Federal Budget and Fiscal Policy,* p. 14.
51. *Ibid.*
52. We are indebted to James Savage's dissertation on the balanced-budget idea
    for elaboration of this point. James Savage, "Balanced Budgets and American
    Politics," dissertation in progress, Political Science Dept., Univ. of California,
    Berkeley, 1983. All serious students of this subject should read his thesis.
53. Kimmel, pp. 27–28; and Forsythe, p. 60.
54. Kimmel, pp. 16–17.
55. *Ibid.,* pp. 17–18.
56. *Ibid.,* pp. 19–21.
57. *Ibid.,* pp. 20–22.
58. *Ibid.,* p. 22.
59. *Ibid.,* p. 23.
60. *Ibid.,* p. 24.
61. *Ibid.,* pp. 24–25.
62. *Ibid.,* pp. 25–26.
63. *Ibid.,* pp. 26–27.
64. *Ibid.,* pp. 65–69.
65. *Ibid.,* pp. 71–73.
66. *Ibid.,* pp. 87–88.
67. *Ibid.,* pp. 84–85.
68. *Ibid.,* p. 88.
69. *Ibid.,* p. 96.
70. Albert Gallatin, Secretary of the Treasury under Thomas Jefferson, quoted in
    Leonard D. White, *The Jeffersonians: A Study in Administrative History,
    1801–1829* (New York: Macmillan, 1951), pp. 474–75.
71. Robert Fulton, quoted, *ibid.,* pp. 474–75.
72. Shultz and Caine, *Financial Development of the U.S.,* pp. 134–35.
73. Myers, *A Financial History of the U.S.,* pp. 106–8.
74. Shultz and Caine, pp. 137–40.
75. Leonard D. White, *The Jeffersonians,* p. 483.

76. Myers, pp. 108–9.
77. Kimmel, *Federal Budget and Fiscal Policy*, p. 19; and White, *Jeffersonians*, p. 483.
78. See Joseph L. Blau, ed., *Social Theories of Jacksonian Democracy* (New York: Bobbs-Merrill, 1954).
79. Louis Hartz, *Economic Policy and Democratic Thought: Pennsylvania, 1776–1860* (Chicago: Quadrangle, 1968).
80. See Henry C. Adams, *Public Debts: An Essay in the Science of Finance* (New York: Appleton, 1887), p. 321; and B. U. Ratchford, *American State Debts* (Durham: Duke Univ., 1941), pp. 77–83. "Creating a Symbol: Balanced Budgets and American Politics, Colonial America to the Civil War," Ch. Three of James Savage's dissertation, is an indispensable guide to the intricacies of this subject.
81. Kimmel, *Federal Budget and Fiscal Policy*, pp. 31–32.
82. *Ibid.*, p. 33.
83. *Ibid.*, pp. 34–35.
84. *Ibid.*, p. 34.
85. *Ibid.*, p. 41.
86. *Ibid.*, p. 52.
87. Leonard D. White, *The Jacksonians: A Study in Administrative History, 1829–1861* (New York: Macmillan, 1954), p. 438.
88. *Ibid.*, pp. 450–51.
89. *Ibid.*, p. 451.
90. *Ibid.*, p. 442.
91. *Ibid.*, pp. 450–51.
92. Myers, *Financial History of the U.S.*, p. 116.
93. *Ibid.*, pp. 115–16.
94. Shultz and Caine, *Financial Development of the U.S.*, pp. 235–36; see also Myers, p. 109.
95. Kimmel, p. 57.
96. Annual Report of the Secretary of the Treasury on the State of the Finances for the Fiscal Year Ended June 30, 1934, pp. 302–3, in Kimmel, p. 57.
97. Kimmel, pp. 71–72.
98. *Ibid.*, pp. 70–71.
99. E. E. Naylor, *The Federal Budget System in Operation* (Washington: Hayworth Printing, 1941), pp. 20–21.
100. Richard F. Fenno, Jr., *The Power of the Purse: Appropriations Politics in Congress* (Boston: Little, Brown, 1966), pp. 43–44. For a revealing analysis of the political forces at work, see James I. Lengle, "The Appropriations Process as a Political Instrument: House Reorganization in 1885," typescript, 1973.
101. Fenno, p. 43.
102. Lucius Wilmerding, Jr., *The Spending Power: A History of the Efforts of Congress to Control Expenditures* (New Haven: Yale Univ., 1943), pp. 143–44.
103. Woodrow Wilson, *Congressional Government: A Study in American Politics* (Boston: Houghton Mifflin, 1892), pp. 168–69.
104. Quoted in Edward A. Fitzpatrick, *Budget Making in a Democracy: A New View of the Budget* (New York: Macmillan, 1918), p. 212.
105. See James Savage, "Republican Party Government: 1860–1932," Ch. Five of his dissertation in progress, "Balanced Budgets and American Politics."

106. Bennett D. Baack and Edward John Ray, "The Political Economy of the Origin and Development of the Federal Income Tax," in Robert Higgs, ed., *Emergence of the Modern Political Economy* (Greenwich, Conn.: JAI Press, forthcoming). See also Baack and Ray, "The Political Economy of Tariff Policy: A Case Study of the United States," *Explorations in Economic History,* Vol. 20 (1983), pp. 73–93.

107. Baack and Ray, "Special Interests and Constitutional Amendments: A Study of the Adoption of the Income Tax in the U.S.," Working Paper No. 84–5, Dept. of Economics, Ohio State Univ., September 1983, p. 2.

108. Douglas C. North, "The Growth of Government in the United States: An Economic Historian's Perspective," typescript, May 1984.

109. William Franklin Willoughby, *The Problem of a National Budget* (New York: Appleton, 1918), pp. 55–56.

110. Leonard D. White, *The Federalists: A Study in Administrative History* (New York: Macmillan, 1961), p. 14.

111. *Ibid.,* p. 29.

112. *Ibid.,* pp. 90–91.

113. Shultz and Caine, *Financial Development of the U.S.,* p. 100.

114. Forsythe, *Taxation and Political Change,* pp. 44–45.

115. *Ibid.,* pp. 39–40.

116. *Ibid.,* pp. 41–46.

117. Shultz and Caine, p. 93.

118. White, *Federalists,* pp. 118–19.

119. Shultz and Caine, pp. 93–94.

120. White, *Federalists,* p. 70.

121. *Ibid.,* p. 94.

122. James Sterling Young, *The Washington Community, 1800–1828* (New York: Columbia Univ., 1966), *inter alia,* esp. pp. 128–31, 163–77.

123. White, *Federalists,* p. 291.

124. White, *Jeffersonians,* pp. 404–5.

125. See Herbert Kaufman, "Emerging Conflicts in the Doctrines of Public Administration," *American Political Science Review,* Vol. 50, December 1956, pp. 1057–73.

126. White, *Federalists,* p. 324.

127. *Ibid.,* p. 329.

128. White, *Jacksonians,* p. 126.

129. *Ibid.,* p. 123.

130. *Ibid.,* pp. 126–27.

131. *Ibid.,* p. 131.

132. *Ibid.,* p. 141, and Bolles, *Financial History of the United States, 1774–89,* pp. 539–40.

133. White, *Jacksonians,* pp. 133–34.

134. *Ibid.,* pp. 134–35.

135. Wilmerding, *Spending Power,* pp. 137–47.

136. Albert S. Bolles, *The Financial History of the United States: From 1861 to 1885* (New York: Appleton, 1886), pp. 530–31.

137. White, *Jacksonians,* p. 138.

138. *Ibid.,* pp. 138–40.

139. Wilmerding, pp. 152–53.

140. *Ibid.,* p. 14.
141. Bolles, *Financial History, 1861–1885,* p. 231.
142. Wilmerding, p. 154.
143. White, *Jacksonians,* pp. 126–27.
144. Bolles, *Financial History: 1861–1885,* pp. 544–45. Senator Ingalls' estimate of $18 or $20 million total costs went up in a few years to $50 million and then to $100 million, an overrun of a kind we have become accustomed to in our time, but which was quite alarming in those days. Yet it had ample historical precedent. The modest veterans' pensions granted by Julius Caesar, when he became Rome's first emperor, established legal claims that, after several centuries of inflation and war, raised Rome's pension obligations to monumental proportions. See Chapter Three, pages 99*n*, 111, 125.
145. Frederick Cleveland, "Leadership and Criticism," *Proceedings of the Academy of Political Science,* Vol. 8 (1918–20), No. 1, p. 31.
146. Wilson, *Congressional Government,* pp. 136–37.
147. A. E. Buck, *Public Budgeting* (New York: Harper, 1929), p. 339.
148. Wilson, *Congressional Government,* p. 156.
149. Wilmerding, *Spending Power,* pp. 151–52.
150. Fenno, *Power of the Purse,* p. 99.
151. See Aaron Wildavsky, *The Politics of the Budgetary Process,* 4th ed. (Boston: Little, Brown, 1984), pp. 47–62, 73.
152. Dwight Waldo, *The Administrative State* (New York: Ronald Press, 1948), p. 105.
153. René Stourm, quoted in A. E. Buck, *Public Budgeting,* p. 285.
154. Frederick Cleveland and Arthur E. Buck, *The Budget and Responsible Government* (New York: Macmillan, 1920), p. 54.
155. *Ibid.,* p. 403.
156. *Ibid.,* p. 68.
157. Nicholas M. Butler, "Executive Responsibility and a National Budget," *Proceedings of the Academy of Political Science,* Vol. 8 (1918–20), p. 46.
158. Wilson, *Congressional Government,* p. 284.
159. *Ibid.,* p. 285.
160. Frederick A. Cleveland, "Need for Re-adjustment of Relations Between the Executive and Legislative Branches of Government," in F. A. Cleveland and J. Schafer, eds., *Democracy in Reconstruction* (Boston: Houghton Mifflin, 1919), p. 443.
161. Willoughby, *Problem of a National Budget,* pp. 29–30.
162. Wilson, *Congressional Government,* p. 283.
163. Woodrow Wilson, *College and State Educational, Literary and Political Papers, 1875–1913,* Vol. 1 (New York: Harper, 1925), p. 357.
164. Willoughby, *Problem of a National Budget,* pp. 116–17.
165. Quoted in Wilmerding, *The Spending Power,* p. 150.
166. Charles Wallace Collins, *The National Budget System* (New York: Macmillan, 1917), p. 3.
167. Willoughby, *Problem of a National Budget,* pp. 56–57.
168. *Ibid.,* p. ix.
169. Wilmerding, *The Spending Power,* pp. 258–59.
170. *Ibid.,* p. 283.

171. Arthur Macmahon, "Woodrow Wilson: Political Leader and Administrator," in Earl Latham, ed., *The Philosophy and Policies of Woodrow Wilson* (Chicago: Univ. of Chicago, 1958), pp. 100–22; reference is to page 113.
172. Wilson, *Congressional Government*, pp. 180–81.
173. Charles Beard, "Prefatory Note," *Municipal Research*, No. 88 (August 1917) (New York: Bureau of Municipal Research), p. iii.
174. Willoughby, *Problem of a National Budget*, p. 55.
175. Dwight Waldo, *The Administrative State*, pp. 105–7.
176. Wilson, *Congressional Government*, p. 282.
177. Cleveland and Buck, *Budget and Responsible Government*, p. 13.
178. Willoughby, *Problem of a National Budget*, pp. 98–99.
179. William Franklin Willoughby, "The Budget as an Instrument of Political Reform," *Proceedings of the Academy of Political Science*, Vol. 8 (1918–20), pp. 59–60; and Willoughby, *Problem of a National Budget*, p. 98.
180. Butler, "Executive Responsibility and a National Budget," *loc. cit.*, p. 49.
181. Willoughby, *Problem of a National Budget*, p. 32.
182. A. E. Buck, "The Development of the Budget Idea in the United States," *Annals of the American Academy of Political and Social Science*, Vol. LXIII, May 1924, p. 36.
183. Willoughby, *Problem of a National Budget*, pp. 33–34.
184. Buck, *Public Budgeting*, p. 482.
185. Willoughby, *Problem of a National Budget*, pp. 59–60.
186. Cleveland and Buck, *Budget and Responsible Government*, p. xviii.
187. Willoughby, *Problem of a National Budget*, p. 405.
188. Cleveland and Buck, *Budget and Responsible Government*, pp. xviii–xix.
189. Collins, *National Budget System*, p. 41.
190. Fitzpatrick, *Budget Making in a Democracy*, p. 55.
191. *Ibid.*, pp. viii–ix.
192. *Ibid.*, p. ix.
193. *Ibid.*, p. 49.
194. *Ibid.*, pp. 50–51, 59.
195. *Ibid.*, p. 54.
196. *Ibid.*, p. 5.
197. *Ibid.*, p. 292.
198. Oscar Kraines, *Congress and the Challenge of Big Government* (New York: Bookman Associates, 1958), pp. 44–45; see also the foreword by Dwight Waldo, p. 7.
199. *Ibid.*, pp. 56–57.
200. Jesse Burkhead, *Government Budgeting* (New York and London: Wiley/Chapman & Hall, 1956), p. 13.
201. Waldo, *The Administrative State*, pp. 193–94.
202. Buck, "The Development of the Budget Idea in the United States," *loc. cit.*, p. 31.
203. Burkhead, *Government Budgeting*, p. 50.
204. Cathryn Secler-Hudson, "Budgeting: An Instrument of Planning and Management. Unit I, The Evolution of the Budgetary Concept in the Federal Government," typescript, American University, 1944.
205. Oscar Kraines, "The President versus Congress: The Keep Commission,

1905–1909, First Comprehensive Presidential Inquiry into Administration," *Western Political Quarterly,* Vol. 23, No. 1 (March 1970), p. 45.

206. Burkhead, *Government Budgeting,* p. 17.
207. Naylor, *Federal Budget System in Operation,* pp. 23–24.
208. Cleveland, "Leadership and Criticism," *loc. cit.,* p. 33.
209. Naylor, *Federal Budget System in Operation,* p. 24.
210. Wilmerding, *Spending Power,* p. 151; and Burkhead, *Government Budgeting,* p. 119.
211. Naylor, *Federal Budget System in Operation,* pp. 24–25.
212. Burkhead, *Government Budgeting,* pp. 20–21.
213. Frederick A. Cleveland, "Constitutional Provisions for a Budget," *Proceedings of the Academy of Political Science,* Vol. 5 (1914), No. 1, pp. 141–62.
214. Buck, *Public Budgeting,* p. 21.
215. Willoughby, *Problem of a National Budget,* pp. 155–56.
216. Naylor, *Federal Budget System in Operation,* pp. 25–26.
217. Fritz Morstein Marx, "The Bureau of the Budget: Its Evolution and Present Role," *American Political Science Review,* Vol. 39, No. 4 (August 1945), pp. 653–84.
218. See Charles G. Dawes's still indispensable book, *The First Year of the Budget of the United States* (New York: Harper, 1923).
219. *Ibid.,* p. 29.
220. Quoted in William Franklin Willoughby, *The National Budget System with Suggestions for Its Improvement* (Baltimore: Johns Hopkins, 1927), pp. 287–88.
221. *Ibid.,* pp. 286–87.
222. Thomas Borcherding, "A Hundred Years of Public Spending, 1870–1970," in Borcherding, ed., *Budgets and Bureaucrats: Sources of Government Growth* (Durham: Duke Univ., 1977), p. 20.
223. *Ibid.,* p. 26.
224. Shultz and Caine, pp. 518–19.
225. Jens P. Jensen, *Property Taxation in the United States* (Chicago: Univ. of Chicago, 1931).
226. See Richard Netzer, *Economics of the Property Tax* (Washington: Brookings Inst., 1966), for a persuasive contrary argument.
227. Sidney Ratner, *American Taxation: Its History as a Social Force in Democracy* (New York: Norton, 1942).
228. L. L. Ecker-Racz, *The Politics and Economics of State–Local Finance* (Englewood Cliffs: Prentice-Hall, 1970).
229. Randolph E. Paul, *Taxation in the United States* (Boston: Little, Brown, 1954).
230. Clinton Yearly, *The Money Machines: The Breakdown and Reform of Governmental and Party Finance in the North, 1860–1920* (Albany: State Univ. of New York, 1970), p. 85.
231. Sidney Ratner, *Taxation and Democracy in America* (New York: Wiley & Sons, 1942), Ch. 5; cited in John Witte, *The Politics and Development of the Federal Income Tax* (Madison: Univ. of Wisconsin, 1985), p. 69.
232. *Congressional Globe,* 38th Congress, 1st Session, p. 1940; quoted in part in Ratner, *Taxation and Democracy,* and in Witte, *Politics and Development.*
233. David Hill in *Congressional Record,* 53rd Congress, 2nd Session, Vol. 26, pp.

3557–68; and a later speech on June 21, 1894, pp. 6611–24 of same volume; cited in Witte, p. 71.

234. *Congressional Record,* 53rd Congress, 2nd Session, Vol. 26, p. 6711, cited in Witte, p. 72.

235. Congressman Bourke Cochran in *Congressional Record,* 53rd Congress, 2nd Session, Vol. 26, Appendix, pp. 462–67, cited in Witte, p. 72.

236. William Jennings Bryan in *Congressional Record,* 53rd Congress, 2nd Session, Vol. 26, p. 1656, quoted in Witte, p. 72.

237. *Congressional Record,* 53rd Congress, 2nd Session, Vol. 26, p. 1656, cited in Witte, p. 73.

238. See Louis Eisenstein, *The Ideologies of Taxation* (New York: Ronald Press, 1961), pp. 16–18.

239. Witte, pp. 74–75.

240. *Ibid.,* p. 79.

241. Charles Gilbert, *American Financing of World War I* (Westport, Conn.: Greenwood Press, 1970), pp. 114–15; cited in Witte, p. 86.

242. Andrew Mellon, *Taxation: The People's Business* (New York: Macmillan, 1924), p. 16; quoted in Witte, p. 89.

243. See Eisenstein, p. 49.

244. Cordell Hull in *Congressional Record,* Vol. 67 (1921), p. 563; quoted in Witte, pp. 91–92.

245. Paul, *Taxation in the United States;* Herbert Stein, *The Fiscal Revolution in America* (Chicago: Univ. of Chicago, 1969); and Frank W. Taussig, *The Tariff History of the United States,* 8th rev ed. (New York: Putnam, 1931).

246. *Report of the Treasurer of the United States for the Year Ended June 30, 1931* (Washington: U.S. Government, 1931), p. 29; quoted in Witte, p. 96.

247. Paul, *Taxation in the United States, p. 203; cited in Witte, p. 103.*

248. *Joseph Pechman, Federal Tax Policy* (Washington: Brookings Inst., 1971), pp. 256–57.

249. *Ibid.,* p. 215.

CHAPTER EIGHT

1. John Maynard Keynes, *The General Theory of Employment, Interest and Money* (New York: Macmillan, 1936), pp. 483–84.

2. R. F. Kahn, "The Relation of Home Investment to Unemployment," *Economic Journal,* Vol. XLI, No. 162 (June 1931), pp. 173–98.

3. Robert Lekachman, *The Age of Keynes* (New York: McGraw-Hill, 1966), pp. 73–75.

4. Harvey Stephen Perloff, *Modern Budget Policies: A Study of the Budget Process in Present-Day Society,* Ph.D. dissertation submitted to the Depts. of Government and Economics, Harvard Univ., Dec. 1, 1939, p. 140.

5. *Ibid.,* pp. 139–40.

6. Dan Throop Smith, "An Analysis of Changes in Federal Finances, July 1930–June 1938," *Review of Economic Statistics,* Vol. 20, November 1938, pp. 149–60; cited in H. Perloff, p. 140.

7. Gunnar Myrdal, *Varning för fredsoptimism* (Stockholm: Bonniers, 1944).

8. For a history of spending in France from 1900 to 1980, see Robert Delorme and Christine André, *L'État et l'économie* (Paris: Seuil, 1983).

9. Jèze Gaston and Henri Truchy, *The War Finance of France* (New Haven: Yale Univ., 1927), p. 177.

10. Source for GNP, J. Carré, P. Dubois, and E. Malinvaud, *French Economic Growth* (Stanford: Stanford Univ., 1975), p. 24; for total expenditure, *Annuaire statistique de la France: Résumé rétrospectif,* 1951, p. 311; for defense, *ibid.,* 1951, p. 310; for taxes, *ibid.,* 1966, pp. 486–89.

11. Gaston and Truchy, p. 121.

12. George Peel, *The Financial Crisis of France* (London: MacMillan, 1926), Ch. III, and Robert M. Haig, *The Public Finances of Post-War France* (New York: Columbia Univ., 1929), Ch. II.

13. Source for GNP, C. H. Feinstein, *National Income Expenditures and Output of the United Kingdom* (Cambridge, Eng.: Cambridge Univ., 1972), Table 3.7; for total expenditures, *ibid.,* Table 14; for defense, A. T. Peacock and J. Wiseman, *The Growth of Public Expenditures in the United Kingdom* (Princeton: Princeton Univ., 1961), Table A-7.

14. Samuel J. Horwitz, *State Intervention in Great Britain* (New York: Columbia Univ., 1949), p. 287.

15. Kathleen Burke, ed., *War and the State* (Winchester, Eng.: Allen & Unwin, 1982).

16. Source for GNP, U.S. Bureau of the Census, *Historical Statistics of the U.S. Since Colonial Times* (Washington: U.S. Government Printing Office, 1976), p. 224; for tax, *ibid.,* p. 1106; for defense, *ibid.,* p. 1114; for total, U.S. Bureau of the Census, *Historical Statistics of the U.S. from Colonial Times to 1957* (Stamford, Conn.: Fairfield Publishing Co., 1960), p. 711.

17. U.S. Bureau of the Census, *Historical Statistics of the United States, Colonial Times to 1970,* Bicentennial ed., Part 2 (Washington, 1975), p. 168.

18. Gaston v. Rimlinger, *Welfare Policy and Industrialization: Europe, America and Russia* (New York: Wiley, 1971), p. 65.

19. "In Financing the War," *Annals of the American Academy of Political and Social Science,* Vol. LXXV, January 1981, p. 14.

20. Cited in Lewis H. Kimmel, *Federal Budget and Fiscal Policy: 1789–1958* (Washington: Brookings Inst., 1959), p. 88.

21. *Ibid.,* p. 89.

22. *Ibid.,* p. 89ff.

23. James Weinstein, *The Corporate Ideal in the Liberal State, 1900–1918* (Boston: Beacon Press, 1968), pp. 40–41.

24. *Ibid.,* p. 61.

25. *Ibid.,* pp. 208–9.

26. Alan Peacock and Jack Wiseman, *The Growth of Public Expenditures in the United Kingdom* (Princeton: Princeton Univ., 1961), pp. xxi, xxxi, and Ch. 1.

27. This section is adapted from a paper by John B. Gilmour.

28. Karl Hardach, *The Political Economy of Germany in the Twentieth Century* (Berkeley, Calif.: Univ. of Calif., 1980).

29. League of Nations, *Memorandum on Public Finance:* 1921, 1922, 1922–1926, 1926–1928, Geneva.

30. John Maynard Keynes, *Essays in Persuasion* (New York: Norton, 1963).

31. Peter Flora and Arnold Heidenheimer, eds., *Development of Welfare States in Europe and America* (New Brunswick: Transaction Books, 1981).

32. Dankwart Rustow, *The Politics of Compromise* (Princeton: Princeton Univ., 1955), p. 91.
33. Suphan Andic and Jindrich Veverka, "The Growth of Government Expenditure in Germany Since the Unification," *Finanzarchiv*, 1964, pp. 169–278.
34. Twentieth Century Fund, *More Security for Old Age* (New York, 1937), p. 29.
35. T. H. Marshall, *Social Policy* (London: Hutchinson Univ., 1965), pp. 64–65.
36. Twentieth Century Fund, pp. 50–51.
37. Sources for German GNP, W. G. Hoffman, *Das Wachstrum der deutschen Wirtschaft* (New York/Berlin: Springer-Verlag, 1965), p. 826; for German expenditure, *Bevolkerung und Wirtschaft, 1872–1972*, Stätistiches Bundesamt, p. 233; for U.K. GNP, C. H. Feinstein, *National Income Expenditures and Output of the UK* (Cambridge, Eng.: Cambridge Univ., 1972), Table 3.7; for U.K. expenditures, *ibid.*, Table 14; for U.S. GNP, U.S. Bureau of the Census, *Historical Statistics Since Colonial Times*, p. 224; for U.S. expenditures, *ibid.*, p. 1115; for Sweden's GNP and expenditures, *Historisk Statistik för Sverige*, p. 265; for France's GNP and expenditures, *Annuaire statistique de la France: Résumé rétrospectif*, 1961.
38. This section is adapted from a paper by Robin Silver.
39. Flora and Heidenheimer, p. 28.
40. Jim Potter, *The American Economy Between the World Wars* (New York: Wiley, 1974), p. 113.
41. Lekachman, *The Age of Keynes*, pp. 122–23.
42. Potter, p. 122.
43. Martha Derthick, *Policymaking for Social Security* (Washington: Brookings Inst., 1979).
44. Potter, p. xxx.
45. William E. Leuchtenburg, *Franklin D. Roosevelt and the New Deal* (New York: Harper & Row, 1963), p. 154.
46. David S. Landes, *The Unbound Prometheus* (Cambridge, Eng.: Cambridge Univ., 1969), p. 394.
47. Sidney Pollard, *The Development of the British Economy: 1914–1967* (New York: St. Martin's Press, 1969), p. 203.
48. *Ibid.*
49. Ursula Hicks, *British Public Finances* (London: Oxford Univ., 1958), pp. 73–76; Pollard, *Development of British Economy*, pp. 204–5.
50. Pollard, p. 206.
51. Landes, *Unbound Prometheus*, p. 400.
52. *Ibid.*
53. Tom Kemp, *The French Economy: 1913–1939* (London: Longman Group, 1972), pp. 115–16.
54. Richard F. Kuisel, *Capitalism and the State in Modern France* (Cambridge, Eng.: Cambridge Univ., 1975), pp. 121–22.
55. Kemp, *French Economy*, p. 128.
56. Charles P. Kindleberger, *Economic Growth in France and Britain: 1851–1950* (New York: Simon and Schuster, 1964), p. 205.
57. Kuisel, *Capitalism and the State in Modern France*, p. 127.
58. *Ibid.*
59. Landes, *Unbound Prometheus*, p. 400.

60. Karl Hardach, *The Political Economy of Germany in the Twentieth Century* (Berkeley: Univ. of California, 1980), p. 59.
61. *Ibid.,* p. 60.
62. Robert A. Brady, *The Rationalization Movement in German Industry* (New York: Columbia Univ., 1937).
63. Hardach, *Political Economy of Germany,* p. 62.
64. *Ibid.,* p. 64.
65. *Ibid.*
66. *Ibid.,* pp. 65–66.
67. *Ibid.,* p. 78.
68. *Ibid.,* pp. 224–25.
69. Jim Potter, *American Economy Between the World Wars,* p. 135.
70. This section was adapted from a paper written by Benny Miller.
71. Derek Wood and Derek Dempster, *The Narrow Margin* (Westport, Conn.: Greenwood, 1975), p. 37.
72. K. Middlemass, *Diplomacy of Illusion* (London: Weidenfeld & Nicolson, 1972), p. 81ff.
73. G. C. Peden, *British Rearmament and the Treasury: 1932–1939* (Scottish Academic Press, 1979), p. 3.
74. War Cabinet minutes, 15 Aug. 1919, quoted in N. H. Gibbs, *Grand Strategy: Rearmament Policy,* Vol. I of *History of the Second World War, United Kingdom Military Series,* ed. J. R. M. Butler (London: Her Majesty's Stationery Office, 1976), p. 3.
75. R. A. C. Parker, *Europe, 1919–45* (London: Weidenfeld and Nicolson, 1967), p. 260.
76. Peden, *British Rearmament,* pp. 60–105.
77. *Ibid.,* p. 180.
78. Bernice A. Carroll, *Design for Total War* (Elmsford, N.Y.: Mouton, 1968), p. 184.
79. *Ibid.,* pp. 179–80.
80. C. J. Bernardo and E. H. Bacon, *American Military Policy* (Harrisburg, Pa.: Military Service Publishing Co., 1955).
81. W. M. Jordan, "The French and British Attitude on the Disarmament Policy," in G. B. Turner, ed., *A History of Military Affairs* (Princeton: Princeton Univ., 1956), pp. 436–47.
82. Parker, *Europe, 1919–45,* pp. 163–89.
83. James Bellini, *French Defence Policy* (London: Royal United Services for Defence Studies, 1974), pp. 5–8.
84. Parker, pp. 187, 189.
85. See Mancur Olson, *The Rise and Decline of Nations; Economic Growth, Stagflation, and Social Rigidities* (New Haven: Yale Univ., 1982).
86. Sources: U.S. Bureau of the Census, *Historical Statistics from Colonial Times to 1957,* p. 711 (for total), and *Historical Statistics Since Colonial Times,* p. 1114 (for defense, which does not include foreign aid).
87. Kimmel, *Federal Budget and Fiscal Policy,* p. 320.
88. Joseph A. Pechman, *Federal Tax Policy* (Washington: Brookings Inst., 1971), p. 255.
89. Peacock and Wiseman, *Growth of Public Expenditure,* passim.

90. W. K. Hancock and M. M. Gowing, *British War Economy,* rev. ed. (Her Majesty's Stationery Office, 1975), p. 195.
91. Peacock, p. 187.
92. Peacock and Wiseman, *Growth of Public Expenditure,* passim.
93. "Trends of social policy health," in Morris Ginsberg, ed. *Law and Opinions in England in the 20th Century* (Westport, Conn.: Greenwood, 1974), p. 318.
94. Sherman J. Maisel, *Macroeconomics Theories and Policies* (New York: Norton, 1982), pp. 288–92, 664.
95. See Aaron Wildavsky, *Budgeting: A Comparative Theory of Budgetary Processes* (Boston: Little, Brown, 1975).
96. Aaron Wildavsky, *The Politics of the Budgetary Process,* 4th ed. (Boston: Little, Brown, 1984).
97. Norman Ward, *The Public Purse* (Univ. of Toronto Press, 1962), p. 165.
98. Chris Argyris, *The Impact of Budgets on People* (New York: Controllership Foundation, 1952), p. 9.
99. Herbert Brittain, *The British Budgetary System* (New York: Macmillan, 1959), pp. 216–17.
100. Willem Drees, *On the Level of Government Expenditure in the Netherlands After the War* (Leiden: Stenfert Kroese, 1955), pp. 61–71.
101. Robert W. Davies, *The Development of the Soviet Budgetary System* (Cambridge, Eng.: Cambridge Univ., 1958), p. 184.
102. Hugh Heclo and Aaron Wildavsky, *The Private Government of Public Money,* 2nd ed. (London: Macmillan, 1981).
103. Aaron Wildavsky, *How to Limit Government Spending* (Berkeley, California: Univ. of California, 1980); and Charles Goodsell, *The Case for Bureaucracy* (Chatham, N.J.: Chatham House, 1983).
104. Drees, *Government Expenditure in the Netherlands,* pp. 61–71.
105. René Stourm, *The Budget* (New York: Appleton, 1917), p. 536.
106. *Ibid.,* p. 69.
107. Richard F. Fenno, "The House Appropriations Committee as a Political System: The Problem of Integration," *American Political Science Review,* Vol. 56 (1962), pp. 310–24.
108. Drees, *Government Expenditure in the Netherlands.*
109. Philip M. Williams, *Crisis and Compromise: Politics in the Fourth Republic,* 3rd ed. (Hamden, Conn.: Archon Books, 1964).
110. Robert E. Scott, "Budget Making in Mexico," *Inter-American Economic Affairs,* Vol. 9 (1955), pp. 3–20.
111. Brittain, *The British Budgetary System.*
112. This section is adapted from Aaron Wildavsky, "A Budget for All Seasons? Why the Traditional Budget Lasts," *Public Administration Review,* No. 6 (Nov./Dec. 1978), pp. 501–9.
113. Heclo and Wildavsky, *Private Government of Public Money.*
114. Naomi Caiden and Aaron Wildavsky, *Planning and Budgeting in Poor Countries* (New York: Wiley, 1974).
115. David Novick, "Program Budgeting: Long-Range Planning in the Department of Defense," Memorandum RM-3359-ASDC (November 1962), prepared for the Office of the Assistant Secretary of Defense/Comptroller.

116. Thomas H. Hammond and Jack H. Knott, *A Zero-Based Look at Zero-Base Budgeting* (New Brunswick, N.J.: Transaction Books, 1979).
117. W. Irwin Gillespie, "Fool's Gold: The Quest for a Method of Evaluating Government Spending," in G. Bruce Doern and Allan M. Maslove, eds., *The Public Evaluation of Government Spending* (Toronto: Butterworth, 1979), pp. 39–59.
118. See Aaron Wildavsky, "The Political Economy of Efficiency: Cost–Benefit Analysis, Systems Analysis, and Program Budgeting," *Public Administration Review,* Vol. 26, December 1966, pp. 292–310.

CHAPTER NINE

1. In 17 OECD nations between 1955 and 1981, Richard Rose finds, combined revenue from income and social-security taxes and VAT more than doubled—from 13 percent of GNP to 27.3 percent. Richard Rose, "Maximizing Revenue and Minimizing Political Costs: A Comparative Dynamic Analysis," paper delivered at Workship on the Politics of Taxation, European Consortium for Political Research, Salzburg, April 1984, p. 37.
2. *Ibid.,* pp. 34–41.
3. Daniel Tarschys, "The Scissors Crisis in Public Finance," *Policy Sciences,* Vol. 15 (1983), pp. 205–24.
4. Joseph White helped us write this section.
5. Stephen Cohen and Charles Goldfinger, *From Permacrisis to Real Crisis in French Social Security* (Berkeley: Institute of Urban and Regional Development, 1976), p. 12.
6. Summarized in Harold Wilensky, *The Welfare State and Equality* (Berkeley: Univ. of California, 1975).
7. See Aaron Wildavsky, *Speaking Truth to Power* (Boston: Little, Brown, 1979), Ch. 4, "Coordination Without a Coordinator," pp. 86–107.
8. National accounts of OECD countries, supplemented by national publications.
9. Thomas Borcherding, "The Growth of U. S. Public Spending: Another Look," Discussion paper 82-02-2, Simon Fraser University, School of Business Administration and Economics, Burnaby, B.C., 1982, p. 6.
10. OECD Studies in Resource Allocations, No. 2, *Public Expenditure Trends* (June 1978), p. 17.
11. Christine André and Robert Delorme, "L'Évolution de longue période des dépenses publiques en France, 1872–1971," in Horst Claus Rectenwald, ed., *Secular Trends of the Public Sector,* Proceedings of the 32nd Congress of the Institut International de Finance Publique (Paris: Éditions Cujas, 1976).
12. Derived from OECD, *Public Expenditure on Education* (except New Zealand); *Public Expenditure on Income Maintenance Programmes.*
13. Dennis Guest, *The Emergence of Social Security in Canada* (Vancouver: Univ. of British Columbia, 1980), pp. 2–3.
14. Quoted in Francis G. Castles, *The Social Democratic Image of Society* (London: Routledge & Kegan Paul, 1978), pp. 66–67.
15. The OECD pamphlets are: *Trends* (cited above) and, from the same series, *Public Expenditure on Income Maintenance Programmes* (July 1976), *Public Expenditure on Education* (July 1976), and *Public Expenditure on Health* (July 1977).
16. OECD, *Trends,* pp. 26, 30.

17. *Ibid.,* p. 27.
18. See Axel Mittelstadt, "Unemployment Benefits and Related Payments in Seven Major Countries," in OECD, *Occasional Studies* (July 1975), for a detailed description of the systems.
19. OECD, *Income Maintenance,* p. 30.
20. Holland survey in *The Economist* (January 30, 1982), p. 8.
21. Aaron Wildavsky, *Speaking Truth to Power,* p. 94.
22. OECD, *Public Expenditure on Education,* pp. 23–24.
23. OECD, *Public Expenditure on Health,* p. 35.
24. See Aaron Wildavsky, "Doing Better and Feeling Worse: The Political Pathology of Health Policy," *Daedalus,* Winter 1976, pp. 105–23.
25. This data is derived from the U.N. Yearbook and National Accounts Statistics, using the 1979, 1970, 1962 and 1958 editions. Where different sources are available for the same year, both are reported. This permits distinguishing change in trend from change in source. The analysis also takes into consideration Table 9.10 from Peter Flora and Arnold J. Heidenheimer, eds., *The Development of the Welfare State in Europe and America* (New Brunswick, N.J.: Transaction Books, 1981), p. 338 and Table 1. These, and sources specific to each country, are used to protect the reliability of the analysis.
26. Swedish submission to OECD conference on public spending (unpublished), May 25, 1980.
27. See Michele Salvati, "May 1968 and the Hot Autumn of 1969: The responses of two ruling classes," in Suzanne Berger, ed., *Organizing Interests in Western Europe: Pluralism, Corporatism, and the Transformation of Politics* (Cambridge, Eng.: Cambridge Univ., 1981), p. 353.
28. Christine André and Robert Delorme, "The Long Run Growth of Public Expenditure in France," *Finances publiques,* Vol. 33, No. 1–2 (1978), p. 49.
29. Robert Delorme, *A New View on the Economic Theory of the State: A Case Study of France* (Paris: Centre d'Études Prospectives d'Économie Mathématique Appliqués à la Planificacion (mimeo, 1984), p. 4.
30. Richard M. Bird, "Trends in Taxation: Calculations and Speculations," typescript, pp. 16–18.
31. See Christopher Leman, *The Collapse of Welfare Reform: Political Institutions, Policy and the Poor in Canada and the United States* (Cambridge, Mass.: MIT Press, 1980), pp. 40–41.
32. Bird, "Trends in Taxation," p. 18. GNE is gross national expenditure, yet another denominator.
33. U.N. data shows an expansion; Bird (p. 9) does not.
34. Leman, *Collapse of Welfare Reform,* pp. 11–15.
35. Federal data are derived from tables based on OMB publications *Payments for Individuals* and *Federal Government Finances* (March 1981), courtesy of Mickey Levy.
36. Australia survey in *The Economist,* Oct. 31, 1981.
37. Richard M. Coughlin, *Ideology, Public Opinion, and Welfare Policy,* Institute of International Studies Research Series, No. 42 (Berkeley: Univ. of California, 1980), p. 68.
38. S. P. Huntington, *The Common Defense* (New York: Columbia Univ., 1969), pp. 278–83.

39. U.S. Department of Commerce, Office of Business Economics; *U.S. Income and Output* (1958), pp. 118–19; *Survey of Current Business,* p. 11 (February 1960), p. 12 (February 1961). For the nature of "national defense spending," see Table 11 in Huntington, *Common Defense,* p. 282.

40. *Budget of the United States Government for the Fiscal Year Ending June 30, 1955,* pp. 1164–65; joint statement, Secretary of the Treasury and Director of the Bureau of the Budget, July 20, 1961, in Huntington, p. 283.

41. Huntington, p. 281.

42. Jerome H. Kahan, *Security in the Nuclear Age* (Washington: Brookings Inst., 1975), pp. 74–75.

43. Robert Osgood, *NATO, the Entangling Alliance* (Chicago: Univ. of Chicago, 1962), pp. 106–7, 151–58.

44. See Edward R. Fried et al., *Setting National Priorities: The 1974 Budget* (Washington: Brookings Inst., 1973), p. 296.

45. Arnold Kanter, *Defense Politics* (Chicago: Univ. of Chicago, 1979), p. 58.

46. *Ibid.,* p. 77.

47. John L. Stromberg, *The Internal Mechanics of the Defense Budget Process, Fiscal 1958–1968* (Santa Monica, Calif.: Rand Corp., 1970).

48. David Greenwood, "Defense and National Priorities since 1945," in John Baylis, ed., *British Defense Policy in a Changing World* (London: Croom Helm, 1977), p. 182.

49. Quoted in W. P. Snyder, *The Politics of British Defense Policy 1945–1962* (Columbus: Ohio State University Press, 1964), pp. 195–96.

50. Greenwood, "Defense and National Priorities," p. 202.

51. R. N. Rosencrance, *Defense of the Realm* (New York, 1962), p. 31.

52. Stockholm International Peace Research Institute Yearbook of World Armaments and Disarmaments, 1978, pp. 144–45.

53. Derived from data in R. Klein et al., *Social Policy and Public Expenditure, 1974* (London: Centre for Studies in Social Policy, 1974).

54. Greenwood, "Defense and National Priorities," *loc. cit.,* p. 202.

55. E. H. Fedder, ed., *Defense Politics of the Atlantic Alliance* (New York: Praeger, 1980), p. 164.

56. *SIPRI* Yearbook, 1974, pp. 125–28.

57. *Ibid.,* 1976, p. 130.

58. *Ibid.*

59. *Ibid.,* 1974, pp. 132–34.

60. The original draft of this section was prepared by Sven Steinmo.

61. See James E. Alt, "The Evolution of Tax Structures," *Public Choice,* Vol. 41 (1983), pp. 181–223.

62. 1880, 1920, and 1935 data from OECD, *Revenue Statistics of OECD Member Countries: A Standard Classification* (Paris, 1976). 1980 data from OECD, *Long Term Trends in Revenue Statistics of Member Nations* (Paris, 1981). The first U.S. entry is from Alt, "Evolution of Tax Structures," *loc. cit.,* p. 193.

63. Joseph Pechman and Benjamin Okner, *Who Bears the Tax Burden?* (Washington: Brookings Inst., 1974), p. 105.

64. OECD, *Revenue Statistics of OECD Member Countries: 1965–1979* (Paris, 1980), p. 42.

65. Pechman and Okner, *Who Bears the Tax Burden?,* p. 117.

66. Irving Kristol, *Two Cheers for Capitalism* (New York: Basic Books, 1978), pp. 210–11.
67. Quoted in Gilbert Burck, "You May Think the Corporate Profit Tax Is Bad but It Is a Whole Lot Worse Than You Think," in H. Camerson and W. Henderson, eds., *Public Finance* (New York: Random House, 1966), p. 61.
68. The data on tax preferences in this and the following paragraphs come from Ronald Frederick King, "Tax Expenditures and Systematic Public Policy: An Essay on the Political Economy of the Federal Revenue Code," *Public Budgeting and Finance*, Spring 1984, pp. 14–31.
69. *Ibid.*, p. 27.
70. An early proposal for a progressive, low-rate income tax is Aaron Wildavsky, "A Uniform Income Tax," *Tax Notes*, Vol. XII, No. 12 (March 23, 1981), pp. 611–12.
71. A. T. Peacock and J. Wiseman, *The Growth of Public Expenditures in the United Kingdom* (Princeton: Princeton Univ., 1961).
72. John Witte, *The Politics and Development of the Federal Income Tax* (Madison: Univ. of Wisconsin, 1985), p. 251.
73. *Ibid.*, pp. 320–21.
74. *Ibid.*, p. 310.
75. *Ibid.*, pp. 343–62.
76. *Ibid.*, p. 364.
77. Charles E. Lindblom, "Decision Making in Taxation and Expenditure," paper for Conference on Public Finances: Needs, Sources and Utilization, National Bureau of Economic Research, April 1959.
78. Witte, *Politics and Development of Federal Income Tax*, p. 141.
79. *Ibid.*, p. 194.
80. Karl Hauser, "West Germany," in National Bureau of Economic Research, ed., *Foreign Tax Policies and Economic Growth* (New York: Columbia Univ., 1966), p. 97.
81. Vito Tanzi, *The Individual Income Tax and Economic Growth: An International Comparison* (Baltimore: Johns Hopkins, 1969), p. 93.
82. Andrew Shonfield, *Modern Capitalism: The Changing Balance of Public and Private Power* (London: Oxford Univ., 1965), p. 296.
83. Alt, "Evolution of Tax Structures," *loc. cit.*, p. 206.
84. Paul Senf, in "Comment," Hauser, "West Germany," *loc. cit.*, pp. 160–61.
85. Robert Wertheimer, "Tax Incentives in Germany," *National Tax Journal*, Vol. X (1957), No. 325, p. 325.
86. Hauser, "West Germany," *loc. cit.*, p. 115.
87. Again, we use this American term, in no small part because we like to emphasize the markedly different perceptions Americans and continental Europeans have toward tax expenditures.
88. Henry Gumpel, *Taxation in the Federal Republic of Germany* (New York: Commerce Clearing House, 1963), p. 507.
89. Fritz Neumark, in "Comment," Hauser, "West Germany," *loc. cit.*, p. 157.
90. Tanzi, *Individual Income Tax and Economic Growth*, p. 91. (See table, p. 93.)
91. Wertheimer, "Tax Incentives in Germany," *loc. cit.*, p. 329.
92. Gumpel, *Taxation in the Federal Republic*, p. 330–31.

93. Joseph Pechman, *Federal Tax Policy* (Washington: Brookings Inst., 1971), p. 32.
94. Gumpel, *Taxation in the Federal Republic of Germany,* pp. 446–47.
95. See John Armstrong, *The European Administrative Elite* (Princeton: Princeton Univ., 1973).
96. Richard Rose and Guy Peters, *Can Governments Go Bankrupt?* (New York: Basic Books, 1978), p. 98.
97. See country graphs in OECD, *Income Tax Schedules, Distribution of Taxpayers and Revenues,* Report by the Committee on Fiscal Affairs, Paris, 1981, pp. 35–38. See also OECD *Tax Benefit Position of Selected Income Groups in OECD Member Countries, 1974–1978,* Report by the Committee on Fiscal Affairs, Paris, 1980, pp. 36–37.
98. This thesis has been challenged. See Erick Nordlinger, *On the Autonomy of the Democratic State* (Cambridge, Mass.: Harvard Univ., 1966), and Anthony King, "Ideas, Institutions, and Policies of Governments: A Comparative Analysis," *British Journal of Political Science,* Vol. 3, No. 4 (October 1974), pp. 291–313.
99. Ken Messere points out that by 1964 Swedish tax makers had a "desire to move from direct to indirect taxation" ("Tax Levels, Structure and Systems: Some Intertemporal and International Comparisons," in Rectenwald, ed., *Secular Trends of the Public Sector,* pp. 194–210). Cf. H. L. Wilensky, "Taxing, Spending and Backlash: An American Peculiarity?,"*Taxing and Spending,* Vol. II, July 1979, pp. 6–12.
100. Nils Elvander, "The Politics of Taxation in Sweden: 1945–1970," *Scandinavian Political Studies,* Vol. 7 (1972), pp. 63–82.
101. Alt, "Evolution of Tax Structures," *loc. cit.,* p. 199.
102. Elvander, "Politics of Taxation in Sweden," *loc. cit.,* pp. 68–69.
103. Martin Norr, Frank Duffy, and Harry Sterner, *Taxation in Sweden* (Boston: Little, Brown, 1959), p. 70.
104. *Ibid.,* p. 73.
105. *Ibid.,* p. 215. Also see Federation of British Industries, *Taxation: In the Proposed European Free Trade Area* (London, 1958), p. 14.
106. Leif Muten and Karl Faxen, in National Bureau of Economic Research, ed., *Foreign Tax Policies and Economic Growth,* p. 353.
107. Sven Steinmo, "Taxation as an Instrument of Public Policy; Sweden—the Carrot and the Stick," paper presented to the European Consortium of Political Research, April 1984, p. 12.
108. For a detailed list, see Norr et al., *Taxation in Sweden,* p. 160.
109. *Ibid.,* p. 70.
110. Steinmo, "Taxation as an Instrument of Public Policy," pp. 23–24.
111. Rose and Peters, *Can Governments Go Bankrupt?,* p. 93.
112. H. L. Wilensky, *"New Corporatism" Centralization and the Welfare State* (Beverly Hills, Calif.: Sage Publications, 1976). See also Philippe Schmitter, "Interest Intermediation and Regime Governability in Contemporary Western Europe and North America," in Charles Maier, ed., *Organizing Interests in Western Europe* (Cambridge, Eng.: Cambridge Univ., 1981).
113. See Elvander, "Politics of Taxation in Sweden," *loc. cit.*
114. J. A. Kay and M. A. King, *The British Tax System* (Oxford: Oxford Univ., 1978), p. 246.

115. Simon James and Christopher Nobes, *The Economics of Taxation* (Oxford: Philip Allan, 1978), p. 135.

116. Kay and King, *British Tax System*, p. 192.

117. See OECD, *The Taxation of Net Wealth, Capital Transfers, and Capital Gains of Individuals*, Report of Committee on Fiscal Affairs, Paris, 1979. See also James and Nobes, pp. 66–67; J. E. Meade, *The Structure and Reform of Direct Taxation* (London: Allen & Unwin, 1978), pp. 58–59; and Kay and King, *British Tax System*, p. 248.

118. See Tanzi, *Individual Income Tax and Economic Growth*, p. 19.

119. E. Gordon Keith, Introduction to National Bureau of Economic Research, ed., *Foreign Tax Policies and Economic Growth*, p. 31.

120. Hugh Heclo and Aaron Wildavsky, *The Private Government of Public Money* (London: Macmillan, 1974), p. 160.

121. See Tanzi, *Individual Income Tax*, pp. 17–21, 103–5.

122. Kay and King, *British Tax System*, pp. 247–48.

123. See Nicholas Kaldor, *Reports on Taxation I: Papers Related to the United Kingdom* (London: Anchor Press, 1980).

124. See Armstrong, *European Administrative Elite*.

125. Arnold Heidenheimer, Hugh Heclo, and Carolyn Teich Adams, *Comparative Public Policies: The Politics of Social Choice in Europe and America* (New York: St. Martin's Press, 1975), p. 237.

126. *Ibid.*, p. 239.

127. Meade, *Structure and Reform of Direct Taxation*, p. 49.

128. André and Delorme, "Long Run Growth," *loc. cit.*, p. 48

129. See Aaron Wildavsky, "The Unanticipated Consequences of the 1984 Presidential Election," *Tax Notes*, Vol. 24, No. 2 (July 9, 1984), pp. 193–200.

130. Alt, "Evolution of Tax Structures," *loc. cit.*, pp. 206–7.

131. Jean-Pierre Balladur and Antoine Coutière, "France," in Henry Aaron, ed., *The Value-Added Tax: Lessons from Europe* (Washington: Brookings Inst., 1981), pp. 19–20.

132. Martin Norr and Pierre Kerlan, *Taxation in France* (Chicago: Commerce Clearing House, 1966), pp. 409–29.

133. Balladur and Coutière, "France," *loc. cit.*, p. 19.

134. Norr and Kerlan, *Taxation in France*, p. 40.

135. *Ibid.*

136. Rose and Peters, *Can Governments Go Bankrupt?*, p. 96.

137. Alt, "Evolution of Tax Structures," *loc. cit.*, p. 206.

138. Tanzi, *Individual Income Tax*, p. 58.

139. Heidenheimer, Heclo, and Adams, *Comparative Public Policies*, p. 236.

140. Douglas E. Ashford, *British Dogmatism and French Pragmatism* (London: Allen & Unwin, 1982).

141. Shonfield, *Modern Capitalism*, p. 165.

142. See Richard Rose, "Maximizing Revenue and Minimizing Political Costs."

143. Daniel Tarschys, "Curbing Public Expenditures: A Survey of Current Trends," paper prepared for the Joint Activity on Public Management Improvement of the OECD (Technical Co-Operation Service), April 1982.

144. *Ibid.*, p. 12.

145. *Ibid.*, p. 12a.

146. See Aaron Wildavsky, "From Chaos Comes Opportunity: The Movement To-

ward Spending Limits in American and Canadian Budgeting," *Canadian Public Administration,* Vol. 26, No. 2 (Summer 1983), pp. 163–81.

147. *Ibid.*

148. See Aaron Wildavsky, *How to Limit Government Spending* (Berkeley: Univ. of California, 1980), and Wildavsky, "Does Federal Spending Constitute a 'Discovered Fault' in the Constitution? The Balanced Budget Amendment," paper prepared for Conference on the Congressional Budget Process at Carl Albert Center, Univ. of Oklahoma, Feb. 12–13, 1982.

149. Tarschys, "Curbing Public Expenditures," pp. 62–63.

CHAPTER TEN

1. David Hume, "Of the Study of History," in Hume, *Philosophical Works,* ed. T. H. Greene and T. H. Grosse (London: Longmans, Green, 1898), Vol. IV, p. 390.

2. Haskell Fain, *Between Philosophy and History: The Resurrection of Speculative Philosophy of History Within the Analytic Tradition* (Princeton: Princeton Univ., 1970), pp. 255–56.

3. John William Miller, *The Philosophy of History, with Reflections and Aphorisms* (New York: Norton, 1981), p. 15.

4. King James Version, I Kings 12.

5. Pharaoh also, the reader of the Bible may recall, had trouble remembering things from one plague to another. See Aaron Wildavsky, *The Nursing Father: Moses as a Political Leader* (University City: Univ. of Alabama, 1984).

6. I Kings 11.

7. On problem succession, see Aaron Wildavsky, *Speaking Truth to Power* (Boston: Little, Brown, 1979).

8. See Aaron Wildavsky, "Budgetary Futures: Why Politicians May Want Spending Limits in Turbulent Times," *Public Budgeting and Finance,* Vol. 1, No. 1 (Spring 1981), pp. 20–27.

9. Letter to Aaron Wildavsky, July 23, 1984.

10. From Patrick D. Larkey, Chandler Stolp and Mark Winer, "Theorizing About the Growth of Government: A Research Assessment," *Journal of Public Policy,* Vol. 1, Part 2 (May 1981), pp. 157–220.

11. See Naomi Caiden and Aaron Wildavsky, *Planning and Budgeting in Poor Countries* (New Brunswick, N.J.: Transaction Books, 1980).

12. Harold L. Wilensky, *The Welfare State and Equality* (Berkeley/Los Angeles/London: Univ. of California, 1975), p. xiii.

13. *Ibid.,* p. 10.

14. B. Guy Peters, "Fiscal Strains on the Welfare State: Causes and Consequences," in Charles H. Levine and Irene Rubin, eds., *Fiscal Stress and Public Policy,* Sage Yearbooks in Politics and Public Policy, Vol. 9 (Beverly Hills/London: Sage Publications, 1980), pp. 23–46.

15. Wilensky, *Welfare State and Equality,* pp. 47–48.

16. Harley H. Hinrichs, *A General Theory of Tax Structure Change During Economic Development* (Cambridge, Mass.: Law School of Harvard Univ., 1966), pp. 8–10.

17. Assar Lindbeck, "Redistribution Policy and the Expansion of the Public Sector," paper prepared for the Nobel Symposium on "The Growth of Government," Stockholm, Aug. 15–17, 1984.

18. James O'Connor, *The Fiscal Crisis of the State* (New York: St. Martin's Press, 1975).
19. Alan Wolfe, *The Limits of Legitimacy* (New York: Free Press, 1977): see the valuable review by Jeffrey Straussman, "Spending More and Enjoying It Less: On the Political Economy of Advanced Capitalism," *Comparative Politics* (January 1981), pp. 235–52.
20. See Ian Gough, *The Political Economy of the Welfare State* (London and Basingstoke: Macmillan, 1979), and "Theories of the Welfare State: A Critique," *International Journal of Health Services,* Vol. 8, No. 1 (1978), pp. 27–40.
21. Richard A. Musgrave, "Leviathan Cometh—Or Does He?" in Helen F. Ladd and T. Nicholas Tideman, eds., *Tax and Expenditure Limitations* (Washington: Urban Institute, 1981), pp. 375ff.
22. Gough, *Political Economy of the Welfare State,* pp. 149–50.
23. Peters, "Fiscal Strains on the Welfare State," *loc. cit.* See also H. L. Wilensky, "Political Legitimacy and Consensus: Missing Variables in the Assessment of Social Policy," in S. E. Spiro and E. Yuchtman-Yaar, eds., *Evaluating the Welfare State: Social and Political Perspectives* (New York: Academic Press, 1983), pp. 51–74.
24. A. T. Peacock and J. Wiseman, *The Growth of Public Expenditures in the United Kingdom* (Princeton: Princeton Univ., 1961).
25. This line of reasoning has been amplified by C. E. Lindblom in *Politics and Markets* (New York: Basic Books, 1977).
26. Rudolf Goldscheid, "A Sociological Approach to Problems of Public Finance," in Richard A. Musgrave and Alan T. Peacock, eds., *Classics in the Theory of Public Finance* (New York: St. Martin's Press, 1967).
27. Joseph A. Schumpeter, "The Crisis of the Tax State," *International Economic Papers,* No. 4 (Macmillan, 1954), pp. 5–39.
28. See Aaron Wildavsky, *How to Limit Government Spending* (Berkeley/Los Angeles/London: University of California Press, 1980).
29. Wilensky, *Welfare State and Equality.*
30. Mancur Olson, *The Rise and Decline of Nations: Economic Growth, Stagflation and Social Rigidities* (New Haven: Yale Univ., 1982).
31. Christopher Hewitt, "The Effect of Political Democracy and Social Democracy on Equality in Industrial Societies: A Cross-National Comparison," *American Sociological Review,* Vol. 42 (1977), pp. 450–64; and Douglas Higgs, "Political Parties and Macroeconomic Policy," *American Political Science Review,* Vol. 71 (1977), pp. 1465–88.
32. Robert Jackman, *Politics and Social Equality: A Comparative Analysis* (New York: Wiley, 1975); and Frank Parkin, *Class Inequality and Political Order* (New York: Praeger, 1971).
33. Frederick Pryor, *Public Expenditures in Communist and Capitalist Nations* (Homewood, Ill.: Irwin, 1968); and Wilensky, *Welfare State and Equality.*
34. Wilensky, *Welfare State and Equality,* pp. 45–46.
35. Harold L. Wilensky, "Leftism, Catholicism, and Democratic Corporatism: The Role of Political Parties in Recent Welfare State Development," in Peter Flora and Arnold J. Heidenheimer, eds., *The Development of Welfare States in Europe and America* (New Brunswick, N.J.: Transaction, 1981).
36. Francis G. Castles, *The Social Democratic Image of Society* (Routledge and Kegan Paul, 1978); and Castles and Sten G. Borg, "The Influence of the Politi-

cal Right on Public Income Maintenance Expenditure and Equality," *Political Studies,* Vol. 29, No. 4 (December 1981), pp. 604–21.

37. Joseph White has contributed this insight.
38. We are indebted to Joseph White for ideas about the differences between Wilensky and Castles.
39. Letter to Aaron Wildavsky.
40. Henry Aaron, "Social Security: International Comparisons," in Otto Eckstein, ed., *Studies in the Economics of Income Maintenance* (Washington: Brookings Inst., 1967).
41. Wilensky, *Welfare State and Equality,* pp. 10–11.
42. Michael Dempster and Aaron Wildavsky, "On Change ... or, There Is No Magic Size for an Increment," *Political Studies,* Vol. 27, No. 3 (September 1979), pp. 371–89.
43. Hugh Heclo, "Toward a New Welfare State?," in Flora and Heidenheimer, eds., *Development of Welfare States,* p. 394.
44. *Ibid.,* pp. 398–99.
45. These categories are adapted from Mary Douglas, "Cultural Bias," in Mary Douglas, *In the Active Voice* (London: Routledge & Kegan Paul, 1982). See also Mary Douglas and Aaron Wildavsky, *Risk and Culture* (Berkeley: Univ. of California, 1982); and Aaron Wildavsky, "Models of Political Regimes or Pluralism Means More Than One Political Culture in One Country at One Time," forthcoming in Ellis Katz, ed., *The Meaning of American Pluralism* (Philadelphia: Institute for the Study of Human Issues Press).
46. Lindbeck, "Redistribution Policy and the Expansion of the Public Sector," *loc. cit.,* pp. 31–32.
47. Steve Rayner and Jonathan Gross, *Measuring Culture: A Paradigm for the Analysis of Social Organization* (New York: Columbia Univ., 1985).
48. Robert T. Kudrle and Theodore R. Marmor, "The Development of Welfare States in North America," in Flora and Heidenheimer, *Development of Welfare States,* p. 89.
49. *Ibid.,* p. 90.
50. Seymour M. Lipset, *Agrarian Socialism: The Cooperative Commonwealth Federation in Saskatchewan* (Garden City, N.Y.: Anchor Books, 1968).
51. Wilensky, *Welfare State and Equality,* p. 61.
52. Kudrle and Marmor, "Development of Welfare States in North America," *loc. cit.,* p. 113.
53. C. Stephen Wolfe and Jesse Burkhead, "Fiscal Trends in Selected Industrial Countries," *Public Budgeting and Finance,* Vol. 3, No. 4 (Winter 1983), pp. 97–102, quotation on p. 102.
54. See Robert Vincent Daniels, *The Conscience of the Revolution: Communist Opposition in Soviet Russia* (New York: Simon and Schuster, 1969); and Leonard Shapiro, *The Origin of the Communist Autocracy: Political Opposition in the Soviet State: First Phase, 1917–1922* (New York: Praeger, 1965).
55. Sam Peltzman, "The Growth of Government," *Journal of Law and Economics,* Vol. 23, October 1980, p. 263.
56. *Ibid.,* pp. 262–63, 265.
57. Olson, *Rise and Decline of Nations,* p. 173.
58. Peltzman, "Growth of Government," *loc. cit.,* pp. 285–86.

59. Richard Rose, "The Programme Approach to the Growth of Government," paper prepared for the American Political Science Association Annual Meeting, Chicago, Sept. 1–4, 1983.
60. *Ibid.*
61. This section is adapted from Aaron Wildavsky's joint work with Michael Thompson.
62. *Government Finance Statistics Yearbook,* Vol. VI (1982); and *International Financial Statistics* (yearbook issue, 1982), both publications of the International Monetary Fund.
63. Gisli Blöndal, "Balancing the Budget: Budgeting Practices and Fiscal Policy Issues in Iceland," *Public Budgeting and Finance,* Vol. 3, No. 2 (Summer 1983), pp. 47–63.
64. *Ibid.*
65. See Rudolph G. Penner, "Forecasting Budget Totals: Why Can't We Get It Right?" in Michael J. Boskin and Aaron Wildavsky, eds., *The Federal Budget: Economics and Politics* (New Brunswick, N.J.: Transaction Books, 1982), pp. 89–110.
66. Allen Schick, "Off-Budget Expenditure: An Economic and Political Framework," paper prepared for Organisation for Economic Co-Operation and Development, Paris, August 1981.
67. *Ibid.* For an insightful effort to get at governmental attempts at self-control, see James Q. Wilson and Patricia Rachal, "Can Government Regulate Itself?," *The Public Interest,* No. 46 (Winter 1977), pp. 3–14.
68. See Wildavsky, *How to Limit Government Spending.*
69. J. H. Plumb, *Death of the Past* (Houghton Mifflin, 1970).
70. Aaron Wildavsky, "From chaos comes opportunity: the movement toward spending limits in American and Canadian budgeting," *Canadian Public Administration,* Vol. 26, No. 2 (Summer 1983), pp. 163–81.

BIBLIOGRAPHY

CHAPTER ONE
BUDGETARY CULTURES

Douglas, Mary. *In The Active Voice.* London: Routledge & Kegan Paul, 1982.
———. *Implicit Meanings.* London: Routledge & Kegan Paul, 1975.
———, and Aaron Wildavsky. *Risk and Culture.* Berkeley and Los Angeles. University of California Press, 1982.
Kettle, Michael, ed. In *Irish Orators and Oratory.* Dublin: Talbot Press, 1916.
Levi, Margaret. "Rule and Revenue Production," paper presented at Western Political Science Association meetings, Sacramento, Calif., April 1984.
North, Douglas C. *Structure and Change in Economic History,* New York: Norton, 1981.
Schmandt-Besserat, Denise. "Decipherment of the Earliest Tablets," *Science,* Vol. 211, No. 16 (January 16, 1981), pp. 283–85.
———. "The Envelopes That Bear the First Writing," *Technology and Culture,* Vol. 21, No. 3 (July 1980), pp. 357–85.
Wildavsky, Aaron. *The Politics of the Budgetary Process,* 4th ed. Boston. Little, Brown, 1984.

CHAPTER TWO
FINANCE WITHOUT MONEY: BUDGETING IN THE ANCIENT WORLD

Adams, Robert McC. *Heartland of Cities: Surveys of Ancient Settlement and Land Use on the Central Flood Plain of the Euphrates.* Chicago and London: University of Chicago Press, 1981.

Asakawa, K. *The Early Institutional Life of Japan: A Study in the Reform of 645 A.D.* New York: Paragon Book Reprint Corp., 1963.

Balasz, Étienne. *Le Traité économique de "Souëi-Chou."* Leiden: E. J. Brill, 1953.

Barth, Frank. *Political Leadership Among the Swat Pathans.* London: Athelone Press, 1959.

Bengtson, Hermann. *An Introduction to Ancient History.* Berkeley: University of California Press, 1970.

Bogaert, Raymond. *Les Origines antiques de la banque de dépôt.* Leyden: A. W. Sijthoff, 1966.

Boutruche, Robert. *Seigneurie et féodalité: Le Premier Age des liens d'homme à homme.* Paris: Éditions Montaigne, 1968.

Breasted, James. *A History of Egypt from the Earliest Times to the Persian Conquest.* New York: Scribners, 1916.

Burn, A. "Hic Breve Vivitur: A Study of the Expectation of Life in the Roman Empire," *Past and Present,* Vol. 4 (1953).

Cambridge Economic History of Europe, Vol. II, *Trade and Industry in the Middle Ages,* ed. M. Postan and E. Rich. Cambridge, Eng.: Cambridge University Press, 1952.

Chang, Kwang-Chih. *Shang Civilization.* New Haven: Yale University Press, 1980.

Childe, Gordon. *What Happened in History.* Baltimore: Penguin, 1964.

Corbin, Paul. "Valeur comparée de per et de l'argent lors de l'introduction du monnayage dans la Grèce ancienne," *Annales: Économies, Sociétés, Civilisations,* Vol. 14, No. 2, April–June 1959, pp. 209–33.

Cotterell, Arthur. *The First Emperor of China.* London: Macmillan, 1981.

Dopsch, Alfons. *Naturalwirtschaft und Geldwirtschaft in der Weltgeschichte.* Vienna: L. W. Seidel, 1930.

Dumont, Louis. *Homo Hierarchicus,* English edition. London: Weidenfeld & Nicolson, 1966.

Eberhard, Wolfram. *A History of China.* Berkeley: University of California Press, 1960.

Encyclopaedia Britannica, 1969 ed. Vol. 1, "Abacus," "Accounting"; Vol. 5, "China"; Vol. 6, "Corvée"; Vol. 15, "Money"; Vol. 16, "Number."

Evans-Pritchard, E. E. *The Nuer.* Oxford: Oxford University Press, 1940.

Fournier de Flaix, E. *L'Impôt dans les diverses civilisations,* Vol. 1. Paris: Guillaumin & Cie., 1897.

Frankfort, Henri. *Ancient Egyptian Religion: An Interpretation.* New York: Harper, 1961.

Ghoshal, U. N. *Contributions to the History of the Hindu Revenue System.* Calcutta: University of Calcutta, 1929.

Glover, T. R. *The Ancient World.* Baltimore: Penguin, 1935.

Gopal, M. H. *Mauryan Public Finance.* London: George Allen & Unwin, 1935.

Hawkes, Jacquetta, and Sir Leonard Wooley. *The Beginnings of Civilization (History of Mankind,* Vol. 1). New York: Mentor, 1965.

Heichelheim, Fritz M. *An Ancient Economic History,* Vol. 1. Leyden: A. W. Sijthoff, 1965.

Heinig, Kurt. *Das Budget,* Vol. 1. Tübingen: J. C. B. Mohr, 1948.

Helck, Wolfgang. *Ägyptologie an deutschen Universitäten.* Wiesbaden: Steiner, 1969.

——. *Untersuchungen zu den Beamtentiteln des Ägyptischen Alten Reiches.* Ägyptologische Forschungen, 18. Hamburg: J. J. Augustin, 1954.

Hicks, John. *A Theory of Economic History.* Oxford: Clarendon Press, 1969.

Jones, A. H. M. *The Roman Economy: Studies in Economic and Administrative History.* Oxford: Basil Blackwell, 1974.

––––––. "The Social Structure of Athens in the 4th Century B.C.," *Economic History Review,* 2nd Series, Vol. III, No. 2 (December 1955).

Kautilya. The *Arthasastra,* Shamasastry translation. Mysore: Mysore Printing & Publishing House, 1961.

Kramer, Samuel Noah. *History Begins at Sumer.* Philadelphia: University of Pennsylvania Press, 1981.

Lapidus, Ira M., ed., *Middle Eastern Cities.* Berkeley: University of California Press, 1969.

Lloyd, Seton. *The Archeology of Mesopotamia, from the Old Stone Age to the Persian Conquest.* London: Thames & Hudson, 1978.

––––––. *Foundations in the Dust.* New York: AMS Press, 1978.

Loewe, Michael. *Imperial China, the Historical Background to the Modern Age.* New York: Praeger, 1966.

Madden, Frederick W. *History of Jewish Coinage and of Money in the Old and New Testament.* New York: Ktav, 1967.

Main, Lucy. *Primitive Government.* Harmondsworth, Middlesex, Eng.: Pelican, 1967.

March, James G., ed. *Handbook of Organizations.* Chicago: Rand-McNally, 1965.

Maspéro, Henri. *China in Antiquity.* Chatham, Mass.: University of Massachusetts Press, 1978.

––––––. *La Chine antique.* Paris: E. de Boccard, 1927.

––––––. *Les Finances de l'Égypte sous les Lugides.* Paris; Presented to the Faculty of Letters for the Diplome d'Études Supérieures, 1905.

––––––, and Étienne Balasz. *Histoire et institutions de la Chine ancienne des origines au XIIè siècle après J.C.* Paris: Presses Universitaires de France, 1967.

McNeill, W. H. *The Rise of the West.* Chicago. Mentor, 1963.

Meissner, Bruno. *Babylonien und Assyrien,* 2 vols. Heidelberg: C. Winter, 1920–25.

Meyer, Eduard. *Kleine Schriften zur Geschichtstheorie und zur wirtschaftlichen und politischen Geschichte des Altertums.* Halle A. S.: Max Neimeyer, 1910.

Oppenheim, A. Leo. *Ancient Mesopotamia: Portrait of a Dead Civilization.* Chicago and London: University of Chicago Press, 1977.

Otto, Eberhard. *Ägypten: Der Weg des Pharaonenreiches,* 3rd ed. Stuttgart: W. Kohlhammer (Urban), 1958.

––––––. *Wesen und Wandel der ägyptischen Kultur.* Stuttgart: W. Kohlhammer (Urban), 1969.

Pareti, Luigi, Paolo Brezzi, and Luciano Petech. *The Ancient World, 1200 B.C. to A.D. 500.* New York: Harper & Row, 1965.

Pirazzoli-t'Serstevens, Michelle. *The Han Dynasty.* New York: Rizzoli International Publications, 1982.

Polanyi, K., C. Arensbert, and H. Pearson, eds., *Trade and Markets in the Early Empires.* Glencoe, Ill.: The Free Press, 1957.

Randles, W. G. L. *L'Ancien Royaume du Congo des origines à la fin du XIXè siècle.* Paris: Mouton & Cie., 1968.

Reischauer, Ernest O., and John K. Fairbank. *East Asia: The Great Tradition. A History of East Asian Civilization,* Vol. I. Boston: Houghton Mifflin, 1960.

Reynier, Louis. *De l'Économie publique et rurale des Arabes et des Juifs.* Geneva: J. J. Paschaud, Imprimeur-Libraires, 1820.

Roux, Georges. *Ancient Iraq.* Harmondsworth, Eng.: Pelican, 1966.

Scharff, Alexander, and Anton Moortgat. *Ägypten und Vorderasien im Altertum,* 3rd ed. Munich: F. Bruckmann, 1962.

Schmoekel, Hartmut. *Das Land Sumer: Die Wiederentdeckung der ersten Hochkultur der Menschheit,* 2nd ed. Stuttgart: W. Kohlhammer, 1956.

————, ed. *Kulturgeschichte des Alten Orient: Mesopotamien, Hethiterreich, Syrien-Palestina, Urartu.* Stuttgart: Alfred Kroener, 1961.

Starr, Chester. *A History of the Ancient World.* New York: Oxford University Press, 1983.

Sterba, James P. "A Report from the Majority of the World," *New York Times Magazine,* Sept. 4, 1971.

Thompson, Michael. *Rubbish Theory.* Oxford: Oxford University Press, 1979.

Von Hagen, Victor W. *World of the Maya.* New York: Mentor, 1960.

Weber, Max. "Agrarverhältnisse in Altertum," in *Gesammelte Aufsätze zur Sozial- und Wirtschaftsgeschichte.* Tübingen: J. C. B. Mohr, 1924.

————. *General Economic History,* translated by Frank H. Knight. Glencoe, Ill.: The Free Press, 1927.

Wirgen, Wolf, and Siegfried Mandel. *The History of Coins and Symbols in Ancient Israel.* New York: Exposition Press, 1958.

Wittfogel, Karl A. *Oriental Despotism: A Comparative Study of Total Power.* New Haven: Yale University Press, 1957.

————, and Feng Chia Sheng. *History of Chinese Society: Liao (907–1125).* Philadelphia: Transactions of the American Philosophical Society, 1949.

Wu, K. C. *The Chinese Heritage.* New York: Crown, 1982.

Yin, Wen-Ching. *Le Système fiscal de la Chine.* Paris: Éditions et Publications Contemporaines, Pierre Bossuet, 1930.

CHAPTER THREE
FROM REPUBLIC TO EMPIRE: TAXING AND SPENDING IN CLASSICAL ATHENS AND REPUBLICAN AND IMPERIAL ROME

Abbott, Frank F., and Allen Chester Johnson. *Municipal Administration in the Roman Empire.* Princeton: Princeton University Press, 1926.

Abel, M. *Histoire de la Palestine depuis la conquête d'Alexandre jusq'à l'invasion arabe,* Vol. I. Paris: Librairie Lecoffre, J. Gabelda & Cie, 1952.

Andreades, A. "The Finance of Tyrant Governments in Ancient Greece," *Economic History,* Vol. 2, No. 5 (January 1930), pp. 1–18.

Aristotle. *The Art of Rhetoric,* translated by John Henry Freese. London: Heinemann, 1926.

Badian, E. *Publicans and Sinners.* Oxford: Basil Blackwell, 1972.

Bengtson, Hermann. *Griesische Geschichte von den Anfängen bis in die römische Kaiserzeit,* 3rd ed. Munich: C. H. Beck, 1965.

Boeckh, Augustus. *The Public Economy of the Athenians,* 2 vols. London: John Murray, 1828.

Bogaert, Raymond. *Les Origines antiques de la banque de dépôt.* Preface by Fritz M. Heichelheim in English. Leyden: A. W. Sijthoff, 1966.

Brown, Peter. *The Making of Late Antiquity.* Cambridge, Mass.: Harvard University Press, 1978.

————. *The World of Late Antiquity from Marcus Aurelius to Muhammad.* London: Thames & Hudson, 1971.

Brunt, P. A. "The Administration of Roman Egypt," *Journal of Roman Studies,* Vol. LXV (1975), pp. 124–47.

———. "The 'Fiscus' and Its Development," *Journal of Roman Studies,* Vol. LVI (1966), pp. 75–91.

———. "Free Labour and Public Works at Rome," *Journal of Roman Studies,* Vol. LXX (1980), pp. 81–100.

———. "Princeps and Equites," *Journal of Roman Studies,* Vol. LXXIII (1983), pp. 42–75.

———. "The Revenues of Rome," *Journal of Roman Studies,* Vol. LXXI (1981), pp. 161–72.

———. *Social Conflicts in the Roman Republic.* London: Chatto & Windus, 1971.

Bullock, Charles J. *Politics, Finance, and Consequences.* Cambridge, Mass.: Harvard University Press, 1939.

Burford, A. "Heavy Transport in Classical Antiquity," *Economic History Review,* 2nd Series, Vol. XIII, No. 1 (August 1960).

Bury, J. B. *History of the Later Roman Empire,* Vols. I and II. New York. Dover, 1958, 1959.

Cambridge Ancient History, Vols. 5, 6, 10, and 12. Cambridge, Eng.: Cambridge University Press. Vol. 5, *Athens, 478–401 B.C.,* ed. J. B. Bury, S. A. Cook, and F. E. Adcock, 1940. Vol. 6, *Macedon, 401–301 B.C.,* ed. Bury, Cook, and Adcock, 1953. Vol. 10, *The Augustan Empire, 44 B.C.–A.D. 70,* ed. Cook, Adcock, and M. P. Charlesworth, 1971. Vol. 12, *The Imperial Crisis and Recovery,* ed. Cook, Adcock, Charlesworth, and N. H. Baynes, 1939.

Cambridge Economic History of Europe, Vol. II, *Trade and Industry in the Middle Ages.* Cambridge, Eng.: Cambridge University Press, 1952.

Cawkwell, G. L. "Athenian Naval Power in the Fourth Century," *The Classical Quarterly,* New Series, Vol. XXXIV, No. 2 (1984), pp. 334–45.

Charlesworth, M. P. *Trade Routes and Commerce in the Roman Empire.* Cambridge, Eng.: Cambridge University Press, 1926.

Coale, Ansley. "A History of the Human Population," *Scientific American,* September 1974, pp. 43–44.

Crawford, Michael. *The Roman Republic.* Hassocks, N.J.: Harvester Press, 1978.

Duff, A. M. *Freedmen in the Early Roman Empire.* Cambridge, Eng.: W. Heffer, 1958.

Duncan-Jones, R. P. *The Economy of the Roman Empire.* Cambridge, Eng.: Cambridge University Press, 1974.

———. Review of Walter Goffart, *Caput and Colonate: Toward a History of Late Roman Taxation* (Toronto and Buffalo: University of Toronto Press, 1974), in *Journal of Roman Studies,* Vol. LXVII (1977), pp. 202–9.

Dureau de La Malle, M. *Économie politique des Romains,* Vol. 2. Paris: Chez L. Hachette, 1840.

Ehrenberg, Victor. *The Greek State.* Oxford: Basil Blackwell, 1960.

Engels, Donald. "The Use of Historical Demography in Ancient History," *The Classical Quarterly,* Vol. XXXIV (1984), No. 2, pp. 386–93.

Ferguson, John. *The Heritage of Hellenism.* New York: Science History Publications, 1973.

Finley, M. I. *The Ancient Economy.* Berkeley: University of California Press, 1973.

———. *Politics in the Ancient World.* Cambridge, Eng.: Cambridge University Press, 1983.

Fournier de Flaix, E. *L'Impôt dans les diverses civilisations.* Paris: Guillaumin & Cie., 1897.

Frank, Tenney. *An Economic History of Rome.* New York: Cooper Square Publishers, Inc., 1962.

———. *An Economic Survey of Ancient Rome,* Vol. 1, *Rome and Italy of the Republic;* Vol. 5, *Rome and Italy of the Empire.* Baltimore: Johns Hopkins, 1933, 1940.

———. "The Financial Activities of the Equestrian Corporations," *Classical Philology,* Vol. XXVIII, No. 1 (January 1933), pp. 1–10.

French, A. *The Growth of the Athenian Economy.* London: Routledge & Kegan Paul, 1964.

Garnsey, Peter, Keith Hopkins, and C. R. Whittaker. *Trade in the Ancient Economy.* London: Chatto & Windus, 1983.

Grady, Eleanor H. *Epigraphic Sources of the Delphic Amphictyony.* Ph.D. thesis, Columbia University, 1931.

Hammond, N. G. L. *A History of Greece to 322 B.C.* Oxford: Clarendon Press, 1967.

Hands, A. R. *Charities and Social Aid in Ancient Greece and Rome.* Ithaca: Cornell University Press, 1968.

Heichelheim, Fritz M. *An Ancient Economic History,* Vol. II, translated by Joyce Stevens. Leyden: A. W. Sijthoff, 1965.

Henderson, Bernard W. *The Life and Principate of the Emperor Hadrian.* New York: Brentano, 1923.

Hignett, C. *A History of the Athenian Constitution to the End of the 5th Century B.C.* Oxford: Clarendon Press, 1952.

Hill, H. *The Roman Middle Class in the Republican Period.* Oxford: Basil Blackwell, 1952.

Hohlwein, Nicholas. *L'Égypte romaine: Recueil des termes techniques relatifs aux institutions politiques et administratives de l'Égypte romaine suivi d'un choix de textes papyrologiques.* Brussels: Hayez, 1912.

Hopkins, Keith. "On the Probable Age Structure of the Roman Population," *Population Studies,* Vol. XX, No. 1 (November 1966), pp. 245–64.

———. "Taxes and Trade in the Roman Empire (200 B.C.–A.D. 400)," *Journal of Roman Studies,* Vol. LXX (1980), pp. 101–25.

Humbert, Gustave. *Essai sur les finances et la comptabilité publique chez les Romains.* Paris: Ernest Thorin, 1886.

Johnson, Allen Chester. *Egypt and the Roman Empire.* Ann Arbor: University of Michigan Press, 1951.

Jones, A. H. M. *Ancient Economic History.* London: H. K. Lewis, 1948.

———. *Athenian Democracy.* Oxford: Basil Blackwell, 1966.

———. *The Greek City from Alexander to Justinian.* Oxford: Clarendon Press, 1966.

———. *A History of Rome Through the 5th Century,* Vol. I, *The Repubic.* New York: Walker & Co., 1968.

———. "Inflation Under the Roman Empire," *Economic History Review,* 2nd Series, Vol. V (1953), No. 3, 293–318.

———. *The Later Roman Empire,* 2 vols. Oxford: Basil Blackwell, 1964.

———. *The Roman Economy.* Oxford: Basil Blackwell, 1974.

———. "The Social Structure of Athens in the 4th Century B.C.," *Economic History Review,* 2nd Series, Vol. VIII, No. 2 (December 1955), pp. 141–55.

———. *Studies in Roman Government and Law.* Oxford: Basil Blackwell, 1960.

Letorneau, C. *Property: Its Origin and Development*. London: Walter Scott, Ltd., 1892.

Littleton, A. C., and B. S. Yamey, eds. *Studies in the History of Accounting*. Homewood, Ill.: Richard Irwin, 1956.

Lombroso, Giacomo. *Recherches sur l'économie politique de l'Égypte sous les Lagides*. Turin: Imprimerie Royale, Bocca Frères, 1870.

Marquardt, Joachim. *Römische Statsverwaltung*, Vol. 2. Leipzig, 1876. Vol. 5 of *Handbuch der römischen Alterthümer*, by J. Marquardt and T. Mommsen.

Maspéro, Henri. *Les Finances de l'Égypte sous les Lagides*. Paris: Presented to the Faculty of Letters for the Diplome d'Études Supérieures, 1905.

Matthews, J. C. "The Tax Law of Palmyra: Evidence for Economic History in a City of the Roman East," *Journal of Roman Studies*, Vol. LXXIV (1984), pp 157–80.

Millar, Fergus. "The Aerarium and Its Officials Under the Empire," *Journal of Roman Studies*, Vol. LIV (1964), pp. 33–40.

————. "The Emperor, the Senate and the Provinces," *Journal of Roman Studies*, Vol. LVI (1966), pp. 156–66.

————. "Empire and City, Augustus to Julian: Obligations, Excuses and Status," *Journal of Roman Studies*, Vol. LXXIII (1983), pp. 76–96.

————. "The Fiscus in the First Two Centuries," *Journal of Roman Studies*, Vol. LIII (1963), pp. 29–42.

————. "The Political Character of the Classical Roman Republic, 200–151 B.C.," *Journal of Roman Studies*, Vol. LXXIV (1984), pp. 1–19.

————. Review of H.-G. Pflaum, *Les Carrières procuratoriennes équestres sous le haut-Empire Romain*, in *Journal of Roman Studies*, Vol. LIII (1963), pp. 194–200.

d'Orgeval, Bernard. *L'Empereur Hadrien: Oeuvre législative et administrative*. Paris: Éditions Domat Montchrestien, 1950.

Ostwald, Martin. *Nomos and the Beginnings of the Athenian Democracy*. Oxford: Clarendon Press, 1969.

Richardson, J. S. "The Spanish Mines and the Development of Provincial Taxation in the Second Century B.C.," *Journal of Roman Studies*, Vol. LXVI (1976), pp. 139–52.

Rogers, R. H. "What the Sibyl Said: Frontinus AQ.7.5," *Classical Quarterly*, Vol. 32, No. 1 (1982), pp. 174–77.

Rostovsteff, Mikhail. *The Social and Economic History of the Hellenistic World*. Oxford: Clarendon Press, 1941.

————. *The Social and Economic History of the Roman Empire*. Oxford: Clarendon Press, 1926.

Scullard, H. H. *From the Gracchi to Nero: A History of Rome from 133 B.C. to A.D. 68*. London: Methuen, 1965.

Seager, Robert, ed. *The Crisis of the Roman Republic*. Cambridge, Eng., and New York: Heffer/Barnes & Noble, 1969.

Serrigny, D. *Droit public et administratif romain*, Vol. 2. Paris: Auguste Durand, 1862.

Seyffert, Oskar. *A Dictionary of Classical Antiquities*, revised and edited by H. Nettleship and J. E. Sandys. New York and Cleveland: World-Meridian, 1961.

————, and Walther Schwann. "Telonai," in *Real-Encyclopädie der Classischen Altertumswissenschaft*, by Pauly-Wissowa, Vol. 5A, No. 1, pp. 418–25. Stuttgart: Metzler, 1934.

Sherwin-White, A. N. "Procurator Augusti," *Papers of the British School at Rome,* Vol. 15 (1939), pp. 11–26.

Sterghiopolous, Constantin D. *Les Finances grèques au VIe siècle.* Athens: Collection de l'Institut Français d'Athènes, 1949.

Syme, Ronald. *The Roman Revolution.* Oxford: Clarendon Press, 1960.

Talbert, Richard A. "Augustus and the Senate," *Greece and Rome,* Vol. XXXI, No. 1 (April 1984), pp. 55–63.

Tierney, Brian, Donald Kagan, and L. Pierce Williams, eds. *Great Issues in Western Civilization,* Vol. 1. New York: Random House, 1968.

Trever, Albert E. *History of Ancient Civilization,* Vol. I, *The Ancient Near East and Greece.* New York: Harcourt, Brace, 1936.

————. *History of Ancient Civilization,* Vol. II, *The Roman World.* New York: Harcourt, Brace, 1939.

Wallace, S. C. *Taxation in Egypt from Augustus to Diocletian.* Princeton: Princeton University Press, 1938.

Watson, G. R. *The Roman Soldier.* Ithaca: Cornell University Press, 1969.

Weber, Max. *General Economic History,* translated by Frank H. Knight. Glencoe, Ill.: The Free Press, 1927.

————. *The Theory of Social and Economic Organization,* translated and edited by Talcott Parsons. New York: Oxford University Press, 1947.

Webster, Graham. *The Roman Imperial Army of the First and Second Centuries A.D.* London: Black, 1969.

Wittfogel, Karl A. *Oriental Despotism: A Comparative Study of Total Power.* New Haven: Yale University Press, 1957.

Woolf, Arthur H. *A Short History of Accountants and Accountancy.* London: Gee & Co., 1912.

CHAPTER FOUR
FINANCE IN THE PRIVATE GOVERNMENTS OF MEDIEVAL EUROPE: POOR KINGS

Andreades, A. "Le Montant du budget de l'empire byzantine," *Revue des études grècques,* Vol. XXXIV, pp. 47–52.

Barraclough, Geoffrey. *The Origins of Modern Germany.* Oxford: Basil Blackwell, 1947.

Becker, M. B. "Economic Change and the Emerging Florentine Territorial State," *Studies in the Renaissance,* Vol. XIII. New York: Renaissance Society of America, 1968.

Bisson, Thomas N. *Conservation of Coinage, Monetary Exploitation and Its Restraint in France, Catalonia, and Aragon, c. A.D. 1000–c. 1225.* Oxford: Clarendon Press, 1979.

————, *Fiscal Accounts of Catalonia Under the Early Count-Kings (1151–1213).* Berkeley: University of California Press, 1984.

Bloch, Marc. *Feudal Society.* Chicago: University of Chicago Press, 1961.

Boissionnade, P. *Life and Work in Medieval Europe: The Evolution of Medieval Economy from the Fifth to the Fifteenth Century.* New York: Harper Torchbooks, 1964.

Bowsky, William M. *The Finance of the Commune of Sienna, 1287–1355.* Oxford: Clarendon Press, 1970.

——. "The Impact of the Black Death Upon Sienese Government and Society," *Speculum,* Vol. XXXIV (1964), pp. 1–34.

——, ed. *Studies in Medieval and Renaissance History,* Vols. II and IV. Lincoln: University of Nebraska Press, 1965, 1967.

Brown, Peter. *The World of Late Antiquity.* London: Thames & Hudson, 1971.

Brucker, Gene. *The Civic World of Early Renaissance Florence.* Princeton: Princeton University Press, 1977.

Cambridge Economic History of Europe, Vols. I–III. Cambridge, Eng.: Cambridge University Press. Vol. I, *The Agrarian Life of the Middle Ages,* ed. M. Postan, 1966. Vol. II, *Trade and Industry in the Middle Ages,* ed. M. Postan and E. Rich, 1952. Vol. III, *Economic Organization and Policies in the Middle Ages,* ed. M. Postan, 1963.

Cambridge Medieval History, Vols. II and III. New York: Macmillan, 1913.

Chamberlain, Carol. "Government Finance in the Italian Communes in the 11th to 15th Centuries" (mimeo), 1971.

Cipolla, Carlo. *Clocks and Culture.* London: Collins, 1967.

——. "Currency Depreciation in Medieval Europe," *Economic History Review,* 2nd Series, Vol. XV, No. 3 (April 1963), pp. 413–22.

——. *Money, Prices and Civilization in the Mediterranean World.* Princeton: Princeton University Press, 1956.

Clagett, Marshall, Gaines Post, and Robert C. Reynolds, eds., *Twelfth Century Europe and the Foundations of Modern Society.* Madison: University of Wisconsin Press, 1961.

Cristiani, Emilio. *Nobilità e popolo nel comune di Pisa.* Naples, Italy: Istituto Italiano per gli Studii Storici 1962 (pbn. 13),

Davies, R. R. "Baronial Accounts, Incomes and Arrears in the Later Middle Ages," *Economic History Review,* 2nd Series, Vol. XXI, No. 2 (August 1968), pp. 211–29.

Davis, R. H. C. *A History of Medieval Europe.* London: Longmans Green, 1957.

Deanesly, Margaret. *A History of Early Medieval Europe.* London: Methuen, 1957.

Douglas, David C., and George W. Greenaway, eds. *English Historical Documents,* Vol. II (1042–1189). New York: Oxford University Press, 1953.

Duby, Georges. *The Early Growth of the European Economy: Warriors and Peasants from the Seventh to the Twelfth Century.* Ithaca: Cornell University Press, 1974.

——. *The Knight, the Lady and the Priest: The Making of Modern Marriage in Medieval France.* New York: Pantheon Books, 1983.

——, "Manorial Economy," in *The New International Encyclopedia of the Social Sciences,* Vol. 9. New York: Macmillan and The Free Press, 1968.

——. *Rural Economy and Country Life in the Medieval West.* London: Edward Arnold Publishers Ltd., 1968.

Einzig, Paul. *The Control of the Purse: Progress and Decline of Parliament's Financial Control.* London: Secker & Warburg, 1959.

Fawtier, Robert. *The Capetian Kings of France.* New York and London: Macmillan, 1962.

Fèbvre, Lucien. *Life in Renaissance France.* Cambridge, Mass.: Harvard University Press, 1977.

Fesler, James W. "French Field Administration," *Comparative Studies in Society and History,* Vol. 5, No. 1 (October 1962), pp. 76–111.

————. "The Political Role of Field Administration," in *Papers in Comparative Administration*. Ann Arbor: University of Michigan Institute of Public Administration, 1962, pp. 117–43.

————, ed. *American Public Administration: Patterns of the Past*. Washington, D.C.: American Society for Public Administration, 1982.

Fichtenau, Heinrich. *The Carolingian Empire*. Oxford: Basil Blackwell, 1957.

Forey, A. J. *The Templars in the Corona de Aragón*. London: Oxford University Press, 1973.

Gimpel, Jean. *The Medieval Machine*. New York: Holt, Rinehart & Winston, 1976.

Girouard, Mark. *Life in the English Country House: A Social and Architectural History*. New Haven: Yale University Press, 1978.

Hall, Hubert. *The Antiquities and Curiosities of the Exchequer*. London: Elliot Stock, 1891.

Harris, G. L. "Fictitious Loans," *Economic History Review*, 2nd Series, Vol. III, No. 2 (December 1955), pp. 187–99.

Harvey, S. "Royal Revenue and Domesday Terminology," *Economic History Review*, 2nd Series, Vol. XX, No. 2 (August 1967), pp. 221–28.

Haskins, Charles Homer. *The Normans in European History*. Boston: Houghton Mifflin, 1915.

Herlihy, David. "Direct and Indirect Taxes in Tuscan Urban Finance," *Finances et comptabilité urbaines du xiie et xive siècles,* International Colloquium at Blankenberge, September 6–9, 1962. Brussels: pro Civitate, 1964.

————. *Medieval and Renaissance Pistoia: A Social History of an Italian Town, 1200–1430*. New Haven: Yale University Press, 1967.

————, Robert S. Lopez, and Vsevolod Slessarev, eds. *Economy, Society and Government in Medieval Italy,* essays in memory of Robert Reynolds. Kent, Ohio: Kent State University Press, 1969.

Hicks, John. *A Theory of Economic History*. Oxford: Clarendon Press, 1969.

Himmelfarb, Gertrude. *The Idea of Poverty: England in the Early Industrial Age*. New York: Knopf, 1984.

Holmes, George. *The Later Middle Ages*. Edinburgh: Norton, 1962.

Hopkins, M. Keith. "On the Probable Age Structure of the Roman Population," *Population Studies,* Vol. 20, No. 2 (November 1966), pp. 245–64.

Howell, Margaret. *Regalian Right in Medieval England*. London: Athelone Press, 1962.

Hunt, R. W., W. A. Pantin, and R. W. Southern, eds. *Studies in Medieval History,* presented to F. M. Powicke. Oxford: Clarendon Press, 1969.

Hurstfield, J. "The Profits of Fiscal Feudalism," *Economic History Review,* 2nd Series, Vol. VIII, No. 1 (August 1955), pp. 53–61.

Jewell, Helen M. *English Local Administration in the Middle Ages*. Newton Abbot: David & Charles, 1972.

Johnson, Chalmers. "La Serenissima of the East," *Asian and African Studies,* Vol. 18, No. 1 (March 1984), pp. 57–73.

Jones, A. H. M. *The Later Roman Empire,* 2 vols. Oxford: Basil Blackwell, 1964.

Kantorowicz, Ernst H. *Selected Studies*. Locust Valley, N.Y.: J. J. Austin, 1965.

Kaeuper, Richard W. *Bankers to the Crown: The Riccardi of Lucca and Edward I*. Princeton: Princeton University Press, 1973.

Landes, David S. *Revolution in Time: Clocks and the Making of the Modern World*. Cambridge: Harvard University Press, 1983.

Lemerle, " 'Roga' et rente d'état aux xe-xie siècles," *Revue des Études Byzantines,* Vol. 25 (1967), pp. 73–97.

Lewis, Ewart. *Medieval Political Ideas,* Vol. I. New York: Knopf, 1954.

Lieber, Alfred E. "Eastern Business Practices and Medieval Commerce," in *Economic History Review,* 2nd Series, Vol. XXI, No. 2 (August 1968), pp. 230–43.

Little, A. G., and F. M. Powicke, eds. *Essays in Medieval History.* Freeport, N.Y.: Books for Libraries Press, 1967.

Littleton, A. C., and B. S. Yamey. *Studies in the History of Accounting.* Homewood, Ill.: Irwin, 1956.

Lopez, Robert. *The Birth of Europe.* London: J. M. Dent, 1967.

Luzzatto, Gino. *Il debito pubblico della Repubblica di Venezia.* Milan: Istituto Editoriale Cisalpino, 1963.

Lyon, Bryce. *A Constitutional and Legal History of Medieval England.* New York: Harper & Brothers, 1960.

———. *From Fief to Indenture: The Transition from Feudal to Non-Feudal Contract in Western Europe.* Cambridge, Mass.: Harvard University Press, 1957.

———. *The High Middle Ages.* Glencoe, Ill.: The Free Press, 1964.

———, and Adriaan Verhulst. *Medieval Finance: A Comparison of Financial Institutions in Western Europe.* Brussels: University of Ghent, 1967.

———. *The Origins of the Middle Ages: Pirenne's Challenge to Gibbon.* New York: Norton, 1972.

Martines, Lauro. *Power and Imagination: City States in Renaissance Italy.* New York: Knopf, 1979.

McEvedy, Colin. *The Penguin Atlas of Medieval History.* Penguin, 1969.

McKisack, May. *The Fourteenth Century, 1307–1399.* Vol. 5 of *The Oxford History of England.* Oxford: Clarendon Press, 1959.

Miskimin, Harry A. *The Economy of Later Renaissance Europe, 1460–1600.* Cambridge, Eng.: Cambridge University Press, 1977.

Moir, Esther. *The Justice of the Peace.* Harmondsworth, Eng.: Penguin, 1969.

Myers, A. R. *England in the Late Middle Ages.* Penguin, 1952.

———, ed. *English Historical Documents,* Vol. IV. New York: Oxford University Press, 1969.

New International Encyclopedia of the Social Sciences. Vol. 2, "Centralization–Decentralization"; Vol. 5, "Feudalism"; Vol. 9, "Manorial Economy." New York: Macmillan and The Free Press, 1968.

Olson, Clair C., and Martin M. Crow, eds. *Chaucer's World.* New York: Columbia University Press, 1961.

Painter, Sidney. *The Rise of the Feudal Monarchies.* Ithaca: Cornell University Press, 1963.

Petit-Dutaillis, Charles. *The Feudal Monarchy in France and England.* New York: Barnes & Noble, 1966.

Pirenne, Henri. *Economic and Social History of Medieval Europe.* New York: Harcourt, Brace, 1937.

———. *Medieval Cities: Their Origins and the Revival of Trade.* Princeton: Princeton University Press, 1948.

Poole, Reginald L. *The Exchequer in the Twelfth Century.* Oxford: Clarendon Press, 1912.

Powicke, Maurice. *The Thirteenth Century, 1216–1307.* Oxford: Clarendon Press, 1970.

Rosenthal, Joel T. *The Purchase of Paradise: Gift Giving and the Aristocracy, 1307–1485.* London: Routledge & Kegan Paul, 1972.

Rubinstein, Nicolai, ed. *Florentine Studies: Politics and Society in Renaissance Florence.* London: Faber & Faber, 1968.

Sayles, G. O. *The Medieval Foundations of England.* London: Methuen, 1964.

Schloss, Aran. "Finance Administration in the Italian Communes, Twelfth to Fourteenth Centuries" (mimeo). 1973.

Stephenson, Carl. *Medieval Feudalism.* Ithaca: Cornell Paperbacks, 1969.

———, and Bruce Lyon. *Medieval History.* New York: Harper & Row, 1964.

Stourm, René. *The Budget.* New York: D. Appleton & Co., 1917.

Strayer, Joseph R. *Medieval Statecraft and the Perspectives of History.* Princeton: Princeton University Press, 1971.

———. *The Reign of Philip the Fair.* Princeton: Princeton University Press, 1980.

———, and Charles H. Taylor. *Studies in Early French Taxation.* Cambridge, Mass.: Harvard University Press, 1939.

Taylor, R. Emmett. *No Royal Road: Luca Pacioli and His Times.* Chapel Hill: University of North Carolina Press, 1942.

Thompson, James Westfall. *Economic and Social History of Europe in the Later Middle Ages.* New York: Frederick Ungar, 1931.

———, and Edgar N. Johnson. *An Introduction to Medieval Europe.* New York: Norton, 1937.

Tierney, Brian, Donald Kagan, and L. Pearce Williams, eds. *Great Issues in Western Civilization,* Vol. I. New York: Random House, 1967.

Tierney, Brian, and Sidney Painter. *Western Europe in the Middle Ages.* New York: Knopf, 1970.

Twitchett, D. C. *Financial Administration under the T'ang Dynasty.* Cambridge, Eng.: Cambridge University Press, 1963.

Vickers, Geoffrey. "Institutional and Personal Roles," *Human Relations,* Vol. XXIV, No. 5 (October 1971), pp. 433–47.

Waldo, Dwight, ed. *Temporal Dimensions of Development Administration.* Durham, N.C.: Duke University Press, 1970.

Waley, Daniel. *The Italian City Republics.* New York: McGraw-Hill, 1969.

White, Lynn T., Jr. *Medieval Technology and Social Change.* London: Oxford University Press, 1964.

Whitlock, Dorothy. *The Beginnings of English Society.* Gretna, La.: Pelican, 1952.

Wolfe, Martin. "French Views on Wealth and Taxes from the Middle Ages to the Old Regime," *Journal of Economic History,* Vol. XXVI (1966), pp. 468–83.

Woolf, Arthur H. *A Short History of Accountants and Accountancy.* London: Gee & Co., 1912.

CHAPTER FIVE
POOR PEOPLE, RICH KINGS:
GETTING AND SPENDING IN EARLY-MODERN EUROPE

Ashley, Maurice. *The Age of Absolutism.* Springfield: Merriam, 1974.

———. *Financial and Commercial Policy Under the Cromwellian Protectorate.* London: Frank Case, 1934.

Ashton, Robert. *The Crown and the Money Market.* Oxford: Clarendon Press, 1960.

———. "Revenue Farming under the Early Stuarts," *Economic History Review,* Vol. VIII, No. 3 (April 1956), pp. 310–21.

Aston, Trevor. *Crisis in Europe, 1560–1660.* New York: Basic Books, 1965.

Aylmer, G. E. *The King's Servants: The Civil Service of Charles I, 1625–1642.* London: Routledge & Kegan Paul, 1974.

————. *The State's Servants: The Civil Service of the English Republic.* London and Boston: Routledge & Kegan Paul, 1973.

Barbour, Violet. *Capitalism in Amsterdam in the 17th Century.* Ann Arbor: University of Michigan Press, 1963.

Behrens, Betty. "Nobles, Privileges and Taxes in France at the End of the Ancien Régime," *Economic History Review,* 2nd Series, Vol. XV (1963), No. 3, pp. 451–75.

Behrens, C. B. A. *The Ancien Régime.* New York: Harcourt, Brace, Jovanovich, 1967.

Beloff, Max. *The Age of Absolutism.* London: Hutchison University Library, 1967.

Berenger, Jean. "Public Loans and Austrian Policy in the Second Half of the Seventeenth Century," *Journal of European Economic History,* Vol. 2 (1973), No. 3, pp. 657–69.

Binney, J. E. D. *British Public Finance and Administration, 1774–1792.* Oxford: Clarendon Press, 1958.

Bland, A. E., P. A. Brown, and R. H. Tawney, eds. *English Economic History: Select Documents.* London: Bell, 1915.

Bosher, J. F. *French Finances, 1770–1795: From Business to Bureaucracy.* Cambridge, Eng.: Cambridge University Press, 1970.

————, ed. *French Government and Society, 1500–1850,* essays in memory of Alfred Cobban. London: Athelone Press, 1972.

Braudel, Fernand. *Capitalism and Material Life, 1400–1800.* New York: Harper & Row, 1974.

————. *The Mediterranean and the Mediterranean World in the Age of Philip II,* 2 vols. New York: Harper & Row, 1966.

————. *The Wheels of Commerce: Civilization and Capitalism, 15th–18th Century.* New York: Harper & Row, 1982.

Break, George, and Joseph A. Pechman. *Federal Tax Reform: The Impossible Dream?* Washington: Brookings Institution, Studies of Government Finance, 1975.

Brittain, Sir Herbert. *The British Budgetary System.* New York: Macmillan, 1959.

Bruun, Geoffrey. *The Enlightened Despots.* New York: Holt, Rinehart & Winston, 1967.

Caiden, Naomi. "Plus Ça Change . . . Financial Administration under the Ancien Régime from the Middle Ages to the Revolution" (mimeo). Haifa, May 1974.

————, and Aaron Wildavsky. *Planning and Budgeting in Poor Countries.* New York: John Wiley, 1974.

Calabria, Antonio. "Taxes and Budgets: The Neopolitan Fiscal System in the Sixteenth and Seventeenth Centuries" (mimeo). Berkeley, Calif.

Cambridge Economic History of Europe, Vol. IV, ed. E. E. Rich and C. H. Wilson. Cambridge, Eng.: Cambridge University Press, 1967.

Cambridge Modern History, Vol. VI, *The Eighteenth Century,* eds. A. W. Ward, G. W. Prothero, and S. Leathes. Cambridge, Eng.: Cambridge University Press, 1934.

Cameron, Rondo. *Banking in the Early Stages of Industrialization.* New York: Oxford University Press, 1967.

Cassirer, Ernest. *The Philosophy of the Enlightenment,* translated by F. C. A. Koelln and J. P. Pettegrove. Boston: Beacon Press, 1961.

Chapman, Brian. *The Profession of Government: The Public Service in Europe.* London: George Allen & Unwin, 1959.

Cipolla, Carlo, ed. *The Economic Decline of Empires.* Oxford: Clarendon Press, 1970.

——. *The Fontana Economic History of Europe,* Vol. III, *The Industrial Revolution.* London and Glasgow: Collins/Fontana, 1973.

——. *The Fontana Economic History of Europe,* Vol. II, *The Sixteenth and Seventeenth Centuries.* London and Glasgow: Collins/Fontana, 1974.

Dakin, Douglas. *Turgot and the Ancien Régime in France.* New York: Octagon Books, 1965.

Darnton, Robert. *The Great Cat Massacre and Other Episodes in French Cultural History.* New York: Basic Books, 1984.

Davenant, Charles. *Discourses on the Public Revenues and the Trade of England.* London: James Knapton, 1698.

Davies, Margaret Gay. "Country Gentry and Payments to London," *Economic History Review,* 2nd Series, Vol. XXIV, No. 1, February 1971.

Dent, Julian. "An Aspect of the Crisis of the Seventeenth Century: The Collapse of the Financial Administration of the French Monarchy, 1653–61," *Economic History Review,* 2nd Series, Vol. XX, No. 2 (August 1967), pp. 241–56.

——. *Crisis in Finance: Crown, Financiers and Society in Seventeenth Century France.* Newton Abbot: David & Charles, 1973.

Dickson, P. G. M. *The Financial Revolution in England: A Study in the Development of Public Credit, 1688–1756.* London: Macmillan/St. Martin's Press, 1967.

Dietz, Frederick C. "The Exchequer in Elizabeth's Reign," *Smith College Studies in History,* Vol. VIII, No. 2 (January 1923).

Dorwart, Reinhold. *The Administrative Reforms of Frederick William I of Prussia.* Cambridge, Mass.: Harvard University Press, 1953.

Earle, Peter, ed. *Essays in European Economic History, 1500–1800.* Oxford: Clarendon Press, 1974.

Ehrenberg, Richard. *Capital and Finance in the Age of the Renaissance.* New York: Augustus M. Kelley, 1963.

Einzig, Paul. *The Control of the Purse: Progress and Decline of Parliament's Financial Control.* London: Secker & Warburg, 1959.

Elliott, J. H. *Imperial Spain, 1469–1716.* London: Edward Arnold, 1963.

Eyre, E., ed. *European Civilization: Its Origin and Development.* Oxford: Oxford University Press, 1937.

Ford, Franklin L. *Robe and Sword: The Regrouping of the French Aristocracy after Louis XIV.* New York: Harper & Row, 1953.

Friedrich, Carl J. "The Continental Tradition of Training Administrators in Law and Jurisprudence," *Journal of Modern History,* Vol. XI (1939), No. 2, pp. 129–48.

Geertz, Clifford. *Peddlers and Princes: Social Change and Economic Modernization in Two Indonesian Towns.* New York and Chicago: University of Chicago Press, 1968.

Geyl, Peter. *The Netherlands in the Seventeenth Century.* London: Ernest Benn, 1961.

Gilbert, Felix, ed. *The Historical Essays of Otto Hintze.* New York: Oxford University Press, 1975.

Gill, Doris M. "The Treasury, 1660–1714," *English Historical Review,* Vol. XLV, No. 184 (October 1931), pp. 600–22.

Goethe's Faust, Parts I and II, translated by Sir Theodore Martin. New York and London: Everyman Library, 1971.

Gunn, J. A. W. *Politics and the Public Interest in the Seventeenth Century.* London and Toronto: Routledge & Kegan Paul/University of Toronto, 1969.

Habakkuk, J. J. "Public Finance and the Sale of Confiscated Property during the Interregnum," *Economic History Review,* 2nd Series, Vol. XV, No. 1 (August 1962), pp. 70–88.

Hacking, Ian. *The Emergence of Probability: A Philosophical Study of Early Ideas About Probability, Induction and Statistical Inference.* Cambridge, Eng.: Cambridge University Press, 1975.

Hagen, E., ed. *On the Theory of Social Change.* Homewood, Ill.: The Dorsey Press, 1962.

Haley, K. H. D. *The Dutch in the Seventeenth Century.* New York: Harcourt, Brace, Jovanovich, 1972.

Harris, G. L. "Fictitious Loans," *Economic History Review,* 2nd Series, Vol. VIII, No. 2 (December 1955), pp. 187–99.

Harris, R. W. *Absolutism and Enlightenment.* New York: Humanities Press, 1966.

Heckscher, Eli F. *An Economic History of Sweden,* translated by Goran Ohlin. Cambridge, Mass.: Harvard University Press, 1963.

Herr, R. *The Eighteenth Century Revolution in Spain.* Princeton: Princeton University Press, 1958.

Hill, B. W. "The Change of Government and 'Loss of the City,' 1710–1711," *Economic History Review,* 2nd Series, Vol. 24, No. 3 (August 1971).

Hill, Christopher. *The Century of Revolution, 1603–1714.* New York: Norton, 1966.

———. *Society and Puritanism in Pre-Revolutionary England.* New York: Schocken, 1972.

Hinrichs, Harley. *A General Theory of Tax Structure Change During Economic Development.* International Tax Program, Harvard Law School, Cambridge, Mass., 1966.

Hinze, Otto. "Die Behoardanorganisation und die allgemeine Staatsverwaltung Preussens im 18. Jahrhundert" (The Organization of the Boards and the General Administration in Prussia During the 18th Century), *Acta Borussica, Die Behoardenorganisation* 6/1. Berlin: Paul Parey, 1901.

Hoon, E. E. *The Organization of the English Customs System.* Newton Abbot: David & Charles, 1968.

Horn, D. B., and Mary Ransome, eds. *English Historical Documents, 1714–1783.* New York: Oxford University Press, 1957.

Hovde, B. J. *The Scandinavian Countries,* Vol. II, *The Rise of the Middle Classes.* Boston: Chapman & Grimes, 1943.

Hurstfield, J. "The Profits of Fiscal Feudalism, 1541–1602," *Economic History Review,* 2nd Series, Vol. VIII, No. 1 (August 1955).

Jago, Charles. "The Influence of Debt on the Relations Between Crown and Aristocracy in Seventeenth Century Castile," *Economic History Review,* 2nd Series, Vol. 26, No. 2 (May 1973), pp. 218–36.

Jennings, Robert M., and Andrew P. Trout. "Internal Control: Public Finance in

17th Century France," *Journal of European Economic History,* Vol. I (1972), No. 3, pp. 647–60.

Joachim-Braun, Hans. "The Economic Theory and Policy in Germany, 1750–1800," *Journal of European Economic History,* Vol. 4 (1975), No. 2, pp. 301–22.

Joslin, D. M. "London Private Bankers, 1720–1785," *Economic History Review,* 2nd Series, Vol. 7, No. 2 (December 1954), pp. 167–86.

Kerr, Alfred Boardman. *Jacques Coeur, Merchant Prince of the Middle Ages.* New York: Scribners, 1927.

Knight, Melvin M., Harry Elmer Barnes, and Felix Flugel. *Economic History of Europe.* Boston: Houghton Mifflin, 1928.

Ladurie, Emmanuel LeRoy. *Carnival in Romans.* New York: George Braziller, 1979.

———. *The Mind and Method of the Historian.* Chicago: University of Chicago Press, 1981.

Lefèbvre, Georges. *The Coming of the French Revolution.* Princeton: Princeton University Press, 1969.

Lennox, Thomas. "The Development of Prussian Financial Administration in the Late 17th and 18th Centuries" (mimeo). Berkeley.

Locke, John. *Two Treatises on Government,* ed. Peter Laslett. Cambridge, Eng.: Cambridge University Press, 1967.

Lodge, Eleanor C. *Sully, Colbert and Turgot: A Chapter in French Economic History.* London and Port Washington, N.Y.: Methuen/Kennikat Press, 1931.

Lublinskaya, A. D. *French Absolutism: The Crucial Phase, 1620–29.* Cambridge, Eng.: Cambridge University Press, 1968.

Manuel, Frank E. *The Age of Reason.* Ithaca: Cornell University Press, 1965.

Mathias, Peter. *The First Industrial Nation: An Economic History of Britain, 1700–1914.* New York: Scribners, 1969.

Matthews, George T. *The Royal General Farms in Eighteenth Century France.* New York: Columbia University Press, 1958.

Maurois, André. *A History of France,* translated by Henry L. Binsee and Gerald Hopkins. New York: Farrar, Straus & Cudahy, 1956.

McCulloch, J. R. *Old and Scarce Tracts on Money.* London: P. S. King, 1933.

Miskimin, Harry A. *The Economy of Later Renaissance Europe.* Cambridge, Eng.: Cambridge University Press, 1977.

Namier, Sir Lewis. *The Structure of Politics at the Accession of George III.* London: Macmillan, 1957.

Neymarck, A. *Colbert et son temps.* Geneva: Slarkine Reprints, 1970 (originally published 1877).

Northrop, F. C. S. *The Meeting of East and West.* New York: Macmillan, 1960.

Outhwaite, R. B. "The Trials of Foreign Borrowing: The English Crown and the Antwerp Money Market in the Mid-Sixteenth Century," *Economic History Review,* 2nd Series, Vol. XIX, No. 2 (August 1966), pp. 289–305.

Palmer, R. R. *The Age of the Democratic Revolution: A Political History of Europe and America,* Vol. I, *The Challenge.* Princeton: Princeton University Paperbacks, 1971.

Pechman, Joseph A. *Federal Tax Policy.* Washington: Brookings Institution, 1973.

Pepys, Samuel. *The Diary and Correspondence of Samuel Pepys,* ed. Richard Braybrooke and M. Bright, Vols. I–VI. New York: Dodd, Mead, 1887.

————. *The Diary of Samuel Pepys: A New and Complete Transcript,* ed. Robert Latham and William Matthews, Vol. I. London: Bell, 1971.

Phelps-Brown, Ernest H., and Sheila V. Hopkins. "Seven Centuries of the Price of Consumables Compared with Builders' Wage Rates," *Economica,* New Series, Vol. XXIII (1956).

————. "Wage Rates and Prices, Evidence for Population Pressure in the Sixteenth Century," *Economica,* New Series, Vol. XXIV (1957).

Plumb, J. H. *Sir Robert Walpole: The Making of a Statesman.* London: Cresset, 1956.

Postlethwayt, Malachy. *Great Britain's True System* (London, 1757). New York: Augustus Kelley, Reprints of Economic Classics, 1967.

Pressnell, L. S. "Public Monies and the Development of English Banking," *Economic History Review,* 2nd Series, Vol. V (1953), No. 3, pp. 378–97.

Pullan, Brian. *Rich and Poor in Renaissance Venice.* Oxford: Basil Blackwell, 1971.

Radian, Alex. "Budgeting in the Cromwellian Protectorate, 1653–1659; From Traditional to Modern Financial and Budget Systems and Procedures" (mimeo). Berkeley, May 1972.

————. "Budgeting in England from the Restoration to the Beginning of the Napoleonic Wars: Impoverished Kings, Affluent Kings and Wasteful Ministers" (mimeo). Berkeley, September 1972.

Ranum, O. A. *Richelieu and the Councillors of Louis XIII; A Study of the Secretaries of State and Superintendents of Finance in the Ministry of Richelieu, 1635–1642.* Oxford: Clarendon Press, 1963.

Redlich, Fritz. *Steeped in Two Cultures: A Selection of Essays.* New York: Harper & Row, 1971.

Rees, J. F. *A Short Fiscal and Financial History of England, 1815–1918.* London: Methuen, 1921.

Richardson, W. C. "Some Financial Expedients of Henry VIII," *Economic History Review,* 2nd Series, Vol. 7, No. 1 (August 1954), pp. 33–48.

————. *Stephen Vaughan, Financial Agent of Henry VIII.* Baton Rouge: Louisiana State University Press, 1953

Robinson, A. T. V. "The Exchequer and Audit Department," *Journal of Public Administration,* Vol. 2, No. 2 (April 1924), pp. 142–52.

Roover, Raymond de. *Business, Banking and Economic Thought in Late Medieval and Early-Modern Europe,* ed. Julius Kirshner. Chicago: Chicago University Press, 1974.

Rosenberg, Hans. *Bureaucracy, Aristocracy and Autocracy: The Prussian Experience.* Cambridge, Mass.: Harvard University Press, 1958.

Roseveare, Henry. *The Treasury: The Evolution of a British Institution.* New York: Columbia University Press, 1969.

————. *The Treasury, 1660–1870: The Foundations of Control.* London and New York: George Allen & Unwin/Barnes & Noble, 1973.

Rothkrug, Lionel. *Opposition to Louis XIV: The Political and Social Origins of the French Enlightenment.* Princeton: Princeton University Press, 1965.

Rotwein, Eugene, ed. *David Hume: Writings on Economics.* Madison: University of Wisconsin Press, 1955.

Sampson, R. V. *Progress in the Age of Reason: The Seventeenth Century to the Present Day.* Cambridge, Mass.: Harvard University Press, 1956.

Schmoller, Gustav. *Umrisse und Untersuchungen zur Verfassungs- Verwaltungs- und*

Wirtschaftsgeschichte besonders des Prussichen Staates im 17. und 18. Jahrhundert (Sketches and Investigations in the Constitutional, Administrative and Economic History Especially of the Prussian State of the 17th and 18th Centuries). Leipzig: Duncker & Humblot, 1898.

Schumpeter, Joseph A. *Economic Doctrine and Method.* New York: Oxford University Press, 1954.

———. *History of Economic Analysis.* New York: Oxford University Press, 1955.

Scott, James C. *Comparative Political Corruption* (especially "Proto Corruption in Early Stuart England"). Englewood Cliffs: Prentice-Hall, 1972.

Scott, William R. *The Constitution and Finance of the English, Scottish and Irish Joint-Stock Companies to 1720,* Vol. I, *The General Development of the Joint-Stock System.* Cambridge, Eng.: Cambridge University Press, 1912.

Scoville, Warren C. *The Persecution of Huguenots and French Economic Development 1680–1720.* Berkeley: University of California Press, 1960.

Sinclair, John. *A History of the Public Revenues of the British Empire.* London: Strahan, 1790.

Slavin, Arthur J., ed. *The "New Monarchies" and Representative Assemblies.* Boston: D. C. Heath, 1964.

Smith, Adam. *Lectures on Justice, Police Revenue and Arms,* ed. Edwin Cannan. New York: Kelley & Millman, 1956.

———. *The Wealth of Nations.* ed. Cannon. New York: Modern Library, 1937.

Stephens, W. Walter, ed. *The Life and Writings of Turgot.* London: Longmans, Green, 1895.

Stone, Lawrence. *The Crisis of the Aristocracy, 1558–1641.* London: Oxford University Press, 1965.

———. *Family and Fortune.* London: Oxford University Press, 1973.

———. *Social Change and Revolution in England, 1540–1640.* New York: Barnes & Noble, 1965.

Swart, K. W. *Sale of Offices in the Seventeenth Century.* Rotterdam: Martinus Nijhoff, 1949.

Temple, Sir William. *Collected Works,* Vol. 1. New York: Greenwood Press, 1968.

Tilly, Charles, ed. *The Formation of National States in Western Europe.* Princeton: Princeton University Press, 1975.

Tilly, Charles. *The Vendée.* Cambridge, Mass.: Harvard University Press, 1976.

Treasure, G. R. R. *Cardinal Richelieu and the Development of Absolutism.* London: Black, 1972.

Usher, A. P. *The Early History of Deposit Banking in Mediterranean Europe.* Cambridge, Eng.: Cambridge University Press, 1943.

Wilson, Charles. *Anglo-Dutch Commerce and Finance in the Eighteenth Century.* Cambridge, Eng.: Cambridge University Press, 1966.

———. *The Dutch Republic and the Civilization of the Seventeenth Century.* London and New York: Weidenfeld & Nicholson/McGraw-Hill, 1968.

Wolfe, Martin. *The Fiscal System of Renaissance France.* New Haven: Yale University Press, 1972.

———. "French Views on Wealth and Taxes from the Middle Ages to the Old Regime," *Journal of Economic History,* Vol. 26 (1966).

Woolf, Stuart. "The Aristocracy in Transition: A Continental Comparison," *Economic History Review,* 2nd Series, Vol. XXIII, No. 3 (December 1970).

CHAPTER SIX
THE WAYS AND MEANS OF PUBLIC GOVERNMENT:
TAXING AND SPENDING IN REPRESENTATIVE STATES OF THE EARLY
INDUSTRIAL AGE

Alber, Jens. *Von Armenhaus zum Wohlfahrtsstaat: Analysen zur Entwicklung der Sozialversicherung in Westeuropa.* Frankfurt: Campus Verlag, 1982.

Alt, James E. "The Evolution of Tax Structures," *Public Choice,* Vol. 41 (1983), pp. 181–222.

Anderson, Eugene N., and Pauline R. Anderson. *Political Institutions and Social Change in Continental Europe in the Nineteenth Century.* Berkeley: University of California Press, 1967.

Ashworth, William. *An Economic History of England, 1870–1939.* London: Methuen, 1960.

Barker, Michael. *Gladstone and Radicalism: The Reconstruction of Liberal Policy in Britain, 1885–1894.* New York: Harper & Row, 1975.

Bastable, C. F. *Public Finance.* London: Macmillan, 1903.

Blake, Robert. *Disraeli.* London: Eyre & Spottiswoode, 1966.

———. *Disraeli and Gladstone* (the Leslie Stephen Lecture, 1969). Cambridge, Eng.: Cambridge University Press, 1969.

Braudel, Fernand. *The Wheels of Commerce: Civilization and Capitalism, 15th–18th Century,* Vol. 2. New York: Harper & Row, 1979.

Briggs, Asa. *Victorian People: A Reassessment of Persons and Themes, 1851–1867.* Chicago: University of Chicago Press, 1970.

Buchanan, James. *Fiscal Theory and Political Economy.* Chapel Hill: University of North Carolina Press, 1960.

Buck, A. E. *The Budget In Governments of Today.* New York: Macmillan, 1934.

Buxton, Sidney. *Mr. Gladstone as Chancellor of the Exchequer,* 2 vols. London: John Murray, 1901.

Caiden, Naomi. "Patterns of Budgeting: The Experience of France, 987–1830," unpublished doctoral dissertation, University of Southern California, May 1978.

Cipolla, Carlo M., ed. *The Fontana Economic History of Europe,* Vol. 4, *The Emergence of Industrial Societies,* Part 1. London and Glasgow: Collins/Fontana, 1973.

———, ed. *The Fontana Economic History of Europe,* Vol. III, *The Industrial Revolution.* London and Glasgow: Collins/ Fontana, 1973.

Cottrell, Philip L. "Anglo-French Financial Cooperation 1850–1880," *Journal of European Economic History,* Vol. 3, No. 1 (Spring 1974), pp. 54–86.

Deane, Phyllis, and W. A. Cole. *British Economic Growth, 1688–1959.* Cambridge, Eng.: Cambridge University Press, 1964.

Dudden, Arthur Power. *Joseph Fels and the Single-Tax Movement.* Philadelphia: Temple University Press, 1971.

Ely, Richard T. *Taxation in American States and Cities.* New York: Thomas Crowell, 1888.

Ferguson, E. James. *The Power of the Purse: A History of American Public Finance, 1776–1790.* Chapel Hill: University of North Carolina Press, 1961.

Fischer, Wolfram. "The Strategy of Public Investment in XIXth Century Germany," *Journal of European Economic History,* Vol. 6, No. 2 (Fall 1977), pp. 431–42.

Flamant, Maurice, and Jeanne Singer-Kerel. *Modern Economic Crises and Recessions,* translated by Pat Wardroper. New York and Evanston: Harper Colophon, 1970.

Forsythe, Dall W. *Taxation and Political Change in the Young Nation, 1781–1833.* New York: Columbia University Press, 1977.

Gay, Peter, and R. K. Webb. *Modern Europe.* New York: Harper & Row, 1973.

Gershenkron, Alexander. *Continuity in History and Other Essays.* Cambridge, Mass.: Belknap Press of Harvard University Press, 1968.

Giffen, Robert. *Essays in Finance.* London: George Bell, 1890.

Gillespie, Frances E. *Labour and Politics in England, 1850–1867.* Durham, N.C.: Duke University Press, 1927.

Gladstone, W. E. *The Financial Statements of 1853, 1860–1863.* London: John Murray, 1863.

Grice, J. Watson. *National and Local Finance.* London: P. S. King, 1910.

Grigg, John. *Lloyd George: The People's Champion, 1902–1911.* Berkeley: University of California Press, 1978.

Guedalla, Philip, ed. *Gladstone and Palmerston.* New York and London: Harper, 1928.

Hamerow, Theodore S. *The Birth of a New Europe: State and Society in the Nineteenth Century.* Chapel Hill and London: University of North Carolina Press, 1983.

Hammond, Bray. *Sovereignty and an Empty Purse: Banks and Politics in the Civil War.* Princeton: Princeton University Press, 1970.

Hartwell, Ronald M. *The Industrial Revolution and Economic Growth.* London: Methuen, 1971.

Heclo, Hugh. *Modern Social Politics in Britain and Sweden: From Relief to Income Maintenance.* New Haven and London: Yale University Press, 1974.

Heidenheimer, Arnold J., Hugh Heclo, and Carolyn Teich Adams. *Comparative Public Policy: The Politics of Social Choice in Europe and America.* New York: St. Martin's Press, 1975.

Henderson, W. O. *The State and Industrial Revolution in Prussia, 1480–1870.* Liverpool: University of Liverpool Press, 1958.

Himmelfarb, Gertrude. *The Idea of Poverty: England in the Early Industrial Age.* New York: Alfred A. Knopf, 1983.

Hirst, Francis W. *Gladstone as Financier and Economist.* London: Ernest Benn, 1931.

Hobsbawm, E. J. *The Age of Revolution, 1789–1848.* New York: Mentor, 1962.

———. "The British Standard of Living," *Economic History Review,* 2nd Series, Vol. X (1957), No. 1, pp. 46–61.

Holmes, Colin J. "Laissez-faire in Theory and Practice: Britain, 1800–1875," *Journal of European Economic History,* Vol. 5, No. 3 (Winter 1976), pp. 671–88.

Knowles, L. C. A. *Economic Development in the Nineteenth Century.* London: Routledge & Sons, 1932.

Kuznets, Simon. *Modern Economic Growth: Rate, Structures and Spread.* New Haven: Yale University Press, 1966.

Lee, W. R. "Tax Structure and Economic Growth in Germany, 1750–1850," *Journal of European Economic History,* Vol. 4, No. 1 (Spring 1975), pp. 153–78.

Llewellyn, Alexander. *The Decade of Reform: The 1830s.* New York: St. Martin's Press, 1971.

Lubenow, William C. *The Politics of Government Growth: Early Victorian Attitudes Toward State Intervention, 1833–1848.* Newton Abbot, Devon: David & Charles, 1971.

Lynd, Helen M. *England in the Eighteen-Eighties: Toward a Social Basis for Freedom.* London: Oxford University Press, 1945.

Lynn, Arthur D., Jr. "Adam Smith's Fiscal Ideas: An Eclectic Revisited," *National Tax Journal,* Vol. XXIX, No. 4 (December 1976), pp. 369–78.

Machlup, Fritz, ed. *Essays on Hayek.* New York: New York Univ., 1976.

MacKenzie, Norman and Jeanne. *The Fabians.* New York: Simon and Schuster, 1977.

Marshall, Dorothy. *Industrial England, 1776–1851.* London: Routledge & Kegan Paul, 1973.

Mathias, Peter. *The First Industrial Nation: An Economic History of Britain, 1700–1914.* New York: Scribners, 1983.

———, and Patrick O'Brien. "Taxation in Britain and France, 1715–1810, a Comparison of the Social and Economic Incidence of Taxes Collected for Central Governments," *Journal of European Economic History,* Vol. 5, No. 3 (Winter 1976), pp. 601–50.

Mill, John Stuart. *Principles of Political Economy.* Boston: Little, Brown, 1848.

Milward, Alan S., and S. B. Saul. *The Development of the Economies of Continental Europe, 1850–1914.* London: George Allen & Unwin, 1977.

———. *The Economic Development of Continental Europe, 1780–1870.* London: George Allen & Unwin, 1973.

Mitchell, B. R. *European Historical Statistics, 1750–1970.* New York: Columbia University Press, 1975.

Morley, John. *The Life of William Ewart Gladstone,* 3 vols. London: Macmillan, 1903.

Murray, Charles. *Losing Ground: American Social Policy, 1950–1980.* New York: Basic Books, 1984.

Myers, Margaret G. *A Financial History of the United States.* New York: Columbia University Press, 1970.

Northcote, Sir Stafford H. *Twenty Years of Financial Policy: A Summary of the Chief Financial Measures Passed between 1842 and 1861.* London: Saunders, Otley & Co., 1862.

Offner, Avner. "Empire and Social Reform: British Overseas Investment and Domestic Politics, 1908–1914," *The Historical Journal,* Vol. 26 (1983), No. 1, pp. 119–38.

Okun, Arthur M. *Equality and Efficiency: The Big Tradeoff.* Washington: Brookings Institution, 1975.

Paine, Thomas. *Complete Works.* Chicago: Donohue Bros., 1870

Peacock, Alan T., and Jack Wiseman. *The Growth of Public Expenditure in the United Kingdom* (National Bureau of Economic Research). Princeton: Princeton University Press, 1961.

Pechman, Joseph A. *Federal Tax Policy.* Washington: Brookings Institution, 1971.

Perkin, Harold. *The Origins of Modern English Society.* London: Routledge & Kegan Paul, 1969.

Plehn, Carl C. *Introduction to Public Finance.* New York: Macmillan, 1896.

Pollard, Sidney. *The Genesis of Modern Management.* London: Edward Arnold, 1965.

Price, Roger, ed. *1848 in France.* Ithaca: Cornell University Press, 1975.

Ratcliffe, Barrie M. "The Tariff Reform Campaign in France, 1831–1836," *Journal of European Economic History,* Vol. 7, No. 1 (Spring 1968), pp. 61–138.

Rees, J. F. *A Short Fiscal and Financial History of England.* London: Methuen, 1921.

Rogers, James E. Thorold. "Local Taxation, Especially in English Cities and Towns," a speech delivered before Parliament on March 23, 1886, published by the Cobden Club. London: Cassell & Co., 1886.

Roseveare, Henry. *The Treasury: The Evolution of a British Institution.* New York: Columbia University Press, 1968.

———. *The Treasury, 1660–1870: The Foundations of Control.* London: George Allen & Unwin, 1973.

Routh, Guy. *The Origin of Economic Ideas.* New York: Vintage Books, 1977.

Sabine, B. E. V. *A History of Income Tax.* London: George Allen & Unwin, 1966.

Schumpeter, Joseph A. *History of Economic Analysis.* New York: Oxford University Press, 1954.

Seligman, Edwin R. A. *Essays in Taxation.* New York: Macmillan, 1925.

———. *The Income Tax.* New York: Macmillan, 1914.

———. *Progressive Taxation in Theory and Practice.* Princeton: Princeton University Press, 1908.

Shehab, F. *Progressive Taxation: A Study in the Development of the Progressive Principle in the British Income Tax.* Oxford: Clarendon Press, 1953.

Sherman, Dennis. "Governmental Responses to Economic Modernization in Mid-nineteenth Century France," *Journal of European Economic History,* Vol. 6, No. 3 (Winter 1977), pp. 717–36.

Smith, Adam. *An Inquiry into the Nature and Causes of the Wealth of Nations,* Vol. 2, ed. Cannon. New York: Modern Library, 1937.

Steinmo, Sven. "Taxation as an Instrument of Public Policy: Sweden—the Carrot and the Stick," paper presented to the European Consortium of Political Research, Salzburg, Austria, April 13–18, 1984 (mimeo).

Stourm, René. *The Budget,* translated by Thaddeus Plazinski. New York: Appleton, 1917.

Tarschys, Daniel. "Government Growth: The Case of Sweden, 1523–1983." University of Strathclyde Center for the Study of Public Policy, Studies in Public Policy No. 121. Glasgow, 1983.

Thompson, E. P. *The Making of the English Working Class.* New York: Vintage Books, 1963.

White, R. J. *Waterloo to Peterloo.* London: William Heineman, 1957.

Wiseman, Jack. "Genesis, Aims and Goals of Social Policy," paper delivered at the 39th Congress of the International Institute of Public Finance, Budapest, Hungary, August 22–26, 1983 (mimeo).

CHAPTER SEVEN
BALANCED REGIMES, BALANCED BUDGETS:
WHY AMERICA WAS SO DIFFERENT

Adams, Henry Carter. *Public Debts: An Essay in the Science of Finance.* New York: Appleton, 1887.

————. *The Science of Finance: An Investigation of Public Expenditures and Public Revenues.* New York: Henry Holt, 1899.

Baack, Bennett D., and Edward John Ray. "The Political Economy of Tariff Policy: A Case Study of the United States," *Explorations in Economic History,* Vol. 20 (1983), pp. 73–93.

————. "Special Interests and Constitutional Amendments: A Study of the Adoption of the Income Tax in the U.S." Working Paper No. 84-5, Department of Economics, Ohio State University, September 1963.

Beard, Charles. "Prefatory Note," *Municipal Research,* No. 88 (August 1917). New York: Bureau of Municipal Research.

Bialer, Seweryn, and Sophia Sluzar, eds. *Sources of Contemporary Radicalism.* Boulder, Colo.: Westview Press, 1977.

Blau, Joseph L., ed. *Social Theories of Jacksonian Democracy.* New York: Bobbs-Merrill, 1954.

Bolles, Albert S. *The Financial History of the United States: From 1861 to 1885.* New York: Appleton, 1886.

————. *The Financial History of the United States, 1774–89.* New York: D. Appleton, 1879.

Borcherding, Thomas, ed. *Budgets and Bureaucrats: Sources of Government Growth.* Durham, N.C.: Duke University Press, 1977.

Bryce, James "Lord." *The American Commonwealth.* London: Macmillan, 1891.

Buck, A. E. "The Development of the Budget Idea in the United States," *Annals of the American Academy of Political and Social Science,* Vol. LXIII, May 1924.

————. *Public Budgeting.* New York: Harper, 1929.

Bullock, Charles. "The Finances of the United States from 1775–1789 With Special Reference to the Budget," *Bulletin of the University of Wisconsin,* Vol. 1 (1894–1896). Madison, Wisc., 1897.

Burkhead, Jesse. *Government Budgeting.* New York and London: John Wiley/Chapman & Hall, 1956.

Butler, Nicholas M. "Executive Responsibility and a National Budget." *Proceedings of the Academy of Political Science,* Vol. 8 (1918–20).

Cleveland, Frederick A. "Constitutional Provisions for a Budget." *Proceedings of the Academy of Political Science,* Vol. 5 (1914), No. 1, pp. 141–62.

————. "Leadership and Criticism," *Proceedings of the Academy of Political Science,* Vol. 8 (1918–20), No. 1.

————, and Arthur E. Buck. *The Budget and Responsible Government.* New York: Macmillan, 1920.

————, and J. Schafer, eds. *Democracy in Reconstruction.* Boston: Houghton Mifflin, 1919.

Collins, Charles Wallace. *The National Budget System,* New York: Macmillan, 1917.

Crecine, Patrick, et al. "Presidential Management of Budgetary and Fiscal Policymaking," *Political Science Quarterly,* Vol. 95, No. 3 (Fall 1980), pp. 395–425.

Dawes, Charles G. *The First Year of the Budget of the United States.* New York: Harper, 1923.

Dewey, Davis R. *Financial History of the United States.* New York: Longmans, Green, 1939.

Ecker-Racz, L. L. *The Politics and Economics of State–Local Finance.* Englewood Cliffs, N.J.: Prentice-Hall, 1970.

Eisenstein, Louis. *The Ideologies of Taxation.* New York: Ronald Press, 1961.

Fenno, Richard F., Jr. *The Power of the Purse: Appropriations Politics in Congress.* Boston: Little, Brown, 1966.

Ferguson, E. James. *The Power of the Purse: A History of American Public Finance, 1776–1790.* Chapel Hill, N.C.: University of North Carolina Press, 1961.

Fitzpatrick, Edward A. *Budget Making in a Democracy: A New View of the Budget.* New York: Macmillan, 1918.

Forsythe, Dall W. *Taxation and Political Change in the Young Nation, 1781–1833.* New York: Columbia University Press, 1977.

Gilbert, Charles. *American Financing of World War I.* Westport, Conn.: Greenwood Press, 1970.

Grayson, Theodore J. *Leaders and Periods of American Finance.* New York: John Wiley, 1932.

Hartz, Louis. *Economic Policy and Democratic Thought: Pennsylvania, 1776–1860.* Chicago: Quadrangle Books, 1968.

———. *The Liberal Tradition in America.* New York: Harcourt, Brace, 1955.

Higgs, Robert, ed. *Emergence of the Modern Political Economy.* JAI, forthcoming.

Huntington, Samuel P. *The Common Defense.* New York: Columbia University Press, 1969.

Jefferson, Thomas. *Works,* ed. Paul Leicester Ford, Vol. VIII. New York: G. P. Putnam's Sons, The Knickerbocker Press, 1904.

Jensen, Jens P. *Property Taxation in the United States.* Chicago: University of Chicago Press, 1931.

Kaufman, Herbert. "Emerging Conflicts in the Doctrines of Public Administration," *American Political Science Review,* Vol. 50, December 1956, pp. 1057–73.

Kimmel, Lewis H. *Federal Budget and Fiscal Policy, 1789–1958.* Washington: Brookings Institution, 1959.

King, Anthony. "Ideas, Institutions and the Policies of Governments: A comparative analysis, Part III," *British Journal of Political Science,* Vol. 3, October 1973, pp. 409–23.

Kraines, Oscar. *Congress and the Challenge of Big Government.* New York: Bookman Associates, 1958.

Latham, Earl, ed. *The Philosophy and Policies of Woodrow Wilson.* Chicago: University of Chicago Press, 1958.

Lengle, James I. "The Appropriations Process as a Political Instrument." Typescript, 1973.

Marx, Fritz Morstein. "The Bureau of the Budget: Its evolution and present role," *American Political Science Review,* Vol. 39, No. 4 (August 1945), pp. 653–84.

Mellon, Andrew. *Taxation: The People's Business.* New York: Macmillan, 1924.

Myers, Margaret G. *A Financial History of the United States.* New York: Columbia University Press, 1970.

Nash, Gary B. *The Urban Crucible: Social Change, Political Consciousness and the Origins of the American Revolution.* Cambridge, Mass.: Harvard University Press, 1979.

Naylor, E. E. *The Federal Budget System in Operation.* Washington: Hayworth Printing, 1941.

Netzer, Richard. *Economics of the Property Tax.* Washington: Brookings Institution, 1966.

North, Douglas C. "The Growth of Government in the United States: An Economic Historian's Perspective." Typescript, May 1984.

Paul, Randolph E. *Taxation in the United States.* Boston: Little, Brown, 1954.

Pechman, Joseph. *Federal Tax Policy.* Washington: Brookings Institution, 1971.

Ratchford, B. U. *American State Debts.* Durham, N.C.: Duke University Press, 1941.

Ratner, Sidney. *American Taxation: Its History as a Social Force in Democracy.* New York: Norton, 1942.

———. *Taxation and Democracy in America.* New York: John Wiley & Sons, 1942.

Savage, James. "Balanced Budgets and American Politics." Dissertation in progress, Political Science Dept., University of California, Berkeley, 1983.

Schultz, William J., and M. R. Caine. *Financial Development of the United States.* New York: Prentice-Hall, 1937.

Secler-Hudson, Cathryn. "Budgeting: An Instrument of Planning and Management. Unit I, The Evolution of the Budgetary Concept in the Federal Government." Typescript, American University, 1944.

Stein, Herbert. *The Fiscal Revolution in America.* Chicago: University of Chicago Press, 1969.

Sumner, William Graham. *The Financier and the Finances of the American Revolution.* New York: Dodd, Mead, 1891.

Taussig, Frank W. *The Tariff History of the United States,* 8th revised ed. New York: Putnam, 1931.

Tocqueville, Alexis de. *Democracy in America.* New York: Alfred A. Knopf, 1945.

Tucker, Robert C., and David C. Hendrickson. *The Fall of the First British Empire: Origins of the War of American Independence.* Baltimore and London: Johns Hopkins Press, 1982.

Waldo, Dwight. *The Administrative State: A Study of the Political Theory of American Public Administration.* New York: Ronald Press, 1948.

Webster, Pelatiah. *Political Essays on the Nature and Operation of Money, Public Finances, and Other Subjects.* Philadelphia: Joseph Crukshank, 1791.

White, Leonard D. *The Federalists: A Study in Administrative History.* New York: Macmillan, 1961.

———. *The Jacksonians: A Study in Administrative History, 1829–1861.* New York: Macmillan, 1954.

———. *The Jeffersonians: A Study in Administrative History, 1801–1829.* New York: Macmillan, 1951.

Wildavsky, Aaron. *The Politics of the Budgetary Process,* 4th ed. Boston: Little, Brown, 1984.

Willoughby, William Franklin. "The Budget as an Instrument of Political Reform," *Proceedings of the Academy of Political Science,* Vol. 8 (1918–20).

———. *The National Budget System with Suggestions for its Improvement.* Baltimore: Johns Hopkins Press, 1927.

———. *The Problem of a National Budget.* New York: D. Appleton, 1918.

Wilmerding, Lucius, Jr. *The Spending Power: A History of the Efforts of Congress to Control Expenditures.* New Haven: Yale University Press, 1943.

Wilson, Woodrow. *College and State Educational, Literary and Political Papers, 1875–1913,* Vol. 1. New York: Harper, 1925.

———. *Congressional Government: A Study in American Politics.* Boston: Houghton Mifflin, 1892.

Witte, John. *The Politics and Development of the Federal Income Tax.* Madison: University of Wisconsin Press, 1985.

Yearly, Clinton. *The Money Machines: The Breakdown and Reform of Governmental and Party Finance in the North, 1860–1920.* Albany: State University of New York Press, 1970.

Young, James Sterling. *The Washington Community, 1800–1828.* New York: Columbia University Press, 1966.

CHAPTER EIGHT

STABILITY AMIDST TURBULENCE: THE HALF CENTURY AFTER 1914

Andic, Suphan, and Jindrich Veverka. "The Growth of Government Expenditure in Germany Since the Unification," *Finanzarchiv,* 1964, pp. 169–278.

Annals of the American Academy of Political and Social Science, Vol. LXXV, January 1981.

Argyris, Chris. *The Impact of Budgets on People.* New York: Controllership Foundation, 1952.

Bellini, James. *French Defence Policy.* London: Royal United Services for Defence Studies, 1974.

Bernardo, C. J., and E. H. Bacon. *American Military Policy.* Harrisburg, Pa.: Military Service Publishing Co., 1955.

Brady, Robert A. *The Rationalization Movement in German Industry.* New York: Columbia University Press, 1937.

Brittain, Herbert. *The British Budgetary System.* New York: Macmillan, 1959.

Burke, Kathleen, ed. *War and the State.* Winchester, Eng.: Allen & Unwin, 1982.

Caiden, Naomi, and Aaron Wildavsky. *Planning and Budgeting in Poor Countries.* New York: Wiley & Sons, 1974. Paperback ed. by Transaction Press, New Brunswick, N.J., 1980.

Carroll, Bernice. *Design for Total War.* Elmsford, N.Y.: Mouton, 1968.

Davies, Robert W. *The Development of the Soviet Budgetary System.* Cambridge, Eng.: Cambridge University Press, 1958.

Delorme, Robert, and Christine André. *L'État et l'économie.* Paris: Seuil, 1983.

Derthick, Martha. *Policymaking for Social Security.* Washington: Brookings Institution, 1979.

Doern, G. Bruce, and Allan M. Maslove, eds. *The Public Evaluation of Government Spending.* Toronto: Butterworth, 1979.

Drees, Willem. *On the Level of Government Expenditure in the Netherlands After the War.* Leiden: Stenfert Kroese, 1955.

Fenno, Richard F. "The House Appropriations Committee as a Political System: The Problem of Integration," *American Political Science Review,* Vol. 56 (1962), pp. 310–24.

Flora, Peter, and Arnold Heidenheimer, eds. *Development of Welfare States in Europe and America.* New Brunswick, N.J.: Transaction Books, 1981.

Gaston, Jèze, and Henri Truchy. *The War Finance of France.* New Haven: Yale University Press, 1927.

Ginsberg, Morris, ed. *Law and Opinions in England in the 20th Century.* Westport, Conn.: Greenwood Press, 1974.

Goodsell, Charles. *The Case for Bureaucracy.* Chatham, N.J.: Chatham House Publishers, 1983.

Haig, Robert M. *The Public Finances of Post-War France.* New York: Columbia University Press, 1929.

Hammond, Thomas H., and Jack H. Knott. *A Zero-Based Look at Zero-Base Budgeting; Or, Why Its Failures in State Government Are Being Duplicated in Washington.* New Brunswick, N.J.: Transaction Books, 1979.

Hancock, W. K., and M. M. Gowing. *British War Economy,* revised ed. Her Majesty's Stationery Office, 1975.

Hardach, Karl. *The Political Economy of Germany in the Twentieth Century.* Berkeley, Calif.: University of California Press, 1980.

Heclo, Hugh, and Aaron Wildavsky. *The Private Government of Public Money,* 2nd ed. London: Macmillan, 1981.

Hicks, Ursula. *British Public Finances.* London: Oxford University Press, 1958.

Horwitz, Samuel J. *State Intervention in Great Britain.* New York: Columbia University Press, 1949.

Kahn, R. F. "The Relation of Home Investment to Unemployment," *Economic Journal,* Vol. XLI, No. 162 (June 1931), pp. 173–98.

Kemp, Tom. *The French Economy, 1913–1939.* London: Longman Group, 1972.

Keynes, John Maynard, *Essays in Persuasion.* New York. Norton, 1963.

———. *The General Theory of Employment, Interest and Money.* New York: Macmillan, 1936.

Kimmel, Lewis H. *Federal Budget and Fiscal Policy, 1789–1958.* Washington: Brookings Institution, 1959.

Kindleberger, Charles P. *Economic Growth in France and Britain, 1851–1950.* New York: Simon and Schuster, 1964.

Kuisel, Richard F. *Capitalism and the State in Modern France.* Cambridge, Eng.: Cambridge University Press, 1975.

Landes, David S. *The Unbound Prometheus.* Cambridge, Eng.; Cambridge University Press, 1969.

League of Nations. *Memorandum on Public Finance:* 1921, 1922, 1922–1926, 1926 1928, Geneva

Lekachman, Robert. *The Age of Keynes.* New York: McGraw-Hill, 1966.

Leuchtenburg, William E. *Franklin D. Roosevelt and the New Deal.* New York: Harper & Row, 1963.

Maisel, Sherman J. *Macroeconomics Theories and Policies.* New York: Norton, 1982.

Marshall, T. H. *Social Policy.* London: Hutchinson University, 1965.

Middlemass, K. *Diplomacy of Illusion.* London: Weidenfeld & Nicolson, 1972.

Myrdal, Gunnar. *Varning för fredsoptimism.* Stockholm; Bonniers, 1944.

Olson, Mancur. *The Rise and Decline of Nations: Economic Growth, Stagflation, and Social Rigidities.* New Haven: Yale University Press, 1982.

Parker, R. A. C. *Europe, 1919–45.* London: Weidenfeld & Nicolson, 1967

Peacock, Alan, and Jack Wiseman. *The Growth of Public Expenditures in the United Kingdom.* Princeton: Princeton University Press, 1961.

Pechman, Joseph A. *Federal Tax Policy.* Washington: Brookings Institution, 1971.

Peden, G. C. *British Rearmament and the Treasury: 1932–1939.* Scottish Academic Press, 1979.

Peel, George. *The Financial Crisis of France.* London: Macmillan, 1926.

Perloff, Harvey Stephen. *Modern Budget Policies: A Study of the Budget Process in*

Present-Day Society. Ph.D. dissertation submitted to the Departments of Government and Economics, Harvard University, December 1, 1939.

Pollard, Sidney. *The Development of the British Economy, 1914–1967.* New York: St. Martin's Press, 1969.

Potter, Jim. *The American Economy Between the World Wars.* New York: Wiley & Sons, 1974.

Rimlinger, Gaston V. *Welfare Policy and Industrialization: Europe, America and Russia.* New York: Wiley & Sons, 1971.

Rustow, Dankwart. *The Politics of Compromise.* Princeton: Princeton University Press, 1955.

Scott, Robert E. "Budget Making in Mexico," *Inter-American Economic Affairs,* Vol. 9 (1955), pp. 3–20.

Smith, Dan Throop. "An Analysis of Changes in Federal Finances, July 1930–June 1938," *Review of Economic Statistics,* Vol. 20, November 1938, pp. 149–60.

Stourm, Renè. *The Budget.* New York: Appleton, 1917.

Turner, G. B., ed. *A History of Military Affairs.* Princeton: Princeton University Press, 1956.

Twentieth Century Fund. *More Security for Old Age.* New York, 1937.

U.S. Bureau of the Census. *Historical Statistics of the United States, Colonial Times to 1970,* Bicentennial ed., Part 2. Washington: U.S. Government Printing Office, 1975.

————. *Historical Statistics of the United States Since Colonial Times.* Washington: U.S. Government Printing Office, 1976.

————. *Historical Statistics of the United States from Colonial Times to 1957.* Stamford, Conn.: Fairfield Publishing Co., 1960.

Ward, Norman. *The Public Purse.* University of Toronto Press, 1962.

Weinstein, James. *The Corporate Ideal in the Liberal State, 1900–1918.* Boston: Beacon Press, 1968.

Wildavsky, Aaron. *Budgeting: A Comparative Theory of Budgetary Processes.* Boston: Little, Brown, 1975. A revised second edition to be published by Transaction, forthcoming 1986.

————. *How to Limit Government Spending.* Berkeley: University of California Press, 1980.

————. "The Political Economy of Efficiency: Cost–Benefit Analysis, Systems Analysis, and Program Budgeting," *Public Administration Review,* Vol. 26, December 1966, pp. 292–310.

————. *The Politics of the Budgetary Process,* 4th ed. Boston: Little, Brown, 1984.

Williams, Philip M. *Crisis and Compromise: Politics in the Fourth Republic,* 3rd ed. Hamden, Conn.: Archon Books, 1964.

Wood, Derek, and Derek Dempster. *The Narrow Margin.* Westport, Conn.: Greenwood Press, 1975.

CHAPTER NINE
**THE GROWTH OF THE WELFARE AND TAX STATES: FROM THE 1960s UNTIL
TODAY**

Aaron, Henry, ed. *The Value-Added Tax: Lessons from Europe.* Washington, D.C.: Brookings Institution, 1981.

Alt, James E. "The Evolution of Tax Structures," *Public Choice,* Vol. 41 (1983), pp. 181–223.

André, Christine, and Robert Delorme. "The Long Run Growth of Public Expenditure in France," *Finances publiques*, Vol. 33 (1978), No. 1–2, p. 49.

Armstrong, John. *The European Administrative Elite*. Princeton: Princeton University Press, 1973.

Ashford, Douglas E. *British Dogmatism and French Pragmatism*. London: Allen & Unwin, 1982.

Baylis, John, ed., *British Defense Policy in a Changing World*. London: Croom Helm, 1977.

Berger, Suzanne, ed., *Organizing Interests in Western Europe: Pluralism, Corporatism, and the Transformation of Politics*. Cambridge, Eng.: Cambridge University Press, 1981.

Bird, Richard M. "Trends in Taxation: Calculations and Speculations." Typescript.

Borcherding, Thomas. "The Growth of U.S. Public Spending: Another Look." Discussion paper 82-02-2, Simon Fraser University, School of Business Administration and Economics, Burnaby, 1982.

Castles, Francis G. *The Social Democratic Image of Society*. London: Routledge & Kegan Paul, 1978.

Cohen, Stephen, and Charles Goldfinger. *From Permacrisis to Real Crisis in French Social Security*. Berkeley: Institute of Urban and Regional Development, 1976.

Coughlin, Richard M. *Ideology, Public Opinion, and Welfare Policy*. Institute of International Studies Research Series, No. 42. Berkeley: University of California, 1980.

Delorme, Robert. *A New View on the Economic Theory of the State: A Case Study of France*. Paris: Centre d'Études Prospectives d'Économie Mathématique Appliqués à la Planification (mimeo), 1984.

Elvander, Nils. "The Politics of Taxation in Sweden: 1945–1970," *Scandinavian Political Studies*, Vol. 7 (1972), pp. 63–82.

Fedder, E. H., ed. *Defense Politics of the Atlantic Alliance*. New York: Praeger, 1980.

Federation of British Industries. *Taxation: In the Proposed European Free Trade Area*. London, 1958.

Flora, Peter, and Arnold J. Heidenheimer, eds. *The Development of the Welfare State in Europe and America*. New Brunswick, N.J.: Transaction Books, 1981.

Fried, Edward R., et al. *Setting National Priorities: The 1974 Budget*. Washington: Brookings Institution, 1973.

Guest, Dennis. *The Emergence of Social Security in Canada*. Vancouver: University of British Columbia Press, 1980.

Gumpel, Henry. *Taxation in the Federal Republic of Germany*. New York: Commerce Clearing House, 1963.

Heclo, Hugh, and Aaron Wildavsky. *The Private Government of Public Money*. London: Macmillan, 1974.

Heidenheimer, Arnold, Hugh Heclo, and Carolyn Teich Adams. *Comparative Public Policies: The Politics of Social Choice in Europe and America*. New York: St. Martin's Press, 1975.

Huntington, S. P. *The Common Defense*. New York: Columbia University Press, 1969.

James, Simon, and Christopher Nobes. *The Economics of Taxation*. Oxford: Philip Allan, 1978.

Kahan, Jerome H. *Security in the Nuclear Age*. Washington: Brookings Institution, 1975.

Kaldor, Nicholas. *Reports on Taxation I: Papers Related to the United Kingdom.* London: Anchor Press, 1980.

Kanter, Arnold. *Defense Politics.* Chicago: University of Chicago Press, 1979.

Kay, J. A., and M. A. King. *The British Tax System.* Oxford: Oxford University Press, 1978.

King, Anthony. "Ideas, Institutions, and Policies of Governments: A Comparative Analysis." *British Journal of Political Science,* Vol. 3, No. 4 (October 1974), pp. 291–313.

King, Ronald Frederick. "Tax Expenditures and Systematic Public Policy: An Essay on the Political Economy of the Federal Revenue Code," *Public Budgeting and Finance,* Spring 1984, pp. 14–31.

Kristol, Irving. *Two Cheers for Capitalism.* New York: Basic Books, 1978.

Leman, Christopher. *The Collapse of Welfare Reform: Political Institutions, Policy and the Poor in Canada and the United States.* Cambridge, Mass.: MIT Press, 1980.

Lindblom, Charles E. "Decision Making in Taxation and Expenditure." Paper for Conference on Public Finances: Needs, Sources and Utilization, National Bureau of Economic Research, April 1959.

Maier, Charles, ed. *Organizing Interests in Western Europe.* Cambridge, Eng.: Cambridge University Press, 1981.

Meade, J. E. *The Structure and Reform of Direct Taxation.* London: Allen & Unwin, 1978.

National Bureau of Economic Research, ed. *Foreign Tax Policies and Economic Growth.* New York: Columbia University Press, 1966.

Nordlinger, Erick. *On the Autonomy of the Democratic State.* Cambridge, Mass.: Harvard University Press, 1966.

Norr, Martin, and Pierre Kerlan. *Taxation in France.* Chicago: Commerce Clearing House, 1966.

Norr, Martin, Frank Duffy, and Harry Sterner. *Taxation in Sweden.* Boston: Little, Brown, 1959.

Organisation for Economic Cooperation and Development (OECD). *Income Tax Schedules, Distribution of Taxpayers and Revenues.* Report by the Committee on Fiscal Affairs. Paris, 1981.

———. *Occasional Studies.* July 1975.

———. *Public Expenditure on Education.* July 1976.

———. *Public Expenditure on Health.* July 1977.

———. *Public Expenditure on Income Maintenance Programmes.* July 1976.

———. *Public Expenditure Trends.* June 1978.

———. *Revenue Statistics of OECD Member Countries: 1965–1979.* Paris, 1980.

———. *The Taxation of Net Wealth, Capital Transfers, and Capital Gains of Individuals.* Report by the Committee on Fiscal Affairs. Paris, 1979.

———. *Tax Benefit Position of Selected Income Groups in OECD Member Countries, 1974–1978.* Report by the Committee on Fiscal Affairs. Paris, 1980.

Osgood, Robert. *NATO, the Entangling Alliance.* Chicago: University of Chicago Press, 1962.

Peacock, A. T., and J. Wiseman. *The Growth of Public Expenditures in the United States.* Princeton: Princeton University Press, 1961.

Pechman, Joseph. *Federal Tax Policy.* Washington: Brookings Institution, 1971.

————, and Benjamin Okner. *Who Bears the Tax Burden?* Washington, D.C.: Brookings Institution, 1974.

Rectenwald, Horst Claus, ed., *Secular Trends of the Public Sector.* Proceedings of the 32nd Congress of the Institut International de Finance Publiques. Paris: Éditions Cujas, 1976.

Rose, Richard. "Maximizing Revenue and Minimizing Political Costs: A Comparative Dynamic Analysis." Paper delivered at the Workshop on the Politics of Taxation, European Consortium for Political Research, Salzburg, April 1984.

————, and Guy Peters. *Can Governments Go Bankrupt?* New York: Basic Books, 1978.

Rosencrance, R. N. *Defense of the Realm.* New York, 1962.

Shonfield, Andrew. *Modern Capitalism: The Changing Balance of Public and Private Power.* London: Oxford University Press, 1965.

Snyder, W. P. *The Politics of British Defense Policy, 1945–1962.* Columbus: Ohio State University Press, 1964.

Steinmo, Sven. "Taxation as an Instrument of Public Policy: Sweden—the Carrot and the Stick." Paper presented to the European Consortium for Political Research, April 1984.

Stromberg, John L. *The Internal Mechanics of the Defense Budget Process, Fiscal 1958–1968.* Santa Monica, Calif.: Rand Corporation, 1970.

Tanzi, Vito. *The Individual Income Tax and Economic Growth: An International Comparison.* Baltimore: Johns Hopkins Press, 1969.

Tarschys, Daniel. "Curbing Public Expenditures: A Survey of Current Trends." Paper prepared for the Joint Activity on Public Management Improvement of the OECD, Technical Co-operation Service, April 1982.

———— —. "The Scissors Crisis in Public Finance," *Policy Sciences,* Vol. 15 (1983), pp. 205–24.

Wertheimer, Robert. "Tax Incentives in Germany," *National Tax Journal,* Vol. X (1957).

Wildavsky, Aaron. "Does Federal Spending Constitute a 'Discovered Fault' in the Constitution? The Balanced Budget Amendment." Paper prepared for the Conference on the Congressional Budget Process, the Carl Albert Center, University of Oklahoma, February 12–13, 1982.

————. "Doing Better and Feeling Worse: The Political Pathology of Health Policy," *Daedalus,* Winter 1976, pp. 105–23.

————. "From Chaos Comes Opportunity: The Movement Toward Spending Limits in American and Canadian Budgeting," *Canadian Public Administration,* Vol. 26, No. 2 (Summer 1983), pp. 163–81.

————. *How to Limit Government Spending.* Berkeley: University of California Press, 1980.

————. *Speaking Truth to Power.* Boston: Little, Brown, 1979.

————. "The Unanticipated Consequences of the 1984 Presidential Election," *Tax Notes,* Vol. 24, No. 2 (July 9, 1984), pp. 193–200.

————. "A Uniform Income Tax," *Tax Notes,* Vol. XII, No. 12, March 23, 1981, pp. 611–12.

Wilensky, Harold. *The Welfare State and Equality.* Berkeley: University of California Press, 1975.

Witte, John. *The Politics and Development of the Federal Income Tax.* Madison: University of Wisconsin Press, 1985.

CHAPTER TEN
A CULTURAL THEORY OF GOVERNMENTAL GROWTH
AND (UN)BALANCED BUDGETS

Blöndal, Gisli. "Balancing the Budget: Budgeting Practices and Fiscal Policy Issues in Iceland." *Public Budgeting and Finance,* Vol. 3, No. 2 (Summer 1983), pp. 47–63.

Boskin, Michael J., and Aaron Wildavsky, eds., *The Federal Budget: Economics and Politics.* New Brunswick, N.J.: Transaction Books, 1982.

Caiden, Naomi, and Aaron Wildavsky. *Planning and Budgeting in Poor Countries.* New Brunswick, N.J.: Transaction Books, 1980.

Castles, Francis G. *The Social Democratic Image of Society.* London: Routledge & Kegan Paul, 1978.

————, and Sten G. Borg. "The Influence of the Political Right on Public Income Maintenance Expenditure and Equality," *Political Studies,* Vol. 29, No. 4 (December 1981), pp. 604–21.

Daniels, Robert Vincent. *The Conscience of the Revolution: Communist Opposition in Soviet Russia.* New York: Simon and Schuster, 1969.

Dempster, Michael, and Aaron Wildavsky. "On Change ... or, There Is No Magic Size for an Increment," *Political Studies,* Vol. 27, No. 3 (September 1979), pp. 371–89.

Douglas, Mary. *In the Active Voice.* London: Routledge & Kegan Paul, 1982.

————, and Aaron Wildavsky. *Risk and Culture.* Berkeley: University of California Press, 1982.

Eckstein, Otto, ed., *Studies in the Economics of Income Maintenance.* Washington: Brookings Institution, 1967.

Fain, Haskell. *Between Philosophy and History: The Resurrection of Speculative Philosophy of History Within the Analytic Tradition.* Princeton: Princeton University Press, 1970.

Flora, Peter, and Arnold J. Heidenheimer, eds., *The Development of Welfare States in Europe and America.* New Brunswick, N.J.: Transaction, 1981.

Gough, Ian. *The Political Economy of the Welfare State.* London and Basingstoke: Macmillan Press, 1979.

————. "Theories of the Welfare State: A Critique," *International Journal of Health Services,* Vol. 8, No. 1 (1978), pp. 27–40.

Hewitt, Christopher. "The Effect of Political Democracy and Social Democracy on Equality in Industrial Societies: A Cross-National Comparison." *American Sociological Review,* Vol. 42 (1977), pp. 450–64.

Higgs, Douglas. "Political Parties and Macroeconomic Policy," *American Political Science Review,* Vol. 71 (1977), pp. 1465–88.

Hinrichs, Harley H. *A General Theory of Tax Structure Change During Economic Development.* Cambridge, Mass.: Law School of Harvard University, 1966.

Hume, David. *Philosophical Works,* eds. T. H. Greene and T. H. Grosse. London: Longmans, Green, 1898.

International Monetary Fund. *Government Finance Statistics Yearbook,* Vol. VI, 1982.

————. *International Financial Statistics.* Yearbook issue, 1982.

Jackman, Robert. *Politics and Social Equality: A Comparative Analysis.* New York: John Wiley, 1975.

Ladd, Helen F., and T. Nicholas Tideman, eds., *Tax and Expenditure Limitations.* Washington: Urban Institute Press, 1981.

Larkey, Patrick D., Chandler Stolp, and Mark Winer. "Theorizing About the Growth of Government: A Research Assessment," *Journal of Public Policy*, Vol. 1, Part 2 (May 1981), pp. 157–220.

Levine, Charles H., and Irene Rubin, eds., *Fiscal Stress and Public Policy.* Sage Yearbooks in Politics and Public Policy, Vol. 9. Beverly Hills/London: Sage Publications, 1980.

Lindbeck, Assar. "Redistribution Policy and the Expansion of the Public Sector." Paper prepared for the Nobel Symposium on "The Growth of Government," Stockholm, August 15–17, 1984.

Lindblom, C. E. *Politics and Markets.* New York: Basic Books, 1977.

Lipset, Seymour M. *Agrarian Socialism: The Cooperative Commonwealth Federation in Saskatchewan.* Garden City, N.Y.: Anchor Books, 1968.

Miller, John William. *The Philosophy of History, with Reflections and Aphorisms.* New York: Norton, 1981.

Musgrave, Richard A., and Alan T. Peacock, eds., *Classics in the Theory of Public Finance.* New York: St. Martin's Press, 1967.

O'Connor, James. *The Fiscal Crisis of the State.* New York: St. Martin's Press, 1975.

Olson, Mancur. *The Rise and Decline of Nations: Economic Growth, Stagflation and Social Rigidities.* New Haven: Yale University Press, 1982.

Parkin, Frank. *Class Inequality and Political Order.* New York: Praeger, 1971.

Peacock, A. T., and J. Wiseman. *The Growth of Public Expenditures in the United Kingdom.* Princeton: Princeton University Press, 1961.

Peltzman, Sam. "The Growth of Government," *The Journal of Law and Economics*, Vol. 23, October 1980

Plumb, J. H. *Death of the Past.* Boston: Houghton Mifflin, 1970.

Pryor, Frederick. *Public Expenditures in Communist and Capitalist Nations.* Homewood, Ill.: Irwin, 1968.

Rayner, Steve, and Jonathan Gross. *Measuring Culture: A Paradigm for the Analysis of Social Organization.* New York: Columbia University Press, 1985.

Rose, Richard. "The Programme Approach to the Growth of Government." Paper prepared for the American Political Science Association Annual Meeting, Chicago, September 1–4, 1983.

Shick, Allen "Off-Budget Expenditure: An Economic and Political Framework." Paper prepared for the Organisation for Economic Co-Operation and Development, Paris, August 1981.

Schumpeter, Joseph A. "The Crisis of the Tax State," translated by W. F. Stolper and R. A. Musgrave. *International Economic Papers*, No. 4. Macmillan, 1954.

Shapiro, Leonard. *The Origin of the Communist Autocracy: Political Opposition in the Soviet State: First Phase, 1917–1922.* New York: Praeger, 1965.

Spiro, S. E., and E. Yuchtman-Yaar, eds. *Evaluating the Welfare State: Social and Political Perspectives.* New York: Academic Press, 1983.

Straussman, Jeffrey. "Spending More and Enjoying It Less: On the Political Economy of Advanced Capitalism," *Comparative Politics*, January 1981, pp. 235–52.

Wildavsky, Aaron. "Budgetary Futures: Why Politicians May Want Spending Limits in Turbulent Times." *Public Budgeting and Finance,* Vol. 1, No. 1 (Spring 1981), pp. 20–27.

———. "From chaos comes opportunity: the movement toward spending limits in American and Canadian budgeting," *Canadian Public Administration,* Vol. 26, No. 2 (Summer 1983), pp. 163–81.

———. *How to Limit Government Spending.* Berkeley/Los Angeles/London: University of California Press, 1980.

———. "Models of Political Regimes or Pluralism Means More Than One Political Culture in One Country at One Time," in Ellis Katz, ed., *The Meaning of American Pluralism.* Philadelphia: Institute for the Study of Human Issues Press, forthcoming.

———. *The Nursing Father: Moses as a Political Leader.* University City: University of Alabama Press, 1984.

———. *Speaking Truth to Power.* Boston: Little, Brown, 1979.

Wilensky, Harold L. *The Welfare State and Equality.* Berkeley/Los Angeles/London: University of California Press, 1975.

Wilson, James Q., and Patricia Rachal. "Can Government Regulate Itself?," *The Public Interest,* No. 46 (Winter 1977), pp. 3–14.

Wolfe, Alan. *The Limits of Legitimacy.* New York: Free Press, 1977.

Wolfe, C. Stephen, and Jesse Burkhead. "Fiscal Trends in Selected Industrial Countries." *Public Budgeting and Finance,* Vol. 3, No. 4 (Winter 1983), pp. 97–102.

INDEX

Aaron, Henry, 581
Aaron of Lincoln, 194
Abacus, 77n–78n, 212
Accountability, 279–82, 330
  in Athens and Rome, 127–28
Adams, Henry Carter, 358
Adams, John, 378, 389, 393
Adams, John Quincy, 373, 378–79
Adam of Stratton, 219
Addison, Joseph, 259
Africa, 22, 89, 110, 144, 268, 305, 352
  sub-Sahara, 39, 44
  see also Central Africa; North Africa
Africa Company, 268
Agricultural Adjustment Acts (U.S.),
  454–55
Agricultural Marketing Acts (British),
  458
Aids, 176–77
  excise, 278
Akkad (Babylonia), 41, 46, 57, 65
Alber, Jens, 350

Aldrich, Nelson, 420
Alexander the Great, 62, 73
Alexius Commenus, Eastern Roman
  emperor, 177
Algeria, 504, 517
Allen, William H., 412
Allen, William V., 419–20
Allied Control Council, 536
Alt, James, 548n
Amenhotep III, king of Egypt, 46
America, see United States
American Revolution, 366
  see also Revolutionary War
Ammisaduqa, king of Babylonia, 75
Amon, Temple of, 48
Ancien Régime, 244, 247, 256, 292
Ancient Near East
  city-states in, 41
  empires in, 41
Ancient World
  barter in, 44, 90
  budgeting in, 38–40

711

Ancient World (*cont.*)
bureaucracy in, 49–53
chronology for finance in, 41
corruption in, 82–88
fiscal management in, 77–90
hierarchy in, 81–83, 86, 87
kings in, 38–39, 43–44, 65–68
money in, 90–92
priest-kings in, 45–48
societies in, 40–45
taxation in, 68–76
see also China; Egypt; India; Mesopotamia
Anglo-Dutch War of 1667, 242, 258
Anglo-German Naval Treaty of 1935,
467
Anglo-Scottish Enlightenment, 313,
325, 355, 436
Anne, Queen of England, 287n
Annona (Rome), 111, 112, 125
Anti-Deficiency Act, (U.S.), 396
Antidosis (Athens), 105
Appropriations budgeting, 486–87
Arabs, 162, 164n, 217
Aragon, 195
Arbitrage, 162–63
Aristotle, 120, 139–40, 270, 376,
598
Arthasastra (Kautilya), 62, 594
Arthur, Chester A., 384–85
Articles of Confederation, 358, 359,
361, 368, 371, 389, 390
Asia, 233, 511
Roman provinces of, 109, 110, 116,
117, 118–19, 176
Asoka, Emperor, 46, 87
Assyria, 41, 48, 64, 92
Athens (classical), 56, 117n, 131, 133,
150, 167, 182, 228, 247, 275
accountability in, 127–28
altruism in, 139
audit in, 128–30, 152, 211–12, 213
crown support in, 140
earmarking in, 121–22, 123, 124, 127
egalitarianism in, 108, 144–45
finance in, 101–7
hierarchy in, 98, 99, 101, 108–13,
118, 121, 123, 127, 135, 140
liturgies in, 102–5, 142–43, 173
moral restraint in, 139–40
political institutions in, 95–97,
100–101
public interest in, 142–43, 144–45

social and economic conditions in,
93–95
spending in, 119–22, 123, 124, 127
taxation in, 107–8, 109n
tax farming in, 113–15, 121, 131, 149
Atlantic Alliance, 517
Auditing, 331
in Athens, 128–30, 152, 211–12, 213
in England, 211n, 213–19, 405
in France, 211n
in Middle Ages, 209–19
Augustus, emperor of Rome, 99, 100,
111n, 118–19, 120, 123, 124, 133,
134, 135, 137–38, 140
Australia, 344, 495, 497, 499, 501, 502,
506, 522, 556, 568, 585
Austria, 253, 337, 344, 348, 431, 461,
470n, 495, 497, 499, 500, 523,
556
Austria-Hungary, 438
Authoritarianism, 25
Authority, legitimate, 33
Avars, 155
Aztecs, 41, 73

Baack, Bennett, 387
Babylon (Babylonia), 44, 45, 46, 66, 92
Babylonia, 41, 48, 52, 57, 60, 65, 72, 75,
213n
Baden, duchy of, 337
Bailiffs, (France), 208
Balanced Budget Act, *see* Gramm-Rud-
man-Hollings Balanced Budget
Act of 1985
Balanced budgets, 355, 592–94
efforts to attain in Prussia (early
modern), 285–6
in early industrial age, 323–32
and income tax, 337
and regimes, 595–98, 608–14
Balfour, Arthur James, 351
Baltic States, 233
Banalités, 170
Bank of Amsterdam, 257, 258, 259, 269
Bank of England, 243, 259, 269, 287n,
288, 290, 448, 457
Bank of France, 448, 459
Bank of Venice, 257
Barbarian invasions, in Middle Ages,
154–55
Bardi, 164, 193, 194
Barnard, Samuel, 259
Barter, 44, 90, 117, 125

Bastiat, Frédéric, 339
Battle of the Budget, The (White/Wild-
    avsky), 610n
Belgium, 69n, 327, 341, 495, 497, 499,
    500, 521, 556
Benefit theory, of taxation, 343
Bentham, Jeremy, 306, 308, 313, 315,
    479
Berlin crisis, 507, 510, 517
Beveridge, William, 435n
Bill of Rights (U.S.), 244
Bills of exchange, 251–52
Binney, J. E. D., 296
Bismarck, Otto von, 309, 351, 432n
Bloch, Marc, 168
Blöndal, Gisli, 600
Blum, Léon, 459–60, 472
Bodin, Jean, 259, 270
Borrowing
    in Germany, 322
    of kings, 192–96, 252–54
    in Middle Ages, 189–90, 192–96
    see also Debt
Brahmins (India), 68, 86, 89
Brecker, Enno, 538
Breviarium totius imperii (Rome), 138
Bribery, 84, 107, 116, 130
    see also Corruption
Britain, 109n, 328n, 382, 386, 410, 438,
    461, 462, 477, 479, 480, 506, 548,
    578, 587n, 590, 602
    budgeting in, 18, 284, 326, 327, 408,
        483–85
    cabinet government in, 403
    class in, 522, 544–47, 551–52
    consols in, 309
    deflation in, 446–47
    in Great Depression, 456–58
    and inflation, 468
    medieval Exchequer of, 23
    military personnel in, 518
    military spending in, 239, 440,
        465–71
    Public Expenditure Survey, 483
    spending in, 289, 329, 349, 448–51,
        515, 555, 558
    taxation in, 451–52
    unemployment in, 305, 339, 432–33,
        458, 464
    welfare spending of, 440, 441, 455,
        495, 497, 499, 500, 502, 503, 504
    and World War I, 439–41
    after World War II, 512–16

    and World War II, 472, 475
    see also England; United Kingdom
Brittan, Samuel, 545
Bronze Age, 39, 42, 44, 45n, 90, 91
Bruere, Henry, 412
Bryan, William Jennings, 420
Bubble Act of 1719 (England), 362
Buchanan, James, 374–75, 381, 396
Buck, Arthur E., 398, 400, 406, 407–8,
    409
Buckingham, Duke of, 19
Budget and Accounting Act of 1921
    (U.S.), 414
Budgetary cultures, itemized, 36
Budgeting, 283–86, 328, 555, 556–57
    in ancient world, 38–40
    appropriations, 486–87
    in Britain, 18, 284, 326, 327, 408,
        483–85
    in cash, 482, 484
    conflict management in, 477–78
    deficits, 590–92, 594, 609–13
    defined, 18
    in early-modern Europe, 283–86
    and egalitarianism, 589
    Europe vs. U.S., 358–60
    exploitative, 30
    in France (modern), 556, 586
    in Germany (19th century), 327n,
        556
    guardian role in, 479–80
    and hierarchy, 596
    and inflation, 482–83, 484
    in Italy (modern), 556
    in Japan (modern), 556
    line item, 30, 404, 480–82, 487–88
    loss of comprehensiveness, 600–606
    in Mauryan India, 80
    in modern times, 490–93
    in Netherlands (modern), 556
    and preferences, 24–31
    and problem succession, 562–67
    procedural, 30
    productivity, 30
    public vs. private, 596
    redistributive, 30
    and sectarian regimes, 583, 596
    and social orders, 17–22, 31–32
    in Sweden (modern), 555, 557
    time span for, 483–85
    transformation of norms, 598–607
    treasury, 486–87
    in twentieth century, 428–30, 434–36

Budgeting (*cont.*)
in U.S., 358–61, 369, 370–76,
400–416, 425–27, 476–78, 480, 509,
511–12, 556, 600, 609–12
by volume, 482–83
after World War II, 476–82
see also Balanced budgets; Department budgets; PPB; ZBB
Budget Making in a Democracy (Fitzpatrick), 409–11
Budget Reform, 394, 395
Budget Reform Act of 1921 (U.S.), 399,
405
Budget Reformers
Buck, A. E., 398, 406–7, 407–8, 409
Collins, C. W., 404, 409
Cleveland, Frederick A., 402, 403,
406, 409
Willoughby, W. F., 402, 405, 407, 408
Wilson, Woodrow, 402, 403, 406
Bullock, Charles, 418
Bureaucracy, 39, 49–64, 330, 444, 479,
565
in ancient world, 49–53
in China, 59–62, 83–84
in Egypt, 54–57
in France, 237, 238
in Mauryan India, 62–64
in Mesopotamia, 57–59
in Middle Ages, 210
Burgundy (France), 240
Burke, Edmund, 17, 21, 291, 295, 306n
Burkhead, Jesse, 566, 586
Bythnia, 116
Byzantium, 29, 113, 119, 126, 148, 153,
162, 166, 177, 276
salaries in, 210n–11n

Caesar, Julius, 99, 111n, 125, 133, 137,
154
Calhoun, John, 378, 381
Caligula, emperor of Rome, 138
Calvin, John, 251
Camphausen, Ludolf, 318
Canada, 478–79, 344, 352, 522, 556,
558, 568, 587n, 609
expenditure control, compared to
U.S., 585–86
welfare spending in, 495, 497, 499,
500, 501, 502, 504–5, 506
Cannon, Joseph G., 385, 399
Capetian kings of France, 180
Capital gains tax, 447, 545

Capital market, 250–53, 256–59, 309
Capitalism, 227, 238, 241, 249, 314–15,
576–78
decay of, 578–79
Capital tax, 457
Caracalla, emperor of Rome, 107, 111n
Carolingian period, 150, 160, 166, 172,
212
Carter, Jimmy, 486
Carter administration, 505
Cass, Lewis, 396
Caste system, 89
Castile, early modern administrative
expansion, 267
Castles, Francis, 579
Catalonia, royal harrowing, 192, 195,
196n
audit, 211n, 213, 216n
Catherine the Great, and Enlighten-
ment, 294
Catholic Church, 49n, 236, 248, 249,
251, 264–65, 549
in Middle Ages, 150, 163, 171,
185–88, 199n–200n
Catholic parties, 579, 580
Cato, Marcus Porcius, 130–31, 140
CCC, *see* Civilian Conservation Corps
Central America, 22, 41, 73
pre-Columbian, 44
Central Banks, 257–59
Centralization, 426
in early industrial age, 317–19
in early-modern Europe, 229–31,
235–41, 276
in Rome, 133–39
CETA, 500
Chamberlain, Neville, 467, 468
Chamberlain government, 469
Chambre de justice (France), 253
Chambre des Comptes (France), 206
Champagne fairs, 162
Charlemagne, king of Franks, 153
Charles I, king of England, 19, 255,
264, 286
Charles II, king of England
borrowing costs, 258
legislative grant of stipend, 286
losses from tax farming, 271
professional administrators under,
290
Charles II, king of Spain, 262
Chautemps, Camille, 460
Cheops, king of Egypt, 69

Child allowances, as welfare spending, 499–500
Childe, Sir Josiah, 258
Chilperic, Merovingian King, 167
China (ancient), 22, 29, 42, 45, 54, 55n, 57, 63, 77, 78, 81, 121, 212
  bureaucracy in, 29, 54, 59–62, 83–84
  centralization-decentralization, 57
  Chin Dynasty, 41
  Chou Dynasty, 41, 59, 60, 66, 70, 71–72, 79, 148
  corruption in, 88
  exemptions in, 74
  Han Dynasty, 39, 41, 43n, 44, 60, 61, 67, 69, 70, 72n, 73, 80, 83, 85, 87, 88, 148
  Shang Dynasty, 39, 41, 44, 52, 72, 168n
  Tang Dynasty, 41, 61, 70, 71, 148
  Warring States period, 41
  see also Communist China; People's Republic
Chin Dynasty (China), 41
Chou Dynasty (China), 41, 59, 60, 66, 70, 71–72, 79, 148
Christians, early, 146, 154
Churchill, Winston, 441, 452, 466, 468, 469, 513
Cicero, Marcus Tullius, 109, 118, 132n, 140, 259
Cilicia, 118n
Cities, in early industrial age, 3, 15–16
Civilian Conservation Corps (CCC), 455
Civil War (U.S.), 313, 383–84, 385
  debt, attitudes toward, 374–75, 387, 442
  income tax during, 418–19
  veterans' pensions, 398
Civil Works Administration (CWA), 455
Claudius, emperor of Rome, 123, 135
Clay, Henry, 378, 380
Cleisthenes (Athenian statesman), 128
Clerical subsidies, 220–21
Cleveland, Frederick A., 398, 402, 403, 406, 409, 412, 413
Cleveland, Grover, 375, 384
Cobbett, William, 309, 339, 347
Cockrell Commission (U.S.), 411
Coeur, Jacques, 220, 253
Coins, 166, 361
  precious metal in, 190–91

    see also Currency debasement, Recoinage
Colbert, Jean Baptiste, 237–38, 242, 259, 278, 431n
Cold War, 473, 507
Collectivism, 25, 36, 204
  and feudalism, 152, 226, 227
  and individualism, 146, 241, 246, 269, 325, 360
  and Protestantism, 249
  in Rome, 146
  and welfare spending, 321
Collins, Charles Wallace, 404, 409
Commission on Economy and Efficiency (U.S.), 404, 413
Commodity Credit Corporation (U.S.), 455
Commodus, emperor of Rome, 11n, 135n
Commons, John, 444n
Communist China, 161, 184, 506, 511
Communists in European politics, 460, 520
Company of the South Seas, 268
Company of Staple, 196
Competitive individualism, see Individualism
Condottiere (Italy), 144
Confiscation
  of land and money, 261
  of property, 264–65, 322, 334
Conflict management, in budgeting, 477–78
Consols (Britain), 309
Constantine, emperor of Rome, 106, 113
Constantinople, 151n
Constitution (U.S.), 244, 247, 358, 359, 369, 370, 371, 372, 397, 402, 410, 420
  amendments to, 413, 421, 558
Constitutional Convention (U.S.), 367, 389
Consumption taxes, 23, 261, 334, 452
  see also Excise taxes; Market taxes
Continental Congress (U.S.), 361, 366–67, 368, 390
Coolidge, Calvin, 376, 415, 471
Copernicus, Nicolaus, 248
Corn Laws (England), 335
Corporate income tax, 521n–22n
  in France, 548

Corporate income tax (*cont.*)
  in Sweden, 541
  in U.S., 420–21, 423, 442, 523–24
Corporation of London, 257
Corporatism, in Sweden, 543–44
Corruption, 565
  in ancient world, 82–88
  in China, 88
  in England, 291
  in Rome, 138–39
  see also Bribery
Corvée, 44, 66n, 68–71, 73, 75, 78,
  109n, 293
  see also Forced labor, *sabotnik*
Cost-cutting, in Middle Ages, 324
Cost effectiveness, 302
  see also Efficiency
Counter-Reformation, 264
Crete, 39, 41
  see also Minoan Crete
Cromwell, Oliver
  centralized tax administration under,
    271, 288, 290
  confiscated royalist property, 264
  new taxes under, 263, 286
  weak taxing authority, 19, 236
Crown gold, in Rome, 111
Crown land and offices, sale of, 261,
  264
Crusades, 431
  cost, and new taxes, 177, 186
  and cultural diffusion, 162
Cultural theory
  applying 585–87
  reconsidered, 587–88
  and tax differences, 550–52
  testing, 584–85
  see also Budgetary cultures
Currency debasement, 261
  in Middle Ages, 190–92
Customs duties, 269–71, 353, 452
  see also Tariff
CWA, *see* Civil Works Administration
Czechoslovakia, 507

Danegeld (tax), 180
Davenant, Charles, 290n–91n
David, king of Hebrews, 561
Dawes, Charles G., 414, 415, 444
Dazio, 199, 200
De Aquaductibus (Frontinus),
  137
Death duties, 349

Debt
  in England, 242–43, 258–59, 287–88,
    446–48, 597–98
  in France, 431, 446–48
  in Germany, 446–47
  and GNP, 445
  short vs. long term, 254–55
  in twentieth century, 445–48
  in U.S., 370–76, 445–47, 597–98
Decentralization, 39, 276–79
  in Egypt, Intermediate period, 55
  in Middle Ages, 206–209
Declaration of Independence (U.S.),
  244
Declaration of the Rights of Man
  (France), 347
Decurions, in Rome, 105–6, 149, 173
Defense spending, and regimes, 519–21
  see also Military spending
Deflation, 446–47
de Gaulle, Charles, 504, 517, 547
Delian League, 97
Delos market, Roman era, 116–17
Democracy, 96, 520
  and income tax, 526–29
  see also Social democracies
Democracy in America (Tocqueville),
  359
Demosthenes, 94n
Denmark
  corporation taxes, 522
  budgetary objectives, 556
  expenditures, 495, 497, 499, 501
  income tax, 327, 344, 501
  tax revolt, 533
  see also Danish tribes
Department budgets, 603, 605
Depreciation, in Sweden, 542
  see also Currency debasement
Depression in 19th century 320, 321,
  339, 340, 341
  see also Great Depression
Descartes, René, 244
Despotism, 28, 39, 40, 46, 87, 88–89, 95,
  240, 241
Devaluation, 265–66
  see also Currency debasement
Developing nations, 315–16
"Dialogue of the Exchequer, The"
  (*Dialogus de Scaccario*), 213n
Dictionary of the English Language
  (Johnson), 390
Diderot, Denis, 436

Diggers, 19, 21, 309
Diocletian, emperor of Rome, 110, 111–12, 113, 125–26, 140–41, 154
Diodorus (Roman chronicler), 133
Displacement-effect hypothesis, 576
Distraint of knighthood, 179
Djoser, pharaoh of Egypt, 54, 71n
Dockery Cockrell Commission (U.S.), 411–12
Domitian, emperor of Rome, 111n, 125
Double-entry bookkeeping, 164, 279, 290
  see also L. Pacioli, *Summa de arithmetica*
Downing, Sir George, 242, 258, 290
Drees, W., 479
Dutch East India Company, 268
Dutch Republic, 233–34, 237, 242, 251–52, 283, 285, 361, 525
  public banking in, 257–58
  see also Holland; Netherlands

Early industrial age, see Industrial age, early
Earmarking, 29, 189, 202, 276–79
  in Athens and Rome, 121–27
Economic individualism, see Individualism
Economic stability, and Keynesians, 476–77
Economy Bill of 1932 (U.S.), 454
Edgeworth, F. Y., 344
Education, expenditures for, 497, 499, 501, 502, 570–71
Edward I, king of England, 168, 185, 186, 187, 188, 193
Edward III, king of England, 193
Edward IV, king of England, 203
Efficient Democracy (Allen), 412
Efficiency, 314, 324, 325–26, 334–35
Egalitarianism, 19, 25, 26, 28, 36, 199n, 201, 245, 377, 588–89
  in Athens, 108, 144–45
  and budgeting, 589
  vs. individualism, 596
  and sectarianism, 20
  in U.S., 360, 416–17, 550
  and welfare spending, 350, 498
Egypt, 17, 22, 29, 39, 40, 42, 49, 59, 62, 63, 68–73, 78, 81, 94, 104, 105, 111
  bureaucracy in, 54–57
  conscript labor in, 109n

first Intermediate period, 45n
Middle Kingdom, 41, 44, 46–47, 48, 54, 55, 56, 67, 71n, 84, 129, 148
New Kingdom, 41, 47, 51, 55, 75, 77, 79, 88, 115
Old Kingdom, 41, 43, 44, 46–47, 54, 56, 57, 60, 74–75
pharaohs of, 46, 65,85, 86
predynastic, 52, 53
Ptolemaic period, 56–57
scribes of, 213n
taxed in kind, 55–57
Eisenhower, Dwight D., 489, 505, 510, 511–12
Eisenhower administration, 509, 512
Eisphora (Athenian tax), 108
Elizabeth I, queen of England, 169n, 268
Elizabethan era, in England, 339
Elvander, Nils, 540
Ely, John, 418
Emergency Jobs and Unemployment Assistance Act of 1974 (U.S.), 500
Employment Act of 1946 (U.S.), 435n
Engels, Friedrich, 301, 309, 314, 321
England, 69n, 233, 236, 237, 255, 270, 271, 280, 281, 283, 290, 334, 361, 370, 372, 421, 423, 570
  Ancient Custom in, 197–98
  audit in, 211n, 213–19, 405
  clerical subsidies in, 220–21
  consumption in, 316
  corruption in, 291
  customs duties in, 353
  debt in, 242–43, 258–59, 287–88, 446–48, 597–98
  economic liberalism in, 308
  Enlightenment in, 324, 436
  excise taxes in, 353, 390–91
  export taxes in, 197–98
  feudalism in, 165–66, 261
  free trade in, 340–42
  humanitarianism in, 432n, 443
  income tax in, 309–10, 337–39, 341–48, 351–52, 420, 440, 465
  individualism in, 318, 431
  inheritance tax in, 344
  land tax in, 263
  legislatures in, 285–86
  manufacturing in, 319
  market taxes in, 341
  mercantilism in, 363

England (*cont.*)
  in Middle Ages, 149, 152, 159, 161,
    170, 174–76, 178–89, 191n, 192–96,
    198, 199n, 204, 206–9, 211n,
    212–21, 223, 224
  Norman, 175
  peasant revolt in, 203
  political institutions in, 245–46
  poverty in, 231
  progressive taxation in, 272, 323,
    351–52
  Protestants in, 248
  Puritan Revolution in, 19, 21, 240,
    264, 286, 288, 309, 417
  reforms in, 294–96
  tariffs in, 312, 335, 336, 340, 341, 457
  transfers in, 394
  in Tudor period, 257
  and United States, 358, 364, 365–66
  see also Bank of England; Britain;
    United Kingdom
Enlightenment, 287, 317, 334, 608
  in England, 324, 436
  and equity, 273–74
  in France, 292–94, 323, 324, 355, 436
  and reform, 243–47, 292–94
  rationalism and empiricism, 355
  see also Anglo-Scottish Enlighten-
    ment
Ensi, in Mesopotamia, 57
Entail, 173
Entitlements, spending for, 487, 601
Ephesus (Greek city-state), 139
Equality, different conceptions of,
    550–51
"Equalizations of Burdens" law post–
    WW II (Germany), 537
Equity
  Athenian liturgies, 103–106
  and budget policy (modern), 591
  and Enlightenment, 273–74, 302–3
  in Germany, post–World War II, 537
  and income tax, 543–47
  and individualism, 550
  and market taxes, 272
  in northern Italian communes,
    198–99
  Roman *munera,* 106–7
Erikson, Erik, 249
Escheat, 173, 209
Essenes, 21
Estaing, Giscard d', 504
Estate tax, 424

Eubulus (Athenian commissioner), 122
Europe (early-modern), 119, 228,
    297–98
  absolutism in, 235–43, 276
  accountability in, 279–82
  administration in, 274–98
  agriculture in, 232
  budgeting in, 283–86
  capital market in, 250–51, 256–57
  centralization in, 229–31, 235–41, 276
  colonial exploration and exploitation
    by, 265
  confiscation of property in, 264–65
  credit in, 255–56
  customs duties in, 269–71
  decentralization in, 276–79
  devaluation in, 265–66
  earmarking in, 276–79
  economic expansion of, 234
  Enlightenment in, 243–47
  excise taxes in, 271–72
  financial control in, 282–83
  food riots in, 273
  government borrowing in, 252–54
  hierarchy in, 241, 249, 283, 298
  joint-stock companies in, 238, 241,
    261, 268–69, 287n–88n
  land taxes in, 261, 262–64
  market taxes in, 269–71, 272–73
  ministers in, 241–43
  population in, 231–32
  poverty in, 234–35
  private loans in, 251–52
  productivity in, 232
  public government in, 247–50,
    286–87
  reform in, 292–96
  revenue in, 259–74
  sale of titles and offices in, 266–68
  short-term vs. long-term debt in,
    254–55
  tax farming in, 230, 255, 271, 278,
    294
  tax revolts in, 273
  and trade, 233–34
European budgets, vs. U.S. budgets,
    358–60
European Common Market, 336
European Economic Community, 548
European Middle Ages, 22, 23, 34, 61n,
    72, 119, 148–52, 228, 236, 244, 271,
    297, 362, 564
  administration in, 156–58, 204–21

audit in, 209–19
barbarian invasions in, 154–55
borrowing in, 189–90, 192–96
bureaucracy in, 210
church in, 150, 163, 171, 185–88, 199n–200n
cost-cutting in, 324
currency debasement in, 190–92
economic revival in, 160–64
feudalism in, 171–81
fiscal control in, 204–21
forced sale of royal assets in, 196–197
legalized taxation in, 197–203
meaning of, 221–27
public loans in, 203–4
purveyance in, 188–89, 191n
recentralization in, 165–67
scarcity economy of, 158–59
6th–10th centuries, 167–71
tax farming in, 184, 194, 202, 208, 217, 221
time frame of, 153–54
12th–14th centuries, 29, 181–204, 239, 253
Excess profits tax, 422, 423, 524n
Exchequer audit, 211n, 213–19, 405
Excise taxes, 271–72, 334, 353, 390–91, 452
see also Consumption taxes; Market taxes
Executive vs. legislative branches (U.S.), 392, 393, 403, 413
Exemptions, from taxation, 74–75
Expenditures
and revenue, 595
in U.S., 384, 415–16, 441, 442, 448–51, 474, 589
see also Government spending; Military spending; Spending; Transfers; Welfare spending
Exploitative budgeting, 30
Export taxes, 270
in England, 197–98
Extortion, 75

Fabians (Britain), 444
"Faculty" tax, 363
Faculty theory of taxation, 343
Fain, Haskell, 560
Far East, 90, 162, 268
Farm Credit Administration (U.S.), 455

Fatalism, 25, 26, 27, 30, 31, 32, 34–35, 40
Federal Emergency Relief Administration (FERA), 455
Federalist papers, 246, 359, 389, 530
Federal Old Age and Survivors Insurance Trust Fund, 474
Fee, administration by, 133
Fenno, Richard, 385
FERA, see Federal Emergency Relief Administration
Ferguson, Adam 324
Feudalism, 148–53, 154, 158, 159–60, 171–81, 182, 184, 185, 191–92, 208, 212, 222–24, 261, 324
and collectivism, 152, 226, 227
and decentralization, 226
in England, 165–66, 261
in Middle Ages, 171–81
and recentralization, 165–67
Fillmore, Millard, 381
Finance
in Athens, 101–7
chronology in ancient world, 41
in Rome, 101–7
Finland, 495, 556
Findley, William, 391
First World War, see World War I
Fiscal equity, see Equity
Fiscal management, in ancient world, 77–90
Fisci, in Rome, 123, 124–25
FitzNigel, Richard, 206, 213n
Fitzpatrick, Edward A., 409–11
Flanders, 152, 161, 177, 180, 189, 203, 211n, 213, 252
Flat-rate income tax, 528
Flemish, see Flanders
Floating debt, 254–55
Florence (Italy), 161–62, 200, 201, 202, 203, 257
Ford administration, 505
Food riots, in early-modern Europe, 273
France, 18, 21, 60n, 233, 236, 242, 253, 264, 271n, 278, 280, 281, 291, 311, 318, 319, 320, 336, 362, 364, 441, 466, 477, 520, 570, 597
audit in, 211n
budgeting in, 556, 586
bureaucracy in, 237, 238
Communists in, 460
confiscation in, 334

France (*cont.*)
  consumption in (early modern),
    234
  corporate income tax in, 548
  customs duties in, 353
  debt in, 431, 446–48
  Enlightenment in, 292–94, 323, 324,
    355, 436
  excise taxes in, 353
  feudalism in, 165–66
  Fifth Republic, 504
  fiscal policy in, 312, 327
  Fourth Republic, 480, 504
  free trade (19th century), 342
  Gaullists in, 548
  in Great Depression, 458–61, 464
  income tax in, 344, 438, 548, 549
  inheritance tax in, 344
  kings in, 186, 219–20, 257, 267
  legislatures in, 332
  mercantilism in, 270
  in Middle Ages, 149, 159, 161, 162,
    174–76, 178–85, 188, 191–96, 198,
    203, 204, 206–10, 213, 218, 221
  military spending in, 239, 440,
    471–72
  national interest in, 539
  Physiocrats in, 239
  poverty in, 231
  production in, 246
  property-in-office in, 256
  see also Sale of Titles and Offices
  reforms in, 292–94, 312
  revolution in, 240
  riots of 1790, 235
  social climate in, 316n
  socialism in, 590
  speculation in (early modern), 288n
  spending cuts, Great Depression, 464
  spending in, 448–51
  tariffs in, 341–42
  taxation in, 262–63, 272, 278, 337,
    354, 451–52, 522, 523
  tax farming in, 282
  Third Republic, 447, 472
  transfers in, 394
  value-added tax in, 547–48
  welfare spending in, 444, 495, 496,
    497, 499, 500, 501, 502, 504
  and World War I, 437–39
  after World War II, 516–17, 547–50
  see also French Revolution; French
    Wars of Religion

Francis I, king of France, 168n–69n,
    238, 253
Franco-Prussian War, 438
Franklin, Benjamin, 22, 244, 362–63,
    368
Frederick II, king of Prussia, 294
Frederick Wilhelm II, king of Prussia,
    535
Frederick William I, elector of Bran-
    denburg-Prussia, 262, 285
Free trade policy, 340–42, 352
French Revolution, 21, 265, 322, 345
French Wars of Religion, 263n
Frescobaldi family, 164, 195n–96n
Fronde, the, 280
Fugger family, 252
Full employment, 371
Full Employment in a Free Society
    (Beveridge), 435n
Funded debt, 254–55

Gabelles, 201–2, 278
Gallatin, Albert, 373, 377, 378, 393–94
Garentibelopp, 542
Gaul, 109n, 110, 126, 154, 155, 156,
    158, 159, 161, 167
Geertz, Clifford, 233
General Accounting Office (U.S.),
    405–6
*General Theory of Employment, Interest,
    and Money, The* (Keynes), 433
Genoa (Italy), 162, 163
George III, king of England, 243
George, Henry, 347, 553
Germanic tribes, 154–55, 157–58, 171
  customs of, 172
  rulers of, 167, 169, 182
Germany, 21, 159, 161, 162, 165, 216n,
    252, 309, 341, 403, 438, 460, 472,
    514, 516, 545, 548, 570, 586, 597
  accounting procedures in, 546
  administration in, 549
  arms limitation in, 466
  borrowing in, 322
  budgeting in, 327n, 556
  constitution of 1871, 353
  customs duties in, 353
  customs union (19th century), 336
  debt in, 446–47
  deficit financing in, 328n
  economic stabilization in, 537–38
  excise taxes in, 353
  Four-Year Plan of 1936, 462

in Great Depression, 461–64
growth in, 320, 535–39, 550, 578
hierarchy in, 319, 551
and Holy Roman Empire, 166
income tax in, 344, 535–37
inflation in, 446, 447
inheritance tax in, 344
military spending in, 465, 467, 468, 469, 470, 471
principalities of, 264, 348
reconstruction in, 536–37, 538–39
Reich Labor Service, 462
and reparations, 439
socialist influence in, 351
spending in, 448–51
stabilization in, 537–38
state capitalism in, 461–63
states of, 312, 335–36
taxation in, 431, 451–52, 522, 523, 538
tax incentives in, 536–37
unemployment in, 461–62
Weimar, 446, 462
welfare spending in, 351, 432n, 495, 497, 499, 500, 502
after World War II, 517
Gladstone, William Ewart, 18, 318, 342, 394, 443
Glass, Carter, 443
Global Strategy Paper of 1952 (Britain), 513
GNP
and debt, 445
and military spending, 469, 470, 471, 508, 509
and spending, 450
and World War II, 509
Godolphin, Sidney, 243, 290
Gold, 191n, 265
Golden Age of Pericles, 97, 100, 107, 120, 129, 145
Goldscheid, Rudolf, 576–77
Goodnow, Frank J., 406, 413
Gough, Ian, 575
Government
growth of, 430–31, 435–36, 567–73, 587–88
regulation of, 306–7
size of, 591, 613
Government spending, in early industrial age, 308, 310
Gracchi brothers, 98–99
Graeco-Persian Wars, 97

Gramm-Rudman-Hollings (GRH) Balanced Budget Act of 1985, 558–59, 609–10
Granaries of constant equalization, 81
Grant, Ulysses S., 375
Great Britain, see Britain; England; United Kingdom
Great Depression, 376, 386, 432–33, 453–64, 471, 473, 477, 562
Greece (ancient), 22, 63, 95, 104, 115, 117n, 128, 138, 139, 563
accounting technology in, 129n
liturgies in, 58n, 102–5, 257n
salaries in, 127
taxation in, 107
see also Athens; Hellenistic period; Mycenaean Greece
Gregorian reforms, 150
Gregory of Tours, 167
GRH, see Gramm-Rudman-Hollings Balanced Budget Act of 1985
Guardian role, in budgeting, 479–80
Gudea, king of Lagash, 48
Guest, Dennis, 498
Guilds, public spending in Middle Ages, 149
Guiscard, Robert, 177
Gustavus Vasa, king of Sweden, 264

Hadrian, emperor of Rome, 120, 135, 136, 168n
Hamilton, Alexander, 370, 371, 372, 389–90, 391, 427
Hammurabi, king of Babylon, 44, 45, 46, 57, 58
Code of, 65
Han Dynasty (China), 39, 41, 43n, 44, 60, 61, 67, 69, 70, 72, 72n, 73, 80, 83, 85, 87, 88, 148
Hanseatic trading towns, 149, 153
Hansen, Alvin, 433
Hapsburg empire, 240, 245, 246, 253, 254, 257, 264, 270, 294, 334
Harappa (Indus Valley), 41
Hardenberg, Karl August von, 18
Harding, Warren, 376, 414–15, 443, 466, 471
Harley, Robert, 287n, 288n, 290
Harmhab, pharaoh of Egypt, 46, 75, 85
Harrington, James, 372
Hartz, Louis, 359, 380
Haskins, Charles W., 411
Hayes, Rutherford B., 375

Head tax, 22, 78, 79, 199
Health care epxenditures, 497, 501
Hearth tax, 187
Heath government (Britain), 503
Hebrew kingdoms, ancient, 41
Heclo, Hugh, 546, 581–82
Hellenistic period, 62, 103, 104, 108, 115, 122, 127–28, 140, 143, 149
    see also Greece (ancient)
Henry I, king of England, 175
Henry II, king of England, 186, 209, 213n, 215
Henry III, king of England, 187
Henry IV, king of England, 196–97
Henry VIII, king of England, 264
Henry IV, king of France, 268
Henry IV, king of Germany, 177
Hervart, Barthelemy, 280
Hierarchical regimes, 20–22, 24–30, 32, 137, 144–46, 199n, 260, 586, 597, 598
    in ancient Israel, 561–62
    and balanced budget, 608–9, 613–14
    and welfare spending, 350
Hierarchy, 34–35, 36, 325, 377, 526
    in ancient world, 81–83, 86, 87
    in Athens and Rome, 98, 99, 101, 108–13, 118, 121, 123, 127, 135, 140
    and budgetary strategies, 596
    complex, 89–90
    and deficits, 361
    and despotism, 39
    in early-modern Europe, 241, 249, 283, 298
    in Germany, 319, 551
    and individualism, 58n, 118
    and inequality, 583
    and Keynesianism, 562–63
    and kings, 66
    and market regimes, 58, 81, 87, 99, 101, 113, 118, 283, 298, 426
    in Middle Ages, 152, 171, 172, 178n, 223, 226–27
    vs. sects. 519–21
    and social order, 89
    supporters of, 305
    and tax differences, 550–52
    in U.S., 400–411, 426–27
Hill, Christopher, 248
Hinrichs, Harley, 572–73
Hitler, Adolf, 461, 467, 468, 469
Hobbes, Thomas, 290

Holland, 337, 344
    see also Dutch Republic; Netherlands
Holmes, Oliver Wendell, 333
Holy Roman Empire, 166, 248, 264
Hospitalers, 193
Hudson's Bay Company, 268
Huguenots, 264
Hull, Cordell, 424
Hume, David, 239, 270, 274, 291, 292n, 339, 560, 591–92
Hundred Years' War, 186

Iceland, balanced budgets in, 566, 590, 600
Import Duties Act of 1932 (Britain), 458
Import taxes, 270
    see also Customs duties, Market taxes, Tariffs
Incas, 39, 41, 69
Income inequality, and government growth, 587–88
Income maintenance expenditures, 497, 499, 500
Income redistribution, 199n, 200n
    see also Welfare spending
Income tax, 199n, 308, 322, 323, 387, 413, 456, 457, 521n–22n, 550
    and balanced budgets, 337
    and democracy, 526–29
    in England, 309–10, 337–39, 341–48, 351–52, 420, 440, 465
    flat-rate, 528
    in France, 344, 438, 548, 549
    in Germany, 344, 535–37
    and individualism, 338
    in Italy, 261, 322, 344, 549
    in Japan, 344
    progressive, 347–48, 352, 452
    in Sweden, 344, 354, 539n, 540, 543
    and tax preferences, 530–34
    in U.S., 278, 344, 387–88, 416, 418–25, 435, 442, 474–75
    and World War I, 422, 438
    and World War II, 425
Incrementalism, 581
Incremental taxes, 201–2
Indexing, 491
India, 29, 42, 55n, 66, 84, 88, 89, 121, 234
    see also Mauryan India

Individualism, 25, 28, 29, 36, 239, 248, 310, 321, 569
and balanced budget, 355
changes in, 314
and collectivism, 146, 241, 246, 269, 325, 360
and earmarking, 121
vs. egalitarianism, 596
in England, 318, 431
and equity, 550
and Great Depression, 432
and hierarchy, 58n, 118
and income tax, 338
and market regimes, 20, 595–96
in Middle Ages, 152, 171, 178n, 181n, 192, 199n, 204, 223, 226–27
and Protestantism, 249
in U.S., 25, 27, 28, 318–19, 431, 445
Industrial age, early
balanced budgets in, 323–32
centralization in, 317–19
change in, 310–23
cities in, 3, 15–16
economizing in, 325–26
efficiency in, 325–26, 334–35
government spending in, 308, 310
legacy of, 355–57
legislative branch in, 299–300, 304, 306–7, 327–29
public finance in, 299–310
taxation in, 332–55
Treasury in, 327–29
welfare spending in, 349–55
Industrial Commission (U.S.), 444n
Industrial Revolution, 204, 300, 305, 313, 384
Indus Valley, 17, 41, 42, 45n
Ine (Saxon king), 170
Inequality, 582
and hierarchy, 583
Inflation, 220, 265, 446–47, 531
in Britain, 468
and budgeting, 482–83, 484
and currency debasement, 191n
in Germany after World War I, 446, 447
Inheritance tax, 323, 344, 349, 422
Inland bill, 281
Inquisition, 264
Institute for Government Research (U.S.), 414
Interest, 193, 204, 253, 254n, 258, 309
see also Debt

Internal Revenue Service (U.S.), 422, 538
Interventionism, in early industrial age, 307, 308–9
Investiture Controversy, 150
Investment tax in Sweden, 541
Ireland, 165, 495, 557
Isabella, queen of Castile, 268
Israel, 160, 525
ancient, 560–62
Italy, 233, 240, 252, 253, 281, 284, 320, 327, 343n, 466, 586
bankers in, 193, 194, 195, 218, 221
budgeting in, 556
city-states in, 144
commercial revival in (medieval), 162–64
deficit spending in, 328n
food supply in (Roman), 94
"gray economy" in post–WW II, 555
income tax in, 261, 322, 344, 549
incremental taxes in N. Italian communes, 201–2
inheritance tax in, 344
merchants of, 197
in Middle Ages, 149, 153–59, 161, 166, 167, 181, 182, 186n, 191n, 196, 198, 203, 204, 206, 220
monte de pietà in, 256–57
peninsula of, 99, 109, 115
property taxes in, 199–201
revenue in, 354, 521, 523
taxing mercantile wealth in N. Italian communes, 198–99
transfers in, 502–3
welfare spending in, 495, 497, 499, 500, 502–3, 504

Jackson, Andrew, 27, 373, 379–80, 392, 396, 426
Jacksonians (U.S.), 26–27, 379, 397–98, 426
James I, king of England, 262
James II, king of England, 286
Jansenists, 21
Japan, 39, 73, 77, 78, 148, 472, 478, 511, 535, 539, 558, 597
budgeting of (modern), 556
feudal, 70–71, 83, 88
growth in (modern), 578
income tax in, 344
industry in, 571
inheritance tax in, 344

Japan (*cont.*)
  and naval treaties, 466, 467
  oligarchy in, 162n
  protectionism in, 270
  tax preferences in, 525
  welfare spending of, 495, 497, 499, 500, 502
Jay, John, 244
Jefferson, Thomas, 244, 370, 372, 373, 378, 381, 384, 391, 393, 426, 427
Jeffersonians (U.S.), 370, 371, 372, 392
Jewish moneylenders in medieval Europe, 194–95
John, king of England, 175, 218
John the Good, 192
John of Salisbury, 205
Johnson, Andrew, 375
Johnson, Lyndon, 510, 511
Johnson, Samuel, 390
Johnson administration, 505, 510, 511, 512
Joint Commission to Inquire into the Status of Laws Organizing the Executive Department, *see* Dockery-Cockrell Commission
Joint-stock companies, 238, 241, 261, 268–69, 287n–88n
  see also Societates publicanorum
Joseph II, Hapsburg emperor, 245, 294

Kahn, R. F., 433
Kaiser, Henry, 435n
Kassite period, in Mesopotamia, 57, 59, 70, 148
Kaufman, Herbert, 580–81
Kautilya (ancient Indian writer), 62, 63, 64, 68, 71, 72, 73, 75, 78, 79–80, 81, 82, 83, 89, 175, 210, 594
  list of devices for raising revenue, 76
  list of techniques for misrepresentation (Mauryan India), 85–86
Keep Commission (U.S.), 412
Kennedy, John F., 510, 511
Kennedy administration, 510, 511, 512
Keynes, John Maynard, 432, 433–34, 435, 447–48, 454, 468, 563
Keynesians, 434, 453, 457, 474, 476–77, 541, 578, 600, 609, 611, 612
  and hierarchy, 562–63
Kimmel, Louis, 381, 383
King, Anthony, 359
King, Ronald, 526, 544
King Philip's War, 363

Kings, 175
  in ancient world, 38–39, 43–44, 65–68
  borrowing of, 192–96, 252–54
  divine right of, 236
  and forced sale of royal assets, 196–97
  in France, 186, 219–20, 257, 267
  and hierarchy, 66
  limitations of, 564
  in Mauryan India, 74, 75
  in Merovingian era, 153, 159, 167
  in Mesopotamia, 65
  ministers to, 241–43
  poverty of, 205–6
  revenues for, 181–98, 215–21
Knighthood, 178
  distraint of, 179
  salable, 197
Knights Templars, 193, 195, 218
Korea, 473, 513, 571
Korean War, 474, 507, 509, 514, 516, 520, 524n
Kraines, Oscar, 411
Kristol, Irving, 524
Kudrle, Robert, 585–86
Kuisel, Richard F., 459–61
Kusch, vice-king of, 55

Labor
  under feudalism, 224n
  forced, 169–70
  see also Corvée
Lagash (Sumer), 41, 42n, 46, 48, 75
Laissez-faire, 247
  see also Market regimes, Individualism
Land
  under feudalism, 224n
  value of, 47–48, 155–56, 347
Landes, David, 456–57, 458, 459
Land taxes, 78, 79, 261, 262–64
  in Middle Ages, 151
  in U.S. cities, 151
  Roman, 170
  single-tax, 347
Lane, Jan-Erik, 448n
Latin America, debt repudiation in, 254n
Law, John, 292n
"Law Promoting Stability and Growth of the Economy" (Germany), 537
Lay subsidies, 198, 220–21
League of Nations, 472

Legislative branch
  in early industrial age, 299–300, 304,
    306–7, 327–29
  executive vs. (U.S.), 392, 393, 403,
    413
  see also Representative government
Leiserson, William M., 444n
Levellers, 19, 21, 309
Levenson, Cy, 17
Levi, Margaret, 33–34
Liberty Loan Acts (U.S.), 376, 442
Libra, see Dazio
Libyans, 47
Lincoln, Abraham, 375, 397
Lindbeck, Assar, 573–74, 583–84
Lindblom, Charles E., 532
Line-item budgeting, 30, 404, 480–82,
    487–88
Liturgies
  in ancient Greece, 58n, 102, 257n
  in Athens, 102–5, 131, 142–43, 173
  in Rome, 102–7, 131, 142–43, 257n
Lloyd-George, David, 351–52, 440
Loan guarantees, 487, 601
Locke, John, 239, 245–46, 290, 292n,
    325
Logic of Collective Action (Olson), 578
Lombard communes, 162
London Naval Treaty (1930, 1936),
    466, 467, 471
Long, Russell, 534
Lorris (France) medieval charter,
    183n–84n
Lotteries in early modern debt funding,
    364
Louis VI, king of France, 183n
Louis IX, king of France, 195, 253
Louis XIV, king of France, 237–38,
    258, 265n, 278, 337, 431n
Louis XVI, king of France, 243, 273,
    293
Lowndes, William, 243, 290
Luther, Martin, 249, 251
Luxembourg, 334, 521, 522
Luxury taxes
  early modern, 272
  in Sweden, 543
Lycurgus (Athenian statesman), 130

Machiavelli, Niccoló, 62
McKinley, William, 376
Macmillan, Harold, 503
McNamara, Robert, 489, 511, 512

Madden, Martin, 415
Madison, James, 244, 373
Magna Carta, 175, 188
Mahan, Alfred, 322
Malthus, Thomas, 431n–32n
Marcus Aurelius, emperor of Rome,
    140
Marginal-utility theory, 323
Market administration, see Tax farm-
    ing, Sale of titles and offices
Market conservatism, 307, 308
Market model, self-organizing, 246–47
Market regimes, 19, 21, 24–28, 30–33,
    36, 144, 181n, 277, 377, 586
  and balanced budgets, 608–9, 613–14
  and economic growth, 550–51
  and hierarchy, 58, 81, 87, 99, 101,
    113, 118, 283, 298, 426
  and individualism, 20, 595–96
  and spending, 325, 361, 597
  and taxation, 598
  and tax preferences, 526
  and welfare spending, 350
  see also Customs, Excise, Tariffs
Market taxes, 23, 269–71, 272–73, 339,
    341, 438, 457
Marmor, Theodore, 585–86
Marshall, T. H., 450, 498
Martin, Joseph W., 534
Marx, Karl, 223, 306, 309, 314, 321
Marxists, 577
Marxist theories, 574–76
Materialism, and rationality, 225
Mauryan India, 39, 41, 43, 46, 65, 68,
    70–73, 77–79, 83, 175, 564
  budget categories in, 80
  bureaucracy in, 62–64
  fiscal management in, 85–87
  job classifications in, 81–82
  kings in, 74, 75
Mayan civilization, barter in, 91
Mellon, Andrew, 423, 424–25
Mendoza, Códice de, 73
Mercantilism, 241, 246, 270, 363
Merovingian era, 167n, 185
  kings from, 153, 159, 167
  warriors from 171–72
Mesopotamia, 21, 22, 39–45, 49, 51–54,
    60, 63, 66–68, 71–73, 77–79, 121
  bureaucracy in, 57–59
  Kassite period in, 57, 59, 70, 148
  kings in, 65
  land tax in, 47–48

Mesopotamia (cont.)
  standard of value in, 90–91, 92
  tax farming in, 21, 57–58, 88
Metals, as standard of value, 91–92
  see also Precious metals
Mexico, 73, 480
Micawber principle in budgeting, 376, 594
Middle Ages, see European Middle Ages
Middle East, 43, 305
Middle Kingdom (Egypt), 41, 44, 46–47, 48, 54, 55, 67, 71n, 84, 129, 148
Military spending, 239
  for World War I, 437–44, 473, 474
  after World War II, 506–11, 512–21
  and World War II, 435, 472–75
  between world wars, 464–72
Mill, James, 308
Mill, John Stuart, 315, 348
Miller, John William, 560, 590
Mills, Wilbur, 531
Mineral rights, 261
  see also Metals
Minoan Crete, 41, 44, 45n
Mitterrand, François, 590
Mobile tax, 541
Mohenjo-Daro (Indus Valley), 41
Mondale, Walter, 612
Money, 260
  in ancient world, 90–92
  intrinsic value of, 191n
  in Middle Ages, 161, 166, 176–78, 180
  quantity theory of, 191n
Moneylending, 73, 163, 192–95, 251
  see also Debt
Monroe, James, 373, 378
Monte de pietà, 256–57
Morrill, Justin, 419
Morrill Act of 1862 (U.S.), 383–84
Morris, Robert, 367–68
Muggletonians, 19
Multiplier principle, 433
Mun, Thomas, 270
Munera, in Rome, 102, 104
Municipal Corporation Act (U.S., 1899), 412
Murray, Charles, 306n
Muskie, Edmund S., 534
Mussolini, Benito, 467

Mycenaean Greece, 41, 44
Myrdal, Gunnar, 436

Napoleon, emperor of France, 311, 312, 337, 338
Napoleon, Louis, emperor of France, 342
Napoleonic Wars, 335, 343
  income tax in, 261, 337, 421
Naram-Sin, king of Sumer, 53
National Association of Manufacturers, 435n
National Industrial Recovery Act (U.S.), 454
National Labor Relations Act (U.S.), 455
National Municipal League, 412
National Recovery Administration (NRA), 454
National Resources Planning Board (U.S.), 435n
NATO, 513, 517
Naval Construction Act (U.S.), 456
Navigation Acts, 363
Nazis, in Germany, 27, 461–63, 471, 475
Near East, 17, 40, 55n, 90, 94
  see also Ancient Near East
Necker, Jacques, 18
Neolithic period, 40
Nepal, 572
Nero, emperor of Rome, 120, 140
Nerva, emperor of Rome, 120
Netherlands, 243, 281, 290, 324, 479, 480, 597, 613
  budgeting in, 556
  legislature in, 327
  public debt in 251–52, 257–58
  revenue in, 523
  tariffs in, 342
  taxation in, 334, 521–22
  welfare spending in, 495, 497, 499, 500, 501
  see also Dutch Republic; Holland
New Deal, in U.S., 444n, 453–56, 464, 611
"New Economics, The," 434
New Guinea, 89
New Kingdom (Egypt), 41, 47, 51, 55, 75, 77, 79, 88, 115
Newton, Isaac, 244, 248, 290, 292n, 324, 325
Newtonian concepts, 245, 609

New York Bureau of Municipal Research, 412
New York City financial crisis (1975), 250, 254, 293, 294
New Zealand, 344, 495, 497, 499, 502, 521, 522, 558
Nicomedeia (Roman), 136
Nixon administration, 505, 510, 511
Nondiscretionary spending, 31
Norman Conquest of England, 166, 176, 214
Normandy, 152, 165, 213, 278
Normandy, Duke of, 179
Norman England, kings of, 175
Normans, 179, 180, 185, 211n, 212
Norsemen, 165
North, Douglas C., 224, 388
North, Lord Frederick, 313
North Africa, 94, 119
Norway, 327, 344, 495, 497, 499, 500, 501, 521, 523, 557
Novick, David, 485
NRA, see National Recovery Administration
Nuhanda, in Mesopotamia, 52
Nubians, 47

O'Connor, James, 574
OECD (Organisation for Economic Cooperation and Development) countries, 495, 497, 498, 499, 501, 521
"Off-budget" expenditures, 601, 603
Offerings, 43
Offices, sale of, 266–68
Oil depletion allowance, 424
Old Kingdom (Egypt), 43, 44, 46–47, 54, 56, 57, 60, 74–75
Olson, Mancur, 578–79, 588
Opramoas (Greek), 104
Ordinance of 1787 (U.S.), 383
Organisation for Economic Cooperation and Development countries, see OECD countries.
Orwell, George, 458
Ottawa Conference (1932), 457
Owen, Robert, 309
Oxenstierna, Count Axel, 272

Pacioli, Luigi, 164n
Paine, Thomas, 306, 309, 347
Paley, William, 347
Palmyra, 119n

Paper money, in U.S., 362–63
Paris Knights Templar, 195, 206
Paris food riots, 316n
Patrimonium, in Rome, 123–24
Paulette, 267
Payment in kind, 22, 38, 43–45, 56–57, 58–59, 74, 79, 83–84, 91, 364
   in Middle Ages, 151, 170, 176
Peacock, Alan, 445, 530, 576
Pechman, Joseph, 524, 538
Peel, Sir Robert, 318, 340, 342
Peloponnesian Wars, 108
Peltzman's law, 587–88
Pensions, spending for, 499, 502
People's Republic of China, 69n
Pepys, Samuel, 233, 277, 283, 290
Pericles (Athenian statesman), 130
Pericles, Golden Age of, 97, 100, 107, 120, 129, 145
Personal property taxes, 363
Peru, 39, 254n, 265n
Peruzzi, the, 164
Peters, Guy, 539, 549, 572, 575–76
Peter's Pence, 187
Petty, Sir William, 270, 271
Philip IV (the Fair), king of France, 180, 185, 192, 195, 197, 206, 207
Philip VI, king of France, 186
Philip II, king of Spain, 257, 281
Philip Augustus, king of France, 177
Physiocrats, 347
Pierce, Franklin, 381
Pindar, Sir Charles, 255
Pipe Roll, 216
Pisa (Italy), 161, 162
Piso (Roman consul), 138
Pistoia (Italy), 200
Pitt, William, the Younger, 243, 309, 345–46
Planning, programming, and budgeting (PPB), 485–86, 511
Planning-Programming-Budgeting System (PPBS), 511
Plehn, Carl, 418
Pliny the Younger, 136
Plumb, J. H., 607
Pluralism, 28
Plutarch, 94n
Plymouth Brethren, 21
Pocock, J. A. G., 152
Poland, 233, 235, 240
Pólis (Greek concept), 95, 96, 128, 167
Political culture, 578–84

Political regimes, 36
  and social orders, 25
  see also Regimes
Politics and Administration (Goodnow),
  406
Polk, James K., 374, 380
Pollock v. Farmers Loan and Trust
  Company, 387
Poll tax, 363, 364
Polybius (Greek commentator), 130
Poor Law (England), 450
Popular Front, in France, 459–60, 472
Population, and feudalism, 224n
Portoria, 110
Portugal, 557
Postelthwaite, James, 291
Potter, Jim, 456
Poujadist rebellion (France), 548
Poverty, in early industrial age, 305–6
  see also Welfare spending
PPBS, see Planning-Programming-Bud-
  geting System
Precious metals, 167n
  in coins, 190–91
Pre-Columbian civilizations, 73
Prévôt, in France, 207, 208, 209
Priest-kings, 45–48
  see also Kings
Priestley, Joseph, 292n
Primogeniture, 173
Prince, The (Machiavelli), 62
Procedural budgeting, 30
Procurators, in Rome, 134–36
Productivity, and welfare spending,
  302, 307
Productivity budgeting, 30
Program budgeting, 29
  see also Planning, programming, and
  budgeting (PPB)
Progressive taxation, 272, 323, 347–48,
  352, 452
Property taxes, 151, 199–201, 221, 349,
  417–18
  see also Personal property taxes
Protectionism, 270, 340, 342
Protestantism, 227, 249, 264
Protestants, 232, 248, 263n
Protestant states, 251, 281
Prussia, 18, 237, 240, 246, 262, 270, 294,
  318, 334, 335, 341, 348, 351, 410,
  535
  army, 238–39
  financial systematization, 285

Public government, 247–49, 286–87
Public interest, 142–44, 245–46, 295–96,
  357
Public-private distinction
  in Greece and Rome, 129–31, 144–47
  in Middle Ages, 148–51, 182–83,
  193–94, 220
  in early modern era, 247–48, 249,
  256–59, 266–68, 269, 274–76, 279
  in 19th century, 319
Ptolemies, in Egypt, 115
Public assistance, 306
Public Works Administration (U.S.),
  454
Punic Wars, 140
  see also Second Punic Wars
Puritan Revolution, in England, 19, 21,
  240, 264, 286, 288, 309, 417
Puritans, in New England, 362
Purveyance, 188–89, 191n

Quesnay, François, 239
Quitrents, 364

Randell, Samuel, 385
Randolph, Edmond, 389
Randolph, John, 378
Ranters, 19
Rational choice theory, 33–34
Rationality, 323–26, 356
  and materialism, 225
  and regimes, 32–34
Rationes imperii, 137
Ray, John, 387
Reagan, Ronald, 506, 523, 534, 590,
  597, 611
Reagan administration, 520
Realm, idea of, 182–83
Recentralization, 223, 240
  and feudalism, 165–67
Recoinage, 190–91, 192
Reconstruction Finance Corporation
  (U.S), 433
Redistributive budgeting, 30
Redundancy, and corruption, 84, 86–87
Reformation, 264
Regimes
  and balanced budgets, 595–98,
  608–14
  budgetary consequences of hybrid,
  28
  and defense spending, 519–21
  and rationality, 32–34

Rehoboam (Hebrew King), 560–61
Renaissance, 144, 160, 162n, 168n, 247, 252, 259, 261, 271n, 280, 322, 337, 566
Rent, interest disguised as, 204
Representative government, 95–98, 228, 239, 243–48, 299–300, 304
 see also Democracy
Resources, and spending, 595
Res privata, 126
Restoration (England), 240–42
Revenue
 below national level in OECD nations, itemized, 523
 direct and indirect, 68–76
 in early-modern Europe, 259–74
 and expenditure, 595
 in Italy, 354, 521, 523
 for kings, 181–98, 215–21
 maximizing, 32, 33, 34
 minimizing, 32
 ordinary and extraordinary, 262
 in Rome, 107–13
 in U S , 336–37, 416–25
Revenue Act of 1909 (England), 352
Revenue-anticipation note, 253
Revolution of 1848, 347
Revolutionary War, 366, 367, 390, 586
 see also American Revolution
Ricardo, David, 381, 432n
Riccardi, the, 164, 193
Richard II, king of England, 196
Richelieu, Duc de, 278, 431n
Rights of Man, The (Paine), 347
Role coordination, and budgeting, 478–80
Romanticism, in early industrial age, 314–15
Rome (republican and/or imperial) 23, 29, 56, 61n, 83, 129, 130, 148, 165, 166, 168n, 182, 185, 187, 213n, 216n, 221–22, 247, 276, 359, 563, 564
 accountability in, 127 28
 centralization in, 133–39
 collectivism in, 146
 corruption in, 138–39
 crown support in, 140
 currency devaluation in, 139, 190
 decline of, 153, 154–57, 167, 171
 decurions of, 105–6, 149, 173
 earmarking in, 121–27
 finance in, 101–7, 131–33

 hierarchy in, 98, 99, 101, 108–13, 118, 121, 123, 127, 135, 140
 imported food for, 151n
 land tax, 170
 latifundia of, 158, 159
 law, 150, 183, 194
 liturgies in, 102–7, 131, 142–43, 257n
 moral restraint in, 140
 munera in, 102, 104
 numerals, 217
 political institutions in, 95, 97–101
 public interest in, 142–43, 145–47
 revenue in, 107–13
 social and economic conditions in, 93–95
 spending in, 119–42
 taxation in, 107–13, 141–42
 tax farming in, 113, 115–19, 121, 131
 treasuries in, 119–27
Roosevelt, Franklin D., 408, 425, 453–54, 455, 456, 462
Roosevelt, Theodore, 376
Roosevelt administration, 425
Rose, Richard, 491, 539, 549, 589
Royal storehouses, 38, 39
Russia, 238, 294, 320, 334, 337, 342
 see also Soviet Union; U.S.S.R.
Rustow, Dankwart, 449

Sabotnik, in Soviet Union, 22
Sales taxes, 202, 528, 537, 541
 see also Excise, Market taxes
Sale of titles and offices, 266–68
Salvian the Presbyter, 142
Samlans, 139 40
Sandwich, Earl of, 277
Sunga, in Mesopotamia, 52
Sargon, king of Akkad, 46
Saxons, 180, 209
Saxony, 341
Say, Jean-Baptiste, 339, 381
Scaeveola, Mucius, 132–33
Scandinavia, 320, 456, 457, 499, 613
Scandinavian tribes, 165
Schlck, Allen, 603
Schmoekel, Hartmut, 41n, 42n
Schumpeter, Joseph, 577
Scotland, 34, 69n, 218, 255, 324
 see also Anglo-Scottish Enlightenment
Scutage, 179–80
"Second American Revolution," 358–59

Second Punic Wars, 100
Second World War, *see* World War II
Sectarian regimes, 21, 24–28, 30, 32, 36,
    89, 377, 577, 598
    and balanced budget, 608–9, 613–14
    and budgeting, 583, 596
    and central government, 426
    and egalitarianism, 20
    vs. hierarchy, 519–21
    and tax differences, 550–52
Sects, in U.S., 21, 28
Secular-stagnation theory, 433, 435
Securities and Exchange Commission
    (U.S.), 455
Selective Employment tax, 546
Seligman, Edwin, 432n
Sells, Elijah W., 412
Semblançay, Beaune de, 253
Septimus Severus, 125, 126
Serfs, leaving for towns, 161
Serra, Junípero, 270
Sesostris III, pharaoh of Egypt, 54
Seti I, king of Egypt, 69, 70
Seven Years' War, 363
Severus Alexander, 110n, 111n
Shang Dynasty (China), 39, 41, 44, 52,
    72, 168n
Sheriff (England), 207, 209, 214, 215,
    216
Shih Huang Ti, 66n
Shonfield, Andrew, 535
Shulgi, king of Sumer, 53
Siberia, 160
Sicily, 94, 109, 110, 166, 212
Sickness benefits, 500
    see also Health care expenditures,
        Social insurance
Sienna (Italy), 200
Silver, 191n, 265
"Sin taxes," 452
Single-tax, 347
Sixteenth Amendment, to U.S. Consti-
    tution, 413, 421
Slavery, 28, 74, 97, 98, 108, 109, 110,
    129, 595, 596
Smiles, Samuel, 321
Smith, Adam, 239, 250, 270, 291, 292n,
    302, 303, 313, 324, 339, 347, 381
Smith, Sidney, 383
Social democracies, 25–28, 145, 199n,
    520, 551, 597, 598
    taxation in, 552–55
Social insurance, 449, 450

Social order, 36
    and budgets, 17–22, 31–32
    and change, 225–26
    and political regimes, 25
Social Security Act (U.S.), 455, 464
Social Security tax (U.S.), 525, 532–33
Societates publicanorum, 116
Solomon (Hebrew king), 560–61
Solon (Athenian lawgiver), 102
South Sea Company, 287n, 288n
Soviet Bloc, 587
Soviet Union, 22, 69n, 160, 184, 473,
    479, 509, 513, 520, 568, 587
    see also Russia, U.S.S.R.
Spain, 94, 109, 116, 126, 195, 231, 233,
    236, 238, 240, 251, 253, 263–64,
    270, 361, 557
    American colonies of, 265
    conquerors from, 73
    towns in, 257
    welfare spending in, 495
Spanish Civil War, 460
Sparta, 139–40
Special Areas Acts (Britain), 458
Special interests, 529n
Spending
    in Athens, 119–22, 123, 124, 127
    in Britain, 289, 329, 349, 448–51, 515,
        555, 558
    in France, 448–51
    in Germany, 448–51
    limits, in modern world, 555–59
    and market regimes, 325, 361, 597
    nondiscretionary, 31
    and resources, 595
    in Rome, 119–42
    in Sweden, 448–51, 583
    and taxation, 23–24, 26–29
    in twentieth century, 428–30, 434–36,
        437, 448–51
    see also Expenditures; Government
        spending; Military spending; Wel-
        fare spending
Sputnik, 509
Stagflation, 477, 530, 563
Standard of value, 90–91
    metal as, 91–92
    see also Barter
State capitalism, 25, 27, 28
Statius (Roman poet), 134n
Stein, Lorenz von, 18
Stipendia, 109
Stourm, René, 401, 405, 407

Student Non-Violent Coordinating Committee (U.S.), 21
Subsidies, *see* Clerical Subsidies; Lay subsidies
Sudetenland, 470n
Suez crisis, 516
Suger, Abbé, 208, 210
Sukkal, in Mesopotamia, 52
Sukraniti, 68, 80
Sulla (Roman general), 99, 100
Sumer, 41, 42n, 44, 52, 53, 57, 65
Summa de arithmetica (Pacioli), 164n
Sumner, William Graham, 368
Switzerland, 341, 344, 495, 557, 583–84
Sweden, 238, 240, 272, 327, 550, 572, 586, 597
  budgeting in, 555, 557
  corporate income tax in, 541
  deflation in, 447
  exports of, 233
  hyperpluralism in, 551
  income tax in, 344, 354, 539n, 540, 542
  inheritance tax in, 344
  Labor Market Review Board, 541
  parties in, 579
  spending in, 448–51, 583
  stabilization in, 539–44
  taxation in, 312, 451–52, 521, 522, 539–44
  welfare spending in, 495, 496n, 497, 499, 500, 501, 502

Taft, William Howard, 376, 404, 413, 414, 420, 421
Taille, 198, 199
Tallies of receipt, 189–90, 212, 214, 215, 219, 253, 263, 278
Tang Dynasty (China), 41, 61, 70, 71, 148
Tanzi, Vito, 536, 549
Tariffs, 322
  in England, 312, 335, 336, 340, 341, 457
  in France, 341–42
  in Netherlands, 342
  in Russia, 342
  in U.S., 387–88, 419, 592
  see also Customs duties
Tarschys, Daniel, 493, 555, 559
Taxation
  in ancient Greece, 107
  in ancient world, 68–76

  in Athens, 107–8, 109n
  benefit theory of, 343
  in Britain, 451–52
  displacement effect hypothesis, 576–78
  in early industrial age, 332–55
  exemptions from, 74–75
  faculty theory of, 343
  in France, 262–63, 272, 278, 337, 354, 451–52, 522, 523
  in Germany, 431, 451–52, 522, 523, 538
  history of, 552–55
  legalized, in Middle Ages, 197–203
  and market regimes, 598
  of mercantile wealth, 198–99
  and morality, 74–76
  in Netherlands, 334, 521–22
  political culture of, 521–23
  progressive, 272, 323, 347–48, 352, 452
  in Rome, 107–13, 141–42
  social theory of, 346–47
  and spending, 23–24, 26–29
  in Sweden, 312, 451–52, 521, 522, 539–44
  in twentieth century, 451–52
  in U.S., 451–52, 474–75
  see also Payment in kind, Corvée
Tax collectors, 39, 75
Tax differences, and culture, 550–52
Taxe professionielle, 549
Taxes
  bargaining on, 184–85
  persuasion for, 185
Tax expenditures, 487
Tax farming, 133
  in Athens, 113–15, 121, 131, 149
  in early-modern Europe, 230, 255, 271, 278, 294
  in France, 282
  in Mesopotamia, 21, 57–58, 88
  in Middle Ages, 184, 194, 202, 208, 217, 221
  in Rome, 113, 115–19, 121, 131
Tax incentives, 525
  in Germany, 536–37
Tax preferences, 524–26, 601
  and income tax, 530–34
Tax revolts, 33, 273
  see also Fronde
Taylor, John, 371, 378

Technology, 19, 225, 564
  in early industrial age, 320
  after World War II, 517–19
Temple, Sir William, 258
Temple of Amon, 48
Tenure-of-Office Act of 1820 (U.S.),
  392
Thatcher, Margaret, 503, 547, 597
Thatcher government (Britain), 484
Thebes (ancient Egypt), 48
Theorica, in Athens, 122
Thiers, Louis, 18, 318, 480
Third World nations, 254n, 327, 329,
  439, 517, 592
Thirty Years' War, 238
Thomas, Robert Paul, 224
Thutmose III, pharaoh of Egypt, 46
Tiberius, emperor of Rome, 111n, 134,
  135, 138
Tingsten, Herbert, 576
Tithes, 51, 71, 109, 118, 119
Titles, sale of, 266–68
Tocqueville, Alexis de, 34, 316n,
  359, 370
Totalitarian regimes, 25, 27
Towns, in Middle Ages, 183–85,
  209
Trajan, emperor of Rome, 136, 137
Transactions taxes, 110
  see also Market taxes, Customs,
  Excise
Transfers
  in England, 394
  in France, 394
  growth of, 495, 496, 499
  in Italy, 502–3
  in U.S., 393–95, 494
Treasury Commission (England), 290,
  295
Treatise on Political Economy, A (Say),
  381
Tribute, 79, 101, 105
Tributum, 108–9, 112
Tributum in Capita, 109
Tributum soli, 109
Trirarchy, in Athens, 103–4, 105
Trollope, Anthony, 315
Truman, Harry, 534
Tudor period (England), 257
Turgot, Anne Robert Jacques, 18, 239,
  263, 273–74, 292–94
Turkey, 267
Tyler, John, 374, 395

Umma (Mesopotamia), 42n
Unemployment, 305, 321
  in Britain, 305, 339, 432–33, 458, 464
  in Germany, 461–62
  in U.S., 464
Unemployment insurance, 449
  economic function of, 500
  growth of, 448, 450
  see also Welfare spending
United Kingdom, 437, 523, 556
  see also Britain; England
United Nations, 473, 496n
United Provinces, see Netherlands
United States, 160, 201, 310, 311, 320,
  429, 437, 438, 546, 548, 558, 570,
  578, 587n
  appropriations in, 358–60
  banks, 254n
  budget absence in, 388–400, 405
  budgeting in, 358–61, 369, 370–76,
  400–416, 425–27, 476–78, 480, 509,
  511–12, 556, 600, 609–12
  vs. Canada, 585–86
  capital gains tax in, 545
  after Civil War, 34
  in colonial period, 69n, 234, 265,
  361–66
  constitutional government in, 563
  corporate income tax in, 420–21, 423,
  442, 523–24
  debt in, 370–76, 445–47, 597–98
  early relations with England, 358,
  364, 365–66
  economic growth in, 300
  egalitarianism in, 360, 416–17, 550
  executive vs. legislative branches in,
  392, 393, 403, 413
  expenditure control compared with
  Canada, 585–86
  expenditures in, 384, 415–16, 441,
  442, 448–51, 474, 589
  Fair Deal in, 507
  foreign policy of, 514, 516, 517
  founders of, 244, 313
  GNP, 508, 509
  government size of, 568
  hierarchy in, 400–411, 426–27
  income tax in, 278, 344, 387–88, 416,
  418–25, 435, 442, 474–75
  individualism in, 25, 27, 28, 318–19,
  431, 445
  inheritance tax in, 344
  internal improvements in, 377–88

Jacksonians in, 26–27, 379, 397–98, 426
Jeffersonians in, 370, 371, 372, 392
loan guarantees in, 601
market conservatism in, 308
military spending in, 441, 442, 469, 470, 471, 474, 506–12, 518, 520–21
and naval treaties, 466, 467
New Deal in, 444n, 453–56, 464, 611
as nonheirarchical country, 535, 539
parties in, 579, 590
Populism in, 387, 419–21, 426, 524
poverty program, 306n
Progressive movement in, 388, 412, 443–44
property taxes in, 151
protectionism in, 342
pump priming in, 433
revenue in, 336–37, 416–25
sects in, 21, 28
spending limits in, 555
and Suez crisis, 516
tariffs in, 387–88, 419, 592
taxation in, 451–52, 474–75
tax history of, 552
tax policies of, 522
tax preferences in, 524–25, 530–34
tax revolt of, 313, 334
transfers in, 393–95, 494
unemployment in, 464
welfare spending in, 495, 497, 499, 500, 502, 505–6
and World War I, 441–43
and World War II, 23, 472–75
after World War II, 506–11
see also Revolutionary War
Ur (Mesopotamia), 42n, 53, 57
Uruk (Sumer), 41
Urukagina, king of Lagash, 46, 48, 75
U.S. Budget Bureau (later Office of Management and Budget), 327, 396, 414, 415, 426, 478, 483
U.S. Constitution, 244, 247, 358, 359, 369, 370, 371, 372, 397, 402, 410, 420
amendments to, 413, 421, 558
U.S. Housing Authority, 455
U.S. Securities and Exchange Commission, 455
U.S.S.R., 506–7
U.S. Supreme Court, 387, 420, 421
U.S. Tax Code, 537–38
Usury, 163n

Value-added tax (VAT), 547–48
Van Buren, Martin, 373, 374
Vanderbilt family, 420
VAT, see Value-added tax
Vauban, Jean, 292n, 337
Venality, see Sale of titles and offices
Venice (Italy), 162n, 202
Verres (Roman governor of Sicily), 115, 132n
Versailles Treaty, 467
Vespasian, emperor of Rome, 125, 136
Vethake, Henry, 381
Vickery, William, 524
Vienna school of economics, 577
Vietnam War, 505, 508, 510, 518
Villèle, Louis de, 318
Voltaire (François Marie Arouet), 245, 436
Volume, budgeting by, 482–83
Voluntary giving, 43

Wages-fund theory, 374
Wagner, Adolf, 432n, 569–70, 571
Wagner's law, 569–71, 587, 614
Waldo, Dwight, 400, 406, 412
Wales, 218, 280
Walker, Robert J., 374
Walpole, Sir Robert, 272–73
Wampum, 361–62
Wardship, 173
War of 1812, 373, 374
War of the League of Augsburg, 242
Warring States period (China), 41
War of the Spanish Succession, 238, 242
Wars of Religion (France), 264, 267
Washington, George, 367–68, 371, 378, 389, 390, 392
Washington Naval Treaty, 466, 467, 471
Wealth of Nations (Smith), 313, 381
Wealth tax (Sweden), 542
Wealth Tax Act of 1935 (U.S.), 456
Webster, Daniel, 381
Webster, Pelatiah, 370
Weimar Germany, 446, 462
Welfare spending, 493–506
in early industrial age, 349–55
and egalitarianism, 350, 498
and hierarchical regimes, 350
in OECD countries, 497
and productivity, 302, 307

Welfare state
  and Great Depression, 453–64
  growth of, 581–82
  and Marxist theories, 574–76
  as synthesis, 310
Welser family, 252
West Germany, 517, 522, 525, 536
Wheat Act of 1932 (Britain), 458
White, Leonard, 397–98
Wicksell, Knut, 577
Wildavsky, Aaron, 299n, 485, 610n
Wilensky, Harold, 571–72, 575, 578,
  579, 581
William III, king of England, 259, 286,
  292n
William the Conqueror, 179
Willoughby, W. F., 388, 403, 405, 407,
  408, 413, 414
Wilmerding, Lucius, 385, 405
Wilson, Sir Horace, 444
Wilson, Woodrow, 375–76, 386, 398,
  400, 402–3, 406, 413
Window tax, 280
Wiseman, Jack, 445, 530, 576
Witte, John, 527, 530, 531
Wolfe, Alan, 574, 575, 576
Wolfe, C. Stephen, 586
Woodbury, Levi, 373

Wool exports, taxed in England,
  197–98
Works Progress Administration (WPA),
  455
World War I, 475, 519, 524n, 587n, 608
  financial policies before, 310
  and income tax, 422, 438
  military spending for, 437–44, 473,
    474
  mobilization for, 437–38
  resources for, 354–55
World War II, 441, 485, 524n
  budgeting after, 476–82
  effects of, 472–76
  and GNP, 509
  income tax in, 425
  military spending after, 506–11,
    512–21
  military spending for, 435, 472–75
WPA, *see* Works Progress Administration

Yaranton, Thomas, 258
Young Man Luther (Erikson), 249

ZBB (zero-base budgeting), 29–30,
  485–86
Zöllverein, 336